THE UNIVERSAL
STANDARD
ENCYCLOPEDIA

SEA LIFE. *Above: Sea anemones swallowing Tobias fishes. Right: A codfish and a jellyfish. Below: Spider crab (top) and sun rays.*

THE UNIVERSAL STANDARD ENCYCLOPEDIA

VOLUME 17

NEGROES—PAN

*An abridgment of The New Funk & Wagnalls Encyclopedia
prepared under the editorial direction of*
JOSEPH LAFFAN MORSE, Sc.B., LL.B., LL.D.
Editor in Chief

STANDARD REFERENCE WORKS
PUBLISHING COMPANY, INC., NEW YORK

THE UNIVERSAL
STANDARD
ENCYCLOPEDIA

LIST OF ABBREVIATIONS USED

abbr., abbreviated
A.D., Anno Domini
alt., altitude
A.M., ante meridiem
anc., ancient
approx., approximately
Ar., Arabic
AS., Anglo-Saxon
A.S.S.R., Autonomous Soviet
Socialist Republic
at.no., atomic number
at.wt., atomic weight
b., born
B.C., before Christ
b.p., boiling point
B.T.U., British Thermal Unit
Bulg., Bulgarian
C., centigrade, syn. Celsius
cent., century
Chin., Chinese
cm., centimeter
Co., County
colloq., colloquial
cu., cubic
Czech., Czechoslovakian
d., died
Dan., Danish
Du., Dutch
E., east, easterly, eastern
ed., edition
e.g., for example
Egypt., Egyptian
Eng., English
est., estimated
et seq., and following
F., Fahrenheit
fl., flourished
fr., from
Fr., French
ft., foot

Gael., Gaelic
Gen., General
Ger., German
Gr., Greek
Heb., Hebrew
Hind., Hindustani
Hon., Honorable
h.p., horsepower
hr., hour
Hung., Hungarian
I., Island
i.e., that is
in., inch
Ind., Indian
Ir., Irish
It., Italian
Jr., junior
kg., kilogram
km., kilometer
lat., latitude
Lat., Latin
lb., pound
lit., literally
long., longitude
m., mile
M., Middle
min., minute
M.L., Medieval Latin
mm., millimeter
mod., modern
m.p., melting point
M.P., Member of Parliament
m.p.h., miles per hour
Mt., Mount, Mountain
N., north, northerly, northern
N.T., New Testament
OE., Old English
OF., Old French
OHG., Old High German
ON., Old Norse

ONF., Old Norman French
O.T., Old Testament
oz., ounce
Phil., Philippine
P.M., post meridiem
Pol., Polish
pop., population
Port., Portuguese
prelim., preliminary
pron., pronounced
q.v., which see
R., River
rev., revised, revision
Rev., Reverend
Rom., Romanian
Russ., Russian
S., south, southerly, southern
sec., second
Skr., Sanskrit
Sp., Spanish
sp.gr., specific gravity
sq., square
S.S.R., Soviet Socialist
Republic
Sum., Sumerian
Sw., Swedish
syn., synonym
temp., temperature
trans., translation, translated
Turk., Turkish
U.K., United Kingdom
U.N., United Nations
U.S., United States
U.S.A., United States of
America
U.S.S.R., Union of Soviet
Socialist Republics
var., variety
W., west, westerly, western
yd., yard

Note.—The official abbreviations for the States of the Union are used throughout. For academic degrees, see article DEGREE, ACADEMIC. Other abbreviations or contractions are self-explanatory.

NEGROES IN THE UNITED STATES
(*continued from previous volume*)

The Negroes did not undertake concerted overt opposition to this system of oppression, but when opportunity afforded they tried to escape from it. About 1880, as industrialization in the United States proceeded at a rapid rate (see INDUSTRIAL REVOLUTION), Negroes began to seek employment in lumber camps, sawmills, mines, and in industry generally. Negro families left the virtual bondage of sharecropping in the hope of achieving a freer life in cities. After 1900 the movement to southern cities increased markedly, and it is still continuing. Urbanization of the Negroes in the South, however, did not end segregation and discrimination, but gave rise to new problems in interracial relations.

Greater hope for a better life in the North gradually pervaded the Negroes, who, about 1880, also began migrating to northern cities. The movement continued on a small but steady scale until about 1910, when it began to increase appreciably. Two great waves of Negro migration to northern cities took place between 1916 and 1919, and 1921 and 1924, when a serious shortage of labor created opportunities for Negroes to seek employment in industry. Important consequences resulted from these movements. By about 1929, Negroes became an integral part of the labor force of the United States, particularly in mines, steel mills, foundries, plants making railroad cars, in the building and construction industry, on docks and piers, and in meat-packing houses. They were almost entirely restricted, however, to unskilled labor. And they were barred from membership in most trade unions, or were organized into segregated locals, in accordance with the exclusionist policy of a majority of the affiliates of the American Federation of Labor, which was permeated with anti-Negro prejudices. Many Negroes became strikebreakers.

Another consequence of the influx of Negroes into cities was the creation, as the result of segregation in the North as well as in the South, of large Negro slum areas, frequently called black belts and Negro ghettos. Overcrowding, poverty, and unwholesome sanitary conditions in these areas resulted in a higher incidence of certain diseases, a higher mortality rate, and a greater frequency of crime and juvenile delinquency than among the population of the country as a whole and among the white population. As a continual stream of newcomers from the South flowed into these slums, Negroes began to seek living quarters in neighborhoods inhabited by white persons. The pressure of the Negroes on white areas generated antipathy. Antagonistic whites strove to prevent the Negroes from expanding by compelling landlords and property owners to refuse to rent or sell to Negroes, and when these means failed threats and physical violence were employed. Interracial friction increased greatly during the acute housing shortage in the United States caused by the suspension during World War I of residential building. It gave rise in the South to the revival of the Ku-Klux Klan. In East St. Louis, Ill., in 1917, and in Washington, D.C., Chicago, and twenty-four other cities in 1919, acute interracial tension exploded into race riots in which hundreds of Negroes and white persons were killed and injured.

Another important consequence of the changes in the situation of the Negroes was the development of a heightened sense of group consciousness, called race consciousness by most Negroes and white persons. Race consciousness assumed a fundamental and antithetical conflict of interest between the Negro and white populations. Under slavery, this view had constituted the basis for the establishment in 1817 of the American Colonization Society which acquired Liberia, in Africa, for the purpose of founding colonies there of freed American slaves. A number of colonies were established, but few Negroes were attracted by the prospect of settling in Africa. Immediately following emancipation, Negro leaders, foremost among whom was the celebrated Abolitionist orator, Frederick Douglass (q.v.), stressed a program of legislative and court action and propaganda to end discrimination against Negroes and to attain full economic, political, and social equality with white persons. During the last two decades of the 19th century, however, when new patterns of discrimination and segregation were fashioned against the Negroes, a struggle for equality appeared to many to be unrealistic, and they inclined in large part to views of interracial conciliation.

Hurok Attractions; Brooklyn National Baseball Club

NEGROES IN THE U.S. *Left: Marian Anderson, singer. Right: Jackie Robinson, ballplayer.*

The ablest and best-known spokesman of this attitude was the educator, Booker T. Washington (q.v.), who counseled that "the agitation of social equality is the extremest folly", and who urged Negroes to depend for whatever privileges they might receive on the good will and philanthropy of upper-class white persons. Washington's position was stigmatized by more militant advocates of the Negroes' cause as an "uncle Tom" attitude, i.e., the attitude of servility before his oppressors displayed by *Uncle Tom* in Harriet Beecher Stowe's famous antislavery novel, *Uncle Tom's Cabin*. It was vigorously denounced by such men as the educator and writer William E. B. Du Bois (q.v.), founder of the National Association for the Advancement of Colored People, who demanded elimination of all social and legal disabilities of the Negroes.

Migration to the North awakened hopes among the Negroes that they could achieve equality, but when these hopes were disappointed in consequence of the situation into which they were forced, a revival of race consciousness followed. Immediately after World War I, sentiments of racial consciousness were intensified by thousands of demobilized Negro soldiers smarting from the disdainful and discriminatory treatment to which they had been subjected in the armed forces. The most striking manifestation of the race consciousness of this period was the "back to Africa" movement, led by the self-styled Provisional President of Africa, Marcus Garvey (1887–1940), which attracted a large following among Negroes in all parts of the country, but which declined sharply in a few years.

A less spectacular manifestation of race consciousness was the idea, propagated also by advocates of other programs for a better life for Negroes, of making Negroes economically independent of the white population. Experience had demonstrated that it is a visionary prospect (the economy of the United States is indivisible); nonetheless, the idea was effective in stimulating the establishment of a large number of enterprises owned and controlled by Negroes. These included banks, insurance and real-estate firms, wholesale businesses, retail stores, hotels, restaurants, cafés, night clubs, and many beauty parlors.

Following the decline of the "back to Africa" movement, the predominant attitude among Negroes was that which centered on the achievement of equality, and the history of the Negroes in the United States in the last quarter of a century has been to a considerable degree a record of their success in hurdling barrier after barrier to fuller participation in the economic, political, and cultural life of the country. As negative evidence of the strength of the tendency toward integration into American life, may be cited the total failure of the Communist Party, very active among Negroes since its formation in 1919–21, to win support for its divisive and separatist scheme of an independent Negro republic in the Southern counties in which Negroes constitute a majority.

A milestone in U.S. Negro and labor history was the formation in the latter part of the 1930's of the Congress of Industrial Organizations (q.v.), the affiliates of which, for the first time, included large masses of Negro workers on terms of complete equality with white workers. Support appeared to be given by this development to views long advocated by the socialist and revolutionary movements that the basic interest of the Negro population lay in unity with white workers against the common exploiters of both white and black workers. But the interest of the Negroes in communism, never very great, declined sharply as a result of a growing conviction that the Communist Party was interested in exploiting the struggle of the Negroes to improve their condition for ends with which most Negroes have no sympathy.

In the political field Negroes gained local influence, particularly in New York, New Jersey, Michigan, and Illinois. A few Negroes were again elected to Congress and occupied positions in various State and municipal governments. A number were appointed to the bench. In Presidential elections, the "Negro vote" became important. A continuing series of Federal court decisions enlarged the opportunities of Southern Negroes to participate in political life; the "grandfather clause" and the white primary were declared unconstitutional. Other decisions by the courts and Federal agencies struck at long-established discriminatory laws and practices, e.g., segregation on conveyances engaged in interstate commerce. A number of Southern States abolished the poll tax. Racial segregation in the public schools was ruled unconstitutional by the U.S. Supreme Court in unanimous deci-

sions rendered on May 17, 1954. Though effectuation of the ruling was postponed until the Court completed hearings on the various practical problems involved, the District of Columbia ended segregation in September and gradual desegregation was instituted in several of the twenty-one States affected by the decisions. In Alabama, Georgia, Mississippi, and some of the other States in which segregation is compulsory, officials vehemently denounced the Court's ruling and initiated legislative measures designed to circumvent it.

A unanimous ruling of the United States Supreme Court on May 31, 1955, declared that desegregation in the public schools must be completed "with all deliberate speed", but established no deadline for this action.

Other outstanding advances include the establishment by the Federal government, during World War II, of the Fair Employment Practice Committee (q.v.) to investigate violations of the Federal prohibition of racial and other discrimination in plants working on government contracts; the establishment by a number of State and local governments of similar committees, as in New York State, to combat discrimination in industry and in various other fields; the institution of measures to end discrimination in the armed forces; and the institution by the Federal, State, and local governments of slum clearance and housing projects in Negro communities.

As the Negroes pressed forward toward integration into American life, they made notable achievements and received recognition in numerous fields. As any listing must be arbitrary and cannot be complete, the following is intended merely to suggest the range and scope of achievements by Negroes. In the field of education, Negroes conduct, among institutions of higher learning, Fisk University, Hampton Institute, Howard University, and Tuskegee Institute (qq.v.). Negroes also serve on the faculties of leading American universities. Outstanding in the field of science was George Washington Carver (q.v.), discoverer of many industrial uses for agricultural products. In the arts, Negroes achieved especial distinction in literature and music. Notable literary artists include, among numerous others, the poets Countee Cullen, Langston Hughes, and James Weldon Johnson (qq.v.), and the novelist Richard Wright. Among outstanding Negroes in the field of music are the composer of serious music, William Grant Still (1895–　　　), and the composer in the jazz (q.v.) idiom, William C. Handy (q.v.), and the singers Marian Anderson (1908–), Dorothy Maynor (1912–), Roland Hayes, and Paul Robeson (qq.v.). The last named also achieved distinction in the theater; another and earlier notable Negro actor was Charles Gilpin (1878–1930). Many distinguished Negro performers have appeared in the realm of sports, among whom may be mentioned the heavyweight boxing champions Jack (John) Johnson and Joe Louis (qq.v.); and, among baseball players, Jackie Robinson, an infielder and the first Negro to play in the major leagues. One of the most notable of all Negro athletes was the Olympic Games (q.v.) track-and-field champion Jesse Owens.

While the achievements and progress of the Negroes in the United States have been considerable, their fundamental position remains unaltered: they still occupy a position or status of economic, social, and political inferiority. Anti-Negro prejudice, although less, continues to be widespread and intense. Discrimination may be giving ground before the exposure of enlightened public opinion, the efforts of interracial movements, and the onslaughts of judicial decisions and legislative enactments, but it is still an ingrained habit of American life; Negroes continue to find their access barred to most occupational, vocational, and professional fields, or so restricted as virtually to constitute exclusion. Segregation is another dominant custom in interracial relations, stubbornly maintained to the disadvantage of the Negroes. Negro slums continue to constitute breeding places of disease and crime perilous to the entire nation, and foci of bitter resentment and potential political disaffection. White mobs still employ violence on occasion against Negroes, but there have been no lynchings in recent years. In the consciousness of the Negro is embedded the realization that he is shut out from U.S. society and that his efforts to become a part of it are beset by multitudinous and, more frequently than not, insuperable obstacles. The resolution of the Negro problem will require the greatest wisdom and statesmanship of which the leaders of both white and black groups are capable; but the greater burden rests on the dominant white population to make true for the Negroes as for itself a politically democratic and economically secure way of life. See RIGHTS, CIVIL.

NEGRO FOLKLORE, AMERICAN, the large and diversified body of anecdotes, ballads, fables, folk tales, legends, myths, and superstitions belonging to the culture of the American Negro. Some features of American Negro folklore are distinctively African in their derivation, while others are taken from the popular traditions of the white man.

The American Negro, like the African Negro, assigns to animals a dominant role in his folk stories. The animals are made to think, talk, and behave like human beings, and are endowed with great cleverness. This species of tale is well exemplified in the *Uncle Remus* tales by the American author Joel Chandler Harris (q.v.). Harris based his stories on authentic folk material collected among Negroes of the South. Uncle Remus, a kindly old Negro who was at one time a slave, has become a faithful family retainer in a larger Southern mansion, and amuses his employer's young son with the droll and exciting adventures of Br'er Rabbit, Br'er Wolf, and Br'er Fox. The animals are endowed with human attributes and portrayed in a series of encounters with Tar Baby, a doll or manikin made of tar. Before Harris wrote down these animal folk tales in his Uncle Remus series they were isolated in American Negro folklore; today children of all races enjoy them.

Another class of American Negro folk tales is that which has to do with work and working conditions. An excellent example of this class is the story of John Henry, a powerfully built Negro laborer employed as a stake driver in the construction of a railroad. Most of the ballads and fables relating to John Henry center about the memorable contest in which he pitted his strength against a steam-operated stake driver. John Henry drove more stakes than did the machine, but he suffered a heart attack and died "with his hammer in his hand". In an alternate version of the story John Henry was a dock hand who beat a steam winch in hoisting bales of cotton from the wharf onto a river boat.

A third type of story found in the folklore of the American Negro is that which relates some love affair, usually tragic. Such stories are customarily cast in the form of a ballad, and have close affinities with the distinctive Negro musical idiom known as the *blues* (see JAZZ). This type of story is admirably represented in the ballad of *Frankie and Johnny,* two lovers who swore always to be true to one another. One night Frankie caught Johnny with another woman, whereupon she drew a pistol from beneath her dress and shot him dead. The ballad, which became current about the middle of the 19th century and was printed for the first time in 1912, is believed to have been based upon the killing of a St. Louis Negro by his sweetheart. In addition to the foregoing, American Negro folklore incorporates an amorphous mass of superstitious beliefs concerning black magic, charms, ghosts, voodoo, and witches. See also FOLKLORE; FOLK TALES; MYTHOLOGY; NEGROES IN THE UNITED STATES; SPIRITUALS; VOODOO.

NEGROPONTE. See EUBŒA.

NEGRO, RIO, river in Argentina, formed by the junction of the Limay and Neuquen. Its length is some 650 m., and it reaches the Atlantic Ocean in latitude 41° 2′ s.

NEGROS OCCIDENTAL, province occupying the N. and W. shores of Negros, an island (area, 4905 sq.m.; pop., about 400,000) in the Philippines between Panay and Cebu. Bacolod is the capital of the province. The country has forests and coal of great value. The soil is fertile and under irrigation yields tobacco, coffee, and sugar cane. Area, 3110 sq.m.; pop., about 310,000.

NEGROS ORIENTAL, province of Negros, one of the Philippine Islands. The capital is Dumaguete. Malaspino, or Canlaon, a volcano 8190 ft. high, is situated in this province. Crops of tobacco and sugar cane are raised. Manufactures are sugar, sugar sacks, and cotton pillows. Area, 1740 sq.m.; pop., about 200,000.

NEHEMIAH, or (in the Douay Bible) NEHEMIAS, Jewish leader during the 5th century B.C. He held a position of honor in the court of the Persian King Artaxerxes I (reigned 464–24 B.C.) and in 445 was appointed by him to the governorship of Judea with authorization to rebuild Jerusalem. The rebuilding of Jerusalem's walls, and the reforms made during his administration of Judea, are recounted in the Old Testament book of Nehemiah. See NEHEMIAH, BOOK OF.

NEHEMIAH, BOOK OF. The Canonical Book of Nehemiah originally formed the closing chapters of an undivided work, Chronicles-Ezra-Nehemiah, for which two of the most important original sources were the memoirs of Ezra and Nehemiah. See EZRA.

NEHRU, SHRI JAWAHARLAL (1889–   ), Indian nationalist leader and statesman, born in Allahabad. He went to England at the age of sixteen, and was educated at Harrow School and at Cambridge University. Returning to India in 1912, he practiced law for some years and in 1919 joined the Indian National Congress, the principal nationalist or-

British Information Services
Shri Jawaharlal Nehru

ganization of India, led by Mohandas K. Gandhi (q.v.). Nehru soon became one of the leaders of the nationalist movement; between 1921 and 1934 he was imprisoned seven times by the British administration for his activities on behalf of Indian independence. He served as secretary of the Congress from 1929 to 1939, and in the latter year was elected its president, a position he subsequently held three times. Although Nehru remained a supporter of Gandhi until the latter's death in 1948, he did not share Gandhi's belief in passive resistance as a means of driving the British from India. Nehru put forth a militant program involving the adoption of all possible measures short of armed resistance to the British.

In 1942 he replaced Gandhi as the recognized leader of the National Congress Party. Four years later, when the British began their preparations for withdrawal from India, Nehru was elected vice-president and minister for external affairs and Commonwealth relations in the interim government which had been set up to organize a permanent, independent Indian government. During the ensuing year Nehru attempted to prevent the partition of India into separate Hindu and Moslem states, but his efforts proved unsuccessful, and a separate Moslem state known as Pakistan was set up. In August, 1947, following the final withdrawal of the British and the establishment of India as a self-governing dominion within the British Commonwealth, Nehru was elected the first prime minister of India. His writings include a collection of letters published under the title *Glimpses of World History* (1936), and an autobiography published in the United States as *Toward Freedom* (1941); his addresses and articles were collected under the titles *The Unity of India* (1937–40) and *Independence and After, 1946–1949* (1950). See INDIA: *History.*

NEIHARDT, JOHN GNEISENAU (1881–   ), American poet, born in Sharpsburg, Ill., and educated at Nebraska Normal College, the University of Nebraska, and Creighton College. From 1901 to 1907 he lived among the Omaha Indians to study their habits. In 1921 he was made poet laureate of Nebraska, and in 1923 he became professor of poetry at the State university. He became literary editor of the St. Louis *Post-Dispatch* in 1926. From 1944 to 1948 he held positions with the Office of Indian Affairs, Chicago. After 1948 he was lecturer in English at the University of Missouri. His poetry, epic and lyric, deals mainly with the American Indians, and includes *Songs of Hugh Glass* (1915), *Song of the Indian Wars* (1925), and *Song of the Messiah* (1935). His prose works, essays, novels, and short stories, include *The River and I* (1910), *Indian Tales and Others* (1926), and *When the Tree Flowered* (1951).

NEJD. See SAUDI ARABIA.

NELSON, BYRON (1912–   ), American professional golfer, born in Fort Worth, Texas, and educated at the public schools there. While still in high school he won the junior championship at the local country club, where he worked as a caddy. He played his first professional match in 1932 in Texarkana, Texas and Arkansas, placing third. The first professional match which he won was the New Jersey Open in 1935. Thereafter he won such notable tournaments as the Professional Golfers' Championship (1940, 1944, 1945), Canadian Professional Golfers' Championship (1945), and All-America Open (1941, 1942, 1944, 1945). He was chosen "Athlete of the Year" by the Associated Press sports writers in 1944 and 1945, and was the leading money winner in those years, setting a record of $52,511 in 1945. His average of 68.33 strokes for 120 rounds set a new record in 1945. He retired from active competition in the United States in 1946, but played in international matches as a member of the United States Ryder Cup team in 1947.

NELSON, HORATIO (1758–1805), British admiral and naval hero, born in Burnham Thorpe, Norfolk, and educated briefly at Norwich, Downham, and North Walsham. He entered the British navy in 1770, serving under his uncle, Captain Maurice Suckling. In the ensuing years Nelson gained much naval experience through service on a merchant vessel, on an Arctic expedition, and in the East Indies and the West Indies. By 1779 he had attained the rank of captain. Subsequently he saw battle service in the West Indies (1780), was chosen to instruct the future King William IV of England in naval tactics, studied naval matters in France, and in 1784 commanded the British frigate *Boreas,* stationed at Antigua, West Indies. In the West Indies Nelson married (1787) Frances Nisbet (1761–1831), the widow of a British physician.

Nelson's important services to the British nation were contributed in the course of the French Revolutionary and the Napoleonic Wars (see FRENCH REVOLUTION; NAPOLEON I). Serving under Rear Admiral Samuel Hood, in 1793 he assisted in the occupation of the city of Toulon by allied British and Spanish forces. In the course of a visit to Naples, from which he convoyed troops to help the British at Toulon, Nelson first became acquainted with Emma Hamilton, wife of the British ambassador at Naples; Lady Hamilton subsequently became Nelson's mistress, and his career was considerably influenced by her advice and help. After the allies were driven from Toulon by Napoleon, Nelson assisted Hood in the taking of the towns of Bastia and Calvi in Corsica, and in the further occupation of the island (1794). At Calvi he was wounded in the right eye, the sight of which he eventually lost.

Nelson was made a commodore in 1796. The following year he played a prominent part in the victory off Cape St. Vincent, Portugal, of the British fleet under John Jervis, later Earl St. Vincent, over the fleet of Spain, then allied to France. In July, 1797, Nelson led a rash attack by small boats on the town of Santa Cruz de Tenerife in the Canary Islands, a Spanish possession; the attack failed and Nelson received a wound in the right arm which led to its amputation. The following year he was sent to discover the purpose of the great French fleet gathering at Toulon. Nelson's ships, reconnoitering off Toulon, were scattered by a storm, and before he could resume his position, the French fleet sailed. Nelson discovered it had gone east, carrying Napoleon's troops for an invasion of

Egypt, and immediately set out in pursuit.

The French fleet had discharged its troops before Nelson came up with it at Abukir Bay; in the Battle of the Nile, August 1, 1798, he destroyed most of the French vessels; the victory cut Napoleon's line of communication with France, and eventually was responsible for Napoleon's withdrawal from the Near East in spite of his military victories there. Nelson then proceeded to Naples, from which the Neapolitan royal family had been driven by French troops and Neapolitan sympathizers with the French Revolution; he was prominent in the action against Naples which resulted in the restoration of the royal family, and for his services he was created (1800) Duke of Bronté by the King of Naples. He returned to England the same year, and the following year was separated from his wife.

In 1801 Nelson became a vice-admiral, but in spite of his rank accepted service under Sir Hyde Parker when the latter was placed in command of the fleet sent to the Baltic Sea to compel Denmark and Sweden to discontinue their economic aid to France. In the Battle of Copenhagen, in which the British fleet destroyed the Danish in the harbor of the capital, Nelson, although second in command, took entire charge of the British operations; when his attention was called at the height of the battle to Parker's signal for the British ships to withdraw, Nelson placed a telescope to his blind eye and declared he could not see the signal. Later that year he was created viscount.

Nelson lived in England during the period of the Peace of Amiens (1802-03) which temporarily ended the fighting between England and France. When war broke out again in 1803 he was appointed commander of the British Mediterranean fleet. He blockaded Toulon, where a large French fleet under Vice-Admiral Pierre Charles de Villeneuve was preparing to invade England. Nelson forced the French fleet to remain in Toulon for two years, but it escaped in 1805 and made for the West Indies. Nelson set out in pursuit, but the French fleet eluded him and, sailing back to Europe, took refuge in Cádiz, where it was joined by a number of Spanish ships. The British blockaded the city, but Villeneuve finally broke out of the harbor and gave battle off Cape Trafalgar, Spain. In the Battle of Trafalgar (q.v.), October 21, 1805, Nelson overwhelmingly defeated the combined French and Spanish fleets, leading the attack himself in his flagship the *Victory*. He was mortally wounded by a French sharpshooter,

Horatio Nelson

however, and died as the battle ended. The British victory put an end to Napoleon's plans for invading England.

Nelson is regarded as the most famous of all British naval leaders and as one of the most noteworthy in world history. He was buried in St. Paul's Cathedral. In November, 1805, in recognition of his services, his brother William (1757-1835) was made Earl Nelson of Trafalgar. In 1849 a monument known as the Nelson Column was erected to Admiral Nelson in Trafalgar Square, London.

NELSON RIVER, river flowing from the N. end of Lake Winnipeg in Canada. It forms the lower course of the Saskatchewan, and falls into Hudson Bay at York Factory, in the estuary of Port Nelson. Length, 500 m.

NEMATHELMINTHES. See THREADWORM.

NEMATOCYSTS. See HYDRA.

NEMATODES or **ROUNDWORMS,** common name for any of the unsegmented terrestrial, fresh-water, or salt-water worms constituting the class Nematoda which includes most of the threadworms (q.v.). Nematodes are almost world-wide in distribution; many of them are economically and medically important, living as parasites in plants and domestic animals, and producing disease in man. Roundworms differ from other threadworms in having an intestinal system, in lacking a proboscis, and in having a long, indented, longitudinal line on each side of the body, marking the course of the excretory ducts. Like other threadworms, roundworms are cylindrical, tapering creatures which secrete an elastic cuticle about themselves. This cuticle is molted four times during the lifetime of a roundworm. Nematodes range in size from species no more than 1/50 in. long to species attaining a length of 4 in. The worms move from place to place by snapping the body up and down; unless the body encounters a projecting obstacle from which it can ricochet it remains more or less in the same place. Nematodes have separate sexes. Fertilization is internal; the young, which resemble the adults, develop without metamorphosis.

Classification of the nematodes is a subject of some controversy among zoologists today. Many include the Gordian worms (see HAIRWORM) as a subclass of nematodes; most zoologists, however, group the Gordian worms in a class by themselves, subdividing the other nematodes into several orders, the most important of which follow.

Ascaroidea, containing almost all of the nonparasitic species. The animal parasites are: *Ascaris* (q.v.); *Toxocara canis,* the common worm of puppies; *Strongyloides* (q.v.); and the pinworm. The plant parasites are: the eelworms, *Heterodera,* producing root knot of cotton (q.v.); and *Tylenchus,* producing earcockle of wheat.

Strongyloidea, containing parasitic species. These are the hookworms (q.v.); *Strongylus* (q.v.); and *Hemonchus,* a common intestinal parasite of sheep.

Filarioidea, the filarians (q.v.).

Trichinelloidea, the trichina worm *Trichinella,* cause of trichinosis (q.v.), and the whipworm.

NEMEAN GAMES, one of the four great Panhellenic festivals of ancient Greece. The Nemean games were held in the valley of Nemea near Cleonae every two years in honor of Zeus, father of the gods. They are said to have been founded originally as funeral games when Opheltes, the infant son of the king of Nemea, was killed by a dragon. The Nemean games consisted of horse races, athletic contests, and poetical and musical competitions. The prize was a wreath of pine or of wild celery.

NEMERTINEA or **NEMERTEA,** a group of unsegmented worms, classified by some zoologists as a separate phylum and by others as a class belonging to the phylum Platyhelminthes, which contains the flatworms. Most nemertine species are marine, but some inhabit fresh water and a few dwell on land.

All nemertineans are characterized by (1) a straight alimentary tract with a mouth at one end and an anal opening at the other end; (2) a closed circulatory system (nemertineans are the most primitive animals with such a system); (3) a long, muscular proboscis used for grasping and defense; (4) an excretory system similar to that of flatworms (q.v.); and (5) a carnivorous diet of living and dead invertebrates. All nemertineans lack a coelom (body cavity). Aquatic nemertine worms are characterized by the presence of many cilia on the surface of the body, which are used for swimming. Separate sexes are present among the nemertineans; unlike normal flatworms, none are hermaphroditic. Many nemertineans possess remarkable powers of regeneration; the process of *autotomy,* or self-fragmentation occurs in certain species, followed by the development of resulting fragments into new individuals. In experiments with a worm about 4 in. long, *Lineus socialis,* the worm was cut into a hundred pieces, each of which developed into a smaller, living worm. The small worms were again cut up, resulting in the production of living nemertineans about 1/50,000 in. long. Many young, sexually produced nemertine worms develop directly into the adult; some undergo a larval stage, called the *pilidium,* which metamorphoses into the adult. Nemertineans range from a minute fraction of an inch to about 15 feet in length. The largest nemertinean is *Cerebratulus lacteus,* a flesh-colored marine species, found in U.S. coastal sands from Maine to Florida. Aquatic nemertineans build burrows in the sand or mud of the ocean bottom, or conceal themselves in clumps of algae; the few terrestrial species are usually parasitic on land crabs or mollusks.

The nemertineans are classified in three orders: Paleonemertina, containing long, slender, marine species, such as *Carinella pellucida* and *Cephalothrix linearis,* which have transverse outer muscular layers; Metanemertina, similar to Paleonemertina, but characterized by a proboscis armed with spines or *stylets,* containing the widespread marine genus *Tetrastemma* and many other marine, fresh-water, and terrestrial species; and Heteronemertina, a marine order having longitudinal outer muscular layers, containing the common genera *Lineus* and *Cerebratulus.*

NEMESIS, in Greek mythology, the personification of divine justice, and later the goddess of vengeance or retribution. The early Greek poet Hesiod describes her as a goddess, the daughter of Night. Nemesis seems originally to have been the distributor of good or bad fortune to mortals, in proportion to the deserts of each. According to the writers of Greek tragedy, Nemesis was the being to whom was entrusted the execution of strict retribution; hence she punished arrogance and avenged crime, and was regarded as akin to Ate (q.v.), the goddess of vengeance, and to the Eumenides, or Furies. Nemesis was sometimes called *Adrastia*, "she from whom there is no escape", and *Rhamnusia*, from the district of Rhamnus, in Attica, where she had a celebrated sanctuary. At Rome, Nemesis was also worshiped as a goddess, especially by gladiators and victorious generals, and was sometimes identified with Fortuna (q.v.), the Roman goddess of chance.

NEMIROVICH-DANCHENKO, Vladimir (1857–1943), Russian theatrical director, dramatist, actor, and novelist, born in Tiflis, Russia. He early manifested an interest in the theater, participating in amateur dramatic productions and subsequently becoming drama and music critic for newspapers and magazines in St. Petersburg (Leningrad) and Moscow. Notable among his novels are *A Drama Behind the Scenes, Literary Pensioners,* and *Mist*. Nemirovich-Danchenko wrote his first play, *The Wild Rose* (1882), in fulfillment of a wager. His succeeding dramas included *The Happy Man, Gold, A New Affair,* and *The Value of Life*. In 1898 he and the distinguished Russian producer Konstantin Sergeevich Alekseev, known professionally as Stanislavski, founded the famous Moscow Art Theater. The history of this institution is recounted by Nemirovich-Danchenko in *My Life in the Russian Theater* (1936).

NEO-CELTIC MOVEMENT, the literary and scholarly activities concerned with the culture and history of the ancient Celtic peoples (see CELTIC PEOPLES AND LANGUAGES). The designation is specifically applied to the Celtic movement in late 19th-century Ireland, otherwise known as the Irish Literary Revival, which included original literary creation in the Celtic vein and translations from ancient Gaelic texts. Associated with this movement was the Gaelic League (q.v.), a society organized to revive, foster, and encourage the use of Gaelic as a spoken tongue. Prominent members of the Neo-Celtic Movement were the Irish poet William Butler Yeats, the Irish dramatist John Millington Synge, the Irish playwright and translator Lady Augusta Gregory, the Scottish poet William Sharp (Fiona Macleod), and the English scholar

Alfred Trübner Nutt. See also CELTIC ART; CELTIC CHURCH; GAELIC LANGUAGE; GAELIC LITERATURE; IRISH LITERATURE.

NEODYMIUM, a metallic element, member of the cerium subgroup of rare-earth elements, atomic number 60, atomic weight 144.27, symbol Nd. It was isolated in 1885 by the Austrian chemist Baron Carl Auer von Welsbach, who separated it from praseodymium (q.v.). Neodymium and praseodymium had previously been regarded as a single element, called didymium. Neodymium ranks twenty-ninth in order of abundance of all the elements in the earth's crust. It is slightly yellow in color, has a specific gravity of 6.9 and melting point 840° C. (1544° F.). It forms trivalent salts, which are rose red or reddish violet in color. The metal and its compounds have no important commercial application. See RARE EARTHS.

NEOLITHIC PERIOD. See STONE AGE.

NEON, a gaseous element, atomic number 10, atomic weight 20.183, symbol Ne. It is one of the inert gases of the atmosphere (q.v.) and constitutes eighteen parts per million in the gaseous portion of the atmosphere. Neon was first separated from other inert gases in 1898 by the British chemists Sir William Ramsay and Morris William Travers. It is a colorless, odorless, monatomic gas, with specific gravity 0.696, m.p. −248.67° C. (−415.57° F.), and b.p. −245.9° C. (−410.6° F.). Neon occurs naturally in three stable isotopic forms, Ne-20 (isotope with mass 20), the most abundant isotope, and Ne-22 and Ne-21. The first demonstration of the existence of stable isotopes (q.v.) in elements was performed with neon in 1912. Like the other inert or noble gases, neon is chemically inactive. It produces a crimson glow in a vacuum electric discharge tube and is used extensively in the familiar neon light of advertising displays. The term "neon light" is often but incorrectly applied to discharge tubes filled with gases other than neon which produce a colored glow; see NEON LAMP.

NEON LAMP. 1. A glass bulb containing the gaseous element neon, at low pressure, and two metallic electrodes. Such neon lamps give a dim orange glow when an electric current, applied across the electrodes, is raised in voltage to the point at which it ionizes the gas in the tube. The voltage at which the glow appears varies with the design of the tube. When gas in the tube is ionized the voltage drop across the tube is nearly constant, no matter how much current flows through the tube. For this reason neon lamps are often used in electronic devices as voltage regulators to provide a constant direct-current voltage. Such lamps are also sometimes used as pilot lamps to indicate whether or not a piece of electrical equipment is drawing current. **2.** A glass tube containing ionized neon, at very low pressure, which shines with a brilliant red glow when a high-voltage alternating current is applied to electrodes sealed in the ends of the tube. Neon lamps of this type, and similar lamps using argon (q.v.), are used extensively for advertising signs.

NEOPLASM (Gr. *neos*, "new"; *plasma*, "formation"), scientific term applied to any region of tissue (see HISTOLOGY) which grows more rapidly than similar normal tissue. Unlike normal tissue, the growth (q.v.) of neoplasms is not self-limiting, and usually continues throughout the lifetime of the diseased organisms. Neoplasms may appear in any tissue of the body.

When tissue in which a neoplasm originates is solid, such as bone, muscle, or connective tissue, the neoplasm is known as a *tumor;* no general name is given to neoplasms originating in liquid tissues, such as blood or lymph. Tumors which spread extensively throughout the surrounding tissues, and which undergo metastasis (q.v.) by sending parts of their substance through the blood stream and lymph vessels are known as *malignant tumors,* and are usually fatal. Tumors which gradually enlarge in their original location, and which do not metastasize, are known as *benign tumors.* Unless the enlargement impedes the function of an important organ, by blocking off a major blood vessel or excretory duct, for example, benign tumors are seldom fatal. Neoplasms of liquid tissues and tumors are specifically named according to the type of tissue originally appearing in the neoplasm, often by adding the suffix "-oma" to the scientific name of the tissue (e.g., granuloma, lymphoma, epithelioma). Malignant tumors are classified in several major groups, chief of which are the *carcinomas* and the *sarcomas.* Carcinoma, or cancer, includes malignant tumors composed of epithelial tissue (see EPITHELIUM). Sarcoma includes malignant tumors made up of connective tissue (q.v.) or of tissues embryologically derived from connective tissue, such as bone and cartilage. Because a large number of the malignant tumors commonly occurring on the surface of the body (e.g., on the skin or breast) are carcinomas, all malignant tumors are popularly but erroneously called "cancer".

Cause of Neoplasms. Neoplasms may be caused by any number of agents. Breast cancer in mice and a type of sarcoma of chickens, for example, are caused by viruses. The method of transmission of the chicken-sarcoma virus is not known; mouse breast cancer is transmitted through the milk ingested by suckling mice. Several other agents are known to cause neoplastic growth: radioactive substances produce several types of malignant tumors in man; beta-naphthylamine, a chemical encountered in factories manufacturing aniline dyes, produces neoplasms of the bladder in man; certain coal-tar derivatives produce neoplasms in man and animals, such as the scrotal carcinoma of chimney sweeps, and one such coal-tar derivative, methylcholanthrene, is closely related to the human sex hormones; chronic inflammation often results in the formation of neoplasms; tobacco-chewing and betel-nut chewing often result in cancer of the mouth; and cancer of the thyroid gland is most common as the result of iodine deficiency in the diet. Other metabolic factors which cause abnormal growth of cells include hormones. Cigarette smoking and smog are considered by many researchers contributory causes of lung cancer (see CANCER). Frequent exposure to small amounts of X rays may produce cancer of the skin or leukemia. Medical studies, reported in 1955, revealed that survivors of the Hiroshima atomic explosion had a high incidence of leukemia as the result of exposure to radioactive radiation.

Incidence of Neoplasms. Neoplasms may appear in persons of any age, but the vast majority appear in those of middle age. Most malignant tumors of persons under fifty occur in women, and most malignant tumors of persons over fifty occur in men. Vegetarians, meat-eaters, and fish-eaters alike are susceptible to the neoplasm-forming diseases; obese persons, and persons with a history of neoplasms in their family, are more likely to develop neoplasms than others. As the span of human life increases, due to the conquest of infectious diseases, the rate of neoplasm incidence goes up; malignant tumors, which were eighth in the list of fatal diseases in 1900, are second in the number of deaths caused in recent years, being surpassed only by heart diseases. Most malignant tumors of women are cancers of the breast or tumors of the reproductive organs; most malignant tumors of men affect the prostate gland and alimentary tract. In 1953 about 229,110 persons died of malignant tumors in the United States. Malignant tumors may usually be effectively arrested if treated soon after they appear, although they may recur after treatment; benign tumors may be removed without recurrences. Ninety-five percent of tumors of the lip and skin, seventy-five percent of tumors of the breast and mouth, and fifty percent of tumors of the rectum and bladder may be cured if treated during the early stages.

Common Symptoms. Malignant tumors produce varying constitutional symptoms according to the sites of the original tumor and of the secondary tumors produced through metastasis. Common symptoms, which can easily be recognized by the layman, include: persistent sores, particularly on or near the tongue; painless lumps or swellings, especially of the breast, tongue, or lips; chronic indigestion and loss of appetite, with abnormal bowel habits; change in appearance (i.e., color or size) of a wart, birthmark, or mole; and bleeding, often painless, from any body opening. Early consultation with a physician when symptoms appear, followed by prompt treatment, usually results in cure.

Diagnosis. The diagnostic procedures vary greatly with the location and type of the neoplasm. Important means of diagnosis include the patient's history; inspection and palpation of accessible tumors; indirect examination of internal tumors by X rays and fluoroscopy; microscopic examination of suspected material after surgery (see Biopsy); and various chemical and clinical tests of the body fluids. Radioactive tracers (q.v.) are also valuable as aids in the detection and diagnosis of tumors. According to medical reports in 1955, radioactive phosphorus is especially effective in cases of stomach cancer. Injected under the skin, the radioisotopes tend to accumulate in cancerous tissue; the presence and location of a malignancy are indicated by a scintillation counter (q.v.), an electronic device which records the radiations.

Because successful treatment often depends upon early diagnosis, i.e., before the appearance of symptoms, numerous attempts have been made to devise a general cancer-detection test that could be used on a mass scale. To be practical such a test must be inexpensive, accurate, and easy to interpret. A new blood test under investigation in 1955 gave promising results in preliminary studies. The test is based on a thickening of the blood serum that occurs in cancer patients. Medical reports indicate that differences between the blood serum of persons with and without cancer can be measured easily by optical methods. Found to be over 90 percent accurate, the test yielded best results in cases of cancer in its early stages.

Treatment. Most benign tumors can be removed by surgery. Malignant tumors are treated chiefly by radiation with X rays or radioactive chemicals or by surgery; sometimes a combination of both methods is used. Analgesics are commonly used to relieve the pain of malignant tumors and psychotherapy is administered to remove the patient's fears. In cases of neoplasm of the breast and ovary in the female and of the prostate gland in the male, administration of the sex hormones which predominate in the opposite sex often relieves pain and temporarily arrests neoplastic growth. Nitrogen mustard, a derivative of mustard gas, has shown remarkable specific action against Hodgkin's disease (q.v.), producing temporary remission of this fatal ailment; although the remissions are only temporary, continuous careful use of the chemical greatly extends the life span of persons afflicted with this neoplasm. Radioactive isotopes of iodine have proved valuable in arresting cancer of the thyroid gland. Folic acid, a vitamin of the B group, has been found essential for the growth of certain neoplasms; folic-acid antagonists, i.e., drugs which inhibit the action of folic acid, such as aminopterin, have been useful in lessening discomfort and prolonging the lives of some patients with leukemia (see Leucocytosis and Leukemia).

History. Fossil remains of the prehistoric Java man indicate that he had a bone tumor. Neoplasms have been recorded for over 4000 years, and were named "cancer" by the ancient Romans (Lat. *cancer,* "crab") because the spreading extensions of carcinoma of the breast and skin resemble the appendages of a crab. Among the ancient and ineffective remedies for neoplasms, some of which are still used in some regions today, are crab flesh, colored salves, clay, tea, laxatives, diuretics, silver, gold, mercury, cold packs, hot packs, acids, alkalis, herbs, toads, and snake venom. One of the first scientific observations on neoplasms was made in 1775 by the English physician Percival Potts, who noted that the incidence of scrotal tumors was highest in chimney sweeps; since that time hundreds of carcinogenic compounds have been isolated and synthesized and carcinomas have been artificially produced in many lower animals. In 1935 the American pathologist John Bittner, working with strains of mice which are highly susceptible to breast cancer, discovered that many young "susceptible" mice suckled by adult mice of "nonsusceptible" strains do not develop cancer, and that "nonsusceptible" young suckled by "susceptible" adult mice develop breast cancer. Bittner postulated a "milk factor" in the transmission of mouse breast cancer. In 1949 this factor was proven to be a virus. The difference in life span between humans and mice, and the difficulty of rearing humans in controlled conditions make application of this discovery to human breast cancer virtually impossible. Current research projects include attempts to produce antibody-like substances in animals by injecting cancerous tissue which would act as an antibody stimulant, attempts to produce antienzymes and chemicals which would interfere with neoplasm nutrition, and work with various radioisotopes in search of substances which will kill neoplastic tissue without damaging normal tissue. Attempts are also being made to produce chemotherapeutic agents which will inhibit the rapid reproduction of malignant-tumor cells by removing certain basic constituents of their chromosomes; 2,6-diaminopurine is such a chemical which neutralizes adenine, a constituent of animal chromosomes; its use has been found effective in arresting the growth of malignant tumors in chickens and other animals.

In 1955 viruses were employed for the first time in experimental cancer therapy. Two types capable of destroying malignant cells in test tubes were grown in human-cancer tissue. Researchers believe that such viruses may lose the ability to multiply readily in normal cells and thus will attack the malignancy in cancer patients without infecting noncancerous tissues. See CANCER; VIRUS.

NEOPLATONISM, the collective designation for the philosophical and religious doctrines of a school of Greco-Alexandrian speculative thinkers who sought to synthesize the metaphysical ideas of the Greek philosopher Plato and conceptions derived from Judaism (see JEWS) and from other Eastern religions and philosophies. By extension the term is applied to similar metaphysical theories expounded in medieval, Renaissance, and modern times. Neoplatonism is a type of idealistic monism in which the ultimate reality of the universe is held to be an infinite, incogitable, perfect One (see IDEALISM; METAPHYSICS; MONISM). From this One emanates *nous* (pure intelligence), whence in turn is derived the world-soul, the creative activity of which engenders the lesser souls of human beings. The world-soul is conceived as an image of the nous, even as the nous is an image of the One; both the nous and the world-soul, despite their differentiation, are thus consubstantial with the One. The world-soul, however, being intermediate between the nous and the material world, has the option either of preserving its integrity and imaged perfection or of becoming altogether sensual and corrupt. The same choice is open to each of the lesser souls. When, through ignorance of its true nature and identity, the human soul experiences a false sense of separateness and independence, it becomes arrogantly self-assertive and falls into sensual and depraved habits. Salvation for such a soul is still possible, the Neoplatonist maintains, by virtue of the very freedom of will which enabled it to choose its sinful course. The soul must reverse that course, tracing in the opposite direction the successive steps of its degeneration, until it is again united with the fountainhead of its being. The actual reunion is accomplished through a mystical experience (see MYSTICISM) in which the soul knows an all-pervading ecstasy.

Doctrinally, Neoplatonism is characterized by a categorical opposition between the spiritual and the carnal (elaborated from Plato's dualism of Idea and Matter); by the metaphysical hypothesis of mediating agencies (nous, world-soul) which transmit the divine power from the One to the many; by an aversion to the world of sense; and by the necessity of liberation from a life of sense through a rigorous ascetic discipline.

Neoplatonism originated at Alexandria, Egypt, early in the 3rd century A.D. Its founder was the philosopher Ammonius, surnamed Saccas ("the sack bearer"), in allusion to his early occupation as a porter. The foremost exponent of Neoplatonism was the Roman philosopher Plotinus (q.v.), whose *Enneads* contain a comprehensive exposition of Neoplatonic metaphysics. Other important Neoplatonic thinkers were Proclus (q.v.), Porphyry, Iamblichus, and Synesius. Although a number of medieval theologians and philosophers, notably the German mystic Johannes Eckhart, were deeply influenced by Neoplatonism, Roman Catholic dogmatists condemned its unorthodox tenets. In the 15th century, however, Neoplatonism became more generally accepted. The Roman Catholic speculative philosopher Nicholas of Cusa and other mystics sought to overcome the doubt arising from the limitations of human knowledge by espousing the theory of man's direct intuition of God, a theory closely akin to the Neoplatonic doctrine that the soul in a state of ecstasy has the power to transcend all finite limitations. The Humanists (see HUMANISM) of the Italian Renaissance, in their reaction against the previously dominant rationalistic philosophy (see RATIONALISM) of the Greek philosopher Aristotle, turned to the idealistic metaphysics of Plato, and thence to Neoplatonism. Notable in this connection was the scholar Marsilio Ficino who, under the patronage of the wealthy nobleman Cosimo di Medici, translated and annotated the works of Plotinus, Porphyry, and Iamblichus. In England, the so-called Cambridge Platonists (q.v.) exhibited marked affinities with Neoplatonic philosophers. The elements of asceticism and unworldliness in Neoplatonism appealed strongly to the Fathers and Doctors of the Christian Church. The great theologian and philosopher St. Augustine, in his *Confessions,* acknowledges the contribution of Neoplatonism to Christianity, and indicates the profound influence exerted by its doctrines upon his own religious thinking.

NEOPRENE. See RUBBER, SYNTHETIC.

NEOPTOLEMUS, also called PYRRHUS, in Greek legend and poetry, the son of the warrior Achilles (q.v.) and Deidamia, daughter of King Lycomedes of Scyros. Neoptolemus was reared at Scyros and, after the death of Achilles, was taken to Troy by the hero Odysseus in the final year of the Trojan War, since it was prophesied that the Greeks could not take Troy without his assistance. When the city was captured, Neoptolemus killed Priam, King of Troy, and sacrificed Polyxena, daughter of Priam and Hecuba, to the spirit of his dead father. In the apportioning of the Trojan captives, Andromache, widow of the slain hero Hector, fell to the lot of Neoptolemus and was taken by him to Greece. He abandoned his father's kingdom in Thessaly, and settled in Epirus. He was later considered the ancestor of the Molossian kings of that region. He married Hermione, daughter of Menelaus and Helen, king and queen of Sparta, and was slain at Delphi by Orestes (q.v.), son of Agamemnon and Clytemnestra, who had been a suitor for the hand of Hermione. Neoptolemus was buried within the precincts of the temple at Delphi, where he was afterward worshiped as a hero. In earlier Greek poetry, such as the *Philoctetes* (about 409 B.C.) of the dramatist Sophocles, Neoptolemus is portrayed as a noble youth of high ideals, but in later Roman works, such as the *Æneid* of Publius Vergilius Maro, usually known as Vergil, and in the *Troades* "Trojan Women", a tragedy by

Lucius Annæus Seneca, he is described as a cruel and bloodthirsty villain; in this latter capacity he is called Pyrrhus.

NEOSHO RIVER, river rising in Morris Co., Kans., and flowing generally S.E., entering Oklahoma, and joining the Arkansas R. near Fort Gibson. Its length is 200 miles.

NEOTROPICAL REGION. See GEOGRAPHICAL DISTRIBUTION OF ANIMALS.

NEPAL, kingdom of Asia, bounded by China on the N. and by the Union of India on the E., S., and W. The main range of the Himalaya extends along the N. border; in this region are Mt. Everest and Kanchenjunga, respectively the highest and third-highest peaks in the world, Mt. Dhaulagiri, and several other peaks with elevations of more than 20,000 ft. The mountainous central portion, with ranges averaging 8000 ft. in height, has small, fertile, and thickly populated valleys, notably the Valley of Nepal, or Katmandu, to the E. In the extreme S., the terrain forms part of the Terai, a region of swampy lowlands, jungles, and areas suitable for cultivation. The Terai abounds with wildlife, including the elephant, rhinoceros, tiger, leopard, black bear, gaur, buffalo, and wolf. The principal rivers, all of which flow southward into the Ganges, are the Kali, Karnali, Gandak, and Kosi. Because of the rugged terrain Nepal is deficient in modern transportation facilities; there are about 65 m. of narrow-gauge railroad lines, about 240 m. of vehicular highways, and airplane service between Katmandu and Calcutta, India. The bulk of freight leaving and entering the country is transported by porters and pack animals.

Nepal has diversified natural resources, particularly timber, limestone, marble, coal, mica, graphite, copper, and deposits of quartz, sapphire, and ruby. Most of the inhabitants are engaged in agriculture. In 1947 more than 7,600,000 acres of land were under cultivation. Wheat, jute, rice, barley, maize, cotton, medicinal herbs, spices, oilseed, and oranges are the chief crops; cattle and sheep are raised. Industrial establishments include jute, sugar, textile, and lumber mills, and factories producing matches, soap, chemicals, and pottery.

The Nepalese are largely of Mongoloid origin; however, the dominant Gurkhas originated in India. The Newar and Sherpa are major native tribes. Hinduism is the leading religion, but Buddhism is common, especially in the remoter areas. Katmandu (q.v.) is the capital and largest city. Other cities of appreciable size are Bhadgaon and Patan (qq.v.). Area, 54,000 sq.m.; pop. (1953 est.) 8,596,000.

H. Davis, from Black Star

Children in the main square of Patan, a town in Nepal

History: Little of an authentic nature is known regarding ancient and early-medieval Nepalese history. Forces under a Rajput raja, in flight from invading Moslems, overran Nepal in 1324, and his descendants continued to rule until 1768. In the latter year the country was seized by invading Gurkhas. Following consolidation of their power, in 1790 the Gurkhas attempted the conquest of Tibet, but they were defeated two years later by a Chinese force, which briefly occupied part of Nepal. Relations between the Gurkhas and the British in India were governed by treaty from 1791 to 1803, when, as a result of frontier disputes, the British withdrew their representative from the Nepalese capital. Friction increased steadily during the next decade, and finally, in November, 1814, the British declared war on Nepal. The ensuing conflict ended in victory (1815) for the British. Under the terms of the peace agreement, ratified in 1816, the Nepalese government relinquished an extensive section of the Terai and other border territories. Pro-British and anti-British groups in the ruling circles of Nepal contended for power during the next thirty years. In 1846 the pro-British army leader Jung Bahadur Rana seized control of the government and became prime minister. Jung Bahadur initiated a long period of political domination by the Rana family, in which the office of prime minister was made hereditary. In 1854 Jung Bahadur launched a successful invasion of Tibet. By the provisions of the peace treaty (1856) Tibet granted diplomatic and commercial rights to Nepal and agreed in addition to the payment of a yearly tribute. Nepal rendered valuable assistance to the British during the Indian Mutiny (1857–59) and during World War I. The British government reaffirmed the independence of Nepal by the terms of a treaty concluded in 1923. Nepal supported the Allied cause during World War II. The Nepalese and U.S. government established diplomatic relations in 1948.

The hereditary Rana regime was subjected to increasing criticism during 1949, particularly by dissidents residing in India. The political-reform movement, which was approved by the Indian Union government and directed by the newly created Nepalese Congress Party, won the support of Maharajadhiraja (King) Tribhuvana. Like his predecessors under the Ranas, he possessed purely nominal powers. However, his intervention in domestic politics deepened the crisis, and on Nov. 7, 1950, Prime Minister Maharaja Mohan Shumshore Rana removed him from the throne. A few days later the king fled to the Union of India and Nepalese Congress insurgents began military operations along the southern frontier. The Indian Union prime minister Jawaharlal Nehru, refusing to recognize King Tribhuvana's deposition, requested the reorganization of the Nepalese government along democratic lines and the election of a constituent assembly.

Prime Minister Rana acceded to Nehru's suggestions on Jan. 8, 1951. Within the next few weeks representatives of the Congress Party were installed in the cabinet. The king returned to the Nepalese capital on Feb. 15.

Friction between the Rana and Congress Party factions culminated (Nov. 16, 1952) in the removal of Prime Minister Rana from power and the formation of a Congress Party-Independent cabinet headed by the Congress Party leader Matrika Prasad Koirala.

As a first step toward the establishment of constitutional rule, the king convened an advisory assembly at Katmandu on July 4, 1952. The cabinet resigned on Aug. 8, as a result of disagreements among the Congress Party leaders, and the king, assisted by five advisers, assumed direct control of the government. On June 15, 1953, former prime minister Koirala, head of the newly created National Democratic Party, formed a new government in coalition with independents. The Indian Union extended substantial economic aid to Nepal during 1953 and helped the Nepalese government suppress a communist uprising in the s.w. border region. Floods and landslides occurred in various parts of Nepal in the summer of 1954, killing almost 1000 persons.

NEPENTHES, genus of climbing herbs, constituting the family Nepenthaceae. Members of the genus are commonly called "pitcher plants", a name applied also to plants of the genus *Sarracenia* (q.v.), or "monkey cups". The genus, which contains about sixty species, is native to bogs in the East Indies, Madagascar, the Philippines, and northern Australia, and is widely cultivated in greenhouses. The flowers, which are inconspicuous, produce capsular fruits. Pitcher plants have long leaves which branch directly from the main stem. The midrib extends beyond the tip of the leaf to form a tendril, which is used for support as the plant "climbs" on larger plants. At the end of the tendril, the midrib expands to form a pitcherlike cup, which varies from the size of a thimble in some species to the size of a quart container in others. The rim of this cup is corrugated, and contains numerous nectar-secreting glands. The interior of the cup just below the rim is slippery, causing insects which visit the pitchers in search of nectar to fall into the interior. The bottom of the cup contains water in which the insects drown, and secretes acid and enzymes to convert the insects' bodies into simple mineral-containing compounds used as food by the plants; see CARNIVOROUS PLANTS.

NEPHELINE or **NEPHELITE,** a mineral composed of sodium-potassium aluminum silicate $(Na,K)(Al,Si)_2O_4$. It crystallizes in the hexagonal system, sometimes in small, prismatic, transparent crystals, but most often in compact, translucent masses called *eleolite*.

The color of eleolite is gray, greenish, or reddish; that of the crystalline variety is white or yellowish. Nepheline has a hardness ranging from 5½ to 6 and a specific gravity ranging from 2.55 to 2.65. The massive variety has a greasy luster and the crystalline variety has a vitreous luster. The mineral shows a distinct prismatic cleavage. Nepheline occurs in igneous rocks; it is present as glassy crystals in some recent lavas, such as those of Mt. Vesuvius, and as eleolite in older rocks. The largest known mass of nepheline rocks is located on the Kola Peninsula, U.S.S.R. Extensive masses are also present in Canada, Norway, and South Africa. In the United States massive and crystalline nepheline are found in Maine, Arkansas, and New Jersey. The mineral is often used in the glass industry in place of feldspar because of its high alumina content.

NEPHRITE. See JADE.

NEPHRITIS, general term for inflammatory and degenerative diseases of the kidney, characterized by edema and by urinary changes. The condition was first described by the English physician Richard Bright (1789–1858) and was therefore originally known as Bright's disease. Nephritis may be acute, chronic, or intermittent, and is generally progressive. Advanced cases are often associated with hypertension and arteriosclerosis. In the United States nephritis ranks high among the diseases which are a direct cause of death. It ranks high also as a contributory cause in such cases as cerebral apoplexy and heart failure. See KIDNEY, DISEASES OF.

NEPOMUK, or POMUK, JOHN OF (1340?–93), patron saint of Bohemia, born in Pomuk, near Pilsen. In 1380 he became pastor and then cathedral canon and vicar-general to the archbishop of Prague. He was later appointed confessor to Queen Joanna, wife of Wenceslaus IV of Bohemia. The king had him tortured and put to death for his refusal to divulge the queen's confessions and for his defense of ecclesiastical rights. He was canonized in 1729 by Pope Benedict XIII. His feast day, May 16, is still observed as a high festival in Bohemia.

NEPOS, CORNELIUS (fl. 1st century B.C.), Roman biographer and historian, born in northern Italy, perhaps in Ticinum or Verona. Although a close friend of the orator and statesman Marcus Tullius Cicero, Nepos had no interest in public affairs and devoted himself entirely to writing. His works included *Chronica,* a chronological outline of universal history in three books, *Lives* of Marcus Porcius Cato the Elder and of Cicero, a geographical treatise, poems, and *De Viris Il-lustribus,* parallel biographies of famous foreigners and Romans in sixteen books. Of this last work, the section on foreign generals is preserved, as are the biographies of the Elder Cato and the literary patron Titus Pomponius Atticus from the section on historians. The extant biographies contain valuable information, but are marred by chronological inaccuracies; according to the manuscripts, they were written by Æmilius Probus, a writer of the 4th century A.D., and formerly some scholars believed that they represented an abridgment by Probus of the biographies of Nepos. Modern authorities, however, accept the biographies as the direct work of Nepos.

NEPTUNE, the third largest of the planets in the solar system. Its mean distance from the sun is about 2,793,000,000 miles; its diameter is about 33,000 miles (slightly more than four times the diameter of the earth); its volume is about 72 times, its mass 17 times, and its mean density about 0.29 times that of the earth. The albedo of the planet is high; 73 percent of the light falling upon it is reflected. The period of rotation is slightly less than 16 hours and the period of revolution about the sun is 164.79 years. The average stellar magnitude of the planet is 8, and it is therefore never visible to the naked eye. In the telescope it appears as a small, round, greenish-blue disk without definite surface markings. The temperature of the observable surface of Neptune is very low; it is estimated to be at least –200° C. (–328° F.). Spectrographic analysis indicates the presence of large amounts of methane in the atmosphere. Neptune has two known satellites. The first satellite, which was discovered shortly after the planet itself, is estimated to approximate the earth's moon in size. The second was discovered in 1949.

The discovery of Neptune was one of the great triumphs of mathematical astronomy. In order to account for perturbations in the orbit of the planet Uranus, the French astronomer Urbain Jean Joseph Leverrier predicted in 1846, purely on the basis of mathematical calculations, the existence and position of a new planet. The same year the German astronomer Johann Gottfried Galle discovered the planet within one degree of the position Leverrier had predicted.

NEPTUNE, or (Lat.) NEPTUNUS, an old Italian deity, about whose original worship little is known. He seems to have been a god of fresh water, who as early as 399 B.C. was identified with Poseidon (q.v.), Greek god of the sea, and hence was worshiped as a sea deity. The festival in honor of Neptune, called the *Neptunalia,* was celebrated on July 23; on this occasion the Romans constructed tents or booths of foliage, in which they indulged in drinking and feasting.

NEPTUNIUM, a radioactive chemical element, atomic number 93, symbol Np. Like other elements heavier than uranium (plutonium, americium, curium, californium, and berkelium), it has not been found in nature but is produced artificially. It was first produced in 1940, and was named after the planet Neptune. Neptunium was produced by bombardment of U-238 (the uranium isotope of mass 238) with neutrons, forming U-239. U-239 decays radioactively by emitting a beta particle to form Np-239. The neptunium isotope in turn emits a beta particle, forming the important isotope plutonium-239, one of the materials of which atomic bombs are made. Seven isotopes of neptunium are currently known, all of them radioactive and artificially produced. The most stable neptunium isotope is Np-237, which has a half-life (q.v.) of 2.25 million years. Several hundred milligrams of this isotope have been made and isolated chemically. Scientists believe that neptunium is part of a second rare-earth (q.v.) series, which begins with the element actinium; the chemical properties of the element, which have been explored by microchemical techniques (see MICROCHEMISTRY), are similar to those of the rare earths.

NERBUDDA. See NARBADA.

NEREIDS, or NEREIDES, in Greek mythology, sea nymphs, daughters of Nereus (q.v.) and Doris, daughter of Oceanus. Their number is variously given, although fifty seems to have been the traditional number. The Nereids were the marine nymphs of the Mediterranean Sea, as distinct from the Oceanides, the nymphs of the great ocean, and the Naiads, or fresh-water nymphs; see NYMPHS. The most famous of the Nereids were Thetis, wife of Peleus and the mother of the hero Achilles; Amphitrite, wife of Poseidon, god of the sea; and Galatea, beloved by the Cyclops Polyphemus (q.v.). The Nereid Panope is mentioned by the English poet John Milton in his elegy *Lycidas.* In art the Nereids are depicted as youthful and lovely maidens, riding on tritons and dolphins; often they appear as spectators in scenes involving sea deities, as at the contest between Nereus and Hercules and at the capture of Thetis by Peleus.

NEREIS, genus of common, marine, annelid worms in the order Polychaeta, popularly known as clamworms. Clamworms are large, greenish-blue, segmented creatures, attaining a length of about 1 ft. and a diameter of about ⅓ in. Each segment bears a pair of short, bristly projections, called *parapodia,* which the clamworm uses to propel itself through the water, and through which it obtains oxygen from the water. The head bears several sensory tentacles and two pairs of simple eyes. The clamworm, which is omnivorous, feeds by extending its two-toothed pharynx through its mouth and engulfing passing organisms. During the day the worm lives in a burrow, which it lines with mucus, in the sand or mud of littoral seas. At night it swims about in search of food. Clamworms are often used as bait in fishing. The common species found off the American Atlantic coast is *Nereis virens.*

NEREUS, in Greek mythology, an ancient sea divinity, the son of Pontus, a sea god, and of Gæa, the personification of the earth. Nereus was the husband of Doris, by whom he was father of the Nereids (q.v.). Nereus, called "the old man of the sea", was a wise and kindly god and, like other deities of the sea, such as Proteus (q.v.), had the power of prophesying the future and of appearing to mortals in manifold shapes. The hero Hercules was obliged to wrestle with Nereus and hold him fast in order to learn the way to the Garden of the Hesperides.

Sculpture of a Nereid in Naples Museum

Ancient sculpture of Nero

NERNST, WALTHER HERMANN (1864–1941), German physical chemist, born in Briesen, West Prussia, and educated at the universities of Zurich, Berlin, Graz, and Würzburg. After serving as professor at the University of Göttingen, he was appointed professor of physics at the University of Berlin in 1905 and later became director of the Physikalische Technische Reichsanstalt at Charlottenburg. In 1925 he was appointed director of the Physical Institute at the University of Berlin. Nernst developed an electric lamp, called the Nernst lamp, which was more efficient than the old carbon-arc lamps, but which became obsolete with the development of modern filament lamps. He made outstanding contributions in chemical equilibria and in the theory of solutions, particularly on the diffusion, hydration, and dissociation of electrolytes, and made important measurements of specific heats of substances at low temperatures. He is best known for his enunciation of the third law of thermodynamics (q.v.). He received the 1920 Nobel Prize in chemistry.

NERO (37–68 A.D.), Roman Emperor from 54 to 68 A.D., and the last of the Cæsars, born in Antium, on the coast of Latium. He was the son of the Roman consul Gnæus Domitius Ahenobarbus and Agrippina the younger, the daughter of Germanicus Cæsar, sister of the emperor Caligula, and great granddaughter of the emperor Augustus. In 49 A.D. Nero's mother married her uncle, the emperor Claudius, who adopted him the following year, changing the boy's name, originally LUCIUS DOMITIUS AHENOBARBUS, to NERO CLAUDIUS CÆSAR DRUSUS GERMANICUS. In 53 A.D. Nero, at the age of sixteen, married Octavia, the daughter of Claudius by his former wife Valeria Messalina, thus allying himself still more closely with the imperial family. After the death of Claudius (54 A.D.), the Prætorian Guards, at the instigation of Sextus Afranius Burrus, their prefect, declared him emperor, instead of Claudius' son Britannicus, and their choice was accepted both by the Roman Senate and by the provinces.

In the opening years of his reign Nero displayed considerable ability and many good qualities. He was noted for his liberality and his clemency. Under the guidance of Burrus and of his tutor, the philosopher Marcus (or Lucius) Annæus Seneca (q.v.), Nero ruled with moderation, the first five years being considered a golden *quinquennium Neronis.* Nero had, however, caused the death by poison of Britannicus, Claudius' son, in 55 A.D., and by 59 A.D. his vanity, selfishness, and cruelty were apparent to all. In this year he caused his own mother Agrippina to be murdered to please his mistress Poppæa Sabina. In order to marry Poppæa, Nero divorced and later had put to death his youthful and neglected wife Octavia, the sister of Britannicus.

The affairs of the empire at this time were in turmoil. In 61 A.D. an insurrection broke out in Britain among the Iceni under their queen Boadicea (q.v.), but the revolt was suppressed by the Roman governor Suetonius Paulinus. In the following year a Roman army fought a costly and unsuccessful war against the Parthians in Armenia. At home both the emperor and the senate were bitterly criticized. Burrus died, and Seneca retired to private life. In July, 64 A.D., two thirds of Rome burned completely. Nero was said to have admired the spectacle from a distance, reciting verses about the burning of Troy, and he was charged in ancient times with being the incendiary, but most modern scholars doubt that he was in any way responsible for the fire. To offset the charge, Nero laid the blame upon the Christians and persecuted them with fury. He rebuilt the city with great magnificence and constructed for himself a splendid palace, known as the Golden House, extending from the Palatine Hill to the slopes of the Esquiline Hill. To provide for this expenditure and also for the gratification of the populace by spectacles and distributions of free grain, he plundered both Italy and the provinces.

A conspiracy of many distinguished persons was organized against Nero in 65 A.D., known usually as the Pisonian conspiracy, from Gaius Calpurnius Piso, one of the leaders. The conspiracy was discovered, and many prominent Romans fell victim to the emperor's vengeance, among them Seneca and his nephew, the epic poet Marcus Annæus Lucanus, usually known as Lucan (q.v.). In a fit of passion Nero kicked his wife Poppæa, who died of the injuries sustained. He then proposed marriage to Antonia, the daughter of Claudius, but was refused, whereupon he caused her to be put to death, and married Statilia Messalina after putting her husband to death. Nero's vanity led him to seek distinction as a poet, a philosopher, an actor, and a musician, and he received applause, not only in Italy but also in Greece, which he visited in 67 A.D. The following year the Gallic and Spanish legions, and after them the Prætorian Guards, rose against him, and Nero fled from Rome. The senate declared him a public enemy and the tyrant saved himself from execution by suicide.

NERVA, MARCUS COCCEIUS (about 35–98 A.D.), Roman Emperor from 96 to 98 A.D., born in Narnia, Umbria, to parents of senatorial rank. He was twice consul, in 71 A.D. with the emperor Vespasian as colleague, and in 90 A.D. with the emperor Domitian as colleague. When Domitian was assassinated in 96 A.D., Nerva was elected emperor by the senate, being the choice both of the people and of the soldiers. As an emperor Nerva displayed great wisdom and moderation; today he is known as the first of the so-called "good emperors". The activities of the informers who had flourished under Domitian were checked. Nerva chose senators as his councilors and allowed the senate to perform its traditional functions. He attempted to reduce the costs of the government. Being interested in the economic welfare of Italy, he had the senate pass an agrarian law which provided for the purchase of land for poor citizens. Even more effective was his legislation to maintain the children of poor parents in the towns of Italy at public cost. Because of his advanced age and feeble health, Nerva was not vigorous enough to repress the demands of the Prætorian Guards, who had favored his predecessor Domitian and now insisted on the execution of Domitian's murderers, retained in office by Nerva. Wishing to place the government in strong hands, Nerva adopted as his son and successor Marcus Ulpius Trajanus, usually known as Trajan (q.v.), who was then in command of

the Roman legions on the Rhine R. Nerva ruled for three months with Trajan as his colleague, but died suddenly in January, 98 A.D. He was accorded divine honors after his death by Trajan, who succeeded him as emperor.

NERVE GAS. See CHEMICAL WARFARE.

NERVOUS DISEASES, functional or organic affections of any part of the nervous system. For functional nervous diseases, that is, those showing no apparent anatomical change, see PSYCHOLOGY, ABNORMAL. For organic diseases, see BRAIN, DISEASES OF THE. See also separate articles on such diseases as APHASIA; APOPLEXY; EPILEPSY; HYSTERIA; MULTIPLE SCLEROSIS.

NERVOUS SYSTEM, the chain or network of tissue which transmits impulses from one part of the animal organism to another and controls the reaction of the impulses. The nervous system correlates the effect of a single impulse with other simultaneous impulses, and with impulses previously received and stored in the nervous system as memories. The structural unit of the nervous systems is the *neuron,* or nerve cell; the functional unit is the *reflex arc.*

The neuron consists essentially of a cell body, a number of afferent conducting fibers called *dendrites,* which carry impulses toward the cell, and usually one efferent fiber called the *axon,* which carries impulses away from the cell. The reflex arc consists of a sensory neuron, the *receptor,* which receives an external stimulus and passes an impulse to a motor neuron, which modifies the impulse and passes it to the *effector,* the muscle or gland which accomplishes the response. The simple reflex arc may be modified by one or several interposed neurons acting as co-ordinators of more complicated responses.

In simple animals, such as the coelenterates, the nervous system consists of a *nerve net,* a network of interconnected, unspecialized nerve cells extending through the organism and producing a generalized or local response when external stimulation is applied. In more complex animals nerve cells are differentiated into sensory and motor neurons which, instead of being continuous with each other, as in the nerve net, are connected through a *synapse* in which the axon of one neuron is in contact with, but not continuous with, the dendrites or cell body of another. The synapse is *polarized,* that is, it permits passage of the nerve impulse in only one direction. The complexity of the nervous system increases with the complexity of the animal. In most arthropods the nervous system consists of a trunk of nerve fibers extending the length of the animal, and containing in each segment of the body a ganglion, or concentration of cell bodies, from which nerve fibers radiate to all parts of the segment and connect with other ganglia of the nerve trunk. Large ganglia occur in the body segments containing the specialized senses, such as sight and orientation, and in those concerned with the control of vital functions, such as heart action and digestion. In the higher animals, such as the vertebrates, this arrangement of nerve trunks and ganglia persists as an autonomic nervous system (q.v.), which controls the automatic functions of the body. The principal part of the nervous system, however, comprises the brain and spinal cord (qq.v.) with the peripheral nerves and specialized end organs; see SPECIAL SENSES. The central nervous system is adapted especially for the reception of impulses from both external and internal stimuli, for evaluation and retention as memories of these impulses, and for control of the responses evoked and of the voluntary activity of the organism.

Twelve pairs of cranial nerves arise from the brain in man and the higher vertebrates, and thirty-one pairs of spinal nerves arise from the spinal cord. The first and second cranial nerves are sensory, for smell and sight, respectively. The third, fourth and sixth are motor to the muscles of the eye. The fifth, or trigeminal, is mixed in function, being motor to the muscles of mastication, and sensory to the face, tongue and teeth; the seventh, or facial, is motor to the muscles of the face and scalp and sensory to the tongue. The eighth cranial nerve comprises two distinct nerve tracts, both sensory, the acoustic from the cochlea of the ear, for hearing, and the vestibular from the semicircular canals, for equilibrium. The ninth, or glossopharyngeal, is mixed motor and sensory to the tongue and throat; the twelfth, or hypoglossal, is motor to muscles of the tongue. The tenth cranial nerve, the vagus or pneumogastric, and the eleventh, or accessory, are sensory and motor to the pharynx, esophagus, and the thoracic and abdominal viscera. The spinal nerves arise from the spinal cord in pairs, each member of each pair being formed from two roots, a dorsal sensory or afferent root, and a ventral motor or efferent root. The distribution of each spinal nerve includes elements to the skin and skeletal muscles. In many cases, the spinal nerves form connections with the sympathetic system; thus providing, with the connections of the vagus and accessory nerves, for co-ordina-

tion of the autonomic with the central nervous system.

NESS, LOCH, long, narrow lake of Inverness-shire, Scotland, situated 6 miles s.w. of Inverness, and forming part of the Caledonian Canal (q.v.). It extends in a N.E. direction for about 24 m. The average breadth of the loch is 1 m. and the greatest depth is 754 ft. Its outlet is the Ness R., which empties into Moray Firth (q.v.).

NESSUS. See HERCULES.

NESTOR, in Greek legend, the King of Pylos in Messenia, the son of Chloris and Neleus. He was the only one of the twelve sons of Leleus to escape death at the hands of the hero Hercules after Neleus had refused to grant Hercules purification for one of his misdeeds. Nestor participated in the fight of the Lapithæ against the Centaurs, in the hunt for the Calydonian boar, and in the expedition of the Argonauts. He went with the Greeks to fight against the Trojans; according to Homer in his *Iliad,* he was the aged counselor of the Greeks, renowned for his wisdom and eloquence and for his role as a peacemaker between the bickering young Greek leaders during the early part of the Trojan War. After the fall of Troy, Nestor returned to Pylos, where he later welcomed Telemachus, the son of Ulysses, when the youth came to seek information concerning the whereabouts of his father.

NESTORIANS, in ecclesiastical history, the adherents of Nestorius (d. about 451 A.D.), Patriarch of Constantinople from 428 to 431. Nestorius preached a variant of the orthodox Catholic doctrine concerning the nature of Jesus Christ. The orthodox Catholic doctrine is that Christ has two natures, one divine and one human, which although distinct are joined in one Person and Substance; Nestorius claimed that in Christ a divine and human person acted as one, but did not join to compose the unity of a single individual. Also, according to Nestorius, the Virgin Mary could not be called "Mother of God", as she was termed by orthodox Catholics, because she bore Jesus as a man, his divine nature being derived not from her but from the Father who begot him. The doctrines of Nestorius spread throughout the Byzantine Empire during the 5th century and caused much argument.

The Council of Ephesus (431) finally declared the Nestorian beliefs to be a heresy, deposed Nestorius and drove him out of the empire, and persecuted his followers. The Nestorians sought refuge in Persia, India,

China, and Mongolia; in early medieval times the Nestorian Church was powerful in those countries. It was greatly reduced by later persecutions, and at the present time the Nestorian or East Syrian Church includes less than 100,000 people, located in Persia, Kurdistan, and Malabar. A monument consisting of a stone table 6 ft. 3 in. high and 3 ft. wide was put up by Chinese Nestorians at Changan in 781 A.D. Its inscription, in Syriac, comprises the only extant record of Nestorianism in China. The monument was excavated in 1625; a reproduction of it is in the Metropolitan Museum of Art, New York City.

NETHERLANDS ANTILLES. See CURAÇAO; WEST INDIES, NETHERLANDS.

NETHERLANDS BORNEO. See BORNEO; NETHERLANDS INDIES; REPUBLIC OF INDONESIA.

NETHERLANDS INDIES, NETHERLANDS or **DUTCH EAST INDIES,** and **NETHERLANDS INDIA,** alternative designations of the former colonial possessions of the Netherlands in the Malay Archipelago (q.v.). Officially, they were called the Netherlands Overseas Territories in Asia and included the large islands of Celebes, Java, and Sumatra (qq.v.); most of Borneo and the w. part of New Guinea (qq.v.); and thousands of small islands. At the end of World War II, a nationalist revolutionary army seized control of the islands of Java, Sumatra, and Madura, and in the summer of 1945 the independent Republic of Indonesia was proclaimed in those islands. By the terms of the Basic Agreement of Linggadjati, or Cheribon Agreement, formally signed at Batavia by the government of the Netherlands and the Indonesian republican government in 1947, provision was made for the inclusion of the Indonesian republic in the United States of Indonesia (U.S.I.) comprising the Netherlands Indies; and for constitution of the Netherlands-Indonesian Union, with the Netherlands and the U.S.I. as equally sovereign states under the Dutch crown. Area of former Netherlands Indies, 735,268 sq.m.; pop., about 70,500,000.

Details of the physiography, climate, flora and fauna, population, economy, and history of the large islands named above will be found in the articles in this encyclopedia on those islands. See also BALI; BANGKA; BILLITON; MOLUCCAS OR SPICE ISLANDS; SUNDA ISLES; TIMOR. A description of the present-day economy and government structure of the islands as a whole is contained in the article REPUBLIC OF INDONESIA.

The known history of the Netherlands Indies begins in the early 16th century with the arrival of Portuguese and Spanish explorers, who were followed by traders and settlers. Accounts of earlier epochs are based on tradition and speculation. Scholars believe that Hindu invaders from India, in the first centuries of the Christian era, established kingdoms on a number of islands. Moslem invaders, in the 15th century, converted virtually all the inhabitants of the islands.

By the terms of a treaty between Spain and Portugal in 1529, the Spaniards, in exchange for a large sum of gold, agreed to abandon their interests in the East Indies. During their long struggle for national independence from Spain, the Dutch, in the 17th century, ousted the Portuguese, then under Spanish rule, from the East Indies. See NETHERLANDS: *History*. Domination by the Dutch East India Company, chartered in 1602, of the lucrative trade in spices grown in the East Indies, was an important factor in the development, in the 17th century, of the Netherlands as the leading commercial and maritime power of Europe, and as an important colonial and imperialist power (see EAST INDIA COMPANY: *Dutch East India Company*). Under the rule of the Dutch East India Company, the cultivation of sugar, coffee, and the opium poppy was fostered in the East Indies. Revolts were severely repressed and huge fortunes were accumulated by Dutch traders and investors.

As a result of the participation of the Netherlands in numerous wars, costly in men and money, its economy and power began to decline in the first half of the 18th century. The Dutch East India Company was disadvantageously affected by these developments and also by the competition of the English East India Company. During the second half of the 18th century, piracy and smuggling became widespread in the East Indies, and the Dutch East India Company paid large dividends to stockholders out of borrowed money. Following dissolution (1798) of the company by the Dutch government, the latter, after 1816, ruled its possessions directly.

For the greater part of the following century, the Dutch government was occupied with the restoration of Dutch power in the East Indies, with wars with native rulers to extend Dutch dominion (Sumatra was subdued between 1903 and 1907), and with the development of the agricultural economy of the islands. The years following World War I witnessed the spectacular development of crude-rubber production, amounting, at the outbreak of World War II, to almost 40% of the world total. In these years, the production

Netherlands Information Bureau

NETHERLANDS INDIES

Above: Male dancers of Java. Left: Female Djanger dancer of Bali, wearing gold crown decked with rolled paper and a buffalo-hide collar covered with gold leaf.

of cinchona bark, from which quinine is made, petroleum, tin, and other mineral products also increased, chiefly as a result of large investments by United States, British, and other capitalists. The prosperity of the Netherlands became dependent on the flourishing state of the economy of the Netherlands Indies.

Intensive exploitation of the Indonesians by the Dutch was a continuing cause of political unrest, engendering sporadic uprisings, which were suppressed. Pressure by the Indonesians for political freedom became particularly intense after World War I, and as a result various reforms in the direction of representative government were introduced. Municipal councils with limited local authority were instituted after 1901. An advisory body, called the Volksrad, or People's Council, was established in 1918 to assist the governor-general of the Netherlands Indies, appointed by the Dutch crown. In 1927 the Volksrad was vested with legislative powers jointly with the governor-general, who had the right of vetoing legislation passed by the Volksrad.

These measures, however, did not satisfy the Indonesians, and their struggle for social equality, economic independence, and political freedom continued. In Dec., 1942, during the occupation of the East Indies by the Japanese in World War II, Queen Wilhelmina of the Netherlands announced the constitutional equality of the Netherlands Overseas Territories and the Netherlands. In 1945, as Japanese power began to crumble under the blows struck by the United States, the Indonesian nationalist revolutionary forces seized a favorable opportunitiy to assert the independence of Indonesia.

NETHERLANDS, THE, or HOLLAND, a constitutional monarchy of Europe, situated in the w. central region of the continental mainland, and forming with Belgium and the grand duchy of Luxembourg what are known as the Low Countries. The Netherlands is bounded on the w. and N. by the North Sea, on the E. by Germany, and on the s. by Belgium. The greatest width of the country, from w. to E., is 125 m., and the greatest length, from s.w. to N.E., is 190 m. The total area of the Netherlands is 15,785 sq.m., including the Ijsselmeer or Ysselmeer, a fresh-water lake formerly comprising the greater part of the Zuider Zee (q.v.), and, since 1932, enclosed by an enormous dike, the Afsluit Dijk. As reclamation of land from the Ijsselmeer progresses, the land area of the Netherlands increases; in 1952 it was 12,510 sq.m.

For administrative purposes, the Netherlands is divided into eleven provinces and 1014 municipalities. The provinces are Drenthe, Friesland, Gelderland, Groningen, Limburg, North Brabant, North Holland, Overijssel, South Holland, Utrecht, and Zeeland (qq.v.). The official capital and largest city of the Netherlands is Amsterdam (q.v.). The administrative center of the country and the site of the royal residence is The Hague (q.v.) or (Dutch) *'s Gravenhage*. In addition to the foregoing, the cities of Rotterdam, Utrecht, Haarlem, Eindhoven, Groningen, Tilburg, Nijmegen, and Enschede (qq.v.) have populations in excess of 100,000. The population of the Netherlands (1954 est.) is 10,568,000.

The overseas units of the kingdom are Surinam (Netherlands Guiana) and the Netherlands Antilles (Curaçao); the units are self-

Netherlands Information Bureau

A street in the northern section of Amsterdam, the Netherlands

governing except in foreign affairs and defense. For information regarding Netherlands New Guinea and former colonial possessions of the Netherlands, see *History* below. See also REPUBLIC OF INDONESIA.

Physical Features. Physiographically, the Netherlands comprises the w. extremity of the North German Plain. With the adjoining coastal region of Belgium, the Netherlands is the lowest part of Europe. Most of the country contains neither rocks, natural springs, nor wild trees. The maximum elevation, attained in the hills of the province of Limburg in the S.E., is about 1050 ft. above sea level. Elsewhere in the E. part of the Netherlands, the highest elevation is several hundred feet. The average elevation of the entire country, however, is only 30 to 33 ft. Approximately 13% of the area of the Netherlands lies between sea level and 3 ft. above the sea, and more than 25% lies below sea level.

The principal coastal feature is the deep indentation made in the N. by the former Zuider Zee as a result of a cataclysmic incursion of the sea in the early part of the 13th century. Realization of the vast reclamation projects under way since 1923 will reduce this gulf to a large inland lake. Another striking coastal feature is the area of sand dunes in the w., formed by the wind and the sea in past ages, and extending southward from the entrance to the former Zuider Zee for a distance of about 75 m. These sandy hills attain a height of 100 to 180 ft. and serve as a natural barrier against incursions by the sea. South of the sand dunes and comprising the extreme s.w. part of the country is the delta area created by the wide estuaries of the Scheldt and Maas (Fr. Meuse) rivers. In the delta are a number of relatively large islands, including Walcheren, Schouwen, (qq.v.), North Beveland and South Beveland (see BEVELAND, NORTH AND SOUTH), and Goedereede (area, 83 sq.m.; pop., about 33,000). From the northern extremity of the w. coast, the West Frisian Islands (see FRISIAN ISLANDS) of the Netherlands extend in a north-easterly direction in the North Sea, forming an irregular arc parallel to the N. coast. A large bay in the N. coast, Lauwers Zee, and a smaller gulf at the mouth of the Ems R., between the Netherlands and Germany, were also formed by catastrophic inundations in past centuries.

On the lee side of the sand dunes is the region of the polders, an area of low, fertile meadows, reclaimed in part from the sea and protected against inundation by a multitude of dikes and dams, some of them 60 ft. high; on the principal dikes are roads and canals which comprise an important part of the communications system of the country. As the polders are too low for natural drainage, they are drained by a vast system of engineering works; in former times the motor power for the drainage system was supplied entirely by windmills.

Large rivers are found only in the southern part of the country. These rivers flow in the direction of the general slope of the land, from E. to w., and are important in the commerce not only of the Netherlands but also of western Europe. The Rhine is the great highway from western Germany to the sea. Entering the Netherlands near the town of Millingen, it divides into two principal arms. The southern and main arm, called the Waal R., merges with the Maas. The northern arm, called the Lek R., flows past Rotterdam and empties into the North Sea at the Hook of Holland (Hoek van Holland). From the Lek, a subsidiary stream, the Kromme Rijn (Crooked Rhine), winds northward, past Utrecht, and empties in the Ijsselmeer. Another branch, Oude Rijn (Old Rhine), flows westward from Utrecht to empty into the North Sea at Katwijk. The Ijssel and Vecht rivers also enter the Netherlands from Germany and empty into the Ijsselmeer. The Maas enters the Netherlands from Belgium in the extreme southeastern part of the country. It flows first in a general northerly direction, forming a part of the border with Belgium; near Kuik, it turns westward and flows parallel to the Waal, with which it merges to empty into the North Sea. Of the Scheldt, which rises in France as the Escaut R., only the mouths lie within Netherlands territory.

Climate. The climate of the Netherlands is moist, with a relatively small range in temperature. The summers are not very warm, nor are the winters often very cold. The mean temperature is 49°F. in the spring and autumn, 64.4°F. in July and August, and 35.6°F. in January. The annual precipitation is about 30 inches, rain falling on about 204 days in the year on the average. Most days are misty and damp. Marsh fevers are prevalent in the boggy districts, where the death rate is about a third higher than in the country as a whole.

Agriculture and Industry. The principal industry of the Netherlands is agriculture. Of a total of about 5,770,000 acres devoted to agricultural pursuits in 1952, approximately 3,278,000 acres were pasturelands and about 2,287,000 acres were employed in raising crops. Over 227,000 acres were devoted to

A well-planned system of canals irrigate a typical Netherlands farm, seen from the air.

market gardening, and close to 22,000 acres were utilized for the cultivation of bulbs and flowers (especially tulips). The principal food crops are wheat (327,165 metric tons in 1952), rye (497,000), oats (482,983), barley (239,625), potatoes (3,302,350), and sugar beets (2,789,211). Beans, peas, buckwheat, turnips, carrots, hops, tobacco, and flax are also cultivated. In 1953 the livestock population included 2,930,000 cattle, 1,965,000 hogs, 244,500 horses on farms, and 423,500 sheep. The production of dairy products is an important agricultural industry, carried on in large part under state control. Butter and cheese are the chief dairy products; in 1952 about 73,625 metric tons of the former and 144,292 metric tons of the latter were produced.

Fisheries comprise an important industry, herring and oysters being the principal products. The annual catch of herring, in the North Sea, was in 1952 more than 182,604 tons, and the quantity of oysters was about 1432 tons.

The manufacturing industries of the Netherlands are of smaller importance than the country's agriculture. Included among the diversified industrial establishments are cotton and linen mills, breweries and distilleries; sugar refineries; iron and steel works; shipbuilding yards; motor, engine, and boiler works; plants making hydraulic pumps, hoists, and cranes, and radio and electrical equipment; chemical works; aluminum plants; oil refineries; factories for the manufacture of scientific and optical instruments; diamond-cutting shops; brick and tile yards and pottery works; tanneries and leather factories; carpet mills; clothing and shoe factories; meat-preserving plants and fruit, vegetable, and fish canneries; flour mills, and cocoa, tobacco, and soap factories. Coal is mined in the southeastern part of the country; in 1952 twelve mines produced 12,532,000 metric tons of coal.

Commerce. The principal countries with which the Netherlands conducts foreign trade, in the order of the value of imports and exports, are Belgium and Luxembourg, West Germany, Great Britain, United States, Indonesia, Sweden, France, Switzerland, and Argentina. Trade with Belgium and Luxembourg was greatly facilitated by the Benelux (q.v.) Customs Union which went into effect on January 1, 1948. Among the principal items of import are textile fibers and manufactures, coal, petroleum, iron and steel manufactures, grain, sugar, coffee, tea, cocoa, and tobacco. The chief exports are milk, eggs, and other dairy products, textile fabrics, machinery, chemicals, and fishery products.

Much of the foreign trade of the Netherlands is carried in ships registered under the Dutch flag. In 1953 the country's sea-going merchant marine numbered more than 1400 vessels totaling about 3,274,000 gross tons. Nearly 17,000 barges and vessels were engaged in inland shipping; these craft, which move a tremendous amount of the country's trade, range in capacity from a minimum of about 20 to over 1500 tons.

Communications. A unique feature of the communications system of the Netherlands is the canals, many of which are built on the larger dikes. The total length of the navigable canals and of the navigable rivers is about 4300 m. Railroad trackage, partially destroyed during World War II, was restored after the war and totaled about 2000 m. in 1952. Communications are facilitated by approximately 2500 m. of first-class roads, and over 14,000 m. of other roads. Many of the roads are constructed on the dikes. The Royal Dutch Air Lines (KLM), 95% of which is owned by the government, provide aerial communication with all parts of the world.

People, Language, and Religion. The Dutch population is of Teutonic origin, a large majority (the inhabitants of the provinces of Gelderland, Utrecht, North and South Holland, and Zeeland) being descendants of the Batavi. In the provinces of Friesland, Drenthe, Groningen, and Overijssel, the people are descended chiefly from the ancient Germanic tribe of the Frisii (q.v.); and in the provinces of North Brabant and Limburg, from the Flemings. The predominant language spoken in the Netherlands is called Nederduitsch (see DUTCH LANGUAGE). Closely allied to it is the Flemish language spoken in the southeastern and part of the southern regions of the country (see FLEMISH LANGUAGE AND LITERATURE). In 1947 nearly one half of the population were of various Protestant faiths, a large majority of these being communicants of the Dutch Reformed Church, which has a Presbyterian government. The second-largest religious group is made up of Roman Catholics, who numbered about one third of the population.

Education. Since 1900, primary-school education has been compulsory in the Netherlands, but private schools, supported by the government, are about twice as numerous as

public schools, which are supported jointly by the national government and the municipalities. In 1952–53 the number of private elementary schools was about 4900, with an enrollment of approximately 950,000 pupils of both sexes, about equally divided. The number of public elementary schools was about 2400, with an enrollment of nearly 370,000 pupils of both sexes, also equally divided. Secondary schools, technical and agricultural schools, and schools for instruction in domestic duties, called housewifery schools, numbered about 2900, and had an enrollment of about 575,000. Institutions of higher learning include a number of world-famous universities, namely those of Leiden (founded in 1575), Groningen (1614), Amsterdam (1632), and Utrecht (1636). In addition to the above institutions, which are public universities, are the Calvinist University of Amsterdam and the Roman Catholic University of Nijmegen, an agricultural university at Wageningen, and three other universities, one technical and two commercial. University enrollment in 1952–53 totaled more than 28,000 students.

Government. By the terms of the constitution of the Netherlands, the central executive power is vested in the crown, which appoints the prime minister, the burgomasters of the municipalities, and all the judges of the kingdom. Legislative power is vested jointly in the crown and the national parliament, called States-General. The latter consists of two houses, called the Upper, or First, Chamber and the lower, or Second, Chamber. The 50 members of the Upper Chamber are elected by the governing bodies of the provinces for six-year terms, half of the Chamber retiring, in rotation, every three years. The members of the Lower Chamber are elected on the basis of universal suffrage and proportional representation for four-year terms; the number varies with the size of the electorate and is approximately 100. Voters must be Netherlands subjects 23 or more years of age. Only the cabinet ministers, who are appointed by the prime minister and may not be members of the States-General, and the members of the Lower Chamber may introduce legislation. The Upper Chamber may not initiate legislation, nor may it amend enactments initiated in the Lower Chamber; its legislative powers are restricted to approval or rejection of measures issuing from the Lower Chamber. Either Chamber or both houses may be dissolved by the crown, on condition that a new election be held within forty days and that a new legislative body be convened within three months of the dissolution. In the Netherlands, as in some other European countries, trial by jury is unknown. Minor offenses are tried in the 62 cantonal courts, each court consisting of a single judge. More serious violations of the law are tried in the 19 district tribunals, consisting, for the most part, of 3 judges each. Appeals from the decisions rendered in these courts may be taken first to one of the 5 courts of appeal (3 judges each) and then if necessary, to the High Court of the Netherlands or Court of Cassation (5 judges).

History. The Germanic tribes inhabiting the territory now comprising the Netherlands were partly conquered by the Romans under Julius Cæsar and Augustus in the 1st century B.C., and were subdued by the Franks beginning in the 3rd century A.D. During the disintegration of the Carolingian empire in the 9th century, nearly the entire region was included in the northern possessions of the Holy Roman emperor Lothair I, and later became known as the Kingdom of Lorraine. In the 10th century, after having been included first in the kingdom of the east Franks and then in the kingdom of the west Franks, the region became the duchy of Lower Lorraine, under German overlordship. During the 9th and 10th centuries the Scandinavians made invasions of the duchy; these invasions were repelled largely because of the efforts of local authorities who, in consequence, became powerful feudal lords. As the power of the feudal lords increased, they opposed the authority of their ducal sovereigns, and the following centuries witnessed the rise of such powerful counties and duchies as those of Gelders, Holland, and Brabant. A notable feature of Dutch history in the 13th century was the development of powerful city communes, which, like their counterparts in Flanders (q.v.), under the leadership of the rising bourgeoisie (q.v.), began to challenge the power of the feudal lords and which thus became the spokesmen for political freedom.

During the 14th and 15th centuries, the Dutch, or Northern, provinces of the Low Countries, commonly called Holland, became part of the realm of the dukes of Burgundy, and in the 16th century passed into the possession of the Spanish branch of the House of Hapsburg (q.v.). Oppressive rule by the Spanish aroused the Dutch to stubborn opposition and engendered rebellion. The current of political disaffection coincided with and was reinforced by the great tide of Protestant revolt against the Catholic Church, which was the state church of Spain. Calvinism established itself among the Dutch; however, the Belgians, in the southern provinces of the Low Countries, remained Catholic. During the eighty years from 1568 to 1648, the Dutch and Belgian provinces of the Low Countries, or Netherlands, as they were then jointly called, were the arena of protracted, bitter, and sanguinary warfare in which William, Prince of Orange, played a leading role in behalf of Dutch freedom. In 1581 the Dutch provinces proclaimed their independence from Spain. In 1585 the English came to the aid of the Belgian and Dutch insurgents, and as a result of the destruction of the Spanish Armada by the English in 1588 and the consequent effect upon Spanish might, the Spanish entered into the Twelve Years' Truce (1609–21), under which the Dutch were virtually assured of their independence. At the termination of the truce the Spanish resumed the war, but were unable to subdue the Dutch, and after almost three decades of further struggle were compelled, in 1648, to sign the Treaty of Westphalia, by the terms of which they recognized the sovereignty of the Dutch Republic of the United Provinces.

The first half of the 17th century, during which the Dutch were fighting for national liberty, was also an era of great commercial prosperity and the "golden age" of the Netherlands in art and literature (see EAST INDIA COMPANY: *Dutch East India Company*; DUTCH LITERATURE; DUTCH PAINTING). By the middle of the century, the Dutch were the foremost commercial and maritime power of Europe, and Amsterdam was the financial center of the continent.

The 17th century also witnessed the ascendancy of the Dutch as a leading colonial and imperialist power. From 1619 to about 1667, the Dutch acquired Batavia, Sumatra, and other islands in the Malay Archipelago, which later became known as the Netherlands Indies, ousted the Portuguese from Ceylon and Malacca, and established a foothold on the African continent at the Cape of Good Hope. In the New World, during this period, they opened settlements in Surinam, engaged in extensive conquests in Brazil, took Curaçao and other West Indian Islands, and established New Amsterdam and other colonies in the present eastern United States.

Inevitably the Dutch came into sharp commercial rivalry and military conflict with the English. The issues between the two countries were not settled by the First and Sec-

Netherlands Information Bureau

THE NETHERLANDS

Above: A windmill bordering a canal in the province of Utrecht. Left: On a street in Volendam, fishing village in North Holland.

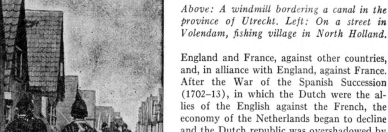

ond Anglo-Dutch Wars (1652–54, 1664–67); see DUTCH WARS. As a result of the latter conflict, the Duch lost New Amsterdam but received Surinam in exchange. Other wars, costly in men and money, followed against England and France, against other countries, and, in alliance with England, against France. After the War of the Spanish Succession (1702–13), in which the Dutch were the allies of the English against the French, the economy of the Netherlands began to decline and the Dutch republic was overshadowed by the expanding might of England.

In 1747 William IV of Orange-Nassau became ruler in all seven provinces of the Netherlands, and the rule was made hereditary in the Orange family; previously the princes of Orange had been provincial rulers. During the French Revolutionary Wars, the French overran the Netherlands and established the Batavian Republic, which was modeled on that of the revolutionary French republic and endured from 1795 to 1806. In the latter year, Napoleon transformed the Batavian Republic into the Kingdom of Holland, and in 1810 incorporated it into the French empire. While the Dutch were under French rule, the British seized the Dutch colonial possessions in Africa and also took Ceylon. By the terms of the Congress of Vienna in 1815, following the downfall of Napoleon, the independence of the Dutch was restored, but the territory now comprising Belgium and then called the Austrian Netherlands was included with the Dutch provinces to form the Kingdom of the Netherlands, under the House of Orange.

Fifteen years later, during the revolutionary tide which engulfed western Europe in 1830, the Belgians revolted and established their independence as a sovereign state. Efforts by the Dutch crown to reconquer the Belgian provinces were frustrated by France and England acting jointly. The second half of the 19th century in Dutch history was marked by the abolition of slavery in the Netherlands West Indies in 1862, by the introduction at home of electoral reforms and social-reform legislation, and by the suppression of revolts in the Netherlands East Indies.

The Netherlands maintained neutrality during World War I, but suffered hardship through loss of trade and the stringent regu-

lations imposed on maritime commerce by the Allies in order to make effective their blockade of the European continent. The principal postwar problems of the country were economic, and these were sharply aggravated by the economic depression of the 1930's. At the outbreak of World War II, the Netherlands again declared its neutrality, but in 1940 was overrun by the Germans, following an aerial bombardment of Rotterdam which destroyed the greater part of the city. Much destruction was also wrought in other parts of the country by the Germans; by the Dutch, who opened many dikes as desperate defense measures; and later, during the war, by the allies in aerial assaults on German-held positions. The Germans occupied the Netherlands until driven out in 1944–45. The years following World War II were marked by intensive efforts to rebuild the country and to restore its trade and industry. In 1945 the Netherlands became a charter member of the United Nations; in 1948 it became a recipient of E.R.P. funds (see EUROPEAN RECOVERY PRO-

THE NETHERLANDS. *Right: Early moated castle at Helmond, North Brabant province. Below: Peace Palace in The Hague.*

Netherlands Information Bureau

Netherlands Information Bureau

IN ROTTERDAM, THE NETHERLANDS

Above: Houses along the Steiger canal.
Left: The Van Nelle tobacco factory.

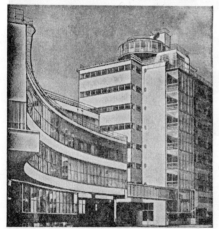

GRAM); and in 1949 it became a signatory to the North Atlantic treaty (q.v.). Meanwhile, during the postwar period, the Netherlands had fought a losing war against Indonesian nationalists in the East Indies. On Feb. 16, 1949, the Dutch agreed to accept in principle a peace plan sponsored by the U.N. Security Council. The plan stipulated that all Indonesian political prisoners be released, that elec-

tions for an Indonesia constituent assembly be held, and that an Indonesian government be established and vested with sovereignty in the Netherlands Indies. The Netherlands and the Indonesians concluded a truce on May 7, 1949, and held a round-table conference between August and November. Agreement was reached on the establishment of the United States (later Republic) of Indonesia, and the Statute of the Netherlands-Indonesian Union was signed. This statute provided for the voluntary association of the two countries in a Union under the Dutch crown. On Dec. 27 the Netherlands formally transferred sovereignty in the East Indies (excluding Netherlands New Guinea) to the Indonesian government. See REPUBLIC OF INDONESIA.

On March 27, 1950, the Netherlands recognized Communist China. Later in the year a contingent of Dutch troops joined the United Nations fighting in Korea. An economic situation marked by high prices and an unfavorable trade balance provoked sharp criticism of the government during the year. There were disagreements also on rearmament, and criticism of official compromise proposals made (December, 1950) to Indonesia on the question of sovereignty over Netherlands New Guinea. As a result the four-party coalition cabinet, headed by Premier Willem Drees (Labor), resigned on Jan. 24, 1951. In March the premier formed another cabinet, which, with the exception of a new defense minister, was identical to its predecessor. On March 19 the Netherlands became a member of the European Coal and Steel Community (q.v.). The government further aligned itself with the Western powers by signing (May 27, 1952) the European Defense Community Treaty, which provided for the creation of a supranational army consisting of French, German, Italian, and Benelux troops.

Meanwhile, early in 1952, negotiations between the Netherlands and Indonesia regarding the permanent status of Netherlands New Guinea had ended in failure; the deadlock resulted from Dutch opposition to Indonesian demands for incorporation of the disputed region into the Republic. In parliamentary elections, held on June 25, the Labor party increased its seats in the lower chamber. A dispute over the proportional representation in the coalition cabinet to be granted the other political parties led to a protracted cabinet crisis. Finally, on Sept. 1, Premier Drees formed his third postwar government.

Early in February, 1953, storm-driven tides, the worst in 500 years, burst dikes and flooded large sections of the country, causing great loss of life and property. Approximately 1800 persons died and almost 400,000 acres were inundated, including fertile farm lands.

The Netherlands completed ratification of the E.D.C. treaty on Jan. 20, 1954, thus becoming the first of the signatory nations to do so. Following rejection of the treaty by France in July the government signed (Oct. 23) the London-Paris accords granting West Germany rearmament rights and membership in the North Atlantic and Brussels treaty organizations. On Aug. 10, meanwhile, Dutch and Indonesian leaders, completing a six-week conference in The Hague, dissolved the Netherlands-Indonesian Union. Several days later Indonesia accused the Netherlands of refusing to negotiate on the New Guinea issue and referred the dispute to the U.N. The General Assembly rejected on Dec. 10 a resolution requesting the two countries to negotiate. On Dec. 15 Surinam and the Netherlands Antilles were formally granted self-rule except in foreign affairs and defense.

On April 28, 1955, Parliament completed ratification of the London-Paris accords. The U.N. General Assembly agreed on Oct. 3 to discuss the long-standing New Guinea dispute.

NETHERLANDS WEST INDIES. See CURAÇAO; WEST INDIES, NETHERLANDS.

NETSCHER, CASPAR (1639–84), Dutch genre and portrait painter, born in Heidelberg, Germany. He studied in Holland under Gerard Terborch and became a member of the Guild of The Hague in 1662. His early work consisted chiefly of skillfully detailed genre scenes. During his later life he devoted himself principally to portraiture. Among his well-known works are "Lady at a Spinning Wheel" (National Gallery, London), "Singing Lesson" and "Violincello Lesson" (Louvre, Paris), and "A Card Party" and "Portrait of a Dutch Lady" (Metropolitan Museum of Art, New York City).

NETTLE, a genus, *Urtica,* of plants of the family Urticaceae, having unisexual flowers, the male and female on the same or separate plants; the male flowers with a four-parted perianth and four stamens; the female flowers with a two-parted perianth and a tufted stigma; the fruit an achene. The species are herbaceous plants, shrubs, or even trees, many of them covered with stinging hairs, which pierce the skin when touched and often cause inflammation and pain.

NETTLE RASH. See URTICARIA.

NETTLE TREE. See CELTIDACEAE.

NEUCHATEL, or NEUFCHÂTEL, a canton in the west of Switzerland, between Lake Neuchâtel and the French frontier. Neuchâtel lies in the midst of the Jura Mountains. Asphalt, absinthe, wine, watches, and lace are produced. Area, 309 sq.m.; pop. (1950) 128,152.

NEUCHÂTEL, chief town of the canton of the same name, situated on the northwest shore of Lake Neuchâtel, 85 miles N.N.E. of Geneva. It is noted for its many charitable, educational, and artistic institutions. There are manufactures of watches and jewelry. Pop. (1950 prelim.) 27,573.

NEUCHÂTEL, LAKE OF, the largest lake entirely within Switzerland. It lies in Neuchâtel canton, 1420 feet above sea level. It is 25 miles long and 500 feet deep.

NEUILLY, TREATY OF, a treaty signed at Neuilly-sur-Seine on Nov. 27, 1919, between the Allies and Bulgaria. It provided that Bulgaria demobilize her army, surrender all arms and ammunition, and carry out certain reparations conditions. In addition Bulgaria ceded small portions of territory on its west-

Ant lion, a neuropteran

ern frontier to Yugoslavia, and gave up part of Thrace. Dobruja, given to Bulgaria in 1878, was restored to Romania.

NEUMANN, JOHN VON (1903–   ), American mathematician, born in Budapest, Hungary, and educated at the Technische Hochschule in Zurich, Switzerland, and at the universities of Berlin and Budapest. From 1927 to 1930 he taught mathematics successively at Berlin and Hamburg universities. He came to the United States in 1930 to join the faculty of Princeton University; in the following year he was appointed professor of mathematical physics there. After 1933 he was associated with the Institute for Advanced Study in Princeton, N.J. He became a U.S. citizen in 1937, and during World War II served as a consultant on the Los Alamos atomic-bomb project. In March, 1955, he became a member of the U.S. Atomic Energy Commission.

Von Neumann is one of the world's outstanding mathematicians. He is noted for his fundamental contributions to the development of electronic computers; see CALCULATING MACHINES. His theoretical work made possible the design of such high-speed calculators as ENIAC and UNIVAC, which played a significant role in the hydrogen-bomb project.

NEURALGIA, term designating the existence of sharp, intermittent pain along a nerve trunk or its branches. The manifold types of neuralgia are distinguished according to the nerve affected or the underlying cause. The pain may be a symptom of a wide variety of diseases, such as neuritis, malaria, influenza, nephritis, arthritis, syphilis, or arteriosclerosis, or it may be the result of toxic conditions caused by alcohol or lead poisoning, or of localized infections of the teeth, ears, tonsils, or sinuses. Neuralgic pain may also be purely psychic in origin, as in the case of hysteria (see PSYCHOLOGY, ABNORMAL: *Hysteria*), and there are certain types of neuralgia, especially those involving the trigeminal or sciatic nerves, for which no adequate organic or psychic cause can be established. Among the

common forms are trifacial neuralgia (also known as *tic douloureux*), intercostal neuralgia, brachial neuralgia, and sciatic neuralgia. The first two types are occasionally associated with herpes zoster (see HERPES). Treatment is mainly palliative, and includes alcohol injection of the nerve and administration of vitamin B_{12}. In *tic douloureux,* an often recurrent neuralgia, permanent relief was formerly obtained only by surgical section of the nerve. In 1954 a synthetic drug called stilbamidine was reported to provide long-lasting relief of the excruciating tic pain.

NEURASTHENIA. See PSYCHOLOGY, ABNORMAL.

NEURITIS, inflammation and degeneration of peripheral nerves, characterized by sensory and motor disturbances, by constant, burning pain, and frequently by numbness or paralysis of the affected parts. There are many types of neuritis, depending upon the causative factors and the distribution and intensity of the disease, but the disorders may be grouped into two broad categories, i.e., simple neuritis and multiple neuritis. Simple neuritis, involving one nerve or a group of adjacent nerves, is generally the result of such localized causes as wounds, pressure from tumors, or prolonged exposure to extreme cold. Multiple neuritis involves several nerves in different parts of the body, tends to be bilateral and symmetrical, and affects the extremities. Infectious diseases, such as typhoid fever, malaria, syphilis, or tuberculosis, heavy-metal poisoning or alcoholism, or vitamin deficiencies associated with pregnancy, beriberi, and pellagra are common causes of multiple neuritis. Discovery and correction of the underlying cause are prerequisite to the treatment of neuritis.

NEUROPTERA, order containing about 1200 species of insects, characterized by possession of four extensively venated wings in the adult, and a larva which undergoes complete metamorphosis and has piercing and sucking mouth parts. The order is almost world-wide in distribution. It is now restricted to the ant lions, golden-eyed flies, and their allies, collectively known as "lacewings". Formerly included in this order, but now classified as separate orders, are the alder flies and hellgrammites (order Megaloptera); the May flies (order Ephemerida); the dragon flies (order Odonata); the stone flies (order Plecoptera); the termites (order Isoptera); the book lice (order Corrodentia); the bird lice (order Mallophaga); the scorpion flies (order Mecoptera); and the caddis flies (order Trichoptera). Insects of these distinct orders have four net-veined wings, but differ in larval development from the true neuropterans.

Adult neuropterans are slow-flying insects which feed on soft-bodied insects or on insect honeydew. Their mouth parts are usually adapted for biting. The large, soft-bodied, active larvae are completely carnivorous and feed on many species of insects economically injurious to man. Most of the larvae are terrestrial; a few species are aquatic in the larval stages. Female neuropterans lay their eggs on the end of a stalklike thread which they secrete and attach to the surfaces of leaves. The newly-hatched larvae fall to the ground or, in the case of the few aquatic species, into the water. All species pupate on land, spinning a cocoon of silk.

In addition to ant lions and golden-eyed flies (q.v.), the order contains the families Hemerobiidae, consisting of brown lacewing insects, and Mantispidae, constituted by the mantis flies. Mantis flies are peculiar tropical and subtropical insects having elongated thoraxes and modified forelegs resembling those of the true mantes.

NEUROSIS. See PSYCHOLOGY, ABNORMAL.

NEUSTRIA, the name given in the times of the Merovingians and Carlovingians to the western portion of the Frank empire, after the quadruple division of it which took place in 511. Neustria contained three of these divisions. It extended originally from the Scheldt to the Loire and was bounded by Aquitania on the south and by Burgundy and Austrasia on the east.

NEUTRALITY, in international law, the complete abstention of a state from giving material aid or encouragement in time of war to any belligerent (q.v.). The doctrine of neutrality as now understood is of comparatively recent growth, dating from the latter part of the 18th century. The principles which gave rise to complicated rules of modern neutrality are in themselves extremely simple. A neutral state, being neither judge nor party, must show absolute impartiality in its dealings with both belligerents; the belligerent must pay scrupulous respect to the sovereignty of his neutral neighbors. Accordingly, throughout a war, neutral states continue diplomatic intercourse with all belligerent states. A neutral state is not permitted to give armed assistance to any belligerent, even though such aid may have been promised before the war; nor to lend money to either side or guarantee a loan; nor to allow the passage of belligerent

troops through its territory. A neutral is bound to prevent and cancel all acts of hostility, either in the neutral territory itself or in adjacent waters.

The relations of belligerent states to the private citizens of neutral states involve greater difficulties. On land the property of neutral individuals is protected from belligerent attack. To this rule, however, an exception is furnished by the Right of Angary under which a belligerent state may seize the property of a citizen of a neutral state when such a property is found in the territory of a hostile belligerent, and make use of it for the purpose of warlike operations. At sea the commercial interests of belligerent and neutral merchants are so interwoven that it is difficult to separate them. Two distinct principles for regulating the maritime capture of neutral property have at different times prevailed. By one principle, the nationality of the ship determined liability to capture, so that neutral goods on hostile ships were liable to confiscation, while hostile goods on neutral ships went free. By the other principle, the nationality of the property determined its liability, so that neutral goods went free even though found on hostile ships, and hostile goods were liable to seizure even though found on neutral ships. In 1856 the Declaration of Paris (q.v.) finally settled the question by providing that the neutral flag should cover an enemy's goods, except contraband of war (q.v.); and that neutral goods, except contraband of war, should not be liable to capture even under the enemy's flag.

Several important exceptions exist to the general rule of maritime capture thus determined. Belligerents continue to have the right of intercepting such articles as are deemed contraband of war, even on board of neutral vessels. The vessels carrying the goods may be condemned along with its contraband cargo, when both belong to the same owner, or when false papers are found, or any other fraudulent device is resorted to. Another instance in which a belligerent is entitled to interfere with the ships and property of neutral individuals is furnished by the law of blockade (q.v.). If, during a war, ships belonging to citizens of neutral states perform certain classes of services on behalf of one of a belligerent state, the other belligerent is entitled to confiscate these ships.

At the conference of The Hague in 1907 (see HAGUE CONFERENCES) conventions were adopted defining the rights and obligations of neutrals further. During World Wars I and

II, however, practically all the rules of war were broken, and all rights of neutrals were violated.

United States. At the outbreak of World War I, this country proclaimed its neutrality. But with the shadow of a new European war on the horizon, Congress, in 1935, passed a Joint Resolution, providing that upon outbreak of war among foreign states, the President shall proclaim such fact. Thereafter the export of arms or implements of war from the U.S. to any belligerent country was prohibited. Traveling of U.S. citizens on vessels of belligerent nations also was restricted. In November, 1939, the arms embargo of 1935 was repealed by a so-called "cash-and-carry" provision, giving every belligerent the right to pay and call for armaments produced in this country. U.S. vessels, aircraft, and citizens were prohibited from proceeding into or through any combat area prescribed as such by the President.

Pressed by continued German submarine attacks on American merchantmen, Congress repealed (Nov., 1941) the sections of the Act of 1939 which prohibited the arming of American merchantmen. At the same time, the ban on carrying cargo into belligerent ports was lifted. With the entrance of the United States into World War II, Section 7 of the Act of 1939, restricting financial transactions of U.S. citizens in favor of any belligerent, was altered.

During the Italian invasion of Ethiopia, the Act of 1935 was enforced and during the Spanish Civil War, the export of arms to the contending factions was prohibited, though in the former case, the government denounced the Italian aggression and the latter was a clear case of rebellion against the legally elected government. See TERRITORIAL WATERS.

NEUTRINO, fundamental nuclear particle which is electrically neutral and of much smaller mass than an electron. In beta-decay processes (see RADIOACTIVITY) the emission of electrons occurs in such a way that the total energy, momentum, and spin (qq.v.) involved in the process are not conserved. The existence and properties of the neutrino were hypothesized in 1933 by the Austrian physicist Wolfgang Pauli (q.v.) in order to account for this inconsistency, and the neutrino hypothesis was widely accepted by physicists even before laboratory experiments proved its existence. Because it has no charge and negligible mass the neutrino is an extremely elusive particle; through the measurement of its recoil effect, however, recent research confirmed the peculiar properties ascribed to it by the hypothesis.

NEUTRON, an uncharged particle, one of the fundamental particles of which matter is composed. The mass of a neutron is 1.00897 on the atomic-weight scale. The existence of the neutron was predicted by the British physicist Ernest Rutherford as early as 1920, but experimental verification of its existence was exceedingly difficult because it bears neither a positive nor a negative charge. It was first detected in 1932 in experiments of the French physicists, Frederic and Irene Joliot-Curie, in which neutrons produced by the interaction of alpha particles with beryllium nuclei were passed through paraffin wax. Collisions between neutrons and the hydrogen atoms in the wax produced protons (q.v.) which were readily detectable.

The neutron is believed to be a constituent particle of all nuclei of mass number greater than 1; see NUCLEUS. Neutrons are produced only in nuclear reactions; they can be ejected from atomic nuclei at various speeds or energies and are readily slowed down to very low or "thermal" energy by collisions with light nuclei, such as those of hydrogen and carbon. For the role of neutrons in the production of atomic energy, see ATOMIC ENERGY AND ATOMIC BOMB. When expelled from the nucleus, the neutron is unstable and decays to form a proton and an electron. Its half life (q.v.) was experimentally determined to be about 12 min. See RADIOACTIVITY.

NEVADA, one of the Mountain States of the United States, bounded on the N. by Oregon and Idaho, on the E. by Utah and Arizona, on the S. by Arizona, and on the s.w. and w. by California. It ranks as the 6th State in the Union in area, 48th (1950) in population, and 36th in order of admission to the Union, having entered on Oct. 31, 1864. The State capital is Carson City (q.v.). In the order of population (1950) the chief cities are Reno and Las Vegas (qq.v.). Area of the State, 110,540 sq.m., including 738 sq.m. of inland water surface. Pop. of the State (1950) 160,083.

Nevada, chiefly a plateau, lies almost wholly within the Great Basin. It is hemmed in on the w. by the Sierra Nevada Mts., and on the E. by the Wasatch and lesser mountains. Numerous mountain ranges from 7000 to 10,000 ft. above sea level and up to 100 m. in length divide the State into a series of elongated parallel valleys extending from N. to s. The highest point is Boundary Peak (13,145 ft. above sea level) in the s.w. portion of the State; the lowest point is in the s.e. and is 470 ft. above sea level. The average elevation of Nevada is 5500 ft.

The chief rivers are the Humboldt, which rises in Elko Co. in the n.e. and flows w. to Humboldt Lake; the Colorado, which forms the s.e. boundary of the State; and the Walker, Carson, and Truckee rivers, which rise in the Sierra Nevadas and flow e. to Walker Lake, Carson Lake, and Pyramid Lake, respectively.

The dominant features of the climate are the low relative humidity and the large daily range in temperature. The rapid radiation, due to the dry air, cloudless skies, and high altitude, make the nights cool. The average temperature during January is 28° F.; during July, 71.9° F. Extremes of 110° F. and —22° F. have been recorded. The average annual precipitation is low, 8.54 inches, and varies from 3 inches in the s.w. corner of the State to 12 inches in the e.

The Federal government owns (1949) 85% of the Nevada lands, the largest percentage in any State. More than 115,000 acres of the Death Valley National Monument (q.v.) are situated in Nevada, and Lehman Caves National Monument, embracing 640 acres, is located entirely within the State. Hoover (Boulder) Dam National Recreation Area occupies about 557,000 acres of the State. National forest land totals (1951) 5,375,000 acres, and about 1,141,000 acres have been assigned to Indian tribes (Indian pop. in 1950, 5025) by the Office of Indian Affairs.

Nevada is rich in mineral wealth. Mining production in 1951 included (in order of value) about 56,000 tons of copper, 17,000 tons of zinc, 121,000 fine ounces of gold, 2,617,000 tons of sand and gravel, 7000 tons of lead, 644,000 tons of gypsum, and 835,000 tons of stone. Uranium, magnesite, vanadium, tungsten, antimony, platinum, cobalt, and nickel also are mined. The total output in 1951 was valued at $57,475,000.

Agriculture rivals mining in economic importance, and the State contains (1950) 3110 farms covering more than 7,000,000 acres. In 1952 the income from crops, livestock, and Federal subsidies amounted to over $54,-000,000. Tenant farmers operated about 9% of the farms and less than 4% of the total farm area. The chief crops are hay, barley, alfalfa, wheat, potatoes, sugar beets, orchard fruits, and vegetables. In the semitropical southern portion of Nevada, figs, grapes, almonds, and pomegranates are grown. In 1953 the livestock population of Nevada included

Ewing Galloway
Nevada State Capitol in Carson City

about 495,000 sheep, 624,000 cattle of all types (including 17,000 dairy cows), 26,000 horses, and 22,000 hogs. In 1952 the wool clip amounted to nearly 4,000,000 pounds from about 443,000 sheep.

Nevada is one of the least important States in the Union in manufacturing. Approximately 125 manufacturing establishments employ (1951) 1825 production workers. Divorce seekers and vacationists add to the State's income. In 1931 the legislature passed a divorce law requiring a minimum stay of six weeks to establish residency. Gambling has been legalized and the State receives two percent of the receipts of each gaming table.

The Southern Pacific, Union Pacific, and Western Pacific railroads cross Nevada from e. to w. and provide (1953) 1646 m. of main-track railway. The State highway system comprises over 3500 m. of roads.

Attendance at the public schools of Nevada is free and compulsory during the entire school year for all children between the ages of seven and eighteen. In the 1952–53 school year 210 elementary and secondary schools employed 1351 teachers who taught over 29,000

Ernie Mack, Reno

IN NEVADA

Above: Virginia Street, the main thoroughfare in Reno, at night. Left: A quiet street in Virginia City, in sharp contrast to bright lights of Reno.

students. The University of Nevada, at Reno, a State-supported school, is the only institution of higher learning in Nevada (see NEVADA, UNIVERSITY OF).

Nevada is governed according to the constitution of 1864, as amended. Executive authority is vested in a governor, lieutenant governor, secretary of state, attorney general, controller, treasurer, superintendent of public instruction, inspector of mines, and surveyor general, all elected for four-year terms. The legislature is composed of a senate of 17 members elected for four-year terms (half every two years) and an assembly of 47 members elected for two-year terms. The judiciary is composed of a supreme court consisting of a chief justice and 2 associates who are elected for six-year terms, 8 district courts, and justices of the peace. The State is divided into 17 counties. Nevada sends 2 senators and 1 representative to Congress.

History. The first European known to have entered the region of Nevada was Francisco Garcés, a Franciscan friar, in 1775. In 1825 Peter S. Ogden, an employee of the Hudson's Bay Company, crossed the territory and reached the Humboldt R. Other trappers followed, though they were constantly harassed by Indians. On Feb. 2, 1848, at the close of the Mexican War (see MEXICO: *History*) the territory from which Nevada was formed was acquired from Mexico by the U.S. in the Treaty of Guadalupe Hidalgo. In 1849 the Mormons (q.v.) founded a trading post in the Carson R. valley near the present site of Genoa. Most of Nevada was included in the Territory of Utah when the latter was formed on Sept. 9, 1850. In 1853 and 1856, the inhabitants of the Carson valley petitioned the Federal government for annexation to California, claiming that the government of Utah was lax in its protection of the settlers.

Until this time, Nevada had been merely a region that gold-seekers passed through on their way to California, but with the discovery of gold at the Comstock lode (q.v.) in 1859, many persons flocked to the area. Nevada became a Territory on March 2, 1861; its eastern border was the 116th meridian. On July 14, 1862, the E. boundary was extended to the 115th meridian, and in 1866 the State achieved its present boundaries. On Oct. 31, 1864, Nevada became a State, joining California and Oregon in being the only States w. of Kansas in this period.

The first transcontinental telegram was dis-

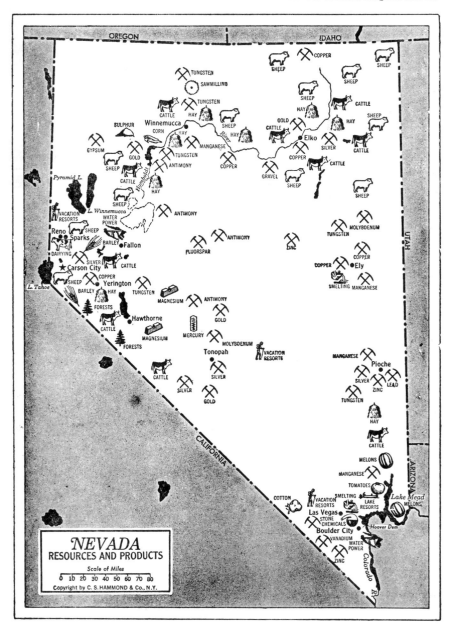

NEVADA
RESOURCES AND PRODUCTS
Scale of Miles
0 10 20 30 40 50 60 70 80
Copyright by C. S. Hammond & Co., N.Y.

Ernie Mack, Reno; International News Service
Above: The Crown Point mine near Virginia City, Nevada. Left: Aerial view of Hoover Dam, Nevada, seen from downstream.

Silver was the chief mineral mined, and when the price of silver fell in 1873 the State suffered a depression which lasted until 1900.

Farming and livestock raising aided the economic recovery of the State. It was discovered that the soil of Nevada was exceedingly fertile when irrigated. The United States Reclamation Act, passed in 1902, was designed to aid in the building of canals and drainage ditches in such States as Nevada. The Truckee-Carson project, which cost $7,-000,000, was the first Federal project constructed in Nevada under the Act. In 1936 the Hoover Dam was completed.

The majority of the people in the State voted for the Republican Presidential candidate in 1872, 1876, 1884, 1888, 1920, and 1928. In 1912 and 1924 third parties polled large votes, but a plurality of the ballots cast was for the Democratic Presidential candidate in the former year and the Republican Presidential candidate in the latter year. In all other Presidential election years through 1948, with the single exception of 1892, when the majority of the ballots cast was for the People's Party candidate, James Baird Weaver, the Democratic Party candidates have received the majority of the votes. In 1952 the Republican candidate Dwight D. Eisenhower received 50,502 votes and the Democratic candidate Adlai E. Stevenson received 31,688 votes.

patched from Nevada to Washington, D.C. in 1864, and it affirmed the loyalty of the State to the Union. In 1868 the Union Pacific and Central Pacific railroads met near Iron Point and the occasion was commemorated by the driving of a gold spike into the ties at the junction of the two lines. In 1879 the Sutro Tunnel, designed to drain the Comstock Lode, was completed. In this period mining camps existed at Eureka, Hamilton, Aurora, Treasure City, Belmont, and Virginia City.

NEVADA, UNIVERSITY OF, a coeducational, State-controlled institution of higher learning, founded as a secondary school at Elko, Nev., in 1874, and established as a university at Reno, Nev., in 1886. It is the only institution offering university-level courses in Nevada. The University confers baccalaureate degrees in the liberal arts and sciences, mining, business administration, and various branches of engineering; master's degrees are offered in the liberal arts and sciences. The mining courses are conducted in a separate division of the University, the Mackay School of Mines; branches of the School are situated at Virginia City and Tonopah, Nev. Accelerated courses are available for students desiring to earn their degrees in three years plus two or three summer sessions. In a recent year, about 1400 men and 500 women were enrolled in full-time courses, and an additional 1000 were taking part-time courses; the faculty numbered about 140 persons.

NEVERS, capital of the French department of Nièvre, at the influx of the Loire, 159 miles s.s.e. of Paris. It has been the seat of a bishop since 506. The *palais-de-justice,* dating from 1475, was formerly the castle of the dukes of Nevers; there is a triumphal arch (1746) commemorating Fontenoy. The industries comprise the manufacture of iron cables, chemicals, cloth, glue, shoes, chains, and porcelain. Pop. (1946) 34,036.

NEVILLE or **NEVILL,** an English noble family, founded in 1131. The outstanding members of the family are the following. **1.** RALPH DE NEVILLE, 2nd BARON NEVILLE (1291?–1367), who supported King Edward III against the invading Scottish barons during the Hundred Years' War, and was the principal commander of the English forces at the victorious battle of Neville's Cross in 1346. In 1355 he became governor of Berwick. **2.** JOHN DE NEVILLE, 3rd BARON NEVILLE (d. 1388), son of the preceding. He fought in the Hundred Years' War, serving in campaigns in France in 1345, 1349, and 1360. In 1370 he became admiral of the fleet, and in 1378 was appointed Edward III's lieutenant in Aquitaine, France. After 1381 he served as warden of the Scottish border. **3.** RALPH NEVILLE, 4th BARON NEVILLE, 1st EARL OF WESTMORELAND (1364–1425), son of the preceding. He was created earl in 1397 for his services as warden of the Scottish border. His second wife, Joan Beaufort, was a daughter of John of Gaunt and a half-sister of Henry of Lancaster (later Henry IV). Neville assisted Henry of Lancaster in his struggle against Richard II in 1399, and was

rewarded by being named marshal of England and, in 1403, warden of the west marches. In 1405 he suppressed a rebellion against Henry IV at Shipton Moor. His daughter Cicely married Richard, Duke of York, and was the mother of King Edward IV and King Richard III. **4.** CHARLES NEVILLE, 6th EARL OF WESTMORELAND (1543–1601), grandson of the preceding. He was an active member of the Roman Catholic uprising in the north of England in 1569. When the revolt failed he fled to the Netherlands and was deprived in absentia of his hereditary estates and titles in 1571.

5. RICHARD NEVILLE, 1st EARL OF SALISBURY in the Neville line (1400–60), son of the 1st earl of Westmoreland. He married Alice, only daughter of Thomas de Montacute, Earl of Salisbury, in 1425. He was appointed warden of the Scottish and west marches in 1434, and chancellor of England in 1454, during the protectorate of Richard Plantagenet, 3rd Duke of York. A supporter of the house of York during the Wars of the Roses, Neville fled to France in 1459 after the battle of Ludford. The following year he returned, and, after his faction had seized the king at Northampton, he was named chamberlain of England. Five months later, after the battle of Wakefield, Neville was captured by the Lancastrian forces and murdered. **6.** RICHARD NEVILLE, 2nd EARL OF SALISBURY in the Neville line, 15th EARL OF WARWICK (1428–71), son of the preceding, and known as "the Kingmaker". In 1449 he married Anne Beauchamp, the daughter of the earl of Warwick, who brought her husband the title and most of the Warwick estates. During the Wars of the Roses he supported the Yorkist faction, and was rewarded with the captaincy of Calais in 1456. He was largely responsible for the Yorkist victories of Northampton in 1460 and Towton in 1461. After Edward IV was proclaimed king, Neville was virtual ruler of England from 1461 to 1464; in 1467, displeased with Edward's favoritism toward his wife's relatives he allied himself with the Lancastrian Queen Margaret. Neville instigated the Yorkshire rebellion led by Robin of Redesdale in 1469, and, joining the exiled Queen Margaret in France, aided her in an invasion of England, during which Edward IV was forced to flee the country. Neville had the weak-minded King Henry VI released from imprisonment in the Tower of London in September, 1470, and actually ruled England himself for the next six months. When Edward IV returned and the Yorkists rallied to his banner, Neville was outmaneuvered and slain at the battle of Barnet on April 14, 1471. He was the hero of Lord Edward Bulwer-Lytton's novel *The Last of the Barons* (1843).

7. JOHN NEVILLE, MARQUIS OF MONTAGUE, EARL OF NORTHUMBERLAND (d. 1471), brother of the preceding. He fought with distinction on the Yorkist side early in the Wars of the Roses. He defeated the Lancastrian forces at Hexham in 1464, and was created marquis and earl. However, he abandoned the Yorkist cause after the earldom of Northumberland had ᴸ᷄ restored to Henry Percy in 1469. He was killed fighting on the Lancastrian side at the battle of Barnet. **8.** GEORGE NEVILLE, (1433?–76), English divine, educated at Oxford University. Through the influence of his father Richard, Earl of Salisbury, then chancellor of England, and of his brother Richard, Earl of Warwick, his preferment was rapid. From 1453 to 1457 he was chancellor of Oxford University. In 1458 he became Bishop of Exeter, and in 1464 he was appointed Archbishop of York. From 1460 until 1467 he was chancellor of England. During the short reign of Henry VI (1470–71), he again held the chancellorship, but surrendered himself and Henry to Edward IV who haɔ returned from Holland and had defeated Warwick at Barnet (1471). Neville was imprisoned in the Tower of London, but was soon pardoned. Edward imprisoned him again from 1472 to 1475, however, on a charge of treason.

NEVIN, ETHELBERT WOODBRIDGE (1862–1901), American composer, born in Edgeworth, Pa., and educated at the Williams Conservatory in Pittsburgh, Pa., and in Berlin, Germany. In 1887 he settled in Boston, Mass., as a music teacher and devoted much of his time to the composition of songs. The first of his songs to gain lasting popularity was "Oh That We Two Were Maying" (1888). In 1891 he moved to Europe for a six-year period, during which he continued to compose songs and piano suites and worked on several orchestral compositions, none of which were ever completed. Of his numerous piano pieces the best known is "Narcissus", from the suite *Water Scenes* (1891). Among his many songs are the popular "The Rosary" (1898) and "Mighty Lak' a Rose" (1901). His completed work was almost entirely confined to short forms, and is characterized by an emphasis upon simple, often sentimental melody.

NEVINS, ALLAN (1890–   ), American educator, historian, and biographer, born in Camp Point, Ill., and educated at the University of Illinois. From 1913 to 1931 he was a member of the editorial staff of various newspapers and periodicals published in New York City. In the latter year he was appointed professor of American history at Columbia University. He was elected a member of the American Academy of Arts and Letters in 1954. Nevins is best known for his historical and biographical writings, which are characterized by their freshness and clarity of style, thoroughness of scholarly research, and liberal social and political outlook. His works include *Life of Robert Rogers* (1914), *America in World Affairs* (1941), *The Ordeal of the Union* (1946), *Emergence of Lincoln* (1950), *The World of Eli Whitney* (with Jeannette Mirsky, 1952), *Statesmanship of the Civil War* (1953), and *Ford: The Times, the Man, the Company* (with Frank E. Hill, 1954). He edited *Diary of John Quincy Adams* (1928), *The Heritage of America* (with Henry Steele Commager, 1939), and *The Diary of George Templeton Strong 1835–1875* (with Milton H. Thomas, 1952).

NEVSKI, ALEXANDER. See ALEXANDER NEVSKI.

NEVUS or **BIRTHMARK,** term applied to any number of superficial benign tumors (see NEOPLASM) on the body surface of a human being. Such tumors are almost always congenital. The term "nevus" when unqualified refers to a cutaneous tumor consisting of blood capillaries, or rarely of venules or arterioles. Such tumors, which rarely spread from their original site, and which consequently are not dangerous to life, vary in color according as the capillaries composing them carry arterial or venous blood. Thus, the popularly termed "cherry marks", and "portwine stains" or "claret stains" are nevi containing arterial blood and venous blood respectively. These nevi are on a level with the surface of the skin. Certain other vascular nevi, commonly known as "strawberry marks" or "raspberry marks", are slightly elevated above the surface of the skin. Vascular nevi comprise most birthmarks; two thirds of the vascular nevi are found on the face and head region. The term "nevus" is also applied with qualifying adjectives to superficial tumors derived from epithelium, nervous tissue, connective tissue, or fat. Among such tumors are pigmented spots and hairy moles. Disfiguring nevi may be removed by electrosurgery.

Birthmarks have been mentioned in the literature of civilized countries for thousands of years. At first, because these marks sometimes resembled in outline animals or familiar inanimate objects, birthmarks were believed to be visitations of divine anger; later, this superstition was replaced by one still current in many regions, that the marks are expressions of wishes or emotions of the mother during her pregnancy. Modern scientists, although they do not as yet know the origin of nevi, tend to search for the causes of nevus-formation in the field of tissue development or histogenesis.

NEW ALBANY, county seat of Floyd Co., Ind., situated on the Ohio R., opposite Louisville, Ky. It is served by four railroads and by river steamers. New Albany is an important manufacturing center, and the commercial center and shipping point of an agricultural area noted for the production of strawberries and dairy products. In the vicinity are extensive coal fields, and the city is provided with extensive hydroelectric power from the falls in the Ohio R. Industrial establishments include one of the largest plants in the U.S. for the manufacture of prefabricated houses. New Albany was settled in 1813, incorporated as a town in 1819, and chartered as a city in 1839. Pop. (1950) 29,346.

NEW AMSTERDAM. See MANHATTAN.

NEWARK, county seat and port of entry of Essex Co., N.J., situated on Newark Bay and the Passaic R., 8 miles w. of the s. end of Manhattan Island. Transportation facilities include six railroads; the Hudson and Manhattan Railroad, operating trains to New York via tunnels under the Hudson R.; a subway system; coastal and overseas steamship lines; and the Newark Metropolitan Airport, until recently the principal air terminal for the New York metropolitan area. Newark, the metropolis of New Jersey and the twenty-first (1950) largest city in the U.S., is one of the principal commercial and manufacturing centers in the country. Among the chief products of the extensive and highly diversified industrial establishments in Newark are paints, varnishes, chemicals, drugs, lubricating oil, electrical machinery and equipment, machinery and machine-shop products, metal products, motor-vehicle bodies and parts, airplanes, radio equipment, phonographs, jewelry, cutlery, leather goods, shoes, celluloid, cosmetics, malt liquors, beverages, bakery products, packed meats and other food products, cigars and cigarettes, furniture, paper boxes, and dressed furs. In addition, the city is an important retail and wholesale trading center and a leading insurance center. The Port of Newark, on Newark Bay, development of which began in 1914, comprises an important part of the New York metropolitan port area. The port has an improved harbor, with a channel 30 ft. in depth and 400 ft. in width. Waterfront facilities include large warehouses, and miles of railroad track, and more than 140 docks and piers. Lumber and paper are the chief exports of the Port of Newark.

Among the educational institutions in the city are the University of Newark, the New Jersey State Teachers College, the Newark College of Engineering, the New Jersey College of Pharmacy (now an affiliate of Rutgers University), Newark Technical School, and Newark Public School of Fine and Applied Arts. Newark is an episcopal see of the Roman Catholic and Protestant Episcopal churches, and the site of several Federal and State governmental agencies. Cultural facilities are provided by the Newark Public Library, noted for its progressive innovations; the Newark Museum, originally part of the library, with exceptional collections on art, science, and industry; and the New Jersey Historical Society, the Newark Art Club, the Griffith Music Foundation, and the Bach Society of New Jersey. Parks and playgrounds within the city cover an area of approximately 1000 acres. The Trinity Episcopal Cathedral, built in 1743, and the First Presbyterian Church (1791) are notable landmarks.

Newark was settled in 1666 by a company of Puritans from Connecticut, under the leadership of Robert Treat. The first settlement was established on a site known as the "Four Corners", now the intersection of the principal business thoroughfares, and was named after Newark-on-Trent, England, the home of one of the religious leaders of the colony. It was incorporated as a township in 1693. From 1747 to 1756 it was the site of the College of New Jersey, now Princeton University (q.v.). The present important leather industry in Newark had its beginning prior to the Revolutionary War. During the war the town and vicinity were the site of several military engagements. After the Revolutionary War Newark entered upon a period of rapid industrial development. It was incorporated as a city in 1836. Pop. (1950) 438,776.

NEWARK, county seat of Licking Co., Ohio, on the Licking River, 33 miles N.E. of Columbus. Its manufactures include table glassware, bottles, and agricultural implements. Indian mounds are found here. Pop. (1950) 34,275.

NEW BEDFORD, city, seaport, and a county seat of Bristol Co., Mass., situated at the confluence of the Acushnet R. and Buzzards Bay, about 50 miles s. of Boston. It is a leading fishing and textile-manufacturing center, and there are shipyards, boatbuilding plants, and factories engaged in the production of machinery, electrical equipment, paper and rubber goods, shoes, clothing, hardware, and glass. New Bedford has an excellent harbor and modern cargo-handling facilities; it is a regular port of call of coastwise steamships and of ferries operating to Nantucket and Martha's Vineyard. Noteworthy points of interest include the Bourne Whaling Museum; the Seamen's Bethel, described by the American author Herman Melville in the novel *Moby Dick* (1851); the Public Library, which contains valuable material relating to the whaling industry; Friends' Academy, founded in 1810; and the old U.S. customshouse.

Bedford, the first permanent settlement on the site of the present-day city, was established in 1760 as part of the township of Dartmouth. Whaling and freight-carrying vessels began operating out of the port a few years later. During the American Revolution many privateers sailed out of Bedford. In retaliation a British force attacked the town in 1778, reducing most of it to ashes. Bedford was incorporated as a separate town and given its present name in 1787. During the first half of the 19th century New Bedford developed into the principal whaling port in the United States and a center of the fishing industry. By 1857, ten years after New Bedford was chartered as a city, the whaling fleet alone aggregated more than 300 vessels. Whaling declined in importance after 1860; textile manufacturing became a leading industry during the 1880's. Pop. (1950) 109,189.

NEWBOLT, SIR HENRY JOHN (1862–1938), English author, poet, and barrister, born in Bilston, and educated at Oxford University. While practicing law, he wrote a historical novel, *Taken from the Enemy* (1892), which he followed with *Mordred* (1895), a tragedy in blank verse, and *Admirals All* (1897), a volume of ballads which established his literary reputation. He gave up law in 1899 and was editor of the *Monthly Review* from 1900 to 1905. From 1911 until 1921 he was professor of poetry at Oxford University, except for the period of his service in World War I as controller of wireless and cables. His other volumes of verse dealing with the sea include *The Sailing of the Long-Ships* (1902), *Songs of the Sea* (1904), and *Drake's Drum and Other Poems of the Sea* (1914). Newbolt is also known for his *Naval History of the Great War* (1920), volume IV of *Naval Operations* (1928), cumulative official history of

the British navy, and critical essays such as *Studies Green and Gray* (1926) and *New Paths on Helicon* (1927).

NEW BRITAIN, city of Hartford Co., Connecticut, 9 miles w. of Hartford. Principal products include hardware, cutlery, jewelry, and hosiery. Pop. (1950) 73,726.

NEW BRITAIN, or (Ger.) NEU-POMMERN, largest island of the Bismarck Archipelago, 50 miles N.E. of New Guinea. It became part of a German protectorate in 1884, and since World War I has been ruled by Australia under a mandate. In the interior there are several volcanoes, the highest being the Father (3900 ft.). The climate is hot and moist. The chief crop is coconuts. The natives are cannibals of the Melanesian division. Area, with adjacent isles, 14,600 sq.m. Pop., about 90,000.

NEW BRUNSWICK, county seat of Middlesex Co., N.J., on the Raritan River, 31 miles s.w. of New York, at the terminus of the Delaware and Raritan Canal. It is the seat of Rutgers University (1766). New Brunswick is noted for its rubber factories, and also has iron and brass foundries, and manufactories of hosiery, lamps, needles, and paper hangings. Here Gen. Howe, the British commander in chief, established his headquarters, June 17, 1777. Pop. (1950) 38,768.

NEW BRUNSWICK, one of the Maritime Provinces of the Dominion of Canada, bounded on the N. by Quebec, on the E. by the Gulf of St. Lawrence and Northumberland Strait, on the s.E. by Nova Scotia, on the s. by the Bay of Fundy, and on the w. by Maine. Its area is 27,985 sq.m.; the population (1951) is 515,697. Fredericton (q.v.) is the capital. The largest city and chief seaport is Saint John (q.v.). Moncton and Edmunston are other important communities.

Except along the Gulf coast and in the river valleys, where the terrain is generally level, New Brunswick is a region of rolling hills and low, rugged highlands. The latter, occupying about two thirds of the total area, are highest in the N. central section. Mt. Carleton (2690 ft.) is the tallest peak. The province is traversed by many rivers, notably the St. John, 450 m. in length, and navigable for vessels of considerable size to Fredericton, a distance of about 80 m. Other important rivers are the Miramichi, Restigouche, Petitcodiac, and Richibucto. Grand Lake, with an area of about 62 sq.m., is the largest lake; the hydrography includes numerous small lakes. The province has many fine harbors, especially in the s.w., on the Bay of Fundy (see FUNDY, BAY OF) and along the Gulf of St. Lawrence.

Typical continental climatic conditions prevail in the N. part of the province. In this region the winter and summer extremes are often —40° F. and 100° F. In the coastal areas the climate is subject to the moderating influence of oceanic winds and currents. Rainfall averages over 40 inches annually.

The province is heavily forested and lumbering, pulp milling, and related industries are of primary importance. Forest production was valued at about $165,000,000 in 1952. New Brunswick has extensive tracts of arable land, particularly in the coastal region and the valley of the St. John R. In 1950 about 926,000 acres were cultivated; hay, clover, cereal grains, potatoes, and fruits are the principal crops, and there are many dairy farms. Fishing is a leading industry. In 1952 the catch, including cod, haddock, herring, and salmon, was valued at approximately $22,-000,000. There are diversified mineral resources, notably appreciable deposits of coal, gypsum, limestone, natural gas and petroleum. Excellent fishing and wild game hunting attract many tourists every year. There are summer resorts on Passamaquoddy Bay and on Grand Manan and Campobello islands in the Bay of Fundy. Transportation facilities include (1952) over 13,000 m. of roads and over 1800 m. of steam-railway lines.

Education is nonsectarian and free. Institutions of higher education number five, including the University of New Brunswick (at Fredericton), founded in 1800.

The provincial government is headed by a lieutenant governor. This official, who is appointed for a five-year term by the governor-general of the Dominion, exercises his authority with the advice of an executive council headed by a premier and responsible to the legislature. Legislative authority is vested in a 52-member legislative assembly elected by universal suffrage for five year terms. The province elects ten representatives to the Canadian House of Commons.

In 1604 French fur traders established a settlement within the region comprising present-day New Brunswick. The settlement was abandoned the next year, but after 1630, when the French constructed Fort St. John on the site of modern Saint John, there was a steady influx of colonists to the coastal area along the Bay of Fundy. The New Brunswick region then formed part of the French province of Acadia (q.v.). Great Britain obtained possession of Acadia under the terms of the Treaty of Utrecht (1713), the peace agreement ending the War of the Spanish Succession. In 1755, when the British expelled the Acadians from Nova Scotia, some 500 of the deportees settled in New Brunswick, bringing its population to about 5000. Many English and Scottish colonists arrived in New Brunswick after 1762, and there was an influx of loyalists from the United States after the American Revolution. In 1784 New Brunswick was separated from Nova Scotia and constituted a province. With Quebec, Ontario, and Nova Scotia, New Brunswick helped to establish the Dominion of Canada in 1867.

NEWBURGH, a city of Orange Co., N.Y., situated on the w. bank of the Hudson R., opposite Beacon and 60 miles N. of New York City. It is served by two railroads, and is connected by ferry with a third railroad at Beacon. The city is the N. terminus of the Storm King Highway along the Palisades (q.v.). The expansion of the Hudson R. at this point is known as Newburgh Bay, and affords a channel deep enough for ocean-going vessels. Newburgh is a manufacturing center, and the trading center and shipping point of a farming, dairying, and fruitgrowing area. The principal industries are the manufacture of woolen, cotton, and leather goods, men's and women's clothing, coated fabrics, felt, carpets, plastics, radio equipment, tile, lawn mowers, and wood-turning machinery; the city contains lumber yards, brickyards, and shipyards. On the outskirts of Newburgh is Stewart Field, a large base of the U.S. Air Force, and in the vicinity of the city is the U.S. Military Academy at West Point. Nearby is Bear Mountain State Park.

Newburgh was settled in 1709 by a group of German colonists from the Rhine Palatinate. It was an early lumbering, shipbuilding, and whaling center. Gen. George Washington made his headquarters at Newburgh in 1782–83, and "Hasbrouck House", the site of his headquarters, is maintained by the State as a national shrine. The Revolutionary Army was demobilized at Newburgh on June 23, 1783, and there Washington delivered his reply to the anonymous letters, known as the Newburgh Addresses, written in protest against the failure of Congress to pay the American troops. Newburgh was incorporated as a city in 1865. Pop. (1950) 31,956.

NEW CALEDONIA AND DEPENDENCIES, Overseas Territory of France, situated in the s.w. Pacific Ocean, and comprising the island of New Caledonia and a number of other islands and groups. Among the latter are the Loyalty Islands, the Wallis and Futuna Islands, and the Huon Islands. New Caledonia

Island, about 875 miles E. of Australia, has an area of 6531 sq.m. Area of Territory, 7756 sq.m.; pop. (1952 est.) 65,400, including about 21,000 Europeans. The territorial capital is Nouméa (1946 pop., 10,466). Coffee, copra, cotton, manioc, corn, bananas, tobacco, and pineapples form the principal agricultural products. The mineral resources include cobalt, chrome, nickel, iron, and manganese; also antimony, mercury, silver, gold, lead, copper, and cinnabar. The leading exports include minerals, coffee, copper, copra, guano, and preserved meats. The principal imports include wine, coal, flour, and rice. Two domains make up the land, the native reserve and that of the state. The colony is administered by a governor aided by a privy council and an elected council-general.

NEW CASTLE, county seat of Lawrence Co., Pa., on the Shenango River, 50 miles N.N.W. of Pittsburgh. It has manufactures of nails, furnaces, flour, dynamite, glass, and paper. There is an extensive shipping trade. Coal, iron, clay, and limestone are found in abundance. Pop. (1950) 48,834.

NEWCASTLE, city of New South Wales, Australia, 75 miles N.E. of Sydney, at the mouth of Hunter River. It is the chief port of the north coast and exports coal and wool. Pop. (1951 est.) 136,480.

NEWCASTLE, DUKES OF, title in the British peerage borne by members of the Cavendish, Holles, Pelham, and Clinton families. The principal holders of this title were the following.

1. WILLIAM CAVENDISH, DUKE OF NEW-CASTLE (1592–1676), English statesman, sportsman, writer, and patron of the arts, educated at Cambridge University. He inherited a vast fortune, and his entertainment of King James I, in 1619, and King Charles I, in 1633, on his estates at Welbeck, Nottinghamshire, were noted for lavish magnificence. Throughout the difficulties which beset Charles I's reign, Newcastle fought valiantly on the king's side, and unstintingly poured out his fortune for military expenses, spending nearly a million pounds during the Great Rebellion. After the Royalists lost the battle of Marston Moor in 1644, Newcastle retired to the Continent, remaining in exile until the Restoration. During this period he established a famous riding school in Antwerp and wrote, in French, *Méthode et Invention Nouvelle de Dresser les Chevaux* (1658, translated as *A General System of Horsemanship*, 1743), describing his original methods of equestrian training. After the Restoration, Newcastle was restored to

his titles and estates, although the latter were burdened by debt. He lived in retirement, devoting himself to horsemanship and writing. Besides several works on the training of horses, Newcastle wrote comedies, including *The Country Captain and the Varietie* (1649) and *The Triumphant Widow* (1677). He was a generous patron to such English writers as Ben Jonson, James Shirley, John Dryden, and Sir William Davenant, and to the philosophers Thomas Hobbes, René Descartes, and Pierre Gassendi. His second wife, Margaret Lucas Cavendish, Duchess of Newcastle (1624?–74), wrote several volumes of poems, plays, essays, and letters, an autobiography, and a life of her husband. **2.** THOMAS PELHAM-HOLLES, 1st DUKE OF NEWCASTLE (1693–1768), English statesman, educated at Cambridge University. He vigorously supported King George I, and was an important member of the Whig party throughout its political ascendancy in the 18th century. From 1724 to 1754 he was secretary of state, leaving this post to become prime minister. Two years later he retired in favor of William Cavendish, Duke of Devonshire. He was again prime minister from 1757 to 1762. During this period Newcastle is credited with holding the Whig party together, in spite of internal dissension and the attacks of George III.

NEWCASTLE UPON TYNE, city of Northumberland, England, on the Tyne River, 10 m. from its mouth. It dates from the Roman Pons Ælii, one of the chain of forts by which the wall of Hadrian was fortified. At Newcastle the railway system had its origin. The manufactures include locomotive and marine engines, glass of various kinds, earthenware, bricks, and grindstones. There are also large shipbuilding yards. Pop. (1951 prelim.) 291,-723. See also GATESHEAD.

NEW COLLEGE, a college of Oxford University, England, founded in 1379 by William of Wykeham (q.v.), lord chancellor of England, as the College of St. Mary of Winchester. The faculty comprises 28 fellows and 2 chaplains, and the student body consists of 39 scholars and 18 choristers.

NEWCOMB, SIMON (1835–1909), American astronomer and economist. He was stationed at the naval observatory, and directed several expeditions for the observation of eclipses. Later he was professor of mathematics and astronomy at Johns Hopkins University (1894–1901). His works include *Popular Astronomy* (1877).

NEW DEAL, a phrase used to describe the program of Franklin Delano Roosevelt during his first two terms as President of the United States. The phrase is derived from Roosevelt's speech accepting the Democratic nomination for the Presidency in 1932, in which he pledged himself to "a new deal for the American people". The New Deal consisted of two main parts. The first included temporary measures designed to provide relief and to counteract the effects of the economic depression which had begun in 1929. The second included permanent measures designed to rehabilitate and stabilize the national economy so as to prevent the recurrence of severe economic dislocations.

Among the temporary measures adopted were the passage of the *Emergency Bank Relief Act* by a special session of Congress on March 9, 1933, to prevent the breakdown of the national banking system (see BANK AND BANKING) ; the creation of the *Federal Emergency Relief Administration* in May, 1933, to allocate relief funds for distribution to needy individuals by the States; the creation of the *Civilian Conservation Corps* in September, 1933, to employ young workers in reforestation and soil conservation projects; and the establishment of the *Federal Civil Works Administration* in November, 1933, which was replaced in 1935 by the *Works Progress* (later *Work Projects*) *Administration,* to create jobs for the unemployed (see WORK PROJECTS ADMINISTRATION).

The New Deal measures intended to be permanent included the *National Industrial Recovery Act* (q.v.), passed in June, 1933, and invalidated by the Supreme Court in 1935; the *Agricultural Adjustment Act,* providing for limitations on crop production, which was passed in May, 1933, and invalidated by the Supreme Court in 1936; the *Securities Act* of 1933 and the *Securities and Exchange Act* of 1934 (see SECURITIES AND EXCHANGE COMMISSION) ; the *Tennessee Valley Authority,* providing for the electrification and industrialization of the Tennessee Valley, which was created in May, 1933 (see TENNESSEE; WATER POWER) ; the *Rural Electrification Act* of 1936, which provided for the financing of rural electricity distributing systems; the *National Labor Relations Act* (q.v.) of 1935; the *Fair Labor Standards Act* (q.v.), passed in June, 1938; the *Social Security Act* of 1935 (see SOCIAL INSURANCE; UNEMPLOYMENT; OLD-AGE PENSIONS) ; and the *National Housing Act* of 1934 which provided for the insurance of bank loans issued for housing construction and development.

The New Deal was attacked by conservatives as destructive of private enterprise and individual initiative; it was defended by its partisans as a balancing mechanism which would eliminate the recurrent economic booms and depressions of capitalist production and insure an equitable distribution of wealth and opportunity. Most scholars now believe that the New Deal helped to introduce into the United States a widespread attitude that governmental regulation of free economy was justified to whatever extent necessary to satisfy the minimum needs of public welfare and continuous employment; see UNITED STATES: *History.*

NEW DELHI, capital of the Union of India, situated on the Jumna R., about 10 miles s. of Delhi (q.v.). The proposed establishment of the city as a new capital of British India was announced in 1911. Building subsequently commenced, and in 1929 the seat of government was moved to New Delhi from Delhi, the former capital of British India. When India received dominion status in 1947, New Delhi became the capital of the Dominion of India. The city was made capital of the newly formed Union of India in 1948.

In the center of the city, on a low acropolis about 30 ft. above the surrounding plain, are the main government buildings, constructed of white stone on a red sandstone foundation. At the foot of the hill is the legislative building. The remainder of the city is laid out in a series of hexagons, radiating from the acropolis and enclosed on the w. by a semicircular road. Several of the chief avenues lead directly to important monuments in Delhi and other neighboring towns; along the broad avenues are located subsidiary government buildings. At the end of the main processional way is a triumphal arch to the Indian armies. Shops, residences of government officials, and the homes of European and Indian inhabitants of the city, as well as the government buildings and palaces, are surrounded by lawns, trees, and flowering shrubs. Most of the buildings are constructed of brick, overlaid with whitewashed stucco, and the architecture of the whole city combines Western classic and native Hindu and Mohammedan forms. Pop. (1951) 276,314.

NEWELL, HOMER EDWARD, JR. (1915–), American mathematician and physicist, born in Holyoke, Mass., and educated at Harvard University and the University of Wisconsin. He taught mathematics at the University of Maryland from 1940 to 1944, when he joined the staff of the Naval Research Laboratory

Screen Traveler, from Gendreau

Shri Lakshminarain, a Hindu temple in New Delhi, India

in Washington, D.C. In 1947 he became head of the laboratory's Rocket-Sonde Research Branch, which investigates upper-air phenomena. The same year he was appointed a member of the Upper Atmosphere Research Panel.

Newell is noted as an expert in high-altitude rocket research. Studies conducted under his direction contributed greatly to present-day knowledge of stratospheric densities and pressures and of cosmic and solar radiation. Newell is engaged in the earth-satellite program announced by the United States in 1955; see SATELLITE, ARTIFICIAL.

NEW ENGLAND, collective name given to the six Eastern States of the United States of America—Maine, New Hampshire, Vermont, Massachusetts, Rhode Island, and Connecticut. Connecticut was formed by the union of

Connecticut and New Haven colonies, and Massachusetts from those of Massachusetts Bay and Plymouth. Out of the territory claimed by New Hampshire and New York was formed, at the beginning of the American Revolution, the future State of Vermont. Maine was part of Massachusetts until 1820.

NEW ENGLAND CONFEDERATION, a military alliance formed in 1643 by the American colonies of Massachusetts Bay, Connecticut, New Haven, and Plymouth. Its members agreed to co-ordinate their military operations, while retaining their independence in internal affairs. The successful achievement of the aims of the alliance was hampered, however, by the development of bitter rivalries among the signatories. Massachusetts Bay, for example, attempted to win a predominant position within the Confederation on the grounds that she had the largest population; failing in this attempt, she refused in 1653 to participate in a projected war against the Dutch colonies in America. The sole major achievement of the Confederation was the successful co-operation of its members in King Philip's War (1675–76), in which the colonies crushed an uprising among the Indian tribes in New England. In 1684, shortly after the charter of the Massachusetts Bay colony had been revoked by the British government (see MASSACHUSETTS: *History*), the Confederation was dissolved.

NEWFOUNDLAND, an island off the coast of N.E. North America, situated between the Gulf of St. Lawrence and the Atlantic Ocean, and forming, with its dependency, Labrador (q.v.), Newfoundland Province of the Dominion of Canada. The island is separated from the mainland by the Strait of Belleisle on the N. and Cabot Strait on the s.w. The provincial capital is St. Johns; other towns include Corner Brook, Grand Falls, and Bell Island. Area of Newfoundland Province, 155,364 sq.m.; Island, 42,734 sq.m. Pop. of province (1951) 361,416.

The island is shaped somewhat like an equilateral triangle. The coastline is extremely irregular and rimmed with rocky cliffs from 200 to 400 ft. in height. Numerous large bays and sheltered harbors, studded with islets, extend into the interior, where they become narrow fiords. In the s.e., between Placentia and Trinity bays, is the Avalon peninsula, which is connected to the mainland by a narrow isthmus. The interior of the island is a low, rolling plateau traversed by ridges extending from s.w. to N.E., the greatest being the Long Range, along the w. coast, with a maximum

elevation of 2540 ft. above sea level. Lakes and rivers are found throughout the island. The chief rivers are the Exploits, Gander, Terra Nova, Humber, and St. George.

Insular temperatures, moderated by ocean currents, have an annual range of from about 0° to 83° F.; the w. coast is more temperate in climate than the E., which is affected by Arctic currents. Mineral resources are considerable and varied, and include iron, zinc, coal, gold, silver, and fluorspar. More than half the island is heavily forested, principally with balsam fir and black and white spruce, the raw materials for the manufacture of newsprint, one of the principal industries. The greatest industry is fishing, and the processing of fish, chiefly cod (by far the most important), halibut, salmon, lobster, herring, and capelin. Codfishing (see GRAND BANKS) is the oldest occupation on the island. In 1953 the total value of fish and fish products amounted to about $28,000,000. Production of newsprint in 1952 amounted to 528,880 tons; production of sulfite pulp amounted to about 46,500 tons. The total value of forest products was $96,000,000. Mineral products were valued at about $33,000,000. Agriculture is not of major importance, but is being encouraged by the government; in 1953 agricultural products, including domestic animals, were valued at about $28,000,000.

The modern Newfoundlanders are the descendants of settlers principally from Ireland, England, and the Channel Islands. The Roman Catholic and Anglican churches have about the same number of communicants, and the third largest religious group belongs to the United Church. Of about 760 m. of railroad, 56 m. are privately owned. Gander Airport, on the shores of Lake Gander, is used by ten international air lines for transatlantic flights (see GANDER). Steamers connect the island with the mainland.

History. The explorer John Cabot (q.v.), in the hire of England, visited Newfoundland in 1497. England made no immediate attempt at colonization, but during the 16th century the coastal waters of the island attracted increasing numbers of French, Portuguese, English, and Spanish fishermen. In 1583 Sir Humphrey Gilbert (q.v.) took formal possession of Newfoundland in the name of England and established a colony which became St. Johns. Another colony was established in 1610 on the Avalon peninsula. During the 17th century the Netherlands and, particularly, France, tried to assume possession of Newfoundland.

National Film Board

NEWFOUNDLAND. *Top: The harbor of St. Johns, the capital. Middle, left: Above the ground at a coal mine on Bell Island. Middle, right: Codfish being dried in the sun, at Pouch Cove. Bottom: Logs of spruce and fir for making paper, afloat at Corner Brook.*

By the Treaty of Utrecht, which ended the War of the Spanish Succession in 1713, France ceded all rights in Newfoundland to Great Britain, except for the islands of St. Pierre and Miquelon (below s. central Newfoundland) and cod fisheries on the w. coast, and other fishing rights later relinquished. During the next hundred years, the population increased considerably as laborers from various parts of the British Isles were brought to work in the fisheries. With this influx of settlers and the growth of towns, resentment arose among the inhabitants against the colonization restrictions of the British government, directed at keeping the island merely a fishing station, and gave impetus to a demand for self-government. In 1832 Great Britain granted the right of representative government and in 1855 Newfoundland became a dominion with a bicameral legislature, a governor, and a cabinet. Mining operations were begun in 1864. However, despite continued financial aid from Great Britain, the economic condition of Newfoundland remained unsound.

International complications concerning fishing rights were occasioned by France when that country refused to allow British colonization on the w. coast because it wanted no intrusion on its exclusive fishing rights. The Newfoundland government retaliated in 1888 by enacting measures which, in effect, prohibited sale of bait to French fishermen. This controversy was settled by an Anglo-French convention in 1904, by which France surrendered the w. coast rights in return for the Los Islands and other territory in Africa. Another controversy was begun in 1905–06, when the Newfoundland legislature passed acts which the United States claimed were in contravention of 1818 and 1854 treaties giving Americans fishing rights in Newfoundland waters. The question was settled in 1910 by the Permanent Court of Arbitration at The Hague, which confirmed American fishing rights. A third dispute, this time with Canada, and concerning the boundary of Labrador, was decided in 1927 by the British Privy Council. Newfoundland had owned part of Labrador since 1763, and its possession of the disputed territory (about 110,000 sq.m.) was confirmed.

The financial condition of the dominion was continually precarious and the adverse effects of the world economic depression which began in 1929 resulted in virtual bankruptcy. In 1933 the British Parliament suspended self-government; a year later the executive authority was vested in the governor and three Newfoundlanders and three British commissioners, subject to Parliamentary control. The commission worked to develop agriculture, employment opportunities, and the educational and social-welfare facilities of Newfoundland. As a result the economic condition was considerably improved. In 1941 the island became one of eight British possessions in the Western Hemisphere leased to the U.S. as aviation bases. The presence of American soldiers and the construction of American air bases became an added factor in the economic recovery. In 1946 a 45-member national convention was elected to investigate whether Newfoundland had accomplished its economic recovery and to ascertain the form of government desired by its people. After the investigation (completed Jan. 31, 1948), the British government directed a referendum by which the Newfoundlanders could choose union with Canada, the restoration of self-government, or the continuation of government by commission. On July 22, 1948, Newfoundland chose to unite itself with Canada by a vote of 78,323 to 71,334 (for self-government). On April 1, 1949, Newfoundland became the tenth Canadian province. By the terms of the union, Canada agreed to give Newfoundland $42,750,000 in cash grants and about $25,000,000 yearly in family allowances, old age pensions, unemployment insurance, and other benefits.

NEWFOUNDLAND DOG, a breed of working dog that originated in Newfoundland from the crossbreeding of native strains with foreign breeds, possibly the great Pyrenees or the boarhound, brought to Newfoundland by Basque or French fishermen. Most thoroughbred Newfoundlands of today are descended from dogs bred in England from specimens imported into that country from Newfoundland. The male is about 28 inches high at the shoulder and weighs from 140 to 150 pounds; the bitch stands 26 inches high and weighs from 110 to 120 pounds. The Newfoundland has a broad, massive head; small, deeply set eyes, dark brown in color; small ears lying close to the head; a deep chest; a flat, dense, coarse, and oily coat, usually a dull black in color, but sometimes bronze, or black and white; a strong neck; and a tail of moderate length plentifully covered with long hair. Newfoundlands are powerful swimmers and are known to have rescued human beings from drowning and to have carried lifelines from shore to ships in distress. They are employed today in Newfoundland and

Newfoundland dog

Labrador to draw carts and carry burdens; in the United States they are in demand principally as watch dogs and companions. Because of their loyalty, intelligence, and tractability, Newfoundland dogs are ideal pets for children.

NEWGATE PRISON, a London prison established, probably in 1218, in the gatehouse of the west gate, then known as the new gate of the city. The prison was rebuilt in the 15th century with funds from a legacy left by Sir Richard Whittington (q.v.), the famous early 15th-century Lord Mayor of London. It was destroyed in the Great Fire of 1666, again rebuilt, and burned down in 1780 by the rioters led by Lord George Gordon (q.v.) in protest against a Parliamentary action favorable to Catholics. Newgate was used at various times to house debtors and persons convicted of heresy or of adherence to Roman Catholicism. The prison was notorious for the executions held outside its walls; after 1868, executions were held inside the prison. Newgate was not used after 1877, and in 1902 it was razed.

NEW GUINEA, or Papua, an island in the Pacific Ocean, the second largest in the world (the first being Greenland), situated N. of Australia, from which it is separated by the Arafura Sea and, at the closest point, by the 80-mile-wide Torres Strait. Politically, the island is divided into three sections: Netherlands New Guinea, occupying almost the entire w. portion (151,000 sq.m.), a Dutch colony which is claimed by the Republic of Indonesia (q.v.); the Territory of New Guinea (see New Guinea, Territory of) in the N.E., a trusteeship of the United Nations administered by Australia (69,700 sq.m.); and, in the s.E., the mainland portion of Papua (q.v.), a territory of Australia (87,786 sq.m.).

The island is generally long and narrow, its greatest length, N.W. to s.E., being 1490 m., and its greatest width, N. to s., being 430 m. A long mountain range extends from N.W. to s.E. and, in the E. portion, forms the approximate boundary between the Territory of New Guinea and Papua. These mountains include peaks which rise to more than 15,000 ft. above sea level. On the N. coast, another mountain group, principally in Netherlands New Guinea, rises to a height of over 10,000 ft. The coasts are swampy and much of the interior is covered with dense rain forests thickly grown with tropical vegetation and containing ebony, sandalwood, cedar, and camphor trees. The plains in the interior are fertile, but difficulties of transportation have retarded their development. The interior is also rich in mineral deposits, notably gold, silver, platinum, copper, and osmiridium.

New Guinea is directly s. of the equator and has a tropical, humid climate; the average temperature at noon is 92° F. and the annual rainfall is from 30 to 130 inches. The

Australian News & Information Bureau; American Museum of Natural History

NEW GUINEA. *Top: Sailing craft in harbor of Port Moresby. Bottom: Left, a human skull with features modeled in clay, a headhunter's trophy; right, a Papuan bridegroom.*

fauna is similar to that of Australia (q.v.), with only a few varieties of mammals, but is notable for the many varieties of magnificently-colored birds, particularly birds of paradise. The plains and coastal swamps are infested with mosquitoes. The indigenous tribes are Negroid, and almost all are members of three principal groups, the Negritoes, Melanesians, and Papuans. Still in a Stone Age culture, the many diverse New Guinea tribes include cannibals and head-hunters. They subsist by hunting, fishing, and primitive methods of cultivating sago, corn, yams, and other tropical foods. The native population is estimated to be over 1,250,000. Settlements of Europeans are located mainly on the coast. Area, 308,486 sq.m.; pop., about 1,200,000.

History. The first European to see the island is considered, by historians, to have been Antonio d'Abreu, a Portuguese navigator, in 1511, and the first to land there was another Portuguese, Jorge de Menesis, in 1526. The Portuguese navigator Ynigo Ortiz de Retez named the island "Novo Guinea" in 1546 because he thought the natives were similar to the West African tribes. New Guinea became a calling place for many later explorers, notably William Dampier, Philip Carteret, Louis Antoine de Bougainville, Comte Jean de la Pérouse, and Captain James Cook, who explored parts of the coast.

The reports of these explorers as well as scientific interest in the region resulted in the exploration of the island by a number of private and governmental expeditions. In 1793 the entire island was claimed by the British East India Company. Its claim was disputed by the Netherlands, and in 1827 the Dutch East India Company established a settlement and took possession of the w. half of New Guinea. Later in the 19th century the German New Guinea Company claimed the N.E. section, comprising all the territory not under British or Dutch sovereignty; in 1885 the German-claimed territory was taken over by the German government and named Kaiser-Wilhelmsland. The S.E. portion was taken over by Queensland, Australia, in 1883, and in 1906 was made part of the federal Territory of Papua. An Australian force occupied the German region in 1914, during World War I, and in 1920 Australia received a League of Nations mandate over the former German colony, renamed the Territory of New Guinea.

During World War II New Guinea was invaded by Japan, as a base for operations against Australia, and during the campaigns

of 1942–43 it became the contested perimeter of Japanese action in the South Pacific. Japanese forces took almost the entire N. portion, but in 1943 the last major Japanese attack was frustrated (see WORLD WAR II). A large Japanese force, however, remained in the interior until its surrender in September, 1945. In June, 1946, both Papua and the Territory were united in a single unit, under a provisional administration.

NEW GUINEA, TERRITORY OF, a territory in the s.w. Pacific Ocean, administered by Australia under a trusteeship of the United Nations since 1946 and formerly (1920–46) under a mandate from the League of Nations. The territory comprises the N.E. portion of the island of New Guinea (q.v.), the Bismarck Archipelago (q.v.), and, in the Solomon Islands (q.v.), Bougainville, Buka, and adjacent small islands. The administrative center of the territory is Port Moresby, on New Guinea; other towns include Rabaul, on New Britain Island, and Lae, Wewak, and Aitape, on New Guinea. The territory contains large mineral resources, chiefly gold, silver, and platinum. The chief crops are coconuts, coffee, cacao, rubber, bananas, yams, taro, and sago. The territory is ruled by a colonial administrator who advises the governor general of Australia on legislative matters. Area, about 93,000 sq.m.; pop., about 1,000,000 (including 7000 Europeans).

NEW HAMPSHIRE, one of the New England States of the United States, bounded on the E. by Maine and 18 m. of the Atlantic Ocean, on the s. by Massachusetts, on the w. by the Connecticut R., which separates the State from Vermont, and on the N. by the Canadian province of Quebec. New Hampshire ranks as the 43rd State in the Union in area, 44th in the order of population (1950), and the 9th in the order of admission to the Union, having entered on June 21, 1788. The State capital is Concord. The principal cities in the order of population (1950) are Manchester, Nashua, Concord, Portsmouth, Berlin (qq.v.), and Dover. The extreme length of the State, from N. to s., is 178 m., and the extreme width, from E. to w., is 88 m. Area, 9304 sq.m., including 280 sq.m. of inland water surface. Population of the State (1950) 533,242.

The surface of New Hampshire ranges from hilly to mountainous. From the seaboard the land rises to uneven hills, which extend to the White Mountains (q.v.), a part of the Appalachian system. The highest point in the State, 6288 ft. above sea level, is Mt. Washington, a peak of the Presidential range of the White Mountains, located in Coos Co., in the N. part of New Hampshire. The lowest point is at sea level, and the average elevation is 1000 ft. The 18 miles of seacoast are without notable features. Sandy beaches stretch from one low cape to the next, sheltering tidal creeks and salt marshes. The estuaries are small except for the Piscataqua R., which at Portsmouth harbor lies half in New Hampshire and half in Maine. A small group of rocky islets, the Isles of Shoals, is situated 8 m. off the coast and is bisected by the New Hampshire-Maine boundary.

The hydrography of New Hampshire includes the Connecticut R. (q.v.), which flows N. to S. and forms the western boundary of the State; the Merrimack, which flows N. to S. through the S. central part of New Hampshire; the Saco and the Androscoggin, both of which flow S. and E. into Maine; and hundreds of lakes, ponds, and streams.

The climate is characterized by long, severe winters and cool summers. The average temperature is about 42° F. in the N. and 47° F. in the S. Extremes of 102° F. and —38° F. have been recorded. The annual amount of precipitation is about 40 inches, and is fairly evenly distributed throughout the year. The State is a popular summer and winter resort.

Coniferous and deciduous trees grow throughout New Hampshire. More than 677,-000 acres of land are part of the National forest system. State forests (99) cover more than 20,000 acres; State parks (44) cover almost 31,000 acres; and community forests (167) cover more than 64,500 acres. In 1947 about 323,000,000 board feet of lumber were produced in New Hampshire.

Fisheries in 1951 produced a catch of approximately 588,000 pounds, valued at more than $215,000. Lobsters form the most important part of the catch. The chief source of mineral wealth in New Hampshire is granite. Feldspar, mica, stone, sand, and gravel are other mineral products. In 1951 the total value of New Hampshire's mineral output came to a little more than $1,296,000. About a third of the area of New Hampshire is devoted to farming, dairying, and livestock raising. In 1950 almost 14,000 farms covered a total area of more than 1,700,000 acres, and were valued at over $124,000,000. Approximately 3% of the farms and farm area were operated by tenant farmers (the smallest percentage in the U.S.). The total cash income from agriculture in 1952 was approximately $70,600,000. Income from livestock

Lloyd Olmstead

New Hampshire State House in Concord

was $58,400,000; from crops, $11,700,000; from Federal subsidies, $500,000. Animals on farms in 1953 numbered 120,000 cattle (including 70,000 dairy cows), 12,000 swine, 7000 horses, and 9000 sheep. The chief crops are apples, potatoes, corn, hay, oats, and maple syrup.

The leading industry of New Hampshire is manufacturing. The total value added by manufacture in 1951 was $407,474,000. In 1950 there were 1075 manufacturing establishments employing about 80,000 workers; 85,000 were employed in 1951, and they earned $245,000,-000. The manufacture of footwear and cotton goods are the chief industries. The value added by manufacture in leather goods industries was about $88,000,000 in 1951, and in the textile industry it was $112,000,00C Other important industries include the manu facture of paper, lumber, and machinery. Th, resort industry is important to the State's economy. In the average year about 1,500,000 people are guests at 444 hotels, 722 tourist homes, and many cabins and camps. Approximately 20,000 summer homes are located within the State.

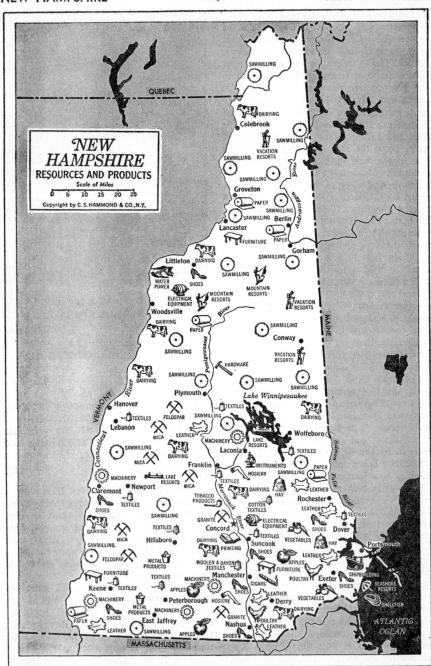

NEW HAMPSHIRE
RESOURCES AND PRODUCTS
Scale of Miles
0 5 10 15 20 25
Copyright by C.S. HAMMOND & CO., N.Y.

Transportation facilities in New Hampshire include (1953) 1351 m. of main-track railway, and the State maintains almost 4000 m. of highway, almost all of which is surfaced. Commercial air lines serve Portsmouth, Keene, Concord, Lebanon, Berlin, and Laconia. In 1953 there were 23 airports, 11 of which were municipally operated.

Attendance at the public elementary and secondary schools of New Hampshire is free and compulsory for all children between the ages of eight and fourteen during the full school year. In 1952–53 there were 581 elementary and secondary schools with an enrollment of more than 79,000 pupils; the latter were taught by more than 3200 teachers. Nine institutions of higher learning are within the State, including Dartmouth College (q.v.), the University of New Hampshire, which is supported by the State, two teachers colleges, and a junior college.

The State is governed according to the terms of the constitution of 1784, as amended. New Hampshire is the only State in the Union in which only a constitutional convention may propose amendments. Executive power is vested in a governor and a five-member executive council, elected for two-year terms. In addition, the legislature elects a secretary of state, treasurer, attorney general, and a comptroller. The executive council shares many of the governor's duties and advises him on many matters of State. The attorney general, judges, coroners, and other State officers are appointed jointly by the governor and the council. The executive council also shares the governor's powers of pardoning, except in the case of impeachment.

The legislature is called the General Court and consists of a senate of 24 members and a house of representatives of 398 members, all elected for two-year terms. The judiciary consists of a supreme court composed of a chief justice and 4 associates, a superior court composed of a chief justice and 5 associates, 10 probate courts (one for each county), and municipal courts. All supreme court, superior court, and probate court justices are appointed by the governor and the executive council to serve until they reach the age of seventy.

Electors in the State of New Hampshire must be twenty-one years of age or more, able to read and write, registered for the election, and not paupers or under sentence for crime. New Hampshire is divided into 10 counties and sends 2 senators and 2 representatives to the Congress of the U.S.

History. The first explorer of the New Hampshire region was an Englishman, Martin Pring, who anchored in Piscataqua harbor in 1603. In 1605 the French explorer Samuel de Champlain sailed along the coast of New Hampshire and discovered the Isles of Shoals. In 1614 the English colonist and soldier John Smith visited the harbor and some of the inland regions of the State. In 1620 the re-

Bernice B. Perry

Taking sap from a maple tree to make maple sirup in Walpole, New Hampshire

Harold Orne; A. N. Bouchard

Top: Skiers on a slope of Mount Cranmore, near Conway, New Hampshire. Bottom: Hikers atop Mount Washington, highest point in New Hampshire, 6288 feet above sea level.

gion was granted to the Council for New England by King James I. The Council, in 1622, granted all the land lying between the Merrimack and Kennebec rivers for 60 m. inland to Sir Ferdinando Gorges and John Mason (qq.v.). The title of the grant was the "Province of Maine" (see MAINE: *History*). In 1623 the town of Little Harbor was established on the present site of Rye. On Nov. 7, 1629, the province was divided and that part lying between the Piscataqua and the Merrimack rivers was given to Mason; the title given to the grant was "New Hampshire".

Several trading stations were established within the grant, the most important of which was Strawberry Bank, later Portsmouth. The Council for New England was dissolved in 1635 and Mason was confirmed in all his grants by the crown and given an additional 100,000 acres w. of the Kennebec R. In 1638 John Wheelwright, a clergyman banished from Massachusetts, founded the settlement of Exeter. Most of the small settlements in this period were practically independent and often lacked an organized government. Massachusetts Bay, the Puritan colony, looked with disfavor upon the settlements of the royalists and churchmen in New Hampshire and laid claim to the territory (see MASSACHUSETTS: *History*). In 1641 all the settlements except Exeter were joined to the Massachusetts Bay Colony. Exeter followed in 1643. Mason's grandson, Robert Tufton Mason, became the sole heir of the province in 1655, and he applied to the crown for the restitution of the territory. Legal difficulties delayed a decision until 1677, when it was decided that Massachusetts had usurped possession of the territory. In 1679 a decree declaring New Hampshire a royal province was issued. From 1686 to 1689 the province of New Hampshire was part of the Dominion of New England, which was under the governorship of Sir Edmund Andros (q.v.).

Attempts of the residents of New Hampshire to establish a provincial authority met with failure, but in 1692 a royal government was established. From 1699 to 1741 New Hampshire was governed by the Royal Governor of Massachusetts. Boundary disputes between the two colonies were frequent. The problem was finally resolved in 1741 when the southern and eastern boundaries of New Hampshire with Massachusetts were permanently fixed. However, boundary disputes with New York, over the question of the possession of Vermont, continued until 1764, when New York succeeded in fixing the western border of New Hampshire at its present limits, the Connecticut R.

In 1776 New Hampshire became the first colony to adopt its own constitution. During the Revolutionary period the overwhelming majority of the State's inhabitants were patriots. At the important Battle of Bennington (see BENNINGTON, BATTLE OF) New Hampshire and Vermont troops inflicted a costly defeat upon the British. New Hampshire became the ninth State to ratify the Constitution on June 21, 1788. With the single exception of 1804, when the majority of the people of the State voted for Thomas Jefferson, Democratic-Republican, New Hampshire was Federalist in national politics until 1816. In the latter year the Democrats gained political control by capturing both State and national elections. The Democrats retained political power in the State until 1855, when the Know-Nothings (q.v.), a third political party, won the electoral votes of the State.

During the years preceding the Civil War reform movements, advocating temperance and the abolition of slavery, gained strength in New Hampshire. From 1856 through 1952 the majority of the people of New Hampshire have usually voted for the Republican Presidential candidate. The Democrats won five elections in that period. In 1912 Woodrow Wilson, Democrat, carried the State with a plurality of less than 1800 votes; in 1916 Wilson defeated the Republican candidate, Charles Evan Hughes, by 56 votes; and in 1936, 1940, and 1944 the Democratic incumbent, Franklin Delano Roosevelt, won the State election by comparatively small majorities. In the 1952 Presidential election Dwight D. Eisenhower, the Republican candidate, received 166,287 votes, and Adlai E. Stevenson, Democrat, received 106,663 votes.

NEW HAMPSHIRE, UNIVERSITY OF, a coeducational, State-controlled institution of higher learning, founded at Hanover, N.H., in 1868, as the New Hampshire College of Agriculture and Mechanic Arts, and moved to Durham, N.H., in 1893. The present name was adopted by legislative enactment in 1923. Baccalaureate degrees are offered in the liberal arts and sciences, technology, and agriculture; master's degrees are offered in the liberal arts and sciences and in education. Courses leading to baccalaureate degrees in music education were instituted in 1947–48, in order to fill the need for music teachers in New Hampshire. Undergraduate students may earn their degrees in three years and five months, instead of the customary four years, by taking accelerated courses. In a recent year, about 2500 men and 930 women were enrolled in full-time courses; an additional 500 students were taking part-time courses. The faculty in the same year comprised more than 300 persons.

NEW HARMONY, a town of Posey Co., Ind., situated on the Wabash R., 22 miles N.W. of Evansville. New Harmony was founded in 1815 by members of a religious sect known as the Harmonists (q.v.), under the leadership of George Rapp (q.v.), who had removed to the site from their earlier settlement at Harmonie, Pa. The colonists, mostly Germans from Württemberg, held their property in common and engaged in agriculture, weaving, and the manufacture of leather goods. In 1825 Rapp sold the entire town to a Welsh socialist and philanthropist, Robert Owen, and returned to Pennsylvania with his adherents, establishing a settlement at Economy, in Beaver Co. Owen and his followers, who were known as "Owenites", attempted to establish a successful socialistic community at New Harmony, but the experiment in communal living was a failure almost from the start, owing perhaps to the dissenting ideas held by the many educators and scientists brought to New Harmony by Owen to share in the practical application of his social and educational theories. The "Owenite" community was dissolved as such about 1828, but during its brief history the settlement was a center of cultural advancement in the Midwest. Many of the original buildings of the Harmonists and their successors are still standing, and a pageant depicting the history of New Harmony is presented biennially by the present inhabitants of the town. Pop. (1950) 1360.

NEW HAVEN, a county seat and port of entry of New Haven Co., Conn., situated at the head of New Haven Bay, on Long Island Sound, and at the mouth of the Quinnipiac, Mill, and West rivers, about 70 miles E.N.E. of New York City. It is served by a railroad, air lines, and coastal steamers, and is the second largest city in the State, and the site of Yale University (q.v.). In addition to its importance as an educational center, New Haven is a manufacturing and commercial center. It is the headquarters of the New York, New Haven, and Hartford Railroad Company, which maintains extensive construction and repair shops there, with a freight-classification yard covering more than 1100 acres. The city, leading distribution point in the State, contains numerous large wholesale houses and storage warehouses, and has a wide retail trading area. In the vicinity are traprock quarries. Among the industrial establishments in New Haven are plants manufacturing guns, ammunition, clocks, watches, hardware, coke, cables, wires, cordage, machinery, machine tools, sewing-machine parts, toys, electrical equipment, rubber goods, corsets, toilet articles, clothing, and razor blades.

New Haven, capital of Connecticut from 1701 to 1873, is the site of several State and Federal agencies, including the Connecticut Agricultural Experiment Station, an office of the U.S. Bureau of Internal Revenue, and a U.S. District Court. In addition to Yale University, educational institutions in New Haven are a State teachers college, established in 1893; Albertus Magnus College (Roman Catholic) for women, founded in 1903; Berkeley Divinity School (Episcopal); Arnold College for Hygiene and Physical Education; Connecticut College of Pharmacy; New Haven Y.M.C.A. Junior College (1920); and Larson Junior College (1911).

New Haven, often called the "City of Elms", maintains a municipal park area covering about 2100 acres. Notable parks are the Green, laid out by the original settlers; East Rock Park; West Rock Park, containing the Judges Cave, where the regicide judges William Goffe and Edward Whalley, who condemned King Charles I to death, are said to have hidden for several weeks in 1661; Lighthouse Point, with a municipal bathing beach; and Nathan Hale Park, in which are the ruins of old Fort Hale, used in the War of 1812. Trinity (Episcopal), Center (Congregational), and United (Congregational) churches, built in the early 19th century, stand on the Green. Other points of interest in the city are the old Grove Street cemetery, containing the graves of many famous Americans, including Noah Webster, Eli Whitney, and Samuel F.B. Morse; and the Pardee Morris House, originally built in 1685 and rebuilt in 1779.

New Haven was settled in 1638 by a group of English Puritans under the leadership of the Rev. John Davenport (q.v.) and Theophilus Eaton. In 1643–44 New Haven Colony admitted the communities of Guilford, Milford, Branford, Stamford, and, on Long Island, Southold, to its jurisdiction. In 1664, however, New Haven and its communities, with the exception of Southold, lost their status as an independent colony to become

Philip Gendreau

New Jersey State Capitol in Trenton

part of the Connecticut Colony, which had received a charter in 1662 entitling it to all lands held by New Haven Colony. From 1701 to 1785 New Haven was a joint capital of Connecticut with Hartford. From 1760 until the War of 1812, it was an important center of the West Indian trade, and later developed a flourishing commerce with Far Eastern ports. New Haven was chartered as a city in 1784. Pop. (1950) 164,443.

NEW HEBRIDES, group of islands in the Pacific Ocean, northwest of Australia. The area is approximately 5700 square miles and the population (1946 est.) 45,000. Some of the islands are composed of coral; others are of volcanic origin with several active volcanoes. The climate is unhealthful. Even the natives are not immune to fever, and dysentery makes great ravages among them. The people of this group of islands are Melanesians, very dark in complexion and below medium stature. The area under cultivation is planted chiefly with coconuts, cacao, cotton, and coffee. Bananas, oranges, and all tropical fruits grow well.

The New Hebrides group was first discov-

ered by the Portuguese in the early part of the seventeenth century. The islands were visited and named by Captain Cook in 1774 and were neutralized in 1778. The group is under the joint administration of France and Great Britain. The capital is Port Vila.

NEW IRELAND, the second largest island of the Bismarck Archipelago, in the Pacific Ocean, N.E. of New Guinea. Area, 3800 sq.m. (plus adjacent islands) ; length, 300 m.; width, 15 m. Pop. (1941) 37,822.

NEW JERSEY, one of the Middle Atlantic States of the United States, bounded on the N.E. by New York, on the E. by the Atlantic Ocean and by the Hudson R., which separates New Jersey from New York, on the S. by Delaware Bay, and on the S.W., W., and N.W. by the Delaware R., which separates New Jersey from the States of Delaware and Pennsylvania. New Jersey ranks as the 45th State in the Union in area, the 8th in population (1950), and the 3rd in order of admission to the Union, having entered on Dec. 18, 1787. The State capital is Trenton. In the order of population (1950) the leading cities of the State having populations over 100,000 are

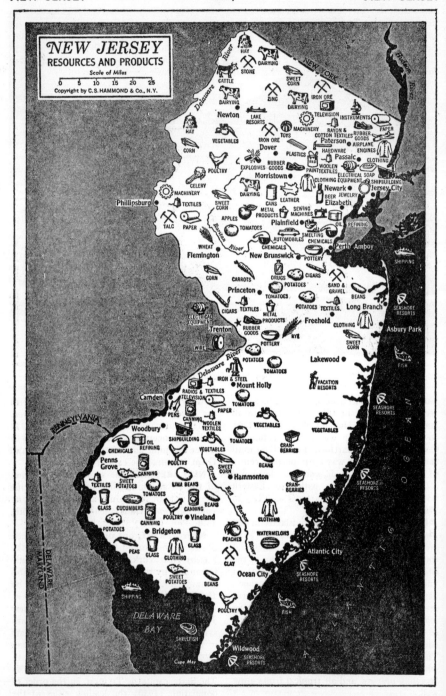

NEW JERSEY
RESOURCES AND PRODUCTS
Scale of Miles

0   5   10   15   20   25

Copyright by C.S. HAMMOND & Co., N.Y.

Newark, Jersey City, Paterson, Trenton, Camden, and Elizabeth (qq.v.). Other important communities include Bayonne, Atlantic City, Asbury Park, and Princeton (qq.v.). Area of the State, 7836 sq.m., including 314 sq.m. of inland water surface. Population (1950) 4,835,329.

Topographically, the surface of New Jersey is divided into four main regions, the Atlantic Coastal Plain, the Triassic Lowland, the Highlands, and the Appalachian Mountains. The coastal plain, which is bounded on the N.W. by a line drawn between Trenton in the w. and Woodbridge in the E., occupies the entire southern half of the State. It is a gently undulating plain drained by sluggish rivers and bordered along the coast by salt marshes. About a third of this region has an altitude of less than 50 ft. above sea level and only about 15 sq.m. of the area has an elevation of 200 ft. above sea level.

The Triassic Lowland is bounded on the S.E. by the coastal plain and on the N.W. by a line which runs roughly parallel to the Trenton-Woodbridge line, and extends through Morristown from the New York boundary to the Pennsylvania boundary. It consists of a rolling plain and constitutes a fifth of the area of the State. It ranges in elevation from sea level in the marshes of the Hackensack valley in the E. to over 900 ft. in the w. The plain is diversified by bold traprock ridges extending in a N.E. to S.W. direction. The best known of these rock ridges is the Palisades (q.v.) extending along the Hudson R. opposite the cities of Yonkers and New York.

The third topographical division, the Highlands, is a continuation of the Berkshire Hills of Massachusetts and the Highlands of New York. They are bordered on the S.E. by the Triassic Lowland and on the N.W. by the fourth topographical province, the easternmost ranges of the Appalachian system. The Highland area consists of rounded, forested hills separated by cultivated valleys. The region encompasses about 900 sq.m., is 60 m. long (N.E. to S.W.), and from 9 to 18 m. wide.

The fourth topographical belt consists of the Kittatinny mountain range and valley, a portion of the Appalachian system. The range enters New Jersey from Pennsylvania and traverses the State in a nearly continuous ridge into New York. At High Point the ridge reaches an elevation of 1809 ft. above sea level, the highest altitude in the State. The lowest point in the State is at sea level, and the average elevation of New Jersey is 250 ft. above sea level. Kittatinny valley borders

the ridge to the N.W. and the Highlands to the S.E. It is about 40 m. long, 12 m. wide, and 700 ft. above sea level. From N. to S. the State possesses an extreme length of 166 m., and an extreme width, from E. to w., of 57 m.

Most of the surface of New Jersey is drained by rivers which flow directly into the Atlantic Ocean. A narrow section along the w. boundary is drained by small rivers and streams which flow into the Delaware R. The chief rivers of the State are the Passaic, Hackensack, Raritan, Mullica, Great Egg, and the Maurice; the last-named stream drains into Delaware Bay. The Delaware R. forms the entire N.W., w., and s.w. boundary of the State for a distance of 245 m. The Hudson R. forms a part of the N.E. boundary of the State and flows along the border of New Jersey for a distance of 22 m. Lakes are confined chiefly to the glaciated northern section of New Jersey; the largest lakes are Hopatcong and Greenwood, the latter lying partly in New York State. New Jersey has a coastline of about 132 m. Measured around bays, inlets, and estuaries reached by tidal water, the coastline has a length of 1660 m.

The prevailing winds of New Jersey, with the exception of a narrow coastal strip, blow from the w. The climate of the State varies considerably between the elevated northern section and the coastal plain. The average annual temperature in the N. is 46° F., and in the s., 54° F. The average annual rainfall is between 41 and 52 inches.

New Jersey contains large resources of clay, zinc, iron, glass sand, green sand, traprock, limestone, sandstone, and granite. In 1951 the total value of mineral products was more than $58,660,000.

Manufacturing is the most important industry in the State. In 1951 the total value added by manufacture in New Jersey's industries was approximately $5,311,000,000. The State led the country in the manufacture of paints, varnishes, chemicals, and in the dyeing and finishing of textiles. In 1952 about 11,300 manufacturing establishments employed over 813,000 workers who earned $3,158,000,000. Other major industrial activities are the smelting and refining of nonferrous metals, petroleum refining, the manufacture of motor vehicles and supplies, wholesale meat packing, shipbuilding and repairing, and the manufacture of electrical equipment.

Cash income from agricultural enterprises in 1952 totaled about $347,500,000. Income from crops was about $124,500,000; from livestock, $222,100,000; from Federal sub-

Port N.Y. Auth.; Gendreau

NEW JERSEY. Above: Aerial view of the United States Metals Refining Company in Carteret. Left: A section of the Pulaski Skyway, elevated highway in northern New Jersey.

sidies, $900,000. Farms in 1950 numbered 24,838, and covered an area of more than 1,725,000 acres. Tenant farmers operated a little more than 7 percent of the total number of farms in the State. The chief crops in New Jersey are apples, peaches, grapes, potatoes, tomatoes, corn, wheat, oats, hay, and asparagus. Livestock in 1953 numbered 225,-000 cattle (including 155,000 dairy cows), 135,000 hogs, 7000 horses, 14,000 sheep, and (1952) 15,850,000 chickens.

The total highway mileage of the State is (1953) 28,692 m.; all but about 6000 m. of this total is improved highway. Railway main-track mileage is (1952) 2059 m. Ten scheduled air lines radiate from Newark and many nonscheduled air lines use the State as a terminus. Four bridges, five tunnels, and a number of ferry lines connect New Jersey to New York. Two cities of New Jersey, Hoboken and Jersey City, form part of the Port of New York, and steamships also use the ports of

Bayonne, Newark, Carteret, and Perth Amboy.

Attendance at the public schools of the State is free for all students between the ages of five and twenty-one, and compulsory during the entire school year for all children between the ages of seven and seventeen. In 1952–53 about 1800 public elementary and secondary schools were attended by almost 763,000 students and staffed by over 27,000 teachers. Thirty-eight institutions of higher learning are in the State. These include thirteen universities and colleges, eight professional and technical schools, ten junior colleges, six teachers colleges, and one institute for advanced study. Rutgers University is operated by the State, as are the New Jersey College for Women, the New Jersey College for Pharmacy, and the various teachers colleges. Other important institutions of higher learning within the State are Princeton University (q.v.) and the Institute for Advanced Study at Princeton, Seton Hall College at South Orange, and the Stevens Institute of Technology (q.v.) at Hoboken.

New Jersey is governed according to the terms of the constitution of 1947. Executive authority is vested in a governor who is elected for a four-year term. The legislature consists of a senate of 21 members, elected for four-year terms, and a general assembly of 60 members, elected for two-year terms. The judiciary is composed of a court of errors and appeals, a court for the trial of impeachments, a court of chancery, a prerogative court, a supreme court, circuit courts, and various inferior courts. Electors are U.S. citizens who have reached the age of twenty-one, resided in the State for one year, the county for five months, and who have registered for the election. New Jersey is divided into twenty-one counties, and the residents of the State send two senators and fourteen representatives to the Congress of the U.S.

History. New Jersey was first claimed by the Dutch as a part of New Netherland, and between 1614 and 1621 the Dutch established settlements in what is now Hudson County. In 1643 a Swedish settlement was established on the New Jersey side of the Delaware R.

In 1644 Charles II of England granted the entire region to his brother James, the Duke of York, who in turn granted the land between the Hudson and Delaware rivers to John Berkeley and Sir George Carteret (q.v.) The State received its name from the Isle of Jersey, which was governed by Carteret from 1643 to 1651.

In 1664, during the Anglo-Dutch Wars, the English seized New Amsterdam from the Dutch and secured the British claim to New Jersey. Berkeley and Carteret promulgated a charter for the government of New Jersey in the following year. In 1673 the Dutch temporarily recaptured the territory, but in 1674, by the Treaty of Westminster, the area was restored to the English. In the same year Berkeley sold his interest to two English Quakers (see FRIENDS, SOCIETY OF), who settled in the western part of the territory. Later, William Penn (q.v.) and some of his associates purchased the area, which was then called West Jersey, from the original buyers and drew up a constitution called "the Concessions and Agreements of the Proprietors, Freeholders and Inhabitants of West Jersey in America" in 1677. The Quaker colony flourished and in 1682 Carteret's heirs sold East Jersey to Wil-

N.J. Council, State Dept. of Economic Development
Boardwalk on the shore of a lake in Sussex County, New Jersey

liam Penn and his associates. In 1702 the proprietors of New Jersey ceded their right of self-government to the crown but retained the right of ownership of the land. New Jersey came under the political jurisdiction of the governor of New York until 1738, when the colony received its own governor. In 1776, during the American Revolution, the royal governor, William Franklin, was deposed and arrested, and on July 18, 1776, a provincial congress ratified the national Declaration of Independence and changed the title of the colony to the State of New Jersey. During the Revolution the State was the site of many important battles.

Canals were constructed in the early part of the 19th century and in 1834 the first railroad, the Camden and Amboy, was completed. In 1860 Abraham Lincoln received four of the State's seven electoral votes. In the Civil War, New Jersey sent approximately 90,000 men to the Union Army. After the Civil War the State was the scene of a bitter railway dispute. In 1871 the Pennsylvania Railway Co. was given a 999-year lease on properties lying between New York and Philadelphia. Other railways were almost eliminated from competition until 1873, when the State legislature passed a bill granting additional railway lines the right of way between New York and Philadelphia.

From 1876 through 1892, a majority of the New Jersey ballots cast in Presidential elections was for the Democratic candidate. From 1896 through 1928 the Republican candidate for President received the majority of the ballots cast in every election but one, the 1912 election when Woodrow Wilson (Democrat) received a plurality. From 1932 through 1944 the Democratic candidate received a majority. The Republican candidate received a plurality in 1948. In the 1952 election Dwight David Eisenhower, the Republican candidate, received 1,373,613 votes and Adlai Ewing Stevenson, the Democratic candidate, received 1,015,902 votes.

NEW KENSINGTON, a city of Westmoreland Co., Pa., situated on the Allegheny R., 18 miles N.E. of Pittsburgh. The city is served by rail, and is a coal-mining and manufacturing center, producing aluminum and aluminum ware, malleable iron, steel, steel conduits, fabricated steel, white lead, car springs, railroad equipment, glass, plastics, electrical equipment, and textiles. In addition, New Kensington is the retail trading center of an area with a population of approximately 200,000. The city was founded in 1891 near the site of an old fort, built in 1778. It was incorporated as

a borough in 1892 and as a city in 1930. Pop. (1950) 25,146.

NEW LONDON, a port of entry and one of two county seats of New London Co., Conn., situated on the w. bank of the Thames R., about 3 m. above its entrance into Long Island Sound and 50 miles E. of New Haven. Transportation facilities include two railroads, steamship lines, and a municipal airport. The city has a deep harbor, and is an important U.S. Naval and Coast Guard base, and a popular summer resort. New London is the site of the U.S. Coast Guard Academy, the Coast Guard Training Station, the Navy Submarine School, Admiral Billard Academy, and Connecticut College for Women. Several yacht clubs are situated in New London, and the annual Yale-Harvard crew races are held on the Thames R., finishing at New London. The city contains many old buildings and points of historical interest. The old cemetery in the city dates from 1653; the old town mill, originally built about 1650, was rebuilt in 1712; Nathan Hale, the Revolutionary hero, taught in the old schoolhouse, built in 1774; and the Shaw Mansion (1756), home of the Connecticut Naval Office during the Revolutionary War, now contains the exhibits of the New London County Historical Society.

The site of New London was settled about 1645, and in 1646 a town bearing the Indian name of *Nameaug* ("fishing-place") was founded by John Winthrop the younger, of the Massachusetts Bay Colony. In 1658 the inhabitants succeeded in having the name changed to New London, and the river, formerly called the Monhegin, was named the Thames. During the Revolutionary War, New London was an important base for privateers, and was attacked and burned in 1781 by a large British military and naval force led by the former American officer Benedict Arnold (q.v.), who then led an attack on Fort Griswold at nearby Groton (q.v.), in which the fort's garrison was massacred. New London was incorporated as a city in 1784 and for some time after the Revolution was a leading whaling center. Pop. (1950) 30,551.

NEWMAN, CARDINAL JOHN HENRY (1801-90), British religious leader, at first in the Church of England and later in the Roman Catholic Church. He was born in London, and educated at Trinity College, Oxford. In 1822 he obtained an Oriel College fellowship, then the highest distinction of Oxford scholarship, and thus was brought into close association with a number of the most illustrious men of the time. In 1826 Newman was appointed a tutor at Oriel, and two years later became vicar of St. Mary's, the church of Oxford University. In this position he exerted a pervasive influence upon contemporary religious thought through his learned and eloquent sermons. He resigned his tutorship in 1832 and in the following year made a tour of the Mediterranean, during which time he wrote the famous hymn *Lead, Kindly Light*.

Newman returned to England in time to hear the memorable sermon on national apostacy preached at St. Mary's by his fellow Oxonian, John Keble (q.v.). This sermon defined the religious issues of the time and marked the inception of the Oxford Movement (q.v.), a movement within the Church of England (see ANGLICAN CHURCH) directed against the growth of theological liberalism, and advocating the return to Roman Catholic theology and ritual (see LAUD, WILLIAM; REFORMATION; RITUALISM; ROMAN CATHOLIC CHURCH; SACRAMENT; TRANSUBSTANTIATION).

Newman, whose own religious thinking had for some time been along similar lines, soon became the acknowledged leader of the Oxford group, a role for which his vital personality, fervent asceticism, and persuasive eloquence pre-eminently qualified him. He was one of the chief contributors to the *Tracts for the Times* (1833–41), for which he wrote twenty-nine papers, including the famous number 90 which terminated the series; the last-named tract provoked a storm of opposition by its claim that the thirty-nine articles of the Church of England (see ARTICLES, THE THIRTY-NINE), which incorporate the creed of the reformed church in England, are aimed primarily at the abuses and not the dogmas of Roman Catholicism. The thesis was repudiated by Anglican dignitaries, who almost universally declared against the Oxford Movement.

In 1842 Newman retired from Oxford to the neighboring village of Littlemore, where he passed three years in seclusion, writing at this time a formal retraction of the adverse criticisms of the Roman Catholic Church which he had made on previous occasions; he also resigned his post as vicar of St. Mary's, and on October 9, 1845, after writing his *Essay on the Development of Christian Doctrine,* which gave final crystallization to his ideas, he became a Roman Catholic. A year later he went to Rome, where he was ordained a priest. Upon his return to England, he introduced the Congregation of the Oratory, a body of priests living in community, but not bound by monastic vows.

Cardinal John Henry Newman

Newman spent most of the remainder of his life in the house of the Oratory which he had established at Birmingham; from 1854 to 1858, however, he served as rector of the Catholic University in Dublin, Ireland. There he delivered a series of lectures, subsequently revised and published under the title of *The Idea of a University Defined,* in which he defined the function of a university as the training of the mind, rather than the diffusion of practical information. In response to a charge by the English novelist Charles Kingsley (q.v.) that Roman Catholicism was indifferent to the truth, Newman published his *Apologia pro Vita Sua* ("Apology for His Life"), a memorable account of his spiritual development. He was elected an honorary fellow of Trinity College, Oxford, in 1877, and Pope Leo XIII created him a cardinal in 1879. Newman's other important writings include the novels *Loss and Gain* (1848) and *Callista* (1856); *The Dream of Gerontius* (1866), a monologue in verse; *Verses on Various Occasions* (1874); and *The Grammar of Assent* (1870), a closely reasoned work on the philosophy of faith.

NEWMARKET, market town of Suffolk, England, 14 miles N.E. of Cambridge. The town owes its prosperity to its horse races, as old at least as 1605; eight race meetings are held annually. Pop., about 10,000. Its rural district,

NEW MEXICO
RESOURCES AND PRODUCTS
Scale of Miles
0 10 20 30 40 50 60 70
Copyright by C.S.HAMMOND & CO.,N.Y.

in Cambridgeshire, has a population of about 19,000.

NEW MEXICO, one of the Southwestern States of the United States, bounded on the E. by Oklahoma and Texas, on the S. by Texas and Mexico, on the w. by Arizona, and on the N. by Colorado. It ranks as the 4th State in the Union in area, 39th in population (1950), and the 47th in order of admission to the Union, having entered on Jan. 6, 1912. The State capital is Santa Fe. The leading cities in the order of population (1950) are Albuquerque, Santa Fe, and Roswell (qq.v.). From N. to S. the State possesses an extreme length of 400

m., and from E. to w. the extreme width is 358 m. Area, 121,666 sq.m., including 155 sq.m. of inland water surface. Population (1950) 681,187.

The surface of New Mexico is a vast, gently undulating plain dotted with steep, rocky mountains, and traversed by occasional valleys and canyons. A southern spur of the Rocky Mountains enters the State from the N. and its isolated ranges and peaks occupy scattered portions of New Mexico. The Sangre de Cristo Mountains occupy the N. central region, various ranges and sierras traverse the western part of the State, and the Guadalupe Mountains in the s. central region of New Mexico extend across the border into Mexico. The highest point in the State is North Truchas Peak, 13,306 ft. above sea level, in Rio Arriba Co. The lowest point, 2876 ft., is located in Eddy Co. The mean elevation of New Mexico is 5700 ft.

The Continental Divide extends through the western portion of the State in a roughly N. to S. direction. Rivers E. of the divide ultimately drain into the Gulf of Mexico and rivers W. of the divide drain into the Gulf of California. The principal rivers are the Rio Grande, which flows roughly N. to S. through the w. central portion of the State, and the Pecos, which flows from the N. central part of the State s.e., then s. into Texas.

New Mexico is often called the "Sunshine State". During an average year almost 60% of the days are cloudless. The winter temperature averages 31° F. and the summer temperature averages 67° F. Extremes of 97° F. and –13° F. have been recorded. At Santa Fe, in the N. central portion of the State, the yearly temperature averages 49° F. Precipitation averages 15 inches a year for the State as a whole. The southern plains receive as little as 6 inches and the northern mountains receive as much as 30 inches.

Animal and vegetable life in New Mexico is extremely diversified because of the nature of the terrain. Mesquite, cactus, cottonwood, and desert willow are among the plants and trees that grow in the southern valleys of the State. Animal life in this area includes rabbits, squirrels, rats, mice, bats, skunks, and varieties of desert fox and weasel. Trout are plentiful in the mountain rivers and streams. Other varieties of fauna found in the State include coyotes, deer, wolves, prairie dogs, elk, mountain lions, bobcats, mountain sheep, black bears, grizzly bears, and minks. Flora includes buffalo and other types of grasses, cacti of several species, and many varieties of deciduous and coniferous trees.

New Mexico is noted for its facilities for hunting, fishing, and winter sports. National forests in the State cover (1952) 8,685,000 acres, and some 4,000,000 acres of heavily forested land is privately owned. The State contains eight national monuments, one national park, and four State parks. Four Indian reservations and eighteen Indian pueblos are located within New Mexico. The Navaho Indian Reservation, the largest in the U.S., covers more than 16,000,000 acres.

Agriculture, aided considerably by irrigation, is the most important industry in New Mexico. In 1952 the cash income from crops, livestock, and Federal farm subsidies amounted to about $212,300,000. In 1950 about 23,600 farms and ranches covered an area of approximately 47,500,000 acres and included lands and buildings valued at more than $633,300,-

New Mexico State Tourist Bureau

The old palace of the governors in Santa Fe, New Mexico, built about 1610

000. The principal crops are cotton, corn, wheat, grain, sorghums, and potatoes. In 1953 about 295,000 acres yielded an estimated 315,000 bales of cotton. Livestock • number (1953) about 1,250,000 cattle (including 55,000 dairy cows), 1,389,000 sheep, 71,000 horses, 60,000 hogs, 3000 mules, and (1952) about 1,015,000 chickens.

New Mexico has many valuable mineral resources. In 1951 over 300,000,000,000 cubic feet of natural gas, 3,307,000 barrels of natural gasoline, and 52,720,000 barrels of petroleum were produced; other minerals were 74,000 tons of copper, 45,000 tons of zinc, 783,000 tons of coal, 6000 tons of lead, 24,-000 tons of fluorspar, and 1,080,000 tons of sand and gravel. The mining of potassium salts, gold, and silver is also important. The total mineral output in 1951 was valued at more than $256,000,000.

The chief manufactures of New Mexico are primarily based upon the natural resources of the State. In 1951 the total value added by manufacture was approximately $121,600,000. The production of lumber, the refining of oil, and printing and publishing are the leading industries. In 1952 about 15,600 wage earners were employed in 626 manufacturing establishments and earned more than $62,000,000.

Six railroads (the most important of which is the Atchison, Topeka, and Santa Fe) maintain about 2500 m. of main-track railway, and the State maintains (1951) 10,403 m. of highway. Albuquerque is a main junction for transcontinental air lines. There are (1951) 16 major airports in the State.

Attendance at elementary and secondary schools in New Mexico is free and compulsory for the full school year for all children between the ages of six and seventeen. In 1952–53 there were 741 public elementary and secondary schools, staffed by about 5700 teachers and attended by more than 166,500 students. In addition, the Federal government maintains 35 special schools for Indians, staffed by approximately 140 teachers and attended by about 4200 students in 1952.

Nine institutions of higher learning are located in the State: six universities and colleges, two teachers colleges, and a professional school. The State supports the University of New Mexico at Albuquerque, the State School of Mines at Socorro, the College of Agriculture and Mechanic Arts at Las Cruces, the New Mexico Highlands University at Las Vegas, the New Mexico State Teachers College at Silver City, Spanish-American Normal at El Rito, Eastern New Mexico Normal at Portales, and the New Mexico Military Institute at Roswell.

New Mexico is governed according to the terms of the constitution of 1911, as amended. Executive authority is vested in a governor, lieutenant governor, secretary of state, auditor, treasurer, attorney general, superintendent of public instruction, commissioner of public lands, and three corporation commissioners, all of whom are elected for two-year terms. The legislature, which meets biennially, is composed of a senate of 32 members, elected for four-year terms, and a house of representatives of 54 members, elected for two-year terms. Judicial authority is vested in a supreme court, which consists of five justices elected for eight-year terms, nine district courts, probate courts, and justices of the peace. The State is divided into 32 counties. Two senators and two representatives, elected by voters of the entire State, represent New Mexico in the U.S. Congress.

History. The first explorers of the region were Spanish. In 1536 Cabeza de Vaca (q.v.) visited the New Mexico and Arizona area, and from 1540 to 1542 Francisco Vásquez Coronado (q.v.) traversed the region, and conquered the Zuñi pueblos (see PUEBLO INDIANS). Other Spanish explorers, priests, and conquerors visited the territory, and in 1598 the first settlement was established at San Juan de los Caballeros in the Chama R. valley. Santa Fe was founded in 1609. The Indians revolted against the Spanish missionaries and settlers in 1680, and drove them out of the territory. The Spanish reconquered the region between 1692 and 1696. The region became a province of Mexico in 1821, when that country gained its independence from Spain (see MEXICO: *History*) Mexico legalized trade (which had been discouraged under the Spanish) between the province and American settlements in the Missouri valley. The Republic of Texas (see TEXAS: *History*) claimed the Rio Grande as its western boundary, and twice sent expeditions to New Mexico (1841 and 1843) in an effort to conquer the region. Both expeditions failed.

After the outbreak of the Mexican War, U.S. forces under the command of Col. Stephen Watts Kearny (q.v.) occupied the province and on Aug. 18, 1846, the entire territory was declared a part of the U.S. A military government ruled the region for five years. The region formed part of the Mexican cession by the Treaty of Guadalupe Hidalgo, on Feb. 2, 1848, ending the Mexican War. On Sept. 9, 1850, the Territory of New Mexico

N.M. State Tourist Bureau

SCENES IN NEW MEXICO
Above: Herd of beef cattle on a range in southwestern New Mexico. Right: Pine and fir logs on train for shipment, near Cloudcroft in the Sacramento Mountains. Below: A flock of sheep grazing in Cumbres Pass, in the north.

Santa Fe Railway

Above: Pueblo Indian village of San Geronimo de Taos, New Mexico. Left: Ranchos de Taos Mission, built in 1776, in the Sangre de Cristo Mountains, New Mexico. Its walls are eight feet thick.

the Territory of New Mexico was added to the newly formed Territory of Colorado.

During the Civil War New Mexico was invaded by Confederate forces. They were defeated by Union forces in 1862 and forced to retire from the Territory. The remainder of the century was marked by the settlement of marauding Apache and Navaho Indians on reservations, and by the expansion of the railways, economic development of the Territory, and range warfare between the cattle and sheep interests.

In June, 1906, Congress passed a Bill providing for the admission of New Mexico and Arizona as one State, on condition that a majority of electors in each Territory approve such a union. A majority of the New Mexico electors approved, but a majority of Arizona electors voted against the proposal, thus leaving the Territorial status of each unchanged. On Jan. 6, 1912, New Mexico was admitted to the Union as a State.

On July 16, 1945, New Mexico was the site of the first atomic bomb explosion (see ALAMOGORDO AIR BASE). Since then, under the guidance of the Secretary of Defense or the Atomic Energy Commission, various proving

was created, including also the present State of Arizona and part of Colorado. In 1853 the Gadsden Purchase (q.v.) was added to the Territory. In 1863 Arizona was set off and established as a Territory, and the western boundary of New Mexico was fixed at its present limits. In 1865 the northern portion of

grounds and research centers have been established in the State for the furtherance of the development of guided missiles and atomic projects.

The majority of the voters of New Mexico have generally cast a plurality or majority of their ballots for the Democratic candidate in Presidential elections. In 1912, 1916, 1932, 1936, 1940, 1944, and 1948 the Democratic candidate carried the State. In 1920, 1924, 1928, and 1952 the Republican candidate received a majority or plurality of the votes. In the 1952 election, Dwight D. Eisenhower, the Republican candidate, received 132,170 ballots, and Adlai E. Stevenson, the Democratic candidate, received 105,661 ballots.

NEW MEXICO COLLEGE OF AGRICULTURE AND MECHANIC ARTS, a coeducational, State-controlled institution of higher learning, founded in 1889 and situated near Las Cruces, N.M. The College offers baccalaureate degrees in the liberal arts and sciences, business administration, agriculture, and in civil, chemical, electrical, and mechanical engineering; master's degrees are offered in the liberal arts and sciences. Specialized technical courses in aircraft and engine mechanics are also available. In 1953 about 1600 students were enrolled, including 1275 full-time students; the faculty numbered 145.

NEW MEXICO, UNIVERSITY OF, a coeducational, State-controlled institution of higher learning, founded in 1892, and situated at Albuquerque, N.M. The University offers baccalaureate degrees in the liberal arts and sciences, the fine arts, business administration, pharmacy, law, and in chemical, electrical, mechanical, and civil engineering; the degrees of master of arts and doctor of philosophy are also conferred. Recently established curricula include courses for teachers of retail selling and merchandising instituted in 1946, and journalism courses instituted in 1947. Accelerated courses are available for students desiring to earn baccalaureate degrees in a period of three years and two months. The buildings of the University are notable for their picturesque architecture, based upon the style of Indian pueblo structures. In 1953 student enrollment totaled 4000, including 3000 full-time students; the faculty numbered approximately 270.

NEW ORLEANS, the parish seat of Orleans Parish, La., with which the corporate limits of the city are co-extensive, largest city and chief port of Louisiana and, in 1950, the sixteenth-largest city in the U.S. It is situated on the Mississippi R., 107 m. from the mouth of the river in the Gulf of Mexico. Most of the city occupies a site between the river and Lake Pontchartrain on the N., which is connected with the river by a canal 5 m. long. The flat site, consisting of soil deposited by the river, is about 10 ft. below the level of the Gulf of Mexico, from 3 to 6 ft. below the high-water level of the Mississippi, and, to a great extent, below the level of the lake. Earthen levees protect the city on all sides from flood, but drainage, sewerage, and sanitation are major civic problems.

New Orleans is popularly called "Crescent City" because the original settlement formed a crescent around a bend in the river. The city is considered one of the most picturesque in the United States, and is famous for the section called the Vieux Carré, or French quarter, with two- and three-story houses, adorned with wrought-iron balconies projecting over the narrow streets. In the heart of the Vieux Carré is Jackson Square, once called the Place d'Armes, surrounded by such historic buildings as the Cabildo, once the administrative center under French and Spanish rule, and the Old Cathedral of St. Louis. Canal Street separates the French quarter from the newer American quarter, containing the commercial buildings and banks and better residential sections. Audubon Park, on the river, and City Park, between the city and the lake, are the largest park areas. The chief institutions of higher learning are Tulane University (1834), its affiliate for women, Newcomb Memorial College (1886), and Loyola University (1912), a Jesuit institution.

New Orleans is the largest center in the U.S. for trade in cotton, cottonseed products, and rice. One of the greatest American ports and able to accommodate the largest ships in its docks, the city has facilities serving over ninety steamship lines which, in a recent year, brought almost a billion dollars worth of goods into the port. Sugar, bananas, coffee, bauxite, and molasses are among the principal imports, and the chief commodities of export trade are petroluem products, iron and steel, corn, and cotton. The city is served by twelve railroads and is the terminus of three canals. The major industrial establishments manufacture sugar and sugar products, clothing, alcohol and spirits, and cottonseed oil.

New Orleans is famous as a cultural center, and the Vieux Carré is the temporary or permanent home of many American writers, painters, and musicians. Thousands of tourists annually visit the city for the carnival season, from Twelfth Night to Lent, which is

Bureau of New Orleans News

In the business section of New Orleans, Louisiana. Canal Street is at right

climaxed by the pageant of the Mardi Gras.

New Orleans was founded about 1718 by Jean Baptiste Lemoyne, Sieur de Bienville, then governor of the French Louisiana colony, who named the settlement for Philippe II, Duc d'Orleans, then regent of France. In 1722 the town was made the capital of the colony. Following the partition of Louisiana between England and Spain in 1762–63, New Orleans (called *Nouvelle Orléans*) became the capital of Spanish Louisiana. The French citizens revolted against Spain and expelled the Spanish governor in 1768. The revolt was short-lived, and a Spanish show of force in 1769 persuaded the citizenry to accept Spanish rule.

New Orleans was ceded secretly to France in 1800 (see LOUISIANA), and in the space of twenty days (Nov. 30-Dec. 20) in 1803, it was formally ceded first to France and then, by the terms of the Louisiana Purchase (q.v.), to the United States. American enterprise soon found expression in the rapid development and growth of the city. At the time of annexation New Orleans had about 10,000 inhabitants; five years later its population had more than doubled. The city was incorporated in 1805, and in 1812 became the State capital. In 1815, at the close of the War of 1812, the city was attacked by a British force. Gen. Andrew Jackson commanded an American army which decisively defeated the invaders in the Battle of New Orleans (q.v.), on Jan.

8, 1815. During the subsequent four decades New Orleans enjoyed great prosperity. Trade was tremendously increased by the advent of the steamboat and railroads, and by 1852 the city was the third largest in the U.S.

During the Civil War New Orleans, as the chief Confederate port and a military center, was a focal objective of Union troops. Admiral David G. Farragut, commanding a Union fleet, captured the city in April, 1862, and the port was held by the Union until the end of the war. From 1865 to 1877 the history of New Orleans was characterized by racial and political strife incited by so-called "carpet-baggers" (q.v.), who encouraged freed slaves to persecute their former masters. Riots became so frequent that the Federal government declared martial law in 1874. The government forces were withdrawn in 1877.

During the reconstruction period the city slowly recovered. The capital was transferred to Baton Rouge in 1880 and civic enterprise devoted itself to commercial development and public works. Among modern projects are the Bonnet Carre Spillway, improved docking facilities, the largest in the U.S., and a large airport, opened in 1934. Pop. (1950) 570,445.

NEW ORLEANS, BATTLE OF, the name of two battles fought near New Orleans, La., one in the War of 1812 and the other in the Civil War.

1. The Battle of New Orleans of the War

of 1812 was fought on January 8, 1815, between American troops numbering about four thousand, under the command of Major General Andrew Jackson, and a British force of about nine thousand commanded by Major General Sir Edward Pakenham (1778-1815). The battle resulted from a British plan to conquer the Gulf of Mexico region of the United States, in pursuance of which an army of ten thousand, carried by a fleet of fifty vessels, sailed from the British base at Jamaica, West Indies, and landed at Lake Borgne, E. of New Orleans, late in December, 1814. Jackson hastily but effectively fortified both banks of the Mississippi River. On January 8, 1815, Pakenham attempted to carry by storm both sides of the river at Chalmette, E. of the city. The British attempt was repulsed with great slaughter on the left bank of the river, although their attack on the right bank met with some success. Over two thousand British were killed, including General Pakenham. The total American casualties numbered about seventy. The defeat caused the British to abandon the attempt to conquer the region; they embarked for England about the end of January. The battle had no effect upon the war, which had already been terminated without the knowledge of the combatants by the signing of a treaty at Ghent, Belgium, on December 14, 1814; see GHENT, TREATY OF.

2. The Battle of New Orleans of the Civil War occurred as a result of the plan of the Federal government to cut the Confederacy in two by capturing all of its strongholds along the entire length of the Mississippi River. The Union plan called for forces under General Ulysses S. Grant to force their way down the river, and for other Union forces, under Admiral David Farragut and General Benjamin Franklin Butler, to take New Orleans and then proceed up the river to meet Grant. To prevent the capture of New Orleans the Confederates placed a barrier of cables across the river below the city; New Orleans was also defended by forts Jackson and St. Philip. The Union West Gulf Blockading Squadron, consisting of forty-three ships under the command of Farragut, entered the Mississippi from the Gulf of Mexico, bombarded Fort Jackson on April 18, 1862, broke the cables and forced its way past the two forts on April 24, defeated the small Confederate flotilla in the river, and took New Orleans on the 25th of April. On May 1 the city was occupied by fifteen thousand Federal troops under Butler. The capture of New Orleans was an important

step in the gaining of complete control of the Mississippi by the Union.

NEWPORT, one of the county seats of Campbell Co., Ky., situated at the confluence of the Ohio and Licking rivers, opposite Cincinnati, Ohio, and Covington, Ky. It is connected by bridges with the latter cities, and adjoins Bellevue and Dayton on the E., and Fort Thomas and Southgate on the S. Transportation facilities include two railroads and river steamers. Newport is a residential suburb of Cincinnati, and also an important manufacturing center. The surrounding agricultural area produces general farm crops, garden truck, livestock, and dairy products. Among the industrial establishments in the city are one of the largest rolling mills and one of the largest steel plants in the State, and a flour mill, a printing and publishing plant, a brewery, bottling works, and factories manufacturing men's clothing, screens, automobile parts, cement, tile, toys, and awnings.

The first settlement on the site of the present city was established in 1789 and the town of Newport was incorporated in 1795. It was an early rallying point for expeditions against hostile Indians in the present States of Ohio and Indiana. Newport was chartered as a city in 1834. Pop. (1950) 31,044.

NEWPORT, county seat and port of entry of Newport Co., R.I., situated at the s. end of the island of Rhode Island in Narragansett Bay, 30 miles S.E. of Providence. Transportation facilities include a railroad, ferries, steamers, and an airport. Newport is a fashionable summer resort and a naval base. It has a deep and almost landlocked harbor, defended by Fort Adams. Other military establishments at Newport and nearby are a naval war college, a naval training station, a naval hospital, a naval torpedo station, and a naval seaplane base. The city comprises an old section, with narrow streets and colonial houses, rising steeply from the harbor, and a modern area, containing five bathing beaches, golf courses, tennis courts, yacht clubs, polo grounds, and the large estates of the summer residents, who are chiefly from New York City. Among the points of interest in the "Old Town" are the Wanton-Lyman-Hazard House, built about 1675 and maintained as a museum; the Friends Meetinghouse, dating in part from 1699, now the Community Center Museum; Trinity Church (1725), with a slender white spire, still topped by the gold crown of England; the colonial State House (1739), a historic shrine; the Redwood Library (1747), with a notable collection of old books and art exhibits; the Touro Synagogue (1763), named for Rabbi Isaac Touro, and said to be the oldest synagogue in the U.S.; and the Vernon House (1756), the residence of Comte de Rochambeau, commander of the French force sent to aid the Continental Army. The interior of the Vernon House is noted for its fine decorative detail, including rare Chinese murals. Also in Newport is an ancient tower believed by some historians to have been erected by Leif Ericson (q.v.) about 1000 A.D.

Newport was settled in 1639 by a group of Antimonians, religious dissenters from the Massachusetts Bay Colony, under the leadership of William Coddington. The shipbuilding industry, for which Newport was noted in the colonial era, was founded about 1646. Newport was an important seaport of that period, rivaling New York and Boston in volume of foreign trade, and engaging in a profitable traffic in slaves, rum, and molasses. In 1758 James Franklin, nephew of Benjamin Franklin, established there a weekly newspaper, the *Mercury*, one of the oldest newspapers still published in the U.S. During the Revolutionary War Newport was occupied by the British from December, 1776, to October, 1779, and its shipping and trade were destroyed. It was chartered as a city in 1784, and until 1900 was one of the capitals of Rhode Island. After the Civil War Newport became the leading summer resort of New York society. Pop. (1950) 37,564.

NEWPORT, municipal and county borough of Monmouthshire, England, on the river Usk, 133½ m. from London. It is one of the principal outlets for the collieries and iron and steel works in the vicinity. Besides its shipping trade, the industries include india-rubber and gutta-percha factories, brass and iron foundries, breweries, and pottery works. Pop. (1951 prelim.) 105,285.

NEWPORT NEWS, a city and port of entry of Virginia, situated in Warwick Co., of which it is politically independent. It lies on Hampton Roads, at the mouth of the James R., opposite Norfolk and Portsmouth. Newport News is the seaboard terminus of a railroad, is served by numerous steamship and ferry lines, and maintains a municipal airport. With the cities of Norfolk and Portsmouth, Newport News forms the Port of Hampton Roads (q.v.), one of the principal commercial ports of the U.S. and an important naval base. It has a commodious and well-protected harbor, with a channel, 35 ft. deep and 600 ft. wide, to the ocean. Harbor facilities include the extensive warehouses, piers, and docks of the railroad terminal, one of the largest single railroad terminals in the world, and the shipbuilding yards and drydocks of one of the largest shipbuilding plants in the world. Coal, tobacco, scrap iron, and lumber are the leading exports; and in addition to shipbuilding yards and railroad shops, the city contains oyster fisheries, tobacco warehouses, and varied industries. Among the ships built or overhauled at Newport News are the passenger liner America, and many of the largest battleships and cruisers of the U.S. Navy.

The site of the present city was first settled in 1621 by a group of Irish colonists. The settlement was fortified by Federal troops during the Civil War, but its present development did not commence until 1881, when it became the terminus of the Chesapeake and Ohio railway. It was incorporated as a city in 1896. Pop. (1950) 42,358.

NEW ROCHELLE, city in Westchester Co., N.Y., 16½ miles from New York City, on an arm of Long Island Sound. It was settled in 1688 by Huguenots, some of whom were natives of La Rochelle. It was the home for several years of Thomas Paine, to whose memory a monument has been erected. Pop. (1950) 59,725.

NEW SCHOOL FOR SOCIAL RESEARCH, a coeducational, privately controlled institution of higher learning, located in New York City, and founded in 1919 primarily as an institution for adult education (see EDUCATION, ADULT). The School is organized in two divisions: the school of politics, and the school of philosophy and liberal arts. The school of politics is subdivided into courses classified into the following groups: the world of today and tomorrow; international relations and foreign affairs; center for the study of the near and middle east; history and political science; economics; housing; sociology and anthropology; and public relations and publicity. The school of philosophy and liberal arts offers courses in philosophy, culture, and religion; science; psychology, psychoanalysis, and education; literature, writing, and speech; linguistics and languages; art; music; gardening; and hygiene, gymnastics, and recreation. The Dramatic Workshop, formerly associated with the New School, received an independent charter in 1949.

The School grants the degrees of bachelor of arts (since 1944); master of social sciences and doctor of social sciences (since 1934); and master of arts and doctor of philosophy (since 1947). The majority of students, however, are enrolled in part-time, noncredit courses. Successful completion of two years of college is required for admission as a candidate for a B.A. degree. In 1953 the enrollment totaled nearly 5000 students, most of whom were on a part-time basis; over 420 were enrolled full-time. The faculty, composed mainly of lecturers who are members of the teaching staffs of various colleges and universities, numbered about 200.

NEW SCOTLAND YARD. See SCOTLAND YARD.

NEW SOUTH WALES, state of the Australian Commonwealth, and the oldest colony of Australasia, named in 1770 by Captain Cook. Area, 309,433 sq.m., including Lord Howe Island; pop. (1952 est.) excluding aborigines, 3,421,768; capital, Sidney (1,621,040). It has the Pacific to the E., S. Australia to the W., Victoria to the S., and Queensland to the N. A series of mountain chains runs parallel to the seacoast at a distance of 20 to 100 m., from near Cape York to the S.E. corner. The principal range attains a height of 7330 ft. in Mt. Kosciusko. The chief rivers are the Murray, Darling, Murrumbidgee, and Lachlan.

Next to grazing, mining is the most important industry. The chief products are gold, silver, coal, copper, tin, coke, lead, zinc, oil shale, opal, diamonds, cobalt, and alunite. Gold was first worked in 1851 near Bathurst. It is found in nearly all parts of New South Wales, but the most important districts are Bathurst, Lachlan, Mudgee, Peel, and Uralla. The silver (discovered in 1883) and lead mining is concentrated mainly at Broken Hill in the Albert Mining District. The main coal-bearing rocks extend over an area of 24,000 to 28,000 sq.m. around the seaport of Sydney.

Acreage under cultivation is (1953) 4,837,-355. The principal crops (with production figures for 1953) are as follows: wheat (56,670,-000 bushels), corn (2,112,672 bushels), barley (340,767 bushels), oats (12,326,016 bushels), potatoes (51,132 tons), tobacco (514,774 pounds), and rice (3,963.787 bushels). Cane sugar and grapes are also grown, wine and sugar constituting important manufactures. Citrus fruits are raised in considerable number, oranges predominating. Grazing and livestock raising are the principal industries, however; in 1953 sheep and lambs in the State numbered 57,461,000; cattle, 3,648,733; horses, 298,367; and pigs, 298,690. Forest area in New South Wales is estimated at 22,500,000 acres.

Manufacturing establishments in New South Wales number (1951–52) 18,144, the principal products being bricks, pottery, glass, chemicals, paint, oil, grease, industrial metals, machinery, conveyances, precious metals, jewelry, and textiles and textile goods.

The balance of trade is fairly even. Principal exports are wool, butter, wheat, flour, fruits, timber, meats, hides and skins, tallow, leather, pig lead, tin, copper, coal, and gold. The bulk of the overseas trade is carried on with the United Kingdom.

Railroad mileage is (1953) 6113, excluding 85 miles of privately-owned line chiefly in the mining districts. Roads and streets cover a total of 126,624 miles in all. The bridge over Sydney Harbor (opened 1932) is the largest arch bridge in the world.

New South Wales joined the other Australian states to form the Commonwealth of Australia in 1901. In New South Wales, government rests with a governor appointed by the imperial government, an Executive Council made up of members of the Cabinet, and a Parliament of two houses, the Legislative Council and the Legislative Assembly. Sixty members, elected by both houses of Parliament for twelve-year terms, make up the Legislative Council. Ninety-four elected members make up the Legislative Assembly. Voting is compulsory for all British subjects (women included) over 21 years of age who have resided six months in the commonwealth, three months in the state, and one month in the electorate. Education is free and compulsory for children between 6 and 15. The University of Sydney (founded, 1850) and its several affiliations, and five denominational colleges provide higher education.

NEWSPAPERS, publications, for the most part issued and distributed daily or weekly, the function of which is chiefly the reporting of news. Newspapers generally also contain comments on the news, advocate various public policies, furnish special information and advice to readers in many fields, and frequently also publish comic strips and cartoons, short stories, and serialized novels. They are in nearly all cases and in varying degrees dependent for their income upon the publication of commercial advertising. Newspapers may be differentiated from news-magazines, which serve many of the purposes of the newspaper, by their format and price. The average size of the sheet of the standard newspaper in the U.S. is sixteen inches by twenty-two inches, and of the small-sized or "tabloid" newspaper, ten inches by fourteen inches; that of the news-magazine is considerably smaller. Furthermore, newspapers

New York Times

PRODUCING A NEWSPAPER. *Top: Editors at the city desk, news department. Left: Searching in the newspaper files. Above: In the art department. Below: Sunday magazine room.*

are printed on rough-surfaced, so-called "newsprint" paper, and their pages are not bound or stapled, as are those of news-magazines, but are printed with two pages on each side of a sheet, and folded down the center. The price of a daily newspaper is also generally considerably less than that of a news-magazine.

Before the invention of printing in the 15th century, and for some time afterward, news was disseminated either by word of mouth, by private letters, or by public notices. The earliest known examples of the last-mentioned form of news distribution were the *Acta Diurna,* daily public news bulletins, most frequently containing military information, posted daily in Rome from the time of Julius Cæsar; copies of the bulletins were sent to the provinces of the Roman Empire. In the middle of the 16th century, the Venetian government posted news bulletins known as *Notizie Scritte;* permission to read them cost a small coin called a *gazetta,* whence later was derived the title or part of the title of many newspapers. After printing came into use, news was often published in pamphlets, or in single sheets devoted to one news item. The first news sheet of this type to be published regularly is believed to have been the German *Avisa Relation oder Zeitung,* which was established in 1609. The earliest daily newspaper in the world was the *Frankfurter Zeitung,* of Frankfort, Germany, which began publication in 1615. The first English newspaper was *The Weekly News* (1622–41), and one of the earliest semi-weekly newspapers in England was the *Oxford Gazette* (established 1665). The last-named newspaper changed its name to *London Gazette* in 1666; it is still published twice a week as an official government journal concerned with the affairs of the royal court. The earliest daily newspaper in England was the *Daily Courant,* which began publication in 1702. Government censorship of the press (see PRESS, FREEDOM OF THE), which began in 1622, tended to discourage the publication of newspapers, but the abolition of government censorship in 1693 gave great stimulus to newspaper publication, and even the heavy government taxation of newspapers which prevailed in the 18th and first half of the 19th century did not prevent a growth in the number of newspapers in England. Notable among 18th-century publishers of and writers for newspapers (see ENGLISH LITERATURE: *The Eighteenth Century*) were Daniel Defoe, with his weekly *The Review* (1704–13), later pub-

lished three times a week; Richard Steele with the *Tatler* (1709); Joseph Addison, who with Steele published and wrote the *Spectator* (1711–12); Jonathan Swift, who was the principal contributor to the Tory newspaper the *Examiner* (established in 1710); Samuel Johnson, with his weekly, *The Idler* (1758), and John Wilkes with the *North Briton* (1761). Notable newspapers of the early 19th century in England were the *Morning Chronicle* (1769–1859); the *Morning Herald* (1781–1869); the *Weekly Political Register* (founded 1802) published by the political reformer William Cobbett (q.v.) at twopence, the first newspaper which sought to gain a wide circulation among the working classes; and the *Examiner* (1808–80), founded by the writer and critic Leigh Hunt, and particularly distinguished for its dramatic criticism.

The abolition (1855) of the government tax on newspapers brought about a general reduction in their prices and an increase in their circulation. The tendency toward low-priced newspapers was increased toward the end of the 19th century by the use of cheaper paper, made of wood pulp rather than of rag; by the use of improved printing machinery, which could print large editions quickly and reasonably; and, as circulation increased, by the growth of advertising in newspapers, which gave the publisher a source of revenue apart from that obtained by sales. The tendency finally resulted in the general establishment in England at the end of the 19th and beginning of the 20th century of the halfpenny daily newspaper. The movement for the establishment of this type of modern newspaper was initiated by Alfred Harmsworth (q.v.), later Viscount Northcliffe, with his newspaper the *Daily Mail* (founded 1896). In the 20th century, also, chains of newspapers were acquired by one publisher or publishing interest. Prominent among the publishing interests of this type in Great Britain were the group of publishers led by Northcliffe's brother Viscount Rothermere; the group controlled by Lord Camrose, formerly Sir William Berry, and his brother Sir Gonner Berry; and the Lord Beaverbrook group. The following is a list of important British newspapers of the 20th century.

The outstanding newspapers of London are *The Times,* founded in 1785 and known until 1788 as the *Daily Universal Register,* and today one of the best-known and most influential newspapers in the world; the *Morning Post* (1772); the *Evening Standard,* a continuation of the *Standard* (1827); the *Daily*

Telegraph (1855); the *Daily Chronicle* (1877); the *Evening News* (1881); the *Daily Mail* (1896); the *Daily Express* (1900); the *Daily Herald* (1912), the newspaper of the British Labor Party; and the *News-Chronicle* (1930). Important British provincial newspapers include the *Manchester Guardian* (1821), the *Liverpool Daily Post and Mercury* (1853), the *Birmingham Daily Post* (1857), and the *Yorkshire Post* (1866). Among the newspapers of largest circulation are the *Daily Express* (nearly four million daily), the tabloid newspaper *Daily Mirror* (nearly four million), the *Daily Mail* (over two million) the *News-Chronicle* (over one and a half million) and the Sunday newspaper *News of the World* (nearly eight million).

In the United States the forerunner of the newspaper was the newsletter written in the 17th century by professional writers for patrons in England or in the American colonies. An immediate predecessor of the newspaper was a newssheet known as *Publick Occurrences,* published for just one issue in Boston in 1690; difficulties with censorship prevented it from actually being the earliest newspaper in the colonies. The first American newspaper was *The Boston News-Letter,* established in 1704 by John Campbell, postmaster at Boston. The paper was the outgrowth of the letters he wrote giving news information to the various colonial governors of New England; it was published until 1776. Among other early American newspapers, which were for the most part published weekly, were the *Gazette* (Boston, established 1719), *The American Weekly Mercury* (Philadelphia, 1719); *The New England Courant* (Boston, 1721); the *Pennsylvania Gazette* (Philadelphia, 1728), edited and partly owned by Benjamin Franklin; and the *New York Gazette* (1725), New York City's first newspaper. The earliest American daily newspaper was the *Pennsylvania Packet and General Advertiser,* established in Philadelphia in 1784. The first daily newspaper in New York City was the *New York Daily Advertiser,* established in 1785 by Francis Childs. It was followed by the *Minerva* (1793), which had as its first editor the lexicographer Noah Webster; this journal later took the name *Globe and Commercial Advertiser,* and under this title was published until 1923.

Notable among American newspapers of the early 19th century were the *Palladium* of Boston, the first in America to make a practice of sending reporters to obtain news instead of publishing merely the news sent to its office from various sources; the New York *Evening Post* (later the New York *Post*), the oldest newspaper in the United States continuously published without change of name, established in 1801 and edited at one time by the poet William Cullen Bryant; the *Daily Evening Transcript* (Boston, 1830); the *Liberator* (Boston, 1831), noted for the strong abolitionist views of its editor William Lloyd Garrison; and the *Sun* (New York, 1833), the first paper selling for one cent and specializing in reporting sensational news for purposes of securing large circulation. The middle and later years of the 19th century are particularly noted in the history of journalism for the work of a number of outstanding publishers and editors. One of them was James Gordon Bennett, who founded the New York *Herald* in 1835 and made it one of the most widely read newspapers of the time, at first by emphasis on lurid and scandalous news items, and later by an unprecedently thorough coverage of foreign news. The most distinguished editor of the period, noted for his editorials in which he supported the rights of labor and of women, fought slavery, and backed the Union cause in the Civil War, was Horace Greeley. He founded the New York *Tribune* in 1841 and was its owner and editor until 1872. Another of the leading publishers and editors of the century was Joseph Pulitzer, noted for his dynamic editing of the New York *World,* which he acquired in 1883 and which until it ceased publication in 1931 was in the front rank of American newspapers supporting the principles of the Democratic Party. *The New York Times,* established in 1851, became in the hands of Adolph S. Ochs, who acquired it in 1896, one of the foremost newspapers in the world, remarkable for the thoroughness of its reporting of all aspects of the daily news, domestic and foreign.

During the last two decades of the 19th century a great increase in department-store and other forms of display advertising, rates for which were based on the number of copies of the newspaper sold, led to unusually intense competition for circulation. To obtain readers, following the example set by the New York *Sun,* newspapers all over the country began to vie with one another in the publication of sensational and scandalous news items. The type of journalism thus created was popularly known as "yellow journalism"; its chief practitioners were two New York newspaper publishers, Joseph Pulitzer, in the New York *World,* and William Ran-

New York Times

PRINTING A NEWSPAPER

Top, left: Linotype operators setting text in type.
Top, right: Putting the type into page form. Above:
In press room the paper is printed on huge presses.
Right: Making an engraving of a photograph.

dolph Hearst in the *New York American* and the *New York Evening Journal,* the last-named of which was edited by Arthur Brisbane.

The first half of the 20th century was marked in American newspaper publication by three outstanding tendencies: one toward the consolidation of newspapers; another toward the establishing of chains of newspapers; and the third toward the small-sized newspaper popularly known as a "tabloid". These small journals featured numerous and vivid illustrations of the news.

The growing competition among newspapers for circulation and advertising and the increasing costs of successfully conducting a newspaper enterprise made it economically unsound for many newspapers to continue operation. In many cases those that were losing money were purchased by publishers of successful newspapers in the same city, who merged them with their own newspaper properties. The New York publisher Frank A. Munsey (q.v.) was particularly noted for the number of consolidations he effected. In 1916 he merged the New York *Press* and the *Sun,* under the name of the latter; in 1923 he consolidated the *Globe and Commercial Advertiser* with the *Sun.* In 1920 he bought the New York *Herald* and four years later sold it to the New York *Tribune,* which thenceforth was published as the *Herald Tribune.* Examples of similar consolidations elsewhere in the United States were the merging in Boston (1912) of the Boston *Herald* with the Boston *Traveler,* and the absorption (1917) by the *Herald* of the Boston *Journal;* and the consolidation in Philadelphia of the *Evening Public Ledger* with the *Evening Telegraph* (1918), the *Press* (1920), and the *Philadelphia North American* (1925). The principal chains of newspapers in the United States are the Hearst, the Scripps-Howard, and the Frank E. Gannett chains. In a recent year the Hearst chain comprised eighteen newspapers in fourteen cities; among the newspapers were the New York *Journal & American* (daily circulation, over 700,000; Sunday, over one million), a consolidation of Hearst's principal morning and evening newspapers, and now the largest afternoon newspaper in the United States; the Boston *Record* (daily, nearly 400,000); the San Francisco *Examiner* (daily, over 200,000; Sunday, over 600,000); and the Chicago *Herald-American* (daily, over 300,000). The Scripps-Howard group comprised at this time twenty-one newspapers in twenty cities; the

papers included the New York *World-Telegram* (daily, over 300,000), the Cleveland *Press* (daily, nearly 300,000), the Cincinnati *Post* (daily, over 150,000), and the Washington *News* (daily, over 100,000). In 1950 the New York *World-Telegram* absorbed the New York *Sun* and was thereafter published as the New York *World-Telegram and The Sun.* The Frank E. Gannett chain comprised sixteen newspapers in New York and New Jersey and one each in Connecticut and Illinois.

The first American tabloid picture newspaper was the *Illustrated Daily News,* established in New York City in 1919; it later changed its name to the *Daily News* and became the largest newspaper in the United States, with a daily circulation of over two million, and a Sunday circulation of nearly four million. Other leaders in the tabloid field are the New York *Mirror* (established 1924), with a daily circulation of over one million and a Sunday circulation of over two million; and the Chicago *Sun-Times* (established 1948 as a merger of the *Times,* founded in 1928, and the *Sun,* founded in 1941), with a daily circulation of over 600,000 and a Sunday circulation of over 700,000.

Among leading newspapers in the United States not members of a chain, exclusive of "tabloid" newspapers, treated above, are the Chicago *Tribune* (daily circulation, nearly one million; Sunday, over one and a half million); the Philadelphia *Inquirer* (daily, nearly 700,000; Sunday, over one million); *The New York Times* (daily, over half a million; Sunday, over one million); the New York *Herald Tribune* (daily, over 300,000; Sunday, nearly 700,000); the Detroit *Free Press* (daily, over 400,000); the Boston *Post* (daily, over 400,000); the Cleveland *Plain Dealer* (daily, nearly 300,000; Sunday, nearly 500,000); and the Boston *Christian Science Monitor* (daily, over 150,000). Among important weekly news-magazines are *Time* (established 1923) and *Newsweek* (established 1933). The Sunday editions of many newspapers contain a magazine or comics supplement which the newspaper does not publish itself but buys from a related or an outside publishing organization. Among the Sunday supplements of this type are *Metropolitan Comics,* which appears in forty Sunday newspapers with a total circulation of about sixteen million; *American Weekly,* which appears in twenty papers with a circulation of over nine million; *This Week,* which serves twenty-four newspapers with a circulation of nearly nine million; *Puck—The*

Comic Weekly, which appears in fifteen newspapers with a circulation of about eight million; and *Pictorial Review,* which serves ten newspapers with a circulation of nearly seven million. The United States has numerous newspapers published in foreign languages. They include the New York *Jewish Daily Forward* (daily circulation, over 80,000; Sunday, over 90,000); the New York *Il Progresso Italo-Americano* (daily, over 75,000; Sunday, over 85,000); the New York *Staats-Zeitung und Herold* (daily, over 25,000; Sunday, nearly 50,000); the Chicago *Svenska Amerikanaren Tribunen* (daily, over 50,000); and the San Antonio *La Prensa* (daily, over 8,000; Sunday, over 18,000).

In a recent year there were approximately two thousand daily newspapers in the U.S. Over four hundred were morning papers and had an estimated combined circulation of over twenty million; nearly sixteen hundred were evening papers, with an average estimated aggregate circulation of nearly thirty-one million. The estimated aggregate circulation of all daily newspapers, including those published all day, was over fifty-two million. At the same time there were in the United States nearly six hundred Sunday newspapers (Sunday editions of daily newspapers), with an estimated aggregate circulation of over forty-five million.

The newspapers of the European continent usually strongly emphasize a political point of view as well as report the news. Freedom of the press is not as highly developed on the Continent as in Great Britain and the United States; the newspapers of many European countries are subject to strict government censorship and to suppression for disagreement with the political point of view of the government. France is a notable exception to the above statement. Among the noted newspapers of France are *Le Temps, Le Matin, Le Petit Parisien,* and *L'Humanité,* all of Paris; *Le Petit Marseillais* and *La Petite Gironde* of Bordeaux; and *La Dépêche de Toulouse.* Other important newspapers of Europe are *Telegraph* and *Der Vorwaerts* of Berlin; *Suddeutsche Zeitung* of Munich; *Frankfurter Rundschau; Osservatore Romano,* an organ of the Vatican, published in Rome; *Stampa* of Turin and *Corriere della Sera* of Milan; the Italian political papers *L'Unità, Avanti,* and *Il Populo,* each published in several cities; *Arbeiter Zeitung* of Vienna; *Szabad Nep* of Budapest; and *Izvestia* and *Pravda* of Moscow. Outstanding non-Continental newspapers are *The Irish*

The crested newt of Europe

Times and the *Dublin Evening Mail* of Dublin, Ireland; the Montreal *Star* and Toronto *Star* of Canada; the Sydney *Daily Telegraph* and Melbourne *Herald* of Australia; *La Prensa* and *La Nación,* published in Buenos Aires, Argentina; *El Mercurio* of Valparaiso, Chile; and *El Excelsior* of Mexico City.

The influence of newspapers in forming public opinion in politics, economics, ethics, and many other aspects of life, has led to an ever-increasing need for thorough training of those who intend to enter the newspaper profession. In answer to this need in the United States, a large number of schools of journalism have been established in American universities and colleges in recent years; see JOURNALISM.

NEWT, EFT, or TRITON, common name applied generally to any small, semiaquatic salamander, and applied specifically to salamanders of the genus *Triturus.* The many species in this genus are widely distributed throughout the temperate regions of the Northern Hemisphere. They are slender, active animals, usually about three to four inches long when adult. The common newt of eastern and central United States is *T. viridescens,* a tannish-green species, spotted on the sides with blotches of red surrounded by black, and spotted below with black. This amphibian inhabits thickly-vegetated ponds and streams, and feeds on aquatic snails and insects. The female attaches its sticky eggs individually to aquatic plants; the newly hatched larvae are equipped with gills which become rudimentary when the larvae are about one inch long. At this time, the larvae, which are brick red in color, and which are consequently known as "red efts", leave the water, and spend the next few years on land, living under stones and logs in damp, wooded regions. The larvae eventually return to the water, and develop the adult coloration, spending the rest of their lives in an aquatic habitat. Another common American species is the giant newt, *T. torosus,* which attains a length of over six inches. Among the common European species are the spotted newt, *T. vulgaris,* the crested newt, *T. cristatus,* the male of which develops a crest during the breeding season, and the palmate newt, *T. palmipes.*

NEW TESTAMENT, the sacred scriptures embodying the covenant of God with man, fulfilled by the coming of Jesus Christ (q.v.) and by the teachings and works of Christ and His disciples; it constitutes, with the Old Testament (q.v.), the authorized dispensation of Christianity known as the Bible (q.v.). The New Testament contains twenty-seven books, usually grouped in the following order. PAULINE EPISTLES, consisting of *Galatians,* in which liberation from the prescripts of the Jewish law (see JUDAISM) is enjoined, and the apostleship of Paul is vindicated; *1 Thessalonians,* in which it is proclaimed that the dead will share in the resurrection (q.v.) of the Messiah; *2 Thessalonians,* in which are corrected several misapprehensions respecting the eschatology (q.v.), or doctrine of final things (death, resurrection, immortality), expounded in 1 Thessalonians; *1* and *2 Corinthians,* in which directions are given on a variety of subjects, including Christian morality, eschatology, and the celebration of the Lord's Supper (q.v.) ; *Romans,* in which are treated the mystery of salvation through Christ, the function of the Jewish law in the preparation for salvation, and the status of Israel in the Christian plan of salvation; *Philemon,* a personal letter in which a master's forgiveness is invoked upon his fugitive slave; *Philippians, Ephesians,* and *Colossians* (known as the Christological Epistles), which treat of the position of Christ in the divine scheme, censure false doctrine, and enjoin a pure life. SECONDARY CANON OF PAULINE EPISTLES (at present regarded as not Pauline), consisting of *1* and *2 Timothy* and *Titus* (known as the Pastoral Epistles), in which the duties of a minister are set forth and heresy is condemned; *Hebrews,* in which the priesthood of Christ is extolled and the nature of faith expounded. CATHOLIC EPISTLES, consisting of *1 Peter,* in which Christians, the redeemed of God, are exhorted to suffer persecution with meekness; *James,* in which the spirit rather than the letter of Christian doctrine is emphasized, and social discriminations are denounced as a violation of the law of love; *Jude,* in which unorthodox religious teachers are condemned, and the Apostolic word is reaffirmed; *2 Peter,* in which the delay in the second coming of Christ is accounted for. HISTORICAL BOOKS, consisting of *Mark,*

in which are recounted the salient events of the public ministry of Jesus, for the most part in Galilee and during a period of one year; *Matthew* and *Luke,* in which the account detailed in Mark is enriched by the addition of further sayings of Jesus; *Acts of the Apostles,* in which is related the founding of the Christian Church by the Apostles Peter and Paul. JOHANNINE EPISTLES, consisting of *Revelation,* in which praise and blame are apportioned among the seven Christian Churches of Asia Minor (namely, those of Ephesus, Smyrna, Pergamum, Thyatira, Sardis, Philadelphia, and Laodicea), and the persecution of the Church, the Last Judgment, and the New Jerusalem (the Heavenly City of the redeemed) are depicted in symbolic visions of compelling grandeur; *1, 2,* and *3 John,* in which Christian charity is extolled and the heresy of Gnosticism (q.v.) refuted; *Gospel of John,* in which the public ministry of Jesus is set against a background of traditional Jewish feasts, the scene of the ministry is laid chiefly in Jerusalem, and the narrative is projected in the form of grand symbolic discourses.

The New Testament dates from the 1st century A.D., but was not vested with canonical authority (see CANON) by the Christian Church until the 4th century. At the outset Christianity was not a scriptural religion. The teachings of Jesus were imparted to His twelve Apostles (see APOSTLE) to be proclaimed by word of mouth as the Gospel (q.v.). The Gospel was regarded as of paramount authority, for it was held to be the very Word of God. Consequently the words of the Apostles, as the accredited expounders of the Gospel, were accorded their highest credence and respect. What was true of their spoken words was also true of what they wrote. Hence, when the Gospel assumed a written form, whether in Apostolic epistle or in narrative of the sayings and works of Jesus transcribed by an Apostle, such writing was certain to be reverentially preserved, widely circulated, and frequently perused. The writings of Justin (q.v.) the Martyr, about 150 A.D., reveal that the memoirs of the Apostles, also called "Gospels", were in common use in the public Sunday devotional services of the Christians, and that these writings were the principal source of information in the Church respecting the teachings and deeds of Jesus. Nevertheless Justin makes no definite pronouncement on the canonical character of the Gospels. Only thirty years later, however, the prelate Saint Irenæus, (q.v.) speaks of the four Gospels as the foundation pillars of the Christian Church. Many collections of the Epistles, particularly those of Paul, are recorded as having been in existence at that time and as having been co-ordinated with the Gospels as a second and equally essential element in the New Testament, which was then coming to be juxtaposed to the Old Testament in the authoritative scriptures of the Church. By 225 the principle of a New Testament conjoined with the Old Testament was quite firmly established.

The two great divisions of the New Testament were designated respectively as "the Gospel" and "the Apostle", corresponding to the Law (Torah) and the Prophets (Nebiim) of the Old Testament, and each division was regarded as divinely inspired. The main components of "the Apostle" section were the Epistles of Paul; 1 Peter; and 1 John, which were almost universally used. The Acts of the Apostles and the Apocalypse (Revelation) were likewise quite generally used. The use of the other books of the New Testament, though they formed part of the collection in some localities, had not yet become widespread. On the other hand, in a number of localities, certain early Christian scriptures, such as 1 Clement, the Epistle of Barnabas, and the Didache (Gr., "teaching"), were accorded quasi-canonical rank. In Rome the principle of Apostolic origin was rigorously applied; in Alexandria, however, the spirit was more liberal, and other writings were admitted into the New Testament. In 367 the uncertainty was dispelled when Saint Athanasius (q.v.), Bishop of Alexandria, decreed that the canon consisted of the twenty-seven books now included in the New Testament. This decree was ratified by the Synod of Carthage in 397 and by the second Trullan Synod in 692. The doctrinal controversies of the Reformation (q.v.) left the New Testament canon virtually untouched, except in various Baptist denominations.

NEW TESTAMENT CHRONOLOGY, the science determining the dates of events mentioned in the New Testament (q.v.) which have not been definitely established because of insufficient data. Two systems of chronology (q.v.) have been used: that of the Jews, for the Gospels, dealing with the life of Christ; and that of the Romans, for the Acts, concerned with the apostolic age. By scholarly comparison of Biblical events with historical and numismatical facts, tentative dates have been fixed for these periods. The Nativity, Baptism, and Crucifixion of Jesus

Christ are respectively 7 or 6 B.C.; 26 or 27 A.D.; and 29, 30, or 33 A.D., possibly on the 14th of Nisan, the 1st month of the Jewish ecclesiastical year, about March 18 in our calendar if 29, the preferred year, is correct. The remaining chronology of the apostolic era extends from 29 to the persecutions of Nero (64) and the fall of Jerusalem (70) and includes the doubtful dating of St. Peter's arrest at Passover (44), the first missionary journey during the famine of Jerusalem (47), the later activities of St. Paul in 55 or 60–61, and the martyrdom of Saints Peter and Paul in 64 or 65.

NEW THOUGHT, the designation for the idealistic movement (see IDEALISM) in religious and philosophical thinking which developed in the United States, particularly in New England, early in the second half of the 19th century. This movement, from which evolved the theosophic and psychotherapeutic systems (see THEOSOPHY; PSYCHIATRY) known as *Higher Thought, Mental Science, Metaphysical Healing,* and *Practical Christianity,* had numerous affinities with the transcendental philosophy (see TRANSCENDENTALISM) of Amos Bronson Alcott, Ralph Waldo Emerson, and Henry David Thoreau, and with the mystical doctrines (see MYSTICISM) of Platonism (see PLATO), Neoplatonism, and Vedanta (qq.v.). The chief tenets of New Thought are that God is omnipotent and omnipresent, that spirit is the ultimate reality, that the true selfhood of man is divine, that divinely attuned thought is a positive force for good, that disease is mental in origin, and that right thinking has a healing efficacy. The therapeutic theories of New Thought received particular emphasis in the Divine Science Church, which taught that God is the sole reality, that sickness is the result of the failure to realize this truth, and that healing is accomplished by the affirmation of man's oneness with God. The first exponent of metaphysical healing in the U.S. was Phineas Parkhurst Quimby (1802–66). Another practitioner was John Bovee Dods (1795–1862), who also wrote several books in which he expounded the thesis that disease originates in the electrical impulses of the nervous system and is curable by a change of belief. New Thought is customarily differentiated from Christian Science (q.v.) and medical psychotherapy.

NEWTON, a city in Middlesex Co., Mass., adjoining Boston, on the Charles River. The industrial establishments include machine shops, fire-alarm-supply works, silk mills,

Sir Isaac Newton

worsted mills, rubber works, manufactories of paper boxes, curtains, railway signals, and cordage. Pop. (1950) 81,994.

NEWTON, Sir Isaac (1642–1727), English mathematician, physicist, and astronomer, born in Woolsthorpe, near Grantham, Lincolnshire, and educated at Trinity College, Cambridge University. He was appointed a Fellow of Trinity College in 1667 and professor of mathematics in 1669.

By the time he was twenty-five Newton had made many of the discoveries and had begun to work on the broad formulations of physical theory for which he later became recognized as one of the greatest scientific geniuses of all time. As early as 1666 he conceived the idea of universal gravitation (see GRAVITATION), and calculated, on the basis of the empirical laws of planetary motion formulated by the German astronomer Johannes Kepler, that the gravitational force between two masses is inversely proportional to the square root of the distance between them. Whether or not the story is true that Newton conceived the idea of universal gravitation after watching an apple fall to the ground in his garden is not definitely known. The story was first circulated by the French philosopher Voltaire who is reputed to have heard it from Newton's grandniece. Newton did not fully work out the law of gravitation until 1685, when he constructed a rigid mathematical proof of the theory, confirming it with known measurements of the masses and

relative distances of the members of the solar system. As a mathematical interpretation of natural phenomena in accordance with well-defined physical principles the law of universal gravitation was the first great systematization of knowledge in the physical sciences; see PHYSICS: *History*.

Newton's investigations of gravitational forces were only a part, although an important part, of his work on the fundamental principles of mechanics (q.v.). The concepts of mass and force were implicit in the work of the Italian scientist Galileo Galilei (q.v.), but Newton made the first successful formulation of the general laws governing the motion of matter; see NEWTON'S LAWS OF MOTION. His work in mechanics was recorded in *Philosophiae Naturalis Principia Mathematica* (1687), which is considered one of the greatest works in scientific literature. Newton's mechanics, as stated in the *Principia,* summed up and systematized the work of the scientists of the seventeenth century and formed the groundwork upon which the sciences of astronomy and mechanics developed for the following two centuries. The mechanistic view of the universe, implicit in Newtonian mechanics and particularly in an orderly system of heavenly bodies rotating in their orbits in accordance with a mathematical law, also greatly influenced the trend of philosophic thinking in the following centuries. A more comprehensive view of the physical universe, which did away with the concepts of absolute space, absolute time, and forces acting at a distance, necessary to Newtonian mechanics, was introduced with the theory of relativity (q.v.). Although the relativistic view is accepted today in explaining ultimate physical concepts, Newtonian mechanics is still adequate in predicting physical phenomena to a high degree of accuracy and in solving practical problems in physics and engineering.

In the field of mathematics Newton established the binomial theorem, developed the theory of equations, and worked out a method of calculus (q.v.), which he called *fluxions.* Although he invented his system of fluxions in 1666 and used it in mathematical investigations of gravitational force, Newton did not publish his work until 1693. The German philosopher Baron Gottfried von Leibnitz, who published a different method of calculus in 1684, claimed prior invention, but it is evident that each investigator independently developed different systems of the calculus.

Newton also made important contributions in the field of optics. He demonstrated, by passing light through two properly arranged prisms, that white light is composed of all the colors of the spectrum. Because he erroneously concluded that the dispersion of light into colors by the lens of a telescope could not be prevented, he invented a new type of telescope, the reflecting telescope, in 1668. He developed the laws of refraction and reflection and proposed a corpuscular theory of light; see LIGHT. His work in optics is summed up in *Optics* (1704).

In 1696 Newton accepted the post of warden of the mint. Three years later he became master of the mint and resigned his professorship at Trinity College. In 1703 he became president of the Royal Society and was re-elected annually until his death. He was knighted in 1705.

NEWTON'S LAWS OF MOTION, the three basic laws of classical mechanics, formulated by the English scientist Sir Isaac Newton (q.v.), on the relation of force to motion. (1) A body at rest remains at rest and a body in motion continues to move at constant speed along a straight line unless, in either case, the body is acted upon by an outside force. (2) An outside force acting on a body causes the body to accelerate in the direction of the force; the acceleration is directly proportional to the force and inversely proportional to the mass of the body. (3) For every action there is an equal and opposite reaction. See MECHANICS.

NEW WESTMINSTER, former capital and one of the chief cities of British Columbia, on the N. bank of the Fraser River, 10 m. from its mouth and 113 m. by railroad and steamer N.N.E. of the present capital, Victoria, on Vancouver Island. It is a busy, progressive seaport with a regular service of coast- and ocean-going steamships. Its principal industries are lumbering and salmon canning. Pop. (1946 est.) 44,359.

NEW YEAR'S DAY, the first day of the year, January 1 in the Gregorian calendar. During the Middle Ages most European countries observed New Year's Day on March 25th (Annunciation Day) in the Julian Calendar (see CALENDAR), but with the introduction of the Gregorian calendar in 1582, all Roman Catholic countries began to celebrate New Year's Day on January 1st. Scotland accepted the Gregorian calendar in 1600; Germany, Denmark, and Sweden about 1700; and England in 1752. Most ancient peoples observed the day with religious feasts, and the custom was continued by the western Christian nations. Today in Scotland, France, and Italy, New Year's Day is observed with more ceremony than Christmas. In the Roman Catholic Church New Year's Day is strictly observed because it falls on the Feast of the Circumcision. Followers of the Julian, or Old Style, calendar, such as members of the Orthodox Church, celebrate New Year's Day on January 13th of the Gregorian calendar. The Feast of Trumpets, or Rosh Hashana, prescribed by the Old Testament as a holy sabbath, is celebrated as the Jewish New Year's Day. It falls on the first and second days of the month of Tishri (generally September). The Chinese celebrate New Year's Day, which falls on the first new moon after the sun enters the Zodiacal house of Aquarius (on January 20th), with the custom of paying or remitting all debts.

NEW YORK, one of the Middle Atlantic States of the United States and the most populous State in the Union, bounded on the N.W. and N. by Lake Ontario and the St. Lawrence R. (which separates it from Ontario, Canada) and by Quebec, Canada; on the E. by Vermont, Massachusetts, and Connecticut; on the S. by the Atlantic Ocean, New Jersey, and Pennsylvania; and on the W. by Pennsylvania, Lake Erie, and the Niagara R. New York ranks as the 29th State in the Union in area. It is the 11th of the original States, having ratified the Constitution of the United States on July 26, 1788. The State capital is Albany (q.v.), the sixth-largest (1950) city of the State. New York City (q.v.), in population the largest city in the United States and the second largest (after London) in the world, contains more than half the inhabitants of the State. In volume and value of foreign and domestic commerce, New York City is the greatest port in the world. The city is also the leading manufacturing city in the United States. Besides the foregoing, five cities of the State have populations of over 100,000. In order of size (1950), these cities are Buffalo, Rochester, Syracuse, Yonkers, and Utica (qq.v.). Cities between 50,000 and 100,000 are Schenectady, Niagara Falls, Binghamton, Troy, Mount Vernon, and New Rochelle (qq.v.). In addition the State has 15 other incorporated cities with populations (1950) between 25,000 and 50,000, 105 incorporated villages with populations from 5000 to 25,000, and nearly 300 unincorporated communities. A number of islands, notably Manhattan Island and Staten Island (qq.v.), both boroughs of New York City, and Long Island (q.v.), comprise part of the State. In shape the mainland portion of New York somewhat resembles a right triangle, with the hypotenuse extending

New York State Capitol in Albany

from the s.w. to the n.w. corner of the State. The maximum width of New York, in an E. and w. direction, is 326.4 m.; the maximum length, from N. to s., is 300 m. The coastline, including that of the islands and all bays and inlets reached by tidal water, totals 1412 m. The coastline of the State on the Great Lakes totals about 275 m. Area of State, 49,576 sq.m., including 1647 sq.m. of inland water surface. Approximately 3627 sq.m. of the surface of Lake Erie and Lake Ontario are under the jurisdiction of New York. Pop. (1950) 14,830,192.

The terrain of New York is highly diversified. North of the valley of the Mohawk R. (q.v.), the dominant topographic feature of the State are the Adirondack (q.v.) Mountains. Mt. Marcy (5344 ft.), a peak of the Adirondacks, is the highest point in the State, and a number of other peaks of the range exceed 4000 ft. in elevation. From the main crest of the Adirondacks, a noted scenic and resort region which is heavily forested and traversed by numerous streams, the mountains slope to peripheral lowlands. In the E. these lowlands comprise the valley of the Hudson R. (q.v.), chief river of the State, and the plains adjacent to Lake Champlain (see CHAMPLAIN, LAKE), which forms part of the Vermont-New York boundary. The N., s., and w. lowlands are respectively those of the St. Lawrence valley, the Mohawk valley, and the Lake On-

tario plain. Most of the region s. of the Mohawk valley falls within the province of the Appalachian plateau. Covering more than one half of the area of the State, the plateau region slopes upward from N. to s. and from w. to E. and attains its maximum elevation in the Catskill Mountains (q.v.) in the s.E. Slide Mountain (4205 ft.) is the highest peak of this uplift. The Catskills contain extensive stands of timber. Unlike the Adirondacks region, the area contains numerous farms. In the w. and N.w. the plateau merges with the plains of Lake Ontario and Lake Erie. Elevations in other sections of the plateau, which is dissected by many river valleys and has several rugged outcroppings, range from 1500 to about 2500 ft. South and E. of the Catskills are the Shawangunk Mountains, with elevations up to 2000 ft., and the Palisades (q.v.), a line of traprock cliffs along the w. side of the Hudson R. The chief topographic feature of that portion of the State E. of the Hudson is the foothills and extensions of the Berkshire Hills (q.v.), which project southward into Manhattan Island. Both Long Island and Staten Island fall within the province of the Atlantic coastal plain, the principal elevations being a belt of low morainic hills.

In addition to the rivers already cited, the principal streams of New York are the Genesee, the Oswego, and Black rivers, which drain into Lake Ontario; the headwaters of the

Delaware R. and the Susquehanna R. (qq.v.), which drain respectively into Delaware Bay and Chesapeake Bay; and a portion of the Allegheny R. (q.v.). The State is traversed by numerous lesser streams, including various affluents of the chief rivers. At many points certain of the rivers pass through precipitous gorges and are broken by rapids and falls. The most spectacular cataract is Niagara Falls (q.v.). Among other famous waterfalls of the State are Portage Falls and Genesee Falls, in the Genesee R., Chittenango Falls, in Chittenango Creek, Cohoes Falls, near the mouth of the Mohawk R., Enfield Falls, in Tompkins Co., and Ausable Falls, in Essex Co. One of the outstanding features of the hydrography of New York is the large number of lakes. Excluding Lake Champlain, which lies partly in Vermont, Lake Erie, and Lake Ontario, the major lakes of New York are Cayuga, Seneca, and Keuka, situated in the w. section of the State and comprising part of the group known as Finger Lakes; Lake Chautauqua, which is situated at an elevation of about 1200 ft. in the s.w. corner of the State; Oneida Lake (q.v.), Lake George (see GEORGE, LAKE), and the three Saranac Lakes. The lakes and ponds

of the State number approximately 2000.

Extensive areas of New York, both in the interior and in the coastal regions, have been reserved for recreational or conservation purposes. The State possesses 337 State forests, totaling more than 501,000 acres; 101 State parks, totaling nearly 2,576,000 acres; and 658 community forests, totaling about 150,000 acres. The major component of the State park system and the second-largest forest preserve in the United States is the Adirondack Forest Preserve, covering more than 2,000,000 acres. Other notable units of the State park system include the Catskill Forest Preserve, which consists of over 230,000 acres in the Catskill Mts.; Allegany State Park, nearly 58,000 acres in the s.w. portion of the State; Palisades Interstate Park, covering 45,000 acres (including about 1800 acres in New Jersey) along the w. bank of the Hudson R.; Jones Beach State Park, approximately 2400 acres along the Atlantic coast of Long Island; and Niagara Reservation, consisting of 425 acres at Niagara Falls.

Climatically, New York lies within the North Temperate Zone. Except in the coastal regions, where the modifying influences of

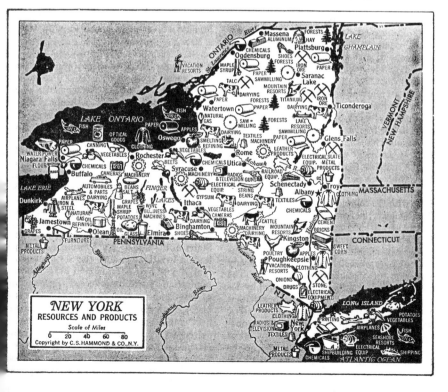

NEW YORK
RESOURCES AND PRODUCTS
Scale of Miles
0   20   40   60   80
Copyright by C.S. HAMMOND & CO., N.Y.

oceanic winds and currents are felt, the State is subject to extreme seasonal variations, with winter temperatures as low as –30° F. and summer temperatures as high as 104° F. Winter extremes of –40° F. are occasionally recorded in the Adirondacks. The respective January and July temperatures for this region average 15° F. and 64° F. In the w. portion of the State the respective January and July temperatures are 26° F. and 72° F. The corresponding figures for New York City are 31.4° F. and 74.2° F. Precipitation, including heavy falls of snow in the interior during the winter season, is abundant, averaging between 40 and 45 inches annually. In the vicinity of New York City precipitation averages about 43 inches.

New York State occupies an unsurpassed position in the Union in the field of finance and banking. In June, 1953, the 356 national banks in New York had assets of more than $14,850,000,000; the 375 banks of other types had deposits totaling nearly $34,802,-000,000. Annual transactions in shares of stock at the New York Stock Exchange, which is situated in New York City, average about 75% of the national total. The commodity exchanges of the State, which are located chiefly in New York City, are the world's principal future markets in coffee, cotton, sugar, cocoa, crude rubber, raw silk, hides, lead, zinc, copper, and tin. Such commodities as wool, eggs, dairy products, lard, rye, wheat, barley, oats, flaxseed, cottonseed oil, peanuts, and tobacco are also traded in huge volume in the produce exchanges of New York.

In terms of value of production, New York ranks as the foremost manufacturing State of the Union. This status, held continuously since 1830, is the result of a number of favorable factors, notably the leading position of New York City as a port and financial center, the commercial advantages that accrued to the State with the completion, in 1825, of the Erie Canal (q.v.), and the subsequent construction of water-level railways to the shores of Lake Erie. In addition, the State possesses the prerequisite natural resources, including abundant supplies of water power, for the steady expansion of manufacturing activity. The process of expansion was accompanied by remarkable diversification, with the result that New York eventually emerged as the leading State in the Union in the variety of manufactures, a status it still retains. Virtually all of the 400-odd manufacturing industries of the United States are represented in New York State.

As noted in the foregoing, New York City is the leading manufacturing city in the United States. More than 75% of the manufacturing establishments in the State are situated in this city, which normally accounts for nearly 60%, by value, of the total manufactures of the State. Five other cities of the State, namely Buffalo, Rochester, Schenectady, Syracuse, and Yonkers, are among the fifty principal manufacturing centers of the country. Troy, Utica, Rome, Binghamton, and Elmira are also important industrial centers. The chief manufacture of the State (and New York City) is clothing and related products. In 1951 the ready-made clothing industry, which was established in New York City in 1835, employed almost 20% of the industrial wage earners in the State. Other major industries of New York are printing and publishing, meat packing, and the manufacture of motor vehicles and parts, baked goods, flour, paper, fur apparel, boots and shoes, chemicals, prepared foods, steel and rolling mill products, carpets and rugs, malt beverages, refined cane sugar, paints and varnishes, and furniture. Other important manufactures are millinery, gloves, artificial flowers, electrical equipment, musical instruments, typewriters, cameras, film, optical instruments, jewelry, airplanes, and aluminum.

New York contains extensive and highly diversified agricultural industries. In 1950 the farms in the State numbered nearly 125,000 and covered more than 16,000,000 acres. Approximately 40% of this acreage is pasturage, and dairying is the chief agricultural enterprise. Annual milk sales in the State in 1949 totaled more than 7 billion pounds. The State ranks high in the Union in the production of cheese and is a leading producer of livestock, including pure bred cattle. In 1953 livestock on the farms of New York included about 2,-311,000 cattle of all kinds, 202,000 hogs, 143,-000 sheep, and 96,000 horses. Poultry raising is also important; in 1953 the number of chickens totaled about 15,119,000. New York is one of the chief egg-producing States of the Union. Truck farming is another leading industry; in 1950 the State was outranked only by California and Florida in the production of garden produce. The production of vegetables for canning and processing is a major farm industry. Among the principal field crops (with estimated yields for 1953) are corn (27,735,000 bushels), oats (25,641,-000 bushels), and wheat (14,322,000 bushels). Hay and barley are also important. New York is surpassed only by Maine, Idaho, and Cali-

Port N.Y. Auth.; Syracuse Chamb. of Comm.

Above: A naval vessel in the harbor of New York City, New York. Right: Office buildings facing Clinton Square, Syracuse, New York.

fornia in the output of potatoes and is a leading onion-producing State. Fruit growing also figures significantly in the rural economy of New York, which has more than 287,000 acres planted to orchards and vineyards. This acreage is exceeded only in California and Florida. The State ranks second (after Washington) in the production of apples and second (after California) in the production of grapes. Central New York is one of the chief wine-producing regions of the nation. Cherries, strawberries, peaches, and pears are among the other important fruit crops. The State ranks next to Vermont in the production of maple sugar and syrup. In 1952 the total cash receipts from farm marketings amounted to more than $947,000,000.

New York contains a variety of valuable and productive mineral deposits, including salt, gypsum, garnet, talc, fire clay, iron ore, wollastonite, limestone, sandstone, granite, marble, bauxite, sand and gravel, cement, petroleum, natural gas, zinc, lead, silver, pyrites, hematite, and magnetite. In 1950 the State ranked first in the U.S. in the production of talc, wollastonite, and garnet, second in the production of salt and gypsum, and fourth in the production of cement. In 1951 the value of the mineral output of the State totaled more than $188,250,000.

Lumbering, an industry in which New York once led the U.S. is now confined mainly to the N. portion of the State. The chief commercial forests consist largely of spruce and hemlock. In 1949 lumber production in New York was about 334,000,000 board feet. The fisheries of the State, particularly the shell-fisheries in Long Island Sound, are another important source of wealth. In terms of value, oysters are the principal catch, and a large volume of clams and scallops is harvested annually. The fisheries also yield shad, alewives, bluefish, butterfish, cod, haddock, and lobsters. The value of the total catch for 1951 was about $15,000,000.

The transportation facilities of New York

are extensive. Intrastate and interstate connections are provided by a vast network of railway, inland-waterway, automotive, and air-transport carriers. In addition to the port of New York, with its tremendous facilities for transoceanic and intercoastal shipping, several ports on the Hudson R. are accessible to ocean-going vessels, and Buffalo is one of the leading ports of the Great Lakes. Thirty-seven railroads, including the New York Central, the Erie, the Pennsylvania, and the Lehigh Valley, operate in the State, maintaining (1950) about 7500 m. of main-track lines. Inland-water transportation is provided by the New York State Barge Canal, a system comprising 525 m. of canals and 382 m. of canalized rivers and lakes. Surfaced highways in the State (1953) total more than 68,000 m. There are (1953) 287 airports, of which more than 30 are equipped for night flying. LaGuardia Field and Idlewild Airport in New York City, which are among the greatest in the world, are terminals for all major national and international air lines.

The public educational system of New York is one of the most advanced in the nation, and the State contains numerous nationally famous institutions of higher learning, museums, and other cultural and educational facilities. Attendance at school throughout a full school year is compulsory for all children from seven to sixteen years of age. In 1951-52 the average expenditure for each public-school pupil was about $340, an amount surpassed in no other State. Elementary schools in New York in 1952-53 numbered 4197, with a total enrollment of about 1,697,000 students; secondary schools numbered nearly 990, with an enrollment of more than 528,000 students. The State also maintains a university, 11 teachers colleges, and a maritime academy. Parochial and private schools in New York number (1951–52) 1200, with about 578,000 enrolled students. More than 100 institutions of higher learning, other than State schools, are situated in the State. Notable among these are Columbia University (q.v.), which includes Barnard College for women; New York University; Fordham University; Cooper Union for the Advancement of Science and Art (qq.v.); College of the City of New York (see NEW YORK, THE COLLEGE OF THE CITY OF; also BROOKLYN COLLEGE and HUNTER COLLEGE); Polytechnic Institute of Brooklyn; St. John's University; Long Island University; and Manhattan College. All of the foregoing are in New York City. Among other notable institutions of higher learning in the State are Col-

gate University, Cornell University, Syracuse University, Rensselaer Polytechnic Institute, Vassar College, Saint Lawrence University (qq.v.), the University of Buffalo (see BUFFALO, UNIVERSITY OF), and the United States Military Academy (see MILITARY ACADEMY, UNITED STATES).

New York is governed according to the provisions of the constitution of 1894, as amended. Executive authority is vested in a governor, lieutenant governor, comptroller, and attorney general, all of whom are elected for four-year terms. Nonelective heads of the State administrative departments are appointed by the governor. Among other powers, the governor has the authority to veto enactments of the State legislature. Legislative power is exercised by a bicameral legislature, consisting of a senate of 58 members and an assembly of 152 members. Members of the legislature serve two-year terms. The legislature meets annually. Supreme judicial authority in the State is vested in the court of appeals, which consists of a chief judge and 6 associate justices, each of whom is elected for a term of fourteen years. Judicial authority in criminal and civil cases is vested in the supreme court, the justices of which are elected for fourteen-year terms. The supreme court has an appellate division, consisting of a presiding justice and a number of associate justices who are selected by the governor from among the justices of the supreme court. Other courts of New York include the court of claims, which has jurisdiction over cases involving private claims against the State, county courts, surrogate's courts, and municipal courts. New York is divided into 62 counties and is represented in the Congress of the U.S. by 2 senators and 43 representatives.

History. The first European of record to visit the coastal region of what is now New York was the Florentine navigator Giovanni da Verrazano, who discovered present-day New York Bay in 1524. Nearly a century elapsed before serious exploration of the region was undertaken. In 1609 Henry Hudson (q.v.), an English navigator in the employ of the Dutch East India Company, piloted his vessel, the *Half Moon,* up the river which now bears his name, reaching the site of modern Albany. The French explorer Samuel de Champlain (q.v.), operating from Quebec, explored the N. portion of the region in the same year. Champlain shortly came into conflict with a powerful Indian confederacy of the Iroquoian linguistic stock, known as the Five Nations and comprising the Onondagas, Cayugas, Oneidas, Mohawks, and Senecas. These tribes occupied most of the region w. of the upper Hudson R. A number of lesser tribes, mainly of the Algonquian stock, inhabited the coastal areas.

In the year following Hudson's expedition, Dutch merchants dispatched a trading vessel to the region, which had been named New Netherland. The vessel returned to Holland with a profitable cargo of furs, with the result that additional voyages to New Netherland were organized. Trading posts were established on Manhattan Island and in the vicinity of present-day Albany about 1613. With the founding of the West India Company in 1621, the Dutch began to colonize New Netherland. The first permanent colonists arrived on the *New Netherland* in May, 1624. Most of the settlers, about thirty families of Walloons, were taken to Fort Orange, which had been established on the site of modern Albany two years earlier. More settlers arrived in 1625, and the next year Peter Minuit (q.v.), the first director general of the colony, purchased Manhattan Island from the Indians for goods valued at 60 guilders (about $24). Under Minuit's direction, a fort, called Fort Amsterdam, was constructed at the s. end of Manhattan. New Amsterdam, the settlement that grew up around the fort, became the administrative center of the colony. Because the West India Company, which had been granted a commercial monopoly in New Netherland by the Dutch government, was concerned chiefly with trade, colonization proceeded very slowly for more than a decade. Attempting to rectify this state of affairs, the company issued, in 1629, a charter of privileges and exemptions. By the terms of the charter, members of the company received the right to buy extensive tracts of land from the Indians. The grantees, who became known as patroons (q.v.), were required to establish no less than fifty settlers on each tract. Among those who acquired vast estates in New Netherland was Kilaen Van Rensselaer (q.v.). Through successful violation of the company trade monopoly, he and other patroons shortly acquired the power and independence of feudal barons.

The West India Company relinquished its commercial monopoly in New Netherland in 1638. This move was followed by an influx of colonists, including English Puritans and French Huguenots. In 1641, as a result of the provocative attitude of the Dutch director general, Willem Kieft, the colony became embroiled in a disastrous war with the Algonquian Indians. Most of the settlements in the

vicinity of New Amsterdam were destroyed during the conflict, which lasted until 1645. In the course of the war the colonists confronted Kieft with demands for a voice in the government. Kieft consented to the establishment of a representative council, but retained effective power in his own hands. The colonists finally forced his removal in 1647, and he was replaced by Peter Stuyvesant (q.v.). Although Stuyvesant's rule was tyrannous in many respects, New Netherland prospered under his administration, growing in population from 2000 to 10,000.

Meanwhile, the British government had taken vigorous exception to Dutch colonial claims in America. In 1650, by the terms of the treaty of Hartford, Stuyvesant agreed to delimitation of the New Netherland-Connecticut frontier, accepting a line generally identical with the boundary between present-day Connecticut and New York. Tense relations between the Dutch and British persisted, and in 1664 the British monarch Charles II established Long Island and all the territory between the Connecticut R. and Delaware Bay as a British province under the proprietorship of his brother James, Duke of York and Albany (later James II). A British expedition, led by the newly appointed provincial governor Colonel Richard Nicolls, was promptly dispatched to New Netherland. On September 8, 1664, Stuyvesant, failing to rally the leading burghers for a defensive stand, surrendered New Amsterdam to Nicolls. In honor of James, the colony and its administrative center were renamed New York and Fort Orange was renamed Fort Albany.

The transition from Dutch to British rule in the colony was accomplished with a minimum of friction. A measure of self-government was authorized in the various settlements, and the Dutch policy of religious tolerance was perpetuated. In August, 1673, the Dutch, then at war with Great Britain, captured New York City and re-established their control of the colony. British rule was restored by the provisions of the treaty of Westminster, concluded in February, 1674. The Dutch withdrew from the colony in the following November.

The period succeeding re-institution of British control was marked by considerable internal unrest caused by the arbitrary acts of the new governor Sir Edmund Andros (q.v.), by the consolidation of close relations with the Iroquois confederacy, and by recurrent border warfare, in the N., with the French. In this fighting the Iroquois tribes, hostile to the

NYSPIX

Above: Bean pickers in field near Rome, New York. Left: Milk cattle grazing in pasture in upper New York.

called the *Gazette,* was published in 1725. Eight years later an opposition sheet, the *Weekly Journal,* appeared. John Peter Zenger (q.v.), editor of the *Journal,* was charged with libel, in 1734, because of his criticisms of the provincial governor, and brought to trial. Supported by the people and the provincial assembly, Zenger won the case, vindicating freedom of the press in New York.

New York figured prominently in the events leading to the outbreak of the American Revolution. As early as 1762, petitions and remonstrances against the oppressive commercial policy of the British government had been submitted to the king and Parliament. The Sons of Liberty, an organization of militant patriots, gave effective leadership to the struggle against the stamp tax (see STAMP ACT). After the refusal of the New York provincial assembly in 1766 to furnish supplies for British troops and the passage by Parliament of the Townshend Acts (q.v.), relations between the anti-British and loyalist factions in the colony deteriorated rapidly. The Sons of Liberty and British troops fought a pitched battle in the streets of New York City in January, 1770. On the refusal, in January, 1775, of the provincial assembly, which had meanwhile passed under the control of the loyalists, to send delegates to the second Continental Congress, New York patriots summoned a provincial congress. The congress met at New York City on April 20, 1775, and elected delegates to the Continental Congress. Following

French since the time of Champlain, gave their support to the British, preventing then, as they did later, French subjugation of upper New York. In 1689, following the outbreak of the Glorious Revolution in the mother country, a colonial Protestant party, led by Jacob Leisler seized power in New York City. The French, taking advantage of the consequent political confusion in the colony, attacked and burned Schenectady in February, 1690. In 1691 Leisler was deposed by Colonel Henry Sloughter, the newly appointed governor of the colony, and executed.

Despite continuing warfare with the French (see FRENCH AND INDIAN WAR), the colony steadily grew and prospered after the turn of the century. By 1720 the population totaled 35,000. The first newspaper, an organ

NYSPIX

NEW YORK. *Above: Fort Ticonderoga, with battlements restored. Right: The Old Dutch Church of Sleepy Hollow near Tarrytown. Below: The Hudson River seen from West Point.*

receipt of the news of the battle of Lexington, the provincial congress assumed control of the government and issued a call for a provincial convention. This body, which was in session from July 10, 1776, to April 20, 1777, drew up a constitution for the State of New York.

Although the Continental Army was shortly forced to relinquish New York City and Westchester County to the British, it strenuously contested British operations in northern New York. The defeat at Saratoga of the British army under General John Burgoyne was one of the decisive engagements of the war (see SARATOGA, BATTLES OF).

In 1783, following the conclusion of hostilities, British forces evacuated New York City. The State had meanwhile (1778) ratified the Articles of Confederation. However, at the Constitutional Convention of 1787, the New York delegation, fearful of Federal interference with the commercial interests of the State, opposed the newly drafted Constitution of the United States. A State convention, which convened at Poughkeepsie in June, 1788, finally voted (30 to 27) for ratification. The Federalist leader Alexander Hamilton (q.v.) played a decisive role at the convention.

The dominant figure in New York politics for more than two decades after Hamilton's death (1804) in a duel with Aaron Burr (q.v.) was DeWitt Clinton (q.v.). An Antifederalist and governor of the State from 1817 to 1821 and again from 1825 to 1828, Clinton contributed substantially to the further expansion of New York as a commercial and financial center. Largely as a result of his efforts, the Erie Canal project was initiated in 1817. The State constitution of 1777 was revised in 1821, with the new document representing a major advance toward more democratic government. Another constitutional revision in 1846 extended this trend.

In the period preceding the beginning of the American Civil War, the mercantile and manufacturing interests of New York advocated peace at any price. A vast majority of the people were Unionist in sentiment, however, and despite serious disturbances in New York City in 1863 (see DRAFT RIOTS), the State was a decisive factor in the Union victory, providing more than 500,000 soldiers for the Federal armies.

After the Civil War the economic development of the State continued at an uninterrupted pace. In the realm of both State and national politics, New York emerged as a key force within the pattern of the traditional two-party system. The State became known as the pivotal State in Presidential elections because of its large electoral vote (47). Between 1900 and 1928 the Presidential candidates of the Republican Party carried the State in seven elections. From 1932 through 1944 the electorate gave majorities to the Democratic Presidential candidate. The Republican candidate received a plurality in 1948. In 1952 Dwight D. Eisenhower, the candidate of the Republican Party, polled 3,952,815 votes, as against 2,687,890 votes for the Democratic candidate Adlai E. Stevenson.

NEW YORK BAY, inlet of the Atlantic Ocean, at the mouth of the Hudson River, on which stands the city of New York. It consists of two parts, the upper and lower bays.

NEW YORK (CITY), the chief city of New York State, commercial and financial metropolis of the Western Hemisphere, largest city in population in the United States, and second largest (after London) in the world. New York is situated in the S.E. corner of the State, on the Hudson R., East R., and New York Bay (qq.v.). Originally consisting of Manhattan Island and, by an act of the New York State legislature, consolidated with adjacent communities on January 1, 1898, New York comprises five boroughs, each of which is coextensive with a county. In the order of area, these boroughs are Queens, which is coextensive with Queens County, one of the four counties of Long Island (q.v.); Brooklyn, which is coextensive with Kings County, another of the counties of Long Island; Richmond, which is coextensive with Richmond County and Staten Island (q.v.); the Bronx, which is coextensive with Bronx County, the only county of the city on the New York State mainland; and Manhattan, which is coextensive with New York County and Manhattan Island. In the order of population (1950), the boroughs rank as follows: Brooklyn, Manhattan, Queens, the Bronx, and Richmond. Each of the boroughs is the subject of a separate article containing pertinent data on industry, cultural institutions, history, and other features. Population of New York City (1940) 7,454,995; (1950) 7,891,957. Area of city, 365.4 sq.m.

Measured from the N. extremity of the Bronx to the s. extremity of Brooklyn, the length of New York City is 36 m.; its maximum width, in an E. and W. direction, is 25 m. The terrain of the city is generally level, but deeply eroded spurs of the Berkshire Hills extend into the Bronx and Manhattan. In these boroughs the maximum elevations are respectively 284.5 ft. and 267.7 ft. The terrain

Gottscho-Schleisner; Edward Ratcliffe

NEW YORK CITY. *Left: New York Stock Exchange. Right: RCA Building, Rockefeller Center.*

of the other three boroughs falls within the province of the Atlantic coastal plain. A range of morainic hills extends in a general E. and W. direction through these boroughs. Maximum elevations in Queens, Brooklyn, and Richmond are respectively 266.4 ft., 182.7 ft., and 409.8 ft. Todt Hill, the last-named elevation, is one of the highest points on the Atlantic coast of the United States.

A number of lesser islands, situated mainly in the East R., form part of New York City. The principal lesser islands in New York Bay are under the jurisdiction of the U.S. government. These islands are Governor's Island (q.v.), a military reservation; Ellis Island (q.v.), the former immigration station; and Bedloe's Island, site of the internationally celebrated Statue of Liberty (q.v.).

One of the outstanding geological features of the site of New York is an underlying formation of metamorphic rock, known as Manhattan schist. This formation, which occurs in several of the boroughs, notably Manhattan, provides solid foundations for the towering skyscrapers of the city. The most unusual feature of the geology is the large variety of precious and semiprecious stones. Among these stones, which occur in veins of granite scat-

tered through the schist, are opals, amethysts, beryls, and garnets.

With only the Bronx situated on the mainland, the major feature of the topography of New York is its insularity in navigable waters. This feature created physical and economic obstacles of unusual severity in the development of the city, particularly in the field of rail and vehicular transportation, but made possible the emergence of New York as the greatest port in the world. Upper New York Bay, the almost completely landlocked N. portion of New York Bay, is one of the safest and largest natural anchorages in North America. The Narrows, a strait separating Richmond and Brooklyn, connects the Upper Bay with the Lower Bay.

New York harbor is traversed by a network of dredged channels. Ambrose Channel, 7 m. long, 40 ft. deep, and 2000 ft. wide, crosses the Lower Bay from the Atlantic Ocean to The Narrows. Main, or Anchorage Channel, which extends across the Upper Bay to the mouth of the Hudson R., is about a half mile wide and from 40 to 90 ft. deep. The Hudson R. estuary, known as the North R., has a channel 40 ft. in depth, and the East R. channel is 35 ft. in depth. By means of these

Port of New York Authority

An early painting showing the harbor of New York City

and other channels all sections of the port, including Jersey City, N.J., Newark, N.J., and Bayonne, N.J., which form part of the port district, are accessible to ocean-going vessels. The North R. water front of Manhattan, the hub of the overseas passenger traffic of the port, is accessible to the largest liners afloat.

The water front of New York City is approximately 578 m. long and is equipped with about 700 piers and wharves, which range up to 1700 ft. in length. Including the side wharfage of these piers, the length of the New York water front is about 770 m. The port areas are equipped with enormous facilities for the loading, discharge, and storage of waterborne freight, with numerous dry docks and ship-repair and shipbuilding facilities, and with immense facilities for intraport transfer of railway freight.

As indicated in the foregoing, the New Jersey communities abutting on New York harbor comprise an integral part of the port economy. In a large degree this aspect of port affairs results from the circumstance that only three of the trunk-line railway systems serving New York have major freight terminals within the city. The terminals of the remainder, totaling seven systems, are situated on the mainland w. of the harbor. As a consequence, a large volume of the cargoes moving in and out of New York must be transshipped

between the city and the New Jersey railheads. Until recent years transshipment was accomplished entirely by means of car floats (barges designed to carry railway cars) and lighters. This system created serious problems, including harbor congestion and the utilization of a disproportionate amount of valuable water frontage for railway marine operations. The Port of New York Authority, established in 1921 as a self-supporting agency of the States of New York and New Jersey, has in recent years completed a number of projects to facilitate the flow of commerce in the port district. Among these projects are the Lincoln and Holland tunnels, vehicular tubes under the North R., and the George Washington Bridge, the second longest suspension bridge in the world. Each of these facilities links Manhattan with New Jersey points.

The magnitude of shipping operations in New York City is indicated by the fact that, in terms of value, more than half of the foreign trade of the United States normally moves through the port. By volume, the foreign trade moving through New York approximates nearly a quarter of the national total. The domestic waterborne commerce of the port is also enormous, usually surpassing the foreign and domestic traffic of San Francisco, Philadelphia, and Baltimore combined.

Port of N.Y. Auth.; Alfred Kleinfeld;
Ewing Galloway

NEW YORK CITY

*Above: Cargo being loaded on a
ship docked in the North River.
Right: Ferry carrying passengers and vehicles to Staten Island.
Below: Brooklyn Bridge, span-
ning the East River.*

In a typical year the combined tonnage of domestic and foreign cargoes handled in the port was more than 90,000,000.

Besides being the financial and commercial center of the Western Hemisphere, with vast banking organizations, commodity exchanges, and related facilities, New York is the foremost manufacturing city of the nation. The chief industry is the manufacture of wearing apparel and accessories. Other leading industries include printing and publishing, meat packing, and the manufacture of foods, confections, and beverages, metal products, textiles other than clothing, wood products, chemicals, stone, clay, and glass products, paper and paper products, jewelry, tobacco products, toys and novelties, and luggage. In a recent year the value of manufactures produced in New York City approximated $15,500,000,000.

New York possesses unsurpassed facilities for the transportation of passengers. Intracity transportation is provided by the largest municipally owned and operated transit system in the nation. Subway and elevated routes included in this system have a total length of 236.6 m., comprising a network that links all of the boroughs except Richmond. Surface routes, consisting of trolley and bus lines, have a combined length of more than 500 m. In addition, the city is served by over 10,000 taxicabs, by numerous privately operated surface lines, by the Long Island Railway, which provides connections between Manhattan and points on Long Island, by the Hudson and Manhattan Railroad, which operates (through tubes underneath the North River) between Manhattan and points in New Jersey, and by the Staten Island Rapid Transit Railway, which services Richmond.

Interstate and intrastate connections are provided by the trunk-line railways with terminals in the metropolitan area. The New York Central, New York, New Haven & Hartford, and Pennsylvania systems, the only trunk-line systems with passenger terminals within the city, maintain direct lines to important points in the South, the Midwest, upper New York State, and New England. The city contains two of the largest airports in the world, namely LaGuardia Field and Idlewild Airport, which are situated in Queens. These airports are the terminals of all the major national and international air lines.

The movement of rapid-transit, railway, vehicular, and pedestrian traffic within and to and from New York City is made possible by a total of 62 bridges, 17 under-river tunnels, and a number of ferry lines, including lines operating between Manhattan and Richmond, between Manhattan and New Jersey, and between Richmond and Brooklyn.

Government. New York is governed according to the provisions of the city charter of 1938, as amended. By the terms of this document the chief executive of the city is a mayor, elected for a four-year term. A comptroller, also elected for a four-year term, is the chief financial officer of the city. Legislative authority is vested in a city council. By the provisions of a charter amendment, adopted in the elections of November, 1948, this body consists of 24 members, one for each State senatorial district of the city. Prior to the elections of November, 1948, members of the city council were elected at large from the boroughs on the basis of proportional representation, with one councilman per 75,000 voters. The mayor of New York has broad powers, including the veto over enactments of the council. He also appoints the heads of the various administrative departments, boards, and commissions of the city, appoints the city magistrates and the justices of the court of special sessions, and enjoys other important prerogatives. To a large degree, the administration of the city is conducted by the board of estimate, which consists of the mayor, comptroller, president of the city council, and the borough presidents. The last-named officials are elected at large from the boroughs for four-year terms. In the deliberations of the board of estimate, the mayor, comptroller, and president of the city council have three votes each, the borough presidents of Manhattan and Brooklyn have two votes each, and the other borough presidents have one vote each. The powers of the board of estimate include control over the fiscal policy of the city, jurisdiction over franchises and the sale or lease of city property, and direction of other major aspects of city affairs. Municipal judicial authority is vested in courts of special sessions, domestic relations courts, magistrates courts, and municipal courts.

Each of the boroughs of the city has a small measure of local autonomy, which is centered in the office of the borough president. These officials are responsible for the maintenance of certain borough works, for various improvements within their jurisdictions, and for other minor functions.

As political subdivisions of New York State, the counties of the city have certain governmental offices, confined mainly to the administration of justice; these include the district attorney, sheriff, and register, and various courts, namely county courts (called the court of general sessions in New York County), surrogate's courts, and city courts.

NEW YORK NAVAL SHIPYARD, better known as the BROOKLYN NAVY YARD, a shipyard of the U.S. Navy, situated in Brooklyn, N.Y., along the shore of Wallabout Bay, an arm of the East River, opposite Corlear's Hook, Manhattan. It occupies an area of 197 acres, 118 on land and 79 on water. The shipyard is operated for the purpose of maintaining, repairing, and building U.S. Navy ships, and is equipped with docks, dry docks, steel shipways, pontoons and cylindrical floats for salvage activity, foundries, warehouses, machine shops, and a railway spur. Also on the area are marine barracks, officers' quarters, a power plant, and a radio station. The site of the shipyard was originally part of an estate owned by the Remsen family until after the American Revolution, when it was purchased by John Jackson, a shipbuilder. Jackson subsequently built two ships, the merchant ship *Canton* and the frigate *John Adams*, at a dock which he constructed on the estate. In 1801 the property was bought for $40,000 by the Federal authorities. The first steamship to be constructed for any navy was built at the Brooklyn Navy Yard in 1814-15 from the plans of the inventor of the steamship, Robert Fulton (q.v.).

During World War II a maximum of 69,000 persons was employed and seventy-two ships, including the battleships *Iowa, Missouri,* and *North Carolina* and the aircraft carrier *Franklin D. Roosevelt*, were built at the New York Naval Shipyard.

NEW YORK PUBLIC LIBRARY, one of the largest and best-equipped libraries in the world, situated in New York City, and established in 1895 by the consolidation of the Astor, Lenox, and Tilden libraries. The first-named library was founded in 1848 by the financier John Jacob Astor, and at the time of the consolidation comprised more than 250,000 volumes valued at nearly $1,000,000. The second was founded in 1875 by the bibliophile James Lenox, and comprised about 86,000 volumes, with a total endowment of more than $500,000. The last-mentioned library, comprising about 20,000 volumes, was created by the terms of the will of the political leader Samuel Jones Tilden, who bequeathed more than $2,000,000 for the establishment of a free library and reading

room in 1895. An act providing for the erection of a building to house the collections was passed by the New York City government in 1897. The new structure, opened to the public in 1911, was executed in marble in the modern Renaissance style; it has a capacity of 3,000,000 volumes and also contains two art galleries and three exhibition rooms for rare and precious books and other materials. Funds for its maintenance are derived entirely from private endowments and contributions.

In the years following the original establishment of the New York Public Library, its collections were expanded by the addition of numerous public and private collections. Notable among these are the New York Free Circulating Library, with eleven branches and a total of 16,000 volumes, merged in 1901; the New York Free Circulating Library for the Blind, merged in 1903; the Aguilar Library, a collection of Jewish Literature, merged in 1903; and the Catholic Free Circulating Library, with five branches, merged in 1904. The Library has also benefited from the liberal financial contributions of various philanthropists, including a gift of $5,200,000 by Andrew Carnegie, in 1901, $3,000,000 given by John S. Kennedy in 1909, and $3,-000,000 given by John D. Rockefeller, Jr., $16,000,000 by Payne Whitney, and $1,000,-000 by Edward S. Harkness in subsequent years. The Carnegie gift enabled the municipal government to erect 39 of the present 65 branches and sub-branches of the main library. The branches, which receive funds for operating expenses from the municipal government, are scattered throughout the boroughs of Manhattan, The Bronx, and Richmond; the remaining two boroughs, Brooklyn and Queens, operate separate library systems.

The New York Public Library is organized into two departments, reference and circulation. In 1953 the reference department had more than 3,500,000 volumes and the circulating department had over 1,900,000. The number of volumes circulated in an average year totals between 8,000,000 and 9,000,000, and more than 3,000,000 persons use the main building. In the fields of American history, New York City history, Semitic languages, the history and culture of the Negro people, art, economics, music, and folklore, the collections of the library are outstanding. The library also has an extensive collection of pamphlets and some 40,000 periodicals, both American and foreign, as well as a comprehensive file of newspapers reproduced on microfilm. It publishes several monthly periodicals: the *Bulletin,* devoted to news of its exhibitions and new acquisitions; the *Branch Library Book News,* to stimulate reading interest; the *Municipal Reference Library Notes* on publications of civic importance; and the bi-monthly *New Technical Books,* listing outstanding recent publications in the field of technology. All material in the Reference Department of the Central Building is for use within the building only, but researchers may purchase, from the Division of Photographic Services, photographs, photostats, or microfilm of desired material.

The facilities of the library in the field of art include the Picture Collection, the largest free circulating picture library in the world, offering a stock of 6,000,000 photographs and printed reproductions; the Print Room, housing a representative collection of 15th- to 20th-century prints from all countries; the Spencer Collection of richly illustrated books; a reference collection comprising books, periodicals, pamphlets, scrapbooks, and clippings on the fine arts in the Art and Architecture Division; and the Theater Collection of material on the stage, the drama, the cinema, the radio, and television.

Since the early years of the 20th century, the New York Public Library has been widely recognized for its pioneering in the field of children's educational and recreational activities. Almost every branch of the library now maintains a separate children's room and a staff specially trained for work with children. Special activities are also offered to teen-age youngsters, while a wide range of activities including current affairs discussion groups, film forums, and book-reviewing and study groups, are available to adults.

NEW YORK, THE COLLEGE OF THE CITY OF, also known as THE CITY COLLEGE, a coeducational, municipally controlled institution of higher learning, founded in New York City as the Free Academy in 1847. The present name was adopted by an act of the New York State legislature in 1866. Baccalaureate degrees are offered in the liberal arts and sciences, business and civic administration, and in civil, mechanical, electrical, and chemical engineering; master's degrees are offered in the liberal arts, the various branches of engineering, education, and business administration. Specialized courses for municipal employees and in food-store management are among the curricula instituted in recent years. The College is administered by the Board of

Higher Education of New York City, and receives its principal financial support from the municipal government.

The College was originally housed in a small building situated on 23rd Street and Lexington Avenue, in the borough of Manhattan. In 1907 the College was moved to a newly erected group of buildings at 139th Street and Convent Avenue; this is now the site of the College of Liberal Arts and Sciences and of the School of Technology. In 1930 the original building was replaced by a sixteen-story structure which now houses the School of Business and Civil Administration. Admission to the College is restricted to residents of New York City; no tuition fees are required. In order to gain admission, applicants must have obtained excellent grades in high school. Undergraduates of the College are required to maintain high scholastic averages; failure to do so may result in either suspension or dismissal. In 1953 more than 29,000 students were enrolled, including about 9300 full-time students; the faculty comprised over 1200 teachers.

NEW YORK UNIVERSITY, a coeducational, nonsectarian, privately controlled institution of higher learning located in New York City, chartered in 1831, and opened for instruction the following year as the University of the City of New York. The present name was adopted in 1896. Divisions of the University, located at various sites owned and rented by the institution throughout the city, are as follows.

At Washington Square, the original site, are the school of law (founded 1835), the graduate school of arts and sciences (1886), the school of education (1890), the school of commerce, accounts, and finance (1900), the division of general education (1908), Washington Square College (1913), the school of retailing (1921), the school of architecture and allied arts (1923), the graduate divisions for training in public service (1938), the institute of public affairs and regional studies (1945), and the educational film institute (1939), of which the film library and the recordings division (1940) are subdivisions. The institute of economic affairs (1946; founded in 1943 as the institute of postwar reconstruction), at 45 Astor Place, and the institute for mathematics and mechanics (1946), at 45 Fourth Avenue, are located nearby.

At University Heights, in the Bronx, on a 45-acre campus of which the first section was acquired in 1891, are the college of arts and pure science (the original college of the University, founded in 1832 and later moved to its present location), the college of engineering (1899), and the Guggenheim school of aeronautics (1925) within the engineering college. The campus is the site of the Hall of Fame for Great Americans (q.v.), founded in 1900, and of the Sanitary Engineering Laboratory erected by the city of New York and operated jointly by the city and the University.

At the Wall Street branch, at 90 Trinity Place, is located the graduate school of business administration (1920). Courses are also given in conjunction with the Washington Square school of commerce, accounts, and finance. At the Bellevue Hospital branch, at First Avenue and Twenty-Sixth Street, is the university medical college (1839), and a public health laboratory erected by the city of New York and occupied jointly by university and municipal services. In addition to medical training, courses in nursing are offered. The institute of rehabilitation and physical medicine (1948), is located at 325 East Thirty-Eighth Street. The college of dentistry (1886), founded as the New York College of Dentistry and in 1925 merged with the University, occupies its own building at 209 East Twenty-Third Street. At 17 East Eightieth Street, near the Metropolitan Museum of Art (q.v.), is the graduate institute of fine arts (1937), a division of the Washington Square graduate school of arts and science.

The University grants bachelor's, master's, and doctor's degrees. The college of arts and pure science and the day division of the college of engineering grant degrees to men only. In 1953 the total student enrollment was approximately 38,600, including about 14,700 students attending classes full time; the faculty numbered more than 3800. The library contained more than 975,000 volumes and the endowment of the University was almost 19 million dollars.

NEW YORK WORLD'S FAIR. See EXHIBITIONS AND EXPOSITIONS.

NEW ZEALAND, a British dominion in the s. Pacific Ocean. It comprises three main islands, named the North Island, the South or Middle Island, and Stewart Island, besides a number of islets near the coast. The total area is 103,736 sq.m., with a population (1953 est.) of 2,037,553, including 123,199 Maoris (comprising 20 clans who were pacified in the 1870's). New Zealand is the scene of considerable volcanic activity, the chief line extending from Write Island, in the Bay of Plenty, to Mt. Tongariro. Wellington (q.v.) is the capital and Auckland (q.v.) is the largest city. Other important cities include Christchurch, Dunedin (qq.v.), Hutt (pop., 1953 est., 80,200), and Hamilton (35,500).

Area under cultivation in 1953 was 20,049,027 acres, the principal crops being wheat, oats, and barley. Dairying and livestock raising are important farm industries. Gold, silver, and coal are the most important minerals of New Zealand; almost all the gold and silver produced is exported.

The balance of trade is favorable to New Zealand, with the total value of exports exceeding the value of imports by about £10,000,000 in 1952. The principal articles of export are wool, butter, casein, cheese, fish, lamb, mutton, beef, milk, apples, peas, potatoes, sheep, hides, tallow, coal, and timber. Imports largely comprise wheat, sugar, tea, alcoholic beverages, tobacco products, apparel, drapery, silk and silk products, iron and steel, yarn, electrical machinery and wireless equipment, motor vehicles and parts, printing paper, books, manure, and rubber tires.

Education is free and compulsory for children between the ages of seven and fifteen. Public primary schools in 1952 numbered 1889, secondary schools 47, and district high schools 112. Native village schools totaled 162, and 9 secondary schools were also maintained for the education of the Maoris. The University of New Zealand with its several branch colleges, offers higher education.

In 1953, 3535 m. of railway were maintained under government operation. About 180 miles of railroad are privately owned and operated.

Government. Executive power rests with a governor general appointed by the crown on recommendation of the dominion government; the latter consists of an executive council (cabinet) headed by a prime minister. Legislative power is exercised by the House of Representatives, a body composed of 80 members popularly elected for three-year terms.

History. New Zealand was discovered and named in 1642 by the Dutch mariner Abel Janszoon Tasman. The English explorer Captain James Cook visited the islands in 1769 and took possession of them for Great Britain, but nearly three quarters of a century elapsed before the British government recognized his claim.

Early in the 19th century English missionaries and whaling men, despite fierce opposition from the native Maoris, established settlements and trading posts in New Zealand, chiefly along the Bay of Islands on North I.

British Info. Ser.

IN NEW ZEALAND. *Above: Boxes of apples for export, in Wellington. Right: Skiing on Mount Cook. Below: A shepherd tending a large flock of sheep.*

Systematic immigration began in 1839–40 under the auspices of the New Zealand Company, which had been organized in London.

By the terms of the Treaty of Waitangi, signed in 1840 by a British representative and fifty Maori chieftains, Great Britain formally proclaimed sovereignty over the islands and agreed to respect the land-ownership rights of the Maoris, who placed themselves under the protection of the British government. At the same time New Zealand was made a dependency of New South Wales, Australia; in the following year it was constituted a separate crown colony.

Colonization continued apace during the ensuing decades. Disputes between the newcomers and the Maoris over land claims led ultimately to violent Maori uprisings, notably in the period between 1860 and 1870. However, after that date colonial authorities pursued a conciliatory policy which resulted in the establishment of permanent peace between the European and native populations.

In the latter part of the 19th century sheep raising and gold mining became the main sources of the country's wealth. Beginning in 1890, when a liberal-labor coalition came to power, the government inaugurated a program of advanced social legislation, a field in which New Zealand earned world renown. The laws included enactments providing for woman suffrage (1893), compulsory arbitration of labor disputes (1894), old-age pensions (1898), and taxation and land reforms.

New Zealand achieved dominion status in 1907. During World War I it furnished 220,099 men for the British forces, of whom 100,471 served overseas. These troops fought in Egypt and at Gallipoli in 1915, the Australian and New Zealand Army Corps being known colloquially as "Anzac". In 1916 New Zealand units arrived in France in time for the battle of the Somme, and the Mounted Rifles later served in the campaign in Palestine. The losses of New Zealand in World War I exceeded 16,000 men killed and 40,000 wounded. German Samoa had been occupied by New Zealand forces on Aug. 29, 1914, and after the war it was administered by the dominion under the mandate of the League of Nations as the "Territory of Western Samoa". New Zealand forces also distinguished themselves in World War II. Casualties totaled 10,130 killed and 19,345 wounded.

The power of the Labor Party, which had controlled the government since 1935, came to an end on Nov. 30, 1949, when the National Party emerged victorious in the general election of that date. The new government, though promulgating a program more favorable to private enterprise, announced that there would be no important reductions in social-welfare services.

In the arena of foreign affairs New Zealand participated (1950) in the Colombo Plan for southeast Asia and in 1952 concluded the so-called "ANZUS" mutual-defense pact with Australia and the United States. Along with seven other countries, New Zealand signed the Southeast Asian collective-defense treaty on Sept. 8, 1954.

NEXT OF KIN. See KIN, NEXT OF.

NEY, MICHEL (1769–1815), Duke of Elchingen and Prince of the Moskwa, one of Napoleon's most famous marshals, born in Saarlouis. He became Kléber's adjutant general at the blockade of Mainz in 1794, and in 1796 general of brigade. For the capture of Mannheim he was made a general of division in 1799. On the establishment of the empire he was made marshal of France. In 1805 he stormed the entrenchments of Elchingen, for which he was created Duke of Elchingen. In 1813 he opened the battle of Lützen. He fought at Bautzen, but was defeated by Von Bülow at Dennewitz. He also engaged in the struggle at Leipzig. In the final campaign he commanded the first and second corps, opposed Brunswick at Quatrebras (June 16), and led the center at Waterloo. After the capitulation of Paris, when Napoleon returned to France after escaping from Elba, Ney was sent to oppose his advance, but he deserted the Bourbons and with his army joined his former commander. For this act of treason he was arrested near Aurillac, tried, and condemned to death for high treason.

NEZ PERCÉS, the leading North American Indian tribe of the Shahaptian (q.v.) linguistic stock. The tribe formerly occupied a large territory in eastern Washington, Oregon, and central Idaho, w. of the Bitterroot Range of mountains and including the lower Grande Ronde and Salmon rivers, with a large part of the Snake River and all of the Clearwater River districts. The name "Nez Percés" (Fr., "pierced nose") was given by French explorers and missionaries to several tribes which practiced nose piercing for the purpose of wearing nose pendants. The appellation was eventually restricted to the Nez Percés proper, although nose piercing was not common among them. They call themselves *Nimapu*, but are called *Shahaptian* by Salish (q.v.) Indian neighbors; the name of

Philip Gendreau, N.Y.

Niagara Falls, a well-known point of interest on the Niagara River

their linguistic stock is derived from the latter title.

The Nez Percés followed an economy based on fishing, especially for salmon, and on vegetable staples such as the bulbs of the camass plant, wild roots, and berries. They also kept horses and hunted buffalo. In winter they lived along river banks in villages of long houses built of bark, mats, and skins; in summer they camped in the mountains and in the great upland camass meadows. They practiced some weaving and the decorating of buffalo skins with paint and porcupine quills. Their principal religious ceremony was a dance in honor of the Guardian Spirit, their presiding deity. War dances were also performed. The entire tribe was divided into more than forty bands, each led by a chief whose power depended upon personal popularity alone. Marriage was generally outside the band or group.

In response to their request for instruction in Christianity, a Protestant mission was established among the Nez Percés at Lapwai, Idaho, in 1837. In 1855 they made a treaty with the United States, ceding the greater portion of their territory to the U.S. government and receiving a reservation which included the Wallowa Valley in Oregon. Subsequently gold was discovered in the region, and they were forced to agree to surrender all their lands and to enter a reservation at Lapwai, Idaho. A band led by a chief called Joseph, whose Indian name was Hinmaton-Yalaktit (1840?–1904), refused to accept the agreement and in 1877 fought a number of engagements with Federal troops. Joseph and his band were defeated and deported to the Indian Territory. In 1884 they were returned to the north and placed on the Colville Reservation in northern Washington, where they were too few in number to retain their tribal identity. The majority of the tribe lives on the Nez Percé Reservation, Idaho.

NIACIN. See VITAMIN.

NIAGARA, a river which forms part of the boundary between New York State and the province of Ontario, Canada, joining Lake Erie to Lake Ontario, with a course of 35 m., during which it makes a total descent of 326 ft. It encloses several islands, the largest being Grand I., which is about 12 m. long, and Goat I., which is situated on the lip of Niagara Falls, and divides the cataract into two. Goat Island is connected with the mainland by bridge.

The Niagara Falls are divided into two sections—the Horseshoe or Canadian fall, which is by far the more majestic, and the American. The Canadian has a descent of 158 ft. and the American a fall of 167 ft. The volume of water is about 15,000,000 cu. ft. per minute. The sight of the falls is equally fine from the bridge on the lip of the fall, or from the Cave of the Winds, below the American fall. The falls were first discovered by Father Hennepin in 1678.

The first hydraulic plant was erected at Niagara in 1853 but was a failure. Successful operations began about 1890. A treaty between the United States and Canada, signed in 1910, fixes the amount of water that can be diverted on the American side at 20,000 feet per second, and on the Canadian side at 36,000 feet per second. On the American side about 400 feet per second were diverted for the Erie Canal. At the present time about 300,000 horsepower is generated on the American side, and on the Canadian, 955,000 horsepower. On the Canadian side is the Queenstown-Chippewa power plant, one of the largest single hydroelectric developments in the world.

A new treaty covering use of the water was signed in 1950, and a joint American-Canadian project was undertaken to control the flow of water over Horseshoe Falls, which had been eroding rapidly. In 1954 a major section of Prospect Point on the American side of the falls collapsed, dislodging 185,000 tons of rock and dirt and leaving a 70-ft.-deep chasm in the crestline.

The first bridge over the Niagara River was erected in 1848, while later ones are the Michigan Central R.R. bridge and the Grand Trunk R.R. bridge completed in 1897. The bridge connecting Niagara Falls (N.Y.) and Niagara Falls (Ont.) has a span of 840 ft.

Parks have been established on the grounds adjacent to the falls on both the Canadian and American banks of the river. The province of Ontario and the State of New York, founders of the park lands, are responsible for their maintenance. It has been estimated that about 2,000,000 people visit the falls annually.

NIAGARA FALLS, city of Niagara Co., N.Y., on the Niagara River. The city's chief products are flour, carbon, paper, graphite, carborundum, emery wheels, machinery, calcium carbide, and bleaching powder. Cantilever, steel-arch, and suspension bridges cross the river to Niagara Falls (Ont.). Pop. (1950) 90,875.

NIBELUNGENLIED, a medieval German epic poem of unknown authorship, written in Middle High German in the late 12th century. The poem is a composite of Norse and Teutonic mythology and the early history of the kingdom of Burgundy. Several other versions exist of the material comprised in the *Nibelungenlied,* the principal one being the Icelandic prose epic *Volsunga Saga,* which emphasizes the mythological and primitive elements of the material common to both; the *Nibelungenlied* stresses the historical material. Parts of both the *Nibelungenlied* and the *Volsunga Saga* were combined by the 19th-century German composer Richard Wagner for his operatic tetralogy the *Ring of the Nibelungen* (q.v.).

NICÆA, or NICE, a city of ancient Bithynia, in Asia Minor, situated on the eastern shore of Lake Ascania. It was built by Antigonus, the son of Philip (316 B.C.), and received the name of Antigoneia, which Lysimachus changed to Nicæa, in honor of his wife. It is famous in ecclesiastical history for two councils held in it. See below.

NICÆA, COUNCILS OF, two ecumenical councils convoked at Nicæa, a city of ancient Bithynia, Asia Minor. **1.** FIRST COUNCIL OF NICÆA (325), the first ecumenical council, convened by the Roman emperor, Constantine I, to settle the Arian (see ARIUS) dispute concerning the nature of Jesus Christ. Of the 1800 bishops in the Roman Empire, 318 attended the council. The *Nicene Creed* (q.v.), which defined the Son as consubstantial with the Father, was adopted as the official position of the Church regarding the divinity of Christ. The council also fixed the celebration of Easter on the Sunday after the Jewish Passover, and granted papal authority in the east to the bishop of Alexandria. **2.** SECOND COUNCIL OF NICÆA (787) the seventh ecumenical council, convened by Irene, empress of the Eastern Roman Empire, and attended by 375 bishops, most of whom were Byzantine. In spite of strong objections by the iconoclasts, the council validated the veneration of images and ordered their restoration in churches throughout the Roman Empire.

NICARAGUA, a republic of Central America, bounded on the N. by Honduras, on the E. by the Caribbean Sea, on the S. by Costa Rica, and on the W. by the Pacific Ocean. The capital and chief city is Managua (q.v.). The best Nicaraguan ports are on the Pacific coast, and include Corinto, San Juan del Sur, and Brito; the Caribbean ports include Gracias a Dios and San Juan del Nort (or Greytown).

Other important cities are Granada (q.v.), León (pop. in 1950, 30,544), Masuya (16,743), and Matalgalpa (10,323).

A mountain range with a mean elevation of about 2000 ft. traverses the country from s.e. to n.w., merging in the n.w. with a smaller range approximately parallel with the n. border. From the n.w. highlands the interior gradually slopes to the low, swampy Caribbean coast. The most distinctive feature of the Nicaraguan topography is a great basin, or depression, which extends diagonally across the country from n.w. to s.e., south of the principal mountain range, and contains two great lakes near the w. coast: Lake Managua, 38 m. long and from 10 to 16 m. wide, and Lake Nicaragua, the largest lake in Central America. The lakes are connected by the Rio Tipitapa, about 100 m. long. In the area between the lakes and the Pacific Ocean is a chain of volcanoes which are frequently the cause of severe Nicaraguan earthquakes. About 70% of the Nicaraguan population live in the great basin, and the w. shores of the lakes are the site of most Nicaraguan cities and industrial activity. The interior of the country is wild and mountainous, and the Caribbean coast, sparsely populated, is overgrown with jungles which border coastal areas cleared for banana plantations. The four principal rivers, the San Juan, Segovia, Rio Grande, and Bluefields, empty into the Caribbean. The climate on the coasts is hot and humid, particularly on the e. coast, which receives as much as 250 in. of rain annually. The soil is extremely fertile; about 2,400,000 acres are under cultivation. Crops include cotton, coffee, sugar cane, cacao, corn, beans, bananas, and tropical fruits. About 17,500,000 acres are forested, and mahogany, cedar, and other valuable woods are exported. Rich deposits of gold and silver are worked, and gold shipments accounted for more than 17% of exports in 1952. Coffee made up nearly 42% of the total exports. The value of all exports in the same year was about $51,373,000, and imports were valued at almost $40,000,000. Most foreign trade is with the United States.

About 68% of the Nicaraguans are *mestizos,* a mixture of Spanish and Indian strains; about 17% are of European and American descent, 10% are Negroes (chiefly from the West Indies), and 5% Indians, principally Zamboes and Mosquitos (q.v.). The prevailing religion is Roman Catholicism, and the official language is Spanish. In 1951 Nicaragua had about 268 miles of government-operated railroads; in 1950 there were about 445 miles of surfaced highways in the country.

Under a constitution promulgated in 1950 Nicaragua is divided into fifteen departments and a national district, each under an administrator. The national executive power is delegated to a president, elected for six years. The bicameral legislature consists of a 42-member house of deputies and 16-member senate, all elected by direct suffrage for six years; ex-presidents become senators for life. The Communist Party is illegal; however, the constitution guarantees representation in the government to other political minorities. Area, 57,143 sq.m.; pop. (1951 est.) 1,088,000.

History. The coast of Nicaragua was seen by Christopher Columbus in 1502 during his fourth and last voyage to the Western Hemisphere. In 1522 the first Spanish expedition of conquest, under Gil Gonzalez Dávila, arrived on the coast. At that time, several Indian tribes inhabited the territory. Along the n.e. coast, on what is now known as the Mosquito Coast, lived the primitive Mosquito Indians. The most powerful tribe, living in the w., was ruled by a chief named Nicarao whose Hispanicized name, Nicaragua, was later given to the entire country. The Dávila expedition was received generally with friendliness, and several Spanish settlements were established. The next notable *conquistador* to penetrate the region was Francisco Fernández de Córdoba (q.v.), for whom the present Nicaraguan monetary unit, the *córdoba,* was named. He founded the cities of Granada and León, and attempted, at Granada, to establish an independent kingdom. Córdoba was killed in battle with Spanish government troops and Nicaragua was later incorporated into the captaincy-general of Guatemala (q.v.). Colonial Nicaragua enjoyed comparative peace and prosperity, although freebooters, notably English navigators such as Sir Francis Drake and Sir Richard Hawkins, continually raided and plundered the coast settlements.

Together with other Spanish-American colonies, the political liberals of Nicaragua began to agitate for independence at the beginning of the 19th century. The country declared itself independent of Spain in 1821. A year later Nicaragua became part of the short-lived Mexican empire of Agustín de Iturbide (q.v.), and after Iturbide's downfall joined, in 1823, the United Provinces of Central America (with Guatemala, Honduras, El Salvador, and Costa Rica).

Factional strife between the Liberals, centered in the city of León, and the Conserva-

Spanish colonial cathedral in Leon, Nicaragua

tives, centered in Granada, became characteristic of Nicaraguan politics. The Liberals fought to establish an independent nation, and the struggle of the two parties became a sanguinary civil war. In 1838 the Liberals obtained control and declared Nicaragua an independent republic. However, civil strife continued.

In 1855 William Walker (q.v.), an American adventurer, arrived in Nicaragua with a small band of followers and was engaged by the Liberals to head their forces. He captured and sacked Granada in 1855, and in 1856 became president of Nicaragua. By arbitrary seizure of boats and other property belonging to a transport company controlled by Cornelius Vanderbilt (q.v.), Walker incurred the latter's enmity. Vanderbilt backed the Conservative opponents of Walker and, as a result of an insurrection, Walker was compelled to flee the country in 1857. Because of the rivalry between León and Granada the capital was established at Managua, between the two cities. The Conservatives controlled Nicaragua from 1863 to 1893. During this period of comparative peace, material advances were made in the economic development of the country.

In 1893 a successful revolution brought the Liberal leader José Santos Zelaya to power. He remained president for the next seventeen years, ruling virtually as a dictator. In 1907 Zelaya tried to set himself up as the leader of a revived Central American union; he succeeded in making his personal candidate president of Honduras by declaring war on that country, and also attacked San Salvador. The tense situation was relieved by a Central American conference, the participants of which agreed on noninterference in each other's domestic affairs. A successful Conservative revolution against Zelaya occurred in 1909. American support was given to the Conservatives, and a succession of presidents took office during the next turbulent years.

After an unsuccessful revolt against the government in 1912, Adolfo Díaz, elected provisional president in 1910, asked the U.S. for military aid to keep the peace. A force of American marines was landed in Nicaragua and remained there until 1925. When the marines were evacuated, revolutions again began and the American force was returned in 1926. To arbitrate the claims and disputes of rival factions, U.S. President Calvin Coolidge sent the statesman Henry L. Stimson to

Nicaragua in that year. Stimson arranged a compromise between the leading factions. An election was held under American supervision in 1928, and Gen. José Maria Moncada, head of the Liberal army, was chosen president. One rebel leader, Augusto César Sandino, refused to accede to Moncada's election. He withdrew into the jungle and from that time on harassed the government troops and American marines. He was pursued unsuccessfully by the marines until they were finally withdrawn in 1933.

Juan Bautista Sacasa, elected president in 1933, was forced to resign in 1936 because of friction with the legislature, and in 1937 Anastasio Somoza, the national guard commandant, was elected president. Somoza collaborated closely with the United States in the field of foreign policy and, accepting U.S. guidance, managed to stabilize the national economy. His regime displayed scant regard for civil liberties, however; opposition parties and trade unions were vigorously suppressed.

Nicaragua declared war on the Axis powers on Dec. 9, 1941, during World War II, and in June, 1945, became a charter member of the United Nations. Somoza was not a candidate in the presidential election of February, 1947, but he retained control of the military establishment. The victor in the election was deposed in May, 1947, as a result of policy differences with Somoza. In August the Congress elected Somoza's uncle Victor Román y Reyes to the presidency. Nicaragua became a signatory in April, 1948, of the charter of the Organization of American States (q.v.).

Román y Reyes died in office on May 7, 1950, and Somoza was elected president on May 21. In 1951 the government secured loans totalling over $5 million from the International Bank for Reconstruction and Development to finance a public-works and industrial-expansion program. The government also obtained Point Four assistance from the United States. In October, 1951, Nicaragua signed the charter of the Organization of Central American States, which was created to solve common Central American problems.

President Somoza imposed martial law on the country on April 5, 1954, following discovery of a plot to assassinate him. Later in April Somoza accused Costa Rica of attempts to foment a Nicaraguan rebellion; Costa Rica leveled similar accusations against Nicaragua. On Jan. 11, 1955, small detachments of rebels launched an invasion of Costa Rica from Nicaragua. Acting on a Costa Rican complaint against Nicaragua, the O.A.S. promptly dispatched an investigating committee to the trouble zone. President Somoza emphatically denied complicity in the revolt, but the O.A.S. subsequently established a neutral zone along the Nicaraguan-Costa Rican frontier. After suffering military reverses the rebels withdrew into the zone and submitted (Jan. 25) to internment in Nicaragua.

NICARAGUA, LAKE, an extensive sheet of water, 100 m. in length, 45 m. in breadth, in the Republic of Nicaragua, Central America. Area, 2975 sq.m. The San Juan River flows from its southeastern extremity into the Caribbean Sea.

NICE (anc. *Nicæa;* It. *Nizza*), capital of the department of Alpes-Maritimes, France, situated on the Mediterranean Sea, at the foot of the Maritime Alps and at the w. extremity of the French Riviera, 140 miles E.N.E. of Marseilles. The city is built around a bay, called the Baie des Anges, and the old and new parts of Nice are separated by a small stream, the Paillon. Embankments and promenades line the sea frontage, and a boulevard extends along the bay shore. The city and bay are protected from severe climatic changes by the mountains on the N.; the dry, mild climate, with a mean annual temperature of 58.6° F., has made Nice a famous winter resort. The port exports oranges, lemons, flowers, and olive oil. Industrial establishments in the city manufacture straw hats, furniture, tobacco products, silks, soaps, confectionery, alcoholic beverages, and perfumes.

Nice was founded by Phocæans from Marseilles (q.v.) about the 4th century B.C. The town became a well-known trading colony in the ancient world. It changed rulers several times during ancient and medieval times, and suffered damage during many wars. In 1388 it acknowledged the supremacy of the House of Savoy, and from 1600 onward it was repeatedly taken by the French. In 1792 the French took it from Sardinian rule (Savoy) and made it a part of France. It was returned to Sardinia after the fall of Napoleon I in 1814, and in 1860 was re-incorporated into France by Napoleon III. During World War II Nice was occupied in 1942 by Italians and from 1943 to 1945 by Germans. Pop. (1946) 211,165.

NICE. See NICÆA.

NICE, COUNCILS OF. See ARIUS; ATHANASIUS; NICÆA.

NICENE CREED, a confession of faith adopted at the Council of Nicæa (325 A.D.) as a settlement of a controversy concerning the persons of the Trinity. It was intended to cover debated questions as to the divinity of Christ, and it introduced the word *homoousian* to correct the error of the *homoiousian* party, and to it were added several minatory clauses concerning Arianism. The creed that is popularly known as the Nicene Creed is more properly called the *Niceno-Constantinopolitan* or *Constantinopolitan Creed*, a profession of faith based on an ancient Jerusalem creed, made under the influence of Cyril of Jerusalem (351–86) and edited in a Nicene sense; it is contained in the *Ancoratus* of Epiphanius of Salamis (373–74), and is traditionally but erroneously attributed to the Council of Constantinople (381). Of the 178 words in the original only 33 are positively taken from the creed of 325 A.D. It is received as ecumenical by the Eastern and Roman communions and by the majority of the Reformed churches. At the Council of Toledo (589) the Western Church added the Filioque clause, the preposition *in* before the words "holy Catholic and Apostolic Church", and employs the singular form of the words used for expressing assent, "I believe", "I hope", "I confess". In the *Book of Common Prayer* the preposition *in* is omitted, and by an accident the word *holy* does not appear as an epithet of the church. See ARIUS; FILIOQUE.

NICHOLAS, SAINT (fl. 4th cent.), Christian prelate and patron saint of Russia. The accounts of his life are confused and historically unconfirmed. According to tradition he was a native of Patara, Asia Minor. He entered the nearby monastery of Sion and subsequently became archbishop of the metropolitan church in Myra, Asia Minor. He is said to have been present at the first Council of Nicæa (325). At the end of the 11th century some Italian merchants transported his remains from Myra to Bari, Italy, where his tomb is now a shrine. He is the patron saint of children, scholars, virgins, sailors, and merchants. In the Middle Ages he was regarded by thieves as their patron saint. Legend tells of his surreptitious gifts to the three daughters of a poor man, who, unable to give them dowries, was about to abandon them to a life of sin. From this tale has grown the custom of secret giving on the Eve of St. Nicholas (December 6). Due to the close proximity of dates, Christmas and St. Nicholas' day are now celebrated simultaneously in most countries. "Santa Claus" is an American corruption of the Dutch "San Nicolaas".

NICHOLAS, the name of five popes and an antipope. **1.** NICHOLAS I, SAINT, known as NICHOLAS THE GREAT (800?–67), Pope from 858 to 867. He succeeded Benedict III and increased the power of the Holy See. His support of St. Ignatius, Patriarch of Constantinople, against his powerful rival Photius, particularly after the former's deposition in 857, contributed to the schism of Eastern and Western churches (see SCHISM, WESTERN OR GREAT). He denied King Lothair II of Lorraine the right to divorce his wife and excommunicated those bishops who supported Lothair. His most significant act was the maintenance of the bishops' right of appeal to the Vatican when he struggled with Hincmar, Archbishop of Reims, on behalf of Rothad, Bishop of Soissons. **2.** NICHOLAS II, born GERARD OF BURGUNDY (980?–1061), Pope from 1059 to 1061. He succeeded Benedict X and directed Vatican policy under the reforming influence of Cardinal Archdeacon Hildebrand, later Pope Gregory VII. His pontificate is known for the progress made toward ending simony and concubinage among the clergy, and for the Lateran Council of 1059 which determined election procedure for popes. **3.** NICHOLAS III, born GIOVANNI GAETANO ORSINI (1216?–80), Pope from 1277 to 1280. He was schooled in diplomacy and during his pontificate decreased civil interference with the papacy. He initiated a law that only Romans could achieve privilege and honor in Rome, and thus rid the city of foreign domination. **4.** NICHOLAS IV, born GIROLAMO MASCI (d. 1292), Pope from 1288 to 1292. He succeeded Pope Honorius after the pontificate had been vacant for ten months. Disinterested in political issues, he did not participate in the contemporary factional struggles in Rome. In 1289 he crowned Charles II, King of Naples and Sicily, when the latter promised to accede to papal authority; in the same year, he promulgated a constitution granting cardinals half of the income of the papal see, thereby establishing independence for the college of cardinals. **5.** NICHOLAS V, born PIETRO RAINALDUCCI (d. 1333), Antipope from 1328 to 1330 in opposition to Pope John XXII. He was installed by Louis the Bavarian, Holy Roman Emperor as Louis IV, who had been excommunicated by Pope John. Nicholas retained his insecure office for two years, during which time he also was excommunicated, and then, having been promised a pardon, confessed to the Pope at Avignor Nicholas, though pardoned, was kept a prisoner in the papal palace until his death. **6.** NICHOLAS V, born TOMMASO PARENTUCELLI (1397?–1455),

Nicholas II of Russia

Pope from 1447 to 1455. He founded the Vatican library. The important events of his pontificate were the resignation of the last antipope, Felix V, in 1449; the crowning in 1452 of Frederick III, the last Holy Roman Emperor to be crowned in St. Peter's in Rome; and the fall of Constantinople to the Turks in 1453.

NICHOLAS I, or (Russ.) NICOLAI PAVLO-VICH (1796–1855), Czar of Russia, third son of Paul I, born in Saint Petersburg. Upon the death of his eldest brother, Alexander I, in 1825, and the abdication of his older brother Constantine Pavlovich because of a nonroyal marriage, he assumed the throne. His domestic policy was autocratic and his foreign policy aggressive. He waged war successfully against Persia (1828–29) and Turkey (1828–29). During 1830 and 1831 Nicholas crushed Polish revolts against Russian authority and abrogated the Polish constitution. In 1849 he aided Austria in the suppression of uprisings in Hungary. His schemes to add Constantinople to his domain led to the Crimean War (1854–56). His regime was severe, and his subjects called him the "Iron Czar".

NICHOLAS II, or (Russ.) NIKOLAI ALEK-SANDROVICH (1868–1918), Czar of Russia, eld-est son of Alexander III, born in Saint Petersburg. He succeeded his father in 1894, and attempted to continue his peaceful foreign policy. At his instigation the International Peace Conference at The Hague met in 1899, and the Permanent Court of Arbitration (q.v.) at The Hague was founded. The unsuccessful war with Japan (1904–05) and his continued reactionary domestic policy occasioned a strong opposition movement in 1905, forcing him to grant a constitution that same year. In the following years he tried unsuccessfully to allay popular discontent by the granting of a number of liberal reforms. In 1914 he attempted to prevent World War I; when his efforts failed, he joined the war on the side of the Allies. The subsequent pro-German intrigues at his court increased the popular opposition to his reign. General dissatisfaction with both the foreign and domestic policies of Nicholas culminated in the Russian Revolution (1917). Nicholas was forced to abdicate (Mar. 15, 1917) and he and his family were imprisoned in Siberia and then executed by the Bolsheviks in July, 1918. See RUSSIA: *History*.

NICHOLAS, or (Russ.) NIKOLAI NIKO-LAEVICH (1856–1929), Russian Grand Duke and soldier, born in Saint Petersburg, and educated at the school for military engineers and the military academy. As a member of the Russian general staff he distinguished himself during the war with Turkey (1877–78) and became inspector general of the cavalry in 1895. During his ten years in the last-named capacity, he introduced training and organizational reforms in the cavalry schools. In 1905 he was appointed commander in chief of the Saint Petersburg military district, and made president of the newly created council for national defense. At the outbreak of World War I he was appointed commander in chief of the Russian Army; the following year Czar Nicholas II personally took command of the Russian armies. After the Russian Revolution of 1917, the Grand Duke went into exile in Paris, France, where he spent his remaining years.

NICKEL, a metallic element, atomic number 28, atomic weight 58.69, symbol Ni. It was used as coinage in nickel-copper alloys for several thousand years, but was not recognized as an elemental substance until 175 when the Swedish chemist Baron Axel Frederic Cronstedt isolated the metal from nic colite ore.

Occurrence and Production. Nickel occur as a metal in meteors. Combined with othe elements it occurs in minerals, such as garnierite, millerite, niccolite, pentlandite, and pyrrhotite; the last two minerals are the principal ores of nickel. Most of the world's supply of nickel is mined in Canada; Cuba and New Caledonia are next in importance as nickel producers. About 180,000 tons of nickel are mined per year all over the world. There are no large deposits in the United States; small amounts of nickel are produced as by-products in copper refining, but most of the nickel used in the United States is imported. Over 160 million pounds of nickel were consumed in the United States in a recent year.

Nickel ores usually contain impurities, chief among which is copper. Sulfide ores, such as pentlandite and nickeliferous pyrrohite, are usually smelted in a blast furnace and shipped in the form of a matte of copper and nickel sulfide to refineries, where the nickel is removed by various processes. In the electrolytic process (see ELECTROCHEMISTRY) the nickel is deposited in pure metallic form after the copper has been preferentially removed by deposition at a different voltage and in a different electrolyte. In the *Mond process* copper is removed by dissolution in dilute sulfuric acid and the nickel residue is reduced to impure metallic nickel. Carbon monoxide is passed over the impure nickel and nickel carbonyl, $Ni(CO)_4$, a volatile gas, is formed. The nickel carbonyl is heated to 200° C. (392° F.) and decomposes, depositing pure metallic nickel.

Properties. Nickel is a silver-white, hard, malleable, ductile metal, capable of taking a high polish. It is magnetic below 345° C. (653° F.), and has a m.p. 1452° C. (2646° F.), b.p. 2900° C. (5252° F.), and specific gravity 8.9. It exists in five stable isotopic forms. Metallic nickel is not very active chemically. It does not oxidize upon exposure to air, and does not tarnish. It is soluble in dilute nitric acid and becomes passive (nonreactive) in concentrated nitric acid; it does not react with alkalis.

Uses. Nickel is used as a protective and ornamental coating for metals, particularly iron and steel, which are susceptive to corrosion. The nickel plate is deposited by electrolysis from a nickel solution. Finely divided nickel absorbs seventeen times its own volume of hydrogen and is used as a catalyst in many processes including the hydrogenation (q.v.) of oils. The greatest amount of the metal is used in the form of alloys. Nickel imparts great strength and corrosion resistance to

steel; nickel steel, containing about 2 to 4 percent nickel, is used in automobile parts, such as axles, crankshafts, gears, valves, and rods, in machine parts, and in armor plate. Some of the important nickel-containing alloys are German silver, Invar, Monel metal, Nichrome, and Permalloy. The nickel coins of currency are an alloy of 25 percent nickel and 75 percent copper.

Compounds. Nickel forms divalent (nickelous) and trivalent (nickelic) compounds. The important compounds are divalent. Most of the salts of nickel, such as nickel chloride, $NiCl_2$, nickel sulfate, $NiSO_4$, and nickel nitrate, $Ni(NO_3)_2$, are green or blue in color and are usually hydrated. Nickel ammonium sulfate, $NiSO_4 \cdot (NH_4)_2SO_4 \cdot 6H_2O$, is used for nickel electroplating solutions. Nickel compounds are often identified by adding an organic reagent, dimethylglyoxime, which reacts with nickel to form a red, flocculent precipitate.

NICKEL PLATING. See NICKEL.

NICKEL STEEL. See NICKEL.

NICOBAR ISLANDS, group of islands in the Indian Ocean, forming with the Andamans, to the south of which they lie, an extension of the great island chain of which Java and Sumatra are the principal links. They consist of Great and Little Nicobar, and a number of smaller islands, with a total area of 635 sq.m. The principal productions are coconuts (about 15,000,000 annually) and copra. The archipelago was occupied by Denmark from 1756 to 1856. In 1869 it was annexed by Britain. There is a permanent assistant commissioner at Car Nicobar. There is a good harbor at Nankauri. Pop., about 10,000.

NICOL, ERSKINE (1825–1904), Scottish genre painter, born in Leith, near Edinburgh. He studied art at the Trustees' Academy, Edinburgh. In 1859 he was elected a member of the Royal Scottish Academy and in 1868 was made an associate of the Royal Academy in London. His vigorous and humorous scenes of Scottish and Irish peasant life were very popular. Characteristic examples of his painting are in the Tate Gallery and Victoria and Albert Museum, London, and the Scottish National Gallery, Edinburgh. Other works by him include "Paddy's Mark" (Corcoran Art Gallery, Washington, D.C.) and "Paying the Rent" (Metropolitan Museum of Art, New York City).

NICOLAS, SAINT. See NICHOLAS, SAINT.

NICOLLE, CHARLES JEAN HENRI (1866–1936), French physician and bacteriologist, born in Rouen, and educated at the University of Rouen. In 1903, after practicing medicine and working at the Pasteur Institute in Paris under the Russian bacteriologist Élie Metchnikoff and the French bacteriologist Pierre Roux, he was appointed director of the Pasteur Institute in Tunis. He subsequently served as a surgeon in the French army in Algeria, and in 1932 became professor of bacteriology at the Cóllege de France. In 1909 Nicolle demonstrated that the body louse is the chief vector of typhus (q.v.); he also showed that cattle plague is caused by a filtrable virus. He was awarded the Nobel Prize in physiology and medicine in 1928.

NICOLLS, RICHARD (1624–72), first British governor of New York, born in Bedfordshire. During the Great Rebellion he commanded a troop of horse in the Royalist forces, and after King Charles II's defeat followed the Stuarts into exile. After the restoration of the monarchy he was appointed to a commission to take New Amsterdam from the Dutch. The town surrendered to Nicolls' forces on September 8, 1664, and he governed the colony as deputy for the Duke of York for four years. He adopted a policy of gradual transition from Dutch to English law and government, renamed the colony and town New York, and with his secretary Mathias Nicolls formulated the legal code known as "the Duke's Laws", which remained in force from 1665 to 1683. Nicolls resigned his post in 1668 and returned to England. He was killed during the war with Holland in the naval battle of Southwald Bay.

NICOMEDES III. See BITHYNIA.

NICOSIA, called also LEVKOSIA, or LEFKOSIA, capital of Cyprus, 23 miles N.W. of the seaport Larnaca, and the residence of the British High Commissioner, and the see of a Greek archbishop. There are manufactures of silk, leather, and cotton. Pop., about 35,000.

NICOTIANA, genus of annual and perennial herbs and shrubs belonging to the Nightshade family. The genus, which contains about forty-five species, is native to the Western Hemisphere; several species are widely cultivated in gardens of warm temperate regions of the world for ornament and as crop plants for commercial use. The genus was named after the 16th-century French diplomat Jean Nicot, who introduced it into France. Nicotiana plants have sticky, hairy, bitter, poisonous foliage; the leaves are large, simple, and alternate. The white, yellow, green, or violet flowers, which are borne in panicles or racemes, have a large, tubular, five-cleft calyx, a large, funnel-shaped, five-lobed corolla from

the interior of which a long tube arises, five stamens, and a solitary pistil. The flowers are usually closed during the day and open at night. The fruit is a two-celled, many-seeded capsule. The domestic tobacco, *N. tabacum*, is the most valuable nicotiana, its leaves being used for tobacco (q.v.), and as a source of nicotine (q.v.).

NICOTINE, a colorless, oily, liquid alkaloid $C_{10}H_{14}N_2$, which constitutes the principal active chemical constituent of tobacco (q.v.). Nicotine turns brown on exposure to air, and boils at 246° C. (475° F.) under an atmospheric pressure of 730 mm. It is soluble in water, and completely miscible in alcohol, ether, chloroform, and petroleum ether. Nicotine is used in agriculture as an insecticide (q.v.), and in chemistry as a source of nicotinic acid (see VITAMIN), which is obtained by the oxidation of nicotine. Because many tobacco smokers habitually inhale nicotine-containing smoke (see DRUG ADDICTIONS), nicotine's greatest importance to man lies in its physiological effects. In small doses, nicotine serves as a nerve stimulant, especially upon the autonomic nervous system, promoting the flow of adrenaline and other internal secretions. In larger doses, nicotine paralyzes the autonomic nervous system by preventing the transmission of nerve impulses across the spaces between adjoining nerve cells. Still larger doses of nicotine may cause convulsions and death. The effects of nicotine upon the nervous system vary among individuals, some persons being capable of inhaling nicotine in tobacco smoke without ill effect, and other persons experiencing nausea, giddiness, depression, and respiratory disturbances upon inhaling the smallest amount of tobacco smoke. In certain individuals nicotine hastens the formation of gastric ulcers. Some physicians claim that nicotine is one of the causes of such diseases as angina pectoris and high blood pressure, but these claims have not been proved.

NICOTINIC ACID and **NICOTINAMIDE.** See VITAMIN.

NICTHEROY, or NITEROY, a town of Brazil, and capital of the state of Rio de Janeiro, on the E. side of the entrance to the bay, and 5 miles E. of the city of Rio de Janeiro. Pop. (1950 prelim.) 190,147.

NIDAROS, or TRONDHJEM, THRONDHJEM, or DRONTHEIM, city of Norway, situated at the mouth of the Nid River on the south shore of the Trondhjem Fiord, 240 miles N of Oslo (q.v.). The new name was substituted for the old on Jan. 1, 1930, and was the name of the city in early times. The principal building is the large cathedral, probably the finest church in Scandinavia. It was founded in the 11th century over the tomb of St. Olaf and consists of a Gothic nave and choir with a Romanesque transept. The industries are represented by sawmills, wood-pulp factories, fish-curing establishments, machine shops, and shipyards. Pop. (1946) 57,128.

NIEBUHR, BARTHOLD GEORG (1776–1831), German historian and statesman, born in Copenhagen, and educated at the University of Kiel. In 1804 he became director of the Danish national bank; in 1806 he resigned to accept a similar post from the Prussian government. He was made professor of history at the University of Berlin in 1810. In 1812 the first two volumes of his *Römische Geschichte* ("Roman History") were published; the final volume appeared posthumously in 1832, and the whole was translated into English between 1847 and 1851. Niebuhr was Prussian ambassador to the Vatican from 1816 to 1823. In 1816 he discovered in the Cathedral of Verona the *Institutes of Gaius*, the first important work to be discovered dealing with Roman private law, and in 1820 he found and edited fragments of the works of Titus Livius Livy and Marcus Tullius Cicero. After 1823 he taught in Bonn. He wrote many historical treatises and a juvenile history of the Greek heroes. Niebuhr's work had a profound influence on the modern critical approach to the study of history.

NIEBUHR, REINHOLD (1892–), American Protestant theologian, born in Wright City, Mo., and educated at Elmhurst College, Elmhurst, Ill., at Eden Theological Seminary, Webster Groves, Mo., and at Yale Divinity School. In 1915 he was ordained in the ministry of the Evangelical Synod of North America and made pastor of the Bethel Evangelical Church of Detroit, Mich. He held that post until 1928, when he joined the faculty of the Union Theological Seminary in New York City. In 1930 he became professor of applied Christianity at the Seminary; he served as dean from 1950 until 1955, when he was appointed vice-president. An outstanding theologian, Niebuhr gave leadership to the Christian struggle against present-day materialist creeds and has also a keen interest in trade-union and political affairs. He was an active member of the Socialist Party in the 1930's, waged a vigorous fight against isolationism and pacifism before and during World War II, and helped to found the Liberal Party in New York State in 1944. Among his many writings are *Moral Man and Immoral Society* (1932), *Interpretation of Christian Ethics* (1935), *The Nature and Destiny of Man* (2 vols., 1941, 1943), *Faith and History* (1949), *Christian Realism and Political Problems* (1953), and *The Self and the Dramas of History* (1955). In addition he edited *Christianity and Society*, a quarterly, *The World Tomorrow*, a Socialist newspaper, and the biweekly periodical *Christianity and Crisis*.

NIEMEYER, OSCAR (1908–), Brazilian architect, born in Rio de Janeiro, and educated at Barnabitas College in the same city. His first important work, done in collaboration with the noted French architect Le Corbusier (q.v.) was the design for University City, Rio de Janeiro. Subsequently Niemeyer designed a great number of buildings and complexes of buildings featuring bold use of ferroconcrete and sheet glass and emphasis on structural elements. He became the best-known architect in Brazil, and achieved a world-wide reputation. Among his outstanding works are the Ministry of Education and Health Building, and a block of duplex apartment buildings, Rio de Janeiro; a theater in Belo Horizonte; a yacht club, restaurant, and casino in Pampulha; and the Brazilian Pavilion for the New York World's Fair of 1939. Niemeyer became the Brazilian member of the United Nations Board of Design Consultants in 1947, and aided in planning the New York City headquarters of the United Nations.

NIETZSCHE, FRIEDRICH WILHELM (1844–1900), German philosopher, born in Röcken, near Leipzig, in the province of Saxony. He studied philology at the University of Bonn under the German classical philologist Friedrich Wilhelm Ritschl. On Ritschl's recommendation, Nietzsche was made professor of classical philology at the University of Basel in 1869. As a student Nietzsche had become acquainted with the writings of the German pessimistic philospher Arthur Schopenhauer, whose metaphysical doctrine of the supremacy of the will profoundly influenced his thinking. Another significant event in Nietzsche's life was his meeting, about 1870, with the German composer Richard Wagner at the latter's villa on the Lake of Lucerne, Switzerland. The two men agreed in their esthetic and artistic opinions, and for a time Nietzsche was an enthusiastic proponent of the Wagnerian music drama, the rationale of which he may be said to have expounded in his essay *Die Geburt der Tragödie aus dem Geiste der Musik* ("The Birth of Tragedy from the Spirit of Music", 1872).

As Nietzsche gradually formulated his own distinctive philosophy, however, he began to doubt the doctrines of both Schopenhauer and Wagner, perceiving in the pessimism of the former a mystical negation of the dynamic life impulse, and in the voluptuous art of the latter a narcotic for an effete and decadent age. The process of Nietzsche's alienation from Wagner was climaxed about 1874 by a violent quarrel, and thereafter they were enemies. In 1889, after a period of sustained and intensive work during which he produced some of his most forceful writings, he suffered a mental collapse. He retired to his mother's home near Weimar, where he was cared for by his sister until he died.

The evolution of Nietzsche's thought, which culminated in the glorification of the *Übermensch* (literally, "overman" or "superman"), and in the doctrine of the ruthless will to power, may be traced in his *Menschliches-Allzu Menschliches* ("Human, All Too Human", 2 vols., 1878–80); *Morgenröte* ("Dawn", 1881); *Die Fröhliche Wissenschaft* ("The Joyous Science", 1882); *Also Sprach Zarathustra* ("Thus Spake Zarathustra", 1883–84); *Jenseits von Gut und Böse* ("Beyond Good and Evil", 1886); *Zur Genealogie der Moral* ("On the Genealogy of Morality", 1887); *Der Fall Wagner* ("The Wagner Case", 1888); *Der Antichrist* ("The Antichrist", 1888); *Der Wille zur Macht* ("The Will to Power", 1888); and *Götzendämmerung* ("Twilight of the Idols", 1889).

Nietzsche's significance in philosophy consists in his attempt to establish a goal for life different from the goals prescribed by traditional ethical and religious systems. According to him the function of philosophy is not to interpret and appraise values but to create them. "The real philosophers," he wrote in *The Will to Power,* "are commanders and lawgivers; they say: 'Thus *shall* it be!' They determine first the Whither and the Why of mankind, and thereby set aside the previous labor of all philosophical workers . . .; they grasp at the future with a creative hand, and whatever is and was, becomes for them thereby a means, an instrument, and a hammer. Their 'knowing' is *creating,* their creating is a lawgiving, their will to truth is *Will to Power."* All life, for Nietzsche, is Will to Power. The established ideals of civilization he holds to be the ends which bold and masterful men have set for themselves; but what was for them the appropriate goal of their own high nature has become for subsequent ages an exalted tradition. Against these self-assertive supermen

stand the weak, the mediocre, the timorous, and the sickly, who, realizing their incapacity for individual achievement on a heroic scale, band together and set up a standard of life glorifying the traits (humility, gentleness, patience, forgiveness, love) which protect their own weakness and make for their common safety. These traits, Nietzsche maintains, are idealized as virtues, such virtues being the marks of a slave morality, which expresses the Will to Power of the inferior. In slave morality "good" and "evil" are reckoned from the viewpoint of the person or persons *affected* by an action; in the morality of the superman "good" and "evil" are reckoned from the viewpoint of the person who *effects* the action. In the latter morality, virtues are regarded as the qualities which give power to the *Übermensch*. The superman, however, is not altogether ruthless. In fact, he has a kind of love which is the overflow of his own power. This love is not controlled by law; it goes out freely to his equals, and may even extend to his inferiors when they do not stand in his way.

According to Nietzsche, slave morality, with its glorification of mediocrity, is to be maintained and encouraged for the vast body of inferior men. It becomes disastrous only when those who are born to be masters permit themselves to be imposed upon by it and so forfeit their birthright of independence and absolute self-determination. Although the mature master is free and accountable to no one but himself, his freedom is attained only through the imposition of a stern discipline in his childhood and youth, this discipline being continued by himself in later years. He is thus hard not alone to others but also to himself. He keeps a strict check on his emotions, allowing himself no passionate outbreaks in small matters. His habitual mien is one of poise, self-containment, and aloofness. Since the superman does not propagate supermen, Nietzsche stipulates a program of selective breeding (see Eugenics) to keep the master class constantly supplied.

Nietzsche's doctrines profoundly influenced the official philosophy and propaganda of National Socialism (q.v.) in the German Third Reich.

NIÈVRE, central department of France. There are fertile plateaus, but the principal wealth of the department consists in its forests and minerals—coal, iron, and gypsum. The river Nièvre is an affluent of the Loire. The other rivers are the Allier, Loire, Aron, Cure and Yonne. The iron industry is important and pottery and glass are manufactured

Nevers is the capital. Area, 2658 sq.m.; pop. (1946) 248,559.

NIGER, river of West Africa. The Niger proper (Joliba or Dhiuliba, Isa, Kworra or Quorra) has a total length of 2600 m., and the area of the entire basin (including that of the Benuë) is estimated at 1,023,280 sq.m. The Tembi is now accepted as the conventional "source". This was discovered by Brouet in 1885. About 300 m. above Timbuktu the river is joined by the Mayel-Balevel. Mungo Park, seeking to complete the discovery of the Niger, was drowned with the last three of his companions at Bussa in 1806. Its delta (14,000 sq.m. in area) is the largest in Africa; it has a coast line of nearly 120 m.

NIGER, Overseas Territory of France, forming part of French West Africa, and bounded on the s. by Nigeria, on the n. by the Sahara, on the w. by Dahomey, and on the e. by French Equatorial Africa. Estimated area, 499,411 sq.m.; pop. (1951) 2,162,099. Of this total, 2149 are Europeans, the remainder being native Tuaregs, Peulhs, and Sudanese Negroes. On the s. from the Niger to Lake Chad the country is wooded and pastoral while on the n. is the desert. The principal products are millet, earthnuts, and manioc. Niamey is the capital. The Territory is administered by a governor with the help of a council and assembly.

NIGERIA, a British colony and protectorate in West Africa; it includes for administrative purposes only the United Nations trusteeship (since 1946) of the British Cameroons (see CAMEROONS). Nigeria is bounded on the n. by the French Niger Colony, on the e. by the Cameroons, on the s. by the Gulf of Guinea, and on the w. by French Dahomey. The colony of Nigeria (area, 1400 sq.m.; pop. in 1952–53, 511,000) in the extreme s.w. portion of the area, is the seat of central government. The capital of both the colony and protectorate, and the chief port, is Lagos (q.v.), in the colony. The protectorate, including the British Cameroons, consists of the Eastern Region (46,000 sq.m.; pop. in 1952–53, 8,000,-00), with a capital at Enugu; the Western Region (45,400 sq.m.; pop. in 1952–53, 6,360,-00), with a capital at Ibadan, the largest city in Nigeria; and the Northern Region (281,-00 sq.m.; pop. in 1952–53, 16,840,000), with capital at Kaduna. Other towns of more than 50,000 population in the protectorate are Kano, Ogbomosho, Oyo, Iwo, and Oshogbo. Total area, about 373,250 sq.m.; pop. (1952–3) 31,200,000.

Along the entire coast line is a belt, extending inland for from 20 to 60 m., of mangrove

Friedrich Wilhelm Nietzsche.

forests and swamps, interconnected by the channels of the delta of the Niger R. (q.v.) and other rivers which empty into the Gulf of Guinea. North of the coastal lowland is a zone, from 50 to 100 m. wide, of tropical rain forest, containing oil palms, African mahogany and other valuable hardwoods, as well as evergreens. Beyond the forests the land rises and changes from open woodland to the grass savannahs of a plateau which cover most of the Northern Region except the extreme n., where desert conditions prevail. The Niger, its principal tributary, the Benue, and the Cross rivers are the most important. Except for Lake Chad (q.v.), in the extreme n.e., Nigeria has no large lakes. The climate in the n. is subtropical and arid, temperatures ascending to about 115° F.; the s. portion is tropical and humid, temperatures averaging about 80° F. and rainfall about 120 in. yearly.

Most of the indigenous population are Negroes (see FULAH; HAUSA; IBO). Christian missions have been successful principally along the coast and in the south; elsewhere Mohammedanism and animism are practiced.

The chief exports are palm oil and palm kernels, cacao, groundnuts, hides and skins, mineral ores, and timber. Exports in 1952 were valued at about £120,289,000, and imports, consisting chiefly of cotton piece goods, iron and steel products, fish, and salt, at £113,-113,000. Trade is almost entirely with Great

British Information Service

IN NIGERIA. *Top: Natives carrying goods across a foot bridge. Bottom, left: The leader of* *village riding a bullock. Bottom, right: Setting out wheat to dry after washing, in Kan*

Britain. Communications include about 1900 m. of railway and about 29,000 m. of roads. The many navigable rivers and creeks are arteries of trade by cargo canoes, rafts, and river boats. In the Northern Region considerable trade is carried on over caravan routes.

History. Portuguese, British, and other traders established slave-trading stations in the Niger delta area during the 17th and 18th centuries. The interior was first penetrated by explorers seeking the source of the Niger R., notably Mungo Park in 1795–96 and Richard and John Lander in 1830–31. In the 19th century palm oil became so important an article of commerce that the delta region became known as "oil rivers". A British consul was sent to Lagos, where British traders were firmly established, and in 1861 Great Britain took full possession of that area.

Of major importance in the opening of Nigeria were the efforts of Sir George Dashwood Taubman Goldie (q.v.). During the last three decades of the 19th century, when the European powers were pursuing imperialist policies in Africa, Goldie determined to unite the British interests in the Nigerian region and take possession of the territory for Great Britain. He organized the United African Company in 1879 and three years later reorganized it as the National African Company. All French interests in Nigeria were bought out by the company in 1884, and at the Conference of Berlin in 1885 on Congo affairs British representatives were able to claim successfully that British interests were supreme on the lower Niger. Nigeria was then internationally recognized as within the British sphere of influence.

After the conclusion of several treaties with native chiefs the British Oil Rivers Protectorate was established in s. Nigeria. In 1886 the National African Company was granted a royal charter; under the charter the company governed the territory N. of the Protectorate, raising an armed constabulary and establishing government services. The name of the Protectorate was changed in 1893 to the Niger Coast Protectorate. The kingdom of Benin was added to the area in 1897, and after further expansion in the s.E., the region became in 1900 the Protectorate of Southern Nigeria. The charter of the Royal Niger Company was revoked in the latter year and the Protectorate of Northern Nigeria was established.

Neither of the two protectorates was under full British control at the time of their establishment. The entire area of present Nigeria was, however, acknowledged to be British by conventions with Germany and France. The greatest military conflicts were with Mohammedan emirs in the N. and Nigerian tribes which raided the area for slaves, although the slave trade was prohibited. The conquest was fairly complete when, in 1914, the two administrations were merged as the Colony and Protectorate of Nigeria. Baron Frederick Lugard, first governor of united Nigeria, instituted the system of indirect rule, whereby the local functions of government are for the most part delegated to the tribal chiefs or councils, acting under the supervision and with the assistance and advice of British administrators. In 1922 the League of Nations mandate of Cameroons was added, administratively, to the protectorate.

NIGGERFISH, common name for a small grouper, *Cephalopholis fulvus,* common off southern Florida and in the Caribbean Sea. The fish, which is about eight inches long, is dark brown, red, or orange in general body color, usually spotted with black. See GROUPER.

NIGHT EFFECT, term applied to errors in radio direction-finding systems (see RADIO AIDS TO NAVIGATION) caused by radio waves reflected from the ionosphere (q.v.). The antennas used for direction finding are usually vertical and the ground wave from the transmitter is vertically polarized. Vertical polarization allows highly accurate directional measurements because radio waves are received by the antenna in a single vertical plane. The sky wave, which is reflected from the ionosphere, however, is horizontally polarized, and makes accurate measurements with vertical antennas difficult or impossible because these antenna may receive radio waves from any part of a broad, horizontal plane. Because the horizontal ionosphere reflection is much stronger during the night than in the daytime hours, its effect is called night effect.

NIGHTHAWK, common name for any goatsucker (q.v.) in the genus *Chordciles,* found throughout North America. Nighthawks, which somewhat resemble the closely related whippoorwill, are about ten inches long and have a wingspread of almost two feet. They feed on insects which they usually catch on the wing at dusk. The common nighthawk, *C. minor,* is tinted in speckled shades of black, gray, and tan, and has a broad white band across its throat and on each wing. The male is recognized by an additional white band traversing the tail. The cry of this bird is a high-pitched nasal note; the bird also produces a hollow, booming sound with its wings as it dives directly downward through

Florence Nightingale

the air in pursuit of food, and thereby derives such popular names as "bullbat" and "mosquito hawk".

NIGHT HERON, common name for any heron (q.v.) in the genera *Nycticorax* and *Nyctanassa,* differing from most other herons in being active only at night, and in hunting, rather than waiting for, its food. The black-crowned night heron, or crabier, *Nycticorax nycticorax,* which is also known as the "night squawk" or "squawk" because of its cry, is common throughout the warmer parts of the Western Hemisphere, and is also found in India, Africa, and southern Europe. The bird, which is about two feet long, is black above, with gray wings and tail, and white below. The yellow-crowned night heron, or fish crane, *Nyctanassa violacea,* is a similar bird with a yellow head, found from the Gulf States to South America.

NIGHTINGALE (AS. *nihtegale,* "night-singer"), common name for any oscine bird in the genus *Luscinia* of the Thrush family. Nightingales are known for the exquisite nocturnal song of the male, especially fine during the breeding season. The birds are native to the Old World, and have been introduced into the United States as cage birds. They are about six inches long, and both sexes are russet brown above, shading into light, reddish chestnut on the rump and tail, and grayish white below. The bill, legs, and feet are brown. The common nightingale of western Europe is *Luscinia megarhyncha.* The name "nightingale" is extended to a number of other singing birds, particularly the Japanese nightingale, *Leiothrix lutea,* a brownish bird with yellow breast, red bill, and red feet, commonly kept as a cage bird in the United States.

NIGHTINGALE, FLORENCE (1820–1910), English nurse, hospital reformer, and humanitarian, born in Florence, Italy. Most of her childhood was spent on her father's estate in Derbyshire, England, where she received from him a thorough classical education. In 1849 she went abroad to study the European hospital system and entered upon a course of training in nursing at the Institute of St. Vincent de Paul in Paris, and at the Institute of Protestant Deaconesses at Kaiserswerth on the Rhine R. In 1853 she became superintendent of the Hospital for Invalid Gentlewomen in London.

When the Crimean War (q.v.) broke out in 1854, Florence Nightingale, stirred by reports of the primitive sanitation methods and grossly inadequate nursing facilities at the large British barracks-hospital at Scutari, Turkey, dispatched a letter to the British secretary of war, volunteering her services in the Crimea. At the same time, unaware of her action, the secretary of war proposed that she assume direction of all nursing operations at the war front, and shortly thereafter she set out for Scutari accompanied by thirty-eight nurses. Under her close supervision efficient nursing departments were established at Scutari and later at Balaklava. Through her tireless exertions the mortality rate among the sick and wounded was cut from 42% to 2% within a period of four months.

At the close of the war, with a fund of $250,000 raised in tribute to her memorable services, she founded the Nightingale Home at St. Thomas's Hospital, London, for the training of nurses. During the Indian (Sepoy) Mutiny, the American Civil War, and the Franco-German War of 1870–71, she was frequently consulted on questions concerning the organization and operation of camp hospitals. She received many honors from foreign governments, and was the first woman upon whom the Prussian Order of Merit (1907) was conferred. In *Santa Filomena,* a verse tribute by the American poet Henry Wadsworth Longfellow, she was immortalized as "The Lady With The Lamp", in allusion to her customary manner of making the rounds of the sick wards during her service in the Crimea. In 1915 a figure of Florence Nightingale was added to the statuary group of the Crimean Memorial in Waterloo Palace, London. Her writings include *Notes on Nursing, Life or Death in India, Notes on Nursing for the Labouring Classes,* and *Health Teaching in Towns and Villages.*

NIGHTSHADE FAMILY or **POTATO FAMILY,** common name applied to the Solonaceae, a family of herbs and small shrubs of the Phlox order, native to most parts of the world, and especially abundant in the tropics. The family contains about seventy-five genera and almost two thousand species. Most nightshades are foul-smelling plants which contain poisonous alkaloids such as hyoscyamine, nicotine, and stramonium. The family, however, also contains such edible plants as the potato, tomato, and eggplant. The flowers have five sepals, five petals, five stamens, and a solitary pistil. The fruit is either a many-seeded berry or a two-seeded capsule. See articles on most of the plants and alkaloids mentioned above. See also BELLADONNA; BITTERSWEET; CAPSICUM; HENBANE; JIMSON WEED; NICOTIANA; PETUNIA; PHYSALIS; SOLANUM; TOBACCO.

NIHILISM (Lat. *nihil,* "nothing"), a Russian movement of the late 19th century, which sought social and political freedom for the individual through rejection of all forms of authority and traditional moral obligation. The word "nihilist" was popularized by the Russian novelist Ivan Turgenev, who used it to describe the hero of his book *Fathers and Sons* (1862). Nihilists were characterized by a thoroughgoing skepticism, coarseness of speech and behavior, and a materialistic, utilitarian, and agnostic approach. A typical summation of the nihilist creed is contained in the following quotation from an essay by the young writer Dmitri P. Pisarev (1840–68), written in the 1860's: "What can be smashed must be smashed; whatever will stand the blow is sound, what flies into smithereens is rubbish; at any rate, hit out right and left, no harm will or can come of it." Some nihilists joined revolutionary groups, such as the one which assassinated Czar Alexander II (q.v.), but many others were principally occupied with the development of their own personalities without interference from any outside source. The Nihilist expression of a youthful urge to freedom encountered bitter opposition from another group of Russian intellectuals, who claimed that it would destroy all possibility of orderly and purposeful existence and was directly contrary to real human needs and desires. Though nihilism is considered by modern scholars to have been a healthy, if exaggerated, reaction to the rigidity and backwardness of contemporary Russian social and intellectual patterns, its basic immaturity and lack of constructive orientation caused the movement to die out by about 1880. Outside of Russia, nihilism was used as a general term erroneously applied to all violently radical groups. This usage eventually became standardized.

NIIGATA, seaport of western Japan, the capital of Echigo Province, on a narrow strip of land at the mouth of the Shinano River, 155 miles N.W. of Tokyo. It was opened to foreign trade in 1859. The apples and watermelons of the province are noted for their excellence. Pop. (1945 est.) 174,740.

NIJINSKY, WASLAW or VASLAV (1890–1950), Russian ballet dancer and choreographer, born in Kiev, and educated at the Imperial Dancing Academy, St. Petersburg (now Leningrad). He made his first public appearance in 1907 with the St. Petersburg Imperial Ballet. He later went to Paris, and after 1909 was a member of the original Ballet Russe under the direction of the Russian ballet producer Sergei Diaghilev. Nijinsky soon attained the rank of *premier danseur.* He was the first to portray the leading roles in *Le Spectre de la rose, Petrouchka, Scheherazade, Les Sylphides, The Afternoon of a Faun,* and *Le Sacre du Printemps.* His unconventional choreography for the two last-named ballets aroused lively comment and many protests in 1912–13, when the ballets were first performed. Ranking among the great male dancers of all time, Nijinsky had remarkable technical powers; his *grands jetés,* for example, created the illusion that he was suspended in mid-air. His spectacular career ended in 1918, when he became the victim of a mental illness from which he never fully recovered. He wrote *System of Annotation of Human Movements* (1919) and *Diary of Nijinsky* (1936).

NIJMEGEN, NIMWEGEN, or **NIMEGUEN,** commune of Gelderland Province, the Netherlands, located on the navigable Waal R., 24 m. by rail E. of Tiel. The city is built in the form of an amphitheater on a series of hills above the river. Its principal landmarks include the square tower on the 13th-century Church of St. Stephen, a museum of Roman antiquities, and the 16th-century Renaissance town hall. The city is the site of a Roman Catholic university. Trade in wine, grain, and cattle from the surrounding agricultural region is maintained, and leather goods, eau de

"Winged Victory," Greek sculpture of Nike

cologne, cigars, silverware, cutlery, and flour are manufactured. Nijmegen is built on the site of a Roman camp and for many years was a residence of the Carolingian emperors. For a period Nijmegen was a town of the Hanseatic League (q.v.). In 1678 peace treaties, terminating the second war of Louis XIV against the Netherlands, were concluded there. Pop. (1947) 105,921.

NIKE, Greek goddess of victory, known by the Romans as Victoria. She is sometimes represented in Greek art as supported by the hands of Zeus and Athena, and as being winged and carrying a wreath or palm. The "Winged Victory" in the Louvre at Paris is fragmentary but superb.

NIKISCH, ARTHUR (1855–1922), Hungarian conductor, born in Lébényi Szent Miklos, and educated at the Vienna Conservatory. Nikisch conducted opera in Leipzig from 1879 until 1889, when he accepted the conductorship of the Boston Symphony Orchestra. In 1893 he became director of the Budapest Opera, and in 1895 he became conductor of the Leipzig Gewandhaus orchestra, a position he held for the remainder of his life. He also conducted the Berlin Philharmonic Orchestra with which he toured Europe from 1897 until his death, and the London Philharmonic Orchestra, with which he toured the United States in 1912.

NIKOLAEV, formerly VERNOLENINSK, city, seaport, and capital of the Region of the same name, Ukrainian S.S.R., situated at the confluence of the Bug and Ingul rivers, about 68 miles N.E. of Odessa. A leading Black Sea port and one of the most important ship building centers in the Soviet Union, it has an excellent harbor, which is kept open in the winter by icebreakers. The chief exports are cereal grains, flour, sugar, iron, coal, manganese ore, and timber. Industrial establishments include factories engaged in the manufacture of textiles and agricultural machinery and in the processing of food products.

In ancient times a Greek settlement occupied the site of the present-day city. Nikolaev developed around a dockyard established by the Russian politician Prince Gregor Potemkin about 1789. In the 1930's it was also known as Vernoleninsk. During World War II the Germans occupied the city and destroyed the naval base there. Area of Region, 7500 sq.m.; pop., about 800,000. Pop. of city, about 200,000.

NILE, the longest river of Africa, to the ancient Egyptians pre-eminently the sacred river. It draws its largest supplies of water from the Victoria Nyanza and Albert Nyanza lakes. Its source is one of the upper branches of the Kagera, which originates in the mountains of Tanganyika. On leaving the Victoria Nyanza it pours over the Ripon Falls, 170 yards wide but only 12 feet high, and then for 300 miles rushes between high rocky walls over rapids and cataracts, at first northwestward, then westward, until it joins the Albert Nyanza. The section between the two nyanzas is called the Victoria Nile or Somerset River. At its southwestern extremity the Albert Nyanza is joined by the river Semliki, which drains the surplus water of the Albert Edward Nyanza (discovered by Stanley in 1889), and this lake drains the slopes of the snowy Ruwenzori and adjacent mountains. The combined rivers leave the northern extremity of the Albert Nyanza as the Bahr-el-Jebel. Various tributaries flow through the Bahr-el Ghazal district.

At Khartoum the White Nile, or Bahr-el Abiad, also called the Bahr-el-Abyad, is joined by the Blue Nile, or Bahr-el-Azrek, the water of the respective streams being of the color indicated in the names. The region adjoining the White Nile above its confluence with the Sobat was for a time known as the Equatorial Provinces. The Blue Nile, 950 miles long, gathers its volume principally from Lake Tsana, on the Abyssinian plateau, in which region it is known as the Abia. From Khartoum the Nile flows northeastward and 20 miles below that city is joined by the Atbara, called also the Bahr-al-Aswad, or Black Nile.

It is the black sediment brought down by this river that settles in the Nile delta, and makes it extraordinarily fertile. During its course from the confluence of the Atbara through the Nubian Desert, the great river makes two deep bends. Below Khartoum navigation is rendered dangerous by cataracts, the sixth occurring not far north of Khartoum, the first near Aswân. The Nile enters the Mediterranean by a delta which separates into two main channels, the Rosetta and the Damietta. Its total length is about 4000 miles, or 3470 miles from its outlet in Victoria Nyanza. Its basin has an area of over 1,000,000 square miles.

In 1858 Speke reached the Victoria Nyanza, and in 1862 discovered Ripon Falls. Two years later Sir Samuel Baker discovered Albert Nyanza, and in 1868–71 Schweinfurth explored the western feeders of the White Nile. Stanley, in 1875, sailed around Victoria Nyanza, and in 1889 traced the course of the Semliki, and discovered Albert Edward Nyanza and Mount Ruwenzori.

Supplementing the previously built Aswân Dam at the heights of the city of Aswân, and providing storage water for the cotton plantations in the Sudan, a dam was built across the Blue Nile south of Khartoum shortly after World War I. Aswân Dam was heightened for a second time in 1936, its storage capacity increasing from 2,500,000,000 to 5,700,000,000 cubic tons. At Gebel Aulia on the White Nile south of Khartoum, another storage reservoir was provided in a dam built in 1937. Storage capacity of this third dam is 2,000,000,000 tons.

NILE, BATTLE OF THE, a naval action fought on August 1–2, 1798, during the Napoleonic Wars, between the British and the French in Abukir Bay, 15 miles N.E. of Alexandria, Egypt. In 1798 a French fleet of seventeen ships under the command of Vice-Admiral François Paul Brueys (1753–98) had sailed from Toulon, France, with Napoleon (see NAPOLEON I) and the army with which he intended to conquer Egypt preliminary to attacking the British in India. From June to August, British Rear Admiral Horatio Nelson (q.v.) and his fleet of fourteen ships searched the central and eastern Mediterranean Sea for the French fleet, and on the afternoon of August 1 found the enemy ships anchored in Abukir Bay.

Brueys disposed his vessels in a line near one shore of the bay. Expecting the British to fight as they came in from seaward, he ordered the guns on the seaward side of his ships prepared for action, neglecting those on the landward side. The battle began about sunset. Nelson, risking the shallows and the reefs near shore, maneuvered part of his fleet between the French ships and the land, and kept part to seaward of the French, who were thus attacked on two sides simultaneously. In addition to being outmaneuvered, the French were short of men, many of their crews having gone to shore earlier in the day to obtain supplies of water. In several hours all of the French vessels, except four which were captured or destroyed in later engagements, either surrendered or were destroyed; several of the British ships were badly damaged. The British casualties were about 200 killed and 700 wounded; the French lost over 5000 killed, wounded, and taken prisoner. The Battle of the Nile was one of the decisive engagements in naval history. Nelson's victory cut off Napoleon's line of communication to France, a circumstance which eventually caused him to abandon his Near Eastern expedition. The victory also gave Great Britain control of the entire Mediterranean Sea and was instrumental in inducing various European powers to join England in a second coalition (1799) against France.

NILGAI, NYLGHAU, or BLUE BULL, a large antelope, *Boselaphus tragocamelus,* of the forests of India and Persia. The nilgai has a large head, a heavy body, and long, slender legs, and is very fleet of foot. It attains a height of about 4½ ft. at the shoulder. The male, which is bluish gray in color, has very short, almost straight black horns, a black mane on the neck, and a fringe of long hair on the throat. The female nilgai, which is tan in color, is hornless, and has neither the mane nor the throat fringe.

NIMBUS, in religious painting, the halo or radiance encircling the head of a sacred personage. The ancient Indians, Egyptians, Etruscans, Greeks, and Romans all used nimbuses in their religious art. In western Christian art the nimbus was not commonly used until the late 5th century. The nimbus is usually circular; less often it is triangular, or consists of rays of light in various shapes.

Another form of radiance is the aureole, surrounding the back of the head and sometimes the entire figure. It was used almost exclusively around figures of Christ, the Trinity, and the Virgin Mary. The combination of nimbus and aureole is called a *glory,* and is often found in Byzantine and early South German art. All three forms of radiances originated in the belief of the ancients in a visible

Official U.S. Navy Photograph

Chester W. Nimitz

aura emanating from the body of a holy person.

NIMES, or NISMES, the capital of the French department of Gard, a fertile plain. It has Roman remains of the ancient *Nemausus* including an amphitheater, 70 feet high, and seating 20,000 spectators. Near by is the Pont du Gard aqueduct. Pop. (1946) 104,109.

NIMITZ, CHESTER WILLIAM (1885–), American naval officer, born in Fredericksburg, Texas, and educated at the U.S. Naval Academy at Annapolis, Md. During World War I, in 1918, he was chief of staff to the commander of the submarine force of the Atlantic Fleet. In 1938, after advancing through the ranks, he was appointed rear admiral. In December, 1941, after the Japanese attack on Pearl Harbor and the entry of the U.S. into World War II, Nimitz was appointed commander in chief of the Pacific Fleet, with the rank of full admiral. He was advanced to the position of admiral of the fleet in 1944. Nimitz's accomplished planning of strategy, bold tactics, and brilliant use of his staff and forces were largely responsible for the successes of the U.S. Navy in the Pacific theater during the war. He was chief of naval operations from December, 1945, to December, 1947, when he retired.

NINEVEH, the modern KOUYONJIK, capital of the ancient kingdom of Assyria, in the valley of the Tigris, 230 miles N. of Bagdad. The original capital was Assur, the ruins of which are now called *Kalah Sherghat,* but the group of cities 60 miles above the Greater Zab, on the eastern side of the Tigris, namely, Nineveh, Calah (*Nimrûd*), and Dur-Sargon (*Khorsabad*), ultimately supplanted it in importance. When Nineveh fell, the whole Assyrian empire, essentially a military power, perished with it. It was not until the excavations of Botta in 1842 and Layard in 1845 that the remains first of Dur-Sargon, then of Nineveh, were revealed to the world. The sculptured monuments of its ancient kings and the relics of its clay-inscribed library yielded their secrets to the investigations of scholars, and the life and history of the ancient kingdom of Assyria became known with almost as much certainty as those of Greece and Rome. See ASSYRIA; CUNEIFORM.

NINGPO, city and port of the province of Chekiang, China, on a fertile plain, 16 m. from the mouth of the Takia (Ning-po) River, and 100 miles s. of Shanghai. It is surrounded by a wall 25 feet high and 16 feet thick, and contains numerous temples and colleges. Manufactures include sedge hats, mats, and cotton goods. Green tea is exported. Pop., about 220,000.

NIOBE, in Greek mythology, the daughter of Tantalus and wife of Amphion, King of Thebes. According to varying accounts, she was the mother of twelve, fourteen, or twenty children, composed of an equal division of sons and daughters. Being proud of her many children, Niobe boasted that she was superior to Leto, the mother of Apollo and Artemis. Leto's two divine children, angered at Niobe's presumption, killed all her children with their arrows. The last son, Ilioneus, begged Apollo for mercy, but the god could not spare him since the arrow had already left his bow. Niobe wept for her children until she was transformed by Zeus, father of the gods, into a stone column which continued to shed tears. The story of Niobe appears frequently in Greek literature and art. A famous marble group in the Uffizi Gallery at Florence shows Niobe holding her youngest daughter on her knee, with thirteen other children grouped about her.

NIPIGON, lake of Ontario, Canada, 30 miles N.W. of Lake Superior, with which it is connected by the Nipigon River. It is 70 miles long, but its deeply indented coast line measures 580 miles.

NIRVANA (fr. Skr. *nis*, "out"; *vana*, "a blowing"), a term denoting a metaphysical concept central to Brahmanism, Buddhism, and Hinduism (qq.v.). The term signifies final deliverance from *samsara*, or transmigration (q.v.), the cycle of births and deaths through which the individual soul must pass. See also MYSTICISM.

NISH (anc. *Niassus*), principal city and commercial center of southern Serbia, in the Republic of Yugoslavia. It is located on the Nishava River, about 130 miles S.E. of Belgrade.

The city, an important center in ancient times, was the birthplace of the Roman emperor Constantine (274 A.D.). It fell in succession to the Huns, Bulgars, Hungarians, Byzantines, Serbs, Turks, and Austrians, and was almost constantly in Turkish possession from the 15th century until the Serbs took it in 1878.

During World War I Nish was temporarily the capital of Serbia, until it was occupied (1915) by the Germans and Bulgars. It was occupied by the Nazis during World War II, and suffered much damage from air raids.

Nish is an episcopal see, with a cathedral. Its main importance is commercial, but it is also an industrial center, producing trucks, iron products, meats, and flour; railway repair facilities are located there. Trains from Belgrade and points north to Greece and Turkey pass through Nish. Pop. (1948) 50,692.

NISHAPUR, town of Khorassan Province, Iran, situated 45 miles w. of Meshed, in a beautiful and fertile valley. There is a trade in turquoises. It was the birthplace, and contains the grave of Omar Khayyám. Pop., about 15,000.

NITER. See SALTPETER.

NITRATES. See NITRIC ACID.

NITRIC ACID, HNO_3, a colorless, corrosive liquid with specific gravity 1.502, m.p. $-42°$ C. ($-44°$ F.), b.p. $86°$ C. ($187°$ F.). Medieval alchemists called it *aqua fortis*, "strong water". Nitric acid is made commercially chiefly by the action of sulfuric acid on sodium nitrate (Chile saltpeter). It is also made by passing air through an electric arc and by the catalytic oxidation of ammonia; see NITROGEN FIXATION. Nitric acid is a very strong acid and a strong oxidizing agent. When dropped on the skin the acid produces a yellow coloration because of the reaction of its acid with protein to form yellow xanthoproteic acid. *Fuming nitric acid*, which is widely used in commerce, consists of nitric

acid with gaseous nitrogen peroxide in solution. It is red or brown in color and more active than colorless nitric acid. Ordinary and fuming nitric acid have wide application. They are used in chemical synthesis, in the nitration of organic materials to form nitro compounds, and in the manufacture of dyes and explosives.

Nitrates. The salts of nitric acid are called nitrates. Potassium nitrate, or saltpeter, and sodium nitrate, or Chile saltpeter, are the nitrates of greatest commercial importance; see SALTPETER. Nearly all nitrates are soluble in water; one of the exceptions is bismuth subnitrate, $BiONO_3 \cdot H_2O$, which is formed by the reaction of bismuth nitrate, $Bi(NO_3)_3$, with water, and is used in medicine for treating intestinal disorders. *Amitol*, a powerful explosive, is a mixture of ammonium nitrate and trinitrotoluene (TNT.). The reaction of nitric acid with organic compounds yields many important nitrates, such as nitroglycerin (q.v.) and nitrocellulose (see CELLULOSE). Ethyl nitrate, formed by the action of nitric acid on ethyl alcohol, is used in medicine and in chemical synthesis.

NITRIFICATION. See NITROGEN FIXATION.

NITROBENZENE, or ARTIFICIAL OIL OF BITTER ALMONDS, a pale-yellow liquid with a characteristic odor of bitter almonds. It is formed by nitration of benzene; see NITRO COMPOUNDS. It has a specific gravity of 1.99, m.p. $5.7°$ C. ($42.3°$ F.), b.p. $210.9°$ C. ($411.6°$ F.), and is soluble in ether and benzene. The most important reaction of nitrobenzene is its reduction to aniline (q.v.), and its chief use is in the preparation of aniline. It is also used in metal polish and shoe polish and is sometimes used in soap.

NITROCELLULOSE. See CELLULOSE.

NITROGEN, a gaseous element, atomic number 7, atomic weight 14.008, symbol N. It was isolated by the Scottish physician Daniel Rutherford in 1772 and recognized as an elemental gas by the French chemist Antoine Lavoisier about 1776. The free gas is found in the atmosphere, of which it composes about four fifths (78.03 percent) by volume. Because it is not chemically reactive it serves in the atmosphere as a diluent for oxygen in burning and respiration processes. It is an important element in plant nutrition; certain bacteria in the soil accomplish the conversion of atmospheric nitrogen to a form, such as nitrate, in which plants can absorb nitrogen, a process called nitrogen fixation (q.v.). Nitrogen in the form of protein (q.v.)

is an important constituent of animal tissue. The element occurs in the combined state in minerals, of which saltpeter, KNO_3, and Chile saltpeter, $NaNO_3$, are commercially important.

Nitrogen is a colorless, odorless, tasteless, nontoxic gas with a specific gravity of 0.967. It can be condensed into a colorless liquid with b.p. $-195.8°$ C. ($-320.44°$ F.), which can in turn be compressed to a colorless, crystalline solid with m.p. $-209.9°$ C. ($-345.8°$ F.). Nitrogen exists in two natural isotopic forms, and four radioactive isotypes have been artificially prepared.

Nitrogen is obtained from the atmosphere by passing air over heated copper or iron. The oxygen is removed, leaving nitrogen mixed with inert gases. Pure nitrogen is obtained by fractional distillation of liquid air; since liquid nitrogen has a lower boiling point than liquid oxygen the nitrogen distills off first and can be collected.

Free nitrogen is chemically inert and combines with other elements only at very high temperatures or pressures; see NITROGEN FIXATION. It is converted to an active form by passing it through an electric discharge at low pressure. The nitrogen so produced is very active, combining with alkali metals to form azides, with the vapor of zinc, mercury cadmium, and arsenic to form nitrides, and with many hydrocarbons to form hydrocyanic acid and cyanides. Activated nitrogen returns to ordinary nitrogen in about one minute.

In the combined state nitrogen takes part in many reactions and forms so many compounds that a systematic scheme of compounds containing nitrogen in place of oxygen was created by the American chemist Edward Franklin (1862-1937). In compounds nitrogen exists in all of the valence states between -3 and $+5$. Ammonia, hydrazine, and hydroxylamine represent compounds in which the valence of nitrogen is -3, -2, and -1, respectively. Oxides of nitrogen represent nitrogen in all the positive valence states. Nitrous oxide, N_2O, a colorless gas with b.p. $-89.5°$ C. ($-129.1°$ F.) is prepared by heating ammonium nitrate. It is popularly called "laughing gas" because it tends to cause hysterical laughter in individuals who inhale it. Mixed with oxygen it is used as an anesthetic in minor operations. Nitric oxide, NO, a colorless gas with b.p. $-151°$ C. ($-239.8°$ F.) is produced commercially by the oxidation of ammonia in the presence of a catalyst. Nitrogen trioxide, N_2O_3, a blue liquid or a

red-brown gas, with b.p. $3.5°$ C. ($36.3°$ F.) is the acid anhydride of nitrous acid. Nitrogen dioxide, NO_2, a yellow liquid or red-brown gas, with b.p. $21.3°$ C. ($70.33°$ F.) is the acid anhydride of nitric acid. Nitrogen pentoxide, N_2O_5, is a white solid with m.p. $30°$ C. ($86°$ F.). Among the other important nitrogen-containing compounds are amines, azo- and diazo-compounds, cyanates, cyanogen, fulminates, nitro compounds, nitric acid and nitrates, nitrous acid and nitrites, and urea. See individual articles on compounds mentioned in this article.

NITROGEN FIXATION, any of the numerous industrial (artificial) or biological (natural) processes in which the inert nitrogen of the atmosphere is converted into a chemical compound which may be utilized for growth by living plants, or used in industrial chemical reactions. Nitrogen fixation is performed industrially in the manufacture of synthetic fertilizers (q.v.) and in the production of nitric acid, cyanides, and ammonia. Nitrogen fixation is carried on in nature by a number of soil bacteria which derive energy for their life functions through the process, and which at the same time enrich the soil by making available utilizable nitrogen. The amount of combined nitrogen produced by such bacteria varies with temperature, moisture of soil, richness of soil, and related factors.

Industrial Processes. The most important method of synthetic nitrogen fixation today is the production of ammonia by combining hydrogen and atmospheric nitrogen at $500°$ to $600°$ C. ($932°$ to $1112°$ F.) in the presence of a metallic catalyst; see HABER, FRITZ; BOSCH, KARL. Direct usage of ammonia as soil fertilizer has come into widespread use in the United States since 1947, and has largely, though not completely, replaced the use of mined nitrates. Among other important synthetic methods are: the production of cyanamide by treating atmospheric nitrogen with calcium carbide at high temperatures in the presence of calcium fluoride, a method devised by the German chemists Nikodem Caro (q.v.) and Adolf Frank; the Birkeland-Eyde process for producing nitric acid from carbonates and atmospheric nitrogen, and processes for making cyanides from carbonates, carbon, and iron heated in a stream of nitrogen, and nitrides from alumina and coal heated with nitrogen in an electric furnace. Synthetic fertilizers containing about 500,000 tons of nitrogen are manufactured yearly in the United States. This tonnage is less than half of the nitrogen drawn from

the atmosphere by bacteria living symbiotically with leguminous plants growing in the
United States.

Biological Processes. All living cells contain
large amounts of protein, a principal constituent of which is nitrogen. Animals obtain
nitrogen in combined form from plants or
from the flesh of other animals which have ingested plants. Plants obtain nitrogen in utilizable form from the soil or from bacteria
living symbiotically in their roots. Such bacteria, typified by those of the genus RHIZO-
BIUM which form tubercles in the roots of
legumes (q.v.), withdraw nitrogen from the
atmosphere and convert it into inorganic compounds, enabling their host to grow in nitro-
gen-poor soils; see HUMUS; SOILS. Farmers usually *inoculate* the seeds of legumes by
placing them in a medium containing large
numbers of nitrogen-fixing bacteria before
planting. Nitrogen is deposited in soil both
by the action of bacteria such as *Clostridium
pastorianum* which draws nitrogen from the
air, and by the action of various other bacteria which break down nitrogenous compounds in dead and decomposing plant and
animal tissues to simple compounds; see
ECOLOGY: *Ecology of Plants.* Many bacteria
break down nitrogenous compounds completely, producing gaseous nitrogen which is
released to the atmosphere; others merely
reduce the organic wastes to ammonia. A
specialized group of bacteria, known as *nitro-
bacteria,* oxidize ammonia to nitrites and
nitrates, a process known as *nitrification.*

NITROGLYCERIN, common name applied
to a powerful explosive derived from glycerin,
containing three nitrate groups, and properly
called *glyceryl nitrate* or *glyceryl trinitrate,*
$C_3H_5(NO_3)_3$. Nitroglycerin is prepared by
treating glycerin (q.v.) with a mixture of concentrated nitric and sulfuric acids. It is a heavy,
oily, colorless or light-yellow liquid with a
specific gravity of 1.6. It solidifies at 12° C.
(53.6° F.). It burns quietly when heated in
air but explodes when heated above 270° C.
(518° F.) or when heated in a closed vessel.
It is very sensitive to shock and therefore
dangerous to transport. Although discovered
in about 1846, nitroglycerin was not used as
an explosive until Alfred Nobel (q.v.) used
it in making dynamite (q.v.) in 1866. Nitroglycerin is a common explosive today, and is
usually mixed with an inert, porous material
such as sawdust. When detonated nitroglycerin produces about ten thousand times its
own volume of gas. Compared with gun-
powder (q.v.) it is eight times as powerful in
proportion to relative weight and thirteen
times as powerful in proportion to relative
volume.

A one-percent solution of nitroglycerin in
alcohol, called *spirit of glonoin,* is used medicinally, particularly in angina pectoris,
asthma, and convulsions.

NITROUS OXIDE. See NITROGEN.

NIXON, RICHARD MILHOUS (1913–),
American legislator and 36th Vice-President
of the United States, born in Yorba Linda,
Calif., and educated at Whittier College and
at Duke University Law School. He began to
practice law in Whittier, Calif., in 1937. For
several months in 1942, during World War II,
he was an attorney with the Office of Emergency Management in Washington, D.C., but
he resigned in August to enter the U.S. Navy.
Following various assignments, including duty
in the South Pacific, he was discharged in 1946
with the rank of lieutenant commander. Nixon
was elected to the U.S. House of Representatives, on the Republican ticket, from the
Twelfth California District in 1946 and again
in 1948. As a member of the House Committee
on Un-American Activities, he figured prominently in the inquiry which resulted in the
trial and conviction on charges of perjury of
Alger Hiss, a former high official in the Department of State. In November, 1950, Nixon
was elected to the U.S. Senate from his home
State. The unanimous choice of the 25th Republican National Convention for the Vice-
Presidential nomination, he was elected in
November, 1952, on the ticket headed by
Dwight David Eisenhower.

NIZAMI, otherwise known as ABU MU-
HAMMAD ILYAS IBN YUSUF SHEIKH NIZAM ED-
DIN (1141–1202), Persian poet and ascetic. His
first poem, *Makhzān al-Asrār* ("The Store-
house of Mysteries"), is didactic and shows
the influence of the mystical Sufi poets (see
SUFISM) and of the *Shāh Nāmah* ("Book of
Kings") by the Persian epic poet Firdausi
(q.v.). Shortly thereafter Nizami wrote
Khusrū u Shīrīn ("Khosrau and Shīrīn"), an
epic of about 7000 couplets dealing with the
rivalry between Khosrau II, a Persian king
of the Sassanid dynasty, and Farhad, a famous architect, for the love of the beautiful
Armenian princess Shīrīn. This romantic poem
won Nizami high favor at the Persian court.
He next composed the *Diwan,* a voluminous
collection of ethical verses. With *Laila and
Majnun,* a poem based upon the Bedouin
tale of two lovers separated by family feud,
their brief joy on earth, and their happy
reunion in Paradise, Nizami returned to the

Alfred Bernard Nobel

field of the romantic epic. His *Iskandar-Nāmah* ("Book of Alexander"), an account of the legendary adventures of the Macedonian king Alexander the Great, is an attempt to rival Firdausi. In 1197 Nizami produced the verse romance *Haft Paikār* ("The Seven Beauties"), in which each of the seven princesses tells a story. These seven princesses symbolized the seven climes into which medieval Moslem geographers divided the world.

NIZHNI TAGIL, city of Sverdlovsk Region, Russian S.F.S.R., situated on the Tagil R., at the E. base of the Ural Mts., about 75 miles N.N.E. of Sverdlovsk. Nizhni Tagil, an important railroad junction and industrial center, lies in a region noted for its diversified mineral resources, including iron ore, manganese, copper, gold, and platinum. Among the large industrial works in the city are steel mills, metallurgical works, and factories producing railroad cars, heavy machinery, chemicals, coke, ceramics, and processed food. The city was founded in 1725 as a mining community. It continued to grow in size and importance, especially in the period prior to and during World War II. Pop. (1948 est.) 250,000.

NOAH, in the Old Testament, son of Lamech, tenth in descent from Adam and, as only survivor of the Deluge (q.v.), the father of all humanity. According to Genesis 6:10, he was spared for his piety when God destroyed the corrupt world by a flood lasting forty days and forty nights. He was forewarned to build an Ark for his safety and

to take on board with his wife and three sons, Sem, Ham, and Japheth, mated specimens of all animals on earth. By Scriptural account he lived 950 years. Xithuthros, Prithu, and Deucalion (q.v.) are heroes of similar flood stories in Chaldaic, Hindu, and Greek cultures. Another text in Genesis (9:18-27) represents Noah as a shameless drunkard, discoverer of wine making, and, describing his sons as progenitors of the three races of mankind, it symbolically denounces Ham (or Canaan), the father, presumably, of the dissolute Canaanites.

NOAH, BOOK OF, a noncanonical part of the Old Testament which gives an account of the laws made by Noah for his children. It was probably written between 200 and 161 B.C. and has not been preserved as an independent work, but fragments of it are incorporated in the Ethiopic Book of Enoch, and it is referred to in the Book of Jubilees (10:13; 30:10).

NOBEL, ALFRED BERNHARD (1833-96), Swedish engineer and inventor, born in Stockholm. He studied mechanical engineering in the United States and in 1867 produced the formula for dynamite. A few years later he produced the first smokeless powder. At the time of his death he controlled nearly a score of factories for the manufacture of explosives in various parts of the world. His will provided that the major portion of his $9,200,000 estate be set up as a fund to establish yearly prizes for merit in Physics, Chemistry, Physiology or Medicine, Literature, and World Peace. The Nobel Foundation is managed by a board of directors, all residents of Stockholm. See NOBEL PRIZES.

NOBEL PRIZES, awards granted annually to persons or institutions for outstanding contributions during the year previous to the grant in the fields of physics, chemistry, physiology or medicine, literature, and international peace. The yearly prizes are awarded from the interest accruing from a trust fund provided by the testament of the Swedish inventor and philanthropist, Alfred Bernhard Nobel (q.v.). According to the will, "The capital [provided by conversion of residue property into money] shall constitute a fund, the interest accruing from which shall be annually awarded in prizes to those persons who shall have contributed most materially to the benefit of mankind during the year immediately preceding. The said interest shall be divided into five equal amounts, to be apportioned as follows: One share to the person who shall have made the most important discovery or invention in the domain of Physics; one share to the person who shall have made the most important Chemical discovery or improvement; one share to the person who shall have made the most important discovery in the domain of Physiology or Medicine; one share to the person who shall have produced in the field of Literature the most distinguished work of an idealistic tendency; and finally, one share to the person who shall have done most to promote the Fraternity of Nations and Abolition or Diminution of Standing Armies and the Formation and Increase of Peace Congresses. The Prizes for Physics and Chemistry shall be awarded by the Swedish Academy of Science in Stockholm; that for Physiology or Medicine by the Caroline Medico-Surgical Institute in Stockholm; the prize for Literature by the Academy in Stockholm and that for Peace by a Committee of five persons to be elected by the Norwegian Storting. I declare it to be my express desire that, in the awarding of prizes, no consideration whatever be paid to the nationality of the candidates, that is to say, that the most deserving be awarded the prize, whether of Scandinavian origin or not."

Control of the entire fund is maintained by the board of directors of the Nobel Foundation, which serves for two-year periods and is composed of five members, four of whom are elected by representatives of the awarding bodies mentioned in the will and the fifth appointed by the Swedish government. Each year about $160,000 is awarded to the prize recipients, the average individual award being approximately $32,000. Each award includes also a gold medal and a diploma bearing the name of the prize winner and his field of achievement. The judges have frequently divided the prize for achievement in a particular field among two or three individuals who have made contributions of comparable significance. Prizes may also be withheld for a year, but if not distributed, the money reverts to the original fund. To further the purposes of the Nobel Foundation, separate institutes have been established, in accordance with Nobel's will, in Sweden and Norway for the advancement of each of the five fields for which the Nobel prizes are awarded.

The first Nobel prizes were awarded on Dec. 10, 1901. The following table contains a chronological listing of recipients of Nobel prizes.

YEAR	PHYSICS	CHEMISTRY	MEDICINE AND PHYSIOLOGY	LITERATURE	PEACE
1901	Wilhelm Konrad Roentgen (G)	Jacobus Hendricus van't Hoff (D)	Emil von Behring (G)	René Francois Armand Sully Prudhomme (F)	Jean Dunant (Swi) and Frédéric Passy (F)
1902	Hendrik Antoon Lorentz (D)	Emil Fischer (G)	Sir Ronald Ross (Br)	Theodor Mommsen (G)	Élie Ducommun (Swi)
1903	Pierre Curie (F), Marie Curie (F), and Antoine Henri Becquerel (F)	Svante August Arrhenius (Swe)	Niels Ryberg Finsen (Dn)	Björnstjerne Björnson (N)	Sir William Randal Cremer (Br)
1904	John William Strutt Rayleigh (Br)	Sir William Ramsay (Br)	Ivan Petrovich Pavlov (R)	Frédéric Mistral (F) and José Echegaray y Eizaguirre (Sp)	Institute of International Law, Hague, Netherlands
1905	Philipp Lenard (G)	Adolf von Baeyer (G)	Robert Koch (G)	Henryk Sienkiewicz (P)	Bertha von Suttner (Aus)
1906	Sir Joseph John Thomson (Br)	Henri Moissan (F)	Camillo Golgi (I) and Santiago Ramón y Cajal (Sp)	Giosuè Carducci (I)	Theodore Roosevelt (A)

Wide World Photo

Ceremony for presentation of the Nobel Peace Prize, University of Oslo, Norway

YEAR	PHYSICS	CHEMISTRY	MEDICINE AND PHYSIOLOGY	LITERATURE	PEACE
1907	Albert Abraham Michelson (A)	Eduard Buchner (G)	Charles Louis Alphonse Laveran (F)	Rudyard Kipling (Br)	Ernesto Teodoro Moneta (I) and Louis Renault (F)
1908	Gabriel Lippmann (F)	Ernest Rutherford (Br)	Paul Ehrlich (G) and Élie Metchnikoff (R)	Rudolf Eucken (G)	Klas Pontus Arnoldson (Swe) and Fredrik Bajer (Dn)
1909	Guglielmo Marconi (I) and Karl Ferdinand Braun (G)	Wilhelm Ostwald (G)	Emil Theodor Kocher (Swi)	Selma Lagerlöf (Swe)	Auguste Marie François Beernaert (B) and Baron d'Estournelles de Constant (F)
1910	Johannes Diderik van der Waals (D)	Otto Wallach (G)	Albrecht Kossel (G)	Paul von Heyse (G)	International Permanent Peace Bureau (Swi)
1911	Wilhelm Wien (G)	Marie Curie (F)	Allvar Gullstrand (Swe)	Maurice Maeterlinck (B)	Tobias Michael Carel Asser (D) and Alfred Hermann Fried (Aus)

YEAR	PHYSICS	CHEMISTRY	MEDICINE AND PHYSIOLOGY	LITERATURE	PEACE
1912	Nils Gustaf Dalén (Swe)	Victor Grignard (F) and Paul Sabatier (F)	Alexis Carrel (A)	Gerhart Hauptmann (G)	Elihu Root (A)
1913	Heike Kamerlingh Onnes (D)	Alfred Werner (Swi)	Charles Robert Richet (F)	Rabindranath Tagore (In)	Henri Lafontaine (B)
1914	Max von Laue (G)	Theodore William Richards (A)	Robert Bárány (Aus)	Not awarded	Not awarded
1915	William Lawrence Bragg (Br) and Sir William Henry (Br)	Richard Willstätter (G)	Not awarded	Romain Rolland (F)	Not awarded
1916	Not awarded	Not awarded	Not awarded	Verner von Heidenstam (Swe)	Not awarded
1917	Charles Glover Barkla (Br)	Not awarded	Not awarded	Karl Gjellerup (Dn) and Henrik Pontoppidan (Dn)	International Red Cross of Geneva
1918	Max Karl Ernst Ludwig Planck (G)	Fritz Haber (G)	Not awarded	Not awarded	Not awarded
1919	Johannes Stark (G)	Not awarded	Jules Bordet (B)	Carl Spitteler (Swi)	Woodrow Wilson (A)
1920	Charles Édouard Guillaume (F)	Walther Hermann Nernst (G)	August Krogh (Dn)	Knut Hamsun (N)	Léon Victor Auguste Bourgeois (F)
1921	Albert Einstein (A)	Frederick Soddy (Br)	Not awarded	Anatole France (F)	Karl Hjalmar Branting (Swe) and Christian Louis Lange (N)
1922	Niels Bohr (Dn)	Francis William Aston (Br)	Archibald Vivian Hill (Br) and Otto Meyerhof (G)	Jacinto Benavente y Martínez (Sp)	Fridtjof Nansen (N)
1923	Robert Andrews Millikan (A)	Fritz Pregl (Aus)	Sir Frederick Grant Banting (C) and John James Rickard Macleod (Br)	William Butler Yeats (Ir)	Not awarded
1924	Karl Manne Georg Siegbahn (Swe)	Not awarded	Willem Einthoven (D)	Wladyslaw Stanislaw Reymont (P)	Not awarded
1925	James Franck (G) and Gustav Hertz (G)	Richard Zsigmondy (G)	Not awarded	George Bernard Shaw (Ir)	Charles Gates Dawes (A) and Sir Joseph Austen Chamberlain (Br)
1926	Jean Baptiste Perrin (F)	Theodor Svedberg (Swe)	Johannes Fibiger (Dn)	Grazia Deledda (I)	Aristide Briand (F) and Gustav Stresemann (G)

Year	Physics	Chemistry	Medicine and Physiology	Literature	Peace
1927	Arthur Holly Compton (A) and Charles Thomson Rees Wilson (Br)	Heinrich Wieland (G)	Julius Wagner von Jauregg (Aus)	Henri Bergson (F)	Ferdinand Buisson (F) and Ludwig Quidde (G)
1928	Owen Willans Richardson (Br)	Adolf Windaus (G)	Charles Jean Henri Nicolle (F)	Sigrid Undset (N)	Not awarded
1929	Louis Victor de Broglie (F)	Sir Arthur Harden (Br) and Hans August Simon von Euler-Chelpin (Swe)	Sir Frederick Gowland Hopkins (Br) and Christiaan Eijkman (D)	Thomas Mann (A)	Frank Billings Kellogg (A)
1930	Sir Chandrasekhara Venkata Raman (In)	Hans Fischer (G)	Karl Landsteiner (A)	Sinclair Lewis (A)	Nathan Söderblom (Swe)
1931	Not Awarded	Karl Bosch (G) and Friedrich Bergius (G)	Otto Heinrich Warburg (G)	Erik Axel Karlfeldt (Swe)	Jane Addams (A) and Nicholas Butler (A)
1932	Werner Heisenberg (G)	Irving Langmuir (A)	Sir Charles Scott Sherrington (Br) and Edgar Douglas Adrian (Br)	John Galsworthy (Br)	Not awarded
1933	Paul Adrien Maurice Dirac (Br) and Erwin Schrödinger (G)	Not awarded	Thomas Hunt Morgan (A)	Ivan Alekseevich Bunin (R)	Norman Angell (Br)
1934	Not awarded	Harold Clayton Urey (A)	George Richards Minot (A), William Parry Murphy (A) and George Hoyt Whipple (A)	Luigi Pirandello (I)	Arthur Henderson (Br)
1935	James Chadwick (Br)	Irène Curie-Joliot (F) and Frédéric Joliot (F)	Hans Spemann (G)	Not awarded	Carl von Ossietzky (G)
1936	Carl David Anderson (A) and Victor Franz Hess (Aus)	Peter Joseph Wilhelm Debye (A)	Sir Henry Hallett Dale (Br) and Otto Loewi (G)	Eugene Gladstone O'Neill (A)	Carlos Saavedra Lamas (Arg)
1937	Clinton Joseph Davisson (A) and George Paget Thomson (Br)	Walter Norman Haworth (Br) and Paul Karrer (Swi)	Albert Szent-Györgyi von Nagyrapolt (H)	Roger Martin Du Gard (F)	Edgar Algernon Robert Cecil (Br)
1938	Enrico Fermi (I)	Richard Kuhn* (G)	Corneille Heymans (B)	Pearl Sydenstricker Buck (A)	Nansen International Office for Refugees at Geneva, Switzerland

Year	PHYSICS	CHEMISTRY	MEDICINE AND PHYSIOLOGY	LITERATURE	PEACE
1939	Ernest Orlando Lawrence (A)	Adolph Butenandt* (G) and Leopold Ruzicka (Swi)	Gerhard Domagk* (G)	Frans Eemil Sillanpää (Finn)	Not awarded
1940	Not awarded	Not awarded	Not awarded	Not awarded	Not awarded
1941	Not awarded	Not awarded	Not awarded	Not awarded	Not awarded
1942	Not awarded	Not awarded	Not awarded	Not awarded	Not awarded
1943	Otto Stern (A)	Georg von Hevesy (H)	Edward Adelbert Doisy (A) and Henrik Dam (Dn-A)	Not awarded	Not awarded
1944	Isidor Isaac Rabi (A)	Otto Hahn (G)	Joseph Erlanger (A) and Herbert Spencer Gasser (A)	Johannes Vilhelm Jensen (Dn)	International Red Cross of Geneva
1945	Wolfgang Pauli (Aus)	Artturi Ilmari Virtanen (Finn)	Alexander Fleming (Br), Ernst Boris Chain (Br), and Howard Walter Florey (Br)	Lucila Godoy de Alcayaga (Gabriela Mistral) (Chi)	Cordell Hull (A)
1946	Percy Williams Bridgman (A)	John H. Northrop, James B. Sumner, and Wendell M. Stanley (A)	Hermann Joseph Muller (A)	Hermann Hesse (G-Swi)	John Raleigh Mott (A)
1947	Edward Victor Appleton (Br)	Robert Robinson (Br)	Carl Ferdinand (A) and Gerty Cori (A)	André Gide (F)	The Friends Service Council, London, England, and The American Friends Service Committee, Washington, D.C., U.S.A.
1948	Patrick Maynard Stuart Blackett (Br)	Arne Tiselius (Swe)	Paul Müller (Swi)	Thomas Stearns Eliot (Br)	Not awarded
1949	Hideki Yukawa (J)	William Francis Giauque (C)	Walter Rudolf Hess (Swi) and Antonio Caetano de Abreu Freire Egas Moniz (Por)	William Faulkner (A)	John Boyd Orr, Lord Boyd Orr (Br)
1950	Cecil Frank Powell (Br)	Otto Diels (G) and Kurt Alder (G)	Philip S. Hench (A), Edward C. Kendall (A), and Tadeus Reichstein (Swi)	Bertrand Russell, 3rd Earl Russell (Br)	Raiph Johnson Bunche (A)

Year	Physics	Chemistry	Medicine and Physiology	Literature	Peace
1951	John Douglas Cockcroft (Br) and Ernest Thomas Walton (Ir)	Glenn Theodore Seaborg (A) and Edwin McMillan (A)	Max Theiler (S.Af)	Pär Lagerkvist (Swe)	Léon Jouhaux (F)
1952	Felix Bloch (A) and Edward Mills Purcell (A)	Archer J. P. Martin (E) and R. Millington Synge (Br)	Selman A. Waksman (A)	François Mauriac (F)	Albert Schweitzer (F)
1953	Fritz Zernike (D)	Hermann Staudinger (G)	Fritz A. Lipmann (A) and Hans Adolph Krebs (Br)	Sir Winston Leonard Spencer Churchill (Br)	George Catlett Marshall (A)
1954	Max Born and Walter Bothe (G)	Linus Pauling (A)	John F. Enders, Thomas H. Wellner, and Frederick C. Robbins (A)	Ernest Hemingway (A)	Office of the United Nations Commissioner for Refugees
1955	Willis E. Lamb and Polykarp Kusch (A)	Vincent du Vigneaud (A)	Hugo Theorell (Swe)	Halldór Kiljan Laxness (Icelandic)	Not awarded

An asterisk (*) indicates that the cash prize was originally declined by the Nobelist; the medal and diploma alone were awarded to Gerhard Domagk in 1947 and to Richard Kuhn and Adolph Butenandt in 1949.

The following abbreviations are used in the above table:

A, American	C, Canadian	Finn, Finnish	Ir, Irish	R, Russian
Arg, Argentine	Chi, Chilean	G, German	J, Japanese	S.Af, South African
Aus, Austrian	D, Dutch	H, Hungarian	N, Norwegian	Sp, Spanish
B, Belgian	Dn, Danish	I, Italian	P, Polish	Swe, Swedish
Br, British	F, French	In, Indian	Por, Portuguese	Swi, Swiss

NOBILITY, a body of persons, within a state, possessing various special hereditary privileges, rights, and honors, including titles; an aristocratic or patrician class. The nobilities of the various modern states of Europe came into existence when feudalism (q.v.), a social system based on land tenure, succeeded the imperial government of Rome after the Germanic invasions. During the unsettled social and economic conditions which followed the fall of the Roman Empire, adventurous men acquired land, usually by conquest. These men then granted parts of their holdings to others, over whom they thereafter exercised certain rights, including that of taxation and the administration of justice, and from whom they were entitled to various services. Those who granted the land were known as lords and those who accepted it were known as vassals. The lords of a nation formed its nobility, their rank depending on the extent of their possessions. The prepositions *de* in the names of French nobles and *von* in the names of German nobles (both meaning "of" or "from") express the idea of ownership of land that is fundamental to the feudal concept of nobility.

The nobilities of Europe flourished from about the 9th to the 19th centuries. Since the French Revolution the tendency in European countries has been strongly toward the abolition of titles of hereditary rank. In France the nobility was first deprived of its special rights and privileges and then, in 1790, all hereditary titles were abolished by decree. Napoleon I, however, created a new nobility, granting titles and estates to those who had served him well, especially in military affairs. After Napoleon's downfall Louis XVIII restored to the pre-Revolutionary nobility its former privileges, rights, and honors. The Second Republic (1848-52) once more abolished nobility in France, but Napoleon III (reigned 1852-1870), restored the aristocratic class. Under the Third Republic (1871-1945) the nobility was once more abolished. In contemporary France, a person who has inherited a title may use it as part of his family name, but possesses none of the special rights or honors of the former nobility.

In Germany titles of nobility existed from early medieval times until they were abolished when Germany became a republic (1918); after 1918, members of the former nobility were permitted to use titles only as part of a name. In Russia titles of nobility similar to those of the nations of Western Europe were instituted by Peter the Great; all such titles were abolished by the revolution of 1917, which established the U.S.S.R. In Spain titles of nobility still exist. Members of the higher nobility bear the title of *grandee*; the lesser nobility are known as *los titulados de Castilla*. In several other European countries, including Italy, Belgium, and Portugal, only courtesy titles exist, as in France and Germany.

In Great Britain the sovereign still grants titles of nobility. The British nobility is divided into an upper nobility and a lower nobility. The upper consists of all those who hold a hereditary rank above that of bar-

onet; it includes those with titles of duke, marquis, earl, viscount, and baron. Among the lower nobility are those holding the rank of baronet, knight, and esquire. The upper nobility composes the British peerage (see PEER), and its members have the right to hereditary seats in the House of Lords.

No nobility exists in the United States; the Federal Constitution specifically states that no title of nobility shall be granted by the United States, and in addition forbids any person holding government office from accepting any such title from a foreign ruler, without the express consent of Congress. A private American citizen who accepts a title of nobility automatically resigns his citizenship.

NOCTURNE (Lat. *nocturnus;* from *nox, noctis,* "night"), in music, a night piece or serenade, usually a languid or meditative instrumental composition. During the 18th century, the Italian term *notturno* was used as a title for compositions similar to the serenade (q.v.), performed as an evening divertissement. Several notturnos were composed by the Austrian composers Josef Haydn and Wolfgang Amadeus Mozart. The current use of the term "nocturne", however, refers almost solely to a type of intimate piano piece. The earliest nocturnes for the piano were written during the 18th century by the Irish composer John Field. The form was subsequently developed in the 19th century during the Romantic era, particularly by the Polish composer Frédéric Chopin. Of a reflective and rather melancholy character, the nocturne is typical of the music of the Romantic period. In its most typical form, a highly expressive melody is played over an arpeggiolike accompaniment.

NODES, in botany. See STEM.

NŌ DRAMA or NOGAKU, a type of Japanese drama which originated in the 15th century as a development of variety of crude popular song-and-dance performance known as *saru-gaku* ("monkey music"). It was originally intended as entertainment for members of the Japanese upper classes. The nō play is written in a combination of prose and verse, and music and dancing are important parts of the drama. Over two hundred and fifty of these plays have been written, mostly in the 15th century.

A nō play is acted on an elevated wooden stage eighteen feet square. The roof of the stage is supported by four pillars, and under the stage earthenware jars are placed in order to increase the resonance of speech and

Various masks worn by performers of the Japanese nō drama

music. On one side of the stage is a narrow extension on which the chorus is seated; a similar extension at the rear is for the use of the musicians. The stage is open on three sides; the rear is closed off by a wooden wall on which is painted the representation of a pine tree, symbolic, it is believed, of the woods in which the nō drama may originally have been given.

The simple scenery used in the nō drama merely suggests the locale of the play. The costumes are elaborate. Each of the two leading actors wears a mask representing the sex, age, and principal emotional expression of the character he is depicting. The chorus consists of from eight to twelve singers; the musicians usually number four, a flutist and a player for each of three different types of drum. The actors not only speak, but occasionally sing. The chorus sometimes sings in unison with an actor, and at times it comments on the action of the play with song of its own.

Nō plays are of five principal types: *waki-nō,* in which the leading characters portray Japanese religious deities; *shura-mono,* about the ghosts of warriors; *kazura-mono,* concerned with the affairs of aristocratic ladies; *senzai-mono,* dealing with contemporary life, and in which situations predominate emphasizing love or insanity; and plays about demons and goblins. The plays are presented in groups of five, consisting of one of each of the types mentioned; a group requires from seven to eleven hours for its performance. Between each two plays of the group a farcical piece known as a *kyogen* is performed.

NOGUCHI, HIDEYO (1876-1928), Japanese physician and bacteriologist, born in Fukushima, and educated at Tokyo Medical College. He emigrated to the United States in 1901, and studied and taught in the pathological laboratory of the University of Pennsylvania from 1901 to 1903. The following year he joined the staff of the Rockefeller Institute for Medical Research in New York City, becoming a member of the Institute in 1914. Noguchi is best known for his diagnostic laboratory tests for syphilis (q.v.). He was the first to obtain pure cultures of the spirochete of syphilis and to demonstrate the syphilitic origin of certain forms of general paralysis and of tabes dorsalis. In 1918 Noguchi discovered the parasite causing yellow fever (q.v.) and subsequently developed a serum and vaccine for combating the disease. He also made important contributions to the etiological study of Oroya fever and trachoma. Noguchi was knighted by the kings of Spain and Denmark in 1913 and by the king of Sweden in 1914; he was awarded the Japanese Order of Merit in 1915. His works include *Snake Venoms* (1909), *Serum Diagnosis of Syphilis and Luetin Reaction* (1910), and *Laboratory Diagnosis of Syphilis* (1923).

NOGUCHI, ISAMU (1904-   ), Japanese-American sculptor, son of the poet Yone Noguchi, born in Los Angeles, Calif., and educated at Columbia University and the Leonardo da Vinci Art School, New York City. In 1927-28 he worked in the Paris studio of the Romanian sculptor Constantin Brancusi. He then traveled and studied in England, China, and Mexico. After executing a 65-foot colored relief sculpture in Mexico City, he won the national competition for the commission to decorate the Associated Press Building in Rockefeller Center, New York City, with the design for a relief sculpture which he executed in 1938. Among his contributions to contemporary art were his imaginative stage sets for the American dancer Martha Graham. His work is represented in the Whitney Museum of American Art, the Metropolitan Museum of Art, and the Museum of Modern Art, all in New York City.

Rockefeller Center, Inc.

Relief sculpture by Isamu Noguchi on Associated Press Building, Rockefeller Center

NOME, seaport of w. central Alaska, situated on the s. side of Seward Peninsula, on the Bering Sea, about 700 m. by plane w. of Fairbanks. It is a commercial center for the surrounding region, in which mining, reindeer grazing, fur farming, and fur trapping are carried on. The town was founded during the rush of prospectors to the area following the discovery of gold at nearby Anvil Creek in 1898. By 1900 it had a population of nearly 20,000. It was first called Anvil City, and its name was later changed to Nome, for nearby Cape Nome. The town is serviced by an air line and by passenger and freight vessels. Gold is still the most important mineral obtained in the area; deposits of silver, tin, antimony, copper, lead, asbestos, coal, cinnebar, iron, graphite, and platinum are also worked in the region. Pop. (1950) 1852.

NOMINALISM (Lat. *nominalis*, "of or pertaining to names"), in medieval scholastic philosophy (see SCHOLASTICISM), the doctrine that abstractions, known as "universals", are without essential or substantive reality, and that only specific individual objects have real existence. These universals, such as *man, animal, nation, beauty, circle*, were held to be mere names, whence the derivation of the term "Nominalism". For example, the name *circle* is applied to things which are round, and is thus a general designation; but no concrete identity exists corresponding to the name. The nominalistic doctrine is opposed to the philosophical theory called *Realism* (q.v.), according to which universals have a real and independent existence prior to and apart from particular objects. Nominalism evolved from the thesis of the ancient Greek philosopher Aristotle (q.v.) that all reality consists in individual things; the theory of Realism was first enunciated by another Greek philosopher, Plato (q.v.), in his doctrine of universal archetypal ideas (see IDEA). The Nominalist-Realist controversy became prominent in the late 11th and 12th centuries, the Nominalist position being expounded by the scholastic philosopher Roscellinus, and the Realist by the scholastic philosophers Bernard de Chartres and Guillaume de Champeau. The issue between Nominalism and Realism was not only logical but also theological, for Roscellinus maintained that the Trinity (Father, Son, and Holy Ghost), conceived in the orthodox theology of the Church as constituting a mystical unity, cannot be understood, according to the individualizing method of Nominalism, except as three distinct and separate gods. The Church was therefore irreconcilably opposed to Nominalism. A theory intermediate between Nominalism and Realism is that of *Conceptualism*, in which universals, though they have no real or substantive existence in the external world, do exist as ideas or concepts in the mind, and are thus something more than mere names. The last defense of Nominalism was undertaken by the 14th-century English scholastic philosopher William of Ockham.

NOMINATION, in politics, the formal selection and presentation of a candidate for an elective office. Four principal methods of nomination have been used in the United States: nomination by convention, by primary election (qq.v.), by caucus, and by petition. Nomination by caucus preceded the development of political parties; before 1800 candidates for office were nominated at private caucuses of leading citizens. By 1800, however, members of Congress chose candidates for President and Vice-President in their own party caucuses, thereby controlling party policy. Local party leaders, however, resented such concentration of power in Congressional hands and insisted upon sharing in the selection of major candidates; between 1830 and 1840, the system of nomination of Presidential and Vice-Presidential candidates at conventions became standard procedure, with delegates from local party organizations convening periodically for this purpose.

The convention system also became the standard method of nomination of State and local candidates, such as governors, senators, congressmen, and State senators and assemblymen. This procedure was in turn attacked as depriving the public of a voice in the choice of candidates, and beginning in the last decade of the 19th century an alternative method of nomination made its appearance. This method was nomination by primary elections, in which the candidates of each party are chosen by the public in State-regulated elections. The first State primary law was enacted in Wisconsin in 1903, and similar laws have since been enacted in most other States. Primary elections are now widely used in the choice of Congressional and State candidates; in some States, they are also used in choosing delegates to the national conventions of the major parties. Because all of the above methods are designed only for the choice of party candidates, most States provide another type of nomination, known as nomination by petition, for nonparty, or independent, candidates. Under this method, the name of any legally eligible candidate can be placed on the ballot by a petition signed by a prescribed number of registered voters.

NONCOMBATANT, in international law, a term used to designate an individual who is a resident of a country involved in war but is not a participant or a combatant in the war. A noncombatant is not permitted to carry arms, and so long as he refrains from participation in military operations, he is not subject to injury or capture as are combatants (see INTERNATIONAL LAW). The term "noncombatant" is also applied to individuals who in time of war are members of the military service, such as the medical corps or chaplains, whose duties do not include fighting. A combatant has been defined as a person who, with the special authorization of his government, takes part, either directly or indirectly, in the operations of war. The term includes, in addition to the troops of the line, all staff officers, surgeons and chaplains, officers and employees of the supply and transport service, all agents, contractors, and others who accompany the army in an official capacity and who assist in its movement, equipment, or maintenance, and all retainers to the camp.

NONCONFORMISTS, a name given generally to all sectaries who, at any period in English history since the establishment of Protestantism, have refused to conform to the Established Church. In Scotland the ordinary name is "dissenters". It is used in a restricted sense to denote the clergy who in 1662 left the Church of England rather than submit to the conditions of the Act of Uniformity.

NOOTKA, the name of a group of closely related North American Indian tribes comprising one of the two major divisions of the Wakashan stock, the other being the Kwakiutl (q.v.). The Nootka inhabit the w. coast of Vancouver Island, southern British Columbia. They are maritime tribes, following an economy based chiefly on fishing. Their principal food is salmon, which is smoked for storage; other fish and shellfish are also eaten. Whaling was formerly practiced, but at the present time only whales stranded on the beach are obtained. The Nootka also hunt deer and mountain goats, and gather berries. They live in permanent villages containing long, rectangular

Museum of the American Indian

Nootka Indian chief (19th-century engraving)

houses built of cedar planks. Cedar is also used to make boxes, and canoes are hollowed out of cedar tree trunks. Carved and painted totem poles are made from logs and erected before the houses as heraldic posts. Bark and root mats and baskets are manufactured, but pottery is unknown. Clothing was formerly made of skins and bark, or was woven from the hair of dogs and mountain goats. Nephrite, a form of jade, was widely used in the making of ceremonial and utilitarian objects, and the possession of copper plaques is still important as a measure of wealth and prestige.

Nootka religion is celebrated in elaborate winter ceremonies, characterized by the custom of the potlatch (q.v.). Their dead are placed in boxes secured high in trees, or, in the case of important families, immured in caves. The leaders of the Nootka hold power through hereditary rank. Prestige depends upon displays of wealth and lavish distributions of gifts. Social rivalry is one of the most important factors in the life of these tribes, and fame is acquired or increased competitively, according to the number of celebrations provided by an individual and his lavishness in bestowing property. The Nootka formerly numbered about 6000;

in a recent year their number was estimated at about 1600.

NORD, the most northerly department in France, corresponding to the former province of French Flanders, and bordering on Belgium and the Strait of Dover. It is watered by the Scheldt and the Sambre, with their affluents, and has many canals. The soil is fertile, the fisheries are productive, the mineral wealth very great, especially in coal; and for manufactures Nord is one of the foremost of French departments. It was almost wholly occupied by German forces during World War I, and in it occurred the most severe battles of the early period of the war. Lille is the capital. Area, 2228 sq.m.; pop. (1952 est.) 2,078,000.

NORDAU, MAX SIMON, originally named SUDFELD (1849–1923), German author and physician, born in Budapest, Hungary, and educated at the University of Budapest. He practiced medicine in his native city from 1878 to 1880 and then went to Paris, where he continued to practice. After 1895 he was a leader in the Zionist movement. As a writer, Nordau was noted for his satirical attacks upon the conventional point of view on ethics, social life, literature, and the arts. His best-known work is *Degeneration* (2 vols., 1892-93), in which he attempted to prove that genius is a form of mental and moral degeneration.

NORDENSKJÖLD, BARON NILS ERLAND HERBERT (1877-1932), Swedish ethnologist, born in Stockholm, and educated at Upsala University. He made extensive journeys of discovery in South America, bringing back large ethnographic collections for museums in Stockholm. He investigated South American Indian life in Patagonia in 1899, in Argentina and Bolivia from 1901 to 1902, in Peru and Bolivia from 1904 to 1905, in Bolivia from 1908 to 1909, and conducted further field trips in the interior of South America in 1913. In the last-named year he became director of the ethnographic division of the Göteborg Museum. In 1927 he made ethnographic studies in Panama and Colombia. Nordenskjöld contributed numerous articles to scientific publications, and wrote a number of books, several of which were translated into English and published under the title *Comparative Ethnographical Studies* (9 vols., 1919-31).

NORDHAUSEN, city of Thuringia, East Germany, on the Zorge R., 36 miles N.N.W. of Erfurt. It is noted for its schnaps (brandy), and there are textile mills, tanneries, chemical works, and food-processing plants. During World War II Nordhausen was the site of a notorious Nazi concentration camp and of the largest underground V-2 rocket plants in Germany. Pop., about 32,000.

NORDKYN, CAPE. See NORTH CAPE.

NORFOLK, a seaport and port of entry of Virginia, situated in Norfolk Co., of which it is politically independent, on Hampton Roads (q.v.) opposite Portsmouth. With the cities of Portsmouth and Newport News it forms the Port of Hampton Roads, one of the greatest natural harbors of the world; the waters of Norfolk and Portsmouth are collectively called Norfolk Harbor. Transportation facilities include nine railroads, two airports, ferries, and coastal, inland waterways, and overseas steamship lines. Norfolk is a leading commercial and manufacturing center, and a popular shore resort. Its harbor is connected with Chesapeake Bay by a channel 40 ft. in depth, and the city has 50 m. of developed water frontage on Chesapeake Bay, Hampton Roads, and the Elizabeth and Lafayette rivers. More than 150 piers line the water front, in addition to warehouses, dry docks, and shipbuilding yards. The chief exports are coal, tobacco, cotton, garden truck, and oil, and the city also has an extensive trade in peanuts, oysters, grain, cornstarch products, and fruits. Among the industrial establishments in the city, in addition to extensive shipbuilding yards, are flour mills, grain elevators, breweries, cottonseed-oil and peanut-oil mills, silk mills, lumber mills, meat-packing plants, automobile assembly plants, railroad repair shops, foundries, fisheries, and factories manufacturing chemicals, fertilizers, peanut candy, beverages, cotton bagging, clothing, hosiery, mattresses, springs, barrels, cement, and machinery.

Within a few miles of the city are several of the most notable recreation areas in the State, including Virginia Beach, Seashore State Park near Cape Henry, and the Great Dismal Swamp, a famous hunting and fishing area. Norfolk is the site of several facilities of the Federal government, of which the most important is the U.S. Naval Base, which includes a training station, a supply depot, a naval air station, and a submarine base. The U.S. Navy Yard, known as the Norfolk Navy Yard, is situated across the Elizabeth R. in Portsmouth. Other governmental agencies in the city are the district headquarters of the U.S. Coast Guard, a branch of the U.S. Hydrographic Office, a U.S. District Court, a U.S. Public Health Service unit, and the headquarters of the Virginia customs district. The principal educational institutions in Norfolk are a branch of the College of William and Mary (q.v.), and a branch of Virginia Polytechnic Institute. St. Paul's Church (Protestant Episcopal), built in 1739, the Myers House (1791), and Fort Norfolk (1796) are among the historic buildings in the city. Embedded in the walls of St. Paul's is a British cannon ball.

Norfolk was laid out in 1682 and incorporated as a borough in 1736. It was an important center of trade with England and the West Indies until the Revolutionary War, when it was bombarded by the British fleet on Jan. 1, 1776, and later burned by Virginia militia to prevent its occupation by the British. The town was rebuilt and was attacked unsuccessfully by the British in the War of 1812. The city of Norfolk was chartered in 1845. An epidemic of yellow fever in 1855 seriously retarded its development. During the Civil War it was captured by Union forces in 1862. After the war the city gradually developed in importance as a commercial, industrial, and naval center. Pop. (1950) 213,513.

NORFOLK, a maritime county of England, bounded on the N. and E. by the North Sea, on the W. by Cambridgeshire, and on the S. by the county of Suffolk. Much of the level land near the coast has been reclaimed from the sea. Norfolk is chiefly an agricultural, stock-, and poultry-raising county. There are manufactures of textiles. The principal rivers are the Ouse, Yare, and Bure. The capital is Norwich. Area, 2053 sq.m.; pop. (1951 est.) 546,550.

NORFOLK, EARLS and DUKES OF, titles held by the highest-ranking member of the English peerage, next in rank to the princes of the royal blood. The earldom of Norfolk was first held by the 11th-century knight Ralph de Guader, upon whom it was conferred by William the Conqueror. In 1075, when De Guader revolted against William, the title was declared forfeit. It was renewed about the middle of the 12th century, when King Stephen (q.v.) awarded it to one of his chief supporters, Hugh Bigod (see BIGOD). The earldom remained in the Bigod family until the death in 1306 of the fifth earl, Roger Bigod, who was childless. Six years later the title was bestowed by King Edward II upon his half-brother Thomas of Brotherton. The latter died without sons in 1338, and the title remained vacant

until Thomas' daughter Margaret was created Duchess of Norfolk in 1397; at the same time her grandson Thomas, 12th Baron of Mowbray, was created the first Duke of Norfolk. The Mowbrays retained the dukedom until the death of the fourth duke, John Mowbray, in 1476, when the dukedom fell vacant. In 1483 it was conferred upon John Howard, a grandson of Thomas Mowbray; the Howard (q.v.) family has retained the title until the present time.

NORFOLK ISLAND, an island in the western Pacific Ocean, situated about halfway between New Zealand and New Caledonia, 400 miles N.N.W. of the former. Formerly governed by the governor of New South Wales, since 1914 it has been under the administration of the Australian Commonwealth. The coasts are high (mean altitude, 400 ft.) and steep, and the surface generally uneven, rising in Mt. Pitt to 1050 ft. The island is 6 m. long, and has an area of 13½ sq.m. The population is about 1100, mostly descendants of the mutineers of the *Bounty* transferred there from Pitcairn Island.

NORMAL SCHOOLS. See TEACHER TRAINING.

NORMAN, county seat of Cleveland Co., Okla., situated 18 miles s. of Oklahoma City. Transportation facilities include two railroads and an airport. The city is the commercial center of an area producing corn, grain sorghums, cotton, oats, barley, wheat, alfalfa, hay, vegetables, fruits and berries, poultry, livestock, and oil. Among the industrial establishments in Norman and the vicinity are oil refineries, cottonseed-oil mills, flour mills, frozen-food lockers, chick hatcheries, and plants processing dairy products and manufacturing mattresses, brooms, furniture, and bicycle seats. Norman is the site of the University of Oklahoma (see OKLAHOMA, UNIVERSITY OF). Also in the city is the Oklahoma Central State Hospital for mental diseases and a U.S. veterans hospital. Norman was settled in 1889 and chartered as a city in 1902. Pop. (1950) 27,006.

NORMAN ARCHITECTURE. See ROMANESQUE ART AND ARCHITECTURE.

NORMAN CONQUEST. See ENGLAND: *History.*

NORMANDY, an ancient duchy and later a province of France, bordering on the English Channel. In area it corresponded approximately to the modern departments of Seine-Inférieure, Eure, Orne, Calvados, and Manche, its capital being Rouen. Under the

French Embassy, Information Division
Normandy, France: ruins of early buildings in Les Andelys, department of Eure

Romans it formed part of *Gallia Lugdunensis Secunda;* after the Franks' invasion it made a constituent part of the kingdom of Neustria, and came to be known as Normandy after Charles the Simple, in 911, had given it to Hrolf or Rollo, the leader of a band of Norse rovers, as a fief of the French crown. From Hrolf (baptized under the name of Robert) and Gisela, the daughter of Charles the Simple, sprang the dukes of Normandy, of whom Richard I (grandson of Hrolf) vigorously maintained his authority against his liege lords, Louis IV and Lothaire. William II, son of Robert II le Diable, became Duke of Normandy in 1035 and in 1066 established a Norman dynasty on the throne of England, thereby politically uniting Normandy with the latter country. In 1077 his eldest son, Robert, wrested Normandy from him, but it was again united to England under Henry I in 1106. With this monarch the direct male line became extinct. Henry II, the son of Henry I's daughter Matilda, after the death of Stephen of Blois obtained in 1154 the government of England and Normandy; but in the reign of his son, John, Normandy was conquered by Philip Augustus of France (1202-04). It remained a portion of the French monarchy for over two centuries, save when conquered by Edward III in 1346; but after the battle of Agincourt (1415) it was reconquered by the English, who held it till 1449. The Channel Islands, which were once a part of Normandy, have remained in possession of England.

NORMAN FRENCH, a French dialect which developed in Normandy after the Scandinavian invaders, under Rollo, had settled there about 911. (See NORMANDY; NORTHMEN.) In adopting French as a medium of communication the Normans retained for purposes of literary expression many Scandinavian words, which are still, though in a greatly changed form, characteristic of this French dialect. The largest class is that of proper names of persons and places. During the early period Norman French played an important part in French literature. Among the most important works written in this dialect are historical accounts, for it was in Normandy that history in the vulgar tongue first made its appearance. Geffrei Gaimar's *Estorie des Engles,* which belongs to the middle of the 12th century, is connected with the achievements of the Anglo-Normans; Wace, who died about 1175, wrote the *Roman de Brut,* drawn from Geoffrey of Monmouth, which purports to give an account of the English from the fall of Troy, and the *Roman de Rou,* a long account of the Norman dukes.

In England, even before the conquest, the influence of French had begun as a result of the strong French sympathies of Edward the Confessor, and for several centuries after the Conquest French continued to be the court as well as the legal language. A considerable French literature was produced, both in poetry and prose. Among the most important works of the 12th century may be mentioned the *Cumpoz* and *Bestiaire* of

Philippe de Thaün, the laws of William the Conqueror, and versions of the Alexis, Roland, and Brandan legends, besides the *Chançun de Guillelme,* which probably belongs to the end of the 11th century. The 13th century was by far the most flourishing epoch. Among the poets belonging to this period are Adgar; Fantosme, who wrote a *Chronique* of the invasions of the Scots in 1173-74; Angier, author of a life of Gregory the Great; Chardri; and Guillaume de Berneville, who wrote a life of St. Gilles. Thomas à Becket, Bevis of Hampton (Bœve de Haumtone), St. Auban, and others are the subjects of anonymous poems, while versions of the *Pèlerinage de Charlemagne,* and the mystery play of Adam, as well as a *Fabliau du Héron,* are also of interest. The 14th century, marking the decline of this literature, is noted for the *Contes Moralisées* of Nicole Bozon and versions of various Biblical legends.

After the decline of the Anglo-Norman literature French continued to be the language of pleadings in the law courts even as late as the period of Henry VIII. When argument was slowly differentiated from out of the mixed process of arguing and pleading, it was done in English, and the precedence of the native tongue became greater and greater until the Revolution, when law French had completely died out.

NORMANS. See NORMANDY; NORTHMEN.

NORODOM SIHANOUK (1922–), King of Cambodia, educated at French schools in Saigon, Cochin China (now South Viet Nam), and in Paris. He succeeded to the throne by vote of the Royal Grand Council in 1941, following the death of his uncle King Sisowath Monivong. Following the expulsion of Japanese occupation forces from Cambodia after World War II, he opposed the Issarak (Free Cambodia) movement, which advocated immediate independence from France, and consented to the reinstitution of French control. In May, 1947, he promulgated a constitution for his realm, until then nominally an absolute monarchy. His government and France concluded (November, 1949) a treaty under which Cambodia became one of the three states of the Associated States of Indochina, an integral part of the French Union. Norodom Sihanouk supported the French war (1946–54) against the Communist-led Viet Minh rebels in Indochina. In exchange he obtained (1953) concessions granting Cambodia greater jurisdiction over its internal affairs. In February, 1955, Norodom Sihanouk abdicated the throne in favor of his father Prince Suramit. When Cambodia withdrew from the French Union in September, Norodom Sihanouk became premier. See CAMBODIA.

NORRIS, CHARLES GILMAN (1881-1945), American author and editor, brother of the author Frank Norris, born in Chicago, Ill. From 1908 to 1913 he was art editor of *American Magazine.* In 1909 he married the writer Kathleen Thompson, who became well known as Kathleen Norris. His writings, principally fictionalized studies of vital American industries, include *The Amateur* (1915), *Brass* (1921), *Bread* (1923), *Pig Iron* (1925), *Seed* (1930), *Zest* (1933), *Hands* (1935), and *Brick Without Straw* (1938).

NORRIS, FRANK, in full BENJAMIN FRANKLIN NORRIS (1870-1902), American novelist, born in Chicago, and educated at the University of California and at Harvard University. He was a correspondent for the San Francisco *Chronicle* during the Boer War and for *McClure's Magazine* during the Spanish-American War. Norris' novels are brutally realistic, describing and analyzing sordid human motives and environments; the influence of the French naturalistic novelist Émile Zola is strong in his work. Norris' principal novels are *McTeague* (1899), a powerful story of the tragedy caused in the lives of ordinary people by greed; a trilogy depicting the human drama arising from the raising, selling, and consumption of wheat, of which two novels, *The Octopus* (1901) and *The Pit* (1903), were written, and the third, *The Wolf,* only projected; and *Vandover and the Brute* (posthumously published, 1914), a story of degeneration. Others of his novels include *Moran of the Lady Letty* (1898), an adventure story; *A Man's Woman* (1900), a tale of arctic exploration; and *Blix* (1900), a semiautobiographical love story.

NORRIS, GEORGE WILLIAM (1861-1944), American legislator, born in Sandusky Co., Ohio, and educated at Baldwin University (now Baldwin-Wallace College) at Berea, Ohio, and at the Northern Indiana Normal School. He settled in Furnas Co., Nebr., in 1885, and entered the practice of law; from 1895 to 1902 he was judge of the 14th Nebraska District Court. From 1902 to 1913 he was a Republican member of the U.S. House of Representatives. During this period Norris was the leader of the group of congressmen who, by effecting a change in the House rules in 1910, ended the arbitrary rule of the Speaker of the House, Joseph G.

Cannon. In 1912 Norris was elected to the U.S. Senate, and he was for some years a member of the Middle Western isolationist bloc which opposed the entry of the United States into World War I and later attacked the Versailles Treaty. He subsequently became prominent as an exponent of Federal regulation of public utilities; he led the campaign which culminated in 1933 in the passage of the act creating the Tennessee Valley Authority (see TENNESSEE; WATER POWER), an act written by Norris. The first T.V.A. dam to be completed was named for him.

Among the other notable enactments sponsored by Norris are the Twentieth Amendment to the U.S. Constitution, popularly known as the "Lame Duck" Amendment (q.v.), passed in 1932; and the Norris-LaGuardia Anti-Injunction Act of 1932, whereby the issuance of injunctions in labor disputes was restricted. Norris' consistent disregard for the narrow limitations of party politics, exemplified by his support of many policies initiated under the New Deal (q.v.) program, eventually deprived him of the support of the Republican Party. In 1942, when he ran for re-election as an Independent, he was defeated by the regular Republican candidate. Norris was the author of an autobiography, *Fighting Liberal* (published posthumously, 1945).

NORRIS, KATHLEEN (1880-   ), American novelist, born in San Francisco, and educated privately. She was the wife of the novelist Charles Gilman Norris. Kathleen Norris began her literary career in 1910 with the sale of short stories to magazines; her first novel, *Mother,* was published a year later. She is best known for her novels dealing with domestic American life and for her love stories; several of her novels were best sellers. Her novels include *Saturday's Child* (1914), *The Story of Julia Page* (1915), *Sisters* (1919), *Certain People of Importance* (1922), *Second Hand Wife* (1932), *Heartbroken Melody* (1938), *The Venables* (1941), *Corner of Heaven* (1943), *The Secret of Hillyard House* (1947), *High Holiday* (1949), *Shadow Marriage* (1952), and *Miss Harriet Townshend* (1955).

NORRISTOWN, borough and county seat of Montgomery Co., Pa., on the Schuylkill River, 17 m. by rail N.W. of Philadelphia. It contains a State asylum for the insane, and has factories making cigars, tacks, wire, screws, and boilers. Pop. (1950) 38,126.

NORRKÖPING, seaport on the E. coast of Sweden, situated at the head of the

Bravik, 75 miles s.w. of Stockholm. There are manufactures of textiles, paper, tapestries, and sugar. Pop. (1952 est.) 87,140.

NORSEMEN. See NORTHMEN.

NORSE MYTHOLOGY. See SCANDINAVIAN MYTHOLOGY.

NORTH, FREDERICK, 2ND EARL OF GUILFORD, by courtesy known as LORD NORTH (1732-92), British statesman, born in London, and educated at Eton School and Oxford University. In 1754 he was elected a member of the House of Commons, in which he served for almost forty years. He was appointed chancellor of the exchequer in 1767, and three years later became prime minister. In the latter post he displayed complete subservience to the wishes of King George III (q.v.), carrying through a number of measures for the taxation of the American colonies which he personally believed unwise. Upon the outbreak of the American Revolution in 1776, he advocated the conclusion of an early peace; by 1779 he had recognized the impossibility of a British victory over the Americans, but was nevertheless persuaded by the king to support the continuation of the war. In 1782, immediately after the surrender of the British forces in America, he resigned his position. In the following year North formed a coalition with Charles James Fox (q.v.), who had formerly led the Whig opposition to his administration, and with whom he succeeded in overthrowing the ministry headed by the second Earl of Shelburne. Thereafter, North was prominent as a member of the opposition to the ministry of William Pitt the Younger (q.v.). He succeeded to the earldom of Guilford in 1790.

NORTH AMERICA. See AMERICA, NORTH.

NORTHAMPTON, county seat of Hampshire Co., Mass., situated on the Connecticut R., 16 miles N. of Springfield. Transportation facilities include two railroads. The city is a manufacturing and educational center, and lies in an agricultural area producing tobacco, potatoes, and onions. The chief products are brushes, plastics, silk hosiery, cutlery, and paper boxes. Northampton is the site of Smith College (q.v.), one of the largest women's colleges in the U.S.; the Northampton School for girls; the Mary A. Burnham School for girls; the Clarke School for the Deaf; a State hospital; and a U.S. veterans hospital. In the vicinity are Mount Holyoke, 954 ft. above sea level, and Mount Tom (1214 ft.), both ascended by electric railroads. Northampton was the birthplace or the residence of many noted Americans, including Jonathan Edwards, leading clergyman and theologian, Timothy Dwight, a grandson of Jonathan Edwards and a prominent educator, and Calvin Coolidge, 30th President of the U.S. Northampton was first settled in 1654 and was incorporated as a city in 1883. Pop. (1950) 29,063.

NORTHAMPTON, capital of Northamptonshire, England, on the River Nen, 66 miles N.W. by N. of London. The principal manufacture is that of boots and shoes, the town being the English center of that industry. A considerable trade is carried on in the dressing of leather, some lace is made, and extensive breweries are also in operation. Pop. (1951 est.) 104,429.

NORTHAMPTONSHIRE, a southern midland county of England. It is principally an iron-producing county, but it manufactures boots and shoes, and in the pastoral districts livestock raising is profitable. Area, 914 sq.m.; pop. (1951 est.) 359,550.

NORTH ATLANTIC TREATY, a pact of alliance for the purpose of promoting "stability and well-being in the North Atlantic area" which was signed in Washington, D.C., on April 4, 1949, by representatives of the governments of Belgium, Canada, Denmark, France, Iceland, Italy, Luxembourg, the Netherlands, Norway, Portugal, the United Kingdom, and the United States. The treaty was designed to counteract the threat of Russian expansion into western Europe, which arose after Russia's establishment of puppet communist regimes in eastern European countries following World War II. The treaty attempted to forestall Russian aggression against any of the signatory powers by declaring that "an armed attack against one . . . shall be considered an attack against them all".

The treaty contains a preamble and 14 articles. Its provisions are as follows: article 1 pledges the parties to seek peaceful settlement of all disputes arising between themselves and other powers; article 2 pledges the parties to promote economic co-operation between themselves; article 3 calls for "continuous and effective self-help and mutual aid" to develop "individual and collective capacity to resist armed attacks"; article 4 provides for mutual consultation whenever "the territorial integrity, political independence or security of any of the parties is threatened"; article 5 pledges the use of armed force in "collective self-defense"; article 6 defines the area covered in the agreement, excluding Asiatic and central or south African colonies of the signatories; article 7 affirms that the obligations of the signatories under the Charter of the United Nations shall take precedence over their obligations under the treaty; article 8 provides against conflict between the treaty and past or future international obligations assumed by the signatories; article 9 calls for the establishment of a consultative Council between the parties, one of the duties of which was the immediate establishment of a Defense Committee; article 10 covers the admission of new powers to participation in the treaty; article 11 outlines the ratification procedure for the treaty; article 12 outlines the amendment procedure for the treaty; article 13 outlines the procedure for withdrawal from the treaty after the passage of twenty years; and article 14 provides for the deposit of the signed treaty in the archives of the government of the United States.

The treaty became effective on Aug. 24, 1949. Later in 1949 the U.S. Congress approved the Mutual Defense Act, legislation providing about $1.31 billion for military aid to the signatory powers, Turkey, Iran, Greece, and South Korea. U.S. aid to the North Atlantic nations was enormously increased after the outbreak (1950) of war in Korea.

Both before and after the signing of the North Atlantic Treaty the Soviet government repeatedly denounced the alliance, describing it as "openly aggressive", in violation of the U.N. charter, and directed against the U.S.S.R. Soviet hostility was especially pronounced following the decision (1950) of the signatories to bring West Germany into the framework of the North Atlantic defense system. The signatory powers, maintaining that the alliance was designed solely to safeguard peace, rejected the Soviet protests.

The provisions of the treaty are implemented through the North Atlantic Treaty Organization (q.v.), often referred to as N.A.T.O. On the invitation (1951) of the signatory nations, Greece and Turkey adhered to the treaty in February, 1952. West Germany adhered to it in May, 1955.

NORTH ATLANTIC TREATY ORGANIZATION, in abbreviated form N.A.T.O., international agency created in 1949 for the purpose of implementing the North Atlantic Treaty (q.v.). The leading body of N.A.T.O., as presently constituted, is the Council. Actually a council of the governments adhering to the treaty, the Council generally consists of the cabinet officers responsible for the con-

Ministers of twelve nations meet in Washington to discuss the North Atlantic Treaty

duct of the foreign affairs of their respective nations and/or the cabinet officers responsible for national defense. Originally the defense ministers comprised the Defense Committee, which was specifically responsible for the implementation of treaty articles 3 and 5, but the functions of this committee were absorbed by the Council as the result of structural changes effected in February, 1952. On the basis of other changes approved in February, 1952, the Council may consist of other cabinet officers or, when appropriate, of the heads of state of the signatories; to insure the continuous functioning of the Council, in the absence of ministerial representatives, each government is represented therein by a permanent delegate; and responsibility for the organization of the Council's activities and for the direction of its secretariat was vested in a secretary-general.

Foremost among the various committees which assist the Council is the Military Committee. This body, consisting of the chiefs of staff of the signatory powers, furnishes policy guidance on military matters. A subcommittee, officially known as the Standing Group and composed of representatives of the United States, Great Britain and France, functions between sessions of the Military Committee.

Leadership of the N.A.T.O. military establishment, which was authorized by a Council decision in December, 1950, is exercised by Supreme Headquarters, Allied Powers in Europe (S.H.A.P.E.). At the head of this organization, activated at Rocquencourt, near Paris, in April, 1951, is the supreme commander, Allied Powers in Europe (S.C.A.P.E.). The first S.C.A.P.E. was U.S. General of the Army Dwight David Eisenhower, later elected 34th President of the United States. At the beginning of 1954 the N.A.T.O. military establishment included about 60 divisions, some 5500 aircraft, and powerful naval detachments. These forces were distributed among central, northern, and southern regional commands. As part of its program of unifying the national units which comprise the international organization, S.H.A.P.E. conducts large-scale military maneuvers annually. In addition, N.A.T.O. maintains a defense college in Paris.

West German participation in the N.A.T.O. defense system was a major objective of the Council almost from its inception. Chiefly because of French fears of a resurgent Germany, the campaign to attain this objective was attended with grave difficulties. The interested powers finally reached agreement late in 1951 on a formula providing for the creation of a supranational west-European army which would form an integral part of the North Atlantic defense system. Approved by the Council in February, 1952, the formula became the basis of the European Defense Community Treaty. The latter, signed by France, West Germany, Italy, Belgium, the

Netherlands, and Luxembourg in May, 1952, included provisions for a 43-division army under the overall command of S.H.A.P.E. Ratification of the treaty by the parliaments of the signatory powers was prerequisite to its effectuation. The French National Assembly rejected the treaty on Aug. 30, 1954. In September the Western powers, meeting in London, reached agreement on a new formula for bringing West Germany into the N.A.T.O. defense system. The accords (signed in Paris on Oct. 23 and effectuated in May, 1955) granted West Germany membership in N.A.T.O. and the Brussels Treaty Organization (q.v.). The latter, to which Italy also was admitted, was renamed "Western European Union".

NORTH BRABANT, province of the Netherlands, situated in the southernmost part of the country. The terrain is generally low and flat and is traversed by numerous waterways, including the Dommel, Donge, and Zuid-Willemsvaart rivers and the Wilhelmina Canal. Agriculture and stock-raising are the chief occupations. Manufactured products include textiles, shoes, pharmaceuticals, and electrical goods. The capital of the province is 's Hertogenbosch (q.v.). Other important cities are Bergen-op-Zoom, Breda, Eindhoven, and Tilburg (qq.v.).

North Brabant originally comprised part of the Duchy of Brabant (see BRABANT, DUCHY OF). In 1648 it was incorporated in the Dutch Republic of the United Provinces. The whole of Brabant (q.v.) was included in the Kingdom of the Netherlands in 1815 and partitioned into the provinces of Antwerp, South Brabant and North Brabant. Following the Revolution of 1830 Antwerp and South Brabant became part of Belgium; North Brabant remained a Dutch province. Area, 1893 sq.m.; pop. (1952 est.) 1,309,597.

NORTH CAPE, a promontory in Europe, in 71°11′ N. latitude, often referred to as the most northerly point of the continent, though it is not on the continent, but on the island of Magerö. The most northerly point in Europe is on the small island, Knivskjaerodden, which is a little to the w. The northernmost point on the continent is Cape Nordkyn, 6 m. to the s. of North Cape.

NORTH CAROLINA, one of the South Atlantic States of the United States, bounded on the E. by the Atlantic Ocean, on the S. by South Carolina and Georgia, on the w. by Tennessee, and on the N. by Virginia. It

N.C. Dept. of Conservation & Development

North Carolina State Capitol in Raleigh

ranks as the 27th State in the Union in area, 10th in population (1950), and 12th in the order of admission to the Union, having entered on Nov. 21, 1789. The State capital is Raleigh (q.v.). The principal cities in the order of population (1950) are Charlotte, Winston-Salem, Greensboro, Durham, and Raleigh (qq.v.). The State possesses an extreme length from E. to W. of 503 m., and an extreme width from N. to S. of 188 m. Area of the State, 52,712 sq.m., including 3570 sq.m. of inland water surface. Pop. (1950) 4,061,929.

North Carolina occupies three main physiographic provinces: the Coastal Plain, which comprises the surface of the eastern half of the State; the Piedmont Plateau, which occupies the center of the State; and the Appalachian Mountain region, which occupies the western portion.

The Coastal Plain, level and sandy, stretches inland for an average distance of 150 m., is nowhere more than 500 ft. above sea level, and covers an area of about 26,000 sq.m. It is bordered by swamps, inlets, estuaries, and a chain of long, narrow barrier reefs, which extend for approximately 325 m. along the coast from the N. border of the State S.S.E. to Cape Hatteras, then S.W. to Cape Lookout, and then W. and S., in a long arc, to Cape Fear. The barrier reefs enclose Albemarle and Pamlico sounds, and form the inner boundary of Raleigh and Onslow bays. The general coastline of the State possesses a length of 301 m. The over-all length of the coastline, measured around bays, inlets, and estuaries reached by tidal water, is 3074 m.

The Piedmont Plateau region is separated from the Coastal Plain by a "Fall Line",

which marks a sharp increase of 200 ft. in elevation. The Fall Line follows a very irregular course across North Carolina in a generally southwesterly direction from the Falls of Roanoke in the N. to Anson Co. on the South Carolina border. The plateau covers an area of about 20,000 sq.m., and rises to the W. at the approximate rate of 3 to 4 ft. per mile until it joins the mountain region, about 1200 ft. above the level of the plateau.

The portion of the Appalachian system which crosses North Carolina covers an area of about 6000 sq.m. and consists of the Blue Ridge Escarpment and the Great Smoky Mts. Some 43 peaks in the Great Smoky Mts. reach elevations exceeding 6000 ft. above sea level, and 4 peaks in the Blue Ridge Escarpment exceed 5000 ft. The highest point in the State, and the highest point E. of the Mississippi R., is Mount Mitchell, 6684 ft. above sea level, in Yancey Co. The lowest point in the State is at sea level along the coast. The average elevation of North Carolina is 700 ft. above sea level.

The Blue Ridge Escarpment forms the watershed for the Atlantic slope. West of the ridge North Carolina is drained by rivers and streams which flow into the Mississippi basin. The principal rivers E. of the Blue Ridge flow in a generally southeasterly direction and include the Roanoke, the Tar, and the Neuse, which flow into Albemarle and Pamlico sounds through deep and wide estuaries; the Cape Fear R., which flows into the Atlantic at Cape Fear; and the Catawba and Yaokin rivers, both of which flow into South Carolina. The mountains to the W. of the Blue Ridge are drained by the headstreams of the Tennessee R., the chief of which are the

Little Tennessee and the French Broad rivers.

The average yearly temperature of the State in the s.E. is 64°F.; along the Coastal Plain, 62°F.; on the Piedmont Plateau, 60°F.; in the mountain region, 55°F.; and in the extreme s.w. corner of the State, 50°F. The yearly average for the State, below an elevation of 4000 ft., is 59°F. Extremes of –19°F. and 107°F. have been recorded. Precipitation is almost all rain, and averages about 50 inches a year.

National forest land in North Carolina totaled 3,592,763 acres in 1953. There are also extensive community forests. About half of the Great Smoky Mountains National Park (q.v.) lies within the State, in addition to which there are two National Military parks, twelve State parks, covering about 17,570 acres, Federal and State wildlife sanctuaries, game farms, and fisheries, and the Cape Hatteras National Seashore Park, which includes the Fort Raleigh National Historical Site and the Kill Devil Hill National Memorial. The Cherokee Indian Reservation is located on the edge of the Great Smoky Mountains National Park. Approximately 3000 Indians live on the reservation, which occupies 60,000 acres.

The State is a major resort area, with excellent mountain vistas in the w. and fine beaches in the E. Duck, geese, and brant are numerous along the waterways and coast. Inland are bears, deer, foxes, raccoons, and game birds. Yachting and fishing are popular along the coast, and the fresh-water fishing in the rivers and streams of North Carolina is among the best in the U.S.

Although agriculture is second to manufacturing in economic value, North Carolina usually ranks high among the States in the value of its farm crops. The State grows, in quantities sufficient enough to be reported, all 100 of the crops that the U.S. Department of Agriculture lists as possible to grow commercially in the U.S. The chief cash crops are tobacco, cotton, and peanuts, and corn is grown in every county in the State. North Carolina usually leads the nation in the production of tobacco and sweet potatoes. In 1952 the production figures were: tobacco, 918,250,000 pounds; corn, 55,616,000 bushels; sweet potatoes, 3,990,000 bushels; and cotton, 569,000 bales. Other important crops include peaches, hay, potatoes, wheat and soy beans. Farm animals (1953) included 1,203,000 hogs, 892,000 cattle (including 399,000 milch cows), 222,000 mules, 75,000 horses, and 48,000 sheep. Cash income in 1952 from crops

and livestock was $942,169,000, and from Federal subsidies $6,790,000. In 1950 a total of 288,508 farms covered an area of 19,317,937 acres, and were valued at (land and buildings) $1,905,714,000. North Carolina usually leads all States in its expenditures for fertilizers.

In 1952 the manufacturing industries of North Carolina turned out products valued at $6,426,000,000. A total of 449,000 wage earners were employed in 7400 industrial establishments and received wages and salaries totaling $1,617,000,000. The leading industries are the manufacture of textiles (more than two thirds of the industrial employees in the State are connected with textile manufacture) and the manufacture of cigarettes (almost three fourths of the entire production in the U.S.). North Carolina leads all States in the manufacture of furniture. Other important industries are the processing of food crops and the manufacture of lumber and timber products. Stands of timber cover approximately 18,000,000 acres of North Carolina, and the State ranks high in the nation in the production of hardwood and softwood; the output in 1950 totaled 1,994,000 board feet. Fisheries are also important to the State's economy. About twenty-five varieties of fish, chiefly menhaden and shrimp and other shellfish, are taken from the waters of the State. In 1952–53 the commercial catch was valued at $11,861,894.

Although North Carolina does not rank among the leading States in the total production of minerals, it possesses the largest variety (289 different types) found in the U.S., and also leads all States in the production of mica, feldspar, silica, olivine, and residual kaolin clays, and is the only producer of pyrophyllite, a substitute for talc. In addition, the world's largest open-face granite quarry is located in North Carolina at Mt. Airy. The State is second in the U.S. in the output of quartz and talc. Other minerals are abrasive garnet, nickel, granite, asbestos, and rare minerals, such as monazite, columbite, wolframite, vermiculite, allanite, and zircon. Total mineral production in 1951 was valued at $29,648,000.

Transportation facilities (1953) include 4531 m. of main-track railway, and 67,409 m. of roads and highways, of which 30,698 m. were paved. In 1952–53 there were 155 airports and airfields within the State, of which 95 were commercial and municipal.

Attendance at the public schools in North Carolina is free for all persons between the ages of six and twenty-one, and compulsory for all children between the ages of seven and sixteen, for the full school year. North Carolina provides separate schools for white, Negro, and Indian children. In 1952 there was a total of 3432 public elementary and secondary schools, staffed by 30,207 teachers and attended by 914,269 students. Institutions of higher learning include 17 State-supported universities and colleges, and 41 private institutions. The University of North Carolina, which consists of the University proper at Chapel Hill, the State College of Agriculture and Engineering at Raleigh, and the Woman's College at Greensboro; 7 teachers colleges (3 white, 3 Negro, and 1 Indian); and 2 other colleges comprise the State institutions. Duke University at Durham, Davidson College at Davidson, Salem College at Winston-Salem, and Wake Forest College at Wake Forest are notable among the private institutions of higher learning within the State.

North Carolina is governed according to the terms of the constitution of 1868, as amended. Executive authority is vested in a governor (not eligible to succeed himself), lieutenant governor, secretary of state, auditor, treasurer, attorney general, superintendent of public instruction, commissioner of agriculture, commissioner of labor, and commissioner of insurance, all elected for four-year terms. The governor has broad powers of appointment, but he has no power of veto, and many of his other executive powers are limited by a council of state, which is composed of the secretary of state, treasurer, auditor, and the superintendent of public instruction.

Judicial authority is vested in a supreme court consisting of a chief justice and six associates elected for eight-year terms, superior courts, and minor courts. Legislative authority is vested in a General Assembly, which consists of a senate of 50 members and a house of representatives of 120 members, all elected for two-year terms. Those eligible to vote in North Carolina are persons who have been citizens of the U.S. for a minimum period of one year, reached the age of twenty-one, resided in the State one year, and the district four months; registration of persons whose ancestors were not voters in 1867 and who were not eligible to vote on Dec. 1, 1908, is limited to those able to read and write any section of the Constitution in the English language. As a result of these qualifications and the interpretation of them, there is a substantial voting disfranchisement in North Carolina, particularly of Negroes. In

the 1952 election only about 50% of the potential voters cast ballots. North Carolina is divided into 100 counties, and the State is represented in the Congress of the U.S. by two senators and twelve representatives.

History. On July 4, 1584, two English explorers, who had been commissioned by Sir Walter Raleigh, dropped anchor off the North Carolina coast. Their glowing reports of the region caused a colonizing expedition to set out from Plymouth the following year. On Aug. 17, 1585, a colony was established on Roanoke Island (q.v.), but abandoned a year later. On July 22, 1587, another colony commissioned by Raleigh landed on the island. The colony of 121 men was led by John White, whose granddaughter, Virginia Dare, born on Aug. 18, 1587, was the first child of English parents born in America. White went back to England for supplies and returned in 1590 to find that the colony had completely vanished (see CROATAN). In 1629 the land s. of Virginia, which was called Carolina, was granted to Sir Robert Heath by Charles I, but the proprietor failed to make use of his land, and in 1663 Charles II granted the Carolina territory to eight proprietors. The proprietors divided the grant into North and South Carolina and set up a system of government drawn up by John Locke (q.v.) and called the Fundamental Constitution. The constitution provided for four houses of parliament and three orders of nobility, but it was never put fully in operation and was finally abandoned in 1693.

The proprietary period of the colony, which lasted from 1663 to 1729, was a turbulent one because of the independence of the settlers, who occasionally drove out a governor whom they regarded as obnoxious. Indian troubles also beset the colony, but in 1713 the Tuscarora Indians were defeated and expelled from the Carolinas. The Carolinas did not prove a success from a financial standpoint to most of the proprietors, and in 1728 seven of the eight proprietors sold their grants to the crown. In 1744 the eighth proprietor relinquished control of his grant in return for a smaller strip of land in North Carolina. The colonists continued to rebel against the authorities, who were now royal governors, and from 1765 to 1771 the Regulators (q.v.), a group of colonists who refused to pay taxes, were in rebellion against royal authority.

The first provincial congress met in defiance of the royal governor in 1774 and sent delegates to the Continental Congress. In

N.C. Dept. of Conservation & Development

INDUSTRY IN NORTH CAROLINA

Above: Apparatus for packaging cigarettes in a tobacco-processing factory. Right: In a textile mill, making cloth from cotton. ,

May, 1775, the Mecklenburg Declaration of Independence was enacted. It declared that the royal commissions of the colonies were null and void, and advocated the setting up of an independent government. On April 12, 1776, North Carolina became the first colony to instruct its delegates in Congress to vote for independence. The first constitution of the State was adopted on Dec. 18, 1776. North Carolina soldiers took part in many of the important battles of the Revolution, and in 1776 and 1781 the State was invaded by the British. Delegates were sent to the Constitutional Convention in 1787, but they refused to ratify the instrument in 1788 on the grounds that the central government was too strong. The State did not vote in the first Presidential election. After the adoption of the Bill of Rights, North Carolina ratified the Constitution on Nov. 19, 1789.

The period between the ratification of the Constitution and the Civil War was marked by internal dissension over the problem of representation in the State government between the eastern and western counties, and by the emigration of many of the State's settlers to western territories. In February, 1861, North Carolina opposed secession from the Union, but when President Abraham Lincoln issued a call for troops in order to coerce the seceding States, sentiment in North Carolina changed, and on May 20, 1861, the State passed an ordinance of secession. During the Civil War, North Carolina provided the Confederacy with more than 120,000 troops, lost more soldiers than any other Southern State, and, during the last year of the war, furnished the Confederate Army with food. In 1867, during the Reconstruction (q.v.) period, the civil authority was superseded by the military. The constitution of 1868 established Negro suffrage and in the same year the Ku-Klux Klan (q.v.) began functioning in the State. The Federal government withdrew its military forces from the State in 1868.

From 1872 through 1948, the residents of North Carolina voted for the Democratic candidate for President in every election year except 1872 and 1928, when Republican candidates carried the State. In the 1952 Presidential election, Governor Adlai E. Stevenson of Illinois, the Democratic candidate, received 652,803 votes, and Dwight David Eisenhower, the Republican candidate, received 558,107 votes.

NORTH CAROLINA, UNIVERSITY OF, a coeducational, State-controlled institution of higher learning consisting of three branches, the University of North Carolina proper, the Woman's College of the University of North Carolina, and the North Carolina State College of Agriculture and Engineering, situated respectively at Chapel Hill, Greensboro, and Raleigh, N.C.; the last two institutions were consolidated with the University proper in 1931 by act of the State legislature.

The University of North Carolina at Chapel Hill was chartered in 1789 and opened for instruction in 1795. For about eighty years the institution operated under grave financial difficulties and with a small student body, the largest enrollment prior to the Civil War being about 460 students; it was twice closed down, in 1868 and again in 1874. After 1875, however, financial conditions improved, and the University continued to expand its enrollment, faculty, and equipment. The present divisions of the University proper include the college of arts and sciences, schools of law, medicine, and pharmacy, the general college, the school of public welfare and social work, the division of public health, the division of education, the library school, and the graduate school. Bachelor's, master's, and doctor's degrees are granted; women are admitted to junior and senior classes and the professional and graduate schools only. In 1953 the total enrollment was 5525, including approximately 5200 full-time students; the faculty numbered about 700; and the endowment was over 4 million dollars.

The Woman's College at Greensboro, opened in 1892 as the State Normal and Industrial School, was known from 1897 until 1918 as the State Normal and Industrial College, and until 1932 as the North Carolina College for Women. Courses are offered in liberal and fine arts, music, home economics, business administration, and physical education, leading to bachelor's degrees. In 1953 the total enrollment was about 2375, including almost 2300 full-time students; the faculty numbered over 195.

The State College of Agriculture and Engineering at Raleigh, a coeducational technological institution, was founded as a land-grant college in 1887 and known until 1917 as the North Carolina State College of Agriculture and Mechanic Arts. The divisions of the College include schools of engineering, agriculture and forestry, science and business, teacher training, and textiles. Bachelor's, master's, and doctor's degrees are granted. In 1953 the total enrollment, including 3300 full-time students, was over 3580. Less than 100 of the students were women; the faculty numbered over 500.

NORTH DAKOTA, one of the North Central States of the United States, bounded on the N. by the Canadian provinces of Saskatchewan and Manitoba, on the E. by the Red R., which separates it from the State of Minnesota, on the S. by South Dakota, and on the W. by Montana. It ranks as the 16th State in the Union in area, 41st in population (1950), and 39th in the order of admission to the Union, having entered on Nov. 2, 1889. The State capital is Bismarck. In order of population (1950) the principal cities are Fargo, Grand Forks, Minot, and Bismarck (qq.v.). From N. to S. the extreme width of the State is 210 m., and from E. to W. the extreme length is 360 m. Area of the State, 70,665 sq.m., including 611 sq.m. of inland water surface. Population (1950) 619,636.

The surface of North Dakota is formed by three plains rising one above the other from E. to W. The lowest plain is in the Red R. valley and varies in elevation from 800 to 1000 ft. above sea level. The plain is remarkably level and once formed a portion of the bed of Lake Agassiz (see AGASSIZ, LAKE), an ancient glacial lake. This part of the State's topography extends 30 to 40 miles W. of the Red R. to the next higher plain, from which it is separated in the N. by an escarpment, and in the S. by a more gradual slope. The second plain varies in elevation from 1200 to 1600 ft., and its width averages from 75 m. in the S. to 200 m. in the N. It is

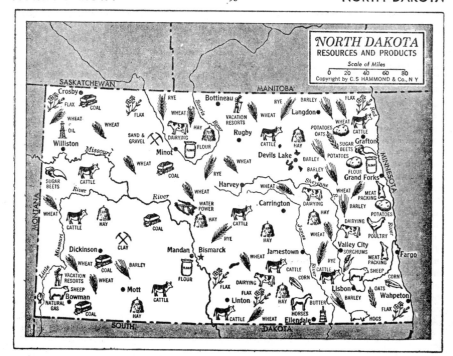

composed primarily of glacial drift, and is bordered on the w. by an abrupt slope which rises to the third plain, the Missouri plateau. The escarpment which separates the intermediate plain from the Missouri plateau bends in a N.W. to S.E. arc across the State, and roughly parallels the Missouri R., which is 50 to 60 miles w. of it. The Missouri plateau occupies almost half of the State and ranges in altitude from 1800 to 2800 ft. above sea level. The s.w. portion of the Missouri plateau is characterized by a series of buttes, sometimes called the "Bad Lands", which rise to elevations of 400 to 700 ft. above the surrounding territory. The highest point in the State, 3468 ft. above sea level, is located at Black Butte in Slope Co. The lowest point, 790 ft. above sea level, is in Pembina Co. The average elevation of North Dakota is 1900 ft. above sea level. Less than one percent of North Dakota is forested. The few trees that are located within the State are found in the Turtle Mts., a small region of high hills, lakes, and streams near the Canadian border in the central portion of the State.

The principal rivers of North Dakota are the Red R., which forms the eastern border and flows s. to N.; the Missouri R., which enters the State in the w. and flows generally southward; the James R., which flows N.W. to S.E. and is located approximately halfway between the Missouri and the Red rivers; the Souris R., which originates in Canada, flows S.E. in the N. central part of the State, S.W., then N.W. in a loop back to Canada; the Little Missouri R., which flows s. to N., paralleling the s.w. border of North Dakota, and then turns E. to join the Missouri; and the Heart, Knife, and Cannon Ball rivers, which flow in a generally easterly direction from the s.w. corner into the Missouri R.

The climate of North Dakota is remarkably uniform throughout the entire State because there are no large bodies of water, mountains, or forest areas to cause variations in temperature. The average temperature of Bismarck in January is 8°F., in July, 70°F. Extremes of –45°F. and 114°F. have been recorded. The yearly average temperature for the State is 39°F. Summers are short and winters are long and severe. The dryness of the atmosphere mitigates the extremes of temperatures. Tornadoes and blizzards are known in the State. Precipitation averages 18 inches a year, most of which is in the form of rain, which falls in the spring and summer. Snowfall is generally light.

Verendrye National Monument (q.v.),

Theodore Roosevelt National Memorial Park, and Fort Berthold Indian Reservation are located in North Dakota. The Federal Bureau of Indian Affairs administered, in 1949, more than 1,000,000 acres of land, of which about 77,500 acres were assigned to Indian tribes. The Indian population of the State in 1950 was 10,766.

Agriculture is the chief pursuit of the people of North Dakota. Over 85 percent of the land is devoted to agriculture. In 1950 there were 65,400 farms covering an area of approximately 41,200,000 acres and valued at (lands and buildings) more than $1,189,000,-000. Cash income from crops, livestock, and Federal subsidies in 1952 was $523,000,000. The State usually leads the nation in the annual production of spring wheat (81,190,000 bu. in 1952), barley (34,580,000 bu.), durum wheat (18,879,000 bu.), and rye (1,575,000 bu.) Other important crops are potatoes, hay, oats, and corn. In 1953 there were about 1,742,000 cattle (including 422,000 dairy cows), 451,000 sheep, 362,000 hogs, and 113,000 horses. The wool clip from 346,000 sheep in 1952 was 3,701,000 lbs.

Manufacturing industries in North Dakota are almost all directly dependent upon agriculture. Flour milling, the manufacture of cream products, butter, cheese, condensed and evaporated milk, and meat packing are the most important industries. North Dakota is the only State in the Union which operates its own flour mill and grain elevator. In 1947 there were about 360 manufacturing establishments. In 1952 the plants employed about 6000 people who earned $16,745,000; the total value added by manufacture in that year was more than $31,000,000. The mineral resources of the State are chiefly lignite coal and clay. In 1951 about 3,244,000 tons of coal valued at $7,784,000 were produced. The total value of mineral products in that year was $10,246,-000.

Transportation in the State includes (1952) 5259 m. of main-track railway, which serves more than 80 percent of all communities (the highest percentage in the U.S.). Two transcontinental railroads traverse the State, a third railroad cuts the s.w. corner, and a fourth joins the Canadian Pacific at the northern border. The State maintains (1952) 6847 m. of highway, and there are (1951) 137 airports in North Dakota, of which 62 are municipally operated.

Attendance at the schools of North Dakota is free and compulsory for all children between the ages of seven and fifteen (seventeen if the eighth grade of elementary school has not been completed). In 1952–53 there were about 3380 public elementary and secondary schools staffed by more than 6700 teachers and attended by about 118,300 students. Three universities and colleges, five teachers colleges, and four junior colleges are in North Dakota. The State supports the University of North Dakota (founded 1883) at Grand Forks, the State Agricultural College (1890) at Fargo, and the five teachers colleges.

North Dakota is governed according to the terms of the constitution of 1889, as amended. Executive authority is vested in a governor, lieutenant governor, secretary of state, treasurer, auditor, attorney general, commissioner of insurance, commissioner of agriculture and labor, tax commissioner, three public service commissioners, and a superintendent of public instruction, all elected for two-year terms. Legislative authority is vested in a senate of 49 members, elected for four-year terms, and a house of representatives of 113 members elected for two-year terms. Judicial authority is vested in a supreme court consisting of 5 justices elected for six-year terms, 15 district judges, and county judges and justices of the peace. Qualified electors in North Dakota are U.S. citizens twenty-one years of age or older who have resided in the State at least one year, the county three months, and the district one month. The State is divided into 53 counties and sends 2 senators and 2 representatives to the Congress of the U.S.

History. A French-Canadian explorer, Sieur de la Verendrye, was the first white man to lead a party into the region of North Dakota, in 1738. In 1742 his sons also explored the territory. In 1803 the Dakotas, containing only a few English fur-trading posts, became a part of the U.S. as a result of the Louisiana Purchase (q.v.). In 1804-05 the Lewis and Clarke Expedition (q.v.) wintered in North Dakota, and soon after the area became the site of the operations of the American Fur Company (see ASTOR, JOHN JACOB). In 1810, however, a Scotchman, Thomas Douglas, 5th Earl of Selkirk, built a fort at Pembina, claiming the region to be a part of British territory. The War of 1812 and the Treaty of Paris in 1818 settled the conflicting boundary claims and established the northern border of the U.S. at the 49th parallel as far w. as the Rocky Mts. In 1823 the U.S. sent an exploring expedition into the Red River valley, and in 1839 John Charles Frémont (q.v.) explored much of the region. In 1849

Greater N.D. Assoc.

NORTH DAKOTA AGRICULTURE

Above: Hardy wheat growing on a typical farm in North Dakota. Right: Spring wheat stacked at harvest time in the Red River valley. Below: A group of grain elevators.

Greater North Dakota Association

Bad Lands in the Theodore Roosevelt National Memorial Park, western North Dakota

the region E. of the Missouri R. was attached to the Territory of Minnesota, and in 1854 the region w. of the Missouri was attached to the Territory of Nebraska. In 1861 the entire region, including present-day Wyoming, Montana, and a large portion of Idaho, was established as the Territory of Dakota. In 1889 the Dakotas were separated, and in November of that year North Dakota was admitted to the Union as a State.

Hostilities with the prairie Indians discouraged immigration, and in 1863 and 1864 Federal troops drove them w. of the Missouri, thus opening eastern North Dakota to settlement. In 1873 the Northern Pacific railroad reached the Missouri R. and in 1887 the Great Northern railroad route was completed across the northern portion of the State. From 1890 to 1915 settlement and expansion increased at a great rate as a result of the land development programs of the railroads. The competing railroads went so far as to induce people to settle in the country by conducting land excursions. Approximately 18,000 persons a year emigrated to North Dakota in this period.

From 1892 through 1948, a plurality or majority of the ballots cast in Presidential elections by the voters of North Dakota have been for the Republican candidate. A coalition of the Democratic and People's parties received a plurality in 1892, and in 1912, 1916, 1932, and 1936 the Democratic candidate received a plurality or majority of the ballots. In all other Presidential election years the Republican candidate received the majority vote. In the 1952 election, Dwight D. Eisenhower, the Republican candidate, received 191,802 votes, and Adlai E. Stevenson, the Democratic nominee, received 76,694 votes.

NORTH DAKOTA AGRICULTURAL COLLEGE, a coeducational, State-controlled, land-grant college, located at Fargo, N.Dak., and founded in 1891. Divisions of the College include agriculture, applied arts and sciences, chemical technology, pharmacy, home economics, and engineering. Bachelor's and master's degrees are granted. In 1953 the total enrollment, all full-time students, was over 1860, including almost 500 women; the faculty numbered about 175.

NORTH DAKOTA, UNIVERSITY OF, a coeducational, State-controlled institution of higher learning, situated at Grand Forks, N.Dak., and founded in 1884. Divisions of the University include colleges and schools of engineering, mines, commerce, liberal arts, science, education, law, and medicine, and a graduate school. Bachelor's, master's, and doctor's degrees are granted. The University is affiliated with Wesley College, a coeducational, privately controlled institution, under the auspices of the Methodist Church, offering courses in applied music and in religion. In 1953 total student enrollment at the University was more than 2350, including approximately 2200 full-time students; the faculty numbered 175.

NORTHEAST BOUNDARY DISPUTE, a long-standing dispute between the United States and England concerning the northeastern boundary line with Eastern Canada. It arose, like the Northwest Boundary Dispute, from the vagueness of the line laid down in Article II of the Treaty of Versailles (1783). By this article the line was to run from the N.W. corner of Nova Scotia, northward from the source of the Saint Croix River to the dividing range of the Quebec Highlands and thence to the N.W. head of the Connecticut River, and along other lines westward. It was difficult to state exactly where the dividing line of the Highlands lay, although it was clear that Great Britain wished that those Highlands should form a buttress to the fortifications of Quebec. This was accordingly the part of the boundary which caused most trouble. The location of the N.W. head of the Connecticut led to much dispute. The Jay Treaty (1794) settled what was meant by the St. Croix line, but neither the boundary terms in the Treaty of Ghent (1814) nor the decision of the king of the Netherlands (1831) made the other lines clear. The quarrel over the islands in Passamaquoddy Bay was easily settled (1817), and the United States obtained Moose, Frederick, and Dudley islands. The Aroostook War between the inhabitants of New Brunswick and Maine (1838–39) made both the United States and British governments wish for a definite boundary. Accordingly, Lord Ashburton was sent by Great Britain to Washington, and after talks of an informal character with Webster, arrived at a satisfactory solution (August 9, 1842). Great Britain secured the Highlands, and a clear though circuitous route between Quebec and Halifax, while the United States secured seven twelfths of the disputed territory, as well as the right to carry timber down St. John's River. In lieu of territory lost to Maine and Massachusetts, it gained Rouses Point on Lake Champlain.

NORTH-EAST PASSAGE. See Arctic Exploration.

NORTHERN BAPTISTS. See Baptist.

NORTHERN IRELAND, a part of the United Kingdom (q.v.) of Great Britain and Northern Ireland, situated in the N.E. portion of the island of Ireland (q.v.). The administrative area consists of the counties of Antrim, Armagh, Down, Fermanagh, Londonderry, and Tyrone, and the parliamentary boroughs of Belfast and Londonderry (qq.v.). The capital and only large city is Belfast (q.v.). Agriculture is the basic occupation. The leading crops are potatoes (1,073,000 tons in 1952), oats (289,000 tons), and turnips (164,000 tons). The principal industries are the manufacture of linens and other textiles, and shipbuilding. The Belfast shipyards, among the largest in the world, launched merchant vessels with a total gross tonnage of 129,977 in 1952. Educational facilities (1952-53) include 1626 public elementary schools, 123 secondary and technical schools, and Queen's University of Belfast (see Education, National Systems of: *United Kingdom*). Over 60% of the population adheres to Protestantism, one of the cultural bases for the political division from the Republic of Ireland (see Ireland, Republic of), which is predominantly Roman Catholic.

Northern Ireland is represented by twelve members in the British House of Commons, and the executive power is vested in a governor appointed by the British king. A large degree of local autonomy is exercised through its parliament, consisting of a senate and a house of commons, and a cabinet responsible to the Parliament. The local government legislates in all fields save those affecting foreign relations, external trade, and a few governmental concerns, such as coinage, postal service, and trade marks, which are reserved to the British Parliament.

In 1920, when Ireland was granted home rule, six counties of the province of Ulster, northernmost of the four Irish provinces, were given the opportunity to separate politically from the rest of the island and preserve a close relation with Great Britain. Under the Government of Ireland Act of 1920, the six counties became a separate political division, with its own constitution. The Irish Free State (later Eire, and now the Republic of Ireland) did not accept the separation of Northern Ireland as permanent, but Northern Ireland steadily refused to consider a reunion. When, in 1949, Eire withdrew completely from the British Commonwealth of Nations, becoming the Republic of Ireland, the partition of Ireland became a major consideration in both divisions. In the elections in Northern Ireland in spring, 1949, the political party supporting union with the Republic was decisively defeated. On May 17 the British Parliament passed a bill retaining Northern Ireland as a part of the United Kingdom until the local parliament decided otherwise. Area, 5238 sq.m.; pop. (1951 prelim.) 1,370,933.

NORTHERN LIGHT. See AURORA.

NORTHERN RHODESIA. See RHODESIA, NORTHERN.

NORTHERN TERRITORY, a territory of the Commonwealth of Australia, situated in the central and northern part of the island continent. Area, 523,620 square miles; population, exclusive of aborigines, 15,527 (1951 est.). The aborigines number 12,200. The principal town and port is Darwin (pop., about 1500). Agriculture has not been developed chiefly because the climate is unsuitable for Europeans. The white ant is a pest, and mosquitoes and sand flies are troublesome, especially in the wet season. Stock raising and mining are the chief occupations. The grasses of the country are especially nutritious for cattle, horses, sheep, and other stock. Though rich in mineral resources, the deposits are little exploited. In recent years, however, mining activity has begun, gold mining leading in production.

NORTH GERMAN CONFEDERATION, the union of the German states north of the Main R. formed in 1886 under the leadership of Prussia and chiefly through the agency of Prussia's foreign minister, Prince Otto von Bismarck. By this union Prussia sought to consolidate the power it had won in Germany through its defeat of Austria (1866) in the Seven Weeks' War (q.v.). The North German Confederation took the place of the German Bund or Germanic Confederation, the loose union of thirty-nine German states which had been established at the Congress of Vienna (1815) at the end of the Napoleonic Wars. Twenty-two of the German states adhered to the North German Confederation. According to the agreement, each retained its own government, but submitted its military forces to the control of the Confederation; the commander in chief of the combined armies was the king of Prussia. A legislative body was created to administer the Confederation; its president was the king of Prussia, but the duties of the office were performed by a chancellor, who was responsible only to the king.

Alliances were entered into between the North German Confederation and the important states to the south of the Main, namely, the Kingdom of Bavaria, the Grand Duchy of Baden, and the Kingdom of Württemberg, under which these states agreed to place their military forces under command of the king of Prussia in case of war against the Confederation. The North German Confederation was an important step toward the unification of Germany, finally achieved in 1871 at the end of the Franco-Prussian War. After Prussia's victory in this war, the states of the North German Confederation and all the remaining states of Germany were combined to form the German Empire. The constitution of the Confederation was adopted with slight modifications as the constitution of the Empire.

NORTH HOLLAND (Dutch, *Noordholland*), province of the Netherlands, situated between the North Sea and Ijssel Lake. The islands of Texel, Vlieland, and Terschelling, in the West Frisian group, Marken and Urk, in Ijssel Lake, and the former isle of Wieringen, now a part of the mainland, are included in the province. Amsterdam, capital of the Netherlands; Haarlem, capital of the province; Alkmaar and Edam, noted for their cheese markets; and Hilversum (qq.v.) are the principal towns. The terrain is flat and low, some of it being land reclaimed from former lakes. Cattle raising, cheese making (chiefly Edam cheese), and market gardening are the most important occupations. Industrial establishments include gristmills, sawmills, oil refineries, and cement and paper works. With what is now South Holland Province, North Holland formed part of the medieval county of Holland. In the 13th century it became a possession of the counts of Hainaut, but was ceded to Philip the Good of Burgundy in 1433. The county passed from Burgundian to Hapsburg control in 1482. It fell under the authority of the princes of Orange, the present royal family of the Netherlands, in 1572, following a revolt against the Spanish Hapsburgs. Area, 1081 sq.m.; pop. (1951 est.) 1,895,242.

NORTH ISLAND. See NEW ZEALAND.

NORTHMEN, or NORSEMEN, sea rovers from Denmark, Norway, and Sweden, whose adventures and conquests, during the period between the middle of the 8th century and the beginning of the 13th, made them famous in European history. They were also known

Above: A typical vessel of the Northmen.
Right: Northmen at sea (from a painting).

as Vikings. Many of them sought fame and booty in distant lands; strong impulses were given to these expeditions when the more powerful chiefs (kings) at home began to subdue their weaker contemporaries and rivals, and the separate kingdoms (Norway, Denmark, Sweden) began to take definite shape, under such rulers as Harold Fairhair (Haarfager) and Canute.

The Northern sea rovers made their first recorded attack upon England in 787, after which they began to raid along the shores of Frisia, Flanders, and France. During the first half of the next century their depredations were more terrible than ever, especially in Frisia and Flanders, during the periods 834-37 and 845-50. From about the middle of the century bodies of Northmen established themselves in permanent camps at the mouths of the French rivers, and repeatedly ascended them to plunder and slaughter. Three times in quick succession they took Paris, though on a fourth attempt they were repulsed. Alfred drove them from England, but Charles the Simple of France, unable to overcome these dangerous and pertinacious foemen, in 912 turned over to Rollo, one of their chiefs, the duchy of Normandy as a feudal fief, on condition that he would become his man or vassal, and be baptized a Christian. Rollo accepted the terms, and thus acquired the nucleus of the duchy of Normandy. There the Northmen were softened into Normans, a name celebrated in history not only by virtue of the conquest of England by Duke William, but also because of their exploits in Italy, Sicily, and the East. About 852 the Danes began to dispute fiercely with

the Northmen. Seventy years before the acquisition of Normandy, Olaf the White of Norway had founded the Scandinavian (chiefly Danish) kingdom of Dublin, which lasted three centuries or more, while two of his followers created the separate kingdoms of Waterford and Limerick. The Faroe, Orkney, and Shetland islands seem to have been frequently visited by Northmen after 825, and were permanently colonized during the next quarter of a century. Iceland was discovered and colonized by the same people between the middle and end of the century; and from Iceland they ventured still farther w., and made settlements in Greenland, and even visited Vinland in N. America.

As early as 860 the Northmen entered the Mediterranean, and eventually founded kingdoms in lower Italy and Sicily. In 862 the tribes who dwelt s. of Lake Ladoga as far as the Southern Dwina invited three Scandinavian chiefs, brothers, of whom Rurik became the most influential, to come and rule over them. These brothers established themselves at Holmgaard (Novgorod) and laid the foundations of the kingdom of Gardarike, out of which grew the subsequent Russia, that was ruled over by Rurik's descendants down to 1598. After Vladimir introduced Christianity into his dominions in 988, the Scandinavian rulers in Russia surrounded themselves with stout and trusty warriors from the north. From the end of the 10th century the emperors of Constantinople had, till the fall of the city in 1453, a picked bodyguard of Varangians (Norse rovers). The men of the north esteemed it a high honor to have served in this chosen cohort at Myklegaard. After the Norman Conquest of England large numbers of English Northmen made their way to Constantinople and enlisted in the Varangian guard. This guard of the Byzantine emperors, made up of Scandinavian warriors, became famous.

NORTH PLATTE, county seat of Lincoln Co., Nebr., situated between the North and South forks of the Platte R., 280 miles w. of Omaha. Transportation facilities include a railroad and a municipal airport, with regular transcontinental air-line service. North Platte is a railroad division point, with extensive railroad shops, and is the center and shipping point of an irrigated agricultural area producing sugar beets, hay, and livestock. Industrial establishments in North Platte are flour mills, grain elevators, meatpacking plants, chick hatcheries, creameries, and ice plants. The city is the site of a U.S. Weather Bureau Station, and in the vicinity is a State Experimental Farm and a ranch established about 1878 by Col. William F. Cody ("Buffalo Bill"). North Platte was settled in 1867. Pop. (1950) 15,433.

NORTH RIDING. See YORKSHIRE.

NORTH RIVER, name applied to the lower course of the Hudson River.

NORTHROP, JOHN HOWARD (1891-), American biochemist, born in Yonkers, N.Y., and educated at Columbia University. He began his career in 1916 as an assistant in chemistry at the Rockefeller Institute for Medical Research in Princeton, N.J., becoming a permanent member of the Institute in 1924. From 1937 to 1939 he served successively as a lecturer in chemistry at Johns Hopkins and Columbia universities, and in 1939 was appointed Hitchcock professor of chemistry at the University of California. In 1941 he became an official investigator of the National Defense Research Committee. Northrop's most notable contribution to the field of biochemistry was his successful isolation of several enzymes (q.v.) and virus proteins; he further demonstrated that these substances were chemical compounds whose structure and functions could be determined by chemical methods. For this work he shared the 1946 Nobel Prize in chemistry with James Batcheller Sumner and Wendell Meredity Stanley (qq.v.). He is the author of *Crystalline Enzymes* (1939).

NORTH SEA, or GERMAN OCEAN (Lat. *Germanicum Mare,* Ger. *Nord See,* Dan. *Vesterhavet,* "west sea"), that part of the Atlantic Ocean between the east coast of Great Britain and the continent of Europe. The Strait of Dover, with the English Channel, forms the southern communication with the Atlantic. The greatest width of the North Sea is 412 miles; its greatest length is 680 miles; and its area is about 200,000 square miles. A number of large rivers flow into the southern part of the North Sea; the chief of these are the Elbe, Weser, Ems, Rhine (which is joined at its mouth by the Meuse), and Scheldt on the Continent, and the Thames and the Humber in Great Britain. The mean depth of the southern portion is about 100 feet, near the middle it is 250, and in the north 400 feet. Along the coast of Norway there runs a trough, The Norway Deep, with a depth of nearly 1000 feet within 20 miles of the shore and a maximum depth of over 2400 feet at the entrance of the Skagerrak. The Dogger Bank occupies a large portion of the south-central part of the sea, with a depth of 60 to 100 feet, the surrounding depths being 150 to 200 feet. The tides of the North Sea are very irregular, owing to the fact that two tidal waves enter it, one from the north and one from the south.

Rain and fogs occur at all seasons, and the violent northwest storms blowing toward the shoals on the southeast coast make navigation dangerous, especially along the coast of Jutland. Its fisheries provide support for inhabitants of the surrounding countries. By means of the Kiel Canal ships enter the Baltic Sea without making the passage around Jutland.

NORTHUMBERLAND, the northernmost county of England. The coast region and the valleys are cultivated, producing barley, wheat, and vegetables; the western part is largely pastoral. The chief industries are the mining of coal, lead, and zinc, and the manufacture of iron, rope, glass, chemicals, and pottery. There are also salmon fisheries. Newcastle-upon-Tyne, the chief city, is a separate county borough. Among the principal towns are Tynemouth, Wallsend, and Cowpen. Northumberland contains remains of Hadrian's Wall and of Roman military roads and famous battlefields of the Scottish wars. Pop. (1951 est.) 798,175.

NORTHUMBRIA, in Anglo-Saxon England, a kingdom of the Heptarchy established by Ida in 593 out of the two earlier kingdoms of Bernicia and Deira. It grew greatly in power during the reign of Ethelfrid (593-617), became the strongest kingdom in the Heptarchy under Edwin (d. 633), and under Oswald (d. 642) it was the champion of Christianity against pagan Mercia. Its separate existence was brought to an end by Egbert in 827. The name survives in the modern county of Northumberland.

NORTHWEST BOUNDARY DISPUTE, a controversy between the United States and Great Britain concerning the northwest boundary of the United States. The United States commissioners proposed the forty-ninth parallel from the Lake of the Woods to the Rocky Mountains as a continuation of the northern boundary between the United States and Canada. By the convention of 1818 the two governments accepted the proposed boundary line. The proposition of the United States to accept a continuation of that line to the Pacific as a suitable division of the Oregon country between the two claimants was rejected by Great Britain on the ground that it would give the Columbia River to the United States. After fruitless negotiations the United States agreed to accept an arrangement by which the two powers were to occupy the Oregon territory jointly for a period of ten years. During the administration of President Tyler negotiations for the permanent settlement of the dispute were carried on between Secretary of State Calhoun and the British minister Pakenham, who offered to accept the forty-ninth parallel as far as the Columbia River, and from thence onward the Columbia River itself, as the boundary. The government of the United States declined to accept this proposition. The popular opposition of the United States public to the making of any concession gave rise to the political watchword, "Fifty-four forty, or fight". The Democratic Party, in its national platform of 1844, asserted the right of the United States to the whole of Oregon, and won the election partly on this issue. Negotiations were resumed, but as Great Britain offered nothing better than the old terms, they were rejected. The President formally withdrew the proposal and reasserted our "rightful claim to the whole of Oregon". Finally the dispute was settled by a treaty concluded in 1846, by which it was provided that the boundary line should be the forty-ninth parallel to the middle of the channel which separates Vancouver Island from the continent, and thence southerly through the channel, and the Strait of Juan de Fuca to the Pacific Ocean, the navigation of the channel and straits to remain free and open to both parties.

NORTHWESTERN UNIVERSITY, a coeducational, privately controlled institution of higher learning, situated at Chicago and Evanston, Ill., chartered in 1851, and opened for instruction four years later; women were first admitted in 1869. The University is nonsectarian, but a majority of the board of trustees must be members of the Methodist Church. Eight of the twelve divisions of the University are located at Evanston, a suburb 12 miles from Chicago, on a 75-acre campus stretching along the shore of Lake Michigan. They comprise the college of liberal arts (founded 1855), the school of speech (1878), the school of music (1895), the school of commerce (1908), the graduate school (1910), the Medill school of journalism (1921), and school of education (1926), and the technological institute (1939, formerly the school of engineering). The remaining four schools, located on the Chicago campus, are the medical school (1859), the school of law (1859), the dental school (1891), and University College (1932); evening courses of the schools of journalism and commerce are also given at the Chicago branch. Bachelor's, master's, and doctor's degrees are granted. The University has connections with the Garrett Biblical Institute and the Seabury-Western Seminary; both institutions are located in Evanston. In 1953–54 the total enrollment in all branches of the University was 16,486, including 7532 students attending classes full time, and members of the faculty numbered 1024. In the same period the library contained a total of 1,031,000 volumes and the University endowment was 70 million dollars.

NORTH-WEST FRONTIER PROVINCE, province of Pakistan, situated between Afghanistan and Punjab (Pakistan). It is composed of so-called settled areas. Interspersed among these areas are the tribal agencies and territories, integral parts of Pakistan and administered through the governor of the North-West Frontier Province. Physiographically, the province is largely mountainous, containing lofty peaks of the Sulaiman, Hindu Kush, and Himalaya ranges. In the region comprising the Khyber Agency lies the Khyber Pass, famed since remote antiquity as a gateway to India. In addition to the valley of the Indus River, there are the plains of Bannu and Dera Ismail Khan, the latter being one of the hottest districts on the subcontinent of India, and the Vale of Peshawar. Agriculture is made possible through irrigation. Wheat, barley, tobacco, fruits, rice, and cotton are the leading crops. Sheep and poultry farming are also important. Hydroelectric power is being developed for industrial projects and there are important resources of coal, oil, salt, and lead. The inhabitants are Moslems and of predominantly Pathan stock. Peshawar (pop. 114,000) is the capital. Other towns are Dera Ismail Khan, Kohat, Mardan, and Abbottabad.

In 1849, following the second Sikh War, the British seized control of the settled areas and attached them for administrative purposes to Punjab. The settled areas were constituted (1901) a separate province, which became autonomous in 1937. In 1947, after the termination of British paramountcy in India, it acceded to Pakistan. Area of province, about 39,200 sq.m.; area of tribal agencies and territories, about 24,900 sq.m. Pop. of province (1951) 5,864,550; pop. of tribal agencies and territories (1951) 2,642,378.

NORTHWEST PASSAGE, a route for ships from the Atlantic to the Pacific in northern America. The effort to discover a navigable sea route from England to Cathay and India via the ocean to the north of America began with the voyages of the Cabots. Sir John Franklin, whose expedition (1845-48) unknowingly came within 3 miles of the passage, is credited with discovering its course. Roald Amundsen was the first to lead an expedition through the passage (1903–06). See ARCTIC EXPLORATION.

NORTHWEST TERRITORIES, vast area in northern Canada, largely uninhabited and only partially explored, lying north and west of Hudson Bay and Strait, north of the Prairie Provinces, and east of Yukon Territory. Fur production is the chief industry. The Territories were divided in 1920 into three provisional districts, namely, Mackenzie, Keewatin, and Franklin. Area, 1,304,903 sq.m.; pop. (1951) 16,004.

NORTHWEST TERRITORY, in American history, that portion of the national domain lying north of the Ohio River, east of the Mississippi, south of the Great Lakes, and west of Pennsylvania, and embracing territory which constitutes the present States of Ohio, Indiana, Illinois, Michigan, Wisconsin, and part of Minnesota—a total area of about 265,878 square miles. This territory was ceded by Great Britain to the United States of America in 1783. The greater part of it was claimed on the basis of their early charters, by Virginia, New York, Massachusetts, and Connecticut. The other States refused to recognize these claims, and insisted that this territory should belong to the country as a whole. New York ceded her claims in 1781, Virginia hers in 1784, Massachusetts hers in 1785, and Connecticut hers in 1786. All of these colonies, however, reserved for special purposes certain lands from the cession. Thus, Virginia retained in southern Ohio a considerable area, known as the Virginia Military District, and Connecticut retained 3,250,000 acres, known as the Western Reserve, in northern Ohio. On the first of March, 1784, Jefferson reported to Congress a temporary plan of government. His scheme contemplated the division of the territory into new States, divided by lines of latitude two degrees apart, and intersected by two meridians of longitude to be drawn through the mouth of the Kanawha and the falls of the Ohio, and to the new States thus created were to be given the names of Sylvania, Michigania, Cheronesus, Assenisipia, Metropotamia, Illinoia, Saratoga, Washington, Polypotamia, and Pelisipia. These names were soon dropped, although they persisted for some time on the maps. The Ordinance of 1784 was a constitution of government for the Northwest Territory, and provided that there should be formed not less than three nor more than five States, and undertook to define their boundaries. In October, 1787, Gen. Arthur St. Clair, a veteran of the French and Revolutionary wars, was appointed the first governor of the Territory. In July, 1800, the western part of the Territory was constituted into the District of Indiana, with William Henry Harrison as governor and with Vincennes as capital. In January, 1805, Michigan Territory was created, with Gen. William Hull as governor; in February, 1809, the Illinois Territory was organized, with Kaskaskia as its seat of government, and in April, 1836, part of Michigan Territory was organized into the Territory of Wisconsin.

NORTON, CHARLES ELIOT (1827-1908), American author and educator, born in Cambridge, Mass., and educated at Harvard College. In 1846 he traveled to India on business for an Oriental trading firm and on his return trip through Europe he became impressed by the richness of Old World culture; he subsequently came to be known as one of the foremost American interpreters and popularizers of European culture. His first published work was a collection of church hymns (1852), followed by a translation of *The New Life of Dante Alighieri* (1859) and *Notes of Travel and Study in Italy* (1860). During the Civil War, he was an editor for the New England Loyal Publications Society. A frequent contributor to the *Atlantic Monthly,* he was coeditor, with his friend James Russell Lowell, of the *North American Review* from 1864 to 1868, and was one of the founders of *The Nation* in 1865. He was appointed a professor at Harvard University in 1873, and offered the first course in fine arts correlated with the study of cultural, social, and literary history. Six years later he formed the Archeological Institute of America, of which he was president for several years. In 1897 he retired from the Harvard faculty as professor emeritus. His works include *Historical Studies of Church-Building in the Middle Ages* (1880), a prose translation (1891-92) of Dante's *Divine Comedy,* and editions of the *Poems of John Donne* (2 vols., 1895) and the *Poems of Mrs. Anne Bradstreet* (1897).

NORWALK, a city of Fairfield Co., Conn., situated on Long Island Sound, at the mouth of the Norwalk R., 14 miles s.w. of Bridgeport and 41 miles N.E. of New York City. Norwalk is a residential community, a summer vacation resort, and an important manufacturing center. Among its diversified industries are the manufacture of men's hats and shirts, felt goods, woven labels, air compressors, pumps, electric signaling devices, automobile tires, and hardware. Oystering, printing, lithography, and bookbinding also are important. In addition, the city has an extensive retail trade.

The site of the present city was purchased from the Indians in 1640, settled in 1649, and incorporated as a town in 1651. A memorial in the city commemorates Nathan Hale, hero of the American Revolution, who started from Norwalk in September, 1776, on his fateful mission to Long Island. Norwalk was burned by British troops from New York on July 12, 1779. The first derby hat in the U.S. was manufactured at Norwalk in 1850. Norwalk formerly embraced the communities of South Norwalk and Norwalk; in 1913 these were consolidated with East and West Norwalk, Winnipauk, and Rowayton to form the present city of Norwalk. Pop. (1950) 49,460.

NORWAY (Norwegian, *Norge*), a constitutional monarchy in N.W. Europe, occupying the w. and N. portions of the Scandinavian peninsula, and bounded on the N. by the Arctic Ocean, on the N.E. by Finland and the U.S.S.R., on the E. by Sweden, on the s. by the Skagerrak, and on the w. by the North Sea and the Atlantic Ocean. Norway has sovereignty over the archipelago of Svalbard (q.v.) and Jan Mayen Island in the Arctic Ocean, Bouvet Island in the south Atlantic Ocean, Peter I Island in the Antarctic Ocean, and the Norwegian Antarctic Continent Dependency, in the Antarctic Continent. The capital, chief seaport, and largest city of Norway is Oslo (q.v.); other important cities, all seaports, are, in order of population, Bergen, Trondheim, and Stavanger (qq.v.). Administratively, Norway is divided into twenty districts, two being the cities of Oslo and Bergen, and the remainder being the *fylker* ("counties") of Akershus, Aust-Agder, Buskerud, Finnmark, Hedmark, Hordaland, Möre og Romsdal, Nordland, Nörd-Trondelag, Opland, Östfold, Rogaland, Sogn og Fjordane, Sör-Tröndelag, Troms, Telemark, Vest-Agder, and Vestfold. Area, 125,031 sq.m.; pop. (1950) 3,278,546.

Physical Features and Climate. Norway is about 1100 m. long from N.E. to s.w., and has a maximum width of 260 m. North Cape, off the N. coast, is the northernmost point in Europe. Most of Norway is a mountainous plateau, separated from Sweden by a barren wasteland and the Kjölen Mts. The plateau, about 1600 ft. above sea level, is intersected in the E. by deep valleys and in the w. by deep fiords and bays. From N. to s. high mountain ridges traverse the country, dividing the area into smaller plateaus, called *fjelds.* More than 67% of Norway is covered by mountains, their tops generally rounded by glacial action. In the extreme N. is a mountain district with peaks rising to more than 6000 ft. Other mountain masses, interspersed with *fjelds* and glacier fields, extend to the s. until, in w. central Norway, the great mountain plateau called the *Dovrefjeld* begins. The Dovre, on which are peaks rising over 7500 ft., extends s. until it terminates in the *Jostedalsbreen,* a glacier which is the largest ice field in Europe. To the N. of the glacier are the Jötunheim Mts. containing *Galdhöpiggen* (8097 ft.), the highest mountain in Norway. The high mountain ridges continue to the s., gradually decreasing in height to the comparatively low s. coast. In the s.e. and continuing to e. central Norway is a belt of dense woodland, rising on the mountain slopes to a height of about 1500 ft. Forests cover about 24% of the total land area of the country.

Along the w. coast the mountains descend sharply into the ocean. The Norwegian coast, measuring about 12,000 m., is noted for the scenic beauty of its fiords and the many islands (estimated at about 150,000) which fringe it. The fiords (q.v.) extend far into the interior; the largest and deepest are Sogne Fiord, Hardanger Fiord, and Nord Fiord. Of the coastal islands, the Lofoten and the Vesteraalen, off the n.w. coast, are the largest, and are famous as fishing bases.

Most Norwegian rivers are in the lower eastern part of the country. Waterfalls and rapids are frequent. A few of the rivers have large basins, notably that of the principal river, the Glomma (16,000 sq.m.), of the Drammenselv (6600 sq.m.), and of the Skienselv (4250 sq.m.). The highlands and valleys contain numerous lakes, tarns, and pools, most of them narrow and long; the largest lake is Lake Mjösen (150 sq.m.) in s.e. Norway. Because of the fiords, mountains, rapids, lakes, and glaciers, Norway is one of the most scenically magnificent countries in the world. Only about 3% of the land is arable and under cultivation.

Norway extends about 300 m. into the Arctic zone, and the northernmost part of the country is included in the range of the so-called midnight sun; true night occurs only from about the beginning of August to mid-May. The Norwegian climate is from 12.6° to 21°F. warmer than indicated by the latitude because of the moderating influence of the Gulf Stream, which flows northward along the w. coast. The e. interior, where temperatures may drop to —40°F. in winter, is the least habitable portion of the country. The s.e. region has a mean annual temperature of from 44° to 31°F., and the temperature at Oslo in July averages about 61°F. The w. coast receives the greatest amount of annual rainfall, from 50 to over 80 inches. Winter rain and summer fog are common, and in the extreme n.w. snow may fall in any month.

Production and Commerce. Despite the small area of arable land, found in the deep valleys and around fiords and lakes, agriculture is a major activity; less than 50% of the Norwegian population lives in cities. The principal crops (with production figures in metric tons for 1952) include hay (2,961,768), potatoes (1,187,491), oats (161,161), barley (147,911), and wheat (39,586). Horses, cattle (for meat and dairy products), sheep, goats, swine, and poultry are raised. Lumbering (chiefly spruce and pine) and the manufacture of wood products, such as wood pulp and paper, are major Norwegian industries. A second major industry is fishing, with a catch in 1952 valued at about $68,671,300, mainly herring and cod.

Norwegian Official Photo

View of Oslo, largest city in Norway

Swedish Trav. Info. Bur.; Nor. Off. Photo

Norway is noted for its scenic fiords, which are surrounded by snow-capped mountains.

Norway produces almost half the world supply of whale oil. Other major activities are the manufacture of machinery and food products, canning, and the electrochemical and electrometallurgical industries. The principal minerals mined are iron, copper, pyrites, zinc, lead, and nickel. Because of its available water power, Norway has an annual production of electricity estimated at about eighty billion kilowatt hours. Manufacturing establishments numbered more than 6300 in 1951, employing about 229,000 workers. Among the principal industrial products are metal products, transport equipment, rubber goods, cod-liver oil, furniture, wood, boxes, and textiles. Paper and pulp products account for about 25% of Norwegian exports. In 1952 the total exports were valued at about $564,859,000; the imports were valued at approximately $871,-817,900.

People, Language, and Religion. The Norwegians are Teutons, predominantly blond and blue-eyed. Their average height, about 5 ft. 8 in., is one of the tallest in Europe. The Norwegian language (q.v.), akin to Swedish and Danish, is written in two idioms, both of which are accepted as official. The Evangelical Lutheran Church is endowed by the state; all religions are tolerated, although Jesuits are not permitted to enter Norway. The clergy, appointed by the king, are given a dominant part in the Norwegian education system, one of the finest in Europe (see EDUCATION, NATIONAL SYSTEMS OF: *Scandinavian Countries*).

Communications. In 1952 Norway had about 28,700 m. of highways and roads, of which about 5% are surfaced. The length of railway tracks in 1953 was 2777 m., of which 51 m. were privately owned, the remainder being owned and operated by the government. Coastal waterways are of great importance. The former national air line, Det Norske Luftfartselskap (D.N.L.), operated on domestic routes and regular flights to all parts of Europe, to South America, and to the United States. In 1946 D.N.L. united with the Swedish and Danish national air lines to form the Scandinavian Airline System (S.A.S.), which controls the entire operational system.

Government. Under the Norwegian constitution promulgated in 1814 and amended thereafter, Norway is a hereditary monarchy, though no peerage exists. The legislative power lies with the Storting, a body of 150 members elected every four years by universal suffrage. The Storting itself is divided by election into the Lagting, of 38 members, and the Odelsting, the remainder. Laws originate in the Odelsting, go from there to the Lagting, and, in case of disagreement, are deliberated in a joint session. The executive power is given to the king who may veto any legislative act twice; any act passed by three different Stortings becomes law despite royal veto. The cabinet, responsible to the Storting and called the Statsraad, is composed of the prime minister and at least seven other ministers.

Norway has one of the most comprehensive programs of social legislation in Europe, including old-age pensions, poor relief, public housing, health insurance, workmen's compensation, and family allowances. The Norwegian labor code provides disability insurance, vacations, arbitration for management-labor disputes, and compulsory vacations, in addition to other benefits.

History. According to archeological research Norway was inhabited during the Stone Age, before 5000 B.C., by a non-Aryan aboriginal population related to the Finns. Most of these aborigines were driven from the region during the 2nd millennium B.C. by successive migrations of Teutonic tribes

coming, probably, across the Skagerrak from Jutland and from Sweden by land. The Teutons settled around the large lakes and along the coasts. Mountains and fiords formed natural barriers around the various settlements which, remote from each other and almost inaccessible by land, became independent, each recognizing only the authority of its chief. In time social life in the separate settlements came to be headed by an aristocracy and, eventually, by petty kings. By the time of the first historical records of Scandinavia, about the 8th century A.D., approximately twenty-nine small kingdoms, called *fylker*, existed in Norway.

Inevitably the kings turned their attention to the sea, the easiest way of communication with the outside world. Ships of war were built and sent on raiding expeditions, initiating the era of the so-called Vikings (q.v.); see also NORTHMEN. The sea rovers were colonizers and explorers as well as plunderers. They established (about 823) a kingdom in Ireland, and during the 9th century colonized the Hebrides, Faeroes, Orkneys, Shetlands, and the Isle of Man. They took possession of Iceland in 874, and about a century later colonized Greenland, from which, about 1000, Leif Ericson set sail on the first voyage to the American coast. The Norwegian Vikings extended their expeditions to Russia, Scotland, England, Spain, France, Italy, and Greece; their fleets visited Rome and Constantinople, and they sailed to Jerusalem and the Orient. Everywhere they became famous as great warriors, and in some cases they settled in foreign countries, notably in France, where Vikings became the ancestors of the Normans. Their complicated religious mythology (see SCANDINAVIAN MYTHOLOGY), in which brave deeds in battle were extolled and Valhalla (Heaven) was entered by warriors killed in combat, symbolized their way of life (see DANISH LITERATURE).

In the 9th century the first successful attempt to create a united Norwegian kingdom was made by the king of a *fylke* near Vestfold. During several generations this royal family acquired all the country s. of the Dovrefjeld through inheritance, marriage, and conquest. Harold I (q.v), called Haarfager ("Fairhaired"), who succeeded to the throne of this kingdom in 860, established his supremacy over all Norway in 872. Norway's unification was short-lived; at Harold's death in 933 about twenty of his sons divided Norway, with Eric Bloodaxe as

Swedish Trav. Info. Bur.

The City of Bergen, Norway

overking. Dissensions and wars among the heirs disrupted the temporary unity. Moreover, many of the petty rulers refused to surrender their independence, and warred continually against the descendants of Harold. In addition to the domestic struggles, both Denmark and Sweden were attempting to acquire Norwegian territory.

In 995 Olaf I, called Tryggvesson, a great-grandson of Harold Haarfager, became king. Olaf had lived in England before his accession and had there been converted to Christianity. He ascended the throne with the firm purpose of forcing Christianity on Norway and was partially successful. Several years after his accession he quarreled with King Sweyn of Denmark; in a naval battle at Svöld, Olaf was defeated by the combined Danish and Swedish fleets, supported by disaffected Norwegian chiefs. Olaf was killed in the battle, and Norway was divided by the coalition. After a short period of disorder the country was reunited by Olaf II Haraldsson (later canonized), who drove out the foreigners and made himself king of Norway in 1016. He continued the religious work of his predecessor, using the sword against all

who refused to be baptized. By about 1025 Olaf was more powerful than any previous Norwegian king had been. He aroused the enmity of the powerful nobles, who, together with the Danish king Canute the Great, in 1028 drove Olaf into exile in Russia.

On the death of Canute in 1035, Olaf's son, Magnus I, known as the Good, was called from Russia by partisans of his father. He became king and then united Denmark and Norway under his rule. For the next three centuries a succession of native kings ruled Norway. Although internal confusion and wars between rival claimants to the throne disrupted the country intermittently, Norway began to emerge as a united nation, enjoying a comparative prosperity brought by its great trading fleets. The Norwegians had become strongly Christian and a powerful clergy was one of the strongest influences in the kingdom. In 1046 Magnus made his uncle Harold Haardrade coruler, and at the death of Magnus one year later, Harold became king. He was killed while participating in the invasion of England in 1066. The last king of the line of Harold Haardrade was Sigurd I, called the Crusader, whose

Norwegian Official Photo

Skiers on a mountain slope at Stalheim, western Norway

rule lasted from 1103 until his death in 1130.

Dynastic conflict followed the death of Sigurd. Of the many later kings, the most notable was Sverre Sigurdsson, king from 1184 to 1202. A statesman of great ability, Sverre built a strong monarchy, and considerably weakened the power of the clergy and the great nobles. Under Haakon IV (ruled 1217-63) Norway reached the apex of its medieval prosperity and political and cultural power. Iceland was completely subjugated and a written Norwegian literature and law code were considerably developed in the 13th century. The royal authority was greatly increased by Haakon and his son, Magnus VI, called Lagaböter ("Law Mender"). The landed aristocracy was virtually crushed and even the title of *lendermaend*, or baron, was abolished in 1308 by Haakon V. The old noble families gradually descended to the economic status of well-to-do peasants, and for the most part the Norwegian people became a nation of peasants. Commercial activity declined because of the increasing power of the Hanseatic League (q.v.) of N. German cities. The death of Haakon V in 1319, without male heirs,

gave the throne to Magnus Eriksson of Sweden, the three-year-old son of Haakon's daughter. In 1343 Magnus was succeeded by his son, Haakon VI, and the latter's son, Olaf V (Olaf II of Denmark), became the ruler of both Scandinavian kingdoms after the death of his father in 1380. The young king (then ten years old) exercised only nominal rule, the power being in the hands of his mother, Margaret (q.v.), the only child of Waldemar IV, King of Denmark. Olaf died without heirs in 1387 and was succeeded by his mother as ruler of Norway and Denmark and, in 1389, of Sweden also. In order to obtain German support against the dukes of Mecklenburg, who claimed the Swedish throne, Margaret had her grandnephew, Eric of Pomerania, elected nominal ruler. By the Union of Kalmar in 1397, the three kingdoms were made a single administrative unit, and for the next four centuries Norway was ruled by Denmark.

Norwegian prosperity and culture declined steadily after the Union. Moreover, the plague, called the Black Death, swept Norway in the 14th century, exhausting the country and decimating the population. Swe-

Norwegian Official Photos

NORWEGIAN INDUSTRY

Above: A whale taken off the northern Norwegian coast, of great commercial importance. Right: Wood-pulp factory at Sarpsborg. Below: Thousands of logs floating in a lake.

den and Denmark were larger and wealthier than Norway, and the kings, for the most part, ruled solely in the interest of Sweden or Denmark. Sweden left the Union in 1523 and during the subsequent three centuries Norway, reduced almost to a Danish province, remained stagnant under the tyranny of Danish officials.

The Napoleonic Wars at the beginning of the 19th century finally occasioned the end of the Union. After the defeat of Napoleon in 1814, Denmark, an ally of France, was compelled to sign the Treaty of Kiel, ceding Norway to Sweden. The Norwegians, however, disavowed the Treaty of Kiel. They declared themselves an independent kingdom, drew up a liberal constitution, and offered the crown to the Danish crown prince Christian Frederick. The Norwegian move was disapproved by the European powers, and, at the head of an army, Marshal Jean Bernadotte (later Charles XIV of Sweden) persuaded Norway to accept the Treaty of Kiel. In return for this acceptance, Norway was allowed to retain the newly promulgated constitution. By the Act of Union of 1815, Norway was given its own army, navy, customs, and legislature, and permitted full liberty and independence within its own boundaries.

The Norwegian Storting was chiefly occupied, in the period after 1814, in stabilizing and improving the financial condition of Norway and in implementing and guarding her newly won independence. Despite the bitter opposition of Charles XIV, an autocratic monarch, the Norwegian legislature passed a law in 1821 abolishing the Danish-created peerage, a vestige of the onerous Danish rule. The Storting held that the true Norwegian nobility were the peasant descendants of the medieval barons. Norwegian nationalism increased, and the movement for greater independence was headed by the Peasant Party, pre-eminent in the Storting. During the post-Union period, the Storting complained that Swedish treatment of Norway was not totally consistent with the spirit of the Act of Union and with the status of Norway as a sovereign state. At length, in 1839, Charles XIV appointed a joint committee of Swedes and Norwegians to revise the wording of the Act of Union. Charles died in 1844, before the committee submitted its report. The new Swedish king, Oscar I, more liberal than his father, admitted the justice of many Norwegian claims and made himself popular by granting Nor-

way a national flag for its navy, though the flag bore the symbol of union with Sweden.

The liberal movement in Norwegian politics, accompanying the surge of nationalism, became more pronounced after the revolutions of 1848 in the major countries of Europe. Political nationalism was bolstered by intellectual and cultural nationalism. The poet Henrik Wergeland (q.v.) became the leader of the nationalistic Young Norway Party. Norwegian folk songs were collected and arranged, becoming extremely popular. Norwegian dictionaries, histories, and grammars were compiled. The literary renaissance, designed to eliminate the lingering Danish culture, included such writers as Henrik Ibsen, Jonas Lie, and Björnstierne Björnson. In their wake came writers such as Knut Hamsun and Sigrid Undset, and the musicians Ole Bull and Edvard Grieg. See NORWEGIAN LANGUAGE; NORWEGIAN LITERATURE; NORWEGIAN MUSIC.

As their national policy, the Norwegians maintained their refusal to permit closer relations with Sweden than those provided by the Act of Union. When, in 1860, Sweden began to propose revisions in the Act designed to give the ruling country additional powers, the two greatest Norwegian political parties, the Lawyers Party and Peasant Party, combined to form the Venstre ("Left") Party, and blocked the revisions. Another significant controversy between the two countries was occasioned by renewed Swedish attempts at constitutional revision, including establishment of the royal right to dissolve the Storting. Led by Johan Sverdrup, president of the Storting, the Norwegian legislature and Oscar II, then king of Sweden, engaged in a long struggle. Oscar was forced to yield in 1884. Norwegian policy then centered on demands for a separate consular service and a Norwegian flag for the merchant marine without the symbol of Union. The flag was approved by Sweden in 1899, but Sweden balked at the demand for a consular service. In 1905, after protracted negotiations, the Norwegian ministry then in office resigned and refused Oscar's request that they withdraw their resignations. As a result the Storting declared that, because the Swedish king had been unable to form a new government, the constitutional royal power had ceased to function and Oscar was no longer ruler of Norway. Norway was proclaimed an independent kingdom and during a plebiscite in August, 1905, the Norwegian people voted overwhelmingly for separation from Sweden. The Swedish Riksdag ratified the separation in October. A month later the Norwegian crown was accepted by Prince Charles of Denmark, who became Haakon VII of Norway.

The Norwegian government, dominated by ministers with liberal politics, became one of the most advanced in Europe in matters of social legislation, education, and political liberties. In 1907 Norwegian women became the first in Europe to be given the voting franchise. Unemployment insurance benefits, old-age pensions, and liberal laws concerning divorce and illegitimacy made Norway famous for its advanced social policies.

After the beginning of World War I in 1914 the sovereigns of Sweden, Norway, and Denmark agreed to maintain the neutrality of the Scandinavian countries and to co-operate for their mutual interest. The policy of neutrality and friendship thus established continued to be joint policy after the war. The world economic depression which began in 1929 affected Norway considerably because of its dependence on commerce, but the crisis was less crucial than it was in larger countries such as the United States and Great Britain. The Socialist Party was elected to power in 1935 and continued the policies of moderation and political liberalism which had dominated Norwegian politics since 1905. Conditions during the late 1930's were economically satisfactory; unemployment was at a minimum, Norwegian national wealth increased, and considerable industrial progress was made.

Norway maintained its traditional neutrality when World War II began in 1939. Despite Norwegian sympathy for Finland during the Russo-Finnish phase of the conflict, Norway abstained from voting in the League of Nations assembly which expelled the U.S.S.R. in December, 1939, and it rejected, in 1940, an Anglo-French demand for transit of troops to aid Finland. German sinking of Norwegian ships and maritime warfare along the Norwegian coast made neutrality increasingly difficult. On April 8, 1940, Great Britain and France announced that they had mined Norwegian territorial waters to prevent shipments of iron ore to Germany. The strong Norwegian protest, however, was deprived of force by the complete surprise of a German invasion of Norway on the night of April 8-9. Aided by "fifth column" elements, made up of German soldiers disguised as tourists, the Norwegian Nazi Party, and

disloyal Norwegian army officers, the Germans attacked all important ports. Major Vidkun Quisling (q.v.), head of the Norwegian Nazi Party, proclaimed himself head of the Norwegian government on April 9. King Haakon and his cabinet, after an unsuccessful attempt to direct resistance to the German army, withdrew to England in June. For five years thereafter, London was the seat of the Norwegian government-in-exile. Norwegian political leaders in Norway refused to co-operate in any way with Josef Terboven, the German commissioner for Norway. On Sept. 25, 1940, Terboven dissolved all political parties except the Nazi Party, set up a so-called National Council composed of Norwegian Nazis and their sympathizers, and announced the abolition of the monarchy and the Storting. Quisling, as head of the government, then began to employ the methods of Nazi terrorism, such as secret police, concentration camps, massacres of Jews, censorship, and mass arrests and executions. These repressive measures did not decrease the mass resistance of the great majority of the Norwegian people.

Large-scale sabotage and espionage by Norwegians on behalf of the Allies, and the increasing resistance to Quisling were met by increasing Nazi terrorism. Martial law was proclaimed by Quisling in September, 1941. Food supplies decreased and strict rationing of the small supply available was instituted. The leaders of the resistance movement in Norway co-operated closely with the government in London, under Foreign Minister Trygve Lie (q.v.), preparing for eventual liberation. During the Allied advance on the European continent in early 1945, the German forces in Norway held out longer than those in other Nazi-occupied countries, but finally surrendered on May 8, 1945. King Haakon returned to Norway on June 7. To punish traitors, the death penalty, abolished in Norway in 1876, was restored. Terboven and other leading Nazis killed themselves, and Quisling was tried and executed for treason. Over 15,000 Norwegians were arrested and punished for collaboration with Germany.

The government-in-exile resigned after temporary order was established. In the general elections of October, 1945, the Labor Party won a majority of votes, and a Labor cabinet was headed by Einar Gerhardsen. The new government was faced with a tremendous task of rehabilitation. As a result of efficient economic planning on the part of the

Norwegian Official Photo

In Norway: The Borgund Stave church, a wooden structure dating from about 1150.

government and the co-operation of the Norwegian people, economic conditions improved steadily in the postwar period.

Norway became a charter member of the United Nations in 1945. In 1947 the kingdom became a participant in the American European Recovery Program (q.v.). In April, 1949, the government signed the North Atlantic Treaty (q.v.). This action, representing abandonment of Norway's traditional neutrality, was approved wholeheartedly by the Norwegian people in general elections held on Oct. 10. The Labor Party increased its parliamentary majority and the Communists, who alone had opposed the North Atlantic alliance, lost all 11 of their seats.

In January, 1950, Norway recognized Communist China. Problems of reconstruction and defense were paramount during 1951. Inflationary pressures, due largely to the excess of imports over exports, caused serious dislocations in the economy. However, E.R.P. dollar aid, which totaled more than $400 million by 1951, and the earnings of the merchant marine lessened the effects of the crisis.

On Nov. 19 Premier Gerhardsen resigned for "personal reasons". He was succeeded by Oscar Torp, a Laborite with 12 years experience in various cabinet posts. Upon taking office the new premier announced that basic domestic and foreign policies would remain unchanged.

During 1952 Norway continued its firm support of the policies of the western democracies. It agreed (February) to abide by the U.S. embargo on shipment of strategic materials to the Soviet bloc of states. The tempo of defense preparations was sharply increased in April, and in June the government disclosed that the armed forces would total 250,000 trained and equipped men within two years. In a general election held in October, 1953, the Labor Party retained its absolute Parliamentary majority. A combination of adverse developments, notably reduced merchant-marine earnings and declining world-market prices for timber, wood pulp, and paper, caused a serious foreign-trade deficit in 1953. Industrial activity remained on a high level, however, and the government launched a four-year program designed to improve social conditions and strengthen the economy.

On Oct. 23, 1954, Norway and the other North Atlantic Treaty Organization powers signed a protocol to the treaty granting membership in N.A.T.O. to West Germany. The protocol was one of several accords providing for West German participation in the Western defense system.

Einar Gerhardsen resumed the premiership on Jan. 14, 1955, following the resignation of Oscar Torp for "personal reasons".

NORWEGIAN ELKHOUND or **ELKHOUND**, a sporting or hunting dog that originated in Norway over six thousand years ago. The breed is noted for its ability to hunt big game, including bear, elk, lynx, mountain lion, and raccoon. Its principal use in Norway today is to hunt elk; it is also frequently employed there as a draft animal. The dog is also greatly valued in Norway and in other countries as a pet with unusual intelligence, friendliness, loyalty, and trustworthiness. The Norwegian elkhound is a medium-sized dog, with a short, compact, strongly built body. The male is about twenty inches high at the shoulder, the bitch about eighteen inches; the dog weighs about forty-five pounds. It has a short head; pointed ears; brown eyes; a powerful neck; a broad and deep chest; straight legs; a thick, fairly smooth coat, gray in color; and a short, curled tail that is carried high.

NORWEGIAN LANGUAGE, the language of the people inhabiting Norway and the Danish Faeroe Islands. It belongs to the North or Scandinavian branch of the Teutonic or Germanic subfamily of the Indo-European languages (q.v.), and is thus closely related to Icelandic, Danish, and Swedish. See DANISH LANGUAGE; SWEDISH LANGUAGE. Old Norwegian, a dead language which was the parent of the modern tongue, was spoken not only in Norway and the Faeroe Islands, but also in parts of western Sweden, Ireland, northern Scotland, the Hebrides, and the Shetland and Orkney islands. It gave way to modern Norwegian after the 12th century. During the period from about 1350 to 1530, Norwegian was strongly influenced first by Swedish and later by Danish. By about 1600, two main dialect groups had emerged: the Eastern, including the Gudbrandsdal and the Trondheim dialects, which resemble Swedish; and the Western, including the Hardanger, Voss, Sogn, and Sætersdal dialects, which are close to Icelandic. Another subdivision of West Norwegian resembles Danish.

After the Norwegians lost their independence in 1397 under the terms of the Union of Kalmar (see KALMAR), Danish was substituted for Norwegian in literature and public business. The Norwegian dialects continued in use, however, as the language of social intercourse and of folk literature in the country districts and among the working and middle classes of the towns. By the beginning of the 19th century, Danish had become the language of upper-class society, and during the 19th century the upper classes, particularly in the towns, developed a spoken language called "Dano-Norwegian", containing a large body of Norwegian words and a characteristically Norwegian construction and intonation. Although pure Danish was used in church services and in the theater until the end of the 19th century, Dano-Norwegian was officially recognized in 1887 as the language taught for reading in the secondary schools. In 1907, 1917, and 1938, changes from the Danish were introduced into the orthography of the language so as to indicate important characteristics of Norwegian pronunciation. Dano-Norwegian is the language of such modern Norwegian literary figures as the poet and dramatist Henrik Ibsen.

A movement to create and adopt a new national language, based on surviving indigenous Norwegian dialects and free of danicisms, was begun in the mid-19th century by the Norwegian philologist Ivar Andreas Aasen (1813–96). The movement gained popular support, and the new language,

called *Landsmaal* (Nor., "national language"), has become an important secondary language in the school system, in literature, and in government. Landsmaal, based on the country dialects, is rooted in Old Norse through Old Norwegian, and contains a number of loan words from Old English, Old French, and Low and High German.

NORWEGIAN LITERATURE, the literature of the Norwegian people, dating from ancient runic inscriptions of about 300 A.D., and written at first in the Old Norse language, and then, from about the end of the 14th century, in the Dano-Norwegian language known as *Riksmaal,* and also, from about 1850, in the form of Norwegian known as *Landsmaal* ("national language"), which is a synthesis of Norwegian peasant dialects and is related to Old Norse; see NORWEGIAN LANGUAGE. Norwegian literature may be divided into five principal periods, as described below. For further information see also separate articles on authors whose names are not followed by birth and death dates.

FROM THE BEGINNING TO ABOUT 1400. The best of Old Norse literature was that written by Icelandic writers (see ICELANDIC LITERATURE), many of whom, however, lived for considerable periods in Norway. Thus Icelandic literature derived from Norway the material for many of its works, particularly the *Poetic Edda* or *Elder Edda* (see EDDA), the famous Icelandic collection of ballads and lays. The earliest known specimens of Norwegian writing, a number of 4th-century runic inscriptions, antedated Icelandic literature. The earliest known Norwegian writer

Norwegian elkhound

Norwegian Official Photo

Henrik Ibsen

of importance was the scald (q.v.) or court poet Bragi (about 800-50), author of the poem *Ragnars-drápa;* it has come down as part of the *Prose Edda* or *Younger Edda* by the Icelandic author Snorri Sturluson (see SNORRI). Among other important Norwegian poets of the medieval period are Thjodolf of Hvin (about 855-930), author of the *Haustlöng,* fragments of which, contained also in the *Younger Edda,* are extant; Thornbjörn Hornklofi *(Glymdrapa);* and Eyvind Finnson *(Hakonarmal).* From the end of the 12th to the 15th century the most important literature in Norway was written in prose. The best-known works of this period, most of which were anonymous translations and adaptations of tales and epics from chivalric and Biblical sources, include the *Thidreks Saga* (about 1250), the story of the Ostrogothic leader Dietrich of Bern (Theodoric the Great); the *Karla Magnús Saga* (13th century), the story of Charlemagne; *Barlaams Saga ok Josaphats* (13th century), a version of the Biblical tale of Barlaam and Josaphat; and the *Konungs Skugg-sjá* or *Speculum Regale* (late 12th century), in which a king gives his son advice on conduct and which is valuable as a source of information on life and manners in medieval Norway.

THE DANISH PERIOD (from about 1400 to 1814). One historical event determined the entire course of Norwegian literature during this period: the Union of Kalmar (see NORWAY: *History*) in 1397, by which Norway, Sweden, and Denmark were united under one ruler. In this union the hegemony belonged to Denmark. Under Danish control Norway was little more than a Danish province; Danish became the official language of Norway, and Norwegian literature was, until 1814, when Norway became free of Danish control, a branch of Danish literature (q.v.).

Some of the most important figures in the Danish literature of these years were Norwegian-born. Among these writers were the great Ludvig Holberg, the father of Danish drama; Christian Braumann Tullin (1728-65), the nature poet; and Johan Herman Wessel (1742-85), the dramatist and poet. During this period, however, Norwegian poets who wrote on native Norwegian themes were not lacking; they include Peter Dass, author of many secular and religious poems, including *Nordlands Trompet,* written for the common people; and Edvard Storm (1749-94), who wrote ballads and songs in Norwegian dialect. The writings of these and other Norwegian authors foreshadowed an important step taken in 1772 to encourage the growth of a national literature in Norway, the formation of the *Norske Selskab* ("Norwegian Society"), which had as its aim the arousing of interest in Norwegian life and the stimulation of a literature based on that life. Among the adherents to the organization were Wessel; Claus Frimann (1746-1829); Claus Fasting (1746-91), noted for his criticism and his epigrams; the playwright Enevold Falsen (1755-1808); and Johan Nordal Brun (1745-1816), the author of many patriotic Norwegian songs.

THE NATIONALIST PERIOD (from 1814 to 1871). The modern national literature of Norway began with the great development of national consciousness produced in Norway by its political separation from Denmark in 1814 by the Treaty of Kiel. Although Norway remained united to Sweden, it was permitted its own political institutions, and developed during the course of the 19th century a spirit of independence which resulted in its separation from Sweden in 1905 and the formation of the independent kingdom of Norway. Under the impact of these events Norwegian literature developed into one of the important modern European literatures.

Among the outstanding writers early in the period were Henrik Anker Bjerregaard (1792-1842), author of the poem *Sons of Norway* (1820), the national anthem of Norway for fifty years; Conrad Nicolai Schwach (1793-1860); and Mauritz Christopher Hansen (1794-1842), noted for his tales of peasant life. The first half of the 19th century, however, was dominated by the literary controversy between two schools of Norwegian literature. One favored the writing of purely national literature; its principal proponent was Henrik Wergeland, the first great poet of modern Norway, author of the long dramatic poem *The Creation, Man, and Messiah* (1830). The opposing so-called internationalist school, which favored the development of a Norwegian culture in harmony with that of Europe, especially Denmark, was led by the poet and critic Johan Sebastian Welhaven; among his works are *Henrik Wergeland's Poetic Art and Poetry* (1832, a pamphlet attacking Wergeland's poetry as provincial and overemotional), the sonnet-cycle *Norway's Twilight* (1834), and the poem *The English Pilot* (1844), generally considered his best work. The principles of the latter school, which, while not neglecting Norwegian life, sought to interpret it in terms of general ideas current in the culture of the world outside, continued to prevail in later Norwegian literature. One of the important early writers who exemplified the international point of view was Andreas Munch (1811-84), particularly in his novel *The Solitary* (1846). The universal problem of freeing women from traditional social and economic restrictions, which was destined to be a theme for much important later Norwegian literature, formed, in the middle of the 19th century, the subject matter for the realistic novels of Camilla Collet (1813-95), particularly in her work *The Governor's Daughters* (1855). Simultaneously with the stressing of a universal rather than a parochial point of view, two factors stimulated the writing of a purely national Norwegian literature. They were, first, an interest in Norwegian folk tales and poetry, as marked by the publication of *Norske Folke-Eventyr* ("Norwegian Popular Tales", 1841-44) by Peter Christen Asbjörnsen and Jörgen Moe, and of the collection *Norwegian Folk Songs* (1853) by Magnus Brostrup Landstad (1802-80). The second stimulus was the writing by Ivar Aasen of a grammar (1848) and a dictionary (1850) of a synthesis of peasant dialects

known as Landsmaal, which he intended to be used in place of the Riksmaal or Dano-Norwegian language. Although most subsequent Norwegian literature continued to be written in Riksmaal, many important Norwegian authors employed Landsmaal, and after the middle of the 19th century its use became more and more general in Norway for both practical and literary purposes.

REALISTIC AND NATURALIST PERIOD (from 1871 to 1900). Modern Norwegian literature reached one of its highest points of development in the last third of the 19th century. The realistic movement in Norway, as in the other Scandinavian countries, was directly inspired by the writings of the great Danish critic Georg Brandes, who through the medium of literary criticism realistically examined the social and economic forces of the time and attacked the social hypocrisies and traditions that stood in the way of the fullest development of the individual. The four outstanding Norwegian realistic writers whose works dominated the 1870's and 1880's in Norway were the dramatist Henrik Ibsen; the dramatist and novelist Björnstjerne Björnson (see DRAMA: *Norwegian Drama*); and the novelists Jonas Lie (1833-1909), among whose works are *The Pilot and His*

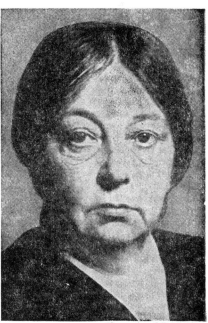

Norwegian Official Photo
Sigrid Undset

Norwegian Official Photo

Edvard Grieg, Norwegian composer

Wife (1874), *Go Ahead!* (1882), and *Matrimonial Life* (1887), and Alexander Lange Kielland (1849-1906), whose works include *Garmann and Worse* (1180) and *Snow* (1886). Among other important Norwegian novels of the 1870's and 1880's are *Tora Trondal* (1879) by Kristian Elster (1841-81), *Dangerous People* (1881) by Amalie Skram (1847-1905), *Peasant Students* (1883) written in Landsmaal by Arne Garborg, and *Town and Harbour Beflagged* (1884) by Björnson. Norwegian fiction of the 1890's was dominated by the works of Knut Hamsun. Among his writings of this decade are the world-famous novels *Hunger* (1890) and *Pan* (1894). Another important novelist whose first works appeared at this time was Hans Ernst Kinck (1865-1926), among whose writings are *Soughing* (1896) and *The Adder* (1898). The last decade of the 19th century was marked also by a revival in Norwegian poetry. Among the notable poets who flourished at the turn of the century was Garborg (*The Hill Innocent*, 1895, written in Landsmaal); Nils Collett Vogt (1864-1937), among whose works are *From Spring to Autumn* (1894) and *The Costly Bread* (1900); Vilhelm Krag, the poet of southern Norway (*Poems*, 1891); and Sigbjörn Obstfelder (1866-1900), whose poetry is remarkable for its delicate musical effects (*Posthumous Writings*, 1903).

THE TWENTIETH CENTURY. The 20th century in Norwegian literature was marked by many diverse tendencies, particularly regionalism, i.e., the description of life in the numerous types of small communities in Norway, particularly of peasant and fishing regions; and a concern with life in various periods of Norwegian history. The following is an alphabetical list of important Norwegian writers of the 20th century, together with the titles of one or more of their characteristic works.

Novelists: Trygve Andersen (1866-1920), author of *Towards Night* (1900) and other novels; Johan Bojer, author of *The Power of a Lie* (1908), *The Great Hunger* (1916), and *Last of the Vikings* (1921); Sigurd Christiansen (1891-   ), whose principal novel is *Two Living and One Dead* (1931); Olav Duun (1876-1939), among whose works is the series of short novels *The People of Juvik* (6 vols., 1918-23, written in Landsmaal); Peter Egge (1869-   ), whose masterpiece is *Hansine Solstad* (1925), the story of a peasant girl; Johan Falkberget (1879-   ), author of novels of life in mining towns (*Black Mountains*, 1907; and *Christianus Sextus*, 3 vols., 1927-35) and of historical novels (*The Fourth Night Watch*, 1923); Hamsun (*Segelfoss Town*, 1915; and *Growth of the Soil*, 1917, awarded the Nobel Prize for literature in 1920); Kinck (*The Avalanche*, 1919-20); Thomas Krag, who depicted the life of the upper classes of southern Norway (*Gunvor Kjeld*, 1904); Gabriel Scott (1874-   ), who wrote of the lives of the poor of southern Norway (*The Fountain*, 1918; and *The Path*, 1925); and Kristofer Uppdal (1878-   ), author, in Landsmaal, of novels dealing with the labor movement in Norway, such as *The Dance Through the Shadows* (10 vols., 1911-24). The greatest Norwegian writer of the 20th century is generally considered to be Sigrid Undset, who was awarded the Nobel Prize for literature in 1928, and among whose works are *Kristin Lavransdatter* (1920-22, a trilogy dealing with 14th-century Norwegian life) and the 13th-century tetralogy *The Master of Hestviken* (1928-30).

Poets: Olav Aukrust (1883-1929), who wrote in Landsmaal (*The Mountain Cairn*, 1916; and *Sunrise*, 1930); Olaf Bull (1883-1933), whose works include *The Hundred Years* (1928); Nordahl Grieg (1902-43), among whose works are the collection of verse *Around the Cape of Good Hope* (1922) and *Norway in Our Hearts* (1929); Vilhelm Krag (*Songs from my Island*, 1918); Tore

Ørjasæter (1886–), author of the epic, written in Landsmaal, *Gudbrand Langleite* (3 vols., 1913-27) and the collection of allegorical poems *Song of the River* (1932); Arnulf Överland (1889-), whose collections of verse include *Bread and Wine* (1919, poems of social protest) and *We Shall Live Through All* (1945, written during World War II, urging resistance to the Nazi invasion and occupation of Norway); Vogt (*Homecoming*, 1917); and Herman Wildenvey (1886–), whose verse includes the collections *Caresses* (1916) and *The Lyre of Autumn* (1931).

NORWEGIAN MUSIC. An indigenous school of Norwegian music did not develop until the growth of the independent national state of Norway in the early 19th century, though historians believe that the European art of polyphony may have originated in Norway and Iceland during the age of the Vikings. The Flemish during the 16th century, the Italians during the 17th century, and the Germans in the early 18th century dominated the art expressions of Norway in their respective eras. The cultural as well as the physical separation of Norway from Sweden, and in the early 19th century from Denmark, may be said to have sponsored the rise of a Norwegian music. Its most striking development is the revivial of a characteristic folk music and dance melody. The elements of early church modes and the whole-tone scale are the distinctive features of the Norwegian folk tune, along with a highly lyrical, romantic feeling. In the 19th century these characteristics attracted the attention of the outside musical world, which was then at the height of the Romantic period. Much Norwegian music was introduced into Europe by the celebrated violinist Ole Bornemann Bull, a leader in the national movement.

The three principal figures of the national school during the second half of the 19th century were Edvard Grieg, Johan Svendsen, and Christian Sinding. Grieg particularly incorporated a larger aspect of romanticism into Norwegian art music, using the popular European instrumental forms in both orchestral and chamber-music compositions, yet reflecting a national and lyrical folk feeling. Norwegian national music reached its zenith in the works of Grieg, declining sharply in importance thereafter. The traditions of the national school have been perpetuated, however, by a small group of composers, notably, Johan Selmer (1844-1910), Ole Olsen (1850-1927), and Gerhard Schjelderup (1859-1933).

NORWICH, cathedral city of England, capital of Norfolk Co., 114 miles N.N.E. of London. The cathedral, almost wholly Norman in style, was founded in 1096; it is surmounted by a noble Norman tower and a decorated spire of 315 ft. Norwich is noted for its textile fabrics. Its principal manufactures are mustard, starch, and ornamental ironware. Pop. (1951 est.) 121,226.

NORWICH TERRIER, a type of small terrier (q.v.) popular in England in the last two decades of the 19th century and introduced into the United States about 1920. The dog is useful in hunting rabbits and other small game, and is popular as a pet. The Norwich terrier is from ten to twelve inches high at the withers and weighs from ten to fourteen pounds. It has dark, bright, and expressive eyes; a strong jaw; a short strong neck; short and powerful legs; and a medium-sized tail. The coat, of hard and wiry hair, is usually red in color, but sometimes is either black and tan or grizzle (bluish-gray). The dog is a hardy, active little animal, and is noted for its loyalty.

NORWOOD, city of Hamilton Co., Ohio, near Cincinnati. It has manufactures of laundry and electric machinery, and office furniture. Pop. (1950) 35,001.

NOSE FLY. See HORSE BOT.

NOSTRADAMUS, assumed name of MICHEL DE NOTREDAME (1503–66), French physician and astrologer, born in St. Remi, Provence, and educated at Avignon and Montpellier. Early in his career as a physician he achieved

Norwich terrier

distinction for his treatment of the plague (q.v.) during outbreaks of the disease in the south of France. He was therefore called to Aix and Lyons in 1545, during a plague epidemic in those cities. Nostradamus subsequently attracted widespread attention by his claim that he could predict the future, and in 1555 he published his famous collection of prophecies, in rhymed quatrains, called *Centuries.* Catherine de' Medici (q.v.) invited him to court to cast the horoscopes of her sons, and upon the accession of Charles IX he was appointed court physician. The name "Nostradamus" is presently used to designate any person who professes to be a seer.

NOTATION, any system of symbols employed in science or art, particularly the symbols used for musical notes (see MUSICAL NOTATION), for chemical compounds and equations (see CHEMISTRY), and for numbers. The history of mathematical notation is discussed under NUMERALS; this article treats the various possible forms of mathematical notation using either Arabic numerals or extensions of the same system.

The generally accepted system of mathematical notation is, at present, a form of positional notation based on the root of ten —i.e., a system in which the digits from one to nine designate the numbers from 1 to 9, the decades from 10 to 90, the hundreds from 100 to 900, and so on, depending upon the position in which they are written. The use of the symbol 0 for zero is a necessary part of any system of positional notation. The use of the number ten as a root for a system of mathematical notation is purely arbitrary. At various times in the history of the world other bases have been used, and, in some cases and for some applications, other bases are more convenient than ten.

The simplest system of numerical notation, the *binary system,* is based on the number two rather than on ten. The binary system has several advantages. The rules for addition, subtraction, multiplication, and division are greatly simplified by the use of the base 2. In the binary system:

$$1 = 1$$
$$2 = 10$$
$$3 = 11$$
$$4 = 100$$
$$5 = 101$$
$$6 = 110$$
$$7 = 111$$
$$8 = 1000$$
$$9 = 1001$$

The rules for addition in the binary system are: $1 + 1 = 10$, and $1 + 10 = 11$. In multiplication $1 \times 10 = 10$, and $10 \times 11 = 110$. The obvious advantage of the binary system is that only two separate number symbols are employed to express any number. Examples of numbers of the binary system, compared to the *decimal* are: decimal 17 is equivalent to 10001 in the binary system, and 21 in decimal is equivalent to 10101 in the binary system. For many years the binary system was regarded as a mathematical curiosity, but when various types of mathematical calculating machines and computers were developed in the 1930's, the binary system was universally employed because it was adapted to electrical relays and electronic tubes which had only two positions, "on" and "off", to represent numbers. On an electronic calculating machine 13 might be represented by a series of relays in the following order: *closed closed open closed,* corresponding to the notation 1101 in the written binary system.

A number of primitive tribes have employed other bases for numeral systems such as systems based on four and five. The *duodecimal system* based on the number twelve has been advocated by many mathematicians. In this system two additional symbols are needed to represent the numbers 10 and 11. If the symbols a and b are used, the first twelve numerals are 1,2,3,4,5, 6,7,8,9,a,b,10; $20 = 24$ in Arabic notation; $100 = 144$; and $1000 = 1728$. An important advantage of using 12 as a base rather than 10 is that 12 can be factored by 1,2,3,4, and 6; 10 can be factored only by 1,2, and 5.

NOTE, in music, the symbol or character representing the pitch and duration of a single musical sound or tone, by use of which a written record of music is made; also, loosely, the musical sound itself. The first note, or tone, of the diatonic scale is called the tonic, the second the supertonic, the third the mediant, the fourth the subdominant, the fifth the dominant, the sixth the submediant, and the seventh the subtonic. A note indicates the pitch of a tone by its positions with respect to the lines and spaces of a staff (q.v.). The duration of tones has been represented by notes only since the 17th century; these time values are indicated by different note forms. The whole note, or full time value, is unfilled and without a stem: The half note, representing half this time value, has a stem; all stems generally extend upward from the right of a note when the note is below the middle line of the staff, and downward from the left when the note is above the middle line. The quarter note is black and stemmed; the eighth note is black, stemmed, and bears a hook or pennant. Still shorter time values are indicated by additional hooks. The most common in musical notations are the sixteenth note, the thirty-second note, and the sixty-fourth note. See MUSICAL NOTATION.

NOTRE DAME (Fr., "Our Lady"), the Virgin Mary. The term has served as the name for Roman Catholic churches and for Roman Catholic abbeys, shrines, and educational institutions dedicated to the Virgin. The most famous of the churches is the cathedral of Notre Dame in Paris, begun in 1163. It is one of the finest existing examples of Gothic architecture (q.v.).

NOTRE DAME, UNIVERSITY OF, a men's Catholic institution of higher education, controlled by the Congregation of the Holy Cross, situated in Notre Dame, a suburb of South Bend, Indiana, and founded in 1842. The divisions of the University comprise the colleges of arts and letters, law, science, engineering, and commerce, and the graduate school. Bachelor's, master's, and doctor's degrees are granted. In 1947 a new curriculum was organized leading to a master's degree in sociology and including courses in criminology and prison administration. The Laetare Medal, granted to American Catholic laymen and women for distinction in beneficent human endeavor, was inaugurated by the University in 1883. Notre Dame is well known for its football team, which for many years headed the list of American teams in an unbroken record of intercollegiate football victories. In 1953–54 the total enrollment was 4958, including 4946 full-time students; the faculty numbered 560 and the endowment was $7,804,859.

NOTTINGHAM, city of Nottinghamshire, England, at the junction of the Leen and Trent rivers, 125 miles N.N.W. of London. The principal manufactures are bobbinet lace, and cotton and silk hosiery. The Saxons called the place *Snottengaham* ("home of the caves") in the 9th century. Nottingham Castle was built by William the Conqueror and was the seat of parliaments. Pop. (1951 est.) 306,008.

NOTTINGHAMSHIRE, or NOTTS, inland county of England, bounded on the N. by Yorkshire, on the E. by Lincolnshire, on the s. by Leicestershire, and on the w. by Derbyshire. Apart from the valley of the Trent River, which is very flat, the general aspect of the county is undulating and well wooded. Area, 827 sq.m.; pop. (1951 est.) 841,083.

NOUN (fr. Lat. *nomen*, "name"), in grammar (q.v.), a word or name denoting a thing, place, person, idea, quality, or action, used in a sentence as the subject or object of a verb, or as the object of a preposition. The noun is one of the four basic parts of speech, the others being the interjection, the pronoun, and the verb (qq.v.); see GRAMMAR. Although the noun is generally distinct from the verb and the pronoun in function and inflection (q.v.), noun and pronoun frequently show similarities, and noun and verb sometimes take the same form, as in the Hottentot and Polynesian languages. Verbal nouns also occur in the Semitic and Indo-European languages (qq.v.) in the form of infinitives which are nouns in form and verbs in function. Because of the similarity of function of nouns and pronouns, in many Indo-European languages pronominal inflection has been extended by analogy to nouns, and nominal inflection has been extended to pronouns.

Nouns may be inflected to indicate gender, case, and number. In modern English, gender has been eliminated, and only three cases occur: nominative, genitive (or possessive), and objective. English nouns have two numbers: singular and plural. The plural is usually formed by adding *s* or *es* to the singular form of the noun. A number of exceptions to this rule exist, however, such as *teeth,* the plural of *tooth,* and *children,* the plural of *child.*

Nouns in modern English are divided into two main classes called "proper" and "common", the latter being further divided into "abstract" and "collective" categories. Proper nouns, always capitalized, denote individuals and personifications, as in *John* and *Liberty;* common nouns denote concrete material things, as in *table* and *horse;* abstract nouns denote qualities, as in *goodness* and *pleasure;* and collective nouns denote masses of units, as in *army* and *majority,* and may usually be the subject of both the singular and plural forms of a verb.

NOVA (Lat. *novus,* "new"), in astronomy, a faint star which, at an unpredictable time and place, suddenly becomes exceedingly bright, reaching its maximum intensity in a few days, and declining to its original brightness over a period of months or years. Many novae at their maximum brightness are about 160,000 times as bright as in their normal state. For a few days very bright novae may appear as the brightest objects in the sky except for the moon and the sun; other novae are too dim to be seen with the naked eye and can be observed only with a telescope. Novae are designated by the constellation to which they belong and the year of outburst. In the years during which systematic astronomic records have been kept novae, such as Nova T Coronae Borealis, have been observed to repeat the outburst of brightness. Some of the novae which have been observed in the Galactic System are Kepler's star in Ophiuchus (1604), Nova Cygni (1876), Nova Aurigae (1891), and Nova Persei (1901). The brightest nova on record appeared in the constellation Cassiopeia (q.v.) in 1572. Over a hundred novae have been identified in the great spiral in Andromeda. In addition to the normal novae found in our Galactic System, extraordinarily bright novae, called *supernovae*, appear in extragalactic systems. Supernovae often attain a brightness about one hundred million times that of the sun.

No completely satisfactory theory has been evolved to account for the appearance of novae. According to present-day evidence, these stars expand until a sudden explosion occurs, releasing vast amounts of radiant energy. A recent theory, postulated by the American physicist Lyle B. Borst, holds that such explosions are caused by thermonuclear reactions, in which radioactive beryllium (q.v.) is formed by nuclear fusion (see HYDROGEN BOMB). Following the explosion, the star contracts and returns to its normal state.

NOVALIS. See HARDENBERG, BARON FRIEDRICH VON.

NOVA LISBOA, formerly HUAMBO, city and capital of Huambo District, Angola (Portuguese West Africa), situated 240 miles from the coast. It lies at an altitude of 5500 ft. and is the trading center for a region producing corn, coffee, sugar, palm oil, and nuts. The repair shops of the Benguela Railway are located in the town. It received its present name in 1928. Pop., about 16,000.

NOVARA, capital of the Italian province of the same name, 60 miles N. of Turin. It has manufactures of silk, cotton, and linen. Pop. (1947 est.) 71,902.

NOVA SCOTIA, the easternmost of the Maritime Provinces of Canada, bounded on

the N.W. by New Brunswick and the Bay of Fundy, on the N. by Northumberland Strait and the Gulf of St. Lawrence, and on other sides by the Atlantic Ocean. The province consists of two portions: Nova Scotia proper, a large peninsula linked to New Brunswick by the narrow Isthmus of Chignecto, and Cape Breton Island (q.v.), separated from the peninsula by the Strait of Canso. The capital, largest city, and chief port of Nova Scotia is Halifax, and other important cities and towns include Sydney, Glace Bay (qq.v.), Dartmouth, and Truro.

The peninsula, consisting of ancient mountain land, has a very irregular coastline (4625 m. long), with excellent harbors. No part of Nova Scotia is farther than 50 m. from the sea. The interior is hilly, with ridges rising above 1000 ft., and traversed by deep valleys. Once mountainous, the surface has been worn by erosion and presents the appearance of an undulating plateau. The climate is temperate, seldom descending below 0°F. in winter and reaching a summer maximum at Halifax, on the S. coast, of 68°F. Annual rainfall is about 45 in. Agriculture is a principal occupation. Fruits, notably apples, are the chief crop; apple production in 1952 totaled 1,500,000 barrels. Dairying and sheep and poultry raising are also important farm industries. Coal, gold, gypsum, and salt are the principal mineral products. Fishing is also a leading occupation; the commercial catch (chiefly cod and lobsters) was valued at $21,398,000 in 1951. Forests cover about 15,900 sq.m., and lumbering is carried on throughout the entire province. Industrial establishments numbered 1474 in the year 1951, and included shipyards and factories producing steel, refined and confectionery sugar, wood, fish, and dairy products, paint and varnish, cordage, clothing, and machinery and foundry products. Coastwise steamships stop regularly at important ports. Communications (1953) include 15,093 m. of highway (less than 1400 m. paved) and 1420 m. of railroad.

Over 75 percent of the Nova Scotians are descendants of English, Irish, and Scottish settlers; about 11 percent are descended from French families. Education is free and compulsory through elementary and secondary school to the age of sixteen; and the educational system includes an agricultural college and a normal college at Truro and the Nova Scotia Technical College at Halifax. The province is governed by a lieutenant governor, appointed by the Canadian govern-

Canadian National Railways

NOVA SCOTIA. *Top: Fishermen unloading their catch from small boats at a dock in Lockport.*
Bottom: The town of Ingonish Ferry, on the coast of Cape Breton Island.

ment, and a 37-member House of Assembly elected by universal suffrage. Nova Scotia is represented by twenty-three members in the Canadian Parliament.

History. The peninsula was discovered in 1497 by John Cabot (q.v.), sailing under the English flag. The first settlements were made by French colonists, who called the region Acadia (q.v.) and founded Port Royal in 1605. England refused to recognize French claims and in 1621 Sir William Alexander was given a royal grant which included Acadia, called Nova Scotia ("New Scotland") by the English. The region was the subject of considerable Anglo-French dispute during the 17th century. New England colonists made many attempts to obtain possession of the region and in 1710, during the War of the Spanish Succession, British forces captured Port Royal. By the Treaty of Utrecht, in 1713, France gave up all claim to the peninsula; Cape Breton Island was ceded to England in 1763, following the Seven Years' War. After the beginning of the American Revolution, about 25,000 American colonists who were loyal to England emigrated to Nova Scotia, where they founded Shelburne. Successive waves of emigration were chiefly from Scotland, notably from the Highland region. During the War of 1812 Nova Scotia was the chief British base in North America. The colony was given responsible government in 1848 after reiterated demands to the British government by the colonists. In 1867 Nova Scotia and Cape Breton Island became a province of Canada. Area of province, including 325 sq.m. of inland water surface, 21,060 sq.m.; pop. (1951) 642,584.

NOVAYA ZEMLYA, archipelago to the north of European Russia, belonging to Soviet Russia, and administered by a Soviet commissioner in Archangel.

NOVEL, fictional prose narrative in which characters and situations typical of real life are depicted within the framework of a plot. Although the novel has served as the instrument of instruction, of satire, of political argument, and of moral edification, its primary purpose is to afford entertainment. It constitutes the third stage in the development of imaginative fiction, the *epic* (see EPIC POETRY) and the *romance* (q.v.) forming respectively the first and second stages. The novel may be divided into four broad categories as follows: (1) the *Novel of Incident,* subdivided into (a) the *novel of adventure,* (b) the *biographical novel,* and (c) the *military, naval,* or *sporting novel;* (2) the *Novel of Artifice,* subdivided into (a) the *detective novel,* in which the chief emphasis is upon the investigation and solution of a baffling crime, (b) the *novel of mystery,* primarily concerned with atmosphere, whether sinister, terrifying, or depressing, and its psychological effects upon the characters involved, (c) the *novel of the unknown,* often indistinguishable from the novel of mystery, dealing with the weird, the occult, and the supernatural in such manner as to make them plausible, and (d) the *novel of suspense,* differentiated from the novel of mystery and the novel of the unknown in that it achieves its effect through the portrayal of characters in realistic situations which almost always involve intrigue, violence, and pursuit, as in themes of espionage, gang warfare, and crime; (3) the *Novel of Ordinary Life,* subdivided into (a) the *novel of purpose,* which points a moral or explores and illustrates a theory of life, and (b) the *realistic* or *naturalistic novel,* which creates the illusion of absolute reality through meticulous attention to detail, great verisimilitude in the dialogue, and the virtual elimination of comments and judgments by the author; and (4) the *Psychological Novel,* subdivided into (a) the *analytical novel* or *novel of character,* which exhaustively investigates the motivation of a character in terms of his background and experience and treats events primarily in their relation to and effect upon character, and (b) the *problem novel,* which is concerned with individual conflicts and with problems in human relations. The length of a novel customarily ranges from about 40,000 words upward; the *novelette,* or short novel, is usually between 10,000 and 40,000 words.

The term "novel" (Lat. *novellus,* dim. of *novus,* "new") appears to have been applied at the outset to any new story. In the 12th and 13th centuries it was a common designation among the Provençal poets of France for a realistic tale of intrigue told in verse form. The term *novella* was popularized in Italy by Giovanni Boccaccio as the title of a short anecdotal narrative in prose. When these Italian tales were translated into English the term itself passed into the English language. The earliest ascertained use of the term "novel" in English literature occurs in *The Palace of Pleasure,* a group of tales translated by William Painter principally from the works of Boccaccio and the Piedmontese writer Matteo Bandello and published in 1566. The Italian novella was then progressively expanded by a succession of English writers down to the 18th century. Despite this development, however, and the multiplication of incidents, the novel remained essentially a formless rambling tale, lacking the structural organization furnished by plot. The English author credited with writing the first novel in the modern sense of the word was Samuel Richardson. His novel *Pamela: or Virtue Rewarded* (1740) is in epistolary or letter form, and recounts the trials and ultimate victory of a maidservant in preserving her virtue against the dishonorable advances of her employer.

In its genesis the novel is as old as the drama (q.v.). Many tales which subsequently became a part of the European literary tradition originated in Egypt. In India the novel began probably with *Daśakumāracarita* ("Adventures of the Ten Princes") by Dandin, a Sanskrit writer of the latter part of the 6th century A.D. The Chinese novel did not begin to develop until the time of the Yüan (Mongol) Dynasty (1260-1368); it is replete with dramatic incidents but deficient in characterization. In Japan the first novel of consequence is the *Genji Monagatari* ("The Tale of Genji", 11th cent.; Eng. trans., 1935), by the Baroness Murasaki. This work is a long love story containing much valuable information on Japanese court society about 1000 A.D. After an extended period of decline, Japanese fiction underwent a renaissance in the 17th century, as exemplified in the works of the novelists Bakin, Kioden, Saikaku, and Tanehiko. Of these authors the greatest is Bakin, whose *Hakkenden* ("Tale of Eight Dogs") is perhaps the most famous of all Japanese novels. Novels had a considerable vogue among the Greeks in the early centuries of the Christian Era. Worthy of mention are the romance *Æthiopica* by Heliodorus of Emesa (Homs), Syria; the *Ephesiaca* (containing the essential features of the story of Romeo and Juliet) by Xenophon of Ephesus, Asia Minor; *Apollonius of Tyre* and *Clitophon and Leucippe* by Achilles Tatius of Alexandria, Egypt; and *Daphnis and Chloë*, the most exquisite of the pastoral romances, generally attributed to the Greek writer Longus. The chief examples of novels written in the Latin language at this time are the *Metamorphoses* or *The Golden Ass* by Lucius Apuleius, a native of Numidia in N. Africa, and the *Satyricon*, generally considered to be the work of the Roman writer Gaius Petronius Arbiter.

The long narrative verse tale, the equally voluminous prose romance, and the *fabliau*, a metrical anecdote frequently cynical in tone and coarse in subject matter, all flourished in Europe during the Middle Ages and contributed to the subsequent development of the novel. This development was notably advanced in Spain during the 16th century by the so-called *picaresque*, or rogue, story, in which the protagonist is a merry scapegrace or vagabond who goes through a series of realistic and exciting adventures. The earliest specimen of the picaresque novel is *Lazarillo de Tormes* (about 1554), sometimes ascribed to the Spanish statesman Diego Hurtado de Mendoza. Another Spanish example is *Guzmán de Alfarache* (part I, 1599; part II, 1604) by Mateo Alemán. Although Englishmen of the age of Queen Elizabeth were well acquainted with the latest innovations in the art of fiction on the Continent, literary activity in England during this period was almost exclusively in the field of the drama. Nevertheless experiments with the novel form were made, as attested by Sir Philip Sidney's *Arcadia* (1580-81), an attempt to combine the idyllic pastoral tale (of the type of *Daphnis and Chloë*) with the medieval romance of chivalry, and to give them the structure of Heliodorus' *Æthiopica*. Other important Elizabethan novels are *Euphues, the Anatomy of Wit* (1579) and *Euphues and his England* (1580) by John Lyly; *Perimedes the Blacke-Smith* (1588) and *Menaphon* (1589) by Robert Greene; *Rosalynde, Euphues Golden Legacie* (1590) and *Euphues Shadow, the Battaile of the Sences* (1592) by Thomas Lodge; and *The Unfortunate Traveller, or The Life of Jack Wilton* (1594) by Thomas Nash. The only novel of consequence in English literature from the Elizabethan age to the Restoration is the *Argenis* (1621) by the Scottish satirist John Barclay, composed originally in Latin and later translated into French and English. This work, cast in the form of a political allegory, is important as a link between the romance of antiquity and the French *roman de longue haleine* ("long-winded novel") as written during the 17th century by Marin Le Roy Gomberville, Gautier de Costes de La Calprenède, and Magdeleine de Scudéry. The best examples of the *roman de longue haleine* are Scudéry's *Grand Cyrus* (1649-53) and *Clélie* (1656), each in ten volumes. Other French novels of the period are *L'Astrée* (1610-27) by Honoré d'Urfé; *La Vraie Histoire Comique de Francion* ("The True Comical History of Francion", 1622), a burlesque on the pastoral and chivalric romances of the day, by Charles Sorel; *Roman Comique* (1651-57) by Paul Scarron; and *La Princesse de Montpensier* (1662), *Zayde* (1670), and *La Princesse de Clèves* (1678) by the Comtesse de La Fayette.

After the Restoration (q.v.) the writing of novels was revived in England. In *The English Rogue* (part one, 1665-71) Richard Head strung together a long series of picaresque episodes which furnish a realistic picture of the life of the lower classes in mid-17th-century London. Another realistic novel of the Restoration is *Oroonoko* (about 1678) by Mrs. Aphra Behn. The realism of the novel, further developed in *Pilgrim's Progress* (1678) by John Bunyan, was brought to a new intensity by Daniel Defoe in his *Robinson Crusoe* (1719). The technique of novel writing was notably advanced by Samuel Richardson in *Pamela: or Virtue Rewarded* (1740), *Clarissa: or the History of a Young Lady* (1747-48), and *Sir Charles Grandison* (1753), and by Henry Fielding in *Joseph Andrews* (1742), *Jonathan Wild* (1743), *Tom Jones* (1749), and *Amelia* (1751). Fielding, unlike Richardson, did not use the somewhat cumbersome epistolary method to tell his story, but let his characters speak directly. His narrative, too, though interspersed with extraneous episodes and digressions, is for the most part in the third person. Another exponent of the realistic novel was Tobias George Smollett, who in *The Adventures of Roderick Random* (1748), *The Adventures of Peregrine Pickle* (1751), *Ferdinand Count Fathom* (1753), and *The Expedition of Humphry Clinker* (1770), furnished a vivid picture of manners in the lower-class society of his time. The salient characteristics of Smollett's work, an easy style and occasional shocking audacity, were taken up and exaggerated by Laurence Sterne in his *Life and Opinions of Tristram Shandy* (1760). About this time Oliver Goldsmith wrote *The Vicar of Wakefield* (1766), the source of many subsequent idyls of village life.

In the following generation a number of writers, influenced by the pedagogic and political ideas expounded in *Émile, ou Traité de l'Éducation* (1762) by the French philosopher Jean Jacques Rousseau, made the novel a vehicle for theories of education and politics. Among these writers, who are some-

times credited with founding the so-called *didactic novel*, were Charlotte Smith (*Emmeline*, 1778; *Celestina*, 1792; and *The Old Manor House*, 1793), Elizabeth Inchbald (*A Simple Story*, 1791; and *Nature and Art*, 1796), and William Godwin (*Caleb Williams*, 1794; and *St. Leon*, 1799). The *novel of manners*, in which the interest centers predominantly on the speech and behavior of the characters as social types formed by peculiar cultural conditions, is well represented in the works of Fanny Burney (*Evelina*, 1778; *Cecilia*, 1782; and *Camilla*, 1796) and Maria Edgeworth (*Castle Rackrent*, 1800; *Belinda*, 1801; *Leonora*, 1806; and *The Absentee*, 1812). This type of novel reached its highest development, however, in the urbane stories of Jane Austen (*Sense and Sensibility*, 1811; *Pride and Prejudice*, 1813; *Mansfield Park*, 1814; and *Emma*, 1816). In Germany, meanwhile, Johann Wolfgang von Goethe, in *Die Leiden des Jungen Werthers* ("The Sorrows of Young Werther", 1773-78), created the vogue of the melancholy, lovelorn young hero preoccupied with his own emotions. This work exerted a pervasive influence on the literature of w. Europe and furnished a powerful impetus to the Romantic movement (see ROMANTICISM) which was then developing on the Continent and in England. One manifestation of the Romantic spirit was the so-called *Gothic novel*, a tale of terror and the supernatural, marked by extended descriptions of ruins (particularly as seen by moonlight) and of nature in its wild and terrifying aspects (such as mountainous regions, waterfalls, thunderstorms, and avalanches). The first Gothic novel was *The Castle of Otranto* (1764) by the British statesman and amateur antiquary Horace Walpole. Other notable exponents of the genre were Clara Reeve (*The Champion of Virtue, a Gothic Story*, 1777), Ann Radcliffe (*The Mysteries of Udolpho*, 1794; and *The Italian*, 1797), William Beckford (*Vathek*, 1782), Matthew Gregory Lewis (*Ambrosio, or the Monk*, 1796), and Mary Shelley (*Frankenstein*, 1818). In the United States the Gothic novel was represented in the work of Charles Brockden Brown (*Wieland*, 1798). In many respects Brown is the precursor of the American novelists Edgar Allen Poe and Nathaniel Hawthorne.

The Gothic novel, which is historical in that its scenes were generally laid in the Middle Ages, was a step toward fictional works in which history became the chief interest. The example set by Sophia Lee, whose *Recess* (1783-86) is a historical romance of the time of Queen Elizabeth, was followed by a number of other writers, the most noteworthy of whom was Jane Porter, author of *The Scottish Chiefs* (1810). This trend culminated in the *Waverley* novels by Sir Walter Scott, the acknowledged master of English historical fiction, who produced about thirty volumes giving a broad panoramic view of English and Scottish history from the closing decades of the 11th century to the turn of the 19th. Among his English followers were Horatio, known as Horace, Smith (*Brambletye House*, 1826; *Reuben Apsley*, 1827; and *Walter Colyton*, 1830), George Payne Rainsford James (*Richelieu*, 1829; and *Philip Augustus*, 1831), William Harrison Ainsworth (*Rookwood*, 1834; *Guy Fawkes*, 1841; *Windsor Castle*, 1843; and *Boscobel*, 1872), and James Grant (*The Romance of War*, 1845; and *Playing with Fire*, 1887). Scott also influenced many novelists abroad, notably Alessandro Francesco Tommaso Antonio Manzoni in Italy, Gustav Freytag in Germany, and Alexandre Dumas, *père*, and Victor Marie Hugo in France. Scott's *The Pirate* (1821) suggested to the American novelist James Fenimore Cooper the series of seafaring tales beginning with *The Pilot* (1823). For his Leatherstocking series, containing *The Last of the Mohicans*, (1826), *The Pathfinder* (1840), and *The Deerslayer* (1841), Cooper became known as the American Scott.

As the 19th century progressed, the vogue of historical romanticism in the novel waned. In France Honoré de Balzac maintained that the novel should be a true-to-life document based upon experience and observation. Balzac's vast and complex *La Comédie Humaine* ("The Human Comedy") in forty-seven volumes, which aimed at realistic depiction of every phase of French society, was a practical demonstration of his thesis, and profoundly influenced the course of the novel both on the Continent and in England. An exponent of the new realism in fiction was the English novelist Charles John Huffam Dickens, who, in such works as *Pickwick Papers* (1836-37), *Oliver Twist* (1837-39), and *Hard Times* (1854), graphically portrayed the life of the middle and lower classes of London. Another eminent English novelist, William Makepeace Thackeray, wrote of the manners of the middle and upper classes with exquisite humor and irony in *Vanity Fair* (1847-48), *Pendennis* (1848-

50), *Henry Esmond* (1852), and *The Newcomes* (1853-55). The social criticism exemplified in the works of Dickens and Thackeray was repudiated by the English novelist Anthony Trollope, who accused his fellow novelists of creating vices in society merely for the purpose of attacking them. Trollope's view of life is presented in the Barsetshire Chronicles (1853-67), comprising *The Warden, Barchester Towers, Doctor Thorne, Framley Parsonage, The Small House at Allington,* and *The Last Chronicle of Barset.* In the imaginary shire of Barset the author describes the clergy and their friends with a benign humor.

The *psychological novel*, which came to occupy a dominant position in the second half of the 19th century, had its distinctive beginnings in such works as Goethe's *Wahlverwandtschaften* ("Elective Affinities", 1809) and *Le Rouge et le Noir* ("The Red and the Black", 1831) by the French writer Stendhal (pseudonym of Marie Henri Beyle). Notable exponents of the novel of psychological analysis include the Russian writers Fëdor Mikhailovich Dostoevski (*Crime and Punishment,* 1866; *The Idiot,* 1868-69; *The Possessed,* 1871; and *The Brothers Karamazov,* 1880), Ivan Aleksandrovich Goncharov (*Oblomov,* 1858), Aleksei Feofilaktovich Pisemski (*A Thousand Souls,* 1858; and *A Troubled Sea,* 1863), Ivan Sergeevich Turgenev (*Rudin,* 1855; *Fathers and Sons,* 1862; *Smoke,* 1867; and *Clara Milich,* 1882), and Count Lev (Leo) Nikolaevich Tolstoi (*Anna Karenina,* 1875-77; *A Confession,* 1884; *The Death of Ivan Ilyich,* 1886; and *The Kreutzer Sonata,* 1889); the French writers Gustave Flaubert (*Madame Bovary,* 1857; and *The Sentimental Education,* 1874), Edmond Louis Antoine de Goncourt and Jules Alfred Huot de Concourt (*Charles Demailly,* 1860; *Renée Mauperin,* 1864; and *Madame Gervaisais,* 1869), Charles Joseph Paul Bourget (*A Woman's Heart,* 1890; *A Divorce,* 1904; and *The Feeling of Death,* 1915), Marcel Proust (*Remembrance of Things Past,* 1926), and André Gide (*Pastoral Symphony,* 1919; and *The Counterfeiters,* 1925); the German writers Thomas Mann (*Buddenbrooks,* 1901; *Death in Venice,* 1912; and *The Magic Mountain,* 1924), Jakob Wasserman (*Casper Hauser,* 1909; *The World's Illusion,* 1919; and *The Maurizius Case,* 1928), and Franz Kafka (*The Trial,* 1925; *The Castle,* 1926; and *America,* 1927); the English writers George Eliot (*Adam Bede,* 1859; *The Mill on the Floss,* 1860; *Silas Marner,* 1861; and

Romola, 1863), George Meredith (*The Shaving of Shagpat*, 1856; *The Ordeal of Richard Feverel*, 1859; *The Egoist*, 1879; and *The Tragic Comedians*, 1880), David Herbert Lawrence (*The White Peacock*, 1911; *The Rainbow*, 1915; *Sons and Lovers*, 1923; and *Lady Chatterley's Lover*, 1928), Virginia Woolf (*Jacob's Room*, 1922; *Mrs. Dalloway*, 1925; *To the Lighthouse*, 1927; and *The Waves*, 1931), and James Joyce (*A Portrait of the Artist as a Young Man*, 1916; *Ulysses*, 1922; and *Finnegans Wake*, 1939); and the American writers Nathaniel Hawthorne (*The Scarlet Letter*, 1850; *The House of the Seven Gables*, 1851; and *The Blithedale Romance*, 1852), Herman Melville (*Moby Dick*, 1851; and *Pierre: or the Ambiguities*, 1852), William Dean Howells (*A Chance Acquaintance*, 1873; *A Foregone Conclusion*, 1875; and *The Lady of the Aroostook*, 1879), Henry James (*Daisy Miller*, 1879; *The Portrait of A Lady*, 1881; *The Bostonians*, 1886; *The Wings of the Dove*, 1902; and *The Golden Bowl*, 1904), and Edith Newbold Wharton (*Ethan Frome*, 1911).

Akin to the psychological novel is the *sociological novel*, which is realistic in subject matter and treatment, employs the technique of psychological analysis, and combines elements of the novel of manners and the novel of purpose. Much sociological fiction illustrates the philosophical doctrine of determinism (q.v.), a theory by which conduct is made to depend wholly upon the factors of heredity and environment, the concept of man as a free moral agent being disavowed. The sociological novel is represented in Russia by the works of Tolstoi (*War and Peace*, 1866), Maksim Gorki (*Foma Gordeev*, 1900; *The Mother*, 1907; and *A Confession*, 1910), Mikhail Evgrafovich Saltykov (*Contradictions*, 1847; and *The Messieurs Golovlev*, 1881), Fëdor Vasilievich Gladkov (*The Fiery Steed*, 1924; and *Cement*, 1926), and Mikhail Alexsandrovich Sholokhov (*The Silent Don; And Quiet Flows the Don; and The Don Flows Home to the Sea*, 1928-38); in France by the works of Honoré de Balzac (*Father Goriot*, 1834; *Memoirs of Two Young Wives*, 1841; *A Shady Affair*, 1841; and *Cousin Pons*, 1847), Émile Zola (*Thérèse Raquin*, 1867; *The Dram Shop*, 1877; *Nana*, 1880; *Germinal*, 1885; and *The Human Beast*, 1890), Guy de Maupassant (*A Woman's Life*, 1883; *Ladies' Man*, 1885; and *Strong as Death*, 1889), Francis Carco (*The Innocents*, 1917; *The Hunted Man*, 1922; and *Perversity*, 1925), Louis Fuch Des-

touches, better known as Louis-Ferdinand Céline (*Journey to the End of the Night*, 1932; and *Death on the Installment Plan*, 1936), and Pierre Hamp (*Flax*, 1924); in Germany by the works of Max Kretzer (*Mister Timpe*, 1888; and *The Betrayed*, 1901), Michael Georg Conrad (*Madame Lutetia*, 1882; *In Complete Darkness*, 1895; and *Majesty*, 1902), Herman Sudermann (*Frau Sorge*, 1887; *It Was*, 1894; *The Whimsical Professor*, 1926; and *The Wife of Steffen Trombolt*, 1927), Bernhard Kellermann (*The Fool*, 1909; *The Sea*, 1910; *The Ninth November*, 1920; and *The Brothers Schellenberg*, 1925), and Hans Fallada (*Little Man, What Now?*, 1932; *The World Outside*, 1934; *and Wolf Among Wolves*, 1937); in England by the works of Samuel Butler (*The Way of All Flesh*; written 1873-85, pub. 1903), Thomas Hardy (*The Return of the Native*, 1878; *Mayor of Casterbridge*, 1886; *Tess of the d'Urbervilles*, 1891; and *Jude the Obscure*, 1895), and Herbert George Wells (*Ann Veronica*, 1909; *Mr. Britling Sees It Through*, 1916; and *The World of William Clissold*, 1926); and in the United States by the works of John Milton Hay (*The Bread-Winners*, 1884), Albion Winegar Tourgée (*A Fool's Errand*, 1879; and *Murvale Eastman*, 1890), Hjalmar Hjorth Boyesen (*Social Strugglers*, 1884; and *The Golden Calf*, 1892), Edward Bellamy (*Looking Backward*, 1888), Mary Eleanor Freeman (*Jane Field*, 1893; *Pembroke*, 1894; and *Jerome, a Poor Man*, 1897), Frank Norris (*McTeague*, 1899; *The Octopus*, 1901; *The Pit*, 1903; and *Vandover and the Brute*, 1914); Stephen Crane (*Maggie: A Girl of the Streets*, 1893; and *The Red Badge of Courage*, 1895), Theodore Dreiser (*Sister Carrie*, 1900; *The Financier*, 1912; *The Hand of the Potter*, 1919; and *An American Tragedy*, 1925), Sherwood Anderson (*Poor White*, 1920; and *Dark Laughter*, 1925), Upton Beall Sinclair (*The Jungle*, 1906; and *King Coal*, 1917), Sinclair Lewis (*Main Street*, 1920; *Babbitt*, 1922; and *Arrowsmith*, 1925), Francis Scott Fitzgerald (*This Side of Paradise*, 1920), John Dos Passos (*Manhattan Transfer*, 1925), William Faulkner (*As I Lay Dying*, 1930), Ernest Hemingway (*A Farewell to Arms*, 1929), Erskine Caldwell (*Tobacco Road*, 1932), James T. Farrell (*Young Lonigan*, 1932), John Ernst Steinbeck (*The Grapes of Wrath*, 1939), and Richard Wright (*Native Son*, 1940).

See also separate entries on most of the authors referred to throughout this article;

the articles NATURALISM and REALISM; and the articles on the literature of the various nations of the world, such as AMERICAN LITERATURE.

NOVEMBER, the eleventh month of the Gregorian calendar, having 30 days. Among the Romans it was the ninth month at a time when the year was composed of ten months. Originally November consisted of 30 days; Julius Cæsar gave it 31; but in the reign of Augustus the number was restored to 30.

NOVENA, in the Roman Catholic Church, a devotion consisting of a prayer asking some special grace, said on one day in each of nine successive weeks, as nine successive Tuesdays. It is in imitation of the nine days spent in prayer by the apostles between the Ascension of Christ and Pentecost. Special novenas of Grace, of the Sacred Heart, and to the Holy Ghost are said for special indulgences. In "flying novenas", those offered in urgent need, as for the recovery of a dying person, the nine prayers may be said in one day.

NOVGOROD ("new town"), a Russian city, capital of the Region of the same name. It is on the Volkhof River, 110 miles S.S.E. of Leningrad. It is rich in relics of the 11th to the 17th centuries and is known as "Museum City". Formerly it had 400,000 inhabitants. Pop., about 31,000.

NOVI SAD, city and capital of Voivodina autonomous province, Yugoslavia, situated on the Danube R., 45 miles N.W. of Belgrade. It is the commercial center of an important agricultural area and has factories engaged in the manufacture of electrical equipment, textiles, chemicals, and pottery. Founded in the middle of the 18th century, the city was the cultural center of the Serbs prior to the collapse of the Austro-Hungarian Empire. Pop. (1948) 77,713.

NOVOCAINE, PROCAINE, or NEOCAINE, a synthetic anesthetic alkaloid, $C_{18}H_{20}O_2N_2\cdot HCl$, derived from anesthesin. Novocaine, or procaine, was synthesized (1905) by the German chemist Alfred Einhorn. Its anesthetic action is similar to, but far less toxic than that of cocaine (q.v.). Fatal doses of novocaine must be six to seven times as large as the dosage of cocaine required to produce death. Novocaine occurs in colorless crystals; it is soluble in water and alcohol, slightly soluble in chloroform, and insoluble in ether. It can withstand boiling without deterioration, and melts at 153° to 156°C. (307° to 313°F.). It is widely used in regional anesthesia, but is ineffective in producing anesthesia of mucous membranes. Novocaine is used in dentistry, surgery, and obstetrics, and is sometimes administered to relieve low-back pain. It is also used in rectal suppositories. In the compound known as procaine penicillin, the anesthetic effect of the procaine permits painless administration of massive doses of penicillin so that one injection of the compound remains effective for several days. Some individuals are sensitive to procaine and develop hives when the drug is injected subcutaneously. More serious after-effects, such as nausea, vomiting, decrease of pulse rate, and even convulsions, may occur if the drug is injected directly into the blood stream. See SPINAL ANESTHESIA.

NOVOCHERKASSK, city of Rostov Region, Russian S.F.S.R., situated on the Aksai R., a tributary of the Don R., about 25 miles N.E. of Rostov. The chief manufactures are machinery and locomotives. Founded in 1805 by Don Cossacks, it was the last stronghold of the counterrevolution (1917-1921). The city is noted as a scientific and cultural center. Pop., about 80,000.

NOVOROSSISK, a port and town of the R.S.F.S.R., Soviet Union, about 65 miles W.S.W. of Krasnodar, on the N.E. coast of the Black Sea. Exports include petroleum, cement, tobacco, and champagne. Pop., about 95,000.

In World War I, the Turkish fleet inflicted great damage in the city by bombardment, October, 1915. It was occupied by the Russian Red army in March, 1920. In World War II it was taken by German forces (Sept., 1942) and reoccupied by Russia a year later.

NOVOSIBIRSK, formerly Novo-NIKOLA-EVSK, capital of a Region of the same name in the Russian Soviet Federated Socialist Republic, one of the constituent republics of the Union of Soviet Socialist Republics. On the right bank of the river Ob, it is the largest transshipment point for produce of the Altai district. Pop., about 405,000.

NOYES, ALFRED (1880-), English poet, born in Staffordshire, and educated at Oxford University. He visited the United States in 1913 as lecturer for the Lowell Institute in Boston, and remained to accept an appointment the following year as professor of modern English literature at Princeton University, at which he taught until his resignation in 1923. His first volume of poetry, *The Loom of Years,* was published in 1902, and his popularity increased with the publication in the following year of *The Flower of Old Japan.* In *Forty Singing Seamen* (1907) and

Combine Photos
Alfred Noyes

followers abandoned his tenets, and in 1881 the flourishing community was incorporated; it became noted for its manufacture of "Community Silverware". Faced with adultery charges, Noyes fled to Canada in 1880. He wrote a number of religious treatises, including *Bible Communism* (1848), *Scientific Propagation* (about 1873), and *Salvation from Sin* (1896).

NUBIA, a region of North Africa, south of Egypt in the Anglo-Egyptian Sudan, between the Red Sea and the Sahara. It is mostly desert. Area, 280,000 sq.m. Under the Pharaohs Nubia was called Cush, but under the twentieth dynasty it was recovered by a series of native rulers. The chief inhabitants are Arab. The "Nubian Desert" lies east of the Nile, opposite the western bend of the river. The most fertile part is near Dongola.

NUCLEUS, in biology. See CELL (in biology).

NUCLEUS, in atomic structure, the central mass of an atom about which the orbital electrons revolve. The nucleus is composed of protons and neutrons (qq.v.) and its mass accounts for nearly the entire mass of the atom. Since the diameter of the nucleus as compared with the diameter of the entire atom is extremely small (most atoms have a diameter of 0.00000001 centimeters and nuclear diameters are roughly 0.0000000000001 centimeters), nuclei are extremely dense. The nucleus was formerly considered a hard, solid sphere of uniform density. In 1953, however, it was discovered that the nucleus consists of particles, that concentration of density exists at the core of the nucleus, and that there is considerable space between particles. The core was found to be 130 trillion times denser than water.

The least stable arrangement of nuclei is one in which an odd number of neutrons and an odd number of protons are present; all except four isotopes (q.v.) containing nuclei of this kind are radioactive. The presence of a large excess of neutrons over protons detracts from the stability of a nucleus; nuclei in all isotopes of elements above bismuth in the periodic table contain this type of arrangement and they are all radioactive. The greatest number of known stable (nonradioactive) nuclei contain an even number of protons and an even number of neutrons.

According to an early conception, nuclei consisted of protons and electrons which were bound together largely by the elec-

Drake (1908) he turned to poetry of the sea. He also wrote verse dramas, of which *Robin Hood* (1927) is the best known; novels, including *The Winepress* (1913); the epic trilogy *The Torch Bearers* (1922, 1925, 1930); and the volumes of verse *Shadows on the Down* (1945) and *Daddy Fell into the Pond, and Other Poems for Children* (1953).

NOYES, JOHN HUMPHREY (1811-86), founder of the Oneida Community (q.v., see also PERFECTIONISTS), born in Brattleboro, Vt., and educated at Dartmouth College and the theological school of Yale College. In 1833 he was licensed as a Congregational minister, but the following year lost his license for professing to a second conversion. He thereafter promulgated the doctrine of the dual sexual nature of God, and preached his belief that no one is bound by any moral code. Noyes attempted a return to the communism of the primitive church in his Perfectionist Community, established in 1836 in Putney, Vt. In 1846 public condemnation of his tenets of free love and "complex marriage" forced him to disband the community; two years later he re-established it in Oneida, N.Y. In 1879 his

trostatic attraction between oppositely charged particles. The electrostatic force theory was discarded when it was demonstrated that nuclei contain neutrons and that electrons are outside the nucleus. In a nucleus composed of neutrons and protons, the only charged particles are the positively charged protons, and according to the theory of electrostatic attraction, protons all carrying the same charge would repel each other. According to the most widely accepted current theory, nuclear particles are held together by "exchange forces", in which mesons (q.v.), common to both neutrons and protons, are continuously exchanged between them. The binding of protons and neutrons by mesons is similar to the binding of two atoms in a molecule through the sharing or exchange of a common pair of electrons (see VALENCE).

Nuclear masses can be accurately determined by use of the mass spectrograph (q.v.). The masses of the constituent particles, the neutrons and protons, are well known. If the sum of the masses of the individual neutron and protons of a nucleus is compared with the measured mass of the nucleus, the mass of the nucleus is found to be smaller than that of its component parts. The difference between these values is believed to have been transformed into energy, called *binding energy*. See ATOM AND ATOMIC THEORY; ATOMIC ENERGY AND ATOMIC BOMB; RADIOACTIVITY.

NUDIBRANCHIA or **ACOELA,** an order of opisthobranch gastropods, characterized by the complete absence of a shell in the adult stages, and commonly known as "sea slugs". Nudibranchiate mollusks are usually marine animals with brightly colored cerata, or respiratory processes. A typical family in this order is Dorididae, which contains the "sea lemons". See also GASTROPODA.

NUDISM, the doctrine and cult of life in the nude. Specifically, nudism is practiced for the physical benefit derived from exposure of the body to healthful qualities of sunlight and fresh air; in a wider sense, however, it is a philosophy and a way of life. The proponents of nudism maintain that when clothing is not absolutely necessitated by the rigors of the weather it should be abandoned, as it serves to focus erotic attention upon the body, thereby exciting an unhealthy sexual prurience. The shame customarily associated with nakedness in modern civilized society results, according to nudists, from centuries of cultural conditioning against complete exposure of the body in public. Nudism, by correcting in its practitioners this false sense of shame, enhances their self-assurance and furnishes them with a new appreciation of the essential beauty and dignity of the human body.

Archeological evidence indicates that nudism, in the form of sun-bathing, was practiced in antiquity by the Babylonians, Assyrians, Greeks, and Romans. In modern times the rise of nudism is identified with the *Nacktkultur* ("culture of nakedness") movement in Germany. The philosophy of Nacktkultur is epitomized in its slogan, "Health, beauty, and purity through nudity and light". The advocates of this movement emphasized its value in relation to preventive hygiene, claiming for their practices a highly tonic effect upon both body and mind. With the advent of National Socialism in Germany, however, Nacktkultur declined as a result of strong government restrictions. Nudist societies are maintained in most European countries, and are particularly prevalent in Norway, Sweden, and Finland. Although nudism has made no great progress in North America, the American Sunbathing Society, with headquarters at May's Landing, New Jersey, has branch organizations throughout the United States and in Canada.

NUEVO LEON, a northern State of Mexico, of which Monterey is the capital. It lies on the northeast slopes of the Sierra Madre. Agriculture, mining, and smelting are the chief industries. Area, 25,134 sq.m.; pop. (1950) 735,692.

NULLIFICATION, in the history of American political theory, the alleged right of a State to suspend operation of a Federal law within its boundaries. The right of nullification was asserted on the basis of a belief that States are the ultimate sources of sovereignty, and that the Federal government is simply a league of freely associated States, the authority of which the State is free to recognize or ignore in accordance with its best interests. This belief stemmed from the beginning of the Republic, when the States, jealous of their sovereignty and fearful of tyranny, agreed to yield certain of their powers to the United States (q.v.), as specifically set forth in the Constitution, only after the looser Articles of Confederation (q.v.) had proved ineffective. The principle of nullification was supported by many of the founding fathers. In 1798 and 1799, the Virginia and Kentucky resolutions (qq.v.), drafted by James Madison (q.v.) and Thomas Jefferson (q.v.), respectively, affirmed the validity of nullification and warned against Federal usurpation of State sovereignty. New England States nullified an unpopular embargo in 1809-10; and fifteen to twenty-five years later, Georgia and Alabama nullified Federal laws relating to American Indians.

As the development of industry and more intensive settlement linked the different parts of the country more closely together, nullification was opposed by advocates of the primacy of the Federal government. One of the foremost of these, Daniel Webster (q.v.), in his most famous speech before the U.S. Senate, warned Robert Young Hayne (q.v.) of South Carolina in 1830 that nullification would cause the Union to fall apart and that the American flag, "stained with the blood of fratricidal war", would wave over "the dismembered fragments of our once glorious empire". Soon after, in 1832, South Carolina called a State convention which declared "null, void, and no law" the high protective tariff of that year. President Andrew Jackson (q.v.) threatened to send troops to enforce the tariff in the port of Charleston. John Caldwell Calhoun (q.v.) of South Carolina, one of the leading advocates of nullification, called on Henry Clay (q.v.) of Virginia to reconcile the claims of South Carolina with those of the Federal government. As a result, a compromise tariff was passed, the South Carolina convention repealed the ordinance of nullification, and both sides of the controversy claimed a victory.

A final resolution of the question of nullification was thus postponed until 1861, when South Carolina, followed by other Southern States, seceded from the Union and precipitated the Civil War (q.v.). Though at the cost of the "blood of fratricidal war" predicted by Webster, this great conflict confirmed the primacy of the Federal government in the authority granted it by the Constitution, and no subsequent attempts have been made by any States to nullify Federal laws. Nevertheless, the question of distribution of powers between the States and the Federal government remains a live issue. The current proponents of "States' rights", still principally from the South, expound a point of view which, in opposing extensions of Federal power, has descended lineally from the original nullification theories of Jefferson and Calhoun. See also UNITED STATES: *History*.

NULLITY OF MARRIAGE, in law, in England and the United States, a void marriage as well as a marriage which is invalidated or annulled by court decision. An action by a married person seeking to have a marriage declared null and void is called a suit of "nullity of marriage", or an action to "annul a marriage". The decision of the court annulling the marriage is called a "decree of nullity".

The annulment of a marriage arises out of two different situations: first, the case of a union which is absolutely void, as for example, an incestuous marriage, a bigamous marriage (see BIGAMY), or in many States of the United States, a miscegenous marriage (see MISCEGENATION); and second, the case of a marriage which is voidable by legal proceedings at the option of the aggrieved party, as, for example, a marriage contracted by an infant, by an insane person, by a sexually impotent party, or a marriage induced by fraud or duress. A decree of the court is not necessary to declare the nullity of a void marriage and the parties to such a marriage are subject to fine or imprisonment. In most States of the United States, however, provision is made for instituting an action to declare by judicial decree the invalidity of such a marriage.

In the case of a voidable marriage, the marriage is a valid marriage for all legal purposes until annulled by the court. Upon annulment, the marriage status is considered to be void *ab initio*. In practical effect, however, the legality of the marriage status and the legal consequences of such marriage, from the time the voidable marriage relationship began until it is annulled, remains undisturbed. Children of such a marriage are legitimate. In the case of a void marriage, however, the marriage is actually void *ab initio;* it never was a marriage. Children of such a marriage are illegitimate and no alimony (q.v.) will be allowed by the court. See MARRIAGE. The statutes of many States however, legitimate the issue of void marriages. See DIVORCE; MARRIAGE; SEPARATION.

NUMBER, a word or symbol used to classify quantities or to represent the ratio of one quantity to another of the same kind. The field of numbers is divided into *real numbers* and *imaginary numbers* (q.v.). This article deals only with real numbers.

The simplest real numbers are the *positive rational numbers*, 1, 2, 3, 4, 5, . . ., which are the natural product of enumeration or counting. Positive rational numbers suffice for the arithmetical processes of addition and multiplication, but subtraction and division are not always possible when only this group of numbers is used. For example: 3 — 5 cannot be expressed as a positive rational number, nor can 3 ÷ 5. This difficulty led to the introduction of two more groups of rational numbers, the *negative rational numbers* such as —3, and the *rational fractions* such as ½. By using these groups of numbers in addition to the positive numbers the processes of subtraction and division are always possible.

The development of geometry (q.v.) by ancient Greek mathematicians led to the discovery that various parts of geometrical figures are often incommensurable, i.e., that they cannot be expressed in the same units. For example the unit value of the diagonal of a square cannot be expressed in terms of the unit values of the sides of the square by any form of rational number if the same units are used to measure both the diagonal and the sides. Similarly the diameter and circumference of a circle cannot be expressed in rational units. Expressed in more general terms, all roots of all rational numbers cannot be expressed in terms of rational numbers. The realization of this fact resulted in the discovery of another group of numbers, the *irrational numbers*. These numbers take such forms as $\sqrt{3}$, $\sqrt{2}$, $3 + \sqrt{2}$. Although irrational numbers can never be exactly expressed in terms of rational numbers, they can always be approximated to any desired degree of accuracy by the use of rational numbers. Thus $\sqrt{2}$ is found to lie somewhere between the rational decimal fractions 1.4 and 1.5, between 1.41 and 1.42, between 1.414 and 1.415.

The number *zero* completes the group of real numbers. This number indicates the operation of subtracting a number from itself, the addition of a positive and a negative rational number having the same absolute or numerical value, such as —5 and 5, or the absence of quantity.

Certain groups of real numbers have special properties. *Odd numbers* are positive or negative rational numbers which are not divisible by the number 2, and *even numbers* are those which are divisible by 2. *Perfect numbers* are defined as those in which the sum of all the divisors of the number are equal to the number itself, for example 6, which is the sum of 1 and 2 and 3. Numbers which are not perfect are classified as im-

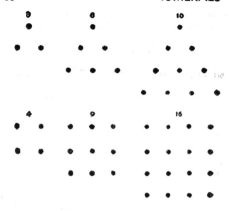

Polygonal numbers

perfect, and either *deficient* or *abundant* depending on whether the sums of their divisors are smaller or larger than the numbers themselves.

Numbers which can be expressed by the arrangement of groups of dots into geometrical patterns were classified by the Greek philosopher Pythagoras as *polygonal numbers*. They include such *triangular* numbers as 3, 6, 10, and 15, and such *square* numbers as 4, 9, and 16.

Prime numbers, which are important in the study of the theory of numbers (q.v.), are numbers which have no integral factors except 1 and the prime number. The first ten prime numbers are 1, 2, 3, 5, 7, 11, 13, 17, 19, and 23.

NUMBERS, BOOK OF, in the Bible, the fourth book of the Pentateuch (q.v.), containing thirty-six chapters and so named for its enumeration of the number of people in each of the tribes of Israel. It deals with the wanderings of the Israelites from Sinai to the hills of Moab, close to the Promised Land, and records the census, character, history, and legal innovations of that period.

NUMBERS, THEORY OF. See THEORY OF NUMBERS.

NUMERALS, signs or symbols used for the graphic representation of numbers. The earliest forms of number notation were simply groups of straight lines, either vertical or horizontal, each line corresponding to the number one. Such a system is inconvenient when dealing with large numbers and as early as 3400 B.C. in Egypt and 3000 B.C. in Mesopotamia a special symbol was adopted for the number 10. The addition of this second number symbol made possible the expression of the number 11 with two instead of eleven individual symbols and of the number 99 with eighteen instead of ninety-nine individual symbols. Later numeral systems introduced extra symbols for a number (usually either 4 or 5) between 1 and 10, and additional symbols for numbers greater than 10. In Babylonian cuneiform notation the numeral used for 1 was also used for 60 and for powers of 60; the value of the numeral was indicated by its context. This was a logical arrangement from the mathematical point of view because $60^0 = 1$, $60^1 = 60$, and $60^2 = 3600$. The Egyptian hieroglyphic system used special symbols for 10, 100, 1000, and 10,000.

The ancient Greeks had two parallel systems of numerals. The earlier of these was based on the initial letters of the names of numbers: the number 5 was indicated by the letter "pi"; 10 by the letter "delta"; 100 by the antique form of the letter H; 1000 by the letter "chi"; and 10,000 by the letter "mu". The later system, which was first introduced about the 3rd century B.C., employed all the letters of the Greek alphabet plus three letters borrowed from the Phenician as number symbols. The first nine letters of the alphabet were used for the numbers 1 to 9; the second nine letters for the decades from 10 to 90; and the last nine letters for the hundreds from 100 to 900. Thousands were indicated by placing a bar to the left of the appropriate numeral, and tens of thousands by placing the appropriate letter over the letter M. The late Greek system had the advantage of conciseness in that large numbers could be expressed with a minimum of symbols but had the disadvantage of requiring the user to memorize a total of twenty-seven symbols.

Roman Numerals. The system of number symbols created by the Romans had the merit of expressing all numbers from 1 to 1,000,000 with a total of six symbols: I for 1, V for 5, X for 10, L for 50, C for 100, M for 1000, $\overline{\text{M}}$ for 1,000,000. The simplicity of Roman numerals was such that almost anyone could learn to use them, and even today, more than 2000 years after their introduction, these numerals are in limited usage. The Roman system had one drawback, however, in that it was not suitable for rapid written calculations. The processes of arithmetic are possible using this notation, but are extremely difficult.

Arabic Numerals. The common system of number notation in use in most parts of the world today is the so-called Arabic system. This system was actually first developed by the Hindus and was in use in India in the 3rd century B.C. At that time the numerals 1, 4, and 6 were written in substantially the same form used today. The Hindu numeral system was probably introduced into the Arab world about the 7th or 8th centuries A.D. The first recorded use of the system in Europe was in the year 976.

The important innovation in the Arabic system is the use of *positional notation,* in which individual number symbols assume different values according to their position in the written numeral. Positional notation is made possible by the use of a symbol for zero. The symbol 0 makes it possible to differentiate between 11, 101, and 1001 without the use of additional symbols, and all numbers can be expressed in terms of ten symbols, the numerals from 1 to 9 plus 0. Positional notation also greatly simplifies all forms of written numerical calculation. See NOTATION.

NUMIDIA, originally the Roman name for that part of northern Africa corresponding nearly to the modern Algeria. The inhabitants of Numidia were a warlike race excelling in horsemanship. In the Punic Wars, between the Carthaginians and the Romans, the Numidians at first fought on the side of the former, but in the second Punic War (208-201 B.C.) Masinissa, King of the Eastern Numidians, joined the Romans and rendered them effective service in the war against Hannibal, the great leader of the Carthaginians. Supported by the victorious Romans, Masinissa united all Numidia under his sway. Of his successors, Jugurtha (q.v.) and Juba I were the most famous. After the victory of Gaius Julius Cæsar over Juba in the African war, Numidia became a Roman province (46 B.C.) under the name of Africa Nova. In 30 B.C. the emperor Augustus restored the western part of Numidia to Juba II, and five years later the eastern part was united with Africa Vetus to form the province of Africa. Under the emperor Septimius Severus (193-211 A.D.), Numidia once more became a separate province. The country was conquered successively by the Vandals in the 5th century, and by the Arabs in the 8th century; it remained under Arab control until the conquest of Algeria by the French in the 19th century.

NUMISMATICS (Gr. *nomisma,* "coin" or "legal tender"), the study of coins, medals, paper money, and objects similar to these in form or purpose. Coins, especially those of antiquity, are the principal subject of inquiry in numismatics. This article deals with coins; for discussion of other subjects of numismatics see MONEY; MEDAL. Coins are pieces of metal stamped with an emblem, portrait, inscription, or any other device showing that they were made under government auspices, and have intrinsic or exchange value as money. The first coins were issued independently both in Asia Minor and in China in the 8th century B.C. Since then they have been in widespread use throughout the civilized world.

The study of ancient coins yields considerable information about commercial and economic history and the art and culture of antiquity. Thus, ancient Roman coins found in India and ancient Arab coins discovered in Scandinavia indicate the extent of international trade between the Roman Empire and India and between the Mohammedan world and northern Europe. The complete chronological series of ancient Greek coins has been utilized by scholars in determining the dating of much of Greek art, as the coins exhibit the same technique, style, and subject matter of contemporary sculpture and other objects. Coins are also one of the principal sources of knowledge concerning such ancient peoples as the Iberians (q.v.), who left few other remains. The metals in which coins are usually minted are gold, silver, copper, and bronze and other alloys, such as electrum (q.v.), a mixture of gold and silver; lead, iron, platinum, nickel, and aluminum have also been used at various times. In the terminology of numismatics, the side of the coin on which the main device is struck is called the "obverse", while the other side is known as the "reverse". The identifying portrait, figure, or scene on either side is called the "type". A small figure or mint mark is called the "symbol", and the principal inscription on either side is called the "legend".

History. The earliest coins, struck in the 8th century B.C. in Lydia, Asia Minor, are of gold and electrum. They are without figures, the obverse having a series of sunken parallel lines or striations, and the reverse a rough triple punch mark. As coinage became a familiar part of everyday life in the cities throughout the Greek world, standard units of value based on the weight of the metal were established. The commonest units included the coin called the *stater,* with its multiples and subdivisions; the *drachma* and its multiples, the *mina* and *talent*; and the subdivision of the drachma, the *obol.* Soon after

coinage was originated, the form of the coins became elaborated, and types, consisting of animal figures and human heads, were stamped on the obverse, while punch marks were retained for the reverse. The punch mark was gradually made more complicated, first with geometrical patterns and then with the addition of a small figure in relief. The coins of the Greek colonial cities of Magna Græcia (southern Italy) do not bear a punch mark; the same type appears in relief on the obverse and is sunk into the surface on the reverse. Athenian coins of the mid-6th century also bear a type on both sides: the head of the goddess Athena on the obverse, and the figure of an owl, the attribute of Athena, on the reverse. Inscriptions generally do not appear on these early coins; when they occur they consist only of the initials of the town where the coins were struck.

The finest Greek coins were issued in the period from the end of the Greco-Persian Wars in 478 to the accession of Alexander the Great in 336 B.C. Athenian coins of this time bear the head of a deity on the obverse and the badge or emblem of the city of origin on the reverse. Symbols are common, and the names of towns and officials are inscribed in full. Well-known artists often executed the designs, and their names often appear on the coins. The silver coinage of Athens had a wider circulation than any other coinage in the Mediterranean region, and was imitated in Asia Minor and Central Asia. In Asia Minor during this period an electrum coinage was issued at Cyzicus. At the same time, gold coins called *darics,* and bearing the portrait of an archer, were produced in Persia; see DARIC. Coinage was also practiced on a large scale in Phenicia and Judea, where the standard unit was called the *shekel* (q.v.), and in Parthia, where the Greek word *"drachma"* was used for the standard coin.

In Greece between 359 and 336 B.C., during the reign of Philip II of Macedon, the first important gold coinage in the world was issued, and the first copper coins appeared, replacing the minute silver coins previously used for small change. In the vast coinages issued under Philip II and his successor, Alexander the Great, the head of a divinity such as Zeus Ammon or Herakles appears as the type. Both monarchs had their names inscribed on the coins, and Alexander also added the word *Basileus* (Gr., "king"). Portraits were first introduced on coins by the successors of Alexander, and in the three

Moneys of the World, Chase Nat. Bank Collec.

EARLY COINS. *Left: Obverse. Right: Reverse.*
Top to bottom: Lydian; Athenian; Egyptian;
Macedonian; Syrian; Roman; Roman.

centuries following the death of Alexander (323 B.C.) the likenesses of the rulers of Macedon, Syria, Egypt, and Bactria were struck on coins. Toward the end of this period many coins were marked with the date and place of mintage, either in letters or monograms. Under Roman domination the Greek towns were allowed to retain their local mints and to issue bronze coins. The special privilege of coining *tetradrachmae* (quadruple drachmae) made of an alloy of silver with copper, tin, or lead was granted to the cities of Antioch in Syria, Cæsaria in Cappadocia, and Alexandria in Egypt. These coins generally bear the head of the reigning Roman emperor on the obverse and a type of local significance on the reverse. All the local mints were closed about the year 268 A.D., except the mint at Alexandria, which was permitted to continue in operation until 296 A.D.

The earliest Roman coinage, dating from the late 4th century B.C., was of bronze, and consisted of a standard unit of currency called the *as* and its subdivisions: the *semis* (1/2 as), the *triens* (1/3 as), the *quadrans* (1/4 as), the *sextans* (1/6 as), and the *uncia* (1/12 as). Silver coins patterned on Greek models were adopted by the Romans at an early date, and in the middle of the 3rd century B.C. a silver coinage representing multiple values of the as was issued. These silver coins, known as the *denarius, quinarius,* and *sesterce* or *sestertius,* were the equivalents respectively of 10 asses, 5 asses, and 2½ asses. The three denominations bear the head of the goddess Roma on the obverse and a sign indicating the value of the coin; the name "Roma" and figures of deities or heroes appear on the reverse. In 217 B.C. the currency was reorganized, and the relation between silver and copper coins was changed so that the denarius equaled 16 asses instead of 10. The right of coinage, originally held by consuls and magistrates, was now exercised by a board of moneyers, who placed their names, initials, or monograms on the coins. About 150 B.C. the types on the silver coins began to be highly varied, each moneyer selecting his own designs to record family traditions, religious cults, or historical events. Gaius Julius Cæsar was the first to place his portrait on a Roman coin. The last important change in the coinage of the Roman Republic took place in 89 B.C. when the as was reduced to the value of half an uncia, or one twenty-fourth of its original value; the silver coin remained unchanged. Gold pieces had been issued irregularly since the 3rd century B.C., and in the last hundred years of the Republic, ending in 27 B.C., gold coins called *denarii aurei* were common.

The coinage of the Roman Empire began with the reign of Augustus Cæsar, and comprised a long and important series of coins with an infinite number of varieties in gold, silver, and bronze. Augustus assumed authority for the coinage of gold and silver; the Senate controlled bronze coinage, and thus the bronze coins from this period until the 3rd century A.D. bear the letters *S.C.*, standing for *senatus consulto* (Lat., "by order of the Senate"). The obverse of imperial coins generally bears the head of the emperor with his name and titles; the reverse is stamped with any of a number of types, such as a deity, personification, group, or monument, with explanatory inscriptions or a continuation of the imperial titles of the obverse. The bronze coins were, in order of value, the *quadrans* (1/4 as), *semis* (1/2 as), *dupondius* (2 asses), and *sesterce* (4 asses). Two coins were minted in silver: the *quinarius* (2 sesterces), and the *denarius* (4 sesterces); and two coins were of gold: the *quinarius aureus* (12½ silver denarii), and the *denarius aureus* (25 silver denarii). Until the end of the 2nd century Roman coinage was of fine quality in design and technique. Subsequently the coins became debased. The silver coins were made of alloys with a high copper, tin, or lead content, and the denarius was often copper merely coated with silver. The large bronze coins, such as the sesterce, dupondius, and as, were no longer issued. In the 4th century, during the reign of the emperor Constantine, a new gold unit called the *solidus* was put into circulation, with the *semissis* (1/2 solidus) and the *triens* (1/3 solidus). Silver coins, the *miliarensis*, and the *siliqua* also appeared; and in bronze the *maiorina* and *centenionalis* were coined. These coins, which generally bear portraits, remained in circulation until the end of the Western Roman Empire in 476 A.D.

In the Eastern Roman or Byzantine Empire the coinage consisted of the gold solidus and lesser values, the silver siliqua and its subdivisions, and the copper *nomisma, centenionalis, denarius,* and *follis.* The portrait of the reigning emperor appears as the usual type on the obverse. After the 10th century the portrait of the emperor is accompanied by a representation of a Christian saint. On the reverse the earlier coins bear such types as a figure personifying Victory, and the

Moneys of the World, Chase Nat. Bank Collec.

EARLY COINS. *Top to bottom: Byzantine; Italian; English; Venetian; Bermudian; colonial New England; early U.S.*

later examples bear images of Christ or the Virgin. In the inscriptions, Latin was gradually superseded by Greek, and disappeared entirely at the end of the 11th century. Byzantine coinage ended in 1453 with the capture of Constantinople (now Istanbul) by the Turks.

In Western Europe the coins of the separate states founded on the ruins of the Roman Empire retained the form and style of late Roman coins. Latin was the universal language for inscriptions. The principal coins in circulation in the early Middle Ages were the silver denarius and its half, the obol. The coins issued by authority of the Ostrogothic, Visigothic, and Vandal kingdoms of Italy, Spain, and North Africa were usually of silver and copper, and rarely of gold. The Visigothic coinage in Spain began at the end of the 6th century, and continued until the Arab conquest in the 8th century, when a Moorish coinage was begun. The numerous Moorish coins of the 8th century bear Latin inscriptions on one side and Arabic inscriptions on the other. Coinage was common throughout the other parts of the vast Mohammedan world. As images were prohibited by the Mohammedan religion, types were usually confined to legends in Arabic.

In England, coinage began in the 7th century, the two principal coins being the silver *sceat* and the copper *styca*. Many early examples have runic letters (see RUNES) accompanying the Latin inscription. In the Frankish Kingdom, the Merovingian kings issued gold solidi and trientes beginning in the 6th century. Beginning in the 8th century, the Carolingian rulers issued portrait coins, chiefly the silver denarius and the gold triens. This coinage spread from the Frankish kingdom and became the standard currency of most of Western Europe. Subsequently a vast number of denominations and issues were produced by local feudal authorities, both lay and ecclesiastical. The finest coins of the Middle Ages were the gold solidi and half-solidi issued by Emperor Frederick II of the Holy Roman Empire. These bear a portrait bust of the emperor on the obverse, and an eagle on the reverse. In 1252 an important gold coin called the *florin* (q.v.) was introduced in Florence; because of the commercial greatness of the city, the florin subsequently circulated throughout Europe and was widely imitated. The imitations included the Dutch *gulden,* and the Venetian *ducat,* or *sequin*; the latter became a world currency and continued

in use until the 19th century. Coins of the 14th century, often richly ornamented, include the French silver *tournois* and gold *mouton,* the German silver *groschen,* and the English *noble* or *rose noble*. Coinage was generally not uniform at this time as a great variety of issues were minted by the innumerable states, kingdoms, and principalities. The German *thaler,* first issued in 1518, became the principal European coin and influenced the form of other coins including the English *crown,* the French *écu,* and the Italian *scudo*. Italian Renaissance coins of the 15th and 16th centuries were often designed by such well-known artists as Benvenuto Cellini.

The earliest coinage of the New World, issued from 1616 to 1624 by the English settlers of Bermuda, consisted of copper *shillings,* and *sixpence, threepence,* and *twopence* pieces. These bear a representation of a hog, and are therefore known as "hog money". In 1652 the Massachusetts colonists issued the first coinage struck by any of the American colonies, a series of shillings, sixpences, and threepences, all of which were coined until 1686. The first regular United States coinage did not begin until 1793. See DOLLAR.

In the Orient, coinage originated in China about the 8th century B.C., or at approximately the same time it was first practiced in Asia Minor. The earliest coins were in the form of small bronze knives and spades, indicating that such utilitarian objects had served previously as articles of barter. Round coins were issued in the 4th century B.C.; in 618 A.D. the definitive form of a round coin with a square hole in the center was established. This form had a strong influence on all the coinages of the Far East until the end of the 19th century. The Japanese learned the art of coinage from the Chinese. The first coins were of bronze, and were issued in the 8th century A.D. Gold and silver coins appeared in the 16th century. India, Siam, Korea, and other countries of the Far East had native coinages of considerable antiquity, but since the late 19th century the minting of silver and copper coins modeled on occidental examples has been universal.

NUN, a member of a religious order for women, not necessarily limited to the Christian religion, living in a convent under vows of poverty, chastity, and obedience. The orders vary in the stipulations of the vows, some being permanent and others only for certain fixed periods of time. Each order varies slightly in dress, function, and regulation, but all follow the same basic principles. The nuns are devoted to a purely contemplative life or to a life of charity, including teaching and nursing. The heads of convents are variously called abbesses, prioresses, and mothers superior, and the nuns are generally called sisters.

NUNEATON, market town of Warwickshire, England, on the Anker River, 8 miles N. of Coventry. It has ribbon manufactures, worsted, cotton, and elastic weaving industries, tool factories, brickkilns, ironworks, and tanneries. Pop. (1951 est.) 54,408.

NÚÑEZ CABEZA DE VACA, ÁLVAR. See CABEZA DE VACA, ÁLVAR NÚÑEZ.

NUNNERIES. See MONASTICISM.

NUREMBERG (Ger. *Nürnberg*), a city of Bavaria, Germany, situated on the Pegnitz R., about 125 m. by rail N.N.W. of Munich. It is a commercial and manufacturing center, served by railroads and the Ludwig Canal, which connects the Danube and Main rivers. Toys are its principal manufacture; electrical equipment, machinery, pencils, needles, chromolithographic items, and novelties in metal, carved wood, and ivory, known collectively as Nuremberg wares, are other important products. The city also maintains a trade in hops.

Nuremberg was first mentioned in a document dating from 1050. After being successively owned by various German nobles, it was made a free imperial town in 1219. It subsequently became noted for its manufactures. During the 15th and 16th centuries the city was a center of culture. Among the celebrated artists who worked there in the 15th century was the painter and engraver Albrecht Dürer (q.v.). Its *Meistersinger*, or members of guilds formed to cultivate music and poetry, included the poet and dramatist Hans Sachs (q.v.) and were the subject of the opera *Die Meistersinger von Nürnberg* by Richard Wagner. In 1806 the city was annexed to the Kingdom of Bavaria. Beginning in 1933 it was the site of the annual September convention of the National Socialist or Nazi Party (see NATIONAL SOCIALISM). During World War II it was extensively bombed by Allied air forces. Following the war the city was incorporated in the U.S. Zone of Occupation, and was the site of the trials of Nazi war criminals by an international tribunal composed of Allied jurists (see NUREMBERG TRIALS.).

Among the buildings for which the city is noted are several medieval Gothic churches; the homes of Albrecht Dürer and Hans Sachs; an 11th-century castle, called the *Kaiserschloss;* a national museum, containing art masterpieces by Dürer, Hans Holbein (q.v.), and others; and a municipal library, in which are found rare manuscripts and books. Pop. (1950) 362,459.

NUREMBERG TRIALS, collective designation of the trials of former Nazi leaders of Germany for war crimes, held in Nuremberg, Germany, after the defeat of the Third Reich in World War II; the first international war-crimes trials in history. The Nuremberg trials were held under the authority principally of two legal instruments. These were the *Agreement for the Prosecution and Punishment of the Major War Criminals of the European Axis* and an annex entitled *Charter of the International Military Tribunal,* both signed in London on August 8, 1945, by representatives of the United States, Great Britain, France, and the Soviet Union; and subsequently ratified by nineteen other nations and then unanimously endorsed in principle by the General Assembly of the United Nations. The London Charter, as these instruments are usually referred to, provided for the establishment of a tribunal, designated as the International Military Tribunal, for the trial of accused persons, defined the jurisdiction, functions, and powers of that tribunal, and prescribed the general procedure to be followed by the tribunal in the conduct of trials.

By the terms of the London Charter, the International Military Tribunal was composed of one judge and one alternate judge from each of the signatory nations. U.S. Attorney General Francis Biddle and Federal Judge John J. Parker were appointed by President Harry S. Truman to serve as judge and alternate, respectively, on the Tribunal. The judges and alternates met in Berlin in October, 1945, to prepare specific rules for the conduct of the trials. On October 18, 1945, the Committee of Chief Prosecutors, also provided for by the terms of the London Charter, and including U.S. Supreme Court Justice Robert H. Jackson, lodged an indictment with the Tribunal against twenty-four individuals. Among the accused were Hermann Göring, economic dictator of the Third Reich and first in line of succession to Adolf Hitler as head of the German state; the diplomat Franz von Papen; Hjalmar Schacht, economic and financial expert and governmental official; Robert Ley, head of the state-controlled German Labor Front; Hans Fritsche,

Wide World Photo

Nazi leaders (seated, in background) hear verdict read at Nuremberg trials, Germany

governmental press chief under Joseph Goebbels, minister of propaganda; Martin Ludwig Bormann, secretary of the Nazi Party; the industrialist Gustav Krupp von Bohlen und Halbach; and a number of military leaders. The indictment contained a large number of specific counts grouped under four general heads: *The Common Plan or Conspiracy* to wage aggressive war, *Crimes against Peace, War Crimes,* and *Crimes Against Humanity.*

As the London Charter also provided that the International Military Tribunal could designate as criminal organizations of which persons tried by it were members, the Committee of Chief Prosecutors asked in the indictment that the following Nazi groups and organizations be adjudged criminal: the cabinet of the Third Reich; the Leadership Corps of the Nazi Party, the Sturmabteilungen (SA) or Storm Troopers, the Schutzstaffeln (SS) or Elite Guard, the Sicherheitdienst (SD) or Security Service, the Gestapo (q.v.) or secret police (see NATIONAL SOCIALISM), and the general staff and high command of the German armed forces.

After the defendants had been served with copies of the indictment, Robert Ley committed suicide in prison, and the case of Gustav Krupp was severed because of his ill health. On November 17 the Tribunal ruled that Martin Bormann, whose whereabouts were unknown, would be tried *in absentia.* The defendants were allowed to select counsel of their own choosing, or, when they so requested, were represented by counsel se-

lected for them by the Tribunal. The indicted organizations were also represented by counsel.

The trial began on November 20, 1945, and was conducted in four languages: English, French, Russian, and German. The Tribunal held 403 public sessions and heard 33 prosecution witnesses against the individual defendants. Most of the evidence submitted by the prosecution consisted of thousands of original documents seized by Allied forces. Among the documents were minutes of topsecret meetings of Hitler and his closest collaborators, secret orders issued by the defendants, and the confidential reports and correspondence of Nazi party, police, and business leaders. 61 witnesses, in addition to 19 of the defendants, gave testimony for the defense. 22 witnesses were heard for the indicted organizations. In connection with the trials of the latter, the Tribunal appointed a number of commissioners who, assisted by a large staff, heard 101 defense witnesses and received into evidence 1809 affidavits from other witnesses. Also submitted to the commissioners, in summarized form, were 38,000 affidavits signed by approximately 313,000 persons in behalf of the indicted organizations and groups. The reports of the commissioners and of their staff were made part of the official record of the trial.

The decisions of the Tribunal, called the Judgment, were handed down on September 30 and October 1, 1946. The Judgment is notable for several reasons, perhaps the most important being the decisions made in it with respect to those points of international law raised by the act of holding the trial itself and vigorously urged in their behalf by the defendants. In declaring its standpoint, the Tribunal declared: "War is essentially an evil thing. Its consequences are not confined to the belligerent states alone, but affect the whole world. To initiate a war of aggression, therefore, is not only an international crime; it is the supreme international crime differing only from other war crimes in that it contains within itself the accumulated evil of the whole." On the basis of its review of the evidence, the Judgment of Nuremberg held that the German government had committed crimes against peace by planning, preparing, initiating, and engaging in wars of aggression against Poland, Denmark, Norway, Belgium, the Netherlands, Luxemburg, Greece, Yugoslavia, the Soviet Union, and the United States; and had also committed acts of aggression against Austria and Czechoslovakia. The Tribunal rejected the contention of the defense that the trial of the accused for acts which had not been defined in international law as crimes prior to their commission, was *ex post facto* (q.v.) law. The Judgment pointed out that the General Treaty for the Renunciation of War of August 27, 1928, known as the Kellogg-Briand Pact (q.v.) or the Pact of Paris, of which Germany had been a signatory, had expressly renounced war as an instrument of policy; and that, therefore, the acts of the defendants in engaging in war in contravention of that treaty, were clearly illegal in international law. To the contentions of the defense that the Pact of Paris did not expressly state that to engage in war was a criminal act, and that the pact had not set up courts to try warmakers, the Tribunal declared that this situation had also been true in regard to the laws of war codified in the Hague Convention of 1907 (see INTERNATIONAL LAW); and that, nevertheless, competent military tribunals had, for many years, and without objections being raised, tried and punished individuals guilty of violating those rules of land warfare.

The Tribunal also rejected the contention made in behalf of a number of the defendants that they were not legally responsible for their acts because they engaged in them on the orders of superior authority. The Tribunal held that that doctrine had never been accepted either in international law or the law of any nation. "The true test," read the Judgment, "which is found in . . . the criminal laws of most nations, is not the existence of the order, but whether moral choice" [in executing it] "was in fact possible."

On the subject of war crimes and crimes against humanity, which the Tribunal considered simultaneously, it found overwhelming evidence of a systematic rule of violence, brutality, and terrorism by the German government in the territories occupied by it. Millions of persons were destroyed in concentration camps, many of which were equipped with gas chambers for the efficient extermination of Jews, Poles, and other non-Germans, and with furnaces for the cremation of their bodies; see GENOCIDE. The slave-labor policy of the German government, the Tribunal found, involved the forcible deportation from their homes to Germany of at least five million persons, many of whom died owing to inhuman treatment. Although the persecution of the Jews in Germany was severe after the seizure of power by the Nazis in 1933, its severity, the Tribunal found, was not as great as that perpetrated on the Jews in the occupied countries; see JEWS. The Tribunal also found that many Allied soldiers who had surrendered to the Germans during the course of the war had been executed, often as a matter of high official policy; the treatment of Soviet prisoners of war, the Judgment declared, was particularly inhumane. In some cases Soviet prisoners of war had been branded; and in others they had been used as subjects for medical experiments in bacteriological warfare.

Of the seven indicted groups and organizations the Tribunal declared criminal only the leadership corps of the Nazi Party, the SS, the SD, and the Gestapo. With respect to the SA, the Judgment declared that although some units of the SA had committed war crimes and crimes against humanity, the members of the SA generally had not participated in, or had no knowledge of criminal acts; after the "blood purge" of 1934 of opposition elements in the Nazi Party, the Tribunal declared, the SA had been reduced to an unimportant group. With the Soviet judge dissenting, the Tribunal ruled that the cabinet of the Nazi government and the general staff and high command of the German armed forces had not constituted criminal groups.

Of the individual defendants, Schacht, Von Papen, and Fritsche were acquitted; seven received prison terms ranging from ten years to life; and the other twelve were sentenced to death by hanging. Pursuant to the terms of the London Charter, the sentences of the convicted offenders were executed by the Allied Control Council for Germany. Sixteen of the defendants appealed their sentences to the Council, which rejected them all on October 10, 1946. On the night of October 15, Göring committed suicide in prison. The others who had been condemned to death were hanged in the yard of the Nuremberg jail in the early morning hours of October 16.

Seen in retrospect, the most important accomplishments of the trial were the establishment of the principle in international law that aggressive war is a crime against humanity, and the establishment of the precedents of the trial and punishment of persons guilty of that crime. A number of authorities on law, however, unconvinced by the reasoning of the Tribunal, consider its decisions as constituting *ex post facto* law in large part, and the Judgment has become the subject of considerable controversy. Other critics of the Tribunal have pointed out that its judgment of the SA was in error, as that arm of the Nazi Party recovered from its decline and reached the zenith of its power and influence in 1943 during World War II.

While the trial of Göring and his coleaders was in progress, the Allied Control Council for Germany issued a law on December 20, 1945, virtually identical in essence with the London Charter, but authorizing the commanders of the occupation zones of Germany to constitute military tribunals in those zones for the trials of persons accused of war crimes. Under this law, the commander of the U.S. Zone of Occupation set up several tribunals composed exclusively of American citizens as judges, which sat in Nuremberg.

Twelve trials of 177 persons were held from the fall of 1946 to the spring of 1949 inclusive. Among the defendants were cabinet ministers under the Third Reich, other government officials, high-ranking police officials, leaders of the armament industry, and a number of leading practitioners of the legal and medical professions under the Hitler regime. All were indicted for atrocities and other offenses constituting war crimes; a few of the defendants were also indicted for crimes against peace. Thirty-five of the defendants were acquitted; 118 received varying prison terms, including sentences to life imprisonment; and 24 were condemned to death by hanging.

NURSERY SCHOOL and **DAY NURSERY,** institutions for the care and development of children of preschool age. In general, the day nursery offers custodial care only, whereas the nursery school affords educational activities

as well. Nursery schools developed as an outgrowth of the day-nursery movement, which arose in Europe early in the 19th century as a reflection of the increasing employment of women in industry. The absence of large numbers of mothers from their homes during the day led to widespread neglect of children, and stimulated various charitable agencies to seek means of caring for the children. The leader in this movement was the French philanthropist Jean Baptiste Firmin Marbeau (1798–1875), whose studies proved that the high rate of infant mortality in France was largely due to the absence of working mothers, and who in 1846 founded the Crèche (Fr., "cradle") Society of France, with the aim of fostering child care. Within a relatively short period, day nurseries had been established in many parts of France and several other European countries had followed suit. Many of these nurseries were wholly or partly supported by local and national governments. A large number of the nurseries were set up in factories, enabling mothers of nursing children to take brief periods from their work in order to tend to the needs of their offspring.

In the United States, the first day nursery was opened in 1854 by the Nursery and Child's Hospital of New York City. Numerous day nurseries were established in various areas during the latter half of the 19th century; most of them were charitable, though a few operated on a commercial basis. Both in Europe and in the United States, the day-nursery movement received great impetus during World War I, when shortages of manpower caused the industrial employment of unprecedented numbers of women. In England, France, Germany, and Italy, nurseries were established even in munitions plants, under direct government sponsorship. Although the number of nurseries in the United States also rose precipitately, this rise was accomplished without government aid of any kind. During the years following World War I, however, Federal, State, and local governments gradually began to exercise a measure of control over the nurseries, chiefly by licensing them and by inspecting and regulating the conditions within the nurseries.

The development of nursery schools occurred after World War I, beginning in England and rapidly spreading to other countries as scientific studies of children revealed the importance of the child's early years in the formation of character. For some years, the chief distinction between the day nursery and the nursery school, besides the difference in activities offered to preschool children, lay in the fact that the former were mainly charitable institutions designed to aid needy families, whereas nursery schools were for the most part commercial enterprises catering to those who could afford their services. More recently, the distinction has gradually been narrowed in most countries, as day nurseries have begun to employ trained personnel capable of giving educational guidance to their charges.

The outbreak of World War II was quickly followed by an increase in the number of day nurseries in almost all countries, as women were again called upon to replace men in the factories. On this occasion the U.S. government immediately came to the support of the nurseries, allocating $6,000,000 in July, 1942, for a day-care program for the children of working mothers. Many States and local communities supplemented this Federal aid. By the end of hostilities, in August, 1945, more than 100,000 children were being cared for in centers receiving Federal subsidies. Soon afterward, the Federal government drastically curtailed its expenditures for this purpose, and later abolished them, causing a sharp drop in the number of nurseries in operation. The expectation that most employed mothers would leave their jobs at the end of the war was only partly fulfilled, however, and the postwar years witnessed the development of a widespread movement, headed by sociologists, social workers, teachers, and other interested groups, which sought renewed government aid to meet the need for a comprehensive day-care program.

NURSING, a profession the members of which provide auxiliary medical care to the sick and disabled under the direction of physicians or other medical specialists. Among the Romans, the nurse was one of a number of attendants that included the bonesetter, the barber, the bath attendant, the masseur, the drug seller, the midwife, and others who specialized early in the medical profession.

In the Middle Ages Christian monasteries were opened to the sick and convent orders were organized especially to care for them. Between the 12th century and the 15th, there was a marked movement for the development of hospitals in Europe, especially in England, where Saint Bartholomew's Hospital and Saint Thomas's date from 1123 and 1215 respectively. The hospitalers were assisted by various bodies of women. In the latter part of the 12th century Hildegarde, abbess of Rupertsburg, organized a school of nurses for service in the hospitals.

At Bresse, in France, three hundred years ago, the first organization for the relief of suffering in France was formed under the name "Servants of the Poor" by Saint Vincent de Paul. Even earlier than this, women were trained to deeds of charity, and the great sisterhoods devoted to this work today, in France and Italy and in Spain, were founded at Rouen, Lisieux, and elsewhere in the 14th century. From these imperfect beginnings grew the modern system of training nurses. In 1840 Mrs. Fry's Nursing Sisters was organized to care for London outcasts. Florence Nightingale in 1853 actively aided the movement for more efficient training of nurses, and raised it from a commonplace, ill-regulated calling to a public profession served by especially trained nurses duly qualified in humanitarian practices. In 1872 the New England Hospital for Women and Children in Boston offered a graded course in nursing, while the Bellevue Training School, New York City, was the first American school organized on the Florence Nightingale plan, graduating its first class in 1875.

The American Hospital Association advocated in 1907 three grades of nurses, the teacher or executive, the bedside nurse, and the attendant. The Rockefeller Association, reporting in 1922 to the American Nurses' Association, made similar recommendations, and suggested 28 months' training for the rank and file, 8 months' additional postgraduate work for teachers, executives, or public health nurses, and an 8 months' course for attendants. Different States provide for different periods of training, but two years is the minimum length required.

Approximately 1300 schools of nursing in the United States meet requirements set by law in their respective States. In general there are two types: hospital schools owned and operated by hospitals, and collegiate schools, affiliated with hospitals and also colleges and universities. These latter provide a degree as well as a diploma in nursing.

Most nursing schools require that candidates be graduated from high school and have two years of science, as well as good health, and a personality suited to the demands of service to the sick.

Opportunities for nurses in addition to hospital and institutional positions include military and civil service positions under Federal auspices, private duty nursing, public health service, and teaching. Nurses' professional registries fill the majority of requests for staff and private duty nurses.

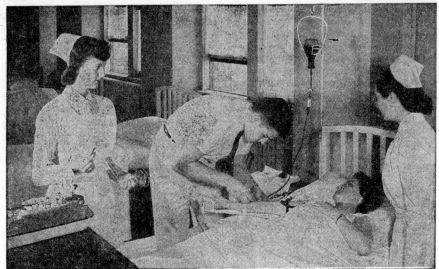

Public Interest Department, Presbyterian Hospital, N.Y.C.

Nurses in a modern hospital assisting a physician at a patient's bedside. A large share of the responsibility for a patient's recovery is placed upon the skilled nurse.

Federal agencies maintaining nursing services include: The U.S. Veterans Administration; the Bureau of Indian Affairs; the U.S. Public Health Service, employing nurses in marine hospitals, prison hospitals, and special institutions for drug addicts; the Children's Bureau; the Office of Vocational Rehabilitation; and St. Elizabeths Hospital; as well as such semiofficial agencies as the American National Red Cross.

NUT, a term commonly and loosely applied to any dry, hard-shelled fruit or seed having a rind which can be easily separated from the internal, edible kernel. In botanical terminology, the term "nut" is restricted to an indehiscent, one-seeded fruit, which has developed from a compound ovary, having external walls hardened to a woody consistency. Such "true nuts" may be edible or inedible; common examples are acorns, beechnuts, chestnuts, and hazelnuts. Examples of fruits or seeds which are incorrectly and popularly termed "nuts" include: almonds and walnuts, which are drupes; horse chestnuts and peanuts, which are pods; and Brazil nuts, which are capsules.

NUTCRACKER, common name for any bird in the genus *Nucifraga* of the Crow family, found in the colder regions of the Northern Hemisphere. The birds are so called because of their long, heavy bills which they use to crack nuts. The birds have long, pointed wings and long, curved claws. The best-known spe-

cies are the European nutcracker, *N. caryocatactes,* about 13½ in. long, and Clark's nutcracker, *N. columbiana,* about 12½ in. long, found in western North America. Clark's nutcracker, which is light gray in general body color, with black and white wings and tail, inhabits high mountains just below the timber line. It is noted for its unusual flying habits, often dropping from a high peak with its wings closed and plummeting several hundred feet before suddenly opening its wings in flight.

NUTHATCH, or NUTPECKER, common name for any of the passerine birds constituting the family Sittidae, widely distributed in the Northern Hemisphere. The birds, which rarely exceed six inches in length, are bluish gray in general body color. They have long, straight, sturdy bills, long wings, short tails, powerful feet, and long powerful claws. They are noted for their curious arboreal habits, creeping about on the trunk or limbs of trees in search of insects. Nuthatches, deriving their sole support from their powerful feet and claws, often move about head downward on the vertical surface of a tree trunk, digging into crevices in the bark for adult insects, larvae, or eggs. The birds also feed on grain and nuts, breaking them by pecking at the hard outer coatings with their bills. Nuthatches have a characteristic, high-pitched, nasal cry. They nest in natural crevices or in

White-breasted nuthatch

nesting holes in trees abandoned by other birds, especially woodpeckers. The nest is lined with bits of bark, rabbit hair, grass, and feathers. Usually four to eight creamy-white eggs, speckled with brown, gray, or purple, are deposited in a clutch.

The North American species are all contained within the genus *Sitta*. The commonest species, *S. carolinensis,* the white-breasted nuthatch, is found throughout the United States east of the Rocky Mountains, and is abundant in winter as well as summer. It is about six inches long, and is grayish blue above and white below, with blotches of brown on the lower abdomen. The adult male is characterized by a black crown. One of the smallest of the American species is the pygmy nuthatch, *S. pygmaea,* of the western portion of the Great Plains. The pygmy nuthatch is about four inches long.

NUTMEG, common name applied to a family, Myristicaceae, of evergreen shrubs and trees, especially to plants of the genus *Myristica.* The family, which comprises about eighteen genera and three hundred species, is native to the Moluccas in the East Indies, and has been widely cultivated in the East Indies, southern Asia, the West Indies, and Brazil for its seeds, which yield various spices, and for its timber Plants in the family are dioecious, with inconspicuous flowers. The fruit is a yellow drupe about 2 in. in diameter, popularly called the "nutmeg apple", which can be split into two equal halves, each containing a seed surrounded by a fleshy outer coating. In plants of the genus *Myristica,* which contains about forty species, this seed is dried to form the culinary spice popularly known as "nutmeg"; the fleshy coating is peeled off and also dried, to form the spice known as "mace". The commonest nutmeg tree is *M. fragrans,* which grows to a height of about fifty feet.

NUTRIA. See COYPU; FUR.

NUTRITION, HUMAN, the processes by which the body obtains, modifies, and utilizes the chemical substances required for growth and health. Nutrition depends on digestion (q.v.) and absorption, and on the more remote functions of respiration, circulation, secretion, and excretion. The secretions of various glands connected with the alimentary system transform food (q.v.) into compounds which are stored for future use or poured directly into the blood stream. The blood stream brings these compounds into contact with the cells, each of which has the power of withdrawing the materials it requires. See METABOLISM.

Food acts in one or more of three ways, i.e., to produce fuel for the body's warmth and energy; to furnish building materials for growth, repair, and reproduction; and to provide regulating substances that enable the body to use other materials for energy production.

Each food contains one or more of the chemical substances termed nutrients, namely carbohydrates and fats, the chief sources of fuel for heat and energy; proteins, which are the building materials for the body's tissues; vitamins, which regulate various body functions; and minerals, required for growth and repair, and also for regulating various processes. See AMINO ACID; PROTEIN; TRACE ELEMENTS; VITAMIN.

The daily diet must include a variety of foods to provide the essential nutrients. An adequate diet consists of daily combinations of foods from seven basic food groups. The groups are leafy, green, and yellow vegetables; citrus fruits and tomatoes; potatoes and sweet potatoes, and other vegetables and fruits not included in the first two categories; milk, cheese, and ice cream; meat, poultry, fish, eggs, dry beans and peas, and nuts; baked goods, flour, and cereals; and fats and oils.

Nutrition is also influenced by such factors as physical environment, dentition, and emotional conditions. Psychic disturbances may cause loss of appetite, poor assimilation of food, or in some cases compulsive eating, which leads to overweight. Obesity is a serious nutritional problem among adults, particularly in the United States. Excess fat, which is a health liability after the age of 35, results from the consumption of more energy foods than the body needs. Proper reducing diets cut down the quantity of food consumed, but provide the minimum daily requirements of essential nutrients.

The excessive use of alcohol may cause malnutrition; see ALCOHOLISM. Nutritional imbalance may also occur as a result of food fads, which give emphasis to certain types of foods and neglect others. Lack of essential nutrients may cause deficiency diseases, such as anemia, beriberi, or pellagra. The importance of three balanced meals daily for normal individuals, whether children or adults, active or sedentary, men or women, has been established by scientific research.

NYASA, LAKE, southernmost and third largest of the great lakes of Africa, situated in the Great Rift Valley, approximately 370 m. from the Indian Ocean. It lies chiefly in Nyasaland Protectorate, and has a maximum length of about 360 m. and an average width of 25 m. The area, variously estimated, is between 11,000 sq.m. and 15,000 sq.m. The surface of the lake is some 1650 ft. above sea level. The northern extremity is shallow, but in the south it reaches a depth of 2400 ft., placing its bed 750 ft. below the surface of the ocean. An outlet of Lake Nyasa extends to the Zambezi R. The lake was discovered in 1859 by David Livingstone (q.v.).

NYASALAND PROTECTORATE, formerly BRITISH CENTRAL AFRICA, now forming part of the Federation of Rhodesia and Nyasaland, established in 1953. Principal exports are tobacco, tea, and cotton. It is a large plateau land, with an area of 37,596 sq.m., and is watered by the Shiré River and several headstreams of the Zambesi. Population (1952 est.) 2,392,000 natives, 4070 Europeans, and 5240 Asiatics. Blantyre and Limbe in the Shiré Highlands are the principal settlements, with a combined population of about 6000. Over 4000 miles of motor roads, all suitable for year round traffic, are maintained, connecting the principal centers of trade and production. Road systems link the Protectorate with South Africa and with Northern Rhodesia, Tanganyika Territory, and Kenya Colony. There are approximately 500 m. of railways, and air service is also in operation.

In World War I, forces from German East Africa invaded the Protectorate upon the outbreak of hostilities in August, 1914, but they were driven out a month later. Naval units with small craft in sections reached Lake Nyasa from England in 1915, having built roads through the forest to transport their vessels from railhead. The German port of Sphinxhaven was attacked and captured on May 30, 1915. German territory was invaded in 1916–17 from the base at Karonga by a force composed of Rhodesian and South Af-

rican Dutch troops. In 1918, the German forces of General von Lettow-Vorbeck invaded Nyasaland but were driven into Northern Rhodesia. The Unknown Soldier of Portugal, whose body is enshrined in the Batalka Monastery in Lisbon, was one of those who fell fighting in the Nyasaland Protectorate.

NYCTAGINACEAE or FOUR-O'CLOCK FAMILY, a family of herbs, shrubs, and small trees containing about one hundred species native to tropical and warm-temperate America. Members of the family have opposite leaves and small, petal-less flowers. The tube-shaped united calyx resembles a corolla in coloration, and the bracts below the calyx form an involucre which closely resembles a calyx, giving to the flower the appearance of having a complete perianth. The flowers usually have three to five stamens and a solitary pistil. The fruit is an achene. The largest genus in the Four-o'clock family is *Oxybaphus*, comprising about forty species of herbs, many of them abundant in the warmer portions of the Great Plains. The four-o'clock, or marvel-of-Peru, *Mirabilis jalapa,* cultivated in gardens all over the United States, has yellow, red, or orange flowers which are closed during the morning and which open in the late afternoon.

NYE, EDGAR WILSON (1850–96), American humorist, born in Shirley, Me., and educated at the River Falls Academy in Wisconsin. He was admitted to the Wyoming bar in 1876 and subsequently held various civic offices in that State, including those of school superintendent and postmaster. Under the name "Bill Nye" he contributed humorous sketches to the Cheyenne *Sun* and Denver *Tribune* until, in 1881, he founded the *Laramie Boomerang;* in the last-named newspaper appeared the comic stories and observations later collected and published in the books *Bill Nye and Boomerang* (1881), *Forty Liars and Other Lies* (1882), and *Baled Hay* (1884). From 1887 to 1891 Nye was a staff member of the New York *World*. He also wrote two farcical histories, *Bill Nye's History of the United States* (1894) and *Bill Nye's History of England* (1896).

NYIREGYHAZA, town of Hungary, 29 miles N.E. of Debreczin. It has grain and tobacco interests, a livestock industry, and manufactures of soap, candles, machines, and cement. Pop., about 56,000.

NYLGHAU. See NILGAI.

NYLON, term applied to a synthetic resin, widely used for textile fibers, characterized by great strength, toughness, and elasticity, and processed also in the form of bristles and molded articles. Nylon was developed in 1935

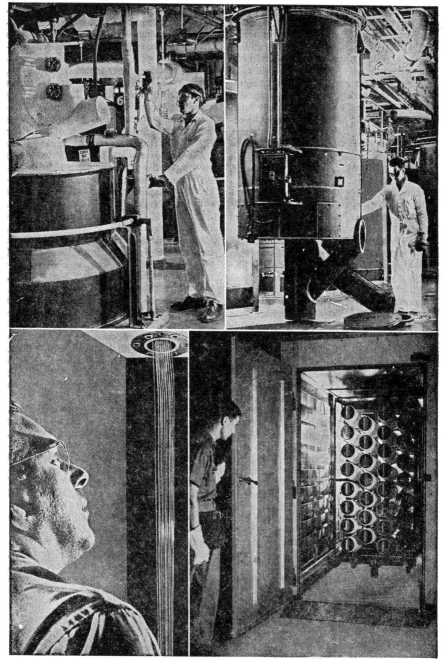

E.I. du Pont de Nemours & Co.

MAKING NYLON. *Top, left: Autoclave in which chemicals polymerize to form nylon. Top, right: Mixer in which nylon flakes are blended to uniform consistency. Bottom, left: Nylon filaments emerging from spinneret. Bottom, right: An oven for baking nylon yarn.*

by scientists of E.I. du Pont de Nemours & Co. It is usually made by polymerizing adipic acid and hexamethylenediamine, an amine derivative; see POLYMER. Adipic acid is derived from phenol; hexamethylenediamine is made by treating adipic acid catalytically with ammonia and hydrogenating the product. The widely circulated slogan that nylon is made from coal, air, and water refers to the processes by which phenol may be obtained from coal, the hydrogen from water, and nitrogen from air. Nylon is insoluble in water and in ordinary organic solvents; it dissolves in phenol, cresol, and formic acid, and melts at 263° C. (505° F.).

In making textile fibers, small chips of the nylon polymer, which is obtained as a tough, ivorylike material, are melted and forced through holes in a metal disk called a spinneret. The filaments are congealed by a blast of air, and are then drawn to about four times their original lengths. The diameter of the filaments is controlled by changing the rate at which the molten nylon is pumped into the spinneret and the rate at which the filaments are drawn away. Filaments much finer than those of ordinary textile fibers can be made from nylon. Nylon fibers have the appearance and luster of silk; their tensile strength is higher than that of wool, silk, rayon, or cotton. Dyes are applied either to the molten mass of nylon or to the yarn or finished fabric. Acetate rayon dyes are usually used for dyeing nylon. Nylon is used in the manufacture of durable fabrics which have the appearance or light weight of silk. It has almost replaced silk in the manufacture of hosiery, and is popular for other articles of clothing, such as night garments, underwear, blouses, shirts, and raincoats. Nylon fabrics are water-resistant; they dry quickly when laundered and do not need ironing. Among the many other articles for which nylon fibers are used are parachutes and insect screening. In addition to its wide application to textile fibers, nylon is used in making medical sutures, strings for tennis rackets, brush bristles, rope, and fishing nets and lines. Articles for which molded nylon is used include insulating material, combs, dishware, and machinery parts.

NYMPHAEACEAE. See WATER LILY.

NYMPHALIDAE, a large family of butterflies, containing about 5000 species, characterized by a rudimentary pair of forelegs which are useless in walking. These butterflies, almost world-wide in distribution, are commonly known as "four-footed butterflies" or, because the vestigial forelegs are tufted, as "brush-footed butterflies". The larvae are usually spiny; and the angular pupae rest upside down, supported at the posterior tip by a filament attached to a branch of a tree or shrub. The pupae are often marked with bronze or silver spots. Nymphalid butterflies have a peculiar odor, and are avoided by insectivorous animals; consequently many species in this family are mimicked by butterflies of other families; see MIMICRY; DANAÏS. Among the common American nymphalids are the fritillaries (q.v.) and the red admiral, *Vanessa atalanta,* which is found throughout most of the Northern Hemisphere. The red admiral is about 1 in. long, and has a wingspread of about 3 in. It is dark purple above, marked with bands of red and spots of white. Other common species in the genus *Vanessa* are the painted beauty, *V. virginiensis,* and the thistle butterfly, *V. cardui.* The zebra butterfly, *Heliconius charithonius,* of southern United States, is black striped with yellow. The wood nymph, *Cercyonis alope,* is a species about ¾ in. long, with a wingspread of about 2¼ in., and is found in wooded regions throughout the United States.

NYMPHS, in Greek and Roman mythology, lesser divinities or spirits of nature, dwelling in groves and fountains, forests, meadows, streams, and the sea. They are usually described as young and beautiful maidens, fond of music and dancing. The nymphs were distinguished according to the various parts of nature which they represented, and included the *Oceanids,* or daughters of Oceanus, the ocean which flows around the earth, the *Nereids* (q.v.), or daughters of Nereus, nymphs of the Mediterranean Sea, the *Potameides,* or river nymphs, the *Naiads* (q.v.), or nymphs of springs and fresh-water streams, the *Oreads* (q.v.), or nymphs of mountains and grottoes, and the *Dryads* (q.v.), nymphs of the forests.

NYSSA. See TUPELO.

O, the fifteenth letter and fourth vowel in the alphabets of western Europe. It was originally a Phenician character representing the Semitic letter *'ayn,* which was consonantal and stood for a guttural breathing sound. The Greeks adopted this sign to represent the short *o* vowel, and added a separate sign for the long sound of *o*; the names *omicron* (Gr., "little o") and *omega* ("big o"), respectively, were given to these letters. The distinction was not continued by the Romans, and only a single letter, standing for both sounds, was incorporated into the Latin alphabet. The upper-case or capital O of the English alphabet changed very little during the course of its development. The Phenician sign in which it originated was approximately circular; in the Greek and Latin alphabets it gradually assumed the oval shape which is its usual form at the present time. In English the letter O represents two principal sounds: the long *o,* as in *old, no,* and *bone;* and the short *o,* as in *nod, hot,* and *golf.* Other sounds for which the letter stands include those heard in *shorn wolf, son,* and *do.* The long *o* sound is indicated by a variety of spellings, such as *oh, sew, dough, tow,* and *foe.*

As an abbreviation the capital O is used for personal names beginning with O, such as Oliver and Olivia, for the month of October, for the States of Ohio and Oregon, and for Ocean. Lower-case o is used as an abbreviation for words such as occidental, oriental, old, order, and octave. As a symbol the capital O is used in chemistry for oxygen, in logic for the particular negative proposition (some A is not B), in mathematics for zero, and in psychology for a person who is both the observer and subject of an introspective demonstration or experiment. O in either upper or lower case stands for the 14th or 15th in an order, class, group, or series. The letter is also used in compound adjectives and nouns to denote circular or oval forms, as in *O-window* and *O-shaped.*

OAHU, one of the Hawaiian Islands. See HAWAII.

OAK, common name applied to trees and shrubs belonging to the genus *Quercus* of the Beech family. The genus, which contains about three hundred species, is native to the North Temperate Zone, and is widely cultivated for its timber and bark, and for shade and ornament. Oak trees are generally deciduous, but are sometimes evergreen in the warmer, southerly portions of their range. These evergreen oaks are commonly called "live oaks". Oak leaves are simple and alternate, and vary in shape among different species. The inconspicuous male and female flowers are borne on the same plant. The staminate flowers are borne in spikes or catkins; the pistillate flowers are usually solitary. The fruit is an acorn, or nut, having characteristic elliptical shape, capped by a persistent, scaly involucre which forms a cup. Oak trees are noted for their great longevity. Their wood is hard, durable, and elastic, and was formerly used extensively in the construction of homes and ships. Although still employed for these purposes, oak-wood is now chiefly used in the manufacture of furniture, panelings, and wooden floors. In Europe, British oak, *Q. robur,* and in the

VARIETIES OF OAK

Common Name	Scientific Name	Habitat	Use
Bartram oak	Q. heterophylla	E. U.S., Texas	c.
bear oak	Q. pumila	S.E. U.S.	fu.
black oak	Q. velutina	Ontario to Texas	d., t.
blue oak	Q. oblongifolia	s.w. U.S.	fu.
British oak	Q. robur	Europe, w. Asia	c.
bur oak	Q. macrocarpa	U.S.	c.
California black oak	Q. kelloggii	w. U.S.	c., cab., t.
California blue oak	Q. douglasii	w. U.S.	d., t.
chestnut oak	Q. sessiliflora	Europe	fu.
chestnut oak	Q. muhlenbergii	E. U.S., Texas	c.
chestnut oak	Q. prinus	E. U.S.	c., fu., t.
cinnamon oak	Q. cinerea	s. U.S.	fu.
cochineal oak	Q. coccifera	Mediterranean region	d.
cork oak	Q. suber	s. Europe	co.
Emory oak	Q. emoryi	s.w. U.S.	
Engelmann's oak	Q. engelmanni	California	
gall oak	Q. lusitanica	Mediterranean region	d.
Georgia oak	Q. georgiana	Georgia	
highland oak	Q. wislizenii	w. U.S.	fu.
holm oak	Q. ilex	s. Europe	c.
iron oak	Q. chrysolepis	w. U.S.	c.
iron oak	Q. marilandica	E. U.S.	fu.
iron oak	Q. stellata	E. U.S.	c.
laurel oak	Q. laurifolia	s.E. U.S.	fu.
live oak	Q. virginiana	s.E. U.S.	c.
live oak	Q. agrifolia	California	fu.
myrtle oak	Q. myrtifolia	E. U.S.	
overcup oak	Q. lyrata	E. U.S., Texas	c., cab.
red oak	Q. rubra	U.S.	c., cab.
red oak	Q. borealis	N. U.S.	c., cab.
scarlet oak	Q. coccinea	U.S.	
shingle oak	Q. imbricaria	U.S.	c.
swamp oak	Q. palustris	N.E. U.S.	c.
swamp oak	Q. lobata	California	fu.
swamp oak	Q. michauxi	E. U.S., Texas	c., fu.
swamp white oak	Q. bicolor	E. U.S.	c., cab.
turkey oak	Q. catesbaei	s.E. U.S.	
Turkey oak	Q. cerris	s.E. Europe, Asia	fu., t.
valonia oak	Q. aegilops	s.E. Europe	d., t.
water oak	Q. nigra	s. U.S.	fu.
white oak	Q. alba	U.S.	c., cab.
white oak	Q. garryana	w. U.S.	c., cab.
willow oak	Q. phellos	E. U.S.	c.

c. = carpentry	co. = cork	fu. = fuel
cab. = cabinetmaking	d. = dyeing	t. = tanning

United States, white oak, *Q. alba,* and red oak, *Q. borealis,* are used for these purposes. The cork oak, *Q. suber,* is the chief source of commercial cork. Tannin, used in leather-tanning and dyeing industries, is derived from the bark of various oak trees; the acorns of such oaks as the valonia oak, *Q. aegilops,* found in southern Europe and Asia Minor, also contain large quantities of chemicals used in leather processing. Acorns are also used as food for swine. The foregoing table contains the popular names, scientific names, and chief uses of various common oaks. Among other trees called oaks are the Australian trees constituting the genus *Casuarina,* and the silk oak of the genus *Grevillea* (q.v.).

OAKLAND, a city of Alameda Co., Calif., on the E. side of San Francisco Bay, 6 miles E. of San Francisco. The principal industrial establishments are shipyards, tanneries, paint works, canning factories, manufactories of cotton and woolen goods, jute, iron, nails, shoes, pottery, carriages, and agricultural implements. The city has one of the largest airports in the country. Pop. (1950) 384,575.

OAKLEY, ANNIE (1866-1926), the greatest woman rifle shot the world has ever produced, born in a pioneer log cabin in Woodland, Darke County, Ohio. Associated with Buffalo Bill's Wild West Show during the nineties, she was the sensation of America and Europe because of her seeming inability to miss any known shot with a rifle, a weapon she used when she was six years old to help provide food for her family. Later her skill made her one of the best-known pot hunters in the country.

At the age of fifteen she met Frank Butler, a traveling stage marksman. After defeating him in a shooting match, she later became his wife, traveling about the country until she was discovered by Sitting Bull, who gave her the name of *Little Sure Shot.* By 1900 she was known throughout the world for her skill in breaking glass balls tossed in the air by the scores. Once she fired 1000 shots in a contest and broke 943 balls. An auto accident caused injuries which resulted in her death.

OAK PARK, a town of Cook Co., Ill., 1½ miles E. of the Des Plaines River. It is a residential suburb of Chicago. Pop. (1950) 63,529.

OAK RIDGE, a town in Anderson County, Tenn., 20 miles w. of Knoxville, occupying about 9 sq.m. of the 93-square-mile government reservation known as the Oak Ridge area. The town was organized in 1942 to provide a residence community for personnel working in the various Oak Ridge plants of the atomic-energy project; see ATOMIC ENERGY AND ATOMIC BOMB. Until 1949 the town of Oak Ridge was confined by guarded barriers and only authorized persons were admitted. All the houses and facilities are government owned, but provision for private ownership of homes is being made. Since 1947 large-scale improvements have been initiated for conversion from a temporary town built in wartime haste to a permanent community. The population, which reached a peak of 75,000 during World War II, dropped to 30,229 (1950) after the war.

Leaves, flowers, and acorns of British oak

OARFISH, or KINGFISH, common name for any of the rare, huge, soft-finned, deep-sea fishes constituting the family Regalecidae, found in the Atlantic and Pacific oceans, and in the Mediterranean Sea. The fishes, which attain a length of about thirty feet, have extremely narrow, flattened, silver-colored bodies, with a dorsal fin running the entire length of the body and prolonged over the head in the form of a crest. The pelvic fins are reduced to long, filamentous projections, swelling at the ends into paddlelike processes. Tail fins are absent. The animals, which resemble huge snakes, are responsible for many of the ancient tales of "sea serpents". *Regalecus banksi* is a representative species.

OATES, TITUS (1649-1705), the principal informer in the so-called Popish Plot in England, born in Oakham. Taking advantage of the hostile state of the public mind toward the Catholics, Oates and Tongue in 1678 induced a Lancashire gentleman, Christopher Kirkby, to reveal to the persons interested fictitious details of a plot of Roman Catholics to murder Charles II and make the Duke of York king.

By the perjured testimony of Oates and his followers about 35 people lost their lives between 1678 and 1681, while Oates himself for a time received a large pension, and lived in Whitehall Palace. A reaction set in for Oates and in 1684 he was imprisoned. Upon the accession of James II he was found guilty

S.C.S.

Harvesting oats on a farm in Minnesota

of perjury and sentenced to be pilloried, whipped, and afterward imprisoned for life. After the Revolution of 1688 he was set at liberty.

OATS, common name applied to the seeds or entire plants of herbs belonging to the genus *Avena* of the Grass family. The genus, which contains about fifty species, is native to most temperate regions of the world; several species, especially the common oat, *A. sativa,* are widely cultivated for their grain, which is used as feed for cattle and horses and in the production of cereals for human consumption, and for their stems and leaves, which are used for hay, silage, and pasturage. Among important species of oats are common oat, wild oat, *A. fatua,* wild red oat, *A. sterilis,* and side oat, *A. orientalis.* These oats are important rotation crops; some of them are grown from fall seedings in various areas as winter crops to prevent soil erosion.

The low cost of oats, which are high in protein and Vitamin B$_1$ content, has made them popular breakfast cereals. For many decades, oats have been highly esteemed as a staple food in Scotland. In recent years, oats have been used in the preparation of processed food products and of industrial products. Among the processed food products are various breakfast cereals which can be served with little cooking, and others requiring no cook-

ing which are served cold. Avenex is an oat flour used as a stabilizer in the preparation of ice cream, chocolate, peanut butter, and lard, and as a preservative inner coating for paper bags used to package salted nuts, coffee, and potato chips. The most important industrial product is furfural (q.v.), a chemical derived from oat hulls, and used as a solvent in various refining industries and for other manufacturing purposes.

In a recent year about 1,268,280,000 bushels of oats were produced in the United States.

OAXACA, or OAJACA, a mountainous State in the south of Mexico bordering on the Pacific, and covering the southern and larger portion of the isthmus of Tehuantepec. The highest peak is Zempoaltepetl (11,145 ft.). Agriculture is the principal industry. The chief products are sugar, cotton, tobacco, coffee, cacao, indigo, cochineal, and dyewoods. Area, 36,371 sq.m. Pop. (1950) 1,414,516.

OBADIAH, the shortest book in the Old Testament canon. The name, meaning "servant of Jehovah", was borne by the chamberlain of Ahab (1 Kings 18:3-16), who protected the prophets from the fury of Jezebel. Delitzsch thinks the author of the prophecy may have been identical with the Obadiah of 2 Chron. 17:7, a Levite sent by Jehoshaphat to teach the law in the cities of Judah. From internal evidence the date of the book may be put after the capture of Jerusalem by Nebuchadnezzar, about 587 B.C.

OBEID, EL, the capital of Kordofan Province, in the eastern Sudan, 220 miles s.w. of Khartoum. Gum arabic, ivory, gold, and ostrich feathers are the chief articles of trade. Near this place, in 1883, a force of Egyptians under Hicks Pasha, with an English staff, was exterminated by a large army of the Mahdi. Pop. (1948 est.) 70,100.

OBELISK, in architecture, a four-sided tapering shaft terminating in a pyramidal or conical top. In ancient Egypt, pairs of these monuments, each hewn from a single piece of hard stone and set on a cubical base, often flanked temple entrances. Associated with sun worship, these monoliths were especially numerous at Heliopolis, the City of the Sun. The pointed tops were frequently sheathed in brass or gold; sculptured dedicatory or commemorative hieroglyphs usually ran down the sides of the shaft. Examples range in size from 2 ft., 1½ in. high (that of Lepsius in Berlin) to 105 ft 9 in. high (that of Pope Sixtus in Rome). They were produced throughout ancient Egyptian history, the dwarf specimens generally dating from the earliest and latest periods, and the giant specimens from the Middle Kingdom. Roman emperors transported many as trophies of conquest, and a number were carved imitatively in Italy as memorial monuments. The two obelisks popularly called Cleopatra's Needles stood at Heliopolis from the 15th century B.C. until the 1st century B.C., when they were moved by the Roman emperor Augustus to Alexandria; in 1877 one was erected on the Thames Embankment, London, and in 1880 the other, a gift of the Khedive of Egypt, was set up in Central Park, New York City. The latter is 69 ft., 6 in. high, and 7 ft., 9 in. thick at the base, and weighs 224 tons.

The obelisk form is still used in monuments and decorations and as an architectural adjunct. It was a popular feature in baroque and neoclassical tombs, and has been used everywhere in the Western world as an ornamental element in parks, gardens, and cemeteries. It has been often added to fountains, balustrades, and gables. The Bunker Hill and Washington monuments are built in the shape of obelisks, although they are not monolithic.

OBERAMMERGAU, a village in Upper Bavaria, situated 45 miles s.w. of Munich. Here the famous Passion Play, which originated in 1634, is performed. It was first presented by the townspeople in gratitude for the end of a plague epidemic. Except for 1870

(Franco-Prussian War), 1920 (when the performance was postponed to 1922 due to the unsettled conditions resulting from World War I), and 1940 (World War II), the play has been performed every tenth year. The earliest known text is that of the Ettal monks; the music was composed in 1814 by Rochus Dedler. The performances are held in a large open-air theater, and last for seven to eight hours. All the actors, nearly seven hundred in number, belong to the village. It manufactures wood and ivory carvings. Pop., about 2000.

OBERHAUSEN, city of the State of North Rhine-Westphalia, West Germany, situated near the right bank of the Rhine, 35 miles N. of Cologne. It has extensive iron foundries, rolling mills, railway shops, chemical works, and manufactures of various iron and tin

Ewing Galloway

Cleopatra's Needle, Egyptian obelisk in Central Park, New York City

wares, soap, chemicals, wire rope, lumber, porcelain, wire, glass, and flour. In the vicinity are important coal, zinc, and iron mines, and coke ovens. Pop. (1950) 202,808.

OBERLIN COLLEGE, a coeducational, privately controlled, nondenominational institution of higher learning, situated at Oberlin, Ohio, founded in 1833, and known as Oberlin Collegiate Institute until 1850, when its present name was adopted. Oberlin was the first coeducational college in the U.S.; two years after the date of its founding the College admitted students "without respect to color", and prior to the Civil War it was known as a center for antislavery activities. Charles Grandison Finney, professor of theology and president of Oberlin from 1851 to 1866, first promulgated at the college his doctrine of evangelical Calvinism which later became known as Oberlin Theology. The divisions of the institution include the college of arts and sciences, the conservatory of music, for which the college is particularly well known, the nondenominational graduate school of theology, and the summer school. Bachelor's and master's degrees are granted. In 1953 the student enrollment was almost 1870, including about 1730 full-time students; the faculty numbered 190; and the endowment totaled more than 24 million dollars.

OBERON, the king of the elves or fairies, and the husband of Titania. Oberon is first mentioned as "Roi du Royaume de la Féerie" in the 13th-century French poem *Huon de Bordeaux.* The name first appeared in English in Lord Berners' translation (Early Eng. Text Soc., 1885), and was adopted in many ballads, and also in Greene's play, *The Scottish History of James IV.* Neither these, however, nor Spenser's use made the name familiar, but Shakespeare's *Midsummer Night's Dream,* where the fairy mythology is an attempt to blend the elves of the village with the fays of romance, did so.

OBESITY, CORPULENCY, or OVERWEIGHT, a body condition associated with a wide variety of physiological disturbances, characterized by excessive transformation of ingested carbohydrates into fat and excessive deposition of fat in the various body storage areas; see METABOLISM. Obese individuals, according to standards set by insurance companies which are interested in obesity because of its relationship to longevity (q.v.), are persons who exceed the average of individuals of the same age and height by twenty percent or more. The mortality rate of obese persons is one and one half times higher than that of either lean

persons or persons of average weight. Over weight individuals comprise the vast majority of diabetics, and are more susceptible to heart disease, high blood pressure, and kidney disease than other individuals. Obese persons also have a lower resistance to infectious diseases than persons of normal or below-normal weight. Operations upon obese persons are difficult because of the large masses of interfering fat, because of increased danger of infection, and because fatty tissues do not heal as well as other tissues.

The direct causes of obesity are not known. Physicians postulate two interrelated groups of factors which encourage deposition of excess fat: the *exogenous factors,* or those arising from outside the individual; and the *endogenous factors,* or those arising from within the individual. Among the exogenous factors are cultural factors, such as national or family customs, which result in overeating, and climatic factors, such as excessive heat, which result in a lethargic, sedentary mode of living. Among the endogenous factors are hereditary predisposition to obesity, endocrine disturbances, particularly of the gonads, lesions in certain portions of the brain, and psychological disturbances which cause overeating as a substitute for unfulfilled wishes or desires. The two most important recognized factors in obesity production are overeating and gonadal disturbances: researches are under way to determine whether or not a definite weight-regulatory center exists in the brain. Disturbances of water metabolism and salt metabolism lead to excessive deposition of water in the tissues, causing an overweight condition resembling obesity.

Because obesity shortens the life span, and because well-established cases of obesity are difficult to treat, physicians place much value on education in proper food habits. This education is especially directed to individuals in families predisposed to obesity. Treatment of obese persons consists of diet suited to the person's individual needs and, in many cases, the administration of hormones.

OBI or **OB,** the westernmost of the great rivers of Siberia. It rises in the Altai Mountains and flows northwest, then north through the Siberian governments of Tomsk and Tobolsk, emptying into the Arctic Ocean through an immense estuary, the Gulf of Obi, which is 600 miles long and 60 miles in average width. The length of the river itself above the estuary is about 2500 miles.

OBLIGATION, DAYS OF, holy days on which Roman Catholics are bound to hear mass and, when possible, to abstain from servile works. The holy days are, for England and Wales, Circumcision, Epiphany, Ascension Day, Corpus Christi, SS. Peter and Paul, Assumption, All Saints, and Christmas Day. Scotland adds St. Andrew's, and Ireland, St. Patrick's Day. In the United States there are six: Circumcision, January 1; Ascension, the 40th day after Easter; Assumption, August 15; All Saints Day, November 1; Immaculate Conception, December 8; and Christmas Day, December 25.

OBOE, in music, the soprano member of the woodwind group of instruments, constructed of wood with a conical bore and a double-reed mouthpiece, and producing a penetrating, rather nasal sound. The oboe consists of three pieces, or joints, with the mouthpiece at the smaller end and fingerholes and stops along its length. Its range comprises two octaves (q.v.) plus a sixth (see INTERVAL). The A tone of the oboe is used to fix the pitch for all other instruments of the orchestra.

The oboe has been traced in the painting and sculpture of ancient Egypt, Greece, and Rome, and was popular throughout Europe by the time of the Middle Ages. During the Renaissance it was frequently called the *schalmei* or *shawm,* and the *pommer* or *bombard,* and appeared in many forms, ranging from soprano to bass. The oboe d'amore and oboe di caccia, or hunting oboe, were popular members of the family during the 16th and 17th centuries. Used extensively in France, the oboe became known as the *hautbois* in contradistinction to the deeper-toned *grosbois,* or bassoon. The present form of the instrument dates from the mid-19th century, when many improvements in construction were effected.

OBREGÓN, ÁLVARO (1880–1928), Mexican soldier and political leader, born near Alamos, Sonora. In 1912 he organized a force of about 400 Indians, as commander of which he entered the service of Francisco Madero (q.v.), then president of Mexico, and crushed a revolt led by Pascual Orozco (1881–1915). After the death of Madero in 1913, Obregón became a supporter of Venustiano Carranza (q.v.), the leader of the Constitutionalist Party. During the ensuing two years Obregón helped defeat the various rebel forces led by Victoriano Huerta, Francisco (better known as "Pancho") Villa (qq.v.), and Emiliano Zapata; in a battle against Villa, he lost his right arm. Upon the election of Carranza to the presidency in 1915, Obregón was appointed commander in chief of the Mexican army. In 1920 he led a successful revolt against Carranza, and soon afterward was elected president. He instituted a number of labor, agrarian, and educational reforms, and in 1923 secured the formal recognition of his government by the United States. Between 1924 and 1928 he was politically inactive. He was re-elected president in 1928, but was assassinated before he could take office.

O'BRIEN, FITZ-JAMES (about 1828–62), Irish-American writer, born in Limerick, Ireland, and educated at Dublin University. After a career as a journalist in London, he emigrated to the United States in 1852, and soon established a reputation as a writer of short stories and plays. In the American Civil War he was an officer in the Union Army; he died of a wound received in battle. O'Brien's short stories deal with the occult, weird, and fantastic. His best-known stories are *The Diamond Lens, The Wondersmith,* and *What Was It?* His most successful play was *The Gentleman from Ireland* (1854).

OBSCENITY, in criminal law, an act of indecency tending to corrupt public morals or to affront public sensibilities, usually punishable as a misdemeanor. The offense may be committed through spoken words, through conduct, through the distribution, exhibition, or publication of pictures, prints, or books, or through exposure of the private parts of the body. In the United States, many States have enacted legislation forbidding the keeping, exhibition, or sale of indecent books and pictures and authorizing their seizure and destruction. Federal statutes have been enacted prohibiting the importation and circulation of obscene literature or articles of any kind. Recent decisions in some jurisdictions emphasize that literary or artistic works must be judged as a whole and in the light of the dominant purpose of the work; a legitimate main purpose may excuse incidental obscenities in some jurisdictions.

OBSERVATORY, a building or series of buildings especially constructed for use in making astronomical observations. The term is also sometimes applied to buildings used for observing magnetic or meteorological phenomena. The earliest known astronomical observatories were created by the Chinese and the Babylonians about 2300 B.C. These observatories were probably little more than high platforms giving an unobstructed view of the heavens. About 300 B.C. the most famous observatory of classical times was built at the city of Alexandria in Egypt. Although no details concerning this observatory remain, it was probably equipped with instruments

Palomar Observatory; Lick Observatory

Left: The Palomar Observatory. Right: Eye end of 36-inch reflector, Lick Observatory.

such as astrolabes by which the celestial latitudes and longitudes of stars and planets could be measured. The Alexandria observatory was in continuous operation for about 500 years.

After the beginning of the Christian Era, the Arabs established a number of observatories at Damascus, Bagdad, and at Mokatta near Cairo in Egypt. The last-named was built about 1000 A.D. The first observatory in Europe was set up in Nuremberg in 1471. The largest and most completely equipped of the early European observatories was built by the Danish astronomer Tycho Brahe (q.v.) on the island of Hven. Brahe's observatory, in which he lived and worked with his students from 1576 to 1596, was equipped with a large quadrant used in making accurate measurements of the altitudes of celestial bodies. The observations which Brahe made at Hven were used by Copernicus (q.v.) in the development of his theory of the solar system.

After the invention of the telescope in 1609, a number of new observatories were built in various European cities. Among the most famous of these were the French National Observatory at Paris, established in 1667, and the British Royal Observatory, often called the Greenwich Observatory (q.v.), founded in 1675. Both of these observatories are still in existence. The first observatory to be constructed in the United States was built at Chapel Hill, N.C., in 1831. The U.S. Naval Observatory (q.v.) at Washington was established in 1843–44. Other famous U.S. observa-

tories which are described in separate articles are the Lick Observatory, the Mt. Wilson Observatory, the Palomar Observatory, and the Yerkes Observatory.

Classification of Observatories. Astronomical observatories are classified into several general types. Government observatories are usually occupied with continuous observations of the stars and planets for the preparation of navigational tables and the determination of standard times. Observatories connected with educational institutions are used chiefly for training students in the techniques of astronomical observation. Certain university observatories and other observatories not connected with institutions are dedicated to purely observational problems such as the discovery of comets and the discovery and measurement of variable stars. Many of the larger observatories are entirely devoted to the problems of astrophysics, the physics of the stars. In addition some observatories have separate apparatus which is used for the study of solar phenomena, and a few observatories make only solar observations.

In the 1950's a new type of observatory was established for the study of radio emanations from the sun and stars. Research in this field, called radio astronomy, is conducted with instruments known as radio telescopes. See also ASTRONOMY.

OBSIDIAN. See RHYOLITE.

OBSTETRICS, also called midwifery, the branch of medical science and practice concerned with the study and care of women during the processes of pregnancy, parturition, and the puerperium, or lying-in. As a department of medical study it embraces the anatomy and physiology of the female organs of generation, the phenomena of conception and pregnancy, of labor, normal and abnormal, and of the puerperium and the return of the organs to their nonpregnant condition. These processes are normal and physiological, and in perfectly natural conditions require little or no skilled help or assistance.

The writings of Hippocrates (400 B.C.) contain the earliest attempt to formulate a practice of obstetrics In 98 A.D. Soranus published a work "on the diseases of women", which shows a considerable advance in the knowledge of the anatomy of the female organs. In the 4th century a remarkable book was published by Moschion, *Peri tōn Gunaikeiōn Pathōn*, which is sometimes called the first obstetric work published. It is based on Soranus, and shows a sound anatomical knowledge. From this time until the beginning of the 16th century it may be said that obstetrics made no progress.

In 1668 Mauriceau published his *Treatise,* which ran through seven editions, and was for long the standard work on the subject. It was translated into English by Hugh Chamberlen in 1672, and it seems to be about this time that men began generally to engage in the practice of midwifery. Harvey, the Chamberlens, and others took it up in England; while La Vallière, the mistress of Louis XIV, by employing Julian Clement, a surgeon of high eminence, in her first confinement in 1663, did much to establish the practice in France.

About the end of the 16th or beginning of the 17th century, the forceps was invented by Dr. Peter Chamberlen, a son of a William Chamberlen, a Huguenot refugee, living in England. The original instrument was modified by Levret of Paris and Smellie and Simpson in Great Britain; subsequently its construction was elaborated by Tarnier of Paris.

In 1847 Sir James Simpson first employed chloroform anesthesia to relieve the pain of labor, and this marks one of the most beneficent advances in the history of obstetrics. Introduction of an anesthesia in 1915, "Twilight Sleep", was thought to have solved the problem of painless labor, but an extensive trial proved it unsatisfactory. An obstetrical analgesia, so called because the woman remains conscious and is able to co-operate, was developed by Dr J. T. Gwathmey and Dr. Asa B. Davis. It was first employed in the Lying-In Hospital in New York, and proved to be an advance over any other method known.

Till 1870 the great scourge of maternity hospitals, and also a frequent cause of disaster in private practice, was the prevalence of outbreaks of puerperal fever or septicemia. In that year the teaching of Lister began to influence obstetric practice, and since then rigorous antisepsis is the rule in all maternity hospitals.

Recent developments in obstetrics include antibiotic and sulfonamide therapy, which reduce considerably the incidence of infection and complications associated with childbirth. Hemorrhages, formerly responsible for many deaths in childbirth, are now controlled by the use of blood transfusions. The discovery of various human-blood types, such as the Rh factor (q.v.), made possible the control of fetal mortality arising from blood anomalies. Among present-day efforts to minimize the pain of childbirth is a program of prenatal training for the type of delivery known popularly as natural childbirth. This program consists of educational lectures on the physiological process involved in birth and of exercises designed to promote relaxation and applied during labor. By the successful application of natural-childbirth techniques the patient may undergo labor and delivery without the need of analgesia medication. Another technique of increasing application in obstetrics is hypnotism (q.v.); it is used to produce anesthesia in childbirth or as an adjunct to chemical anesthesia.

OCARINA, a small, egg-shaped musical instrument, introduced into Europe early in the 19th century by wandering German or Tyrolese musicians. In the course of the 19th century, the ocarina gained great popularity among street players, particularly in Italy. The modern ocarina is made of hollow metal or earthenware, with fingerholes and a protruding spout which serves as a mouthpiece. It produces a sweet, whistlelike tone, the pitch of which is controlled by the number of holes which are left open. The ocarina has also been called a "globular flute"; and in America, in colloquial usage, a "sweet potato", which it resembles in size and shape.

O'CASEY, SEAN (1890–), Irish playwright, born in Dublin. As a youth he lived in the slums of Dublin and worked as an unskilled laborer. In 1916 he participated in the Easter Rebellion, a Dublin uprising against English rule. O'Casey was the outstanding Irish dramatist of the second quarter of the 20th century. His plays are characterized by a

Macmillan

Sean O'Casey

lyrical prose style, realistic and tensely dramatic situations, a deep sense of the tragedy of commonplace lives, rich humor, and a hatred of political oppression. Many of his dramas were first produced at the noted Abbey Theatre in Dublin. Among his plays are *The Shadow of a Gunman* (1923), *Juno and the Paycock* (1924), *The Plough and the Stars* (1926), *The Silver Tassie* (1928), *Within the Gates* (1933), *The Star Turns Red* (1940), and *Cock-a-doodle Dandy* (1949). He also wrote autobiographical works in which he reviewed the course of his personal life, the movements in which he engaged, and the political and literary personages with whom he had dealings. These works include *Knock at the Door* (1939), *Pictures in the Hallway* (1942), *Drums Under the Window* (1946), *Inishfallen, Fare Thee Well* (1949), *Rose and Crown* (1952), and *Sunset and Evening Star* (1954).

OCCASIONALISM, the term employed to designate the philosophical system devised by the followers of the 17th-century French philosopher René Descartes (q.v.) in an attempt to explain the interrelation between mind and body. The occasionalists begin with the assumption that certain actions or modifications of the body are preceded, accompanied, or followed by changes in the mind.

This assumed relationship presents no difficulty to the popular conception of mind and body, according to which each entity is supposed to act directly upon the other, but it has long furnished philosophers with a vexing question. Asserting the principle that cause and effect must be similar, the philosophers could not conceive the possibility of any direct mutual interaction between substances as dissimilar as mind and body. According to the occasionalists the action of the mind is not, and cannot be, the cause of the corresponding action of the body. They maintain, however, that whenever any action of the mind takes place, God directly produces in connection with that action, and by reason of it, a corresponding action of the body; the converse process is likewise true. This theory did not solve the problem, for if the mind cannot act upon the body (matter), then God, conceived as mind, cannot act upon matter; and if God is conceived as other than mind, then He cannot act upon mind. A proposed solution of the problem is furnished by the exponents of the philosophical system known as radical empiricism (see EMPIRICISM). They dispose of the dualism (q.v.) of the occasionalists by denying the fundamental difference between mind and matter.

OCCULTISM (Lat. *occulere*, "to hide"), a belief in hidden or mysterious powers not explained by known scientific principles of nature, and the attempt to bring these powers within human control by scientific methods. The medieval concept of occult properties included only those properties which may be revealed by experimentation. The alchemists, astrologers, seers, and others who practiced this "science" of experimentation were a small group, usually in conflict with orthodox theology. Consequently their work was considered mysterious, and the term "occultism" gradually came to denote the study of supernatural forces. Nevertheless, all the so-called natural sciences stemmed from occultism, and early scientists were frequently considered magicians and sorcerers because of the mystery attributed to their investigations by most of their contemporaries. Modern occultism is generally considered to have begun with the concept of animal magnetism, first developed by the Austrian physician Franz Anton Mesmer (q.v.) in the late 18th century. Mesmer believed that certain individuals possess occult powers, comparable to the magnetic powers of the magnet, which can be used to invoke the supernatural. In the mid-19th century occultism took the form of spiritualism (q.v.), a belief that the spirits of the dead may manifest themselves through the agency of living persons called mediums. After the turn of the century occultism included serious investigation of phenomena such as mental telepathy which, although still not within the usual area of scientific research, are considered by some to be valid natural phenomena explicable by accepted scientific methods.

OCCUPATIONAL DISEASES, in medicine, maladies resulting from specific working conditions, and generally caused by poisons, irritants, radiation, exposure to specific infections, or an unhealthful environment. In law the meaning of the term is limited to diseases which are specifically recognized as compensable under workmen's compensation (q.v.) laws or court decisions.

The ancients recognized particular diseases as incident to such employment as lead or quicksilver mining, but these diseases were regarded as ills of slaves, and as of no general interest. Even the guilds of the Middle Ages did little to protect their members from the hygienic hazards incident to the stone and metal trades. This characteristic indifference to the health of the worker persisted after the establishment of the factory system (see FACTORIES AND THE FACTORY SYSTEM). In the U.S. and most countries of western Europe during the 19th century a few factory laws were enacted, but these affected only the employment of women and children, forbidding night work and barring their employment in certain exceptionally hazardous or unhealthful occupations. With the development of preventive medicine in the last two decades of the century, social agencies initiated a movement aimed at extending protection to all workers by establishing minimum hygienic standards of heating, ventilation, and sanitary facilities, and eliminating or controlling hazardous processes. This movement made little headway at first; after 1910 various States of the United States enacted workmen's compensation laws, factory inspection acts, and other legislation aimed at eliminating dangerous conditions in industrial plants, and providing compensation for employees suffering from occupational diseases on the same basis as compensation for industrial accidents.

Various methods of classifying occupational diseases have been advocated, but no single method has been generally adopted. They may be divided into diseases caused by air-borne agents, contact agents, abnormal physical surroundings, and psychogenic factors. Air-borne agents include smoke fogs, dusts, gases, or sprays carrying toxic material such as mercury, lead, carbon bisulfide, phosphorus gases, and arsenic dust. They also include clouds of such chemically inert material as coal dust, sand, and other abrasives which, by mechanical irritation, cause the various forms of pneumoconiosis, such as anthracosis and silicosis (qq.v.). Bacterial diseases prevalent in certain trades, such as anthrax, formerly called "woolsorters' disease", also belong in this category. Contact agents include chemical irritants which cause various forms of dermatitis (q.v.) and cancer of the skin. Abnormal physical surroundings cause such ailments as the bends (q.v.), from variations of air pressure; radiation burns from X rays or radioactive materials; heat exhaustion and heat stroke; and glass blowers' cataract. Psychogenic factors cause such ailments as neuromuscular fatigue and migraine.

OCCUPATIONAL THERAPY, branch of physical medicine involving regulated activities designed to promote recovery and rehabilitation (q.v.) in the treatment of mental illness and physical disability. Occupational therapy was first used by the Greek physician Asclepiades (fl. 1st cent. B.C.) and thereafter became an intrinsic part of the most advanced treatment of psychiatric patients throughout the centuries. Present-day mental hospitals consider the occupational-therapy programs of great value not only as therapy but also for diagnostic purposes. The behavior of the patient in relation to his task, his instructor, and his fellow patients helps to confirm the diagnosis and to chart the course of the cure. The prescribed activity depends upon the type of illness and its stage of development. Equipment for loom weaving, painting, clay modeling, and leather tooling is made available for some patients; others are assigned to chores in the wards, such as sweeping and bed making; even such passive recreations as concerts, motion pictures, and television are considered part of the occupational-therapy program.

In the 20th century medicine extended the use of occupational therapy to the treatment of physical illness, such as infantile paralysis, tuberculosis (qq.v.), or other diseases confining the patient to prolonged bed-rest. The most recent development is an occupational-therapy program for the rehabilitation of the physically disabled.

OCEAN AND OCEANOGRAPHY, the great body of water which covers the major portion of the earth's surface, and the scien-

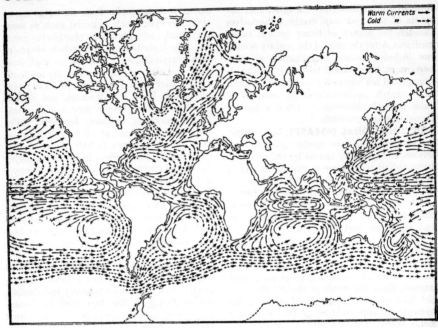

Diagram showing the currents of the ocean

tific study of this body of water. The study of the ocean includes measurement of its shape, size, and depth; chemical and physical analysis of the water of which it is comprised; examination of the various marine deposits which lie on the ocean's floor; exploration of various ocean currents; and classification of the forms of vegetable and animal life found in the ocean.

Dimensions of the Ocean. Although the ocean is commonly considered to be divided into a number of smaller oceans, it is actually a single body of water. The total oceanic area of the earth is approximately 361,059,000 sq.km. or 139,478,770 sq.m., and the total land area of the earth is approximately 148,-892,000 sq.km. or 54,672,310 sq.m. The ocean, therefore, covers approximately 71 percent of the earth's surface, and the land 29 percent. The ocean is distributed unevenly between the Northern and Southern hemispheres of the earth. In the Northern Hemisphere only about 61 percent of the surface is covered by water, but in the Southern Hemisphere approximately 81 percent is water. Of the total area of the ocean 43 percent lies in the Northern Hemisphere and 57 percent in the Southern. Because of this unequal distribution the Northern Hemisphere is sometimes called the "land hemisphere" and the Southern Hemisphere the "water hemisphere".

The large land masses of the continents separate the ocean into three major divisions: the Atlantic, Pacific, and Indian oceans. These oceans, in turn, are joined in the neighborhood of the Antarctic continent, and the water surrounding this continent is often known as the Southern or Antarctic Ocean. Along the shores of all the continents large bays and gulfs exist and capes and peninsulas partially set off bodies of water from the rest of the ocean. These partially separate portions of the oceans are usually referred to as seas. They range in character from almost totally enclosed bodies of water such as the Mediterranean and Black seas to comparatively open "bays" such as the Arabian Sea. In some areas the seas are themselves divided into subordinate seas such as the Adriatic in the Mediterranean.

Ocean Depths. The depth of the ocean varies considerably more than the land surface of the earth. The highest point on the land portion of the globe is the summit of Mt. Everest in Tibet, which is 29,141 ft. above sea level and the deepest portion of the ocean lies in the Marianus Trench southwest of Guam, 35,641 ft. below sea level. The average depth o the entire ocean is approximately 12,460 ft. below sea level, and the average height of the continents is only about 2750 ft. above sea level. Ocean depths were formerly determined by the use of sounding lines, strong, small-diameter lines of hemp or wire which were lowered with weights at their ends. The modern method of sounding, introduced about 1920, is *echo sounding*. In this method of depth finding, a sound signal is directed toward the ocean floor from which it is reflected, and the echo is then received aboard the sounding vessel. The depth is computed by multiplying half the time of the signal's travel from the vessel to the bottom and back by the speed of sound in salt water (about 4950 ft. per second). For the apparatus used in echo sounding, see SONAR.

Surrounding most land masses are belts of comparatively shallow water known as *continental shelves*. These shelves slope gradually from sea level to a depth of about 650 ft. and then drop off to greater depths at a much sharper slope. The continental shelves represent portions of continents and islands which have been submerged in comparatively recent times and are areas in which both the erosive action of the waves and tides and the building up of the bottom by coral animals and other reef-building agents are greatest. The area of the continents and their shelves, down to 650 ft. below sea level, amounts to almost 35 per cent of the entire surface of the earth.

Composition of Sea Water. From the chemical viewpoint sea water is composed of a mixture of dilute solutions of several salts. The total salinity of the water is usually expressed in terms of the number of parts of salts present per thousand parts of water. An average value of salinity for all the oceans is 35 parts per thousand, of which about 27.2 parts are sodium chloride, 3.8 parts magnesium chloride, 1.65 parts magnesium sulfate, 1.26 parts calcium sulfate, and less than 1 part per thousand each of potassium sulfate, calcium carbonate, and magnesium bromide. In addition, sea water contains minute traces of more than twenty other chemical elements. Gold is present in a concentration of about 2.5 parts per ten billion parts of water. The salinity of sea water differs from the salinity of the various salt lakes and seas, which contain comparatively more magnesium sulfate and calcium sulfate and less magnesium chloride. The saltiness of the ocean has direct effect on several of the physical properties of ocean waters. The freezing point of ordinary sea water is 1.91° C. (3.4° F.) lower than that of fresh water and

the boiling point is .56° C. (1° F.) higher. Also, the vapor pressure of sea water is lower than that of fresh water.

The salinity of the ocean varies both at different locations on the surface and at different depths at the same localities. In general, sea water contains most salt in the region of the tropics, less salt in the equatorial region, and least salt in the regions closer to the poles. The Red Sea is the saltiest portion of the ocean, containing about 41 parts per million of salt in the Gulf of Suez. The Baltic Sea has the least salt, with the content ranging from about 28 parts per thousand at Skagerrak to almost nothing in the Gulf of Bothnia. These variations in salinity depend upon meteorological conditions in the various areas. Where evaporation is at a maximum, salinity is highest, and where evaporation is minimal and the sea water is diluted with the fresh water from rivers, as in the Baltic, salinity is low.

The distribution of saltiness in depth differs in the Northern and Southern hemispheres. In northern latitudes, salinity decreases with depth; but in high southern latitudes, salinity decreases to a depth of about 800 meters (2620 ft.), then increases to a depth of about 1000 meters (3280 ft.), and again decreases to the ocean bottom. This variation in saltiness is caused by the circulation of undersea currents.

Ocean Temperatures. The general range of the surface temperature of the ocean is between 96° F. in the Persian Gulf to 29.5° F. (just above the freezing temperature of sea water) in the polar regions. The daily range of temperature variation in all parts of the ocean is never large, being less than 1° F. (.56° C.). The annual temperature change of the surface water of the ocean is greatest in the North and South Temperate zones. At 40° N. the annual range is about 18° F. (10° C.), near the equator about 4° F. (2.2° C.), and in high latitudes about 5° F. (2.8° C.). The temperature of ocean waters in general decreases with depth except in polar seas. In polar areas, surface waters are cooled by the atmosphere and by floating ice (see ICE), and increase in temperature with decreasing depth to depths of about 1000 meters (3280 ft.). Reversals of the temperature trend also occur in the Atlantic Ocean near the Strait of Gibraltar and in the Gulf of Aden near the mouth of the Red Sea. In these cases warm undersea currents flow out of the Mediterranean and the Red Sea. The effect of the Mediterranean subsurface current is measurable from Ireland to the Canary Islands. The abyssal depths of the ocean have a uniform temperature sufficiently cold to reduce the mean temperature of the entire ocean to approximately 39° F. (3.9° C.).

Ocean Currents. The surface currents of the ocean, which are of great importance in navigation and piloting, are almost entirely caused by surface winds. Undersea currents, on the other hand, are chiefly the result of convective circulation of bodies of cooled and heated sea water, and of the circulation of portions of the ocean having differing salinity.

In the Atlantic Ocean two westward-flowing equatorial surface currents occur in the regions in which the trade winds blow. The South Equatorial Current, extending from the equator to about 6° S., is deflected southward because of the rotation of the earth, and flows along the eastern coast of South America, where it is known as the Brazil Current. The Brazil Current, in turn, reaches the region of prevailing west winds between 30° and 45° S. and becomes an eastward-moving drift which flows roughly from the mouth of the Plata River to the Cape of Good Hope. The North Equatorial Current, which lies between the equator and the Tropic of Cancer, is deflected north. Part of this current enters the Caribbean Sea and the Gulf of Mexico and the region of the Atlantic north of the Greater Antilles and flows from thence northward through the Straits of Florida and along the eastern coast of North America as the Gulf Stream. At about 40° N. the Gulf Stream, partially mingling with the colder waters of the Labrador Current, is driven eastward by the prevailing westerly winds, becoming the North Atlantic Drift or West Wind Drift. Part of this drift goes northward, reaching the British Isles, Norway, and Iceland; and a portion of the current turns again from Iceland and flows to the shores of Greenland.

Both the equatorial Atlantic surface currents are warm currents. The Atlantic Ocean also has three important cold-water currents. In the Northern Hemisphere, the Labrador Current arises in Baffin Bay and flows southward along the coasts of Labrador, Newfoundland, Nova Scotia, and northeastern U.S. This current forms a so-called "cold wall" between the shores of the U.S. and the Gulf Stream from Maine to Cape Hatteras. In the Southern Hemisphere the Atlantic has two cold coastal currents flowing from the Antarctic Ocean. One of these begins in the vicinity of Cape Horn and runs northward along the east coast of South America to the southern part of Brazil. The other, the Benguella Current, flows north from the Cape of Good Hope along the coast of s.w. Africa almost to the equator, where it merges with the South Equatorial Current.

The undersea currents of the Atlantic flow chiefly from north to south and from south to north. The Antarctic Undercurrent consists of cold water which sinks below the surface at about 60° S. in the vicinity of the Falkland Islands and flows northward at a depth of approximately 900 meters (2950 ft.), passing the equator and reaching about latitude 20° N. In the area of the Sargasso Sea (q.v.), approximately 30° N., no regular surface currents exist and evaporation is consequently high. Warm, heavily saline water in the region sinks to depths of from 1500 to 3000 meters (4900 to 9800 ft.) and flows southward as the North Atlantic Undercurrent, continuing to about 50° S. In both the Northern and Southern hemispheres bottom currents in high latitudes originate at 4000 meters (13,100 ft.) or deeper and flow toward the equator.

In the North Pacific, the flow of surface currents resembles that of the North Atlantic. The Pacific North Equatorial Current flows westward at about 15° N. and separates into two streams east of the Philippine Islands. The southern stream makes up part of an Equatorial Countercurrent which flows eastward at about 7° N. The northern stream flows northeastward along the edge of the China Sea and the coast of Japan, where it is known as the Kuroshio Current. Between this current and the coast of Japan, a cold current, the Oya Siwo, flows southward from the vicinity of Kamchatka. At about 40° N. the Kuroshio comes under the influence of the westerly winds of that latitude and moves eastward as the West Wind Drift. Reaching the coast of southern Alaska this drift splits, part flowing north and west along the coast of Alaska and the Aleutian Islands, and part, mingling with cold coastal waters, moving south along the west coast of Canada and the U.S. as the cold California Current. In the southern portion of the Pacific, the South Equatorial Current, impelled by the southeast trade winds, flows westward. This current also divides, part flowing northward to join the countercurrent and part turning to the southwest toward the South Sea Islands, New Zealand, and Australia. The West Wind Drift of the Antarctic Ocean, which flows around the entire world in high southern latitudes, sends a branch current along the west coast of South America as far north as the equator. Although the surface currents of the Pacific have been accurately charted, little is known of the undersea currents of this ocean.

U.S. Coast & Geodetic Sur.

STUDYING THE OCEAN

Above: A naval officer reading fathometer in plotting room on a launch. Right: Taking sounding with hand lead. Below: Apparatus for sounding on a ship.

N.Y. Zoological Society

The ocelot, about three feet in length, found from Texas to Peru

The surface currents of the Indian Ocean are greatly affected by the seasonal monsoon winds which blow off the continent of Asia in the winter and from the ocean to the continent in the summer. The current of the Arabian Sea, the Bay of Bengal, and the northern Indian Ocean is called the Monsoon Drift. In the Northern Hemisphere summer this drift flows along the coast of Africa northeastward from Zanzibar, into the Arabian Sea, then southeastward along the west coast of India, and eastward toward Sumatra. In the winter the flow of the drift is almost completely reversed. South of the Monsoon Drift along the line of the equator two countercurrents flow in an easterly direction all year round; and south of these countercurrents the Equatorial Current of the Indian Ocean moves westward from about 5° S. to 15° S. A well-defined current of cold water flows north from the Antarctic Ocean to the western coast of Australia. Like the undersea currents of the Pacific, those of the Indian Ocean are little known.

See also GEOLOGY; TIDES.

OCEANIA, a name sometimes given to the fifth division of the globe, comprising all the islands which intervene between the south-eastern shores of the continent of Asia and the western shores of America. It naturally divides itself into three great sections—the Malay Archipelago, Australasia or Melanesia, and Polynesia.

OCEANIA, FRENCH ESTABLISHMENTS IN, a French colonial possession consisting of groups of small islands scattered throughout a wide area of the eastern Pacific. The total area of the Establishments is estimated at 1520 square miles; pop. (1948 est.) 60,000. The principal island is Tahiti, which contains the chief town, Papeete. Tahiti forms a part of the Society Islands. The other groups are the Marquesas Islands, Tuamotu Islands, Leeward Islands, the Gambier, Tubuai, and Rapa groups, and a number of outlying islands. Various tropical fruits are grown and exported. Pearls, mother-of-pearl, and phosphates are important products. A New Zealand steamship service connects Tahiti with San Francisco, New Zealand, and Australia. The administration is in the hands of a governor assisted by an administrative council.

OCEAN ISLAND or BANABA, island in the s. Pacific, administrative center of the Gilbert and Ellice Islands Colony (q.v.) of Great Britain. It is situated near the equator, between the Gilbert Islands and Nauru. Ocean Island is the only island in the colony which is not a coral atoll. It contains rich deposits of high-grade phosphate, which have been worked since 1921. Ocean Island was claimed by Great Britain in 1901 and formally annexed to the Gilbert and Ellice Islands Colony fifteen years later. Area, 2 sq.m.; pop. (1951) 2307.

OCEAN SPRAY, IRONWOOD, or ARROW-WOOD, common name applied to shrubs of the genus *Holodiscus,* belonging to the Rose family. The genus, which is native to western United States, is cultivated as an ornamental shrub throughout the United States. The shrubs, which attain a height of about nine feet, have slender, curving branches which bear small leaves. The small white flowers, which are borne in large, drooping panicles, usually have five sepals, five petals, numerous stamens, and several pistils. The flowers turn tan in the fall. The common ocean spray is *Holodiscus discolor.*

OCEANUS, in Greek mythology, the eldest of the Titans (q.v.), son of Uranus, or Heaven, and of Gæa, or Earth, and father, by his sister Tethys, of the 3000 Oceanids, or ocean nymphs, and of all the rivers of the earth. According to the Greek poet Homer, Oceanus was the beginning of all things and was also the everflowing stream surrounding the plain of the earth. In the art of the Hellenistic period he is depicted, like the river gods, as a venerable old man, often with horns, and is characterized by a steering oar or by the sea animals surrounding him.

OCELOT, TIGER CAT, SPOTTED CAT, or LEOPARD CAT, a wild, carnivorous mammal, *Felis pardalis,* of the Cat family, found from Texas to Peru. The ocelot, which resembles the domestic cat in form, attains a length of about three feet. The back of the animal is tinted with olive tan or chestnut, marked with stripes and spots of black. The belly is usually white, marked with black. Ocelots inhabit forests, and are expert in climbing trees. At night they search for their food, which consists of birds and small mammals. Two kittens are produced in a litter.

OCHS, ADOLPH SIMON (1858–1935), American newspaper publisher, born in Cincinnati, Ohio, and educated in the primary schools of Knoxville, Tenn. He was a newsboy and printer's apprentice (1869–73), serving (1872–73) as the latter on the Knoxville *Chronicle.* Subsequently he was a compositor on the Louisville, Kentucky, *Courier-Journal;* and in 1877 became a member of the staff of the Chattanooga *Dispatch* and then its editor in chief. The following year he became publisher of the Chattanooga *Times,* which he made one of the outstanding newspapers of the South. Ochs gained control in 1896 of the New York *Times,* then bankrupt. As its publisher he followed a policy of thorough, nonpartisan, and unsensational coverage of news, in contrast to the "yellow journalism" (see NEWS-PAPER) prevailing at the time, and by his journalistic method developed the *Times* into one of the leading newspapers in the world. From 1902 to 1912 he was the owner of the Philadelphia *Times* and of the *Public Ledger* of the same city; he consolidated the two newspapers, retaining the latter name, and in 1913 sold the newspaper to Cyrus H.K. Curtis. Ochs was one of the founders of the Chicka-mauga-Chattanooga National Park, and the founder of the Lookout Mountain and Chattanooga Park. The New York *Times* under his direction gave financial backing to various noted explorers, particularly to Admiral Richard Byrd, and underwrote (1925) the publication of the *Dictionary of American Biography.*

OCIMUM. See BASIL.

OCKHAM or **OCCAM,** WILLIAM OF, known as DOCTOR INVINCIBILIS and VENERABILIS INCEPTOR (1300?–49?), English scholastic philosopher, born in Ockham, Surrey, England. He entered the Franciscan order, and

Adolph Simon Ochs

studied at Oxford and Paris, being a pupil, and afterward the rival, of Duns Scotus. But in the revolt of the Franciscans against Pope John XXII at Perugia (1322) he took a prominent part. After four months' imprisonment at Avignon he repaired to Munich, and found there a defender in the emperor Louis of Bavaria. In 1342 he seems to have become general of the Franciscans. Ockham won fame as the reviver of Nominalism, for which he obtained a final victory over the rival Realism.

OCMULGEE NATIONAL MONUMENT, a national monument in Georgia, adjoining the city of Macon. It was established in 1936 to preserve some of the most important prehistoric Indian mounds in the Southeast, and covers an area of 683 acres. Within the area are the remains of many centuries of Indian occupation, representing the settlements of successive tribes of Indians believed to have lived there as far back as the 13th century. The ruins include earthwork fortifications, burial mounds, and ceremonial mounds. A museum in the area contains relics of the early inhabitants of the region.

O'CONNELL, DANIEL (1775–1847), Irish national leader, called "the Liberator", born near Cahirciveen, in County Kerry, and educated at the colleges of St. Omer and Douai, in France. After completing his education in France, he returned to Ireland, studied law, and was admitted to the bar in Dublin in 1798. He soon gained a reputation as a leading constitutional and criminal lawyer. At the same time his interest in the Irish national problem led him to begin a career of political activity. O'Connell led a group of lawyers in reviving the Irish Catholic Committee, which grew into a strong movement containing almost all Catholic Irishmen under the leadership of O'Connell and the priesthood. The purpose of this movement was to oppose British rule through continuous agitation by the whole population, and thus to force concessions from every British party while operating solely within constitutional limits. By 1813, the Irish Catholic Committee had succeeded in making the British Parliament agree to allow the seating of Irish Catholics if the Church would give the Parliament the right to veto the choice of Catholic bishops. When O'Connell opposed this compromise, his movement lost momentum and collapsed. He revived it in 1823 by organizing the Catholic Association, which was run on a democratic basis. Elected to Parliament in 1828 from County Clare, O'Connell refused to serve until the anti-Catholic oath had been repealed. This refusal stimulated such formidable agitation that the Catholic Emancipation Act (q.v.) was passed the following year, abolishing all obstacles to Catholic representation in Parliament. O'Connell was re-elected, and he entered the House of Commons for County Clare in 1829, retaining his seat until his death. In England, O'Connell helped to pass the Reform Bill of 1832 (see REFORM BILLS), and often allied himself with the Radicals in Parliament.

As head of the Catholic Association, O'Connell received a large yearly income from voluntary contributions by the Irish people, who supported him in a series of demonstrations in favor of Irish Home Rule. Beginning in 1841, meetings were held for this cause throughout the country, and assumed such huge proportions that O'Connell and several other leaders were arrested in 1843 and convicted of seditious conspiracy in 1844. O'Connell's conviction was subsequently reversed by the House of Lords, and he resumed his career. At this time, a great famine descended upon Ireland; and younger elements in O'Connell's party began to advocate revolutionary doctrines which he had always opposed. Their arguments in favor of violent opposition to British rule led to an open split in Irish ranks in 1846, and O'Connell, distressed by this disaffection and suffering ill health, moved to Genoa, Italy, to rest. He died there the following year. See IRELAND: *History*.

O'CONNELL, CARDINAL WILLIAM H. (1859–1944), American prelate, born in Lowell, Mass. He was appointed rector of the American College in Rome (1896), and five years later was consecrated bishop of Portland, Me. He was chosen papal envoy to the Mikado (1906), and shortly after made coadjutor to Archbishop Williams of Boston. A year later he succeeded to the archiepiscopal see of Boston, and in 1911 was created cardinal.

OCTANE NUMBER. See DETONATION.

OCTAVE, in music, an interval consisting of eight notes embracing eight diatonic intervals. It is the interval common to all scales in the history of Western music. The term "octave" is also applied to the eighth note of the scale. This meaning of the term was first introduced about 550 B.C. by the Greek mathematician and philosopher Pythagoras, who discovered the octave to be that tone which is produced by twice the vibration frequency of the first note of the scale. The frequency ratio of the octave to the tonic or key note is thus 2:1.

OCTAVIA (d. 11 B.C.), Roman matron, daughter of Gaius Octavius and Atia, and sister of Gaius Octavius, who, after his adoption by his great-uncle Gaius Julius Cæsar, was known as Octavian until he became the emperor Augustus (q.v.). Octavia was distinguished for her beauty and her virtue. In 416 B.C., upon the death of her first husband, the consul Gaius Claudius Marcellus, she consented to marry Mark Antony (see ANTONIUS, MARCUS), to make secure the reconciliation between him and her brother. When Antony deserted her for the Egyptian queen Cleopatra (q.v.), Octavia remained loyal to her husband, even aiding him with reinforcements on occasion. Octavian was indignant at the treatment she received and wished her to leave her husband's house. When war broke out between Octavian and Antony in 32 B.C., the latter crowned his insults by sending Octavia a notice of divorce. After her husband's death in 30 B.C., Octavia brought up not only her own children, but also Antony's children by Fulvia, his first wife, and by Cleopatra. Octavia herself had five children, two daughters by Antony, and a son and two daughters by her first husband, Marcellus. The son, Marcus Claudius Marcellus, was adopted by Augustus and apparently intended to succeed the latter as emperor, but died in 23 B.C. Among the descendants of Octavia's two daughters, Antonia Major and Antonia Minor, were four rulers of the Roman Empire: the empress Livia and the emperors Claudius I, Nero, and Caligula.

OCTAVIA (42?–62 A.D.), Roman Empress, the daughter of the emperor Claudius (q.v.) and Messalina, and wife of the emperor Nero (q.v.), to whom she was married when he was sixteen and she eleven. He deserted her for Acte, and then for Poppæa Sabina, at whose request she was divorced and sent to Campania. Through Poppæa's jealousy, a charge of adultery was brought against her and she was sent to the island of Pandataria and there killed when she was only twenty years old. She is the heroine of *Octavia*, the only extant Roman historical play, or *fabula prætexta*. This tragedy has been attributed, probably wrongly, to Lucius Annæus Seneca (q.v.); the characters in the play include Octavia, Nero, Poppæa, and Seneca himself.

OCTAVIAN. See AUGUSTUS.

OCTAVIUS, GAIUS. See AUGUSTUS.

OCTOBER (Lat. *octo*, "eight"), formerly the eighth month of the so-called year of Romulus. It became the tenth when Numa changed the commencement of the year to the

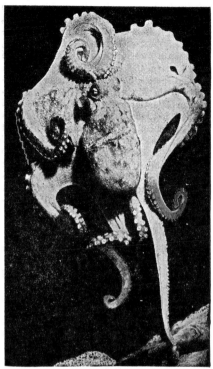

N.Y. Zoological Society

Octopus (Octopus americanus)

first of January, though it retained its original name.

OCTOPUS, DEVILFISH, POULP, or POLYPUS, common name for any of the eight-armed, dibranchiate, cephalopod mollusks constituting the family Octopodidae, especially those in the genus *Octopus*. The octopus has a large, soft, elliptical head, containing a pair of huge eyes with oblong pupils, and a large, horny beak. The head is attached to the membranous foot, from which the arms radiate, by a short, rounded, saclike body. The creature spends most of its life living in caves or crevices among the rocks or coral deposits of the ocean bottom, creeping over the bottom by means of two rows of suckers on each arm. The suckers are also utilized to grasp the octopus' prey, which consists chiefly of crabs. The octopus occasionally leaves its lair at night, propelling itself backward through the water by means of water which it ejects through the *swimming funnel* or *siphon*, a tube opening into and through the foot from the body. Like the squid and the cuttlefish (qq.v.), the octopus is capable of ejecting a murky fluid, commonly called "ink", through its siphon to darken the water about it, screening it from enemies. Contrary to popular belief, most octopuses are small creatures, less than a foot in diameter from the tip of one arm to the tip of the opposite arm. Several species, however, are larger; *O. vulgaris,* of the Mediterranean Sea and the European Atlantic coast, attains a diameter of about 7 feet, and *O. punctatus,* of the American Pacific coast, attains a diameter of about 14 feet. These octopuses are ferocious, and often attack divers, entwining their prey in their long arms; they are responsible for the popular belief that all octopi are "man killers". Large octopuses are used as food by the peoples of the Mediterranean and Pacific regions. See CEPHALOPODA.

OCULAR. See MICROSCOPE.

OCULIST. See SIGHT, DEFECTS OF.

ODD FELLOWS. See INDEPENDENT ORDER OF ODD FELLOWS.

ODE, originally, a poem arranged to be sung to the accompaniment of a musical instrument, such as the lyre. Among the ancient Greeks, lyric odes fell into two broad categories, those to be sung by a single voice and those to be sung by a group, or choir. The simpler form of the Greek ode, for a single voice, was cultivated by Sappho, Alcæus, Anacreon, and other early poets who wrote in the Æolic or Ionic dialect. The choral ode, composed to be sung by a group, was invented by the Dorians. To Alcman of Sparta belongs the innovation of dividing the chorus into two parts, called the *strophe,* or turn, and the *antistrophe,* or counterturn, in which the two groups of performers turn, respectively and successively, to the right and to the left, the one group turning to face and answer the other. Stesichorus of Sicily added a third part called the *epode,* or aftersong, which was sung by the entire chorus after their movements to the right and to the left. The choral ode, consisting thus of the *strophe,* the *antistrophe,* and the *epode,* was adapted by Simonides of Ceos to the warlike Dorian music. He was followed by Pindar (q.v.), the greatest lyric poet of Greece. Of Pindar's work there are extant, besides several fragments, forty-five *epinician* or victory odes, composed for the victors at the four great Panhellenic festivals, the Olympian, Pythian, Isthmian, and Nemean games. The poems of Bacchylides (q.v.), which were discovered on papyri in 1896, include thirteen epinician odes and six *dithyrambs,* or odes connected originally with the worship of Dionysus, god

of nature and of wine. Each ode of Pindar and Bacchylides has its own complicated metrical structure corresponding to its music. The simpler Greek measures of the odes for a single voice were imitated by the Roman lyric poets Gaius Valerius Catullus and Horace (qq.v.), who used the ode as a purely literary form which, if read aloud, was declaimed rather than sung. Horace modeled his odes upon those of Alcæus particularly, and Catullus was influenced by Sappho. The Romans made no attempt to imitate the elaborate measures of the odes of Pindar and Bacchylides.

The modern ode, dating from the Renaissance, is written as pure poetry, without musical accompaniment; it is exalted in tone, more impersonal than the ordinary lyric, and it deals progressively with a single dignified theme. The earliest English odes are the *Epithalamion* and the *Prothalamion* of Edmund Spenser. Among other English writers of odes are Ben Jonson, Richard Crashaw, John Milton, Abraham Cowley, Andrew Marvell, John Dryden, William Collins, and Thomas Gray. Cowley sought to imitate the structure and content of the Pindaric ode; he failed to understand the fundamental division into *strophe, antistrophe,* and *epode,* but he stamped his conception of the ode as a lofty and tempestuous piece of poetry upon later English literature. Gray had a better understanding of Pindaric structure; he divided his *Progress of Poesy* into three stanzas, each stanza being subdivided into *strophe, antistrophe,* and *epode.* But the English ode, as usually composed, is merely a succession of stanzas in lines of varying length and meter. Of musical settings for odes the most famous are those by Henry Purcell, twenty-eight in number, and the four by George Frederick Handel.

Among the great English odes of the 19th century are William Wordsworth's *To Duty* and *Intimations of Immortality;* Samuel Taylor Coleridge's *To France;* Percy Bysshe Shelley's *To the West Wind, To Liberty, To Naples,* and *To a Skylark;* John Keats' *To a Nightingale, To Autumn,* and *On a Grecian Urn;* Alfred, Lord Tennyson's *On the Death of the Duke of Wellington;* and Algernon Charles Swinburne's *To Victor Hugo.* Among American odes is James Russell Lowell's great *Commemoration Ode* to the Harvard students and graduates who fell in the Civil War.

ODENSE, the largest city on the island of Fünen, Denmark, capital of Odense Amt, and the third city in population in the kingdom.

The most notable building is the cathedral of St. Canute, built in the 13th century, the best example of Gothic architecture in Denmark. The church of Our Lady, built in the 12th century, is the oldest in the town. The industrial establishments are breweries, distilleries, glass, chemical, and tobacco factories, machine shops, textile mills, and sugar refineries. It is the birthplace of Hans Christian Andersen. Pop. (1950) 100,940.

ODER, one of the principal rivers of Germany. It rises in the Oderberg of Moravia, traverses Prussian Silesia, Brandenburg, and Pomerania, and flows into the Stettiner Haff, whence it passes into the Baltic by the triple arms of the Dievenow, Peene, and Swine, which enclose the islands of Wollin and Usedom. It has a course of 550 m., and a basin of 50,000 sq.m. Canals connect the Oder with the Havel and the Elbe, and the Friedrich Wilhelm Canal connects it with the Spree. The chief cities on the Oder are Stettin, Frankfort (Brandenburg), Breslau, and Oppeln.

ODESSA, capital of the Odessa Region of the Ukrainian Soviet Socialist Republic (q.v.), and leading seaport of the republic, situated on the Black Sea, 32 miles N.E. of the mouth of the Dniester R. The city is built on terraces which rise above a semicircular bay. Its five harbors are protected by breakwaters and provide 4 m. of quay space. Situated on the coast of one of the largest grain-producing regions in the Soviet Union, Odessa is a principal Soviet center for the export of flour and grain. Other exports are sugar, wool, lumber, and cattle. Imports include machinery, iron, coal, raw cotton, tea, tobacco, and coffee.

Odessa was the site of an ancient Greek settlement which ceased to exist by the 3rd century A.D. No further effort was made to exploit the site until the 14th century A.D., when a Tatar chief, Khaji Bey, built a fort there. Turks captured it in the 16th century, and in 1789 the town, which had developed around the fort, was taken by the Russians and heavily fortified. During the Crimean War, Odessa was bombarded by combined French and British naval forces. In 1876–77 it successfully fought off a Turkish attack. Odessa was the site of a workers' revolution in 1905, supported by the crew of the Russian battleship *Potemkin*. During World War I the city was frequently shelled and occupied successively by Austrians and Germans, French, Serbs, and Poles. In 1917 the provisional government of Aleksander Kerenski (q.v.) was recognized there. In 1920 the city was taken by Bolshevik forces. During World War II Odessa was captured by the Germans on Oct. 16, 1941, after a six-week siege, and retaken by the Soviet army on April 10, 1944. Pop., about 604,000.

ODETS, CLIFFORD (1906–), American playwright, born in Philadelphia, and reared in New York City. He was educated in public schools there but left school at the age of fifteen to become an actor. He later participated in Theatre Guild productions and in 1931 was one of the founders of the Group Theatre in New York City. Most of his plays were produced by the Group Theatre, including *Waiting for Lefty* (1935, a one-act play which established his fame), *Awake And Sing* (1935), and *Till the Day I Die* (1935). After the unsuccessful production of his *Paradise Lost* (1935) Odets went to Hollywood, Calif., where he wrote the motion-picture scenario of *The General Died at Dawn* (1936). Returning to New York after two years, he wrote more plays for the Group, including *Golden Boy* (1937), *Silent Partner* (1938), *Rocket to the Moon* (1939), *Night Music* (1940), and *Clash by Night* (1941), all concerned with the frustration of individual potentialities by economic insecurity and the materialistic ideals of middle-class society. Odets subsequently spent several years in Hollywood, and wrote many motion-picture scenarios, including *None But The Lonely Heart* (1943). He is the author also of the plays *The Big Knife* (1948), *The Country Girl* (1951), and *The Flowering Peach* (1954).

ODIN (ON. *Odhinn,* AS. *Wōden,* OHG. *Wōdan, Wuotan*), the chief god of Northern mythology. Odin rules heaven and earth and is omniscient. His seat is Valaskjálf, whence his two black ravens, Huginn (Thought) and Muninn (Memory), fly daily to gather tidings of all that is being done throughout the world. As god of war, he holds his court in Valhalla, whither come all brave warriors after death to revel in tumultuous joys. His greatest treasures are his eight-footed steed Sleipner, his spear Gungner, and his ring Draupner. By drinking from Mimir's fountain he became the wisest of gods and men, but he purchased the distinction at the cost of one eye. Frigga is his queen and the mother of Balder, but he has other wives and favorites and numerous sons and daughters. See SCANDINAVIAN MYTHOLOGY.

ODONTOLITE. See IVORY.

ODYSSEUS. See ULYSSES.

ODYSSEY, an epic poem by the Greek poet Homer (q.v.), recounting the wanderings of the Greek hero Odysseus after the fall of Troy (see ILIAD). Like the Iliad, it is regarded as one of the greatest literary works ever produced. Particularly noteworthy in the *Odyssey* are the majesty of language, the sagalike descriptions of Odysseus' desperate efforts to return to his home in Ithaca, and the detailed delineation of the hero's character.

The Homeric narrative begins with the victorious Greeks returning to their homes after sacking Troy. Odysseus' ships are driven by a storm on the coast of Thrace, where he plunders the land of the Chicones but loses a number of his crew. When he re-embarks, a north wind blows his vessels to the country of the Lotophagi (the Lotos eaters; see LOTOS), on the coasts of Libya, where some of the companions of Odysseus eat of the wondrous fruit and wish to rest forever. But their leader compels them to leave the land, and, sailing north again, they touch at the Island of Goats, where Odysseus leaves his fleet. Thence, with one ship, he proceeds to the land of the Cyclopes (see CYCLOPS), where occurs the adventure in the cave of Polyphemus (q.v.). With his reunited fleet he now visits the island of Æolus, ruler of the winds, who gives him a favoring breeze and the unfavorable winds tied in a skin His companions, in search of treasure, open the skin, and at once they are swept back to the island, from which they are now sternly excluded. They then reach the land of the Læstrygonians, a race of cannibals who destroy all the ships but one, in which Odysseus escapes, landing next on the island of Ææa, inhabited by the sorceress Circe. After a year's sojourn there he is sent by Circe to the Kingdom of Hades, to inquire about his return from the seer Tiresias (q.v.). Tiresias discloses to Odysseus the implacable enmity of the sea god Poseidon, whose son, Polyphemus, Odysseus has blinded, but encourages him at the same time with the assurance that he will yet reach Ithaca in safety, if he does not meddle with the herds of the sun god Helios in Thrinacia.

Odysseus next passes in safety the perilous island of the Sirens (q.v.), but, when he sails between the monsters Scylla and Charybdis (q.v.), Scylla devours six of his companions. He next comes to Thrinacia, where his crew insists on landing; while they are stormbound and while Odysseus is asleep, they kill, in spite of their oath, some of the cattle of Helios. When they sail away a fierce storm arises and Zeus sends forth a flash of lightning that destroys the ship. Everyone on board is drowned except Odysseus, who clings to the mast and is finally washed ashore on the

island of Ogygia, the abode of the nymph Calypso (q.v.), with whom he lives for eight years. The nymph offers him immortality if he will remain, but his love for his wife Penelope and longing for his home is too deep, and at the entreaty of his special guardian, Athena, Zeus sends Hermes, messenger of the gods, to command his release. Sailing eastward in a skiff of his own building, he is seen by the implacable Poseidon, who rouses against him a terrible storm which wrecks his skiff. He barely escapes, by the aid of the sea goddess Leucothea, to the land of the Phæacians. Naked and worn by fatigue, Odysseus falls asleep, but is found by Nausicaa, daughter of the king, Alcinous; she receives him kindly and brings him to the city. Entering the palace under Athena's protection, he is entertained by the king, who promises him safe convoy to his home. On the magic Phæacian ship he falls asleep, and is landed, at Ithaca, with the rich presents of the Phæacians, while still unconscious.

Disguised as a beggar, he goes to the hut of the swineherd Eumæus, and there meets and reveals himself to his son Telemachus. The next day he is brought by Eumæus to the palace, where he is recognized only by his old dog, Argus, and is harshly treated by the suitors of his wife, who during his long absence have been living riotously on his estate. After an interview with the unsuspecting Penelope, to whom he foretells her husband's return, he is recognized by his old nurse, Eurycleia, whom he binds to silence. When the suitors all fail to string the great bow, the test Penelope has proposed for her suitors, Odysseus takes it, easily strings it, and shoots the arrow through a row of twelve axes. Then, aided by Telemachus, Eumæus, and the cowherd Philœtius, he slays all the insolent suitors. The last book of the *Odyssey* records his recognition by his father, Laërtes, and a final reconciliation with the friends of the suitors, brought about by Athena's aid.

OEDEMA. See DROPSY.

ŒDIPUS, in Greek legend, the son of Laïus and Jocasta, king and queen of Thebes, and the hero of one of the most famous Greek tales. The story as it appears in Greek drama, and especially in the well-known tragedies of Sophocles (q.v.), *Œdipus Tyrannus* and *Œdipus Coloneus,* is as follows. Laïus had learned from an oracle that he was destined to perish by the hands of his own son, and so he ordered the infant exposed on Mount Cithæron after his birth, with his feet pierced through. The child, however, was found by a herdsman of Polybus, King of Corinth, and was named Œdipus from his swollen feet. Polybus and his wife Merope reared him as their own son. Œdipus was taunted by a drunken companion about his origin and went to the oracle at Delphi to have his suspicions allayed. Being told by the oracle that he was destined to slay his father and commit incest with his mother, and believing Polybus to be his father, he fled in horror from Corinth, but proceeded to Thebes and the fulfillment of his destiny. At a crossroads he met Laïus and his attendants and, in a quarrel which ensued, he unwittingly killed his father. Next he freed Thebes from the presence of the Sphinx (q.v.) by solving its riddle. In gratitude the Thebans made Œdipus their king and gave him Jocasta as his wife. From this incestuous union were born four children, Eteocles, Polynices, Antigone, and Ismene. At length a terrible pestilence visited Thebes, and the oracle declared that the murderer of Laïus must be expelled from the country. Œdipus began the search and by degrees the awful truth became known. Jocasta committed suicide by hanging, and, in his horror, Œdipus blinded himself. He was driven from Thebes by his sons and, attended by his faithful daughter Antigone, wandered until he found a destined place of refuge at Colonus, near Athens, where the Eumenides charitably conducted him to the other world without death. His sons by their deeds had brought upon themselves their father's curse, and they ultimately fell by each other's hands. See ANTIGONE.

OEDIPUS COMPLEX. See PSYCHOANALYSIS: *Freud.*

OEHLENSCHLAGER, ADAM GOTTLOB (1779–1850), Danish poet and dramatist, born in Vesterbro near Copenhagen. After unsuccessful attempts at a career first in business and then as a comic actor, he took up a literary career in 1802. His poetry and dramatic works were influenced by those of the Romantic movement in Germany and by the Old Norse sagas. His first published volume of verse, *Digte* (1803), established his reputation. He traveled throughout Europe from 1805 to 1809, returning to Denmark to become professor of esthetics at the University of Copenhagen. Oehlenschlager was the leader of the Romantic movement in Danish literature. Most of his plays are based on Danish history or Norse folklore. They include the lyric drama *Sanct-Hansaftern-Spil* (1803); the historical tragedies *Hakon Jarl* (1807), *Baldur hin Gode* (1808), and *Axel og Valborg* (1810); and the epic cycle *Nordens Guder* (1819).

Others of his important works are the fantasy in verse *Aladdin* (1805), the tragedy *Correggio* (written in German, 1809), and the epic *Regnar Lodbrok* (1848).

OENOTHERA, genus of biennial and annual herbs in the family Onagraceae, commonly known as evening primrose. The genus, which contains about forty species, is native to North America, naturalized in Europe, and widely cultivated as ornamental plants. Evening primroses have alternate leaves, and yellow, white, or pink flowers, which open in the evening. The flowers, which are borne in racemes, have four sepals, four petals, eight stamens, and a solitary pistil. The fruit is a many-seeded capsule. *Oenothera biennis* is the best-known species.

OERSTED, HANS CHRISTIAN (1777–1851), Danish physicist, born in Rudkjöbing, Langeland, and educated at the University of Copenhagen. In 1806 he was appointed professor of physics at the University of Copenhagen and twenty-three years later director of the newly founded Copenhagen Polytechnic Institute. In 1812 he demonstrated the identity of chemical and electrical forces, and on the basis of this finding was able in 1819 to make his most important discovery, concerning the basic relationship existing between magnetism, electricity, and galvanism. His experiments were described by him in *Experimenta Circa Effectum Conflictus Electrici in Acum Magneticam,* published in 1820, and established Oersted as the founder of electromagnetism; see ELECTRICITY.

OERTEL, ABRAHAM. See ORTELIUS.

OFFALY, formerly KING'S, a county of Leinster Province, Republic of Ireland. It is situated chiefly in the coastal plain of Ireland, and is bounded on the w. by the Shannon R. Besides the Shannon, the principal streams are the Brosna and Boyne. The county is crossed by the Grand Canal (see CANAL), and in the central portion is the Bog of Allen. The terrain in the S.E. is mountainous. Tullamore (pop., about 5000) is the county seat. Agriculture is the principal occupation. Oats, rye, barley, potatoes, and turnips are grown and livestock is raised; dairying is carried on in the N. Danish raths, or hill fortresses, and remains of ancient churches and monasteries, some dating from the 5th century, are found. Area, 772 sq.m.; pop. (1951 prelim.) 52,555.

OFFENBACH, town in the Republic of Hesse, situated on the Main, 3 miles E. of Frankfort. It has a palace, the residence of the princes Isenburg-Birstein, and a ruined castle belonging to the same family. It is celebrated

Jacques Offenbach

for its manufacture of fine leather articles. There are machine shops, tanneries, and manufactures of saddlery and tobacco. Pop., about 80,000.

OFFENBACH, JACQUES (1819–80), French composer, born in Cologne, Germany, and educated at the Paris Conservatory. In 1837 he became cellist in the orchestra of the Paris Opéra Comique, and in 1847 was made conductor at the Théâtre Français. His first complete opera, *Pepitò*, was performed at the Opéra Comique in 1853. From 1855 to 1861 he rented a theater, which he named the Bouffes Parisiens, and there produced a large number of one-act operas of his own composition. The success of this venture so enhanced his reputation that more of his longer operas were performed at the Opéra Comique and the Paris Opéra. From 1872 to 1876 Offenbach managed the Théâtre Gaieté in Paris. By 1875 he had written ninety operas, many of them to texts supplied by the French playwright and novelist Ludovic Halévy. Among these operas were *Orphée aux Enfers* (1858; revised 1874), *La Grande Duchesse de Gérolstein* (1867), and *La Vie Parisienne* (1866). His best-known work, the four-act comic opera *The Tales of Hoffmann,* which contains the popular "Barcarolle", was not performed until 1881, after his death. Offenbach's operas were enormously popular in his time, but with the exception of *Tales of Hoffmann* are rarely performed today. His musical style is prevailingly light, witty, and gay.

OFFICE OF DEFENSE MOBILIZATION, agency of the Executive Office of the President of the United States, established in 1950, and reorganized in 1953. The agency is headed by a director, an appointee of the President by and with the consent of the Senate. There are six assistant directors, namely for Financial Policy, Production Requirements and Programs, Materials, Stabilization, Non-Military Defense, and Manpower. In the performance of his duties the director is further assisted by various boards and committees. Generally stated, the Office of Defense Mobilization is responsible for policy planning, co-ordination, and leadership in the national mobilization effort. Specific functions of the agency include the development of policies or programs to insure the maximum utilization of U.S. manpower in the event of war; to insure the most effective use in time of war of the nation's natural and industrial resources for military and civilian needs; to insure economic stabilization in wartime; to determine the relationship between potential supplies of and requirements for manpower, resources, and productive facilities in wartime; to establish adequate reserves of strategic and critical material; and to minimize the effects of enemy attacks on cities, industries, and government. Responsibility for the proper functioning of telecommunications in the Executive Branch of the Federal government is also vested in the Office of Defense Mobilization.

OFFICE OF INTERNATIONAL FINANCE, an agency of the U.S. Treasury Department, created by departmental order in July, 1947. It is responsible for advising and assisting the secretary of the treasury in the formulation and execution of policies and programs relating to the international financial and monetary fields. Specifically, the Office helps formulate policies affecting the following fields: the financial aspects of all international treaties, agreements, organizations, and operations in which the U.S. government participates, including such bodies as the International Monetary Fund and the International Bank for Reconstruction and Development (qq.v.); the liquidation of the Foreign Funds Control program conducted pursuant to the Trading With the Enemy Act of 1917 as amended; statutes and regulations relating to gold, silver, exchange rates, exchange stabilization agreements and operations, acquisition and disposition of foreign currencies, and similar matters; and the administration of all international loans and financial assistance programs initiated by the U.S. government. The Office of International Finance is also charged with obtaining current information concerning the financial position of foreign countries, and with the preparation of analyses and recommendations based on such information.

OFFICE OF PRICE ADMINISTRATION, a World War II agency of the U.S. government, created as the Office of Price Administration and Civilian Supply by a Presidential order issued in April, 1941. This agency, popularly known as "OPA", was charged with forestalling the development of a national economic inflation by stabilizing rents and prices and by preventing speculation, hoarding, profiteering, and price manipulation. Its name was changed to Office of Price Administration in August, 1941, by a Presidential order which also transferred its functions relating to civilian supply to another government agency. Subsequently, the powers of the OPA were expanded by several Congressional enactments to include the rationing of scarce commodities to consumers and various other regulatory functions. The OPA was notably successful in performing its responsibilities during World War II, but soon after the conclusion of hostilities in 1945 it became the center of a bitter controversy, as many producers' groups demanded the abolition of all price controls and a number of consumers' groups fought for their retention. In December, 1946, the OPA was consolidated with several other Federal agencies into the newly established Office of Temporary Controls; the latter agency was abolished in June, 1947.

O'FLAHERTY, LIAM (1896–   ), Irish novelist, born in the Arran Islands, County Galway, and educated at University College, Dublin. He was one of the leading Irish novelists of the second quarter of the 20th century (see IRISH LITERATURE). His works are characterized by unsparing realism and powerful drama. Among his books are *Thy Neighbor's Wife* (1924), *The Informer* (1925, subsequently made into a motion picture of the same name), *Mr. Gilhooley* (1926), *The Mountain Tavern and Other Stories* (1929), *Famine* (1937), *Land* (1946), *Two Lovely Beasts* (1950), and *Insurrection* (1951).

OGDEN, county seat of Weber Co., Utah, situated at the confluence of the Ogden and Weber rivers, 35 miles N. of Salt Lake City. Ogden is the second-largest city in the State, and the leading railroad center between the Rocky Mountains and the Pacific coast. Among its industrial establishments are large railroad shops, stockyards, meat-packing plants, flour mills, fruit and vegetable canneries, creameries, powdered-milk plants, an oil refinery, and factories manufacturing beet sugar, candy, overalls, knit goods, dresses, aprons, tin cans, and cement. Ogden is the site of Weber Junior College, established in 1889, and of a regional headquarters of the U.S. Forest Service. The city lies at the foot of the Wasatch Mountains, at an elevation of 4300 ft. above sea level. Towering above it are Mount Ogden (10,100 ft.) and Mount Ben Lomond (10,900 ft.), and nearby is a canyon of the Ogden R., in which is Pine View Lake, a recreational area impounded by Pine View dam. The site of the present city was first settled by the Mormons in 1847 and in 1851 the settlement was incorporated. Pop. (1950) 57,112.

OGLETHORPE, JAMES EDWARD (1696–1785), English philanthropist and colonist, founder of the colony (now State) of Georgia, born in London. He was elected to the House of Commons in 1722, and subsequently interested himself in prison reform, particularly in alleviating the condition of those imprisoned for debt. He formulated a plan for the resettlement of debtors in America, and in 1732 was granted a royal charter for the purpose of realizing this plan. With a band of 120 emigrants, Oglethorpe landed at the present site of Savannah in February, 1733. established a colony there, and for almost two years acted as its administrator, after which he returned to England. He revisited the colony in 1735–36 and from 1738 to 1743; during the latter period he defeated a Spanish force which had invaded the Georgia colony from Florida. In 1743 Oglethorpe returned to England, where he was commissioned a major general two years later. He returned the charter of the Georgia colony to the British government in 1752, whereupon the colony came under the direct control of the crown.

OGPU. See GPU.

O'GRADY, STANDISH JAMES (1846–1928), Irish man of letters, born in Castletown, County Cork, and educated at Trinity College, Dublin. O'Grady's studies and writings, both historical and fictional, dealing with the people, and heroes of ancient Ireland, were one of the forces that brought about the Celtic or Irish literary renaissance of the late 19th and early 20th century (see IRISH LITERATURE). Among O'Grady's works are *History of Ireland: the*

Random House

John O'Hara

Heroic Period (2 vols., 1878), and *History of Ireland, Critical and Philosophical* (1881); and the historical romances *Finn and His Companions* (1892), *The Coming of Cuculain* (1894), *Ulrich the Ready* (1896), and *The Passing of Cuculain* (1917).

O'HARA, JOHN (1905–), American novelist and short-story writer, born in Pottsville, Pa., and educated at Niagara Preparatory School, Niagara Falls, N.Y. He was successively a newspaper reporter, a dramatic and motion-picture critic, and (from 1934) a motion-picture writer. His first novel, *Appointment in Samara* (1934), brought him wide public recognition. He is best known for his novel *Butterfield 8* (1935), a tragic story of life in the night clubs and underworld of New York City; and for his short stories *Pal Joey* (1940), in the form of letters by a cynical night-club singer. The latter were made into a musical comedy of the same name (1940), for which O'Hara helped write the libretto. O'Hara's fiction is distinguished for satiric, ironic, and tragic realism; stress on characterization rather than plot; and a style marked by simplicity and power. Other works are *The Doctor's Son and Other Stories* (1935), *Rage to Live* (1949), *Sweet and Sour* (essays, 1954), and *Ten North Frederick* (1955); and the collections of short stories

Files on Parade (1939), *Pipe Night* (1945), and *Hellbox* (1947).

O'HIGGINS, BERNARDO (1778–1842), Chilean soldier and statesman, born in Chillán, the son of Don Ambrosio O'Higgins (1720?–1800), governor of Chile from 1778 to 1795 and viceroy of Peru from 1795 to 1801. After spending several years studying in England and Spain, Bernardo O'Higgins returned to Chile in 1802. He took part in the nationalist revolution against Spain in 1810, and was made commander of the patriot army in 1813. Defeated by royalist troops at Rancagua in 1814, O'Higgins fled across the Andes to Argentina with most of his followers. There he joined José de San Martín (q.v.), with whom he returned to defeat the Spaniards at Chacabuco in 1817 and Maipú in 1818. O'Higgins was made dictator of Chile in 1822, but resigned and retired to Peru the following year when discontented revolutionists demanded a constitutional government.

OHIO, river of the United States and second-largest affluent (after the Missouri R.) of the Mississippi R., formed by the confluence of the Allegheny and Monongahela rivers at Pittsburgh, Pa. About 980 m. long, it flows in a generally w.s.w. direction, forming the boundaries between Ohio and West Virginia, Ohio and Kentucky, Indiana and Kentucky, and Illinois and Kentucky, and joins the Mississippi at Cairo, Ill. The chief tributaries of the Ohio are the Tennessee, Cumberland, Wabash, Kentucky, Great Kanawha, Green, Muskingum, Scioto, and Licking. By means of a system of locks and dredged channels the Ohio is navigable by shallow-draft boats throughout its length.

OHIO, one of the North Central States of the United States, bounded on the N. by Michigan and Lake Erie, on the E. by Pennsylvania and the Ohio R. (q.v.), which separates it from West Virginia, on the S. by the Ohio R., which separates it from West Virginia and Kentucky, and on the w. by Indiana. Ohio ranks as the 34th State in the Union in area, the 5th (1950) in population, and the 17th in the order of admission to the Union, having entered on March 1, 1803. The capital is Columbus (q.v.), the third-largest city of the State. Cleveland (q.v.) is the largest city. Besides the foregoing, six cities of Ohio have populations over 100,000. In the order of size, these cities are Cincinnati, Toledo, Akron, Dayton, Youngstown, and Canton (qq.v.). Twenty-five cities of the State have populations ranging from 25,000 to over 70,000. Among the largest of these are Springfield,

Lakewood, Cleveland Heights, Hamilton, Lorain, Lima, Warren, Mansfield, Euclid, Zanesville, and East Cleveland (qq.v.). In shape, Ohio somewhat resembles a square, with the principal irregularities occurring along the s.e. and s. boundaries. The extreme length, in an E. and w. direction, is about 220 m.; the maximum width, from N. to S., is about 210 m. The coastline along Lake Erie is about 230 m. Area of the State, 41,222 sq.m., including 100 sq.m. of inland water surface. The population of the State (1950) is 7,946,627.

The terrain of Ohio consists predominantly of rolling hills and glaciated, undulating plains, the only level portion of the State being in the N. This portion, a strip of ancient lake bottom adjacent to Lake Erie, varies in width from 5 m. in the E. to 70 m. in the w. South of the lake plain and E. of a line extending generally southwestward from Trumbull Co., the terrain falls within the province of the Allegheny Plateau. The plateau region is hilly, with elevations ranging from 500 ft. along the Ohio R. to 100 ft. in the w. Except where dissected by deep river valleys, the terrain of the plains region, to the w. of the Allegheny Plateau, is gently undulating. Campbell Hill (1550 ft.) in Logan Co. is the highest point in the State. The lowest point, along the Ohio R. in Hamilton Co., is 425 ft. above sea level. The average elevation of the State is 850 ft.

Ohio possesses two drainage systems, the basin of the Ohio R. and the basin of Lake Erie. The streams of the Ohio basin are the principal rivers of the State, and include the Muskingum, Scioto, Mahoning, and Hocking. Among the chief rivers flowing into Lake Erie are the Sandusky, Cuyahoga, Huron, and Portage. Most of the lakes within the State are small.

The forests of Ohio cover about 6000 sq.m., approximately 16% of the area of the State. Extensive wooded tracts and areas along Lake Erie are reserved for recreational purposes. Ohio contains 20 State forests totaling more than 145,281 acres, 55 State parks totaling about 22,000 acres, and, in addition, many large community forests. Among the outstanding units of the State park system are the Shawnee State Forest (60,000 acres) in the vicinity of Portsmouth; Scioto Trail State Forest (9000 acres) near Chillicothe; Pymatuning Reservoir State Park (5100 acres) in Ashtabula Co.; and Portage Lakes State Park (2250 acres) near Akron.

Climatic conditions in Ohio are typical of the central areas of the United States. Except in the region under the modifying influence of Lake Erie, the State is subject to extreme seasonal variations of temperature, with maximum temperatures as high as 104° F. in the summer and as low as —32° F. in the winter. The average annual temperature for the entire State is about 51° F. Precipitation averages about 39 inches annually. The heaviest rainfall occurs in the s.e.; the area of minimum precipitation is in the N.w. Precipitation in the form of snow is heaviest in the vicinity of Lake Erie, where the annual fall averages nearly 4 ft.

Almost 80% of the total area of Ohio is devoted to agriculture. In 1950 more than 199,000 farms covered an area exceeding 20,900,000 acres and were valued (land and buildings) at more than $3,808,000,000. The chief crops (with production figures for 1952) are corn (189,000,000 bushels), oats (49,900,000 bushels), winter wheat (55,100,000 bushels), and tobacco (27,450,000 pounds). Other important crops are potatoes, sugar beets, hay, and grapes. The livestock population in 1953 numbered about 2,729,000 swine, 2,416,000 cattle (including 1,019,000 dairy cows), 1,328,000 sheep, 94,000 horses, and 4000 mules. The wool clip in 1952 from 1,062,000 sheep was 9,027,000 pounds. Cash income from livestock and crops in the same year totaled $1,085,000,000.

Ohio Devel. & Publicity Comm.

Ohio State House in Columbus

OHIO
RESOURCES AND PRODUCTS
Scale of Miles
0   10   20   30   40
Copyright by C. S. HAMMOND & Co., N. Y.

Ohio possesses extensive mineral resources. The total value of mineral production in 1951 was about $302,613,000. The chief minerals were coal (37,949,000 tons), stone (25,190,000 tons), cement (11,872,000 barrels), lime (2,289,000 tons), sand and gravel (19,431,000 tons), petroleum (3,140,000 barrels), natural gas (38,879,000,000 cubic feet), clays (5,147,000 tons), and salt (3,112,000) tons.

Ohio is one of the leading manufacturing States of the U.S., with 11,956 industrial establishments in 1953, employing about 1,400,000 workers. The value added by manufacture in 1951 was more than $9,396,000,000. The manufacture of nonelectrical machinery is the most important of these industries, and ac-

counted for more than $1,739,000,000 of the total. Primary metal industries accounted for more than $1,575,000,000. The making of rubber tires and tubes is also a major industry, Akron alone producing most of the auto tires used in the U.S. Other important industries include the manufacture of pig iron, ferroalloys, electrical machinery, motor-vehicle parts and bodies, grindstones, and cement, meat packing, printing and publishing, and petroleum refining.

Transportation facilities in the State include (1953) 8865 m. of main-track railway, 450 airports and landing fields, and more than 102,000 m. of roads, of which about 48,400 m. are surfaced highways.

Attendance at the public schools of Ohio is free and compulsory during the full school year for all students between the ages of six and eighteen. In 1952–53 there were about 4100 public elementary and secondary schools staffed by over 48,000 teachers and attended by more than 1,387,000 students. Ohio supports five State universities and a number of teachers colleges and municipal universities; in addition, more than 60 privately endowed junior colleges, colleges, and universities are in the State. The leading institutions of higher learning include Ohio State University at Columbus, Antioch College at Yellow Springs, the University of Cincinnati at Cincinnati, Miami University at Oxford, Ohio Wesleyan University at Delaware, Western Reserve University at Cleveland, Bowling Green State University at Bowling Green, and the Case Institute of Technology at Cleveland.

Ohio is governed according to the constitution of 1851, revised in 1912, and since amended. Executive authority is vested in a governor, lieutenant governor, secretary of state, treasurer, and attorney general, all elected for two-year terms; a board of public works and a school commissioner elected for three-year terms; an auditor, who is elected for a four-year term; and various appointed officials. Legislative authority is vested in a senate of 33 members and a house of representatives of 136 members, all elected for two-year terms. Judicial authority is vested in a supreme court of seven justices elected for six-year terms, 9 judicial courts of appeals, courts of common pleas, probate courts, juvenile courts, municipal courts, and justices of the peace. Electors are U.S. citizens who have resided in the State at least one year, the county forty days, and the precinct forty days. The State is divided into 88 counties and is represented in the Congress of the U.S. by 2 senators and 23 representatives.

History. The first European to explore the territory of what is the present State of Ohio was, probably, the French explorer Robert Cavelier, Sieur de La Salle, who claimed to have discovered and ascended the Ohio R. in 1669. When, in 1682, La Salle claimed the entire valley of the Mississippi R. for France, the territory between the Great Lakes (to Lake Erie) and the Ohio R. was considered a French possession. French claims were not acknowledged by contiguous British colonies, particularly Virginia, which claimed the territory N. of the Ohio R. and W. of the Mississippi. After about 1730, traders from Pennsylvania and Virginia came into the area and in 1749 George II of Great Britain awarded a royal grant to the Ohio Company (q.v.), organized by Virginia planters and London merchants, to settle and trade in the valley of the Ohio. The French governor of

Ohio Devel. & Publicity Comm.

The Ohio River at Cincinnati

United Airlines

Above: Aerial view of Toledo, Ohio.
Left: Aerial view of Cleveland, Ohio.

Canada, in the same year, sent an officer, Pierre Joseph de Céloron de Blainville, to bury lead markers in the name of France along the river banks. Settlements by the Ohio Company inevitably caused French resentment and in 1756 clashes between the French, their Indian allies, and the British precipitated the French and Indian War (q.v.), the American phase of the Seven Years' War (1756–63) in Europe. By the terms of the Treaty of Paris in 1763, the victorious British acquired undisputed title to the territory. The Indian allies of France, however, refused to acknowledge British supremacy; they revolted in 1763 in the so-called Conspiracy of Pontiac (see PONTIAC). The Indian war was ended by treaty in 1765.

In 1774 Great Britain made the territory part of Canada, by the Quebec Act. The resentment of the American colonies at the annexation of land which they claimed was one of the causes of the American Revolution. During the Revolution the American frontier leader George Rogers Clark invaded and held the region from 1779 to 1783. In the latter year Great Britain ceded its rights to the area, known as the Northwest Territory (q.v.), to the United States. By 1786 all the States had ceded their separate claims in the Northwest Territory to the Federal government, except for Connecticut, which retained its claim to the area known as the Western Reserve (q.v.) until 1800, and Virginia, which retained its claim to the so-called Virginia Military District, between the Little Miami and Scioto rivers, until 1852. In 1785 the Congress enacted the Land Ordinance, establishing conditions for sale of land in the Territory, and in 1787 passed the Northwest Ordinance providing for administration of the Territory. The Ohio Company of Associates was organized in 1786 by officers and soldiers of the Revolutionary army to facilitate land sales.

The first authorized permanent settlement was founded at Marietta in 1788. Cincinnati was established in 1789 and in 1796 Cleveland was founded in the Western Reserve. Hostile Indians, alarmed at the increasing number of settlers, rose in a series of frontier wars which were ended in 1795, when the Indians, defeated by American forces, ceded rights to most of present Ohio. The augmented home-steadings after the cessation of Indian hostilities resulted in a population large enough to demand organized government. Territorial government, under a Federal governor, was instituted in 1799. Ohio was divided from the remainder of the Northwest Territory in 1800 and in 1803 became the first State of the Territory to be admitted into the Union. The capital was first established at Chillicothe and, after several moves, was fixed at Columbus in 1816.

Ohio became continually more prosperous and populous after the acquisition of statehood; its population, about 42,000 in 1800, increased to over 230,000 by 1810. The invention of the steamboat by Robert Fulton made Cincinnati a great river port; and the completion of the Erie Canal from Lake Erie to the Hudson R. in 1825, and of the Ohio and Erie Canal from Portsmouth, on the Ohio R., to Cleveland, in 1835, gave the State access to the Atlantic Ocean and inaugurated an era of great prosperity. A famous episode during this period was the arrival of the Mormons (q.v.) under Joseph Smith at Kirtland, and until 1838 Ohio was the center of Mormonism.

The State was strongly antislavery from its inception, and its cities became famous stops on the so-called Underground Railroad (q.v.) for runaway slaves. During the American Civil War Ohio furnished large contributions of money and troops to the Union forces. Though no major battles were fought on Ohio territory, in 1863 Morgan's Raid, a series of at-tacks by Confederate troops under Gen. John Morgan, caused severe damage in s. Ohio.

Following the Civil War manufacturing activity gradually replaced agriculture as the leading Ohio industry. Cleveland, with its lake port facilities, became a center for oil refining and the iron industry. Lorain, Ashtabula, and Youngstown became centers for the manufacture of steel. Akron was established as a rubber-goods center, and Dayton became famous for steel products. Ohio politics were gradually dominated by the industrialists, notably by George B. Cox, political leader of Cincinnati, and Mark Hanna (q.v.) in Cleveland. Corruption in Ohio politics was notorious until the 1890's, when Ohio citizens demanded reform measures. An era of good government ensued and in 1912, during a constitutional convention, thirty-four amendments were adopted, including initiative and referendum and recall. Also among these amendments was the constitutional authorization of measures to prevent floods in s. Ohio. Floods devastated the Ohio valley several times, notably in 1913, 1915, and 1937. Ohio has expended more than $85,000,000 for flood protection during recent years.

Since the Civil War, and the organization of modern American political parties, the Ohio electorate has usually voted for candidates of the Republican Party in Presidential elections, except in 1912, 1916, 1932, 1936, 1940, and 1948, when Democratic candidates received a majority of the votes. Control of the State administration alternated between the two major parties during this period. In the 1952

Ohio Devel. & Publicity Comm.

An Ohio farmer working in his oat field at harvest time

Presidential elections, Dwight D. Eisenhower, the Republican candidate, received 2,098,481 votes, and Adlai E. Stevenson, the Democratic candidate, 1,602,739 votes. Eight Presidents of the U.S. have been born in or have been residents of Ohio; these are William Henry Harrison, Ulysses S. Grant, Rutherford B. Hayes, James A. Garfield, Benjamin Harrison, William McKinley, William Howard Taft, and Warren G. Harding.

OHIO COMPANY, name of two companies organized in the 18th century for the colonization of the Ohio country. The first company was organized in 1749. King George II granted the company 500,000 acres of land between the Kanawha and Monongahela rivers. The company was finally merged in the so-called Walpole Company in 1772.

The second company, the Ohio Company of Associates, was formed in 1786. In 1787 a large tract of land was purchased, and in the following year Marietta was founded by colonists sent out by the company from New England.

OHIO STATE UNIVERSITY, a coeducational, State-controlled, land-grant institution of higher learning, situated in Columbus, Ohio. It was chartered in 1870, and opened for instruction three years later; until 1878 it was known as Ohio Agricultural and Mechanical College. The divisions of the University comprise the college of arts and sciences, offering courses in the humanities, journalism, languages, sciences, and optometry; the college of education, offering courses in academic, commercial, and physical education, and in the fine arts, industrial arts, and music; the college of agriculture; the college of commerce and administration; the college of dentistry; the college of medicine, offering also a four-year nursing course; the college of pharmacy; the college of engineering, offering courses in various branches of engineering and also in architecture; the college of law; the college of veterinary medicine; and the graduate school. Bachelor's and master's degrees, and the degree of doctor of philosophy are granted. In 1953 the total student enrollment at the University was more than 16,400, including about 15,000 full-time students; the faculty numbered approximately 2000; and the endowment was over 3 million dollars.

OHIO UNIVERSITY, a coeducational, State-controlled institution of higher learning, situated at Athens, Ohio, and organized in 1804, shortly after the admission of Ohio as a State of the Union. The University was opened for instruction in 1809 as a college of arts and

sciences. Present divisions of the University include the college of arts and sciences, the college of commerce, the college of fine arts, the college of education, university college, the college of applied science, and the graduate college; and the division of military science and tactics, the extension division, the division of physical welfare, and freshman branches located at Portsmouth and Zanesville (since 1938) and at Chillicothe (1946). Bachelor's and master's degrees are granted. In 1953 the total enrollment at the University was 4260, including 3800 full-time students; the faculty numbered 300.

OHIO WESLEYAN UNIVERSITY, a coeducational, privately controlled institution of higher learning, situated at Delaware, Ohio, and founded in 1841 under the auspices of the Methodist Episcopal Church and opened for instruction in 1844. To its original nucleus, the college of liberal arts, were added the Ohio Wesleyan Female College (founded in 1853 and incorporated into the University in 1877) and the Cleveland College of Physicians and Surgeons (established in 1863 and incorporated in 1896); the last-named division was disassociated from the University in 1910, when it was merged with Western Reserve University. The college of liberal arts is at present divided into the schools of business administration (organized in 1921), fine arts (1927), and music (1929). Bachelor's and master's degrees are granted. In 1953 enrollment numbered over 2000 students, of whom almost all were full-time students; the faculty totaled more than 140; and the endowment was almost 6 million dollars.

OHM. See ELECTRICAL UNITS.

OHM, GEORG SIMON (1787–1854), German physicist, born in Erlangen, and educated at the University of Erlangen. He became professor of mathematics in the Jesuit College at Cologne in 1817 and in the Polytechnic School of Nuremberg in 1833. From 1852 until his death he was professor of experimental physics in the Hochschule of Munich. Ohm investigated many problems in physics, but he is best known for his research on electrical currents. His formulation of the relationship between current, electromotive force, and resistance, known as *Ohm's law,* is the basic law of current flow. The unit of electric resistance was named the *ohm* in his honor; see ELECTRIC CIRCUIT. Ohm was awarded the Copley medal of the Royal Society in 1841 and was made a foreign member of the society the following year. He wrote *Text Book of Physics* (1854).

Left: Pouches with bandoliers made by the Ojibway Indians. Right: An Ojibway man.

OHM'S LAW. See ELECTRIC CIRCUIT.

OIL AND GASOLINE ENGINES. See INTERNAL-COMBUSTION ENGINE.

OILBIRD. See GUACHARO.

OILFISH. See ESCOLAR.

OILS. See FATS AND FIXED OILS; PETROLEUM.

OISE, a river of northern France, rising in the Ardennes in s. Belgium and flowing through the French departments of Nord, Aisne, Oise, and Seine-et Oise, with a length of 189 m. In World War I, French troops in March-April, 1918, were heavily attacked on the Oise, the Germans forcing them back at Chauny and capturing Landricourt and Coucy. In June the last great German effort was made on this sector, when some progress was achieved but no break-through accomplished. The German supreme effort had been spent and their line was now fifty miles longer, a serious matter for Ludendorff's dwindling armies but of good omen to the Allies, to whose aid the Americans were now coming in great numbers. Foch's great offensive in October, 1918, drove back the Germans on the Oise, his preponderance of strength gradually wearing down their resistance.

OISE, a department in the N. of France, separated from the English Channel by Seine-Inférieure. The rivers are the Oise, tributary to the Seine, 189 m. long, with the Aisne and Therain, affluents of the Oise. The soil is mostly fertile, producing cereals, potatoes, sugar beets and fruit, including grapes. There are manufactures of iron, porcelain, paper, chemicals, beet-sugar, woolens, cottons, and lace (at Chantilly). The capital is Beauvais. Area, 2272 sq.m.; pop. (1952 est.) 421,000.

OITA, seaport in Kyushu, Japan, on the E. coast, 110 miles E.N.E. of Nagasaki. From the 13th century Oita was the seat of the Otomo daimyos, the most powerful of the Kyushu lords. It was at Oita, formerly called *Funai,* that the Portuguese navigator Mendes Pinto landed in 1543 and introduced firearms to the Japanese. Here the Jesuits established a mission soon after. Pop., about 66,000.

OJIBWAY or **OJIBWA,** also called CHIPPEWAY or CHIPPEWA, the largest and most important North American Indian tribe of the Algonquian linguistic family (see ALGONQUIN) formerly inhabiting an extensive territory bordering the Great Lakes in Michigan, Minnesota, the Canadian provinces of Ontario and Manitoba, and adjacent regions. According to Ojibway tradition the tribe originally emigrated from the region of the St. Lawrence River in the east. in company with the related **Ottawa** and **Potawatomi** tribes (qq.v.). The three tribes separated at Mackinaw, the Ojibway spreading westward along both shores of Lake Superior, while the two other tribes went southward. The tribe was scattered over a vast territory. It comprised a large number of bands collectively divided into permanent clans said to have numbered more than twenty. The clans were divided into five phratries, or groups, representing the original clans from which the later number developed. One of the clans claimed the hereditary chieftainship of the entire tribe; another claimed precedence in the councils of war.

The Ojibway followed an economy based chiefly on hunting, fishing, and the gathering of wild fruits and seeds, particularly the abundant wild rice of the lake region; they also made sugar from maple syrup. Their houses were built on pole frames in wigwam or tepee shape, and were usually covered with birch bark. Birch-bark sheets were also used for keeping simple pictographic records of tribal affairs. Ojibway mythology was elaborate; the chief religious ritual centered about the Mide Society, a secret organization.

Although the Ojibway were the largest Indian tribe north of Mexico, they did not have extensive relations with the early European explorers and settlers. They became known to Europeans in the mid-17th century, when they were confined within a narrow area along the shore of Lake Superior by the hostile incursions of the Sioux and Fox tribes (qq.v.). They acquired firearms from the Europeans, drove off their enemies, and subsequently greatly expanded their territory. The Ojibway supported the French against the English in the various wars fought in North America, namely King William's War (1689–97), Queen Anne's War (1702–13), King George's War (1743–48), and the French and Indian War (1754–63). In the War for Independence and the War of 1812, they sided with the English against the Americans. In 1815 they joined with the other belligerent tribes in signing a treaty of peace with the U.S. government. Under the terms of subsequent treaties, they sold the greater part of their former territories. At the present time they live on a number of reservations in Michigan, Minnesota, Wisconsin, North Dakota, and Montana; and in Canada. In a recent year the total Ojibway population in the United States numbered more than 32,000.

OKA, an important navigable river of central Russia, the principal affluent of the Volga.

It rises in the government of Orel, and flows in a generally N.E. direction, joining the Volga at the city of Nijni-Novgorod, after a course of about 900 m. Its basin comprises the richest and most fertile region of Russia, and extends over 120,000 sq.m.

OKAPI, an artiodactyl mammal, *Ocapia johnstoni,* belonging to the Giraffe family, and found in the forests surrounding the Semliki River in central Africa. The okapi resembles the giraffe in the structure of its torso and legs, but differs from the giraffe in having a shorter, thicker neck and larger, broader ears. The okapi stands about 4½ ft. high at the shoulders. It has a yellowish-white face and is chocolate brown in general body color, with white legs striped with purplish black at the thighs. The male has a pair of small bumps, in lieu of horns, on its forehead. Okapis roam the woods in pairs, feeding on leaves.

OKAYAMA, seaport and capital of the prefecture of the same name, Japan, on the Inland Sea. Area of prefecture, 2720 sq.m.; pop., about 1,565,000. Pop. of city, about 93,000.

OKEECHOBEE, lake of s. central Florida, situated on the N. edge of the Everglades. The second-largest lake wholly within the United States, it is 40 m. long and about 25 m. wide, and has an area of about 1250 sq.m. See EVERGLADES.

O'KEEFFE, GEORGIA (1887–   ), American painter, born in Sun Prairie, Wisconsin. In 1904 she studied at the Art Institute of Chicago, and the following year attended classes at the Art Students League, New York City. During the year 1918 she was the head of the art department of West Texas State Normal College. She began to exhibit her still lifes of flowers and city scenes in 1916, and the American photographer and editor Alfred Stieglitz (q.v.), later her husband, launched her first full-scale exhibition in 1917 at his gallery, an American Place, New York City. O'Keeffe became noted for the purity and originality of her style, combining a precise and formal treatment with decorative and abstract elements of design, such as flowers, animal skulls from the New Mexican desert, barns, and skyscrapers. Her work is represented in the Metropolitan Museum of Art, Museum of Modern Art, Whitney Museum of American Art (all in New York City), and the Phillips Memorial Gallery, Washington, D.C.

OKEFINOKEE SWAMP, formerly OKEFENOKEE SWAMP, a large swamp situated in S.E. Georgia and N. Florida, between 40 and 70 m. from the Atlantic coast. It is drained by the

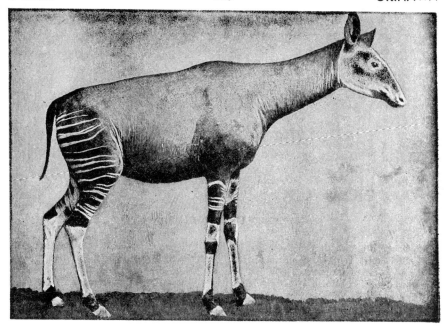

The okapi of the Congo forests

St. Marys and Suwannee rivers. A lake in the
E. part of the swamp contains several floating
islands. Some portions of the area are densely
covered with swamp trees and low vegetation,
others are grassy, and in still others, where the
sandy soil comes above the surface of the
swamp water, are pine groves. Okefinokee
Swamp is 40 m. long and covers an area of
about 660 sq.m.

O'KELLY, SEÁN THOMAS (1882–   ), Irish
journalist and political leader, second president of Eire, born in Dublin, and educated at
the O'Connell Schools, Dublin. O'Kelly was a
frequent contributor to Irish and American
newspapers on the subject of Irish politics,
and, to disseminate his views on Irish independence, he founded and edited in Dublin
the newspaper *The Nation.* For many years
O'Kelly was vice-president of the Fianna
Fáil, or Republican Party, and he was one
of the founders of the Sinn Fein (q.v.). O'Kelly was elected a deputy to the first Dail Eire-
ann, or independent Irish parliament, in 1919,
and served as deputy continuously until 1945.
From 1924 to 1926 O'Kelly was also envoy
from Ireland to the United States, and minister of finance and of education from 1929
until, on June 14, 1945, he was elected president of Eire, now the Republic of Ireland.

He was re-elected to office in May, 1952.

OKI ARCHIPELAGO, off the w. coast of
Hondo, Japan, in lat. 36° 10′ N. and 133° E.
Area, 130 sq.m.; pop., about 40,000. The larg-
est island is Dogo, whose capital is Saigo.

OKINAWA, the largest island and, prior
to the end of World War II, the seat of
the Japanese administration of the Ryukyu
Islands (q.v.), part of which formed the
prefecture of Okinawa (see JAPAN). The capital, chief port, and largest city is Naha (pop.,
about 65,000) on the w. coast. Extending generally N.E. to S.W., the island is approximately
60 m. long and from 2 to 18 m. wide. The
entire coast is fringed with coral reefs. The terrain of the N. two thirds of Okinawa is mountainous and forested. The S. third is hilly, rolling country and contains most of the Oki-
nawan population. Agriculture is the major
occupation; crops include sugar cane, sweet
potatoes, rice, soybeans, and sago. Area, 485
sq.m.; pop., about 440,000.

Japan annexed Okinawa in 1879. Before
that time, the island was semi-independent,
though it paid tribute to China. Little commercial development was undertaken by the
Japanese, who fortified the island and, between the two World Wars, built large airfields in the s. third, particularly around

Oklahoma Planning & Resources Board

Oklahoma State Capitol in Oklahoma City

Naha. On April 1, 1945, during World War II, the United States Tenth Army forces landed on the w. coast of Okinawa. The object of the attack, the largest and last amphibious operation of the Pacific war, was to secure a nearby base for air attacks on the Japanese home islands (distance, 352 m.). The initial resistance was slight, but after about a week the Allied forces reached the main Japanese fortification, in caves and behind heavy fortifications. The Japanese resisted with fanatical tenacity, and the battle became one of the most bitter of the Pacific campaigns. Of the 36 Allied ships sunk during the campaign, 26 were destroyed by *Kamikaze* (suicide) pilots. On June 18, Lieut. Gen. Simon Bolivar Buckner, Jr., commander of the Tenth Army, was killed by Japanese shellfire. On June 21, after 82 days of fighting, organized Japanese resistance ceased. Japanese deaths amounted to 110,071; American losses were 12,281. The Japanese lost 7830 airplanes, the American forces, 763. The Okinawa airfields were quickly reconstructed and developed by the American army, and the AAF bombed the Japanese main islands daily beginning in late June (see WORLD WAR II). Okinawa remained under American control following the surrender of Japan in August, 1945.

OKLAHOMA, a West South Central State of the United States, bounded on the E. by Missouri and Arkansas, on the s. by the Red R., which separates the State from Texas, on the w. by Texas and New Mexico, and on the w. by Colorado and Kansas. It ranks as the 17th State in the Union in area, 25th in population (1950), and 46th in the order of admission to the Union, having entered on Nov. 16, 1907. The capital and largest city in the State is Oklahoma City (q.v.). Other leading communities, in the order of population (1950), are Tulsa, Muskogee, and Enid (qq.v.). Area of the State, 69,919 sq.m., including 636 sq.m. of inland water surface. Population (1950) 2,233,351.

The topography of Oklahoma includes isolated groups of mountainous wooded highlands and treeless plains and prairies. The highest elevation, 4978 ft. above sea level, is at Black Mesa in Cimarron Co., in the extreme N.W. tip of the panhandlelike projection forming Oklahoma's western extremity. The lowest point in the State, 300 ft. above sea level, is at the Red R. in McCurtain Co., in the extreme s.E. The average elevation of the State is 1300 ft.

The highland areas of the State include the Ozark Mts. in the N.E., the Ouachita Mts. in the s.E., the Arbuckle and Wichita Mts. in the s. part of the State, the Chautauqua Mts. in the w. central region of Oklahoma, and the Great Plains, which form a lofty tableland in the N.W. A level to gently rolling plain is situated in the s.E. portion of the State, and w. of the Ozarks, in the N.E., the region consists of prairies traversed by deep-cutting streams. The important rivers are the Canadian, which flows roughly w. to E., joining the Arkansas; the Arkansas, which flows N.W. to s.E. through the middle of the State; the Cimarron, which flows in a southeasterly loop from the N.W. portion of the State to the Arkansas; the Red R., which flows along most of the State's southern border; and various tributaries of the foregoing rivers.

The climate of the State is temperate. The average temperature during the summer is 81°F., and during the winter, 41°F. Extremes of 114°F. and -17°F. have been recorded. The average precipitation is 32 inches.

More than 20 tribes comprising almost a fifth of the Indian population of the U.S. live on reservations in Oklahoma. The State contains 10 State parks, 1 national park (see PLATT NATIONAL PARK), and more than 344,000 acres of national forest land.

The mineral wealth of Oklahoma exceeds that of most States in the Union, and is based primarily upon oil and natural gas. In 1951 there were 55,000 oil wells in the State; production of crude petroleum totaled 194,885,519 barrels in 1952–53; 9,458,000 barrels of natural gasoline were produced in 1951 and 333,228,633,000 cu. ft. of natural gas in 1952–53. Other minerals, and their production figures for 1952–53, were 2,161,326 tons of coal, 359,671 tons of gypsum, and 2,855,772 tons of zinc. The total value of the mineral output in 1951 was $607,485,000.

Approximately 80% of the total area of Oklahoma is devoted to agriculture. In 1950 a total of 142,246 farms had a combined area of 36,006,603 acres, of which 11,896,040 acres were under cultivation; the total value of lands and buildings was more than $1,851,460,000. Soil erosion is a serious problem in the State and about 90% of the total farm area needs continual curative or preventive treatment. The principal crops and their production in 1952 were wheat, 107,115,000 bushels; corn, 10,101,000 bushels; oats, 8,442,000 bushels; and grain sorghums, 4,248,000 bushels. Other important crops are broom corn, cotton, pecans, potatoes, and soybeans.

In 1954 livestock within the State numbered 3,315,000 cattle (including 558,000 dairy cows), 346,000 hogs, 119,000 horses, 159,000 sheep, and 19,000 mules. The wool clip amounted to 999,000 pounds in 1951. The total cash income (1952) from crops and livestock was $673,251,000.

Petroleum refining is the most important of the manufacturing industries of Oklahoma, which are based upon the natural resources and agricultural industries of the State. The refineries account for a large portion of the total value of the manufacturing output. Meat packing, the processing of grains, the manufacture of machinery, and printing are other important industries. In 1952 the industrial establishments of the State employed about 84,000 workers, who earned $275,000,000 in wages. The value added by manufacture was $493,379,000.

Transportation in the State includes (1952) 5973 m. of steam railway, 10,218 m. of State-maintained highway, and 285 airports, of which 46 were municipal and 41 equipped for night flying. Attendance at the elementary and secondary schools of Oklahoma is free and compulsory during two thirds of the school year for all students between the ages of seven and eighteen. In 1950 there were 2844 public elementary and secondary schools; in 1952–53 the total enrollment was 513,018 and the teaching staff numbered 19,477. The State maintains separate schools for white (Indian included) and Negro children. Eleven colleges and universities (including a university for Negroes),

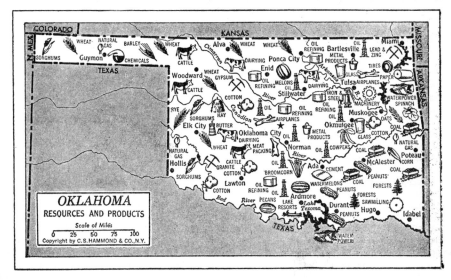

OKLAHOMA
RESOURCES AND PRODUCTS
Scale of Miles
0 25 50 75 100
Copyright by C.S.HAMMOND & CO.,N.Y.

Okla. Plan. & Res. Bd.

AGRICULTURE IN OKLAHOMA

Above: A farmer inspecting his broomcorn crop, Lindsay, Oklahoma. Left: Prize steers in southeastern Oklahoma.

and one professional school, 6 teachers colleges, and 16 junior colleges are in the State. Among the leading institutions of higher education are the University of Tulsa, Oklahoma Agricultural and Mechanical College at Stillwater, and the University of Oklahoma at Norman. The two last-named schools are supported by the State.

Oklahoma is governed according to the terms of the constitution of 1907, as amended. Executive authority is vested in a governor, lieutenant governor, secretary of state, auditor, treasurer, attorney general, superintendent of public instruction, commissioner of insurance, commissioner of labor, chief mine inspector, president of the State board of agri-

culture, and commissioner of charities and corrections, all of whom are elected for four-year terms. The governor, secretary of state, auditor, and treasurer cannot immediately succeed themselves in office. Other members of the executive department include 3 members of a corporation commission, 4 assistant mine inspectors, the clerk of the supreme court, and various appointed officials. Legislative authority is vested in a senate of 44 members, half elected every two years for four-year terms, and a house of representatives of 118 to 123 members, elected for two-year terms. Judicial authority is vested in a supreme court consisting of 9 justices elected for six-year terms, a criminal court of appeals,

31 district courts, 77 county courts, justice-of-the-peace courts, and municipal courts. Electors are U.S. citizens who have resided in the State at least one year, the county six months, and the precinct one month. Oklahoma is divided into 77 counties and is represented in the Congress of the U.S. by 2 senators and 6 representatives.

History. The Spanish explorer Francisco Vásquez Coronado was the first European to enter Oklahoma, in 1541. French traders and trappers visited the region in the 16th and 17th centuries. In 1803, as a result of the Louisiana Purchase (q.v.), all of Oklahoma, except the extreme western panhandle portion of the present State, became a part of the U.S. In 1817 the Federal government began sending the large Indian population of Alabama, Georgia, Florida, and Mississippi to the region. Oklahoma was divided among the Five Civilized Nations, consisting of the Creek, Cherokee, Chickasaw, Chocktaw, and Seminole (qq.v.) Indian tribes. In 1834 the region was established as the Indian Territory (q.v.), and the tribal authority of the Indian Nations within the Territory was assured.

During the Civil War, the Indians of the Territory, many of whom owned slaves, sided with the Confederacy. After the war, by a series of treaties from 1866 to 1883, the Indian Nations were forced to cede the western half of the Territory to the U.S. as a home for other Indian tribes. Great tracts of land still remained unoccupied and though white men were forbidden by law to settle on these lands, colonization schemes were developed by various groups, as a result of which President Rutherford B. Hayes issued proclamations in 1879 and 1880 forbidding settlement in the Territory. Violations occurred frequently and agitation for the opening of the lands to white men increased to the point at which Congress in 1885 authorized the President to open negotiations with the Creek and Seminole tribes for the purpose of opening the unoccupied tracts for settlement. The negotiations were successfully concluded in 1889, and at noon on April 22 the land was opened to the public. A race for the best lands and town sites ensued as nearly 50,000 persons flooded the Territory the first day. Tent towns were laid out, farms sprang up, and the population of the area increased at an extraordinary rate.

On March 2, 1890, the Federal government established the Territory of Oklahoma, which consisted of lands in the southern part of the region, and the western portion of the Indian

Oklahoma Planning & Resources Board
Oil wells in Oklahoma City, seen from the entrance to the Oklahoma State Capitol

Territory, in addition to the panhandle strip N. of Texas. Additional lands were laid open to settlement in 1891, 1892, 1893, 1895, 1901, and 1906. The Territory of Oklahoma agitated for statehood as early as 1891. Indian Territory did not seriously try to gain statehood until 1905. In 1906, after prolonged debate in Congress, a bill was passed which provided that both Oklahoma and Indian territories were to be admitted to the Union as one State, if such union were approved by each Territory. On Nov. 16, 1907, the combined Territories entered the Union as the 46th State.

From 1908 through 1948 a majority or plurality of all the ballots cast in Presidential elections by the voters of Oklahoma has been for the Democratic candidate, with the single exception of 1928, when the Republican candidate received the majority of votes. In the 1952 election Dwight D. Eisenhower, the Republican candidate, received 518,045 votes, and Adlai E. Stevenson, the Democratic candidate, received 430,939 votes.

OKLAHOMA AGRICULTURAL AND MECHANICAL COLLEGE, a coeducational, State-controlled, land-grant institution of higher learning, situated at Stillwater, Okla., and founded in 1891. The divisions of the College include schools of agriculture, engineering, arts and sciences, education, home economics (offering courses in restaurant management and hotel administration), and commerce, and a graduate school. Bachelor's and master's degrees are granted. In 1953 the total enrollment, consisting entirely of full-time students, was 7417, and the faculty numbered approximately 650.

OKLAHOMA CITY, capital of the State of Oklahoma, and county seat of Oklahoma Co., situated on the North Canadian R., near the center of the State. It is the largest city in population in Oklahoma, and the leading commercial, manufacturing, and financial center. It is one of the principal markets for cotton and livestock in the U.S., the chief distributing and shipping point of the State, and the headquarters of an extensive natural-gas and oil-producing area. The city contains large wholesale and retail houses, insurance offices, a branch of the Federal Reserve Bank, and meat-packing plants, flour and feed mills, cotton gins, cotton and cottonseed-oil mills, automobile-assembly plants, machine shops, ironworks, printing and publishing plants, and factories manufacturing airplanes, steel, oilfield equipment, storage tanks and batteries, asphalt, and furniture. Within the city limits and in the adjoining area are numerous producing oil wells. Oklahoma City is served by five railroads and by major air lines.

Educational institutions in the city and vicinity include Oklahoma City University (Methodist), established in 1904, the University of Oklahoma School of Medicine (see OKLAHOMA, UNIVERSITY OF), and the Oklahoma City Law School. The State Capitol, surrounded by a landscaped area of 100 acres, is of white limestone in Roman Corinthian design.

The site of the present city, a part of the fertile central portion of Oklahoma Territory, was purchased from the Indians in 1889 and was opened to settlement on April 22 of that year. By nightfall of the same day a tent colony of 10,000 settlers had been established. Oklahoma City was chartered in 1890 and made the State capital in 1910. Pop. (1950) 243,504.

OKLAHOMA, UNIVERSITY OF, a coeducational, State-controlled institution of higher learning, situated at Norman and Oklahoma City, Okla. It was founded in 1890 by act of the first Oklahoma Territorial legislature, and opened for instruction two years later. The divisions of the University, the main part of which is situated on a 120-acre campus at Norman, are the graduate school, and the college of arts and sciences which includes schools of fine arts, law, medicine and nursing (at Oklahoma City), education, journalism, engineering, business administration, and pharmacy. Bachelor's, master's, and doctor's degrees are granted. In 1953 the enrollment was 8031, including 7373 full-time students, and the faculty numbered about 550.

OKMULGEE, county seat of Okmulgee Co., Okla., situated 44 miles s. of Tulsa. It is served by two railroads and maintains a municipal airport. The city is surrounded by one of the richest oil-producing areas in the world. Natural gas, coal, cotton, general farm crops, and livestock are other products of the region. Among the industrial establishments in the city are large oil refineries, plants processing natural gas, cotton gins, and factories manufacturing window and sheet glass, bottles, and fruit jars. Okmulgee is the site of the College of Technical Training of the Oklahoma Agricultural and Mechanical College. Buildings of interest include the Council House of the Creek Indians (see CREEKS). Pop. (1950) 18,317.

OKRA or **GUMBO,** common name applied to an annual herb, *Abelmoschus* (or *Hibiscus*) *esculentis,* belonging to the Mallow family; see HIBISCUS. The okra, which is native to

Africa, is extensively cultivated in southern United States and the West Indies for its long, many-seeded pod, which, when still young and green, is used as a thickening for soups and stews and as a cooked vegetable. The okra bears large, yellow flowers, similar in structure to typical *Hibiscus* flowers, and is occasionally planted in flower gardens in warm regions of the United States.

OKUMA, COUNT SHIGENOBU (1838–1922), Japanese statesman, born in Saga, Hizen, Japan. Mastering English and Dutch by the help of some missionaries, his mind was completely revolutionized by Western ideas, and he determined to devote himself to the overthrow of the feudal system and the substitution of constitutional government. His opinions bore fruit in the revolution of 1868, and he was appointed chief assistant of foreign affairs in the Mikado's first constitutional government. Always devoted to the promotion of education, he established during the eighties the Semmon Gako, a school for special studies. As premier he declared war on Germany in 1915.

OLBERS, HEINRICH WILHELM MATTHÄUS (1758–1840), German physician and astronomer, born in Arbergen, and educated at the University of Göttingen. He practiced medicine at Bremen after 1780, but is best known for his astronomical studies. Using an original method of calculation, which is still employed by astronomers, he determined the orbit of the comet of 1779 and thus established his reputation. Between 1798 and 1815 he discovered five comets, the last of which was named after him. In 1781 he identified Uranus as a planet rather than as a comet, as had previously been supposed; and in 1802 discovered the planetoid Vesta and in 1807 the planetoid Pallas. He also first proposed the hypothesis, called Olber's hypothesis, that all planetoids are fragments of a primordial planet which formerly revolved about the sun.

OLD-AGE PENSIONS, the provision of annuities for the aged. Old-age pensions, granted by the government to government employees, first appeared in England about 1810; they were instituted in Germany in 1873, after the unification of that country; and they spread to many other European countries in the first decade of the 20th century. In the United States, the railroads were until 1913 the only important groups to provide old-age pensions for their employees. Today, in the United States, three principal sources of old-age pensions exist. The most important is the social-security system established by the

The okra plant

Social Security Act of 1935; see SOCIAL SECURITY ADMINISTRATION; SOCIAL INSURANCE: *Old-Age Assistance*. Under this law, employers and employees contribute to a government fund which is used to provide monthly allowances for employees who have passed the age of sixty-five. The second type of old-age pension is that provided directly by many employers, often with the assistance of employee contributions, to people who have been employed by them for specified minimum periods of time. This type includes pensions provided by both industrial employers and State and Federal government agencies. The third major source of old-age pensions stems from the increasing tendency of trade unions to demand financial provision for retiring workers in the drawing up of a labor contract. Such provision is usually implemented with funds contributed by the employers and administered by the unions or by a neutral trustee.

Under this multiplicity of sources, it often is possible for aged persons to receive financial support from two or more agencies, while self-employed persons or those who have spent their lives working in fields such as agriculture and domestic service, which are not covered by pension programs, may receive no assistance at all. Finally, a frequent supplement to old-age pensions is provided by the veterans' pensions (q.v.) issued to certain classes of veterans of past wars.

OLD BAILEY, the name of a street in London, England, on which is located the sessions house in which the sittings of the Central Criminal Court are held. Prior to 1834 "Old Bailey" was the name of a historic criminal court whose jurisdiction was at that time assumed by the Central Criminal Court. Old Bailey was the scene of many famous English criminal trials; it is graphically described in Charles Dickens' novel *A Tale of Two Cities.* The name "Old Bailey" is derived from its situation in a "bailey", a term applied to the open space inside the old fortifications of London.

OLDBURY, a town of Worcestershire, England, 5 miles w.N.w. of Birmingham. It has iron and steel works, besides factories for edge tools, chemicals, and lenses for lighthouses. Pop. (1951 est.) 53,895.

OLDCASTLE, SIR JOHN (d. 1471), known as the "good Lord Cobham". He was the first author and the first martyr among the English nobility. In 1413 he was condemned as a heretic. He escaped from the Tower into Wales, but after four years' hiding was captured. He was brought to London, and hanged. Oldcastle wrote *Twelve Conclusions Addressed to the Parliament of England.* Halliwell-Phillips first proved in 1841 that Shakespeare's Sir John Falstaff was originally Sir John Oldcastle.

OLD CATHOLICS, those Catholics who at Munich protested against the new dogma of the personal infallibility of the pope in all *ex cathedra* deliverances, proclaimed by the Vatican Council in 1870. The Munich protest by forty-four professors, Dr. Döllinger and Professor Friedrich at their head, was directed against the binding authority of the Vatican Council. To this protest a number of professors at Bonn, Breslau, Freiburg, and Giessen declared their adhesion. At Cologne in 1873 Professor Reinkens of Breslau was elected bishop of the Old Catholics in the ancient fashion, by "clergy and people"—by all the Old Catholic priests and by representatives of the Old Catholic congregations. He was consecrated at Rotterdam by the bishop of Deventer, and acknowledged by Prussia, Baden, and Hesse.

The mass is said in the vernacular. Priests are allowed to marry. Intercommunion with the Anglican communion was accomplished at a conference in Bonn, Germany, in July, 1931, the concordat being ratified later by the Vienna congress of the Old Catholic Church and by the convocations of Canterbury and York of the Church of England.

OLD CHURCH SLAVIC LANGUAGE AND LITERATURE, the oldest language and literature of the Slavic group of Indo-Germanic languages, presenting one of the most important dialects for the study of comparative linguistics. Formerly called Old Slovenian, and now frequently termed Old Bulgarian, the best name seems to be Old Church Slavic. Old Church Slavic is written in two alphabets, called Glagolitic and Cyrillic. The oldest manuscripts of this language date from the end of the 10th or the beginning of the 11th centuries. The literature, which is of considerable extent and consists altogether of translations, is entirely religious. Besides the Bible there are versions of the Euchologium, homilies, legends of saints, some apocryphal books, and various liturgical pieces by Cyril and Methodius, apostles to the Slavs in the middle of the 9th century.

OLDENBURG, former German republic, founded in June, 1919, previously the duchy of Oldenburg, with an area of 2480 sq.m. and a population of about 545,000. It is principally an agricultural district but has manufactures of tobacco, cork, woolen yarn, linoleum, and knitted goods. The grand duke abdicated on Nov. 11, 1918, the state becoming a German republic. In 1946 it was incorporated into the State of Lower Saxony.

OLDENBURG, city of the State of Lower Saxony, West Germany, on the Hunte River, 30 miles N.w. of Bremen. The manufactures include leather goods, soap, machinery, and musical instruments. Pop. (1950) 122,809.

OLD ENGLISH. See ENGLISH LANGUAGE.

OLD ENGLISH SHEEP DOG, a breed of medium-sized working dog used primarily for guarding herds of sheep or cattle. The breed is believed by some authorities to have originated in Britain about the 1st century A.D.; others believe it developed in western England in modern times. The animal was used in England at the beginning of the 18th century for assisting drovers in driving sheep and cattle to market, and was then known as the "drover's dog". The old English sheep dog also can be trained as a retriever and as a draft animal, and its even temper makes it a good companion for children. The male varies in height from about twenty-one to twenty-five inches at the shoulder; the height of the bitch is somewhat less. The animal has a square-shaped skull, dark eyes, a tapering nose with a blunt end, medium-sized ears lying flat to the side of the head, straight forelegs and muscular hind legs, and moves with a characteristic rolling gait. Many of the breed have no tail; some have tails that are between one and a half and two inches in length. The coat is profuse, usually either gray or blue and sometimes with white markings; it is occasionally so shaggy that its hair conceals the eyes.

OLDFIELD, BERNA ELI or BARNEY (1878–1946), American automobile racer, born in Wauseon, Ohio. A bicycle racer in his youth, Oldfield in 1902 began a career in automobile racing which made him famous as one of the foremost racing drivers in the world. In that year he was the first to test Henry Ford's racing model, the "Ford 999", with which he won a five-mile race near Detroit in the near-record time of 5 min., 28 sec. In 1903, driving the "Ford 999" at the Indianapolis Fair Grounds, he was among the first to drive an automobile at the speed of one mile per minute. He achieved his greatest success in 1910 when he established an official world's speed record for automobile races (131.7 m.p.h.) in a "Blitzen Beng" model at Daytona Beach, Fla. In 1918 he retired from racing and became president of the Oldfield Tire Manufacturing Co. In 1946, shortly before his death, he was honored by appointment to the Automobile Hall of Fame in Detroit, Mich.

OLDHAM, a municipal, parliamentary, and county borough of Lancashire, England, 7 miles N.E. of Manchester. It has cotton mills and manufactures of fustians, velvets, silks, and hats, besides huge weaving-machine works. There are collieries in the district. Pop. (1951 est.) 121,212.

OLD KASAAN NATIONAL MONUMENT, a national monument in s. Alaska, situated on Prince of Wales Island in the Alexander Archipelago. It is 38 acres in area, and was established in 1916 to preserve an abandoned village of the Haida Indians. There are several totem poles and an old graveyard in the village. See NATIONAL MONUMENTS.

OLD RED SANDSTONE. See DEVONIAN SYSTEM.

OLDS, RANSOM ELI (1864–1950), American manufacturer, born in Geneva, Ashtabula Co., Ohio, and educated at Lansing Business College in Lansing, Mich. He began his early experiments in the automotive field as a mechanic in 1885, and the following year built the first American three-wheeled horseless carriage. In 1895 he constructed a four-wheeled

Old English sheep dog

automobile powered by gasoline. He became president of the Olds Motor Vehicle Co. in 1897, and of the Olds Motor Works in 1899. In 1904 he became president of the newly organized Reo Motor Car Company, serving as chairman of the board from 1924 to 1926. In 1932 he was appointed president of the R.E. Olds Co., and in 1936 became chairman of the board.

OLD SAYBROOK, a town of Middlesex Co., Conn., situated on Long Island Sound, at the mouth of the Connecticut R., about 30 miles E. of New Haven. Transportation facilities include a railroad and steamboat lines. The principal industry is the packing of maraschino cherries and Spanish olives. The town is chiefly a residential community and a summer resort. Nearby is the town of Old Lyme, a noted art center. Old Saybrook, one of the oldest settlements in Connecticut, contains several fine colonial buildings, and at Saybrook Point is an ancient cemetery in which is buried Lady Alice Fenwick, wife of George Fenwick, one of the original settlers of Old Saybrook. The region of the present town was the site of a Dutch trading post as early as 1623. The first permanent settlement in the area was established in 1635 by a group of English colonists under the leadership of John Winthrop, acting as agent for an English land-grant company in which Lords Saye and Brooke were the chief officers; the settlement was named Saybrook in their honor. In 1644 the Saybrook Colony became a part of the Connecticut Colony. The Collegiate School, from which Yale University developed, was founded there in 1701. In the early days of the settlement it was an important center of trade with the West Indies and was noted for its shad-fishing industry.

David Bushnell (q.v.) built the first submarine there in 1776. Saybrook and Old Saybrook were separated in 1852 and the town of Old Saybrook was incorporated in 1854. In 1947, to prevent confusion of names, the town of Saybrook was renamed Deep River. Old Saybrook now includes several unincorporated communities and the borough of Fenwick. Pop. (1950) 2499.

OLD TESTAMENT, the sacred Scriptures embodying the covenant of God with the Hebrews (q.v.); with the New Testament (q.v.), it constitutes the authorized religious dispensation of Christianity known as the Bible (q.v.). The main sections of the Old Testament recognized as having canonical authority (see CANON) are the Law (Heb., *Torah*), the Prophets (*Nebiim*), and the Hagiographa (*Ketubim*). Of the fourteen books collectively designated as Apocrypha (q.v.) by Protestant sects, all but two, namely the *Prayer of Manasses* and *1 & 2 Esdras,* are admitted as canonical by the Roman Catholic Church. The Old Testament is usually arranged in the following order.

LAW includes *Genesis* 1 to 11, detailing the creation of heaven and earth from primal chaos, and the formation of Adam, his descendant Noah, and the offspring of Noah; *Genesis* 12 to 50, setting forth the genealogies of the patriarchs Terah, Ishmael, Isaac, Esau, and Jacob; *Exodus* 1 to 13, recounting the deliverance of the tribes of Israel from Egypt; *Exodus* 13 to 18, describing the passage of the Israelites across the Red Sea to Sinai; *Exodus* 19 to 40, relating the transmission to Moses of the Ten Commandments (see DECALOGUE) on Mount Sinai, and the construction and consecration of the Tabernacle (q.v.); *Leviticus* 1 to 7, expounding the law of divine sacrifice; *Leviticus* 8 to 10, describing the consecration of the Hebrew priesthood; *Leviticus* 11 to 16, proclaiming the dietary law of clean (*kosher*) and unclean (*tref*) and establishing the Day of Atonement (*Yom Kippur*); *Leviticus* 17 to 27, setting forth the law of holiness; *Numbers,* relating the calculation of the Israelite population, together with various episodes from the forty-year sojourn of the Israelites in the wilderness; and *Deuteronomy,* containing three lectures delivered by Moses in the land of Moab, his parting exhortations, and an account of his death.

PROPHETS includes *Joshua* 1 to 12, recounting the invasion and subjugation of Canaan by the Israelites; *Joshua* 13 to 21, describing the distribution of the land; *Joshua* 22 to 24, detailing the story of Reuben and the final days of Joshua; *Judges,* setting forth the history of the Israelites under the rule of the Judges, particularly Deborah, Gideon, Jephthah, and Samson; *1 & 2 Samuel* (*1 & 2 Kings* in the Roman Catholic Bible), divided into *1 Samuel* 1 to 12, chronicling the birth of Samuel and his accession to the judgeship following Eli, *1 Samuel* 13 to 31, relating the institution of the Kingdom of Israel and the rule of Saul, and *2 Samuel,* recounting the reign of David; *1 & 2 Kings* (*3 & 4 Kings* in the Roman Catholic Bible), divided into *1 Kings* 1 to 11, setting forth the reign of Solomon, *1 Kings* 12, narrating the disintegration of the Kingdom of Israel during the reign of Rehoboam, and *1 Kings* 13 to the end of *2 Kings,* describing the downfall of the kingdom, the creation of two separate kingdoms (Israel and Judah), and the careers of Elijah and Elisha, extending to the Babylonian capture of Judah in 586 B.C.; *Isaiah* 1 to 35, containing discourses on the kingdoms of Israel and Judah, and domestic, foreign, and Messianic (see MESSIAH) prophecies; *Isaiah* 36 to 39, chronicling the events of the reign of Hezekiah; *Isaiah* 40 to 66, comprising prognostications relative to the Babylonian captivity (q.v.) and to the Messiah; *Jeremiah,* in which is delivered the prophecy concerning the downfall of Jerusalem and the exile of the Judæans in Babylon, together with events from the life of Jeremiah; *Ezekiel* 1 to 24, setting forth visions and prophecies of judgment on Israel for its defection from the orthodox faith; *Ezekiel* 25 to 32, expounding prophecies of judgment on the foes of Israel and predicting the ultimate redemption of the Israelites; *Hosea,* in which Israel, symbolized by the figure of a faithless wife, is rebuked for its apostacy; *Joel,* containing prognostications of judgment on Judah, an appeal for repentance, and the assurance of ultimate benediction; *Amos,* in which Israel is visited with rebukes and exhortations to reform; *Obadiah,* in which Edom is condemned for siding with the foes of Israel; *Jonah,* containing an account of the journey of Jonah to the ancient city of Nineveh; *Micah,* prophesying imminent judgment on Judah and Israel, but holding forth the hope of salvation through the Messiah; *Nahum,* setting forth God's judgment in the destruction of Nineveh; *Habakkuk* 1, comprising a dialogue between Jehovah and the prophet Habakkuk on the persecution endured by the faithful; *Habakkuk* 2, setting forth a prophecy of divine judgment on the persecutors of the faithful; *Habakkuk* 3, constituting a prayer for the deliverance of the faithful from their oppressors; *Zephaniah,* addressing to Judah a prophetic admonition with the ultimate promise of redemption; *Haggai,* expounding four prophecies, directed to the Jewish leader Zerubbabel and the people at large, exhorting them to finish construction of the Temple; *Zechariah* 1 to 8, containing visions of the Messiah and various exhortations addressed to the Jews newly returned from their Babylonian exile; *Zechariah* 9 to 14, in which is envisioned the deliverance of Zion by the Messiah; and *Malachi,* in which the Jewish priesthood is censured for being remiss in the performance of its sacerdotal functions and the people are rebuked for intermarrying with foreigners.

HAGIOGRAPHA includes *Psalms,* comprising five books of hymns (1 to 41, 42 to 72, 73 to 89, 90 to 106, and 107 to 150), predominantly devotional in character, and representing the work of various writers; *Proverbs* 1 to 9, comprising homilies on practical wisdom; *Proverbs* 10 to 22, containing the proverbs attributed to King Solomon on the proper conduct of life; *Proverbs* 22 to 24, known as the "words of the wise"; *Proverbs* 25 to 29, containing the proverbs compiled by Hezekiah, King of Judah; *Proverbs* 30 and 31, a collection of wise sayings and counsels; *Job,* a dramatic poem describing Job's patient endurance of the trials which God permits him to undergo as a test of his faith; *Song of Songs,* also known as the *Song of Solomon* and the *Canticles,* a series of highly figurative amatory poems susceptible of allegorical interpretation; *Ruth,* setting forth the history of the Moabite forbear of David, King of Israel; *Lamentations,* comprising five poems (of which four are in the form of acrostics) relative to the sufferings of the inhabitants of Jerusalem and Judah; *Ecclesiastes,* composed of homilies on the vanity of human existence, together with apothegms for the development of wisdom; *Esther,* containing an account of the Jewish heroine Esther, her cousin Mordecai, and Ahasuerus, King of Persia, and his wicked chief minister Haman; *Daniel* 1 to 6, narrating the adventures of the prophet Daniel at the court of Nebuchadnezzar, King of Babylon; *Daniel* 7 to 12, detailing the prophecies of Daniel; *Ezra* (designated as *1 Esdras* in the Roman Catholic Bible), describing the return of the Jewish exiles from Babylon, the reconstruction of the Temple under the leadership of Zerubbabel, and the return of another group of Babylonian exiles headed by Ezra; *Nehemiah* (designated as *2 Esdras* in the Roman Catholic Bible), setting forth the reconstruction of the walls of Jerusalem despite the opposition of Sanballat the Horonite, and describing the administration and reforms of Nehemiah; *1 Chronicles* 1 to 9, containing tables of genealogies; *1 Chronicles* 10 to 29, narrating the salient events of the reign of King David; *2 Chronicles* 1 to 9, recounting the chief occurrences of the reign of Solomon, the son of David; and *2 Chronicles* 10 to 36, relating the history of Judah down to the conquest of Jerusalem.

THE PROTESTANT APOCRYPHA (of which all but the last two books are regarded as canonical by the Roman Catholic Church) includes *Tobit,* setting forth the history of a Jewish captive in Assyria, and enjoining submission to the law and proper interment for the deceased; *Judith,* the story of the heroine Judith, who killed Holofernes, general of the Babylonian king Nebuchadnezzar, and delivered her people from bondage; *Esther,* a miscellany of prayers, visions, and letters introduced into the Book of Esther; *Wisdom of Solomon,* a treatise on Wisdom as the divine instrumentality operative in the creation and ordering of the world; *Ecclesiasticus,* or *Wisdom of Jesus, Son of Sirach,* a collection of proverbs; *Baruch,* comprising a recital of the sins presumably leading to the Babylonish Captivity, a panegyric of Wisdom, and the Epistle of Jeremy (Jeremiah), addressed to the captive Jews at Babylon and inveighing against the worship of idols; *Song of the Three Children,* containing the prayer of the devout youth Azarias (Abednego) and the hymn of thanksgiving offered up by Azarias and his companions Ananias (Shadrach) and Misael (Meshach) for their deliverance from the fiery furnace into which they had been cast by Nebuchadnezzar (in Daniel 3); *Susanna,* the story of the false accusation of adultery brought against the beautiful and virtuous matron Susanna by three elders who had vainly solicited her favors, and of the judicial action of Daniel in acquitting Susanna and condemning the guilty elders to death; *Bel and the Dragon,* in which Daniel is portrayed allegorically as the vanquisher of heathenism (in the Roman Catholic Bible the three foregoing books form part of the Book of Daniel); *1 Maccabees,* chronicling the history of the Maccabees (q.v.) from 175 to 135 B.C.; *2 Maccabees,* recounting the history of the Jews from 187 to 161 B.C.; *1 & 2 Esdras* (or *3 & 4 Esdras* if the Books of Ezra are reckoned as 1 & 2), an alternate version of Ezra, including the account of the triumph of Zerubbabel in a contest of wit, and visions and sermons vouchsafed to Ezra by an angel; and *Prayer of Manassas,* purporting to be the prayer referred to in 2 Chronicles 33.

As in the New Testament, the finally established canon of the Old Testament was the result of a critical process involving the gradual reduction of the number of books authorized for use in devotional services. At the end of the 2nd century A.D. the canon recognized by most synagogues contained twenty-four books, divided into three sections, namely, the *Law,* the *Prophets,* and the *Hagiographa.* The *Law,* which had been the first section of the Hebrew Scriptures to acquire rabbinical authority, remained ever after the supreme authority, all other books being regarded as commentary on the Law and classed together as Cabala (q.v.), or traditional lore. At a very early date, various writings of a religious character were held in high esteem, their contents strongly suggesting a divine origin, and were made part of the canon. Subsequently, however, Hebrew critics and scholars, inquiring whether many of these books merited the sanctity with which tradition had invested them, felt themselves constrained to answer in the negative. Some of these books, the inspirational authenticity of which was generally impugned, were accordingly dropped from the canon; others were not eliminated, though strong efforts were made to withdraw them from public use. Among the books that had been traditionally regarded as sacred, but were finally rejected, a certain number continued to be read and quoted as Scripture in different quarters. Among the Hellenistic Jews (see HELLENIST) several of these allegedly apocryphal works were preserved and quoted as Scripture, and consequently formed a part of the Greek Bible which the Christian Church received from the Jewish Synagogue.

OLEANDER, genus of plants of the Dogbane family. The species are evergreen shrubs with leathery leaves, which are opposite or in threes; the flowers are in false umbels, terminal or axillary. The common oleander, *N. oleander,* is a native of the south of Europe, the north of Africa, and parts of Asia.

OLEFINES. See HYDROCARBONS.

OLEOMARGARINE or **MARGARINE,** a food product, used as butter, now made from refined vegetable or animal oils which are churned with skim milk to the consistency of butter. In its original form oleomargarine was accidentally developed about 1870 by the French chemist Hippolyte Mège-Mouries in an attempt to make butter from beef fat, and was introduced into the United States in 1874. Since that time improvements in refining, deodorizing, and hardening of oils by hydrogenation (q.v.), and the incorporation of skim milk have greatly improved the flavor of oleomargarine. When mixed with a yellow vegetable dye, oleomargarine, which is almost white in color, simulates butter in appearance. The nutritional value is the same as that of butter, except for the Vitamin A content, and most margarine sold in the United States is fortified with Vitamin A to correct the deficiency. Because of its nutritional value and low cost, margarine is used as a butter substitute in cooking and baking and as a spread for bread. In 1953 per capita consumption in the U.S. was 8.2 lbs.

When margarine was introduced into the United States in the 1870's, discriminatory taxes were immediately levied on the product by many States to protect the price of butter. Subsequently Federal legislation was enacted in order to curtail the use of margarine. Passed in 1886, the Federal law continued in effect until 1950, when public pressure from farm, labor, and consumer groups, and the margarine interests, finally succeeded in having the law repealed. By 1953 discriminatory legislation in the large majority of States had likewise been repealed, and the sale of margarine was restricted only by such legal provisions as production and packaging requirements, designed for the protection of the consumer.

OLIBANUM or **FRANKINCENSE,** a gum resin which flows from incisions in several species of *Boswellia* (q.v.), growing in northeastern Africa and in southern Asia. It occurs in commerce in semitransparent yellowish tears and masses; has a bitter, nauseous taste; is hard, brittle, and capable of being pulverized; and diffuses a strong aromatic odor when burned. It is employed for fumigation, and is used as incense in Roman Catholic churches and Indian temples. See FRANK-INCENSE.

OLIGOCENE EPOCH, the division of the Cenozoic Period which followed the Eocene and preceded the Miocene in geological history. The epoch is generally believed to have begun about 36,000,000 years ago and to have endured for about 16,000,000 years.

No great upheavals of the earth's crust occurred during Oligocene times, and most of the rocks belonging to this epoch were originally marine sediments. Oligocene deposits are found along the Atlantic seacoast in South Carolina and Florida and along the coast of the Gulf of Mexico. Other Oligocene formations, not of marine origin, occur in Oregon, Wyoming, and the Dakotas. The Bad Lands and Black Hills regions are particularly rich in the remains of fossil mammals which lived in Oligocene times. In Europe, rocks of Oligocene origin are found in France, Germany, and Switzerland. Deposits left by the sea and by fresh-water streams during the Oligocene epoch are characteristic of the Alps and the Carpathian Mountains, both of which were low plains at the time. The climate of the Oligocene epoch in the area now occupied by the continental United States was subtropical in nature; palm trees and other subtropical species flourished as far north as the present Canadian border. The climate farther to the north was correspondingly temperate; dense deciduous forests covered many parts of Alaska, Siberia, Greenland, and Spitzbergen. Beginning in this epoch, however, the climate gradually became cooler and the temperate and tropical vegetation groups gradually moved farther south.

The fauna of the Oligocene included modern types of reptiles such as alligators which, during this period, lived as far north as Wyoming and the Dakotas. Mammals were represented by various primitive types of horses and rhinoceroses. One Oligocene rhinoceros, the Baluchitherium, is believed to be the largest land mammal that ever existed. This animal, remains of which have been found in s. Asia, was about 13 ft. in height, 25 ft. in length, and had a skull 5 ft. long. Another Oligocene group related to both the horse and the rhinoceros were the Titanotheres, which resembled rhinoceroses but had two, rather than one, bony horns on the nose. No descendants of the group are extant. Other Oligocene animals included mastodons, primitive dogs and cats, and early primates.

OLIVE, common name for plants of the genus *Olea,* type genus of the family Oleaceae in the order Gentianales. The Olive family, Oleaceae, is characterized by usually opposite leaves and four-parted flowers; the fruits may be berries, drupes, or capsules. In addition to the typical genus, the most important genera are *Franxinus* (ash), *Syringa* (lilac), *Ligusrum* (privet), *Jasminum,* and *Forsythia.* See ASH; LILAC; PRIVET; JASMINE; FORSYTHIA. The name "olive" is particularly applied to the plants, fruit, and wood of *Olea europaea* var. *ativa,* the variety of the wild olive which has been cultivated since the early days of civiliza-

tion in Asia Minor and s.e. Europe for its fruit and the oil expressed from the fruit. It is a native of Syria, and in its wild state is a low, thorny shrub, with opposite, simple, entire leaves, small white axillary flowers, and a drupaceous fruit with a thin, hard pericarp. In cultivation the plant is a tree, seldom exceeding thirty feet in height; the fruit is oval, purple when ripe, and rich in oil. Many varieties of the species are cultivated in the regions surrounding the Mediterranean Sea, the subtropical regions of South America, and the State of California. In these regions the best grades of fruit are harvested for pickling in brine when green or for preserving when ripe; the balance of the crop is pressed for olive oil, which is an important export commodity of Greece, Italy, France, and Spain.

In its native habitat of ancient Syria, the possession of a strain of cultivated olive, yielding much more oil and commercial wealth than the wild variety, was regarded as a symbol of cultural and economic advancement; the offer of an olive branch, from which such trees were propagated, was regarded as a symbol of friendship and came to be accepted as a token of peace. Among the ancient Greeks the olive was regarded as the gift of the goddess Pallas Athena, to whom it was sacred, and a crown of olive branches was a symbol of the highest honor bestowed by the state. The Roman writer Pliny reported that a long and pleasant life depended upon "wine within and oil without"; later the use of olive oil came to be regarded more as a necessary substitute for butter and other animal oils than as a luxury.

The wood of the olive is hard, often variegated, and is valued for cabinetwork. Other species of the genus are important timber trees of Australia, and are known collectively as *maire.* The hard wood of *O. laurifolia* is the black ironwood of Natal.

OLIVES, MOUNT OF, called also MOUNT OLIVET, a limestone ridge, lying north and south on the east side of Jerusalem, from which it is separated only by the narrow Valley of Jehoshaphat. It takes its familiar name from a grove of olive trees which stood on its western flank, but has now in great part disappeared. The ridge rises in three principal summits; the central summit is crowned with a village (Olivet proper). It is around the central peak, which is the Mount of Olives properly so called, that all the most sacred associations of Christian history converge. On the summit stands the Church of the Ascension, on the site of a church built by St.

Sir Laurence Olivier in "Henry V"

Helena. Near it are shown the various places where, according to tradition, our Lord wept over Jerusalem, where the apostles composed the Apostles' Creed, and where our Lord taught them the Lord's Prayer. Near the Church of the Ascension is a mosque and the tomb of a Mohammedan saint.

OLIVETANS, a religious order of the Roman Catholic Church; its full title is the Congregation of Our Lady of Mt. Olivet. It was founded in 1313 by Giovanni Tolomei, professor of philosophy in the University of Siena. The order was confirmed by Pope John XXII, Tolomei being the first general.

OLIVIER, SIR LAURENCE (1909–), English actor, theatrical producer, and director, born in Dorking, Surrey, and educated at St. Edward's School, Oxford. At the age of fifteen he made his first stage appearance in a special boys' performance of *The Taming of the Shrew* at the Shakespeare Festival Theatre, Stratford-on-Avon. He became a member of the Birmingham Repertory Company in 1926 and took important parts in productions on tour and in London theaters. As Hugh Bromilow in *Murder on the Second Floor,* he made his American debut in New York City in 1929. Two years later he went to Hollywood, Calif., and appeared in such motion pictures as *Westward Passage* (1932) and *Friends and Lovers* (1932). After 1933 he appeared on the London and New York stage, playing leading roles in *The Green Bay Tree* (1933), *Biography* (1934), *Queen of Scots* (1934), *Theatre Royal* (1934), *Romeo and Juliet* (1935 and 1940), and *No Time For Comedy* (1939). He was first associated with the Old Vic company in London in 1937, playing many Shakespearean roles, and in 1944, after several years devoted to the making of motion pictures in England, he was appointed co-director of the Old Vic. In 1946 he appeared with the Old Vic company in New York City, playing leads in a repertory series. Heading his own company, Olivier starred in *Caesar and Cleopatra* by George Bernard Shaw and *Antony and Cleopatra* by Shakespeare in New York City in 1952. He is most notable as the producer, director, and star of the British movies *Henry V* (1943, for which he was knighted), *Hamlet* (1947), and *The Beggar's Opera* (1953). American films in which he starred include *Wuthering Heights* (1939), *Rebecca* (1940), *Pride and Prejudice* (1940), and *Carrie* (1952).

OLIVINE, a mineral composed of magnesium and iron silicate, $(Mg,Fe)_2SiO_4$. It crystallizes in the orthorhombic system and usually occurs in the form of granular masses. The color ranges from olive green or grayish green to brown. Olivine has a hardness ranging from $6\frac{1}{2}$ to 7 and a specific gravity ranging from 3.27 to 3.37; it exhibits conchoidal fracture, has a glassy luster, and is transparent or translucent. It is found principally in ferromanganese igneous rocks, such as basalt and peridotite, and occurs in the lavas of Mt. Vesuvius, in Norway, Germany, and in Arizona. A rock called *dunite* is composed almost entirely of olivine. A transparent, green variety of olivine, called *peridot,* and a greenish-yellow variety, called *chrysolite* are used to some extent as gem stones. Peridot is found on St. John's Island in the Red Sea and in Arizona and New Mexico.

OLMSTED, FREDERICK LAW (1822–1903) American landscape architect, born in Hartford, Conn., and educated at Yale College. He traveled throughout Europe and the United States, studying landscape gardening and agricultural methods. In 1857 he was appointed superintendent of Central Park, New York City, the first great metropolitan park in the United States. In collaboration with the landscape architect Calvert Vaux (q.v.) he designed new plans for the park, which had a strong influence on park design throughout the country; see LANDSCAPE ARCHITECTURE. Subsequently he planned a large number of city parks, including Prospect Park

Brooklyn, N.Y.; Riverside and Morningside parks, New York City; Washington and Jackson parks, Chicago; and the grounds of the Capitol, Washington, D.C. He was the first commissioner of the national reservation, Yosemite Park, Calif. Olmsted was one of the first landscape architects in America to preserve the natural features of the terrain and to add naturalistic elements when lacking.

OLSZTYN (Ger. *Allenstein*), city and capital of the voivodship of the same name, Poland, situated on the Lyna R., about 80 miles S.E. of Gdansk (Danzig). An important railroad and industrial center, the city has a large trade in livestock, grain, and leather and plants engaged in the production of diversified manufactures, including stoves, machinery, cement, furniture, gloves, and matches. Olsztyn was founded about the middle of the 14th century. With the surrounding region, it became a Polish possession in 1466 and passed to Prussian sovereignty in 1772. The city subsequently became part of the Prussian province of East Prussia. Following World War II it was transferred to Polish control under the provisions of the Potsdam Conference. Area of voivodship, 8106 sq.m.; pop. (1946) 441,651. Pop. of city (1946) 29,053.

OLYMPIA, capital of the State of Washington and county seat of Thurston Co., situated at the s. end of Puget Sound, 60 miles s.s.w. of Seattle. Transportation facilities include four railroads, coastwise and overseas steamships, and a municipal airport. Lumbering, oyster culture, stock raising, poultry raising, and the growing of beans, hay, fruits, and berries are the chief industries of the Olympia area. The Olympia oyster, a small oyster indigenous to the s. waters of Puget Sound, is a famous product of the city's oysterages. Among the industrial establishments in the city are shipbuilding yards, sawmills, woodworking shops, knitting mills, machine shops, foundries, breweries, canneries, oyster-packing plants, and factories manufacturing veneer and plywood. Traffic of the port of Olympia is largely in lumber and lumber products, floated logs, oysters and oyster shells, canned fruits and vegetables, sand and gravel, salt, and sugar.

Olympia is situated amid low green hills, with the Olympic Mountains towering on the w. horizon and Mount Rainier on the E. The group of State buildings, including the Capitol, the Temple of Justice, and other public buildings, stand on a promontory above the sound, and are constructed of white stone in a classic design. The city is headquarters of the Olympic National Forest, and the terminus of the Olympic Highway.

The site of the present city was first settled in 1846, and in 1851 a town was laid out. It became the Territorial capital in 1853, was chartered as a city in 1859, and was made the State capital in 1889. Pop. (1950) 15,819.

OLYMPIA, the scene of the celebrated Olympian games (q.v.), celebrated every four years by the ancient Greeks. Olympia was situated in a valley in Elis, in western Peloponnesus, through which runs the river Alpheus. It was not a town, but only a sanctuary with buildings connected with games and the worship of the gods. Olympia was a national shrine of the Greeks, and contained many of the choicest treasures of Greek art, such as temples, monuments, altars, theaters, statues, and votive offerings of brass and marble. The *Altis,* or sacred precinct, enclosed a level space about 660 ft. long by nearly 580 broad, and in this space were the chief centers of religious worship, the votive buildings, and the buildings connected with the administration of the games. The most celebrated temple was the *Olympieion,* or *Olympium,* dedicated to Olympian Zeus, father of the gods; in this temple was a colossal statue of Zeus made of ivory and gold, the masterpiece of the Athenian sculptor Phidias (q.v.). Next to the *Olympieion* ranked the *Herœum,* dedicated to Hera, the wife of Zeus. In this temple, probably the oldest Doric building known, stood the table on which were placed the garlands prepared for the victors in the games. The *Metroum,* or temple of the Great Mother of the Gods, was much smaller than the *Herœum.* The votive buildings included a row of twelve treasure houses and the *Philippeum,* a circular Ionic building dedicated by Philip II of Macedon after the battle of Chæronea (338 B.C.). Outside of the *Altis,* to the east, were the *Stadium* and the *Hippodrome,* where the contests took place, and on the west were the *Palœstra,* or wrestling school, and the *Gymnasium,* where all competitors were obliged to train for at least one month. Explorations conducted from 1875 to 1881, under the auspices of the German government, threw much light upon the plans of the buildings. Many valuable objects were discovered, the most important of which was the famous Hermes of Praxiteles (q.v.).

OLYMPIAD, in Greek chronology, an interval of four years between two successive celebrations of the Olympian games (q.v.). The use of Olympiads as a convenient system of chronological reckoning appears chiefly in lit-

OLYMPIA, GREECE. *Left: Sculpture of Apollo in the Olympieion. Right: Ruins of the Herœum.*

erature, beginning about 300 B.C., in the writings of the historian Timæus. This method of dating is not used on coins and is found only rarely on inscriptions, and those of a late date. Although the Olympian games were celebrated in much earlier times, the first Olympiad began in 776 B.C., the year in which the official list of victors began with Corœbus.

OLYMPIAN GAMES, the most famous of the four great national festivals of the ancient Greeks, the other three being the Isthmian, Nemean, and Pythian (qq.v.) games. The Olympian games were celebrated every four years in the sanctuary of Zeus at Olympia, in the western part of the Peloponnesus, Greece; the time of the festival varied from the beginning of August to the middle of September. At first the athletic contests occupied only a single day, but in later times five or six days were required to present all of the sports attractions. The origin of the games goes back to remote antiquity. The official list of victors in the athletic competitions began in the year 776 B.C. with a certain Corœbus, who won the foot race. The list is not generally regarded as authoritative, however, for any period prior to the 5th century B.C. According to the accepted belief, the earliest and for long the only

contest was the *stadion,* or short-distance foot race, run over a course of about 630 ft. In 724 B.C. the *diaulos,* or race covering two stadia, was introduced; and at the next celebration of the Olympian games the *dolichos,* a long race of about 15,120 ft., was instituted. At that time also, the contestants discarded the loincloth and appeared naked, a custom which prevailed from then on. In 708 B.C. both wrestling and the *pentathlon* (in which each athlete participated in five different events, such as throwing the discus, throwing the javelin, foot racing, jumping, and wrestling) were introduced, in 688 B.C. boxing, and in 680 B.C. the race for four-horse chariots. Two more contests were added in 648 B.C., the horseback race and the *pancratium,* a combination of boxing and wrestling. In 632 B.C. contests for boys were established, which from 616 B.C. were standardized in separate events of boxing, wrestling, and running. The foot race for men in armor was added in 520 B.C., and during the 4th and 3rd centuries B.C. other novelties, particularly in horse racing, were from time to time attempted. A contest of trumpeters and heralds was inaugurated in 396 B.C., the successful contestant being permitted to demonstrate his skill in announcing the victors in the athletic competitions. During the greater part of their history the Olympian games were held at Elis, although the city of Pisa, in the territory of which Olympia was situated, frequently disputed this honor, until early in the 6th century, when Pisa was destroyed by Elis and Sparta.

The chief officials of the Olympian games were the Hellenodikai, whose number varied from one or two to twelve, though the usual number seems to have been ten. Early in the year of the games envoys from Elis were sent throughout the Greek world to invite the city-states to join in paying tribute to the Olympian Zeus. At first the games had merely a local character, but they soon became national in scope. The city-states thereupon dispatched *theoriæ*, or sacred deputations, to bring their offerings to Zeus and to vie with one another in the splendor of their equipment and the proficiency of their athletic feats. The competitions were open only to men of Greek descent who were free from the taint of impiety, bloodguiltiness, or grave infraction of the laws. All contestants were required to train assiduously for ten months before the games were held. The last thirty days the athletes were obliged to spend at Elis under the close supervision of the Hellenodikai, though it is possible that this condition applied only to novices. Shortly prior to the commencement of the games the list of entrants was prepared, and thenceforth withdrawal was punished with heavy fines.

The order of the events is not precisely known, but the first athletic contest was almost certainly the stadion. The first day of the festival was devoted to sacrifices, especially to Zeus. At this time both the officials and contestants took a solemn oath, the former to judge fairly, the latter that they had faithfully observed the prescribed conditions of their training period and would compete with fairness. The second day began, in all probability, with foot races, for which the spectactors gathered in the stadion, an oblong plain enclosed by sloping banks of earth. The course was marked at both ends by a marble sill about 80 ft. long and 18 in. wide, in which were two grooves to give the runners a foot-hold in starting. The terminus was always at the same end, but the starting point varied for the single and double courses. Another group of contests was formed by wrestling, boxing, and the pancratium. In the first of these sports the object was to throw the antagonist to the ground three times; the struggle was

never continued on the ground. Boxing became more and more brutal throughout the course of the Olympian games; at first the pugilists wound straps of soft leather over their fingers as a means of deadening the blows, but in later times hard leather, sometimes weighted with metal, was used. Despite this fact, the highest praise was reserved for athletes who achieved their success through a defense so perfect that they were able to exhaust their opponents without striking a blow or receiving a cut. In the pancratium, the most rigorous of the sports, both wrestling and boxing were employed, the contest being continued until one or the other of the participants acknowledged his defeat.

The horse races were run in the hippodrome. This sport, in which each entrant owned his horse, was by its nature confined to the wealthy, but was nevertheless a very popular attraction. The successful owner-racer was accorded high honors in his native city-state, and princes commemorated their victories on the coins they issued, and employed such poets as Pindar (q.v.) to sing their praises. After the horse racing came the pentathlon. The exact sequence of the events in this competition, and the method employed to determine the winner, are unknown. In the throwing of the discus, the object used was a plate of bronze, probably lens-shaped; see Discus Throwing. In the throwing of the javelin, the implement was hurled with the aid of a strap which was wound about the shaft, thereby producing a rotary motion which secured greater distance and accuracy. The jumping event was always judged for distance, not for height.

The last event of the Olympian games was frequently the race in armor, the distance being twice the length of the stadion. At first the runners wore the full panoply of a *hoplite*, or completely equipped infantry soldier, but later they carried only the shield. On the last day of the festival the victors were awarded crowns of wild olive from the sacred olive tree, which constituted the only official prize, and were banqueted by the State of Elis at the Prytaneion, or public hall consecrated to Hestia, goddess of the hearth. The victor returned home in triumph, entering the city in a chariot at the head of a chanting procession. He was celebrated in the panegyrics of poets, and in many cities lived for the remainder of his life at public expense.

The Olympian games reached their highest development during the 5th and 4th centuries B.C. Gradually, however, the festival took on a professional character, and in Roman times, although the spectators were as numerous and the splendor as great as in the earlier period, the competitors were virtually all professional athletes, against whose irregular mode of life physicians and moralists alike directed their censure. Yet the games continued until 394 A.D., when they were finally suppressed by the Roman emperor Theodosius, on the ground that they violated the spirit of Christianity. For an account of the modern games, see OLYMPIC GAMES.

OLYMPIC GAMES, designation applied to an international athletic contest, held quadrennially and restricted to amateurs. A modified revival of the Olympian games (q.v.), one of the great festivals of ancient Greece, the Olympic Games were inaugurated, in 1896, largely as a result of the efforts of the French sportsman and educator Baron Pierre de Coubertin (1863–1937). The initial moves of his revival campaign, which included wide circulation of a colorful account of the ancient festival, gained little popular support. However, in 1894, with the help of a few individuals, he succeeded in establishing the International Olympic Committee. This committee enlisted the aid of sports organizations and individuals of various countries, chiefly European at first, drafted plans and policy for the projected games, and selected Athens as the site of the first contest (Olympiad). Among basic features of Olympic policy, as originally formulated, the amateur athletes of all nations are eligible to participate in the games and the various events are regarded as competitions among athletes as individuals rather than as representatives of nations. To a large degree the last-named feature of Olympic policy has been obscured since the first Olympiad, through the emphasis given by newspapers and various other news media to the over-all performance of the participating countries.

The first Olympiad, which took place in April, 1896, attracted athletes from the United States, Great Britain, and seven European nations. Only fourteen events were scheduled for that Olympiad, held on the site of the Athenian stadium of antiquity. Among these events were six track contests, namely, the marathon, four runs (100, 400, 800, and 1500 meters), and the 110-meters hurdle; and six field contests, namely, the pole vault, high jump, broad jump, sixteen-pound shot put, hop, step, and jump, and discus. Contestants from the U.S. were victorious in nine of the events. The marathon race, which originated

in ancient Greece, was won by S. Loues, a Greek.

The second Olympiad (1900) took place at Paris. St. Louis, Mo., was the site of the games in 1904. A special Olympiad, usually classified as the fourth, was held at Athens in 1906. Thereafter, the Olympic Games were held at London (1908), Stockholm (1912), Antwerp (1920), Paris (1924), Amsterdam (1928), Los Angeles (1932), Berlin (1936), and London (1948). The Olympiad schedule for 1916, at Berlin, was canceled because of World War I and those scheduled for 1940 and 1944 were canceled because of World War II. The games of 1940 were awarded originally to Tokyo, but the place was subsequently changed to Helsinki, Finland. London was the scheduled site of the Olympiad of 1944.

Following the Olympiad of 1904, which had little international significance because the contestants were mainly from the U.S., more and more nations have entered teams in the Olympic Games. In the 1936 Olympiad forty-three nations were represented. Athletes from fifty-nine nations competed in the Olympic Games of 1948. The number of participating athletes has also grown greatly, increasing from the relative few who competed at Athens in 1896 to more than 5000 in 1948. Since the inception of the games over 29,000 athletes have competed in the various contests. A similar development has been the competitive struggle in many countries among qualified athletes for membership on the Olympic teams. The Olympic tryouts, elimination games conducted for aspirants quadrennially under the auspices of the various national Olympic Committees, are outstanding occasions in the realm of amateur athletics, particularly in the United States.

The period since the first Olympiad has been marked by several other significant developments. Of major importance, competition among women athletes was instituted in the Olympiad of 1928. Secondly, there has been a steady increase in the number of sports and events open to competition at the Olympiads. Winter sports, including hockey, figure skating, and skiing, became a part of the Olympic program in 1924. Excluding the winter games the number of sports on the program of the 1948 Olympiad totaled seventeen, namely basketball, boxing, canoeing, cycling, equestrian, fencing, soccer, gymnastics, field hockey, modern pentathlon (riding, fencing, shooting, swimming, and cross-country running), rowing, shooting, swimming, track and field, weight-lifting, wrestling, and yachting. The

OLYMPIC GAMES. *Top, left: Robert Mathias of the United States throwing the discus. Top, right: Jesse Owens of the United States starting 200-meter sprint, which he completed in record time of 20.7 seconds. Bottom: Runners in the 4 × 400-meter relay race.*

combined events of the foregoing sports numbered 134.

A third development has been the progressively superior performance of successive generations of Olympic athletes. For example, the winning time for the 100-meters run in the Olympiad of 1896 was 12 seconds; the time for the same event in 1936 was 10.3 seconds, an Olympic record. The winning distance for the discus throw in 1896 was 95 ft. 7½ in.; the winning distances in 1928 and in 1936 were respectively 155 ft. 3 in. and 165 ft. 7⅜ in. In the games of 1948 an Italian athlete threw the discus 173 ft. 2 in., setting a new Olympic record. Old or original marks have been similarly bettered in many other events. Finally, popular interest in the Olympic Games has kept abreast of the growth of the institution itself. By decision of the International Olympic Committee, the Olympic Games of 1952 were held in Helsinki, Finland.

OLYMPIC GAMES OF 1952
Unofficial Scores of the Competing Nations

Country	Points
United States	614
Soviet Union	553.5
Hungary	308
Sweden	267
Germany	170.5
Finland	162.5
Italy	158.75
France	156.25
Great Britain	117
Czechoslovakia	113.5
Australia	97
Switzerland	92.5
Japan	71
South Africa	67
Denmark	58
Argentina	55
Norway	54
Netherlands	44
Iran	40
Jamaica	39
Turkey	36.75
Belgium	34
Romania	31.75
Canada	30
Brazil	30
Poland	26.5
Austria	23
Egypt	22
Yugoslavia	22

Scores of 19 points or less were made by 21 other nations; 16 nations scored no points. In this tabulation of national placings, 10 points are credited for first place in the various events, 5 points for second place, 4 points for third place, 3 points for fourth place, 2 points for fifth place, and 1 point for sixth place.

OLYMPIC NATIONAL PARK, a national park in N.W. Washington, containing an area of 846,719 acres in the heart of the Olympic Peninsula. The park embraces the Olympic Mountains, one of the finest remaining areas of virgin forest in the Pacific Northwest, and a variety of unusual wildlife. Mount Olympus, the highest peak of the mountains, reaches an altitude of 7954 ft. above sea level. On the slopes of Mount Olympus and several of the other high peaks are numerous active glaciers and glacial streams and lakes. Stands of Douglas fir, western hemlock, western red cedar, Sitka spruce, western white pine, and white fir extend up the sides of the mountains, from 1500 ft. to 3500 ft., beyond which the forests gradually lessen in density to the 5000-ft. elevations, where they give way to alpine meadows. In the lower valleys of the w. slopes, where the rainfall averages 142 inches annually, are the noted "rain forests", resembling jungles, with thick undergrowth and deep carpets of moss. The most noted species of wildlife in the park is the Roosevelt elk, now nearly extinct in other regions. More than 3000 Roosevelt elk roam the w. slopes of the mountains. Other forms of wildlife in the park are black-tailed deer, Rocky Mountain goats, black bears, cougars, coyotes, beavers, minks, raccoons, otters, wolves, eagles, hawks, ravens, and grouse.

Mount Olympus National Monument was established by President Theodore Roosevelt in 1909, and in 1938 the area was increased and established as Olympic National Park by President Franklin Delano Roosevelt.

OLYMPUS, the ancient name of several mountains or chains of mountains in Asia Minor and Greece. The most famous range, situated between Thessaly and Macedonia and overlooking the valley of Tempe (q.v.), was regarded by the ancient Greeks as the chief abode of the gods, and the palaces of Zeus and the other divinities were thought to stand upon its highest summit, Mt. Olympus (9571 ft.). The ten major Olympian deities were Zeus, father of the gods and lord of the sky, weather, and thunderbolt; Hera, his wife and the goddess of marriage and domestic affairs; Athena, his daughter, who sprang from his brain, and hence was the goddess of wisdom; Ares, god of war, and Hephæstus, god of fire, both sons of Zeus and Hera; Apollo, god of medicine, music, and light, and Artemis, goddess of the moon and of wild life, the twin children of Zeus and Leto; Aphrodite, goddess of love, the daughter of Zeus and Dione; Hermes, god of commerce, invention, and athletics, and the messenger of the other gods, the son of Zeus and Maia; and Hestia, sister of Zeus and goddess of the hearth. Usually associated with these major gods were Demeter, goddess of the earth and of agriculture, and Poseidon, god of the sea, sister and brother of Zeus respectively. Later Greek writers transferred the home of these Olympian deities from Olympus to a heavenly region free from snow and storm and filled with dazzling light.

OLYNTHUS, a city of ancient Macedon, situated on the Chalcidice peninsula, at the head of the Toronaic Gulf. Founded by the Chalcidians and Eretrians of Eubœa, the city first becarje prominent as the result of its leading role during the revolt of the Chalcidians against Athens in 432 B.C. For some time Olynthus was the head of a powerful confederacy, called the Chalcidic League, but the city was subdued by Sparta in 379 B.C. and totally destroyed by Philip II, King of Macedon, in 348 B.C. The Olynthiac orations, three speeches delivered by the famous orator Demosthenes (q.v.) when, in 349 B.C., Philip laid siege to the city, requested the Athenians to aid the citizens of Olynthus.

OMAGUA or **CAMBEVA,** a South American Indian tribe of the Tupian (q.v.) stock, formerly inhabiting the territory drained by the Marañón River between the Javarí and Ica rivers on the border between Peru and Brazil. Both names of the tribe signify "flathead", and are derived from the custom of flattening the heads of Omagua infants. The Omaguas are of fine physique and light complexion. Their economy is based on agriculture, hunting, and fishing. In the 16th century, at the time of the Spanish conquest in South America, an erroneous report credited the Omaguas with having rich stores of gold, and in 1536, 1541, and 1560, unsuccessful attempts were made by the Spanish to conquer their country. In the 17th century, the Jesuit missionaries established forty villages of Omagua converts along the Amazon River. These tribesmen prospered despite frequent attacks by Portuguese slave hunters. After the expulsion of the Jesuits from the Spanish colonies in 1767 the mission settlements broke up, and the Omaguas returned to their former way of life. Today most of them live in the region of the headwaters of the Japurá and Uaupés rivers in southeastern Colombia. Many of them are employed as rubber gatherers.

OMAHA, county seat of Douglas Co., Nebr., port of entry, and the largest city in population in the State, situated on the Missouri R., opposite Council Bluffs, Iowa. The city is the site of Creighton University, the University of Nebraska College of Medicine, the Municipal University of Omaha, the Presbyterian Theological Seminary, and the State School for the Deaf. One of the outstanding buildings in the city is the Joslyn Memorial, an art and cultural center and concert hall, opened in 1931. Industrial activities in Omaha include the manufacture of locomotives, paints and varnishes, machinery, linseed oil, and food products. The city is a market for the grain of the surrounding region, and one of the most important livestock and meat-packing markets in the U.S. It is the industrial and commercial center of the State. Ten railroads serve the city, and the Omaha Municipal Airport is the central airport on the New York-San Francisco air route and the terminus of the Omaha-Kansas City route.

Omaha was first settled in 1846–47, and was laid out as a town in 1854. Its site, close to the geographical center of the U.S., soon made it an important transportation and trading center. Before the completion of the Union Pacific Railroad in 1869, Omaha was the most northerly outfitting point for overland wagon trains to the West. Until 1867, when Nebraska became a State, Omaha was the capital of the Territory of Nebraska. On March 23, 1913, the city was devastated by a tornado during which 142 persons were killed. Pop. (1950) 251,117.

OMAHAS, a North American Indian tribe of the Siouan stock (q.v.), closely related to the Kansa, Ponca, Osage, and Quapaw tribes (qq.v.), and formerly inhabiting an extensive territory on the west side of the Missouri River, between the Platte and Niobrara rivers, within the present boundaries of Nebraska. They followed an economy based on the cultivation of corn and vegetables and the hunting of buffalo. Their dwellings were generally earth-covered lodges, but they also built bark lodges, and carried skin tepees with them on their hunting expeditions. In 1802 the Omahas were greatly reduced in number by an epidemic of smallpox. Subsequently they were further reduced by incessant warfare with the Sioux, which was terminated through the intervention of the United States government. In 1854, the tribe ceded a large part of their territory to the United States; the remainder was retained as a reservation, part of which was later sold to the government as a reservation for the Winnebago tribe. The Omahas were granted the right to hold their land in severalty in 1882. In a recent year the population of the tribe was about 1800.

OMAN, SIR CHARLES WILLIAM CHADWICK (1860–1946), British historian, born in Mozufferpore, India, and educated at Oxford University. In 1905 he became professor of modern history at Oxford, and was also appointed a fellow of the British Academy. From 1917 to 1921 he served as president of the Royal Historical Society. In 1920 he was knighted. His most important writings were

George Palmer, from Black Star

The Mosque of Omar, famous Mohammedan shrine in Jerusalem

on military history, and include *History of the Art of War in the Middle Ages* (1898) and *A History of the Peninsula War 1807-13* (7 vols., 1902-30). He was also the author of *Napoleonic Studies* (1929) and *On the Writing of History* (1939).

OMAN AND MUSCAT, independent Arabian Sultanate extending 1000 miles along the south coast of the Gulf of Oman and inland to the Great Desert or Ruba al Khali. Three physical divisions make up the Sultanate: the coastal plain; a range of hills; and a plateau. Areas of cultivation are in the high regions of Jebel Akhdar, where some parts are 9000 feet above sea level; a few oases in the plateau; the coastal plain northwest of Muscat known as Batineh; and along the southeastern coast of Arabia, the province of Dhofar. Dates are the principal product.

Area of the Sultanate is estimated at 82,000 square miles; the population is about 500,000. Arabs constitute the principal portion of this total, but Negro blood is strong along the coast. Capital city is Muscat, with a popula-

tion of about 4000. Matrah, the other principal city, has a population of about 8000.

The principal imports are rice, coffee, and sugar. Exports include dates, pomegranates, fresh and dried limes, and dried fish. Muscat is the only port of call.

OMAR (b. about 581), the second Mohammedan caliph. He was the organizer of the Mohammedan power, as from a mere sect he raised the followers of Islam to the rank of a conquering nation and left to his successor an empire that included Syria, Palestine, Persia, Egypt, Alexandria, Jerusalem, Tripoli, and many other cities and kingdoms. He was the founder of many excellent institutions; he assigned a regular pay to his soldiers and made some excellent regulations for the more lenient treatment of slaves. He originated the practice of dating from the era of the Hejira. In 644 he was assassinated by a Christian slave in Medina. See CALIPH; HEJIRA.

OMAR KHAYYÁM (d. 1123?), famous Persian mathematician, astronomer, and poet, born in Nishapur, Khurasan. On the accession as sultan of Jalal ad Din Malik Shah, Omar received the appointment of astronomer royal to the court. He was engaged with seven other scientists to reform the calendar, which resulted in the adoption of a new era, the Jalalian, or Malik-Shāhī. This mode of reckoning dated from March 15, 1079 (tenth Ramazan, 471 A.H.). As an algebraist Omar stands out as the most notable mathematician of his time. He was the first to attempt a systematic classification of types of equations of the first three degrees and to consider cubics from the standpoint of the general equation. He also composed three different books on subjects of natural science and three on metaphysics. But it is in his verse as the author of the *Rubáiyát*, or quatrains, that his name will live. Edward FitzGerald was the first to introduce Omar to the West through a version of 100 of the quatrains. The version is indeed a paraphrase, yet often very close, and it has caught almost exactly the spirit of the original. About 1000 of these four-line stanzas are found, in different works and manuscripts, ascribed to him.

OMAR, MOSQUE OF, also known as the "Dome of the Rock", a Mohammedan place of worship built in the Byzantine style in 691 A.D. on the rock at Jerusalem from which, according to Mohammedan belief, the angel Gabriel carried the Prophet Mohammed through the heavens while the latter was dreaming. According to a Jewish tradition, now discarded, the rock was the site of the intended sacrifice of Isaac by Abraham. The building was restored many times. A central dome, built over the sacred rock, is supported on columns and arches; it rises 97 ft. above the pavement, and is 65 ft. in diameter. The plan of the entire structure is octagonal, each side measuring 66 ft. in length. Brilliantly colored Persian tiles cover the exterior and marble slabs line the interior. These decorations were added in the 16th century.

OMDURMAN, former capital of the successor of the Mahdi, situated on the left bank of the White Nile opposite Khartum, in the Anglo-Egyptian Sudan. Omdurman is noted as the place where the dervishes were overwhelmed by the Anglo-Egyptian troops under Gen. Kitchener on Sept. 2, 1898. Pop., about 115,000.

OMMIADES. See CALIPH.

OMSK, district city in Siberia, U.S.S.R., at the confluence of the Om with the Irtish, 1800 miles E. of Moscow. It is an important commercial center of the steppe belt, on the Trans-Siberian Railway and with steamer trade down the Irtish. During the Russian Revolution the city was the scene of severe fighting and became Kolchak's capital after a slaughter of Communists. In 1919, with the establishment of the Soviet government, Omsk became temporarily the Siberian capital. It has a regional museum, the Siberian Agricultural Academy, the Medical Institute, the Veterinary Institute, and the Central Pushkin Library. In the former fortress the great novelist Dostoevski was confined for four years; he described it in his *House of the Dead.* Pop., about 280,000.

OMUTA, city of Fukuoka Prefecture, Kyushu I., Japan, situated on Shimbara Bay, 22 miles N.W. of Kumamoto. It is the shipping and supply center for the nearby Mitsui coal fields. The area was heavily bombed during World War II. Pop., about 128,000.

ONA, a South American Indian tribe, probably comprising an independent linguistic stock, and formerly inhabiting the interior of Tierra del Fuego, except for the southeastern and southwestern regions. According to some authorities, the Onas are closely related to the Tehuelche (q.v.) tribes and thus belong to the Tsonecan (q.v.) stock. They followed an economy based on hunting, their principal food being the meat of the guanaco, a mammal related to the llama. Other elements of their diet included birds, shellfish, fish, and berries. Despite the cold climate of their region, the Onas rarely built houses, but sheltered themselves behind windbreaks of hides and brushwood, and rubbed their bodies

with protective coats of grease. Their clothing consisted of guanaco fur, and they manufactured bark canoes, bows and arrows, clubs, fishing spears, slings, baskets, simple tools, and ornaments.

The tribe was divided into groups of relatives, who hunted together. Each group had its own hunting territory, and encroachments on the territory of another group generally marked the beginning of a family feud. The hunting groups performed initiation ceremonies for the young men, who were also required to spend two years in solitude so as to develop self-reliance. Ona mythology was rich, and religion centered about a supreme deity and a number of malevolent spirits. The tribe formerly numbered about 3000; in recent years they have become almost extinct.

ONCKEN, HERMANN (1869–1946), German historian. He was professor of history at the universities of Heidelberg, Munich, and Berlin. The views expressed in his writings are markedly liberal and free from all traces of nationalism; on this account his works were subjected to bitter criticism by the National Socialists after their accession to power in 1933. Among his works are a notable biography of the German socialist leader Ferdinand Lassalle (1909); and a penetrating analysis of the history of Germany after 1870, *Das Deutsche Reich und die Vorgeschichte des Weltkrieges* (2 vols., 1933).

ONEGA, LAKE, in the N. of Russia, after Ladoga, to the N.E. of which it lies, the largest lake in Europe, 50 m. in greatest breadth, 146 m. in length, and 500 ft. in depth in parts. Area, 3764 sq.m. It is fed by numerous rivers, but its only outlet is the river Svir, which flows s.w. into Lake Ladoga.

ONEIDA, a North American Indian tribe belonging linguistically to the Iroquoian family and forming part of the Iroquois confederacy (qq.v.). The name by which the tribe is known is a corruption of *Oneyotkaono,* meaning "people of the stone", and referring to a boulder sacred to the tribe and situated near the site of their ancient village on Oneida Lake, New York. Their territory included the region about the lake, and extended south to the Susquehanna River. The tribe was friendly toward the French and Jesuit colonists and missionaries, although most members of the confederacy were hostile toward them. During the Revolutionary War the Oneida sided with the Americans, while their fellow tribes took the part of the English, and they were obliged to take refuge within the American settlements. After the

Eugene O'Neill (from a drawing)

war, most of the Oneida returned to their former territory, but a considerable number emigrated to Canada and settled in the region of the Thames River, Ontario, where their descendants still remain. Between 1820 and 1835, most of the Oneida who had returned to their homes in New York State sold their land, and moved to a reservation at the head of Green Bay, Wisconsin. In a recent year the Oneida numbered about 3500 in Wisconsin and about 350 in New York.

ONEIDA COMMUNITY, a communistic society established at Oneida, New York, in 1847, and dissolved about 1880. The community was founded originally at Putney, Vermont, by John Humphrey Noyes (q.v.) in 1838. Its members, who were called Perfectionists (q.v.), believed that Jesus Christ had returned to earth and completed His work of saving Christians from the necessity of sin. They also held that perfect freedom from sin could be obtained on earth by communion with God, followed by a renunciation of personal property and of binding personal relationships, including marriage. After being expelled from Putney, where its practices had aroused opposition, the group settled at Oneida, where it established several successful manufacturing enterprises; the operating capital of the community increased from $67,-000 in 1847 to about $600,000 in 1880. All properties, including farms and industries,

were held in common; and the community government was conducted by committees which met weekly in public sessions. Cohabitation was permitted freely according to individual tastes; but conception was directed, theoretically, by the community leaders, who attempted to impose eugenic principles in order to produce healthy and intelligent offspring. Children were reared by the community, which in many cases provided them with professional and technical training.

Despite its economic success and the relative lack of friction that marked its administration, outside antagonism to the system of "complex marriage" maintained by the community forced Noyes to move to Canada with a few followers in 1880. Most of the remaining members contracted individual marriages; and, soon afterward, they voluntarily agreed to abandon their communal property system. A joint-stock company, known as Oneida Community, Limited, was formed to carry on the various manufacturing establishments. The company still exists; but it has gradually narrowed its activities from the manufacture of silk and steel traps and the canning of fruits and vegetables, to the manufacture of fine plated and sterling silverware, for which it now is known.

ONEIDA LAKE, situated on the boundaries of Oswego, Oneida, and Onondaga counties, N.Y., about 22 m. long by 6 m. wide. The Oneida and Fish rivers are the chief affluents. A canal connects it with Lake Ontario on the north, and with the New York State Barge Canal on the east.

O'NEILL, EUGENE (GLADSTONE) (1888–1953), American playwright, born in New York City, the son of James O'Neill, a well-known actor. He studied under Professor G. P. Baker, of Harvard, later became associated with the Provincetown Theatre, and after 1914 devoted himself to playwriting. One of America's most forceful playwrights, he brings to the stage revolutionary methods of presentation and startling insight into human nature. He wrote *The Moon of the Caribbees* (1919); *Beyond the Horizon* (1919; Pulitzer Prize, 1920); *Emperor Jones* (1921); *Diff'rent* (1921); *The Straw* (1921); *Gold* (1921); *Anna Christie* (1922; Pulitzer Prize, 1922); *The Hairy Ape* (1922); *The Fountain* (1923); *All God's Chillun Got Wings* (1924); *Desire Under the Elms* (1924); *Marco Millions* (1924); *The Great God Brown* (1925); *Lazarus Laughed* (1926); *Strange Interlude* (1927; Pulitzer Prize, 1928); trilogy, *Mourning Becomes Electra* (1931); *Ah, Wilderness*

(1932); *Days Without End* (1933); and *The Iceman Cometh* (1946). In 1935, O'Neill began work on a 9-play cycle to be called *A Tale of Possessors Self-Dispossessed,* a dramatic history of an American family from 1775 to 1932. He received the Nobel Prize for literature in 1936.

ONION, common name applied to any biennial herb of the genus *Allium,* belonging to the Lily family, but usually restricted to *A. cepa,* native to Asia, and cultivated in temperate and subtropical regions for thousands of years. The true onion is a bulbous-rooted plant with long, hollow leaves, thickened near the base of the stem. It contains sulfurous, volatile oils which give it a pungent taste. The white or pink flowers, which are borne in umbels, have six sepals, six petals, six stamens, and a solitary pistil. In the varieties known as "top onions", the flowers are supplanted by small bulblets which may be grown to obtain new plants. The fruit is a loculicidal capsule. Onion bulbs and stems are eaten raw or cooked, and are used as seasoning in cookery. Onions raised in warm areas are planted as winter crops, and are milder in taste and odor than onions planted in cooler regions. Yellow Bermuda and white Spanish onions are among the mildest cultivated onions. In 1951 976,000 tons of onions were raised in the United States, and brought a market value of $54,072,000. The onion grows well in rich, moist soil; when the crop ripens, the bulbs are pulled and spread thinly on a dry surface in the open air until dry. They are stored in slotted or open-mesh bags to keep them dry enough to prevent sprouting.

Other plants in the genus *Allium* also called onions include: the wild onion, *A. cernuum;* the shallot, *A. ascalonicum;* and the green onion or common leek, *A. porrum.* Both the shallot and the green onion, which have small bulbs, are also known as "scallions". Compare GARLIC.

ONNES, HEIKE KAMERLINGH. See KAMERLINGH ONNES, HEIKE.

ONONDAGA, an important North American Indian tribe belonging linguistically to the Iroquoian family, and by alliance to the Iroquois confederacy (qq.v.). The territory they occupied centered about Onondaga Lake in central New York State, and extended north to Lake Ontario and south to the Susquehanna River. Their principal village, which contained 140 houses in the 17th century, was called Onondaga or Onondaga Castle. This village served as the capital of the Iroquois confederacy, and the Onondaga were the official guardians of the council fire of the league. The tribe ranked as the chief member of the confederacy, although the Mohawk and the Seneca (qq.v.), living on the frontier of the league's territory, were more warlike and became more prominent in Iroquoian relations with European settlers and other tribes. During the American Revolutionary War, the Onondaga sided with the British, and after the war most of the tribe emigrated to a reservation on the Grand River, in Ontario, Canada, where their descendants still live. The rest of the tribe were placed on reservations in the region of their former territory. In a recent year the Onondaga of New York State numbered more than 700.

ONTARIO, the most populous and wealthy province of the Dominion of Canada. It is bounded on the N.E. and E. by Quebec, on the S.E., S., and S.W. by the St. Lawrence and the Great Lakes, on the N. by James and Hudson bays, and on the N.W. and W. by Manitoba. The area is 412,582 sq.m.; the population in 1951 was 4,597,542, with cities (1951) as follows: Toronto, the capital, 675,754; Hamilton, 208,321; Ottawa, capital of the Dominion, 202,045; Windsor, 120,049; London, 95,343.

The Laurentian Hills run westward from the Thousand Islands near Kingston, and extend N. of Lake Simcoe, forming the coasts of Georgian Bay and Lake Huron. In the middle of the province the high land forms a watershed, separating the rivers flowing into the Great Lakes from those entering the Ottawa and the St. Lawrence. The principal rivers of Ontario are tributaries of the Ottawa, which forms part of its northeastern boundary. The St. Lawrence forms the boundary of the eastern portion of the province, dividing it from the United States. Bounded by the Great Lakes, among its smaller lakes are Simcoe, Nipissing, Nipigon, and many others. Ontario is largely an agricultural country, and its resources are very great.

Area under cultivation (1952) is 8,298,000 acres. The principal products are wheat, oats, barley, rye, flax, mixed grains, potatoes, hay and clover, and fodder corn. Fruit production is extensive and dairying constitutes one of the principal farm industries. In 1952 the estimated value of all agricultural products was $868,319,000. Productive forest area in the province in 1952 totaled 159,812 square miles, the principal timber found there being spruce, pine, birch, and poplar.

National Film Board; R.C.A.F. Photo

IN ONTARIO PROVINCE

Above: Office buildings in the business section of the city of Toronto. Right: Cable car carrying sightseers across the Niagara Glen. Below: Power plant on the Kananaskis River.

Manufacturing establishments in 1950 numbered 12,809, and employed 566,513 wage earners, who received a total of $1,412,999,000 in wages and salaries.

Ontario is the leading Canadian province in mineral production; gold production in 1952 totaled 2,514,000 fine ounces. Ontario is also the foremost nickel producer in the world; output in 1952 was 281,117,000 pounds. Also produced are silver, copper, platinum metals, uranium, tellurium, iron ore, magnesium, quartz, salt, asbestos, Portland cement, calcium, cobalt, feldspar, gypsum, mica, crude petroleum and natural gas. Total mineral production value was $453,294,000 in the year 1952.

Road mileage (1951) in the province is 74,009; steam railway mileage is about 10,500.

Elementary and secondary schools number 7356 (in 1952), including day and evening classes. Student enrollment is about 900,000 per year, with certified teachers numbering about 30,000. Institutions for higher education include the following: University of Toronto, Queen's University (Kingston), Western Ontario University (London), McMaster (Hamilton), and Ottawa University, in addition to the Royal Military College maintained at Kingston by the Dominion government.

A single chamber of 90 members elected for five-year terms, a lieutenant governor, and a cabinet hold the legislative and executive power of the province. Women have the franchise and may be elected to the chamber.

History. Ontario was largely founded by the immigration of United Empire Loyalists into Canada after the Declaration of Independence of the United States. It was divided into two separate provinces, called Upper and Lower Canada, in 1792. The two provinces were reunited in 1842, as a result of the disturbances in 1837 and 1838, and remained in that position until confederation in the year 1867, when the province received the name of Ontario.

ONTARIO, LAKE, the easternmost and smallest (7246 sq.m.) of the five Great Lakes of North America. It receives at its s.w. corner the waters of the upper lakes by the Niagara River, and at its N.E. corner it issues into the St. Lawrence. Its surface is 326 ft. below the surface of Lake Erie and 247 ft. above the ocean level. Its mean depth is about 300 ft.; and its maximum depth, 738 ft. It is 190 m. long, 55 m. in its widest part, and over 500 m. in circumference.

There are many convenient harbors and thriving ports, chief among which are Kingston, Port Hope, Cobourg, Toronto, and Hamilton on the Canadian shore, and Oswego, Sacketts Harbor, and Charlotte in New York. Many lighthouses along the coasts facilitate navigation, and the lake is connected with Lake Erie by the Welland Canal, with the Erie Canal and the Hudson River by the Oswego Canal, and with the Ottawa River by the Rideau Canal. See GREAT LAKES.

ONTOLOGY, the science or systematic discussion of real being; the philosophical theory of reality; the doctrine of the categories or universal and necessary characteristics of all existence. (1) The science of being (τὸ ὄν), or the Absolute or First Cause, as the ultimate principles underlying and explaining all other existences; the ultimate philosophy. Compare PHILOSOPHY. (2) The science of the most general and fundamental principles involved in all beings (τὰ ὄντα) or existences constituting the universe. See METAPHYSICS.

The name "ontology" seems to have been first made current in philosophy by Wolf. He divided metaphysics into four parts: ontology; psychology; rational cosmology; and theology. It was chiefly occupied with abstract inquiries into possibility, necessity, and contingency, substance, accident, and cause, without reference to the laws of our intellect by which we are constrained to believe in them.

ONYX, a quartz mineral composed of alternating bands of chalcedony and opal (qq.v.). The bands are straight and parallel and usually colored black and white in alternating layers. Onyx is used as a gem stone, particularly for cameos. Compare AGATE.

OPAH, KINGFISH, SUNFISH, or MOONFISH, a soft-finned, edible, marine teleost fish, *Lampris lune,* the only species in the family Lamprididae, found in the Atlantic Ocean. The opah, which attains a length of about five feet and a weight of several hundred pounds, is a deep, compressed fish with a forked tail. It is purplish green above and on the sides, and yellowish green below, with numerous gilt and silver spots over the surface of its body. Its fins are bright red. The fish feeds on mollusks.

OPAL, a noncrystalline gem mineral consisting of hydrated silica in the gel state. Opal has a hardness of between 5.5 and 6.5, and a specific gravity of 2 to 2.3. Its fracture is conchoidal and its luster varies from glassy to dull. In color the opal also shows extreme variations from white to black, and in transparency from transparent to opaque.

One of the chief characteristics of the opal

is the brilliant play of colors which may be seen in superior stones. These colors result from the cracking of the original stone as it hardens and the deposition of additional opal in the cracks. The indices of refraction of the original stone and the additional deposits are frequently different and result in light interference causing a play of colors. Opal has been used as a gem stone for many centuries in spite of a superstition that the gem brings bad luck to its owners.

A large number of different types of opal are known, but usually only the transparent or translucent varieties are used as gems. Gem opals include: white opals; black opals; fire opals, which are yellow to red in color; girasol, which has a bluish-white opalescence; harlequin opals, which show uniform patches of contrasting colors; and lechosos opal, which has a deep-green play of color within the stone. Other types of opal include: moss opal, which has inclusions of foreign material which resemble moss; hydrophane, a porous white opal which is cloudy when dry and transparent when its pores are filled with water; and hyalite, a colorless and transparent form which looks like glass. Diatomaceous earth, sometimes called tripolite, is a chalky form of opal which is sometimes used for polishing and other industrial purposes.

Opals are found chiefly in Australia, Czechoslovakia, Honduras, Nevada, and Mexico.

OPEN DOOR, in modern diplomacy, a doctrine or policy advocating equal trading rights in the nation to which it is applied for all other nations. The open-door doctrine was first enunciated by the United States with respect to China at the end of the 19th century. Russia, Germany, France, and England had at that time already obtained control of important areas of China, and it appeared that the country would soon be divided into spheres of influence into which other trading nations would have no access. The United States was unwilling to compete for territory, but desired access to China for trading purposes. Accordingly, on September 6, 1899, Secretary of State John Hay (q.v.) sent notes to England, France, Germany, Russia, Italy, and Japan, asking them for formal declarations to the effect that they would not interfere with the rights of other nations in any treaty port, or with the vested interests of other nations in territories under their control. Recognizing that they themselves could lose more than they would gain by restrictive and mutually exclusive arrangements, all of the recipients of the note indicated their willingness to make such declarations. On July 3, 1900, therefore, Secretary Hay sent another note to eleven nations, defining the American position and requesting adherence to principles of "equal and impartial trade with all parts of the Chinese Empire" and preservation of "Chinese territorial and administrative" integrity. All eleven nations answered with formal approval of these principles.

The open-door doctrine was not successful in preventing extension of monopolistic Russian control of Manchurian ports and other facilities in 1902 and again in 1946, or of monopolistic Japanese control in the same area prior to World War I and again in the 1930's. However, it expressed the real interests of the western European powers and of the United States, and it served as a yardstick of their Chinese policies for almost half a century. The open-door policy has been followed by France, England, and Belgium in territories which they control on the west coast of Africa; and France is pledged to observe it in Morocco.

OPEN SHOP, in labor relations, a business establishment or factory in which workers may be employed without regard to their membership or nonmembership in a labor union. The abolition of the open shop is usually one of the primary demands made by labor unions when they engage in collective bargaining with employers, as the ability of employers to hire and retain nonunion help generally has the effect of vitiating all attempts at unionization. The alternatives to the open shop are the closed shop and the union shop; see CLOSED-SHOP AGREEMENT; UNION-SHOP AGREEMENT.

OPERA, a drama set to music, and sung throughout or almost throughout with orchestral accompaniment. The origins of opera are of necessity closely bound with the development of the drama. Though only fragmentary remains of ancient Greek music dramas are now extant, music is known to have been an essential element of the Greek theater, especially as sung by the choruses in the tragedies of Æschylus, Sophocles, and Euripides. It is also believed that the dialogue of these dramas was declaimed in a lyrical, musical spirit. During the Middle Ages religious plays developed in which Biblical stories were illustrated with action and music. Music served only incidentally in the religious mystery plays (so-called from the Latin *ministerium,* "service") of the 14th to the 16th centuries, in which Biblical events, such as the life of Christ and the creation of the world, were staged with great pageantry and dramatic elaboration.

Unaccompanied polyphonic choral music was the prevalent expression of the 16th century. Desiring to break away from this practice, a group of artists and musicians met at the home of the Florentine nobleman Giovanni Bardi, Conte del Vernio, in the last years of the century, to discuss the possibilities of forming a new style based upon the musical declamation used in the ancient Greek lyric drama. Members of the group included Giulio Caccini and Jacopo Peri. The work of this group marks the beginnings of the opera, oratorio, and cantata, and, technically, the beginning of the new monodic style, consisting of a single voice with bass accompaniment which adheres to the natural rhythms of spoken words (see RECITATIVE). In 1600 the group offered their first public production, that of Peri's opera *Euridice;* Caccini set the same libretto to music in the same year. These early experiments led to the recognition of opera as a medium of true esthetic expression. Its full possibilities were first realized by Claudio Monteverdi in such operas as *Orfeo* (1602) and *Arianna* (1608). Monteverdi's bold use of a larger and more varied orchestra, enriched harmonies, expressive recitatives, and highly dramatic characterizations established the value of opera in the musical world. In 1637 the first public opera house, the Teatro di San Cassiano, was opened in Venice, where it enjoyed an enormous popular success, chiefly through the works of Monteverdi, Francesco Cavalli, Marc'Antonio Cesti, Antonio Sartorio, and Giovanni Legrenzi. More characters were introduced, plots grew in complication, comic episodes abounded, soloists were featured, and arias developed a distinctive form. Many of these features were designed to appeal specifically to popular taste. This movement culminated in the development of the comic opera (q.v.) which made its appearance in Rome in the latter part of the 17th century.

In the 18th century, opera was dominated throughout Europe by the Neapolitan school, led by Alessandro Scarlatti. The recitative and the aria (q.v.), highly developed by Scarlatti, the vocal art of *bel canto,* and the reform of the librettos to treat classical historical subjects in a unified three-act form of a rigid dramatic structure, gave opera a new character and style, which became known as *opera seria,* and was cast in a prevailingly tragic mood. From 1711 to 1740 the greatest exponent of *opera seria* was George Frederick Handel.

Others included Alessandro Stradella, Antonio Caldara, and Antonio Lotti. Later composers to use this style were Antonio Salieri, Wolfgang Amadeus Mozart, and Christoph Willibald Gluck.

In the middle of the 18th century, Naples also contributed the classical Italian two-act comic opera style called *opera buffa,* which evolved from the intermezzi (see INTERMEZZO) performed between the acts of *opera seria.* Most famous in its day was Giovanni Battista Pergolesi's *La Serva Padrona* (1733), which was played throughout the capitals of Europe. Niccolò Piccini, Giovanni Paisiello, Domenico Cimarosa, and Mozart excelled in this form as well as in the *opera seria.*

In France, Jean Baptiste Lully and Robert Cambert founded French serious opera (called *grand opera*). It was closely connected to the ballet, which was the most popular form of court entertainment during the 17th century. The works of Lully, Cambert, and Jean Philippe Rameau received the full support of royalty. Lully obtained a monopoly of the Académie de Musique, where French opera developed its distinctive features, such as the elaborate use of ballets and choruses, the use of short, simple songs, and the integration into the action of independent instrumental music. The characteristic French *opéra comique,* the French form of comic opera, developed in the early 18th century.

During the 16th and 17th centuries English stage works known as *masques* (q.v.), which combined the arts of poetry, dancing, acting, and music, were performed for the nobility. Music for masques was composed by William and Henry Lawes and Thomas Campion, among others. Out of the masque grew the first English opera, John Blow's *Venus and Adonis* (1680?–87). The greatest figure in English opera was Henry Purcell, who combined French theatrical and musical practices with characteristically English features; his most celebrated work is *Dido and Æneas* (1689?). During the 18th century the popular stage entertainment known as *ballad opera* developed, in which popular ballad tunes and melodies by such composers as Handel and Purcell were fitted to comic lyrics and alternated with spoken dialogue; the form was most successfully realized by John Gay's *Beggar's Opera* (1728).

The historical turning point of 18th-century opera was occasioned by the reforms of the great Christoph Willibald Gluck. In his famous preface to his Italian opera *Alceste* (1767), he argued for dramatic unity within an opera rather than purely musical considerations, for the avoidance of composing merely to display vocal gymnastics, for simple, unadorned plots, and for a greater flexibility of musical forms than that allowed by Italian opera. *Alceste,* which illustrated his theories, met with vigorous opposition. In 1774, Gluck's first French opera, *Iphigénie en Aulide,* was received triumphantly in Paris by an audience less imbued in the established Italian tradition. Following Gluck, Mozart brought a new level of perfection to the medium of opera. *Le Nozze di Figaro* (1786), *Don Giovanni* (1787), and *Così fan Tutte* (1790) are in the height of the tradition of Italian *opera buffa.* Along with these three masterpieces set to Italian texts, Mozart's German opera *Die Zauberflöte* (1791) achieved a greater subtlety of musical characterization, control of juxtaposed comic and dramatic elements, and integration of voice and instrument than had theretofore appeared.

Gluck's ideas were welcomed in Germany, where they became an integral part of German operatic style. They are best exemplified, in the 19th century, by the works of Luigi Cherubini, and by Ludwig van Beethoven's only opera, *Fidelio* (1805). In France Étienne Nicolas Méhul, André Ernest Modeste Grétry, and François Adrien Boieldieu, gave to the *opéra comique* a new popularity, developing a form which dispensed with spoken dialogue and with the musical and dramatic sacrifices made for the sake of humorous situations. The concepts of Gluck continued to influence French serious operas, including those written by comic-opera composers. Thus, Gioacchino Antonio Rossini, who wrote the masterful opera buffa *Il Barbiere di Siviglia* in 1816, turned to *opera seria* thirteen years later with *Guillaume Tell.* His fame, in turn, was surpassed by Giacomo Meyerbeer's *Les Huguenots* (1836), *Le Prophète* (1849), and *L'Africaine* (1865). The greatest success in serious opera was achieved by Charles François Gounod's *Faust* (1859). It was followed, in 1875, by Georges Bizet's *Carmen.* Léo Delibes, Alexis Emmanuel Chabrier, Ambroise Thomas, and Jules Émile Massenet continued the tradition of serious French opera into the late 19th century. In Italy, Vincenzo Bellini and Gaetano Donizetti retained the conventional forms of 18th-century Italian opera. They were succeeded by the prolific and ever-popular Giuseppe Verdi, whose most successful works are *Il Trovatore* (1852), *La Traviata* (1853), *Aïda* (1871), *Otello* (1887), and *Falstaff* (1893). Verdi's emphasis upon melody

and upon melodramatic plots was continued in the operas of Pietro Mascagni, such as *Cavalleria Rusticana* (1890), in Ruggiero Leoncavallo's *I Pagliacci* (1892), and in Giacomo Puccini's *La Bohème* (1896), *Tosca* (1900), and *Madame Butterfly* (1900).

The 19th century also ushered in German Romantic opera, based upon national legend. *Der Freischütz* (1821) and *Euryanthe* (1823) of Karl Maria von Weber mark the beginning of this style, which led to the "music drama" as conceived by Richard Wagner. In his essay *Oper und Drama* (1850–51) Wagner's theory of the music drama is expounded; he contended that historical legends, because of their symbolic meanings, were the best subjects for music drama. Leitmotivs, which are short melodic phrases or passages used to identify each person, situation, and idea of the drama, were also described as a major stylistic feature of the projected music drama. Wagner's musical application of his ideas first appeared in the four operas which constitute the *Ring des Nibelungen: Das Rheingold* (1854), *Die Walküre* (1856), *Siegfried* (1871), and *Gotterdämmerung* (1874). In his earlier works, *Der Fliegende Holländer* (1841), *Tannhäuser* (1845), and *Lohengrin* (1848), the evolution of these ideas is apparent. Together with *Tristan und Isolde* (1859), *Die Meistersinger von Nürnberg* (1876), and *Parsifal* (1882), the *Ring* embodies Wagner's concept of the fusion of all arts into one new form. Wagner's great command of the orchestra, his skillful and expressive harmonic devices, and the intensity of his dramatic expression marked the apex and culmination of the Romantic period.

Slavonic opera first came into its own in Bohemia and Russia in the 19th century. Prague welcomed the new Bohemian national style of Bedřich Smetana's *Bartered Bride* (1866) and Anton Dvořák's *King and Collier* (1874). The development of national opera in Russia began with Mikhail Ivanovich Glinka's two most famous operas, *A Life for the Czar* (1836) and *Russlan and Ludmilla* (1842). The greatest of Russian operas was Modest Petrovich Musorgski's *Boris Godounov* (1868–69); other national operas were composed by Aleksandr Porfirevich Borodin (*Prince Igor,* 1869–89) and Nikolai Andreevich Rimski-Korsakov (*The Snow Maiden,* 1880–81). Tchaikovsky's operas *Eugene Onegin* (1878) and *Pique Dame* (1890) were, however, in the European Romantic tradition.

Wagner's influence was felt strongly in the 20th century. In Germany, for example, Richard Strauss produced two operas in a com-

Metropolitan Opera Co.

OPERA. *Above: Elizabeth Rethberg, Bidu Sayao, John Brownlee, and Ezio Pinza in scene from "The Marriage of Figaro." Right: Risë Stevens as Carmen. Below: Scene from "Aïda."*

pletely Wagnerian style, *Salome* (1905) and *Elektra* (1909). Strauss' best-known opera is the tragi-comic *Der Rosenkavalier* (1911). Achille Claude Debussy's only opera, *Pelléas et Mélisande* (1902), was one of the first operas to abandon the Wagnerian spirit in favor of a new style known as Impressionism (q.v.). Also in the new style was Maurice Ravel's *L'Heure Espagnole* (1907). Developments in music after World War I gave rise to a renewed interest in opera. Among the best-known works of this period are Alban Berg's *Wozzeck* (1914–21), Paul Hindemith's *Cardillac* (1926), Ernst Křenek's *Jonny Spielt Auf* (1925–26), and Igor Stravinsky's opera oratorio *Œdipus Rex* (1927). Another important operatic work by Stravinsky is *The Rake's Progress* (1951). Among noteworthy operas by modern composers are the works of Benjamin Britten (*Peter Grimes,* 1945; *Billy Budd,* 1951) in England; and Douglas Moore (*The Devil and Daniel Webster,* 1938; *Giants of the Earth,* Pulitzer Prize, 1951), Deems Taylor (*The King's Henchman,* 1927), and Virgil Thomson (*Four Saints in Three Acts,* 1934; *The Mother of Us All,* 1947) in America. The merger of theater and opera was accomplished with a high degree of success by the Italian-American composer Gian-Carlo Menotti, in such works as *The Medium* (1946), *The Telephone* (1947), *The Consul* (1950), and *Amahl and the Night Visitors* (1951), the first opera composed for television presentation.

For additional information, see biographies under names of individual composers.

OPERATIONS RESEARCH, a field of scientific activity in which highly trained scientists, and scientific institutions, contribute to the supervision, conduct, and co-ordination of research on scientific problems related to the conduct of modern warfare. Although scientists have frequently contributed their skills and knowledge to the military branches of their countries in times of war, their efforts were not organized and co-ordinated with those of the military in the definite form of operations research until World War II. Operations research, as conducted by Great Britain and the United States, was first developed in England by the British physicist Patrick Maynard Stuart Blackett. In 1940 he supervised an investigation of the operational effectiveness of radar sets, and shortly thereafter organized operations-research sections attached to the various branches of the British military and naval forces rather than to separate research laboratories. In the United States the first body for the conduct of operations

research was established in 1940 by the Council of National Defense, and was known as the National Defense Research Committee (NDRC). The first chairman of the Committee was the American electrical engineer Vannevar Bush, and its twelve members included representatives from the War and Navy departments and from the National Academy of Sciences. The function of the NDRC, as stated in the act of Congress by which it was officially constituted, was to supervise scientific research on problems related to "the development, production, and use of mechanisms and devices of warfare". In the spring of 1941 President Franklin D. Roosevelt issued an executive order creating the Office of Scientific Research and Development to further coordinate the conduct of scientific research related to the defense program. By this order the NDRC was made an advisory body to the newly created organization, but retained large discretionary powers.

The earliest important research projects of NDRC were in the field of antisubmarine warfare. Scientists from universities, industry, and government agencies investigated problems in this field by directly observing combat operations, and this pattern of activity was repeated with the formation of other specialized groups conducting operations research for aircraft, antiaircraft, and amphibious operations. In 1942 the U.S. Army Air Forces established additional research groups known as operations analysis sections. The following year Bush organized the Office of Field Service (OFS), a subdivision of the OSRD, to insure an adequate liaison between the research laboratories and operations on the field of battle. The functions of OFS included: sending specialists to supervise the use of such equipment as guided missiles, radar devices for the detection of submarines and airplanes, and explosives; making special studies and recommendations on such matters as radio field communications, malaria control, and engineering operations; and providing other operations-research groups with personnel needed by these groups for special assignments. During World War II more than fifty industrial and nonindustrial contractors co-operated with the work of operations research, including General Electric Co., Radio Corporation of America, Western Electric Co., Massachusetts Institute of Technology, Harvard, Columbia, and Johns Hopkins universities, and the Woods Hole Oceanographic Institute.

OPERETTA, a short opera of light or comic character, originally closely related to comic

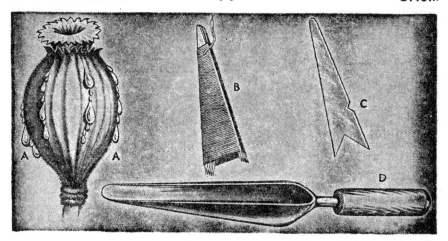

OBTAINING OPIUM FROM THE POPPY. *A, drops of crude opium exhuding from green poppy head; B, eight-bladed knife for scratching poppy; C, one blade; D, spoon for collecting drops.*

opera (q.v.), and originated in the 18th century as a one-act afterpiece or intermezzo (q.v.). Early examples of such operettas are *Schauspieldirektor* (1786) by Wolfgang Amadeus Mozart and *L'Inganno Felice* (1812) by Gioacchino Antonio Rossini. The form was expanded in the 19th century to two acts, and was performed as an independent entertainment. In the second half of the century the Viennese composer Franz von Suppé (*Light Cavalry,* 1866) and the French composer Jacques Offenbach (*La Vie Parisienne,* 1866) originated the modern operetta, characterized by light themes and by spoken dialogue or recitative between musical selections. The operettas of Johann Strauss the younger, particularly *Die Fledermaus* (1874), achieved popularity throughout the world. The most famous of all operettas, however, are among those written by Sir William Schwenck Gilbert (q.v.), with music by Sir Arthur Seymour Sullivan (q.v.). Among 20th-century composers of operettas are Victor Herbert (*Naughty Marietta,* 1910), Sigmund Romberg (*The Student Prince,* 1924), Rudolf Friml (*The Vagabond King,* 1925), and Noel Coward (*Bittersweet,* 1929).

OPHTHALMOLOGY. See SIGHT, DEFECTS OF.

OPIE, JOHN (1761–1807), English historical and portrait painter, born in St. Agnes, Cornwall. Self-taught, he went to London in 1780 with an established reputation as a fashionable portrait painter. He was elected an associate of the Royal Academy in 1786 after the successful showing of his historical painting

"Murder of David Rizzio", and in the following year was made a full member. His work was characterized by broad and vigorous treatment. There is a self-portrait by Opie in the Royal Academy and other works by him in the National Portrait Gallery, London.

OPIUM, a milky exudation from the unripe capsules of the poppy, produced chiefly in Hindustan, Iran, Egypt, Turkey, and Bulgaria. China produced probably double the amount grown in other countries, all of which was consumed at home. Opium is imported into Europe and America chiefly from Egypt and the Levant, while China absorbs most of the surplus of India and Persia. As found in commerce it is a chestnut or reddish-brown globular mass, sticky and rather soft, but hardening from within with age. It has a heavy narcotic odor and in taste is disagreeable and bitter. Chemically it is a mixture of alkaloids, the chief of which are codeine, morphine, and narcotine, with various organic acids, chiefly meconic acid. These are valuable in medicine for their sedative and narcotic properties, as is the gum itself, which is also smoked as an intoxicant. The greater part of the opium produced is used illicitly as an intoxicant. It produces agreeable dreams, profound sleep, and, in sufficiently large doses, death. Its antidotes are strong tea and other stimulants and sharp electric shocks. An opium agreement between the Chinese and British governments was signed on May 8, 1911. It provided that China should annually diminish the production of opium proportionately with the Indian export until extinction of both in

The common American opossum

1917. This agreement, however, did not bring the expected results and was superseded by the League of Nations conventions, effective 1928 and 1933, which limited production of and regulated trade in narcotics. Gen. MacArthur forbade all activities in opium and other narcotics, and ordered crops destroyed in Japan in October, 1945.

OPIUM WAR, a war between Great Britain and China, 1840–42, resulting from the attempt of the Chinese government to prevent the importation of opium from India. By the Treaty of Nanking, which closed the war, China opened certain ports to foreign trade and ceded Hong Kong to Great Britain.

OPOLE (Ger. *Oppeln*), city and capital of the voivodship of the same name, Poland, situated on the Oder R., about 52 miles S.E. of Wroclaw. It is a cattle-trading, railroad, and manufacturing center. Industries include the manufacture of iron products, cement, cement blocks, chemicals, cigars, tile, and soap. The chief points of interest are the Church of St. Adalbert (10th cent.) and a 14th-century church in the late-Gothic style. A prosperous Polish community in late medieval times, it became an Austrian possession in 1532 and passed to Prussian sovereignty in 1772. Oppeln was the capital of Upper Silesia until the partition (1919) of that province. In January, 1945, during World War II, the Red Army captured the city from the Germans. It was transferred to Polish control later that year by the terms of the Potsdam Conference. Area of voivodship, 3633 sq.m.;

pop. (1946) 792,234. Pop. of city (1946) 27,666.

OPORTO, second city of Portugal, standing on the steep, rocky, right bank of the Douro, high above its waters, which reach the sea 3 m. to the w. Owing to the bar at the mouth of the Douro, an Atlantic harbor has been constructed at Lexoes, 4 m. further N. There are seven principal churches, including the cathedral (built by Henry the Navigator), the old Gothic church of Cedofeita (originally founded in 559), and the Torre dos Clérigos. Oporto possesses a polytechnic academy, an observatory, scientific collections, medical school, art academy, commercial museum, industrial institution, library, and two picture galleries. The inhabitants are engaged chiefly in the manufacture of woolen, cotton, and silk fabrics; in tanning, brewing, distilling, cork-cutting, sugar-refining, and brickmaking; and in commerce and shipping. Oporto is the principal place of export for port wine. Pop. (1950) 284,842.

OPOSSUM, name applied to any of over eighty species of American marsupial mammals constituting the family Didelphidae. Opossums are found throughout the Western Hemisphere. Opossums range in size from about six inches to about thirty inches in total length, and usually have long, naked, scaly, prehensile tails two to ten inches long. Several species possess the birth pouch characteristic of marsupials; in most species, however, this pouch is rudimentary or absent. Opossums have as many as twenty-five nipples in the pouch region. Each foot contains five digits, the outer four of which bear sharp claws; the inner digit, which is opposable, has a nail instead of a claw. Fifty teeth are present in the opossum's jaws, consisting of ten incisors in the upper jaw, eight in the lower jaw, four canine teeth, twelve premolars, and sixteen molars. Four to fourteen young are produced in a litter; three litters may be brought forth in a year. Many species are omnivorous, some are completely insectivorous, and others subsist only on aquatic animals. Most opossums are arboreal animals which sleep in trees during the day, and hunt for food at night. A few species are strictly terrestrial and some are aquatic. Opossums habitually feign death when frightened; this habit has given rise to the popular expression "playing possum". Opossums are edible and are also valued by man for their fur.

The largest opossum is the common American species, *Didelphis virginiana*, found throughout eastern United States. The body

length of this beast is twenty inches; the tail
is ten inches long. The animal, which possesses
a well-developed birth pouch, has a covering
of long, sleek, gray hairs with an undercoating
of soft, woolly fur. It has a pointed, slender
face, and large, broad, naked ears. American
opossum baked with sweet potatoes is a
Southern culinary delicacy; the animal is
hunted with the aid of dogs and, when treed,
is commonly captured by means of a forked
stick. The lowlands opossum of tropical America, *D. marsupialis*, is a foul-smelling animal
which often invades villages and farms. Its
outer coat is usually black; its inner coat is
creamy white. Adult males of this vicious,
carnivorous species develop a pair of long,
sharp tusks in each jaw. The uplands opossum,
D. paraguayensis, is found at heights of about
12,000 feet in the Paraguayan Andes.

OPOSSUM SHRIMP, common name applied to any of the small, shrimplike mala-
costracan crustaceans constituting the genus
Mysis of the order Mysidacea. Opossum
shrimps differ from true shrimps chiefly in
having six pairs of legs instead of ten. The
animals, found in salt water and fresh water
in most temperate regions, reach a length of
about one inch. The female opossum shrimp
carries its eggs in a pouch between its legs,
whence the common name of this creature.

OPPELN. See OPOLE.

OPPENHEIM, E(DWARD) PHILLIPS (1866–
1946), English author of over 150 novels,
mostly "thrillers", many short stories, plays,
and the autobiographic *Pool of Memory*
(1941). The *Great Impersonation* (1920) is
his best-known novel.

OPPENHEIMER, J. ROBERT (1904–   ),
American physicist, born in New York City,
and educated at Harvard, Cambridge, and
Göttingen universities. After serving as a fellow with the National Research Council
(1927–28) and with the International Education Board (1928–29), he was assistant professor of physics (1929–31), associate professor
(1931–33), and full professor (1933–47) at
the University of California and at the California Institution of Technology, both institutions sharing his services during these years.
During a leave of absence (1943–45) he served
as director of the atomic-bomb project at
Los Alamos, N.M. In 1947 he became director of the Institute for Advanced Study
in Princeton, N.J. He was chairman of the
General Advisory Committee of the Atomic
Energy Commission from 1947 to December,
1953, when he was suspended pending a review of charges that long association with

communists made him a poor security risk.
In June, 1954, the A.E.C. upheld the charges
and denied him clearance for access to restricted information. Internationally known
for his leadership at Los Alamos, Oppenheimer is noted also for his contributions relating to the quantum theory, cosmic rays,
and relativity. Among his writings is *Science
and the Common Understanding* (1954) and
Open Mind (1955).

OPPER, FREDERICK BURR (1857–1937),
American illustrator and cartoonist, born in
Madison, Ohio. He first contributed to comic
papers and later was on the staffs of *Frank
Leslie's Magazine* and the New York *Journal*.
He was associated with the humorous weekly
Puck from 1880 to 1899. Noted for his sharp,
humorous drawings, he illustrated books by
Edgar Wilson (known as Bill) Nye and by
Mark Twain, and the *Mr. Dooley* series by
Finley Peter Dunne. The popular comic-strip
characters Happy Hooligan and Alphonse and
Gaston were created by Opper.

OPPIAN, the name of two Greek didactic
poets of antiquity. **1.** A poet, born in Corycus
in Cilicia, who flourished in the 2nd century
A.D. He composed a work in five books on fishing, entitled *Halieutica*, which is extant. The
poem, written in an ornate and artificial style,
was dedicated to the Roman emperor Marcus
Aurelius and his son Commodus. **2.** The author of a poem in four books on hunting, entitled *Cynegetica* and probably composed
early in the 3rd century A.D. This poet speaks
of his home as Apamea, in Syria. The metrical
structure of the poem, which is extant, is inferior to that of *Halieutica*.

OPTIC, OLIVER. See ADAMS, WILLIAM
TAYLOR.

OPTIC NEURITIS. See EYE, DISEASES OF
THE.

OPTICS, subdivision of the science of
physics relating to the study of light. The
study of optics is usually divided into two
parts: *geometrical optics,* the study of reflection and refraction of light; and *physical optics,* the study of the spectral composition of
light and of such phenomena as absorption,
diffraction, and polarization of light.

For the purpose of basic optics, light can
be regarded as a form of electromagnetic
radiation consisting of vibrations of waves
which are transverse to the line of travel of
the radiation. Light radiation or light rays are
assumed to travel in straight lines from the
point at which they originate, and to move
at a speed of 186,000 m. per second in a vacuum. Visible light consists of radiations having

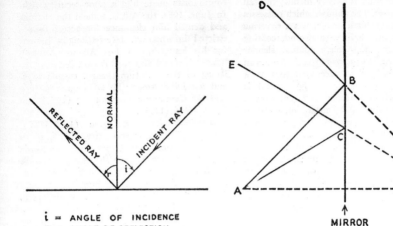

i = ANGLE OF INCIDENCE
r = ANGLE OF REFLECTION

Fig. 1

MIRROR

Fig. 2

wave lengths from .00004 cm. to .00007 cm. Ultraviolet radiation, which is usually regarded as a form of light, has wave lengths between .000001 and .00004 cm.; and infrared radiation, or heat radiation, which is also regarded as a form of light, has wave lengths between .0007 cm. and .1 cm. For further discussion of the nature of light, see LIGHT; QUANTUM THEORY; RADIATION; SPECTRUM.

Geometrical Optics. When a light ray traveling through air or some other homogeneous medium impinges on an object, the light is either reflected by the object, transmitted through the object, or absorbed by the object. A transparent material, such as glass, transmits a large part of the light which falls on it, absorbing the remainder. Opaque surfaces reflect part of the light and absorb the remainder.

The reflection of light is governed by two fundamental laws. The first law states that, for a single ray of light, the *incident ray* (the ray of light impinging on the surface), the *reflected ray,* and the *normal to the surface* (the line perpendicular to the surface at a given point) all lie in the same plane. The second law states that the angle of incidence is equal to the angle of reflection. These laws are illustrated in fig. 1. The angles of incidence and reflection are the angles between the paths of the incident and reflected rays and the normal.

A source of light placed in front of a smooth, polished, opaque surface such as a mirror appears to an observer to lie behind the surface. The reason for this appearance

can be understood by reference to fig. 2. A point on the light-source A sends out rays in all directions. As shown in the figure, two of these rays strike the mirror at B and C and are reflected as the rays BD and CE. To an observer in front of the mirror both of these rays seem to come from the point F behind the mirror. Light from all the other points of the light source is similarly reflected and similarly appears to come from specific points behind the mirror. An observer seeing all these points sees an image of the original light source lying behind the mirror at a distance equal to the distance between the original source and the surface of the mirror.

Opaque objects which do not have smooth surfaces do not show reflected images. Instead, the incident light is scattered on reflection, because the normals to the surface at different points are not parallel to each other as they are in the case of a smooth surface. Such diffuse reflection is characteristic of most opaque objects.

Curved Mirrors. The laws of reflection are applicable to curved mirrors as well as to flat ones, and mirrors of this type reflect images which are either enlarged or diminished in size and either upright or inverted, depending upon the relative positions of the mirror and the object reflected. The images are also *real* or *virtual,* depending on the relation between object and mirror. (A real image is one formed when the rays of light from a point pass through another point after reflection or refraction. A virtual image of a point is a point from which such rays apparently diverge after reflection or refraction. The reflection in a flat mirror is a virtual image; and the image of the sun when focused on a piece of paper with a magnifying or burning glass is a real image.)

The characteristics of a curved mirror are determined by the distance between the mirror and the point, called the *principal focus*, at which parallel rays of light (for example, light from a very distant object such as the sun) meet after reflection. In a curved mirror with a spherical surface, the principal focus is located halfway between the mirror and the center of curvature of the mirror surface, as shown in fig. 3.

The image reflected in a concave spherical mirror is real, inverted, and diminished in size, if the object reflected is outside the center of curvature. If the object is between the principal focus and the center of curvature, the reflected image is real, inverted, and enlarged; and if the object is between the surface of the mirror and the principal focus, the image is virtual, upright, and enlarged. Images reflected in convex spherical mirrors are always virtual, upright, and diminished, and mirrors of this kind are often called reducing mirrors. A series of simple algebraic relations exists between the focal length (the distance from the surface of the mirror to its principal focus), and the distances of object and image from the mirror, and the sizes of the object and the image. The relation between the distances is expressed by the equation $\frac{1}{u} + \frac{1}{v} = \frac{1}{f}$; when u is the distance from the object to the mirror, v the distance from the mirror to the image, and f the focal length of the mirror. The relation between the sizes of the image and the object is given by the equation $\frac{a}{b} = \frac{v}{u}$; when a is the size of the image and b is the size of the object.

Spherical mirrors which are of comparatively large size compared to their focal lengths suffer from a defect known as *spherical aberration*. Parallel rays of light striking the surface of such mirrors are not reflected exactly through the principal focus, except for those reflected from a small area around the center of the mirror, and as a result the images of distant objects formed by such mirrors are not sharp. In cases in which concave mirrors are used as optical magnifying devices, as in astronomical telescopes, or as reflectors to produce light beams with parallel rays, as in automobile headlights and searchlights,

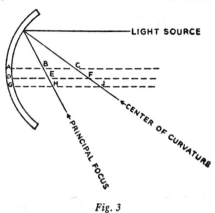

Fig. 3

parabolic mirrors are used. In such mirrors, in which the concave surface is a portion of a paraboloid of revolution, parallel light rays striking all portions of the mirror are reflected exactly to the focus without spherical aberration. When a light source is placed at the focus, the light is reflected from the mirror as a beam of parallel rays.

Refraction of Light. The speed of propagation of light is at a maximum in a vacuum and is less than maximum in transparent substances and still less in translucent substances. The direction of rays of light is unaffected by passage from one medium into another medium in which the speed of propagation differs if the rays are perpendicular to the boundary between the two media. If, however, the rays strike the boundary obliquely, they are bent or *refracted* from their straight-line path to a degree proportionate to the difference between the light velocities in the two media. An everyday example of refraction is the appearance of objects underwater to an observer looking obliquely at the surface of the water. Because of refraction the objects appear closer to the observer than they actually are. Light rays entering a medium in which the velocity of propagation is slower are bent toward the normal, and rays entering a medium in which the propagation speed is faster are bent away from the normal, as shown in fig. 4.

The amount of refraction in any instance depends on the ratio of the speeds of light in the two media. This ratio is called the *index of refraction* of the second medium with respect to the first. The index of refraction of any substance with respect to a vacuum is known as the absolute index of refraction. For practical purposes the speed of light in air

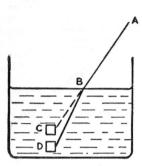

Fig. 4

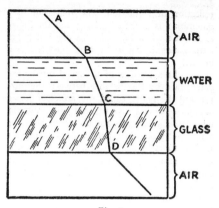

Fig. 5

is almost identical with the speed in a vacuum (speed of light in air = 1; speed of light in a vacuum = 1.00029) and therefore indices of refraction are commonly regarded as the ratios between air and other substances.

The two basic laws of refraction resemble those of reflection. The first law states that the incident ray, the refracted ray, and the normal to the surface of the boundary between the two media lie in the same plane. The second law (sometimes called *Snell's law*) states that the sine of the angle of incidence is equal to the sine of the angle of refraction multiplied by the refractive index. The index of refraction for any substance varies somewhat for different wave lengths of light, so that when such indices are stated accurately, the specific wave length must be given.

A ray of light passing through layers of media with differing refractive indices having parallel faces behaves as shown in fig. 5. The incident ray A is refracted to B as it passes into the water layer, and refracted still farther to C as it enters the glass. Leaving the glass at D, it is refracted in the opposite direction and is parallel to the incident ray but displaced.

When light falls on a *prism,* a wedge-shaped transparent body with flat faces, it is refracted as shown in fig. 6. The angle CBD between the path of the incident ray and the path of the emergent ray is called the *angle of deviation.* When the angle which the incident ray makes with the normal is equal to the angle made by the emergent ray, the angle of deviation is at a minimum. By measuring the angle of minimum deviation of a prism and the angle between the prism's faces, the index of refraction of the prism material may be determined.

Light passing from a denser medium into a thinner one, as from water to air, is bent away from the normal so that the angle of refraction is greater than the angle of incidence. If the angle of incidence is increased the angle of refraction is also increased, until the refracted light is at 90° to the normal and travels along the boundary between the two media. The angle of incidence corresponding to a 90° angle of refraction is known as the *critical angle.* If the angle of incidence is increased beyond the critical angle, the light rays will not leave the denser medium, but will be reflected back into it at the surface. Such reflection is known as *total reflection* and occurs only in the case of light passing from a denser to a thinner medium. The three drawings in fig. 7 show respectively ordinary refraction, refraction at the critical angle, and total reflection.

Lenses. The refraction of light is practically utilized chiefly by means of *lenses,* which are transparent objects having either cylindrical or spherical surfaces. All lenses can be divided into two general types according to the way in which they refract incident light. Lenses having one or two convex surfaces bend incident parallel rays of light inward toward the axis of the lens so that they converge at a

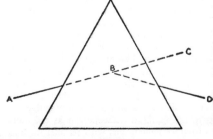

Fig. 6

focus. Such lenses are called *converging* lenses. Lenses having one or both surfaces concave refract incident parallel rays of light outward from the axis so that the rays are apparently radiating from a focus or focal point behind the lens. Such lenses are called *diverging* lenses. The focus of a converging lens is a *real focus* and that of a diverging lens a *virtual focus,* because in the latter the light rays do not actually pass through the focus. The distance from the center of any lens to its focus is called its *focal length.* The focal length of a lens varies with the curvature of its surfaces. A lens with strongly curved surfaces makes the light rays converge or diverge rapidly and therefore has a short focal length. A lens with surfaces curved to a long radius converges or diverges more slowly and has a long focal length. As in the case of spherical mirrors, only light rays from the central portion of the lens are brought together accurately at the focus. Light rays from the outer zones of the lens converge at a point inside the focus, producing a blurred image. In lenses of long focal length and small diameter this spherical aberration is not important, but in large diameter lenses having shorter focal lengths, the curvatures of the lens surfaces must be varied to give less refraction in the outer zones of the lens so that the incident rays will all converge at the focal point.

The images produced by convex or converging lenses vary with the relative distance between the lens and the object. When the object is at a considerable distance from the lens, the image is real, inverted, and diminished. When the object is close to the lens but still farther away than the focal distance the image is real, inverted, and magnified. When the object is closer to the lens than the focal distance the image is virtual, upright, and magnified. Concave lenses form only virtual, erect, and diminished images, regardless of the distance between the object and the lens.

The relationships between the size of an object and of the image formed of it by a lens, and of the distance between the object and the image and the lens, are similar to those for spherical mirrors. The size of the image divided by the size of the object is equal to the distance of the image divided by the distance of the object. The ratio of the size of image and the size of object is called the *magnifying power* of the lens. When an object is being examined by a magnifying lens, it is placed inside the focus of the lens to produce an enlarged virtual image as indicated above. Such an arrangement is a simple microscope, and its magnifying power varies inversely with the focal length of the lens. Thus a simple microscope with a focal length of $\frac{1}{2}$ in. will give an image twice the size of one having a focal length of 1 in. When lenses are used to produce real images of distant objects, as in cameras and telescopes, the size of the image varies directly with the focal length of the lens, and hence the *magnification* increases as the focal length increases. The term "magnification" in such cases is misleading because it refers to the comparative size of the image given by the instrument and the image given by the human eye of the same object at the same distance. As the focal length of the human eye is approximately 1 in., the "magnification" given by viewing an object through a simple lens is approximately equal to its focal length in inches.

The entire amount of light passing through a lens depends upon its diameter, but the intensity of light in each portion of the image formed by a lens is dependent also on the focal length of the lens, because the area of the image increases in area in proportion with the square of the focal length. Thus a lens of 1 in. diameter and 4 in. focal length will admit the same total amount of light as a lens of 1 in. diameter and 8 in. focal length; but the image produced by the 8 in. lens will only be one quarter as bright as that produced by the 4 in. lens. The light-gathering power of lenses

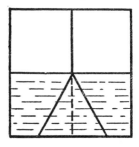 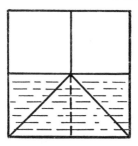 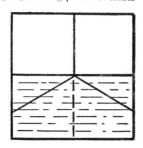

Fig. 7

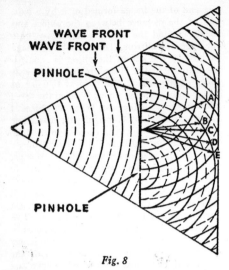

WAVE FRONT
WAVE FRONT ↓
PINHOLE

A
B
C
D
E

PINHOLE

Fig. 8

is expressed in terms of *relative aperture* (the ratio of the focal length to the effective diameter of the lens). Lenses having the same relative aperture have the same light-gathering power, whatever their diameters and focal lengths.

Physical Optics. As mentioned above, the amount of refraction of light passing through a prism varies for different wave lengths. The refraction of light of short wave lengths is greater than that of long wave lengths. If a narrow beam of white light passes through a prism this variable refraction or *dispersion* breaks up the beam into a spectrum or band of light of different colors, indicating that white light is composed of lights of various colors. If a second prism is set behind the first in a reverse position, the dispersed colors are recombined as white light.

The dispersion power of transparent substances varies widely. Some substances produce comparatively short spectra and others comparatively long ones. In addition, there are certain substances which exhibit the phenomenon of *anomalous dispersion,* dispersing certain portions of the spectrum more than others.

The dispersion of light of different colors makes it impossible for a simple converging lens to produce an absolutely sharp image of an object, as the focus of the lens differs for different colors. This defect of lenses is termed *chromatic aberration.* It is overcome by *achromatic lenses* made up of two elements, one converging and one diverging, so designed that the dispersions cancel each other. The

refractive power of the converging lens is greater than that of the diverging lens, so that the net effect of the compound lens is the same as that of a simple positive lens. For further discussion of colored-light phenomena, see COLOR; SPECTRUM; VISION.

Interference of Light. Two beams of light both having the same wave length but traveling different distances can interfere with each other and cancel each other out. This phenomenon, known as interference, was first demonstrated by the English physicist Thomas Young (1773–1829). In Young's original demonstration a narrow beam of light passing through a pinhole illuminated an opaque surface having two pinholes pierced in it, as in fig. 8, and shone on a screen beyond. Instead of being uniformly illuminated, the screen showed a pattern of alternating bright and dark circles. The explanation for this pattern is that at regular intervals, the light waves from the two pinholes arrive at the screen 180° out of phase, as at A, C, and E in the diagram, and neutralize each other. At other points, such as B and D in the diagram, the waves arrive in phase and reinforce each other. These alternations of neutralization and reinforcement produce the observed pattern of interference fringes. See INTERFERENCE.

A thin, transparent film such as an oil film also exhibits interference between light reflected from the front and back surfaces of the film. This type of interference has been put to practical use by coating of the lenses of cameras and other optical instruments with extremely thin oxide films to avoid reflection from their surfaces. In this manner any piece of glass or other transparent solid may be made completely nonreflecting. Another practical application of the interference principle is the testing of flat surfaces. If two absolutely flat pieces of glass are placed in contact and illuminated (preferably by light of a single wave length) interference fringes appear, caused by the thin layer of air remaining between the glass surfaces. If the illuminating source is in the form of a pinhole, the fringes appear in the form of regular concentric circles. If both the surfaces are not absolutely flat, the fringes are distorted and irregular. By using perfectly flat test plates of glass, the flatness of any surface may be tested by this method. Such test plates are known as *optical flats* and are widely employed for precision work in industry. Interference can also be used to measure distances in terms of a known wave length of light by means of an instrument called an *interferometer* (q.v.)

Diffraction. Although light rays generally travel in straight lines, this is not the case when a beam of light passes through a small opening or past the edges of an obstruction. In such cases the light is slightly bent or diffracted in passing the obstruction in the same way that ripples in the water are bent by a solid obstruction in the water. The bending is the result of a fundamental principle of wave motion, *Huygen's principle,* which states that every point on the front of an advancing wave behaves as a source of waves and sends these secondary waves out radially. As shown in fig. 9 a wave front reaching an obstruction will therefore produce a secondary wave that travels in a direction different from that of the original wave motion. The diffraction of light at a straight edge produces a series of shadow bands by interference. See also DIFFRACTION.

Polarization of Light. Ordinary light rays vibrate in all directions around the axis of propagation, and these vibrations persist when the light traverses all ordinary transparent media. If, however, a ray of light is passed through certain crystalline substances such as tourmaline, only vibrations in one plane are passed. The action of the crystal is analogous to the mechanical effect of a barrier with a single narrow slit placed over a stretched rope which is vibrating transversely in all directions. Beyond the barrier only those vibrations parallel to the slit appear, and if a second slit set at 90° to the first is placed over the rope behind the first slit, no vibration at all appears behind the second slit.

Light which has passed through a polarizing substance such as tourmaline appears to the naked eye identical to ordinary light, but

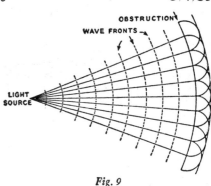

Fig. 9

if a second tourmaline crystal is placed behind the first and is rotated, a point is found at which almost all light disappears. This phenomenon occurs when the optical axes of the two crystals are at right angles to each other, and the second crystal passes none of the polarized light produced by the action of the first crystal. This effect is illustrated in fig. 10. Light reflected from a flat surface is also polarized in a plane parallel to the plane of the surface.

Some transparent substances, particularly sugar solutions, have the property of rotating the plane of polarization of a beam of polarized light. This fact is utilized in an instrument called the *polarimeter* to measure the concentration of sugar solutions. The solution to be examined is placed between two polarizers which are so oriented that no light passes them. After the solution is introduced, the light is no longer totally extinguished and one of the polarizers is rotated until extinction again occurs. As the amount of rotation varies

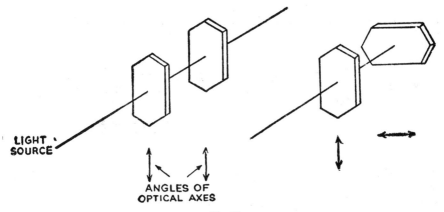

LIGHT
SOURCE

ANGLES OF
OPTICAL AXES

Fig. 10

with the strength of the solution, the strength can be calculated from the amount of rotation of the polarizer necessary to produce extinction of the light.

In the 1930's a patented polarizing material called Polaroid was introduced which eliminated the necessity of using elaborate devices such as the Nicol prism to produce polarized light. Polaroid is essentially a transparent plastic sheet containing a large number of minute polarizing crystals all oriented in the same direction. Polaroid has been employed in a number of ways, particularly in photographic and technical apparatus. One of the simplest applications of this material is for sunglasses. Polaroid glasses are so oriented that they pass only vertically polarized light. The light reflected from the surface of the water or from roads and pavements is strongly polarized in the horizontal direction and therefore the glasses reduce the glare from such surfaces without cutting down the illumination from other objects.

OPTIMISM, the doctrine that the existing order of things is, as a whole, the most perfect or the best which could have been created, or which it is possible to conceive. Some advocates of optimism maintain the position that, although God was not bound to create the most perfect order of things, yet the existing order is *de facto* the best; others contend that the perfection and wisdom of God necessarily require that His creation should be the most perfect. The philosophical discussions of which this controversy is the development are as old as philosophy itself, but the full development of the optimistic theory as a philosophical system was reserved for Leibnitz, in his *Théodicée*. The work was designed to meet the skeptical theories of Bayle, and its theories were ridiculed in Voltaire's *Candide*. The opposite doctrine is *Pessimism*.

OPTOMETRY. See Sight, Defects of.

OPUNTIA. See Prickly Pear.

ORACLE, the response delivered by a deity or supernatural being to a worshiper or inquirer; also the place where the response was delivered. The responses were supposed to be given by divine afflatus, either through means of mankind, or by their effect on certain objects, as the tinkling of the caldrons at Dodona; or by the actions of sacred animals. Oracles date from the greatest antiquity. Among the Egyptians all the temples were probably oracular. In later days one of the most renowned oracles was that of Ammon in the Oasis. Oracles were used by the Hebrews, as in the consultation of the Urim and Thum-

min by the high priest. There were oracles in Phenicia, as that of Beelzebub, and others of the Baalim. They were also in use throughout Babylonia and Chaldæa. The most renowned Greek oracle was the Delphic oracle. In Asia Minor the most celebrated was the oracle of Branchidæ, close to Miletus.

ORADEA, or Oradea Mare, city and capital of the Region of the same name, Romania, situated on the Körös R., near the Hungarian border. It is a railway junction, the commercial center of an important grape-growing area, and has potteries, distilleries, and food-processing plants. Among the noteworthy features are the churches of seven religious groups, notably the parish church containing the remains of St. Ladislaus, who founded a bishopric in 1080. Oradea was ceded by Hungary to Romania following World War I. Occupied by Hungarian forces during World War II, it again passed to Romanian control after 1945. Pop., about 82,000.

ORAN, a fortified seaport of Algeria, the capital of Oran department, on the Gulf of Oran, 261 miles s.w. of Algiers. Alfa, iron ore, and cereals are the chief exports. Pop. (1948) 256,661. Oran was built by the Moors. The French took possession of it in 1831. The department of Oran has an area of 23,500 sq.m. Pop. (1948) 1,990,729.

ORANG. See Orangutan.

ORANGE, the fruit of several trees of the genus *Citrus*, especially the sweet orange, *C. sinensis*, the bitter orange, *C. aurantium*, and the mandarin orange, or tangerine, *C. nobilis*. The fruit is technically a berry; it consists of several easily separated carpels, each containing several seeds and many juice cells, covered by a leathery epicarp, or skin, containing numerous oil glands. Orange trees are evergreens, seldom exceeding 30 feet in height; the leaves are oval and glossy; the flowers are white and fragrant. Three different essential oils are obtained from the orange: oil of orange, or oil of orange peel, obtained from the rind of the fruit, and used principally as a flavoring agent; oil of petitgrain, obtained from the leaves and twigs, and used in perfumery; and oil of neroli, obtained from the blossoms, and used in flavorings and perfumes. See Curaçao; Bergamot.

The orange is of great commercial importance. The tree is a native of s.e. Asia, and was introduced to cultivation in the countries of the Mediterranean region by the Arabs about the 10th century. It is now cultivated in most of the warm regions of the world. In the United States the principal orange-producing States are Florida (the orange blossom is the official State flower of Florida), California, Texas, and Arizona. In a recent year the production of oranges in the United States was almost 5,000,000 tons. The principal varieties of the sweet orange cultivated by orange growers of eastern U.S. are the Hamlin and Parson Brown, both early-maturing, seedy varieties with thin, russet skin and juicy pulp. Both eastern and western growers cultivate the Valencia, a late variety which is commercially "seedless", having two to five seeds. The principal crops of the western growers consist of the Valencia and the Bahia or Washington navel orange, imported from Bahia, Brazil, in 1870, and developed in Washington, D.C., by the U.S. Department of Agriculture. The navel orange is a seedless orange, with medium-thick rind, in which a second small, or abortive, orange grows. A variety of the Washington navel orange is the principal orange product of Texas. The bitter orange is cultivated to a limited extent for preserving fruit and to provide root stock for less vigorous strains. About thirty percent of the total crop of oranges is sold as whole fruit; the remainder is used in making canned juices, extracts, and preserves.

ORANGE, a city of Essex Co., N.J., 12 miles w. of New York, with diversified manufactures. It was settled about 1666. Pop. (1950) 38,037.

ORANGE, Prince of. See William I, the Silent; William III, King of England.

ORANGE FREE STATE, a province of the Union of South Africa (q.v.), situated between the Vaal R. on the N. and the Orange R. on the s. The capital and largest city is Bloemfontein (q.v.). The province is largely a plateau, lying from 4000 to over 5000 ft. above sea level. Mountains in the E. descend gradually to great plains, with very few trees except along the rivers. The Orange Free State is primarily pastoral, and cattle, horses, goats, and sheep are raised in huge herds. Farming districts are chiefly in the E.; crops include wheat, corn, oats, potatoes, tobacco, apples, and plums, and Kaffir corn. Diamonds are mined in the s.w., and coal in the N. A government-owned railroad extends for 1663 m. in the province. Education is free and compulsory for children between the ages of seven and sixteen. The University College (founded 1855) of the Orange Free State is situated at Bloemfontein. English and Afrikaans (South African Dutch) are both official languages.

The first European settlements in the region were made between 1810 and 1820. In 1836,

Florida Citrus Commission
Florida oranges

to this area, occurred the great emigration, called the "great trek", of Boers (q.v.) from the Cape Colony, where they were dissatisfied with British government. The Boers created a republic which, in 1848, was annexed by force by the British, who named it the Orange River Sovereignty. Six years later Great Britain relinquished the territory, which then became known as the independent Orange River Free State. In 1899 the republic joined itself with the Transvaal (q.v.) in the South African War (q.v.) against Great Britain. The country was occupied by the British in March, 1901, and in May of that year was annexed by Great Britain as the Orange River Colony. During the settlement of peace terms in 1902, the State acknowledged British sovereignty. In 1907 the colony was granted responsible government similar to that of the Transvaal. In 1910, as the Province of the Orange Free State, the region was incorporated into the Union of South Africa. Area, 49,647 sq.m.; pop. (1951 prelim.) 1,018,207.

ORANGEMEN, members of the Orange Society, formed by Protestants in County Armagh, Ireland, after the battle of the Boyne in 1690, which was fought between Protestant and Roman Catholic forces. The name of the Society is based upon the Protestant support of William III (former Prince of Orange), who succeeded to the British throne in 1689 after Protestants succeeded in ousting the Catholic Stuart king, James II. The Society grew rapidly, establishing many lodges in both England and North America. The Orangemen were, however, charged with anti-Catholic bigotry, and were forced by Parliament to suspend their activities in Ireland from 1813

Ringling Bros. and Barnum & Bailey

Dizzy Dean, a performing orangutan with the Ringling Brothers and Barnum & Bailey Circus

to 1828. At the present time the Society enjoins toleration and good will toward Catholics upon its members, and has become principally a fraternal order. The most important holiday of the Society is celebrated on July 12, the anniversary of the battle of the Boyne.

ORANGE RIVER, the principal river of South Africa. Its farthest head stream rises on the slope of Champagne Castle, about 120 miles from the Indian Ocean. It flows in a general westward course, first southwestward through Basutoland, then forming the south boundary of the province of the Orange Free State, after which it flows across the northern part of the province of the Cape of Good Hope, and finally forms the boundary between the latter and the protectorate of Southwest Africa, until it empties into the Atlantic Ocean. Its total length is over 1300 miles. The chief tributary is the Vaal.

ORANGUTAN, ORANGOUTANG, or ORANG (Malay, *oran,* "man"; *utan,* "wild"), an anthropoid ape, *Pongo pygmaeus,* found in the moist forests of Borneo and Sumatra, and characterized by reddish-brown hair which attains a length of over a foot on the arms and thighs. The orangutan, which attains a standing height of four and one half feet, lacks hair on its face, hands, and feet. The animal's head is large; its forehead is high; its ears are small; its nose is manlike; its chin recedes. Natives call the beast the "man of the woods". The orangutan has a thick neck, a robust body with a corpulent abdomen, long arms, and short, bowed legs. It lives alone or with a mate and leads an arboreal existence, swinging from branch to branch during the day, feeding on leaves and fruit, and constructing platforms of branches and leaves high in the trees as a resting place. The beast virtually never attacks man, and is docile in captivity. It can be tamed and trained, but is not as intelligent as the chimpanzee.

ORATORIO, a musical composition of a religious or epic character, performed by solo voices and chorus accompanied by a full orchestra, and in modern times usually presented without stage action, costumes, or scenery. Like the opera (q.v.), the oratorio developed out of the medieval liturgical dramas and miracle plays. The earliest oratorios were a form of sacred opera; they were performed with elaborate scenic effects, and were sponsored by the Roman Catholic Church. They differed from the opera only in that the subject matter was of a prescribed religious nature. With the introduction, in the mid-17th century, of a narrator to present each personality and to explain the action, scenery was no longer necessary, but dramatic and narrative qualities were retained. The oratorio is now distinguished from opera by this lack of theatrical settings, by the presence of a narrator, and by an emphasis on the chorus.

In the middle of the 16th century, the Italian priest San Filippo de' Neri founded the Congregation of the Oratory and lectured on Biblical history in the oratory (chapel) of his church in Rome. These lectures were illustrated by the singing of religious poems, and the practice eventually led to the development of the musical form subsequently known as the oratorio. Many such "oratorios" were composed throughout the 16th century, especially by the Italian composer Giovanni Palestrina, but only that of Emilio de' Cavalieri is extant; his *Rappresentazione di Anima e di Corpo* (about 1600) is considered the first known oratorio. Until the following century the form remained much like that of the opera, with elaborate staging and display. In the middle of the 17th century Giacomo Carissimi, Kapellmeister at Assisi and later at Rome, created the role of the narrator, and the oratorio proper was born. Carissimi's disciple was Alessandro Scarlatti, eighteen of whose works in this form are preserved. The oratorios of Scarlatti's contemporaries, including Antonio Lotti, Antonio Caldara, Alessandro Stradella, and Leonardo Leo, flourished along with their operas, and usually exhibited a characteristically operatic style and secular emphasis.

"Passion" music, dramatizing the suffering and death of Jesus Christ, was first composed in Germany at about this time, and restored to the oratorio much of its original religious emphasis. In this respect, the works of Heinrich Schütz were outstanding. The German tradition initiated by Schütz was continued by Johann Sebastian Bach, particularly in his *Christmas Oratorio* (1733–34) and five Passion oratorios, of which only the *Passions According to the Gospel of St. Matthew* (1729) and *St. John* (1723–29) remain. George Frederick Handel revived the elements of operatic style in the oratorio, making of it a theatrical entertainment rather than the deeply religious work composed by his German contemporaries. Handel wrote oratorios to Italian, German, and English texts, the most popular of which are *The Messiah* (1720), *Saul* (1730), *Israel in Egypt* (1739), *Belshazzar* (1744), *Judas Maccabeus* (1746), and *Solomon* (1748).

The oratorio form gained great popularity, particularly in England and Germany, during the 18th and 19th centuries. Joseph Haydn wrote many; his *Seven Words on the Cross* (1797) and *The Creation* (1797–98) are perhaps the best known. In the 19th century the oratorios of greatest artistic merit are probably those of Felix Mendelssohn, whose works in the form include *St. Paul* (1836) and *Elijah* (1846). Richard Wagner in Germany, and Hector Berlioz, Charles François Gounod, Jules Massenet, and César Franck in France were among others in the 19th century to compose oratorios. Special mention may be made of Johannes Brahms' *Deutsches Requiem* (1857–68), which, though it is a musical paraphrase of Scriptural passages rather than an oratorio in the strict sense of the term, nevertheless is often considered an extension of the religious oratorios of the time of Bach.

The oratorio tradition has been continued in the 20th century in many countries, and modern vocal and orchestral techniques peculiar to this century have been applied to the form. Popular examples, among others, are the Swiss-born Arthur Honegger's *Le Roi David* (1923), the Englishman William Turner Walton's *Belshazzar's Feast* (1931), the Frenchman Vincent d'Indy's *Legend of St. Christopher* (1915), the Russian-born Igor Stravinsky's *Œdipus Rex* (1927), and the German Paul Hindemith's *Das Unaufhörliche* (1931).

ORATORY, CONGREGATION OF THE, either of two religious associations. **1.** The Oratory of Saint Philip Neri, rules of which were codified under Baronius, and approved by Pope Paul V, 1612. Its essential constitution is that of a body of priests living in community, but without monastic vows. This order became celebrated in England by the accession of Newman (afterward cardinal). **2.** The Oratory of Jesus, a French congregation founded in 1611 by Pierre de Berulle. It was involved in the Jansenist troubles, and suffered great losses in the French Revolution, but was revived later.

ORCAGNA, real name ANDREA DI CIONE (1308?–68?), Italian painter, sculptor, mosaicist, and architect, born in Florence. In 1343 he became a member of the painters' guild of Medici e Speziali. A follower of the painting tradition of the Florentine artist Giotto, Orcagna was regarded as one of the leading masters of the period. The only painting known to be an entirely independent work by Orcagna is an altarpiece, "Christ Enthroned with Saints", created for the Strozzi Chapel in Santa Maria Novella in 1357; in this work the firmly drawn figures stand out in bold relief from the background. The same chapel contains frescoes by Orcagna which became injured and were later, in the 15th century, reworked by the Florentine painter Ghirlandajo. In 1355 Orcagna began work on the famed sculptured tabernacle at the church of Or San Michele, Florence, intermittently visiting Orvieto to direct the construction of, and also execute mosaics for, the cathedral there. From 1364 to 1367 he was occupied with the construction of the cathedral of Florence. He became a member of the sculptors' guild in 1352, and carved many fine works that anticipated the style of the High Renaissance.

ORCHARD, term applied to an area of land on which fruit trees are cultivated. Fruit cultivation began in the United States in colonial days as an adjunct of common farming. The ground surface of farm orchards, generally covered with grasses, was valued primarily for its utility in grazing small livestock such as sheep, and the fruit was chiefly used for home consumption. The development of scientific methods of fruitgrowing, storage, and transportation led, in the 19th century, to the emergence of orchards as primary commercial crop sources.

Climate is the critical factor determining which fruits may be grown in a given area; citrus fruits and most commercially cultivated nuts are grown in warm regions and protected by artificial heat against unseasoned frosts. The quality of the yield is dependent on soil conditions. Fertility of the surface layer is necessary, but adequate depth and drainage of the surface layer are of greater importance. Trees separated by only a few hundred feet, but growing in soils with different drainage conditions, may vary in yield by ratios of 3 or 4 to 1. Most fruit trees are planted in rows spaced 20 feet apart in both directions; in apple orchards, however, this distance is increased to 40 feet. In orchards composed of dwarf trees, the intervening space is reduced. Many trees bear fruit in greater abundance when fertilized by pollen from other varieties of the same species; some varieties of apple, cherry, and plum bear practically none unless cross-pollinated. A common way of effecting cross-pollination is to intersperse several varieties throughout the orchard; pollen from each tree is dispersed at random and usually fertilizes fruits on a tree of a different variety.

Maintenance of orchard soil at maximum efficiency requires careful attention to soil moisture and supply of nitrogen. In late summer and early fall, maturation of fruit and development of resistance to low temperatures are hastened by reduction of nitrogen and moisture supply. This reduction is best accomplished by the growth of surface crops, such as legumes or cereal grains, which further serve to replenish the supply of humus and nitrogen when mowed in late fall. Irrigation is commonly employed in fruitgrowing in dry areas of northwestern United States and parts of California.

Heavy pruning, especially of young trees, was formerly performed to concentrate growth in branches which could be reached easily. This practice has been modified because of the discovery that heavy trimming delays bearing by several years. Young trees are now pruned sufficiently to retain their shape. Weak, diseased, or shading wood is always removed and, as the trees mature, crowding or crossing branches are eliminated. Additional pruning of mature trees is necessary to confine them to their allotted space and to keep fruit-bearing branches within practical picking distance. A few fruits, especially peaches and apricots, require extensive pruning to force proliferation of shoots and to increase the

size of fruit. Individual growers usually prune mature fruit trees severely, despite consequent reduction of total yield, because quality is usually sufficiently improved to justify the total cost, and because pruned trees produce hardier buds.

Distribution. The major fruit crop of the United States is the apple crop; apples are grown commercially in most parts of the country, the chief centers being the Great Lakes region, New England, and the Northwest. Apples also form the major Canadian fruit crop, being grown in Ontario, the chief fruit region of Canada, and in British Columbia and Nova Scotia. The chief grape-producing areas in the U.S. are California, the Great Lakes region, the Hudson Valley, and the Gulf States. The commercial production of pears is chiefly confined to the Pacific-coast States, Michigan, and New York; apricot growing is chiefly confined to California; and plum raising is chiefly confined to California, Oregon, and Washington. Citrus fruits are grown principally in California, Florida, and Texas, California producing most of the lemons and oranges and Florida and Texas most of the grapefruit. The chief center of sweet-cherry production is along the Pacific coast; sour cherries are grown in New York, Michigan, and Wisconsin.

Semitropical fruits other than citrus fruits, such as olives, dates, and avocados, are produced in small quantities in California, Arizona, and Florida; they are also imported from Mediterranean countries, chiefly France and Italy. Tropical fruits are not extensively cultivated in the United States. Small quantities of nuts are grown in the U.S.; pecans are grown in southern U.S. from Florida to Texas; walnuts are chiefly raised in California and Oregon; almonds are chiefly cultivated in California; filberts are raised in Washington and Oregon; and chestnuts are grown in a few isolated areas of the U. S.

See FRUIT.

ORCHESTRA, a large group of musicians playing various instruments as a unit, as distinct from the smaller chamber group or from the ensemble of special instruments, such as those consisting of wind instruments and drums and called a band. The word originally signified the section in the Greek theater which was reserved for the chorus of dancers; this use of the word is evident in the modern term for the space allotted to musicians in a theater, immediately in front of the stage, and by extension to the entire ground floor of a theater. The modern symphonic orchestra con-

N.B.C. Photo

Arturo Toscanini conducting the National Broadcasting Company Symphony Orchestra

sists of four sections: strings (violins, violas, cellos, and double basses), woodwinds (piccolos, flutes, oboes, English horn, clarinets, and bassoons), brass (horns, trumpets, trombones, and tuba), and percussion (drums and specialized percussion instruments such as cymbals and triangles). The strings generally carry the melodic line of a composition and are capable of playing most uninterruptedly; the woodwinds and brass instruments, each of which has a characteristic timbre, provide a great deal of the color and harmonic effects; the percussion group contributes many special color effects as well as a strong rhythmic support or emphasis.

The invention of many of the instruments of the modern symphonic orchestra, as well as the realization of the various capabilities of each, is of fairly recent origin. The prevalent musical medium during the Middle Ages was wholly or largely vocal. The Renaissance saw the growth of concerted instrumental music designed primarily for small chamber groups. By the 16th century, orchestras were commonly attached to the royal courts of Europe and provided entertainment for many occasions. The first composition written for orchestra in which various instruments had independent parts was *Sacrae Symphoniae* (1600) by the Italian composer Giovanni Gabrieli. A still greater instrumental differentiation was introduced by the Italian composer Claudio Monteverdi in his opera *Orfeo* (1607). String playing was emphasized in the 17th-century court orchestra of Jean Baptiste Lully in France. Instruments and standards of performance were greatly developed by the time of Johann Sebastian Bach and George

Frederick Handel. The number of instruments and their specific roles remained interchangeable, however, and the total effect was generally one of mass rather than of differentiation in color. Moreover, little attempt was made to exhibit the dramatic resources to each section of the orchestra.

The modern symphonic orchestra and modern styles of orchestration were introduced in Mannheim, Germany, in the middle of the 18th century. The conductor of the orchestra there was Johann Stamitz (q.v.); he was responsible for the exploitation of a new dynamic range, for the sharp differentiation in tempo between the slow and fast movements of a work, for the development of an individual character for each instrument, and for the practice of having the strings carry most of the melody. Orchestral parts were written out for the first time, replacing the thorough-bass method (see ORCHESTRATION). Joseph Haydn and Wolfgang Amadeus Mozart were greatly influenced by this orchestra, and in their works, and later in those of Ludwig van Beethoven, the foundations of modern symphonic orchestral practices were largely systematized.

Two other types of orchestra besides the symphonic are the chamber orchestra and the jazz orchestra. In the 18th and early 19th centuries the chamber orchestra consisted of a small ensemble of strings and woodwinds designed for the rendition of appropriate music in the intimate surroundings of the drawing room or private audience hall. At the present time, however, the chamber orchestra may include any combination of instruments so long as the essential condition of the inti-

British Information Services

INSTRUMENTS OF THE MODERN SYMPHONY ORCHESTRA. *Top: The violin section. Middle, left: French horn, a part of the brass section. Middle, right: Trumpet, also in the brass section. Bottom, left: Bassoon, a woodwind. Bottom. right: Piccolo and flute, woodwinds.*

mate setting is satisfied. Thus the diversity of the instruments may approximate those of a standard symphony orchestra, and the ensemble still be considered a chamber orchestra. Many compositions have already been written for this modern expanded type of chamber orchestra.

Jazz orchestras were originally known as jazz bands, since they seldom if ever contained any strings. The distinctive instruments of the old jazz ensembles were the trumpet and the cornet (see JAZZ). The jazz band became the jazz orchestra with the growth of so-called "symphonic jazz"; strings were made an integral feature of the new ensemble, and the number of brasses and woodwinds was considerably augmented. Present-day jazz orchestras, such as those of Andre Kostelanetz and Paul Whiteman, are virtually as large as the standard symphony orchestra.

ORCHESTRATION, or INSTRUMENTATION, in music, the art of combining instruments in the composition of orchestral music in order to achieve particular effects of tonal balance and color. Prior to the 16th century, the greater part of music was vocal, and methods of instrumentation were not well developed. On occasion, however, motets (q.v.) were accompanied by an organ bass part, from which the organist evolved fitting harmonies during a performance. This improvisational method led to the use of the thorough-bass method, prevalent during the 17th and 18th centuries, in which numerals inserted under the bass part indicated the principal intervals and chords which were to be played above the bass. The principal parts were those of the bass and the melody; all instruments which were not of a bass quality were usually considered suited only for melodic parts, with no regard for their individual timbres or the full effect of the combination of their colors. The strings, however, were diversified by Johann Sebastian Bach and George Frederick Handel, and organized into well-defined groups of first and second violins, violas, and cellos, supported by the harpsichord or organ and by double basses. With the 18th century wind instruments, particularly the woodwinds, began to stand out as obbligato and color relief; the functions of the brass instruments were comparatively limited because of their poor construction. Many instruments had been improved upon, however, by the time of Bach and Handel, and instrumentation itself had become of more concern to composers.

Symphonic orchestration was given its greatest impetus by the Mannheim orchestra (see ORCHESTRA) of the mid-18th century. The strings, particularly in the works of Joseph Haydn and Wolfgang Amadeus Mozart, developed as the backbone of the orchestra, carrying the melodic line and constituting the largest section. Each of the woodwinds developed a distinct character and became capable of carrying the melody when necessary. Brasses were gradually improved and their ranges extended. Moreover, composers developed the dramatic exploitation of each instrument's capabilities.

In the 19th century orchestration became more and more complex, especially in the hands of Hector Berlioz and Richard Wagner, who sought to add to the dramatic force and tonal quality of the orchestra. Instrumentation in the 20th century still further exploited instrumental potentialities. One school of composers, typified by Claude Debussy and Maurice Ravel, emphasized the sensuous and pictorial color effects available to the modern orchestra (see IMPRESSIONISM). Another school became known for extreme experiments in orchestration, breaking completely with classical methods; Igor Stravinsky, for example, one of the masters of modern orchestration, often gave the melody to the brass section and transferred the percussive function to the strings.

Orchestration in the sphere of modern popular music is closely associated with the history of jazz (q.v.). The characteristic dance ensemble of the early part of the 20th century represented a simplified form of the symphony orchestra, being composed of strings, brasses, and woodwinds on a greatly reduced scale. This orchestra was designed for the performance of popular music of European derivation, and had too many strings and too few percussion instruments for the dynamic requirements of the jazz idiom. These requirements were completely satisfied by the jazz band, which achieved standard form around 1912. The instruments of this ensemble were divided into three broad types, namely, *rhythm* (banjo or guitar, string bass, piano, and drums); *reeds* (clarinets and saxophones); and *brasses* (cornets, trumpets, and trombones). The rhythm instruments provided an insistent, throbbing accompaniment to the melodic line carried by the reeds and brasses.

In recent dance music, orchestra leaders have employed so-called "arrangers" who compose sets of free variations on popular melodies and provide the instrumentation specifically adapted to the resources of a particu-

Panama National Tourist Commission
The Holy Ghost orchid

lar orchestra. Notable among these arrangers have been Fletcher Henderson, Cy Oliver, and Teddy Wilson for the Benny Goodman Orchestra, and Billy Strayhorn and Edward Kennedy ("Duke") Ellington for the Duke Ellington Orchestra.

ORCHID, common name applied to perennial epiphytes and herbs constituting the family Orchidaceae of the order Orchidales. The family, which contains about 550 genera and almost 8000 species, is native to tropical and subtropical regions throughout the world, and is widely cultivated for the showy flowers of its members. Orchids of the genus *Vanilla* (q.v.) bear pods which yield the vanilla flavoring of commerce. Orchid flowers, which are usually solitary, are unlike the flowers of any other family of plants. They have three petal-like sepals and three petals, only two oi which are alike; the third petal, known as the *labellum,* may have any of a number of shapes; in the butterfly orchid the labellum resembles a butterfly. The stamens and pistils are united with the floral axis. The fruit is a dry capsule or pod. For further information on familiar cultivated orchids, see CATTLEYA; EPIDENDRUM; LADY'S-SLIPPER; ORCHIS; PHALAENOPSIS.

ORCHIS, common name applied to terrestrial herbs of the genus *Orchis* belonging to the Orchid family. The genus, which contains numerous species, is native to Eurasia; one species, *O. rotundifolia,* is found in North America. Orchises are especially abundant in Great Britain, adorning meadows and pastures with their red, lilac, white, or green flowers in summer. The orchid commonly called "showy orchis" in the United States is *Galeorchis spectabilis,* a species of a different genus than the true orchises, and characterized by deep-violet flowers borne in a spike.

ORCZY, BARONESS EMMUSKA (1865-1947), English novelist and playwright, born in Tarnaors, Hungary. From the age of sixteen she made her home principally in London. Her literary reputation was established with the novel *The Scarlet Pimpernel* (1905), a tale of French Revolutionary times featuring the exploits of a mysterious and daredevil titled Englishman in saving French aristocrats from the revolutionists. The novel was made into a successful play (1905) by Baroness Orczy and her husband Montagu W. Barstow, and was later filmed as a motion picture (1934); popular sequels to this work were *The League of the Scarlet Pimpernel, The Way of the Scarlet Pimpernel,* and *The Triumph of the Scarlet Pimpernel.* Among her other writings are the novels *Castles in the Air* (1921), *The Emperor's Candlesticks* (1937), and *Will-o'-the-Wisp* (1946).

ORDEAL, practice of referring disputed questions to the judgment of God, determined either by lot or by the success of certain experiments.

Throughout Europe the ordeal existed in various forms under the sanction of law, and was closely related to the oath. The most prevalent kinds of ordeal were those of *fire, water,* and the *wager of battle. Fire ordeal* was only allowed to persons of high rank. The accused had to carry a piece of red-hot iron for some distance in his hand, or to walk 9 ft. barefoot and blindfolded over red-hot plowshares. The hand or foot was bound up and inspected three days afterward; if the accused had escaped unhurt he was pronounced innocent; if otherwise, guilty. *Water ordeal* was the usual mode of trial allowed to bondsmen and rustics, and was of two kinds, the ordeal of *boiling water* and of *cold water.* The ordeal of *boiling water,* according to the laws of Athelstan, consisted of taking a stone out of boiling water, where the hand had to be inserted as deep as the wrist; the triple ordeal deepened the water to the elbow. The person allowed the ordeal of *cold water,* the usual mode for trial for witchcraft, was flung into a pool; if he floated he was guilty; while if he sank he was acquitted. In the *wager of battle* the defeated party, if he craved his life, was allowed to live as a "recreant", that is, on retracting the perjury to which he had sworn.

In the ordeal of the *bier,* a suspected murderer was required to touch the body of the murdered man, and pronounced guilty if the blood flowed from his wounds. The ordeal of the *eucharist* was in use among the clergy: the accused party took the sacrament in attestation of innocence. A similar ordeal was that of the *corsned,* or consecrated bread and cheese: if the accused swallowed it freely he was pronounced innocent; if it stuck in his throat he was presumed to be guilty.

In England the ordeal seems to have been continuous till the middle of the 13th century. On the Continent it was, generally speaking, abolished rather earlier, although as late as 1498 a Franciscan friar proposed that he and Savonarola undergo an ordeal by fire as a test of the truth of the doctrines preached by the latter.

ORDER. See COLUMN.

ORDERS, HOLY, sacrament by which ministers are set apart for the service of the Church of God. In the Roman and Greek churches a distinction is made between the major and minor orders. The major orders are bishop, priest, and deacon. A fourth rank of subdeacons is generally regarded as one of the major orders, for its functions closely resemble those of the deacon. Some theologians regard the episcopate not as a separate order, but as the completion and extension of the priesthood. The minor orders in the Roman Catholic Church are four, doorkeeper, exorcist, reader, and acolyte. To none of these is a vow of celibacy annexed. In the Greek Church there is one minor order, that of reader (*anagnōstēs*).

In the Anglican and other Reformed Episcopal churches the three higher orders of bishop, priest, and deacon are alone retained.

The New Testament contains frequent reference to the ceremonial of "laying on of hands" (Acts 6:1–7, 13:1–4, 14:23; 1 Tim. 4:14, 5:22; 2 Tim. 1:6). In the Roman, Greek, and eastern churches this rite is sacramental, and it is reserved to bishops. In the Anglican Church the rules of the ancient canon law are retained.

In other Reformed churches ordination is performed by the presbytery by imposition of hands, or by one or more ordinary ministers. Some smaller Protestant denominations have no ceremony of ordination whatever.

ORDERS IN COUNCIL. See CONTINENTAL SYSTEM.

ORDERS OF CHIVALRY, or **KNIGHTHOOD,** in modern usage, honorary societies, membership in which is generally conferred by a monarch, head of a government, or national legislature, on noblemen or persons who have performed some unusually meritorious service. Three categories of orders may be distinguished: royal orders, generally limited to noblemen of royal blood or of the highest grade; noble or family orders, open to noblemen generally; and orders of merit, bestowed on persons of all classes as a reward for distinguished service. Persons admitted to membership in an order generally receive a badge or medal and a formal title, such as "Knight Commander" or "Knight of the Grand Cross". The orders are believed to have originated during the age of feudalism (q.v.), when many noblemen, impoverished by their heavy expenditures during the Crusades or virtually disinherited through the operation of the law of primogeniture (q.v.), became professional soldiers in the service of various kings or other nobles. These knights formed organizations known as orders, which had special uniforms and insignia and were given distinctive names. The orders of the present day use the symbols and nomenclature of the feudal orders, but serve a purely honorary function.

The following list of the chief orders of knighthood, arranged by countries, gives (where obtainable) the date of foundation, name of founder, purpose of foundation, and description of badge.

BELGIUM. (1) *African Star* (1888) ; Leopold II; services to Belgian Congo and African civilization; 5-pointed star and laurel wreath. (2) *Iron Cross* (1867); Leopold II; civil merit; a black cross bordered in gold, with a lion on a gold field in the center. (3) *Leopold* (1832); Leopold I; civil and military merit; 8-pointed white cross edged with gold on a wreath of oak and laurel, suspended from a royal crown; in the center, a medallion bearing a golden lion on a black field, surrounded by a red fillet bearing the motto *L'Union Fait la Force* ("In Union There is Strength").

DENMARK. (1) *The Dannebrog* (1219); Waldemar II; reinstituted (1671) by Christian V; white cross patté edged with red and gold bearing the letter W in the center and the motto *Gud og Kongen* ("For God and King") on the arms. (2) *The Elephant* (1462) ; Christian I; renewed (1693) by Christian V; limited to princes of the blood and 30 knights; a silver star bearing a purple medallion on which is mounted a silver or diamond cross surrounded by a silver laurel wreath.

FRANCE. *Legion of Honor* (1802) ; Napoleon I; civil and military merit; 5-rayed white enameled star, having on the obverse a female head representing the republic and on the reverse two crossed flags.

GREAT BRITAIN. (1) *Bath* (1725) ; George I ; military and civil ; for the military, a gold Maltese cross botoné, enameled white ; in each of the four angles a lion of England ; in the center the rose, thistle, and shamrock ; for the civil, a gold oval, the external filled, containing a motto, and encircling the same device as the military. (2) *British Empire* (1917) ; George V ; for wartime services by men and women ; varies for different classes. (3) *Distinguished Service* (1886) ; Victoria ; military officers ; a white and gold cross with a red center bearing the imperial crown surrounded by a laurel wreath. (4) *Garter* (1350) ; Edward III ; limited to sovereigns, the Prince of Wales, and 25 knights. See GARTER. (5) *Merit* (1902) ; Edward VII ; two classes, one naval and military, the other science, art, or literature ; red-and-blue enamel cross, central blue medallion bearing the motto *For Merit* in gold, and encircled by wreath of laurel. (6) *Royal Victorian* (1896) ; Victoria ; for personal services to the sovereign ; white Maltese cross with crimson oval containing the royal and imperial cipher and the inscription *Victoria*. (7) *St. Michael and St. George* (1818) ; George IV ; for high colonial officers and services relating to foreign affairs ; varies for different classes. (8) *St. Patrick* (1788) ; George III ; for sovereign, governor of Northern Ireland, and 22 knights companions of noble rank ; white shield with cross of St. Patrick, shamrock, and three gold crowns with motto *Quis Separabit?* ("Who Will Divide Us?"). (9) *Star of India* (1861) ; Victoria ; motto *Heaven's Light Our Guide*. (10) *Thistle* (1687) ; James II ; revived in 1703 by Queen Anne ; for royalty and 16 Scottish nobles ; 8-pointed star with figure of St. Andrew and cross, and motto *Nemo Me Impune Lacessit* ("No One Harms Me With Impunity"). (11) *Victorian* (1896) ; Victoria ; personal services to the sovereign ; white Maltese cross with crimson oval containing the royal and imperial cipher.

GREECE. *Redeemer* (1829) ; National Assembly ; services in War of Liberation ; 8-pointed white cross with wreath ; in center, circle of blue containing figure of Christ.

ITALY. (1) *Annunciation* (1362) ; Amadeus VI ; restricted to 15 nobles ; gold medal, representing the Annunciation, entwined in chain of knots, with roses. (2) *St. Maurice and St. Lazarus* (1434) ; Amadeus VI ; service to the state, especially charities ; white enameled cross botoné against an 8-pointed green cross.

LUXEMBURG. *Oak Crown* (1841) ; William II ; general order of merit ; white, gold-edged cross patté, with oak crown around medallion.

NETHERLANDS. (1) *Netherlands Lion* (1815) ; William I ; civil merit ; 8-pointed cross with a gold W between the arms and a lion in the center. (2) *Orange-Nassau* (1892) ; Wilhelmina ; service to country or sovereign ; 8-pointed cross, blue and white, edged with gold ; national arms in laurel wreath. (3) *William* (1815) ; William I ; military ; white cross on a green laurel Burgundian cross, with Burgundian flint-steel in the center.

NORWAY. (1) *Norwegian Lion* (1904) ; Oscar II ; foreigners who obtain the order must be members of reigning houses or heads of states. (2) *St. Olaf* (1847) ; Oscar I ; civil and military merit ; 8-pointed white cross botoné, national arms on red ground.

PORTUGAL. (1) *Christ* (1318) ; Diniz ; for Catholic nobles ; gold-edged Latin cross of red and white enamel, surmounted by 8-pointed star. (2) *St. Benedict of Aviz* (1162) ; military ; green enamel cross with gold fleur-de-lis. (3) *St. James of the Sword* (1175), see under SPAIN ; introduced into Portugal in 1290 ; since 1862, for merit in science, literature, and art ; lily-hilted sword, red with gold border. (4) *Tower and Sword* (1808) ; John VI ; civil and military ; 5-pointed white star, tower, and medallion with sword.

ROME, SEE OF. (1) *Christ*, see PORTUGAL. (2) *Holy Sepulcher* (about 1496) ; Alexander VI ; awarded to noble pilgrims by Guardian of the Holy Sepulcher at Jerusalem ; red enamel cross potent, with small crosses between the arms.

SPAIN. (1) *Alcantara* (1156) ; the brothers Don Suarez and Don Gomez de Barrientos ; since 1835 a court order ; crest, a pear tree. (2) *Calatrava* (1158) ; Sancho III ; military ; red fleur-de-lis cross. (3) *Golden Fleece* (1429) ; Philip the Good of Burgundy ; restricted to royalty and highest nobility, for protection of the Church ; golden fleece suspended from flaming flint stone in enamel, with motto *Pretium Laborum non Vile* ("Not Cheap is the Reward of Labor"). (4) *Isabella the Catholic* (1815) ; Ferdinand VII ; general order of merit ; cross patté indented, center medallion, pillars of Hercules. (5) *St. James of the Sword* (about 1170) ; general order of merit ; gold shield, with broad red sword in cruciform.

SWEDEN. (1) *Pole Star* or *North Star* (1748) ; Frederick I ; civil merit ; 8-pointed white cross and crown, with polar star. (2) *Seraphim* (1285) ; Magnus Ladulas ; for 24 Swedish and 8 foreign members ; 8-pointed white cross, seraph's heads in angles ; blue medallion with *I.H.S.* (3) *Sword* (1522) ; Gustavus Vasa ; military merit ; white cross with golden crowns between points, in the center a blue medallion bearing a sword. (4) *Vasa* (1772); Gustavus III; services to national industries; white cross with blue center charged with a golden sheaf shaped like a vase with two handles.

ORDERS, RELIGIOUS, religious bodies, especially of the Christian Church, whose members live under a distinctive rule or discipline. The members of the greater part of Christian religious orders are ordained priests, although lay brothers and women are admitted to several orders. See BENEDICTINES; CARMELITES; CISTERCIAN; DOMINICANS; FRANCISCANS; JESUITS; KNIGHTS TEMPLARS; MERCY, FATHERS OF and SISTERS OF; PAULISTS; SAINT JOHN OF JERUSALEM, KNIGHTS OF; TRAPPISTS; see also MENDICANT FRIARS; MONASTICISM; NUNS.

ORDINARIES. See HERALDRY.

ORDOVICIAN, or LOWER SILURIAN SYSTEM, division of geologic time following the Cambrian and preceding the Upper Silurian or Silurian proper. The typical strata of the American Ordovician are found in New York State, and consequently the names of many of the subdivisions are locality terms used in New York. It is subdivided into (*a*) *Upper* (Richmond, Lorraine, Utica); (*b*) *Middle* (Trenton, Black River, Lowville); and (*c*) *Lower* (Chazy, Beckmantown, or calciferous).

The Ordovician rocks are chiefly limestones, with the exception of the upper and lower members, which may be very shaly. There are belts of Ordovician rocks around the New York Adirondacks; from central New York westward to Wisconsin and Minnesota; along the line of the Appalachians on the eastern and sometimes on the western slope from Vermont to Alabama; around the V-shaped Archean or Laurentian of Canada; and in the Central States, in Ohio, Kentucky, Indiana, and Tennessee. Ordovician rocks are also known in the Uinta, Wasatch, and Rocky mountains. In Europe the Ordovician rocks form a large area extending from Iceland into Russia. They are of considerable thickness in Great Britain and Wales. Additional areas are found in Bohemia, Germany, France, Portugal, Spain, and northern Africa.

Among the useful minerals of the Ordovician are great quantities of building stone, including limestone, slate, and marble. In Ohio and Indiana supplies of petroleum and natural gas occur in the rocks of the Cincinnati arch. Zinc and lead ores are mined in southeastern Missouri and the Upper Mississippi valley in Wisconsin, Iowa, and Illinois. Along the contact between the Cambrian and Silurian in rocks in many parts of the Appalachians are found deposits of limonite ores, some of which are mined.

OREADS, in Greek mythology, nymphs (q.v.) of grottoes and mountains. One of the most famous Oreads was Echo, who was deprived by the goddess Hera of the power of speaking unless she had first been spoken to.

OREBRO, a seaport of Sweden, situated at the entrance of the Svarta-Elf into the Hjelmar Lake, 135 miles w. of Stockholm. The town has manufactures of machinery, tobacco, matches, and chemicals. These industrial products, together with the minerals obtained from the neighboring silver, copper, and iron mines, are conveyed to Göteborg and Stockholm by means of the extensive system of canals which connects the lakes of the interior with the maritime ports. At the Diet of Örebro, held in 1529, Lutheranism was established as the state religion of Sweden. Pop. (1952 est.) 67,939.

OREGON, one of the Pacific States of the United States, bounded on the N. by Washington, on the E. by Idaho, on the s. by Nevada and California, and on the w. by the Pacific Ocean. It ranks as the 9th State of the Union in area, 32nd in population (1950), and the 33rd in order of admission to the Union, having entered on Feb. 14, 1859. The capital of the State is Salem. The principal cities in order of population (1950) are Portland, Salem, Eugene (qq.v.), Medford, and Corvallis. From N. to s. the State has an extreme width of 280 m., and from E. to w. the extreme length is 380 m. Area, 96,981 sq.m., including 631 sq.m. of inland water surface. Population (1950) 1,521,341.

Topographically, Oregon consists of two distinct regions, the larger of which occupies about two thirds of the area of the State. This region, a generally arid tableland with rugged mountainous outcroppings, is bounded on the w. by the Cascade Mountains (q.v.), the chief mountain system of the State. The average elevation of the tableland is about 5000 ft. above sea level. The Cascade Mountains, about 110 m. inland from and parallel to the coast, extend from the N. to the s. extremity of Oregon. Mt. Hood (11,245 ft.), the highest summit of the Cascades, is the highest point in the State. The lowest elevation of the State is sea level, and the average elevation is 3300 ft. A lesser mountain system, known as the Coast Range, traverses the second topographical area of the State, which extends from the Cascades to the coast. Maximum elevations of this system rarely exceed 4000 ft. Most of the

Oregon State Capitol in Salem

region between the Coast Range and the Cascades is occupied by the valley of the Willamette R. (q.v.), the most fertile portion of Oregon.

The coastline of the State, about 300 m. in length, is generally regular. Spurs of the Coast Range project into the ocean at infrequent intervals, but for the most part the major indentations are river estuaries. A number of these estuaries are excellent natural harbors. The Columbia R. (q.v.), which forms three fourths of the Oregon-Washington boundary, is the principal river of the State. Besides the Columbia and the Willamette, other important rivers are the Snake, the John Day, the Klamath, and the Deschutes. The hydrography of the State includes numerous lakes, mainly situated in the s. portion of the tableland region. This part of Oregon falls within the province of the Great Basin (q.v.). Crater Lake, 6161 ft. above sea level, is the most famous lake of Oregon.

Climatic conditions in Oregon are characterized by sharp regional and seasonal variations. West of the Cascades the climate, largely under the influence of oceanic factors, is mild and humid. The annual range of temperature in this region is between 102° F. and —2° F. Annual precipitation in the areas contiguous to the coast amounts to 138 inches. East of the Cascades the annual range of temperature is between 104° F. and —32° F. Precipitation in the tableland region varies from 10 to 20 inches annually.

Oregon has more standing timber than any other State in the Union. Forests, chiefly in the w., cover nearly 50% of the total land area. Conifers, mostly firs, pines, and spruces, are predominant. In the w. section four fifths of the trees are Douglas firs. In the e. the ponderosa pine is predominant. Redwoods are found in the s.w. The Oregon fauna includes the deer, antelope, elk, gray wolf, panther, black bear, coyote, raccoon, beaver, muskrat, rabbit, and squirrel. The lakes and rivers teem with salmon, trout, smelts, and other fish. The Columbia R. is one of the most famous salmon streams on the American continent.

Oregon is noted for its hunting and fishing facilities. National forests, grouped in thirteen units, cover almost 50% of the wooded area (about 14,817,000 acres). The State parks comprise about 61,000 acres. Oregon contains Oregon Caves National Monument and Crater Lake National Park (qq.v.). Several Indian reservations are located within the State.

Agriculture is a principal industry, particularly in the w. part of the State, where almost any crop grown in the temperate zone can be cultivated. In e. Oregon livestock-raising is the principal occupation. In 1952 the total agricultural income comprised $226,323,000 from crops, $181,770,000 from livestock, and $2,994,000 from Federal subsidies. In 1950 a total of 59,827 farms covered an area of 20,327,683 acres, and included lands and buildings valued at over $1,200,000,000. Cereal grains, hay, potatoes, fruits, and nuts are among the principal crops. The fruit and nut crop includes apples, peaches, cherries, pears, prunes, walnuts, and filberts. Other leading crops are flax and hops. In 1952 the production of winter wheat amounted to 32,016,000 bu. Livestock in 1953 numbered 1,374,000 head of cattle (including 233,000 milch cows), 734,000 sheep, and 140,000 hogs. Grazing lands for cattle and sheep totaled about 39,000,000 acres. Oregon is an important producer of poultry, notably turkeys, which numbered 2,091,000 in 1953. Fur farming and apiculture are also carried on in the State.

Timber industries are among the major industrial activities of Oregon. In the year 1950 8,239,000 board ft. of lumber, the greatest State production in the U.S., were produced. Wood industries, including the felling of timber, the production of paper and pulp, and the production of furniture, are a main source of income. Oregon ranks high among the States in value of fishery products. In 1951 the commercial fish catch, chiefly salmon, halibut, sole, crabs, tuna, and sturgeon, amounted to 53,045,900 pounds and was valued at $7,138,878.

Oregon has great mineral resources, particularly in the s.w. portion of the State, where gold, silver, copper, platinum, and coal are found in quantity. Oregon is also one of the leading producers of mercury. Iron, lead, chromite, manganese, nickle, and zinc are also mined. In 1952 a total of 6,000 fine oz. of gold and 4000 fine oz. of silver were produced. Nonmetallic minerals, including clay, black and white marble, granite, and limestone, are abundant. The total value of all minerals produced in the year 1951 amounted to $28,401,000.

Prior to 1939, the beginning of intensified production for war, manufacturing activity in Oregon was primarily concerned with State-produced raw materials. Manufacturing dependent on timber resources, such as the production of shingles, pulp, paper, veneers, plywood, doors, spars, and furniture, comprised 60% of all industrial activity. Manufacturing concerned with agricultural products, such as the production of canned and frozen fruits and vegetables, dairy products, prepared feed, flour and grain processing, and meat packing,

comprised 20%. Other manufactures were canned fish, Portland cement, woolens and worsteds, tin cans, and machinery. War-production needs rapidly advanced Oregon industry, which now includes large shipyards, electrochemical and electrometallurgical factories, and prefabricated-housing plants. Added impetus to industrial advancement was given by the completion of the Bonneville Dam in 1943 and hydroelectric power supplied by the nearby Grand Coulee Dam in Washington (see DAMS). In 1952 manufacturing establishments in the State numbered 5022 and employed 155,000 workers who received wages and salaries totaling $675,000,000.

Transportation facilities of Oregon (1953) include 57,100 m. of highway; over 7300 m. are State-maintained and of these about 6900 m. are surfaced. The State has about 5100 m. of railway, of which about 65 m. are electrified. Of the 154 airports in Oregon in 1953, a total of 59 were municipally owned and 35 were equipped with lighting for night flying. Many trucking lines, both interstate and intrastate, served inland communities. The

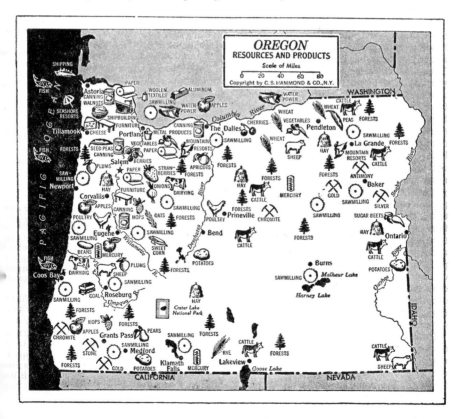

Dalles and Celilo Canal between the town of The Dalles, on the Columbia R., and Celilo, on the Snake R., makes navigation on these rivers possible up to 570 m. inland. Portland, 108 m. inland, can be reached by ocean-going vessels by means of a deep-water channel in the Columbia and Willamette rivers. Coos Bay and Astoria are important river ports.

Education is free and compulsory for children between the ages of seven and sixteen, or until the twelfth-grade curriculum has been satisfactorily completed. The State Board for Vocational Education supervises education in agriculture, home economics, and trades. A separate department of higher education controls the State-supported institutions of higher learning: Oregon State College at Corvallis; the University of Oregon at Eugene; the University of Oregon medical and dental schools at Portland; and three teachers training schools, at Monmouth, Ashland, and La Grande. In 1951–52 the 1317 public elementary and high schools were attended by 304,-876 pupils, taught by 12,073 teachers. The State education budget, in 1951–52, totaled $104,604,875.

The constitution of Oregon, which went into effect in 1859 and was frequently amended thereafter, provides for a governor, elected for a four-year term, but no lieutenant governor. Other administrative officials elected are a secretary of state, treasurer, attorney general, superintendent of public instruction, dairy and food commissioner, and labor commissioner. Legislative authority is vested in the Legislative Assembly, composed of a senate of 30 members, elected for four-year terms, and a house of representatives of 60 members, elected for two-year terms. The Assembly regularly meets in January of odd-numbered years. The judicial power is vested in a supreme court of 7 judges elected for six-year terms, circuit courts, county courts, and justices of the peace. Every elective public officer is subject to recall by the voters of his district and recall elections may take place on petition of 25% of the electorate. Oregon is divided into 36 counties, each of which, by constitutional direction, must have an area of at least 400 sq.m. The State is represented in the Congress of the U.S. by 2 senators and 4 representatives.

History. In 1543 a Spanish navigator, Bartolome Ferrelo, sailed from Mexico to a point near southern Oregon. In 1603 his exploit was duplicated by another Spanish mariner, Sebastian Vizcaino. In the meantime, in 1579, the English navigator Sir Francis Drake

sailed as far north as the 43rd parallel. Other Spanish explorers made intermittent voyages to Oregon coastal waters during the 17th and 18th centuries. In 1775 the Spanish navigator Bruno Heceta discovered the mouth of the Columbia R. In 1788 the English sea captain, James Cook, saw the Oregon coast near the mouth of the Alsea R. Within the next decade various English and American vessels frequented the northern Pacific coast. In 1788 occurred the first known landing of white men on the Oregon coast by seamen of the American vessel *Lady Washington,* commanded by Captain Robert Gray (q.v.). On a second voyage, in 1792, Capt. Gray discovered the great river, which he named the Columbia, after his ship; the U.S. later claimed the entire region drained by the Columbia, basing its claim on Gray's voyage. George Vancouver, a British captain, was at this time exploring Puget Sound. Fur traders entered the region in 1793. The immense wilderness, inhabited only by Indian tribes, was explored in 1804–05 by the Americans Meriwether Lewis and William Clark (see LEWIS AND CLARK EXPEDITION).

The first trading post in the Columbia R. region was established in 1811 by members of John Jacob Astor's Pacific Fur Company, at Astoria. After the declaration of the War of 1812 between Great Britain and the U.S., Astoria was sold to the British North West Company and renamed Fort George.

Negotiations in 1818 led to the establishment of the 49th parallel as the boundary between the U.S. and British possessions as far west as the Rocky Mts. However, as agreement could not be reached regarding the boundary west of the Rocky Mts. and north of the 42nd parallel, the two countries agreed to a ten-year period of joint occupancy. In 1819 Spain, which also had laid claim to the Oregon country, relinquished its claims to all Pacific coast territory north of the 42nd parallel; and in 1824 and 1825, by treaties with the U.S. and Great Britain, claim to territory south of the parallel 54°40' was relinquished by Russia. The Anglo-American convention was extended in 1827.

The rich Oregon fur trade was controlled by the British Hudson's Bay Company, which had absorbed the North West Company. During the 1820's organized American immigration to the Oregon territory began, and the so-called "Oregon question" came to occupy the attention of Congress. By the late 1830's many Americans were demanding that Great Britain relinquish all jurisdiction s. of 54°40' latitude;

Oregon State Highway Dept.

AGRICULTURE IN OREGON

Above: Stacks of oats in field at harvest time. Mount Hood is in the background. Right: Flock of sheep crossing road in eastern Oregon. Below: Rich grazing land near Ontario, Oregon.

Winter scene at a chromium-mining installation in Oregon

in 1844 the Democratic Party slogan, on which James K. Polk was elected President of the U.S., was "Fifty-four forty, or fight". At length, in 1846, the two countries agreed, in the Oregon Treaty, on the 49th parallel as the boundary from the Rockies to the coast, and a line along the mid-channel between Vancouver Island and the mainland to the Pacific Ocean. In 1848 Oregon was established as a Territory of the U.S. The Territory, as originally established, covered all the area between the 42nd and 49th parallels, from the Rocky Mts. to the Pacific Ocean, and included present-day Washington and parts of Idaho, Montana, and Wyoming. Many Oregon settlers left for California after the discovery of gold there in 1849, but the depopulation was more than compensated for after the passage by Congress of the Donation Land Act in 1850, giving large tracts of land free to settlers in Oregon. The increase of population and prosperity prompted the settlers to hold a convention in 1857 and request Statehood, which was granted in 1859. Indian rebellions and wars became increasingly serious after the American Civil War (1861–65). The Modoc War (1864–73) and the Shoshone War (1866–68) were marked by fierce battles and widespread destruction. Many Indian engagements were fought in the 1870's, when the tribes

were being forced to move to reservations.

With the completion of the Union Pacific Railroad in 1869 a new era of expansion in population and economic activity began for the State. In the three decades between 1870 and 1900 the population increased from 90,923 to 413,536. Oregon was among the first States to enact many presently accepted devices of government, such as the initiative and referendum (1902), the direct primary (1904), recall (1908), and woman's suffrage (1912).

In Presidential elections the majority of the Oregon electorate has voted for candidates of the Republican Party, except for the elections of 1868, 1912, 1932, 1936, 1940, and 1944, when Democratic candidates received the majority of votes. In the 1952 Presidential election, Oregon voters cast 418,956 ballots for Dwight D. Eisenhower, the Republican candidate, and 226,059 votes for Adlai E. Stevenson, the Democratic candidate.

OREGON CAVES NATIONAL MONUMENT, a national monument established in 1909 in Josephine Co., s.w. Oregon, situated in the Siskiyou Mountains, about 6 miles N. of the California boundary. Its area of 480 acres includes a group of limestone caverns noted for their beautiful rock formations. The most famous of the caves is Paradise Lost, a chamber 60 ft. in height, with stalactites in the shape of flowers festooning the walls. The caves are lighted by indirect electric lighting. See NATIONAL MONUMENTS.

OREGON GRAPE, common name applied to an evergreen shrub, *Mahonia aquifolia,* belonging to the Barberry family. The shrub, which is native to western North America, is the State flower of Oregon. It grows to a height of about ten feet, and bears large, glossy, pinnate leaves with spiny, dark-green leaflets. The yellow flowers, which are borne in racemes, have six sepals, six petals, six stamens, and a solitary pistil. The fruit is an attractive, bluish-black berry. The plant is cultivated as a hedge shrub in the United States.

OREGON QUESTION, the name given in American history to the dispute between the United States and Great Britain over the delimitation of their possessions on the northwest coast, leading to the determination of the present boundary. See OREGON.

OREGON RIVER. See COLUMBIA RIVER.

OREGON STATE COLLEGE, a coeducational, State-controlled, land-grant institution of higher learning, situated at Corvallis, Ore. It was founded in 1858 as Corvallis College, a 'men's institution under the auspices of the Methodist Episcopal Church. In 1868 it was designated a State agricultural college, and in 1885 came under complete State control. By order of the State Board of Higher Education in 1932 it became a part of the Oregon State System of Higher Education (see OREGON, UNIVERSITY OF), of which it is the scientific and technical center. Divisions of the College include schools of agriculture, forestry, science, engineering and industrial arts, pharmacy, education, arts and sciences, secretarial science, and home economics, and a graduate school and summer session. Bachelor's, master's, and doctor's degrees are granted. In 1953 the student body, including 4186 full-time students, numbered 4332 and the faculty about 440.

OREGON TRAIL, an emigrant route, about 2000 miles in length, from Independence, Mo., to the Columbia River. For 41 miles it followed the Santa Fe trail, leading up the Platte to Fort Laramie, thence to South Pass by the Sweetwater, across Green River, up Black River by Muddy Creek to a pass into the Bear River valley, and thence to Port Neuf River and Fort Hall on the Snake. Following Snake River, below Salmon Falls it cut across to Fort Boise and on to Burnt River, then turned off to the upper Powder River, went over the divide of the Blue Mountains, and down the Umatilla to the Columbia.

Originally, like many of the main roads of the country, it was made in some parts by the Indians and trappers. A part of it was blazed by Vérendrye in 1742, and the expedition of Lewis and Clark in 1804 made more of it known. In 1810 Astor, in establishing his trading posts, dispatched a party overland under W.P. Hunt to follow in the trail of these explorers. This party, returning in 1812 under Robert Stuart, missed the headwaters of the Missouri and, following the Platte, established another link of what became the accepted trail.

U.S.D.I.

Scotts Bluff National Monument on the Oregon trail

OREGON, UNIVERSITY OF, a coeducational, State-controlled institution of higher learning, situated at Eugene and Portland, Ore. It was founded in 1872, and opened for instruction four years later. In 1932, by order of the State Board of Higher Education, it became part of the Oregon State System of Higher Education, which includes, in addition to the University proper, Oregon State College (q.v.) at Corvallis, Ore., and three State normal schools, situated respectively at Monmouth, Ashland, and La Grande, Ore. Divisions of the University include schools of arts and letters, law, medicine, education, social science, music, architecture and allied arts, journalism, business administration, and physical education, and a graduate school and summer session. Bachelor's, master's, and doctor's degrees are granted. In 1953 the total enrollment, including full-time and part-time students, was about 3800 and the faculty numbered about 460.

OREL, capital of the province of the same name, R.S.F.S.R., on the Oka, 222 miles s.w. of Moscow. The town has agricultural trade and bootmaking and metal-working industries. Pop., about 110,000.

ORENBURG. See CHKALOV.

ORENSE, the capital of the Galician province of Orense, Spain, on the Minho, and 60 miles from its mouth. It has hot sulfurous springs, and manufactures woolens, linens, and chocolate. Pop. (1950) 55,574.

ORESTES, in Greek legend, the son of King Agamemnon (q.v.) of Mycenæ and Clytemnestra, and the brother of Electra and Iphigenia. When Agamemnon, on his return from the Trojan War, was murdered by Clytemnestra and her paramour Ægisthus, Orestes was saved from death by Electra or, according to another version, by his nurse. Sent secretly to Phocis, he was reared at the court of King Strophius, husband of Agamemnon's sister Anaxibia. Orestes became an intimate friend of the king's son Pylades. After attaining manhood Orestes, accompanied by Pylades, returned to Mycenæ, revealed his identity to Electra, and avenged his father's death by killing both Ægisthus and Clytemnestra. Orestes was shortly after seized with madness and pursued by the avenging deities, the Erinyes. He sought refuge at the temple of Apollo at Delphi, and was finally acquitted at Athens by Athena, goddess of wisdom, who had established the court of the Areopagus (q.v.) to hear the case. Following his acquittal Orestes, again accompanied by Pylades, traveled to the land of the Taurians.

They were about to be sacrificed by the natives to Artemis, goddess of the moon and of wild life, but were rescued by the priestess of Artemis. The priestess proved to be Orestes' sister Iphigenia (q.v.). The three escaped to Greece, where Orestes took possession of his father's kingdom at Mycenæ. He married Hermione, daughter of the rulers of Sparta, after slaying at Delphi Neoptolemus (q.v.), the son of Achilles, who had earlier married Hermione.

The story of Orestes afforded a favorite theme to the great Greek tragedians, namely, to Æschylus in the extant trilogy, the *Oresteia;* to Sophocles in his *Electra;* and to Euripides in his *Electra, Orestes,* and *Iphigenia among the Tauri.* The versions vary in details according to the dramatic ideas which influenced the different playwrights.

ORGAN, in music, originally a wind instrument consisting of pipes which are opened or closed from a keyboard and are sounded by compressed air forced through them by a mechanical apparatus. Such an organ is frequently called a pipe organ to distinguish it from the reed organ. (A discussion of reed organs, and of electric and electronic organs is at the end of this article.) The pipes, made of wood or metal, are so arranged that all pipes of the same tone quality are in a single row, or rank. Each rank contains as many pipes as there are keys on the keyboard. The pipes set on one rank are called, collectively, a *stop,* or *register,* because they are brought into play by a single "stop knob". Many modern organs are built so that stops can be transferred from one keyboard to another. Tone is produced by means of reed pipes or flue pipes. In the former, a column of air causes a tongue to vibrate and strike against a reed; in the latter, the air impinges upon a sharp edge. The *action* is the mechanism that controls the actual playing of the instrument. The keys or keyboards played by the hands are called *manuals;* those played by the feet are called *pedals.* In a modern organ are also crescendo, sforzando, and swell pedals, controlling the volume rather than the pitch of the sound. The *console* is the desk in which the keys, stop knobs, and all mechanical levers manipulated by the performer are placed.

In the 2nd century B.C., the Greek engineer Ctesibius developed the earliest known form of the organ, an instrument known as the *hydraulis,* in which compressed air was obtained through water pressure developed in cumbersome, hand-pumped receptacles. Compressed air was generated pneumatically by bellows by the 4th century A.D., and gigantic organs were built in the 10th century in England for churches and monasteries. These early instruments had no means of registration (i.e., the manner of choosing a stop or combination of stops). A keyboard with a range of three octaves and containing some chromatic tones was introduced in the 14th century. Before this period, the organ was used in the course of the church service, probably to reinforce the singing of liturgical chants, and, later, in arrangements of vocal music. Organ-playing and improvising led to independent compositions, particularly by Arnolt Schlick in Germany and Claudio Merulo and Francesco Landino in Italy, where smaller, portable instruments were built.

The modern organ dates from the 15th century, with the introduction of reed pipes, pedals, and solo stops. More than two hundred notable organ-builders flourished in Saxony from 1359 to 1780, including Gottfried Silbermann, Zacharius Hildebrand, and Johann Andreas Herbst. With the 17th- and 18th-century "baroque" organ, often called Prætorius organ after Michael Prætorius, who described its specifications, the organ reached its first peak of technical perfection, and the finest music of the organ literature was composed for it. The baroque organ had a light, clear tone, a low wind pressure, pedals, two manuals, and from twelve to thirty-five flue stops. Tonal contrasts were achieved by alternating between the manuals, but the lack of a swell pedal allowed little dynamic range. In churches, a smaller organ was often used along with the main organ to accompany the choir. Led by Girolamo Frescobaldi in Italy, Louis Claude Daquin in France, John Blow in England, Jan Pieters Sweelinck in Holland, and Dietrich Buxtehude, Johann Pachelbel, Johann Kuhnau, and Hans Leo Hassler in Germany, organ music of the period reached its culmination in the works of Johann Sebastian Bach.

Devices were perfected in the 19th century enabling the organ to produce the varied and expressive color effects necessary for the performance of the romantic music of the time. The 19th-century school of organ composers was led by Felix Mendelssohn; other 19th-century composers for the organ were Franz Liszt, César Franck, and Max Reger. Principles of construction of the organ were revolutionized about the beginning of the 20th century by the inventions of Robert Hope-Jones (1859–1914). A complete modern organ, incorporating Hope-Jones' innovations,

consists of from three to six separate organs, each controlled by a separate keyboard and stops. The most important of these "partial organs" are: the *great organ*, which contains the main group of pipes and stops; the *solo organ*, which contains a large group of solo stops; the *swell organ*, which has the same stops as the great organ, but on a smaller scale; and the *choir organ*, which contains softly voiced stops suitable for vocal accompaniment. Very large instruments also have an *echo organ*, the pipes of which are placed at the greatest possible distance from the rest of the organ.

Reed Organs. Related to the organ proper is a family of pipeless instruments in which tones are produced by the action of wind upon a set of free metal reeds. One of the most popular types of reed organ is the *melodeon*, developed in the United States about 1825. In a melodeon, air pressure is generated by bellows operated by the feet. The reeds to be sounded are selected by a keyboard, and the range of most instruments is about three octaves. As in the case of the modern pipe organ, many devices have been added to vary the tone color and expressive qualities of the sound. Another similar reed organ is the *harmonium*. One of the earliest instruments of this type was the *orgue expressif*, invented in 1810. Modern harmoniums use air suction rather than air pressure to make the reeds vibrate. The first such instrument was made in Hamburg, Germany, in 1836 by Friedrich Buschmann. Similar instruments were first made in America in 1856, and were produced commercially starting in 1860. This type of harmonium is often called the American organ. The harmonium was used by many composers of the 19th century, including Felix Mendelssohn, Robert Schumann, Franz Liszt, and César Franck.

Electric and Electronic Organs. In recent years, a number of organlike instruments have been developed which do not depend on either pipes or reeds for their sound production. In some, tones are generated electronically by vacuum-tube oscillation and then amplified; in others, complex electrical devices are used to produce the tone. A typical example of the latter type is the *Hammond Organ*, in which the tones are produced by mechanism centering around a toothed, metallic disk similar to a gear. As the disk rotates, the teeth pass a coil-wound permanent magnet, inducing a tiny electric current in the coil. If, for example, the gear teeth pass the magnet at the

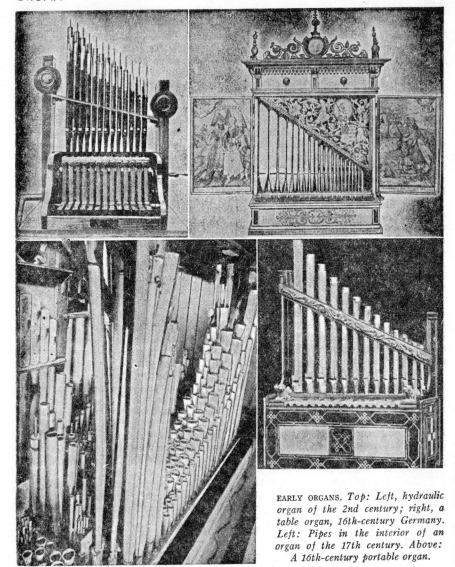

EARLY ORGANS. *Top: Left, hydraulic organ of the 2nd century; right, a table organ, 16th-century Germany. Left: Pipes in the interior of an organ of the 17th century. Above: A 16th-century portable organ.*

rate of 440 per second, when this current is transformed into sound it becomes a pure tone with a frequency of 440 vibrations per second, the note "middle A" on the international scale. There is a separate disk or "tone wheel" for each note of the full range of the organ; the speed of rotation of the disk is constant, and the frequency of the note is determined by the number of teeth on the disk. A separate cabinet containing an amplifier and speaker is attached to the instrument.

The term "electric organ" is also applied to a type of reed organ using electrically operated bellows and an amplifier and speaker to increase the volume of sound.

ORGANIC CHEMISTRY. See CHEMISTRY ORGANIC.

ORGANIZATION OF AMERICAN STATES, a regional alliance comprising the United States and the twenty nations of Latin America, concluded on April 30, 1948, at an international conference held at Bogotá, Colombia. The principal aims of the alliance were to provide machinery for the peaceful settlement of disputes and for military and economic co-operation among the signatories. The Governing Board of the Pan-American Union (q.v.) was designated as the permanent consultative council, secretariat, and central economic, social, juridical, and cultural agency of the Organization. The political functions of the Organization were entrusted to a Council of Foreign Ministers, which was also charged with supervising the activities of a newly created Inter-American Defense Council; the latter agency was assigned the task of formulating plans for mutual military assistance.

ORGANOGRAPHY. See MORPHOLOGY OF PLANTS.

ORGAN PIPE CACTUS NATIONAL MONUMENT, a national monument in s.w. Arizona, on the Mexican border. It is 328,162 acres in area, and was established in 1937 to preserve several rare forms of flora and fauna, including the organ pipe cactus, *Pachycereus marginatus,* second-largest species of cactus native to the U.S. Other varieties of unusual flora and fauna found in this arid desert region are mesquite or desert ironwood, giant saguaro, ocotillo, and the Gila monster. See NATIONAL MONUMENTS.

ORGANUM, in music, a style of polyphonic composition practiced from the 9th to the middle of the 13th century. Essentially consisting of one voice, usually the tenor, to which one or more polyphonic parts were added, its development was rigidly prescribed by the practices of the Church. In the 9th and 10th centuries, for example, the plain song, or liturgical chant, carried by the main voice was doubled note for note by another voice at the lower octave, fifth, or fourth interval (see INTERVAL). In the 11th and the early 12th centuries a more varied motion of the second voice was allowed, no longer following the plain song exactly. Later, a group of notes were sung against the one note of the tenor voice. Around 1175 a strict, measured rhythm was introduced for the first time.

ORGIES, a name given in ancient Greece to secret rites and ceremonies connected with the worship of various divinities, particularly the worship of Demeter (q.v.), the goddess of the earth and of grain, and the festival of Dionysus (q.v.), or Bacchus, god of wine. The latter ceremony was frequently accompanied by dances. By extension, the word "orgy" is used, in modern times, to designate a drunken revel or other form of wild festivity. See ELEUSINIAN MYSTERIES; MYSTERIES, CLASSIC.

ORIEL COLLEGE, a college of Oxford University, England, founded in 1326 by King Edward II as the College of St. Mary. The present name is a corruption of "La Oriole", the name of a building presented to the College in 1327. The enrollment of the College comprises two professorial fellows, twelve ordinary fellows, and the holders of sixteen scholarships.

ORIGANUM. See MARJORAM.

ORIGEN, or (Lat.) ORIGENUS, surnamed ADAMANTIUS (185?–254? A.D.), celebrated Christian writer, teacher, and theologian of antiquity, born in Alexandria, Egypt, of Christian parents. His father Leonidas suffered a martyr's death in 202 A.D. during the persecutions under the Roman emperor Lucius Septimius Severus. Origen had studied under Titus Flavius Clemens, usually known as Clement of Alexandria (q.v.), and at the age of eighteen he was appointed to succeed Clement as head of the Alexandrian catechetical school. He taught at Alexandria for about twenty-eight years with great success, with pagans as well as Christians thronging to his classes. During this period he composed the chief of his dogmatic treatises, and began his many works of textual and exegetical criticism (see EXEGESIS). His labors were occasionally interrupted by journeys to Rome, Arabia, Antioch, Greece, and Palestine.

During a visit to Palestine in 216 A.D. Origen, a layman, had been invited by the bishop of Jerusalem and the bishop of Cæsarea to lecture in the churches on the Scriptures. About 230 A.D. the same bishops ordained him a presbyter without consulting Origen's own bishop, Demetrius of Alexandria. Out of personal jealousy and for other reasons, Demetrius had long been hostile to Origen, and these events heightened his antagonism. By the decision of a synod held at Alexandria under Demetrius, Origen was forbidden to teach in that city. A second Alexandrian synod, consisting of bishops only, deprived him of the office of presbyter. This decision was based on opposition to certain of Origen's doctrinal teachings and practices. However, the churches of Palestine, Phenicia, Arabia, and Achæa declined to concur in the sentence.

Origen then (about 232 A.D.) settled at Cæsarea in Palestine, his home for the next twenty years. He founded there a school which afforded training in literature, philosophy, and theology. During the persecutions of the Christians under the emperor Decius (250 A.D.), Origen was imprisoned and tortured. He was released on the death of the emperor in 251, but, weakened by his injuries, he lived only about three years thereafter.

Origen was probably the most accomplished Biblical scholar produced by the early Church. He was a voluminous writer, the estimated total of his works being 6000. These works included letters, treatises in dogmatic and practical theology, apologetics, exegeses, and textual criticism. Among the writings which have survived are a long apologetic work, *Contre Celsum* ("Against Celsus"), considered the most important Greek apology extant, and a theological treatise preserved, in a somewhat altered form, in a Latin version made by Tyrannius Rufinus in the 4th century A.D. and bearing the title *De Principiis*. Origen's accomplishments as an exegete and student of the text were outstanding. The exegetical works have been preserved mostly in Latin translations. In his *Hexapla* Origen presented the Old Testament in the original Hebrew, with a Greek transliteration, and four previously translated Greek versions of the Septuagint, all arranged in six parallel columns. Of this work numerous excerpts were made by scholars of the 4th century A.D., who thus preserved a large portion of the work.

Origen is sometimes called the father of the allegorical method of interpreting the Scriptures. He taught the principle of the threefold sense, corresponding to the threefold division of man into body, spirit, and soul, which was then a common concept. Like his teacher Clement, Origen was a Platonist and endeavored to combine Greek philosophy and the Christian religion. He developed the idea of Christ as the Logos, or Incarnate Word, who is with the Father from eternity, but he taught also that the Son was subordinate to the Father in power and dignity. This latter doctrine, and others, such as that of the pre-existence of the soul, were severely criticized by many contemporaries and later writers. Origen's disciples and followers were long regarded as heretics, and theories developed from his doctrines became the subject of considerable theological controversy during the Middle Ages.

ORIGINAL SIN, in the Bible and theology, the first sin committed by Adam as related to or manifested in its consequences to his posterity of the human race. See EVIL, ORIGIN OF.

ORIHUELA, a town in the Spanish province of Alicante, on the Segura, 38 miles N. of Cartagena. It has a noted cathedral, and manufactures of silk, linen, and hats, and has trade in wine, cereals, fruit, and oil. Pop., about 35,000.

ORINOCO, one of the great rivers of South America. It has its origin on the slopes of the Sierra Parima, in the extreme southeast of Venezuela. It flows at first west by north, a mountain stream. A little below Esmeralda it divides and sends off to the south an arm, the Cassiquiare, which, after a course of 180 miles, enters the Rio Negro, a tributary of the Amazon. The other branch on reaching San Fernando is met by the strong current of the Guaviare. The united stream then turns due north, and, after passing over the cataracts of Maypures and Atures, and picking up the Meta on the left, meets the Apure. Below the confluence with the Apure the Orinoco turns east, and traverses the llanos of Venezuela, its waters, with an average breadth of 4 miles, being augmented from the right by the Caura and the Caroni. About 120 miles from the Atlantic, into which it rolls its milk-white flood, its delta (8500 sq.m.) begins. The total length of the river is some 1500 miles, of which 900, up to the cataracts of Atures, are navigable, besides a farther stretch of 500 miles above the cataracts of Maypures. The total area of the drainage basin is approximately 388,600 sq.m.

In 1930 the Museum of the American Indian sponsored an expedition by Dr. Herbert S. Dickey to seek the source of the Orinoco. The party proceeded up the river in June and July, and after suffering great hardships reached the headwaters of the Orinoco, having traversed a region never before penetrated by white men. The first explorer of the river was the Spaniard Ordaz who got to within 150 miles of the present Colombian boundary. Previous to the Dickey expedition no one, during the past 400 years, had traced the Orinoco to its source.

ORIOLE, common name applied to passerine birds of the family Oriolidae, especially those in the genus *Oriolus,* confined entirely to the Old World, and characteristic of the Oriental and Ethiopian regions. The members of the family are generally of a bright-yellow or golden color, which is set off by the black of the wings. Twenty-four species are enumerated under the genus. The best known is the golden oriole *O. oriolus.* The adult male is about 9 in. long. Its general color is a rich golden yellow: the bill is dull orange red;

a black streak reaches from its base to the eye; the iris is blood red; the wings are black, marked here and there with yellow, and a patch of yellow forms a conspicuous wing spot; the two middle feathers of the tail are black, inclining to olive at the base, the very tips yellow, the basal half of the others black, the distal half yellow; legs, feet, and claws are dark brown. In central and southern Europe it is common in summer in certain localities; it is abundant in Iran, and ranges through central Asia as far as to Irkutsk. It winters in South Africa. The American "orioles" belong to the family Icteridae which includes the Baltimore bird (q.v.).

ORION, the brightest constellation in the heavens, located on the celestial equator east of Taurus. It is an oblong configuration with three stars in line near its center. It is represented on pictorial charts as the figure of Orion (q.v.), the hunter in Greek mythology, standing with uplifted club. Three bright stars represent his belt and three fainter stars aligned south of the belt represent his sword. *a* Orionis, or Betelgeuse (q.v.), one of the brightest stars in the heavens, is located in the left corner of the oblong, corresponding to Orion's shoulder. β Orionis, or Rigel, is diagonally opposite Betelgeuse. A nebula (q.v.) surrounding the three stars marking Orion's sword is one of the most conspicuous bright nebulae in the heavens.

ORION, in Greek mythology, an unusually handsome giant and hunter of Bœotia and the protagonist of numerous legends. Being in love with Merope, daughter of Œnopion and granddaughter of Dionysus, he attempted to seize her by force, after her father had refused to consent to their marriage. He was blinded by Œnopion, but regained his sight by exposing his eyes to the rays of the rising sun. He loved and was beloved by Artemis, goddess of the moon and of wild life. The accounts of his death vary. According to one version, he was killed by a scorpion. Among other accounts, he was killed by Artemis when he attempted to assault her, or he was killed accidentally by Artemis when, at the suggestion of her brother, the god Apollo, she shot an arrow at a distant mark in the sea and hit the head of Orion as he was swimming. After his death Orion was placed among the stars, where he appears as a giant with a sword, girdle, lion's skin, and club. Another legend relates that he pursued the Pleiades (q.v.) until both they and he were transformed into constellations; hence they still flee from him across the sky.

ORISKANY, BATTLE OF, a battle of the American Revolution. It was fought near Oriskany, New York, on August 6, 1777, between a force of Royalists under Sir John Johnson and Joseph Brant, and Americans under General Herkimer, who was mortally wounded. More than a third on each side were killed or wounded, and the British were forced to retreat. It was the first engagement of American troops under the Stars and Stripes. The event was celebrated on Aug. 6, 1927, when the battlefield was dedicated as a public park.

ORISSA, an ancient kingdom of India, the authentic history of which goes back to about 474 A.D. It extended from Bengal on the north to the Godavari on the south. By the repeal of the "partition" of Bengal, carried out in 1905, Orissa became part of the new province of Bengal. In 1912, Bihar, Chota Nagpur, and Orissa were separated from Bengal and were constituted into the province of Behar and Orissa. The entire district is sacred ground to the Hindus; evidences of the worship of Siva and Vishnu meet the eye at every turn. The most interesting of the aboriginal races are the Kandhs (Kondhs, Khonds).

ORIZABA, or CITLALTEPETL, a volcanic cone 20 miles N.W. of Orizaba, Mexico, a noble pyramid rising to an elevation of 18,700 ft., the highest peak in Mexico (Popocatepetl being 17,500). Its last severe eruption was in 1566. It was ascended for the first time in 1848 by two Americans, Maynard and Reynolds.

ORIZABA, city in the Mexican State of Veracruz, 68 miles s.w. of Veracruz City. It lies in a fertile garden country, largely sugar plantations, 4030 ft. above the sea, and contains textile and tobacco factories. Pop., about 40,000.

ORKNEY ISLANDS (anc. *Orcades*), a group of ninety Scotch islands, islets, and skerries, of which only twenty-eight are inhabited, and which have an aggregate area of 376 sq.m., the largest being Pomona or Mainland (207 sq.m.), Hoy (53 sq.m.), Sanday (26 sq.m.), Westray, S. Ronaldshay, Rousay, Stronsay, Eday, Shapinshay, Burray, and Flotta. The surface is generally low and treeless. The mean annual temperature is 45°, the rainfall 34.3 in. Agriculture and fishing are the principal industries. Kirkwall and Stromness, the only towns, and the standing stones of Stennis and the tumulus of Maeshowe are the chief places of interest. Pop. (1951 prelim.) 21,258.

ORLANDO, county seat of Orange Co., Fla., situated 125 miles s. of Jacksonville. Transportation facilities include two railroads. Orlando is the largest inland city of Florida, a noted winter resort, and the center and shipping point of an agricultural area producing citrus fruits and garden truck. Among the industrial establishments in the city are extensive fruit and vegetable packing and canning plants. Within the city are 31 freshwater lakes, and the surrounding region contains a total of 1000 lakes. Orlando contains numerous parks, noted for their semitropical foliage and flowers. The city is the site of the annual Central Florida Exposition. Rollins College, established in 1885, is at Winter Park, 4 miles N.E. of the city. Orlando was settled in 1843 and incorporated in 1875. Pop. (1950) 52,367.

ORLANDO, VITTORIO EMANUELE (1860–1952), Italian statesman, born in Palermo, and educated at the University of Palermo. He was minister of education from 1903 to 1905, of justice from 1907 to 1909 and from 1914 to 1916, and of interior in 1916–17. He favored the entry of Italy into World War I on the side of the Allies, and in 1917 was elected prime minister. Orlando headed the Italian delegation to the Paris Peace Conference in 1919. His failure to obtain the territorial concessions which had been secretly promised to Italy by the Allies in 1915 under the Treaty of London (see ITALY: *History*) caused the downfall of his ministry in June, 1919. Six months later he was elected president of the Chamber of Deputies. He was at first a supporter of the Fascist government established by Benito Mussolini in 1922, but after the slaying of the Socialist leader Giacomo Matteotti (1885–1924) by the Fascists in 1925 he withdrew his support, and three years later resigned from the Chamber. From 1944 to 1946 he was again president of the Chamber of Deputies, and served thereafter in the Constituent Assembly. Orlando's writings include over one hundred works on juridical subjects.

ORLEANS, capital of the department of Loiret, France, on the Loire R., 77 miles S.W. of Paris. The public edifices include the cathedral, destroyed by the Huguenots in 1567, and rebuilt from 1601 onward by Henry IV and his three successors; the *Mairie* (1530); and the 15th-century *Musée* (till 1853 the hôtel-de-ville). The commerce is more important than the industries (of which the chief is market gardening). Orléans is on the site of Genabum, the Gallic town burned in 52 B.C. by Cæsar to avenge the murder of Roman traders. It was rebuilt by the emperor

Aurelian and named Aurelianum, whence its modern name. In 1428–29 the city was besieged by the English under the duke of Bedford, but was delivered by Joan of Arc, called therefore the Maid of Orléans. The town figured prominently in the wars of the Huguenots; in the Franco-German War it was occupied by the invaders, October 11 to November 9, 1870, and from December 5 to the end of the war. Pop. (1946) 70,240.

ORLEANS, DUKES OF, a title borne by three dynasties of French princes of the blood. It was first, in 1392, given by Charles VI to his dissolute brother Louis (1371–1407), who was murdered in the streets of Paris at the instigation of the duke of Burgundy. His successor was his son Charles (1391–1465), the poet. Charles' son Louis succeeded to the throne as Louis XII in 1498, whereupon the dukedom of Orleans merged in the crown. It was revived in 1626, when Louis XIII created his brother, Jean Baptiste Gaston (1608–60), Duke of Orléans. He died without male issue. Louis XIV revived the title in favor of his brother Philippe (1640–1701), whose grandson was Philippe *Egalité,* and great-grandson, Louis-Philippe. The eldest son of Louis-Philippe took the title; but it was not borne by his son, the Comte de Paris (1838–94), who in 1883 became head of the French Bourbons, his son, Louis Philippe Robert (1869–1926), assuming the old ducal title. For the Orleanist party, see BOURBON; FRANCE.

ORLEANS, CHARLES, DUKE OF (1391–1465). He commanded at Agincourt (1415), was taken prisoner and carried to England, where he employed himself in hunting and writing verses. He was ransomed in 1440. His son became Louis XII of France.

ORLEANS, ISLE OF, situated in the St. Lawrence River, in the province of Quebec, Canada, its southern extremity being about 5 miles N.E. of Quebec; it is about 20 m. long and has an area of 69 sq.m. The island, which contains several villages, is a popular summer resort. Wolfe camped on this island during the siege of Quebec.

ORLEANS, MAID OF. See JOAN OF ARC.

ORMANDY, EUGENE (1899–   ), American orchestral conductor, born in Budapest, Hungary, and educated at the Royal State Academy of Music, in Budapest, and at the University of Budapest. In his fourth year he was recognized as a child prodigy, and as such he gave violin concerts throughout Hungary and Central Europe until 1914. He received his B.A. degree from the royal Academy at the age of fourteen, and at twenty was appointed head of the master classes at the State Conservatorium of Music in Budapest. In 1921, when he removed to the United States, he joined the orchestra of the Capitol Theater in New York City; he later served as its conductor. In 1927 he became a naturalized citizen of the United States. He conducted the Minneapolis Symphony Orchestra from 1931 to 1936, when he was named co-conductor, with Leopold Stokowski, of the Philadelphia Orchestra; he was in complete charge of the latter after 1941. Beginning in 1949 he made guest appearances each summer with European orchestras.

ORMER. See ABALONE.

ORMOC, a town on the w. coast of Leyte, Philippine Is., 34 miles s.w. of Tacloban. It is an important hemp port. Pop., about 72,000.

ORMONDE, EARLS, MARQUISES, and DUKES OF, titles held in the Irish peerage (that of duke existing also in the English peerage after 1682) by members of the Butler family. From the 14th century, when James Butler was created earl after his marriage to Eleanor de Bohun, granddaughter of King Edward I of England, the earls of Ormonde were prominent in English history as statesmen, scholars, and soldiers. Among the most important members of the Butler family who held the title were the following.

1. JAMES BUTLER, 12th EARL and 1st DUKE OF ORMONDE (1610-88), Irish statesman and soldier, born in London. From 1640 he supported Sir Thomas Wentworth, the Earl of Strafford, who was then lord lieutenant of Ireland, in his campaigns against the Irish who were rebelling against English domination; in 1642 he was created a marquis and two years later became lord lieutenant of Ireland. In 1649, after a series of negotiations with the Irish, he concluded a peace granting them the right of free exercise of the Catholic religion. Meanwhile, the English Civil War (see GREAT REBELLION) had been in progress, and in 1650, when Ireland was conquered by the Parliamentary forces of Oliver Cromwell, he went to France to join Charles II in exile. After the Restoration of the Stuarts to the English throne in 1660, Ormonde received honors and important posts from Charles, and in 1661 again became lord lieutenant of Ireland; in this post he encouraged learning and manufacturing in Ireland. In 1669, having fallen from the king's favor, he was dismissed, and became chancellor of Oxford University. Shortly afterward, an attempt was made on his life by Thomas Blood (q.v.), an Irish

adventurer. Ormonde was restored as lord lieutenant by Charles in 1677 and served until 1682, when he was raised to the English peerage as Duke of Ormonde. After the death of Charles in 1685 and the accession of James II he retired to Cornbury, in Oxfordshire, refusing to support many of the policies of James. See JAMES II; GREAT BRITAIN: History.

2. JAMES BUTLER, 2nd DUKE OF ORMONDE (1665-1745), son of Thomas Butler, Earl of Ossory, and grandson of the 1st duke, born in Dublin, and educated in France and at Oxford University. He joined the forces of William III, Prince of Orange, in 1688, and two years later, after William had been declared king of England by Parliament (see GLORIOUS REVOLUTION), commanded a regiment at the battle of the Boyne (q.v.) in which the deposed king, James II, was defeated. Ormonde subsequently served under William in wars on the Continent, and after the accession of Queen Anne in 1702 he served with the English forces in Spain (see SPANISH SUCCESSION, WAR OF THE). He was lord lieutenant of Ireland from 1703 to 1705 and again in 1710-11, and subsequently succeeded John Churchill (q.v.), Duke of Marlborough, as commander in chief of the combined armies of England and Holland, holding the latter post until 1714, when he was dismissed by the newly crowned George I, the first of the Hanoverian kings. Ormonde was known to hold strong Jacobite (see JACOBITES) sentiments, and was impeached and forced to flee to France; in 1716 his estates were confiscated by Parliament. He took part in the unsuccessful Jacobite invasion of England from Spain in 1715, and thenceforth lived at the Spanish court, where he was held in high favor.

ORNE, a department in northwestern France, formed from part of ancient Normandy. A range of wooded hills, nowhere rising above 1370 ft., extends across the south of the department from east to west. Although the soil is fertile, agriculture is not in an advanced state. Cattle and horses of Norman breed are raised. Textile manufacture is the chief industry. The department is divided into four arrondissements, Alençon, Argentan, Domfront, and Mortagne. The capital is Alençon. Area, 2371 sq.m.; pop. (1952 est.) 281,000.

ORNITHOLOGY, the scientific study of birds (q.v.).

ORNITHORHYNCHUS. See PLATYPUS.

OROBANCHACEAE. See BROOMRAPE.

ORONTES, the ancient name of a river in Syria, now called Nahrel-Asi. It rises in the

Collection The Museum of Modern Art, N.Y.C.

"Zapatistas," painting by José Clemente Orozco

Lebanon Mountains, and flows northward as far as the city of Antioch, and then westward to the Mediterranean Sea, through a total course of 250 miles. Its valley formed a highway to and from Egypt.

OROZCO, JOSÉ CLEMENTE (1883–1949), Mexican muralist and painter, born in Zapotlan in the State of Jalisco, and educated at the National University, Mexico City. In 1922 he became one of the leaders of the Syndicate of Painters and Sculptors which sought to revive the true art of fresco painting, under the patronage of the Mexican government. Orozco's most important early work was a series of frescoes for the National Preparatory School in Mexico City, commemorating the revolutionary uprisings of peasants and workers in Mexico. The set of murals at the New School for Social Research in New York City, entitled "The Dispossessed", portrays the desirable identification of intellectuals and professionals with workers under the capitalistic system. In Pomona College in Claremont, California, he painted a fresco on the theme of the Greek hero Prometheus. His mural panels for the Baker Library at Dartmouth Col-

lege, New Hampshire, depict the "Coming of Quetzalcoatl", the "Return of Quetzalcoatl", and "Modern Industrial Man". Orozco contributed to the revival of fresco technique, design, and subject matter, and is regarded as one of the foremost mural painters in the Western Hemisphere.

ORPEN, SIR WILLIAM NEWENHAM MONTAGUE (1878–1931), British portrait painter, born in Stillorgan, County Dublin, Ireland. He studied at the Slade School in London from 1897 to 1899. Orpen became an associate of the Royal Academy in 1910, and was elected a full member in 1919. Noted for his penetrating, dignified portraits, he was in great demand by English society and American notables. His portraits of President Woodrow Wilson and the American banker Otto Kahn are distinguished examples of his work. He also executed paintings illustrating Irish folk tales and battle scenes of World War I, the latter painted for the British government. He was knighted in 1918. His work is represented in the museums of Belfast, Durban, Oxford, London, and Liverpool. In America, paintings by him may be seen at the Metropolitan Museum of Art, New York City, and the Carnegie Institute, Pittsburgh, Pa.

ORPHAN, in law, a minor (q.v.) who has lost one or both parents. In ancient times the care of orphans was a purely private matter. The responsibility of the community for the care of orphans was recognized by the early Christians and collections to raise funds were taken among the members of congregations. Later church charity provided for the establishment of orphan asylums as well as for the care of orphans in monasteries. The duty of the state to provide for orphans was first recognized in the early part of the seventeenth century, in England, where they were frequently placed in workhouses (q.v.). The abuses of the workhouse system led in the 18th century to the establishment by the government of separate residential schools, called barrack schools, for the housing and instruction of orphans, and to a substantial growth in the number of orphan asylums founded by private groups. In recent years the emphasis has shifted to care in foster homes and to provision by the state for financial assistance in the form of pensions paid to widowed mothers.

In other countries, including the United States, orphans are also recognized as wards of the state and governmental provision is made for their care. In the United States both State and Federal legislation provide for aid to orphans in various forms, including their total support when necessary in such institutions as orphanages and foster homes. Liability for the care of an orphan with one surviving parent is, as a general rule, included in the various State statutes regulating the responsibilities of parents for the care of their children. In addition, in needy cases, monthly money allotments are also given to the parent to aid in the support of the child. The amount of such aid varies from State to State. Under the Federal Social Security Act of 1935, the Federal government contributes one half of whatever the State pays, up to a maximum of nine dollars a month for the first dependent child and six dollars a month each for other dependent children in the same home. See MATERNAL AND CHILD WELFARE; SOCIAL INSURANCE.

ORPHANAGE, an institution for the care of orphaned, and also dependent or neglected, children, who have passed infancy but are not yet able to support themselves. An orphanage is distinguished from a foundling hospital in that the latter cares only for infants. Most orphanages admit children who are not or-

phans; according to a recent world estimate the proportion of actual orphans in such institutions is only ten percent. Physically or mentally handicapped children and delinquent children were at one time reared in orphanages, but separate institutions are now maintained for them in most civilized countries. The first institutions for the care of children were foundling homes established by the Roman Catholic Church during the Middle Ages as a deterrent to infanticide by destitute parents. Orphanages developed in England and the United States principally during the 19th and early 20th centuries; they became favorite objects of philanthropy as a result of growing concern at the ill-treatment of children exposed by such books as *Oliver Twist* by the English novelist Charles Dickens (q.v.).

Most orphanages in the United States are maintained by religious organizations, by social or fraternal organizations, or by private endowment; only one tenth of the total number are government institutions. In recent years, governmental authorities have tended to favor foster home care with State assistance over institutional care, as a result of growing criticism of the effects of institutional regimentation on the personalities of children. This criticism also led to the establishment of research bodies, such as the Child Welfare League of America, to find means for eliminating the harmful effects of institutional life. As a result, a tendency has arisen toward organization of orphanages on a "cottage" system, in which children live together in small groups under the care of a house mother, ordinary clothing is worn rather than uniforms, and efforts are made to integrate the lives of the children with the life of the community. All Jewish institutions and most Protestant institutions, for example, make provision for the education of their charges in public schools in which they can meet and associate with other children. In addition, increasing emphasis is given to securing qualified supervisory personnel; and increasingly high salaries are offered by most institutions to attract people with medical, psychiatric, dietetic, and social-work training. See ORPHAN.

ORPHEUS, in Greek mythology, a celebrated Thracian musician and hero. He was generally considered the son of Œagrus, King of Thrace, and of a Muse, either Calliope or Polyhymnia; in time he came to be considered the son of Apollo, god of music, medicine, and light. Orpheus was said either to have invented the lyre, or to have received it from Apollo, and such was his skill that he was credited with the power of taming wild beasts and moving trees by the excellence of his music. He played an important part in the expedition of the Argonauts (q.v.), and with his lyre he enabled the Argonauts to resist the lure of the Sirens. More famous was his journey to the lower world to recover his wife Eurydice (q.v.). She was permitted to follow him back to earth, on condition that he did not look back until they reached the upper world. Overcome by love and anxiety, Orpheus did look back, and Eurydice vanished; Orpheus thereupon killed himself in grief. According to a more common legend, he was torn to pieces by Thracian women, in their gigantic worship of the god Dionysus (q.v.), because, mourning for Eurydice, he had rejected their advances. His head floated across the sea to the island of Lesbos, which became renowned for its lyric poetry. For the importance of Orpheus in Greek religious history, see ORPHISM.

ORPHISM, in classical religion, a mystery or mystic cult of ancient Greece, supposedly founded by the legendary poet and musician Orpheus (q.v.). The doctrines of Orphism, dating from about the 6th century B.C., were derived from the large body of sacred poetry ascribed to Orpheus. Although the exact nature of these writings is not clearly known, certain fragmentary passages, including inscriptions on gold tablets found in the graves of Orphic followers, provide considerable reliable data on the origins and nature of the cult. The Orphic doctrines exercised a profound influence on Pythagoras (q.v.), who is credited with developing the principles of metempsychosis. Plato and Socrates also were probably influenced by Orphism.

The Orphic teachers attempted to combine the Bacchic worship of Dionysus, a suffering god who was supposed to have died for humanity and to have been reborn through many incarnations, with the later Hellenic conception of the supremacy of Zeus. Dionysus was conceived to be the creator of the material world, but also by a curious myth, he was a silver egg which was swallowed by, and therefore became part of, Zeus. He was then born of the union of Zeus and Persephone, as Dionysus Zagreus, and was devoured and eaten by the Titans. However, Athena, goddess of wisdom, brought to Zeus Dionysus' heart, which Zeus swallowed and which was reborn as Dionysus the son of Zeus and Semele. Zeus then destroyed the Titans with his thunderbolt and scattered their ashes throughout the world. Humanity thus became pervaded both with Titanic

(evil) and with Dionysiac (good) elements.

From this myth the Orphics developed a doctrine of sin and regeneration, of heaven, purgatory, and hell. According to their tenets, mortals should endeavor to rid themselves of the Titanic element and should seek to preserve the Dionysiac, or divine, nature of their being. The Orphics believed in a long series of reincarnated lives, accompanied by rewards and punishments for good and evil deeds and culminating in the liberation of the completely purified soul. They held that ascetic living would enable the soul eventually to achieve a blissful eternity. See MYSTERIES, CLASSIC.

ORR, JOHN BOYD, 1st BARON BOYD ORR (1880–   ), British nutritionist and agricultural scientist, born in Kilmaurs, Ayrshire, and educated at Glasgow University. Following distinguished service in World War I he conducted fundamental research in the field of nutrition. During the 1930's he was a member of various official commissions on problems connected with nutrition and animal health. He was knighted in 1939. From 1942 to 1945 he served as professor of agriculture at Aberdeen University. Sir John was prominent in the movement for a world federal government after World War II. Glasgow University appointed him rector in 1945, and the same year he was elected director general of the U.N. Food and Agriculture Organization for a two-year term. In 1946 he became chancellor of Glasgow University. He was raised to the peerage and awarded the Nobel Prize for peace in 1949. His writings include *Food, Health, and Income* (1936), *Fighting for What* (1943), *Food and the People* (1944), and *The White Man's Dilemma* (1952).

ORRISROOT. See IRIS.

ÖRSTED, HANS CHRISTIAN. See OERSTED, HANS CHRISTIAN.

ORTEGA Y GASSET, JOSÉ (1883–1955), Spanish writer and philosopher, born in Madrid, and educated at the University of Madrid and at the University of Marburg, in Germany. In 1910 he was appointed professor of metaphysics at the University of Madrid. His articles, lectures, and essays on philosophical and political issues contributed to a Spanish intellectual renaissance in the first decades of the 20th century and to the fall of the Spanish monarchy in 1931. He was a member from 1931 to 1933 of the Cortes which promulgated the republican constitution. After the outbreak (1936) of the Spanish Civil War he lived abroad until 1949. His solution for the

Religious News Service

Archbishop Damaskinos of the Orthodox Church leading a procession in Athens, Greece

problems of modern civilization is stated in *The Revolt of the Masses* (Eng. tr., 1932), the work which earned him an international reputation. In it he decries the influence for evil of mass-minded (i.e., mediocre) men, who, if not directed by the intellectual minority, encourage the rise of totalitarianism. His many writings include (in English translation) *The Modern Theme* (1933), *Invertebrate Spain* (1937), *Toward a Philosophy of History* (1941), *Concord and Liberty* (1946), and *The Dehumanization of Art* (1948).

ORTELIUS, Lat. name of OERTEL or ORTELL, ABRAHAM (1527–98), Flemish geographer, born in Antwerp. His early years were spent as a map engraver, but while traveling on business in Europe in 1560, he was influenced by another Flemish geographer, Gerhardus Mercator (q.v.), to devote himself to the study of geography. Ortelius' subsequent contributions to geographical science established his reputation as one of the greatest geographers of the 16th century. His most famous work, *Theatrum Orbis Terrarum* (1570), generally considered the first modern atlas, served for many years thereafter as the basis of geographical studies. In 1575 Ortelius was appointed royal geographer to King Philip II of Spain. Three years later he published a critical treatment of the work of ancient geographers entitled *Synonymia Geographica*, republished in 1596 as *Thesaurus Geographicus*.

ORTHOCLASE. See FELDSPAR.

ORTHODOX CHURCH, the body of Christians who use the Byzantine rite (see LITURGY) in their various native languages, are united with the Ecumenical Patriarch of Constantinople, and reject the supremacy of the pope. They agree in accepting the authority of the first seven ecumenical councils (see COUNCIL) of the Roman Catholic Church, but reject all later councils. The Orthodox Church, after six centuries of disputes of authority and theology with the Roman pontiffs, began its separate existence after a complete schism in 1054, when Pope Leo IX excommunicated Michael Cærularius, Patriarch of Constantinople from 1043 to 1059, and the whole Eastern Church.

The doctrinal differences between the Orthodox and Roman Catholic churches consist chiefly in the rejection by members of the Orthodox body of the word *Filioque* (q.v.; "and from the Son") in the creed, in the interest of the supremacy of the Father in the Trinity; in their rejection of the use of the word "purgatory", although they believe in a state of purgation after death and in the efficacy of prayers for the dead; in their repudiation of the authority of the pope; and in the fact that their priests are permitted to marry, although bishops are chosen from the celibate monastic orders.

The principal divisions of the Orthodox Church include the Great Church or Patriarchate of Constantinople, the Patriarchate of Alexandria, the Patriarchate of Antioch, and the Patriarchate of Jerusalem, all established in the early centuries of Christendom; the Church of Russia, established in 1598 and deprived of its political rights as a national church by the Soviet government in 1918, although the constitution of 1936 later guaranteed complete religious freedom in the U.S.S.R.; the Church of Greece, established as an independent body in 1850; the Church of Bulgaria, established in 1872; the Church of Yugoslavia, established in 1920, absorbing the former churches of Serbia, Montenegro, and Bosnia-Herzegovina; and the Church of Romania, established in 1885.

The Orthodox Church, with a world membership of about 100,000,000, ranks third among the divisions of Christendom. In the United States, according to figures for 1954, there are a total of over 2,690,000 members of the Orthodox Church, divided into Albanian, American, Armenian, Assyrian, Bulgarian, Greek, Romanian, Russian, Serbian, Syrian-Antiochian and Ukrainian Orthodox churches, the Apostolic Episcopal Church, and the Holy Orthodox Church in America.

ORTHOGRAPHY. See SPELLING; SPELLING REFORM.

ORTHOPEDICS, branch of surgery devoted to the prevention, correction, or alleviation of deformities, especially of the human spine and of the extremities. It is distinguished from general surgery by the extensive utilization of mechanical appliances. In the 20th century the art has developed greatly, keeping pace with the advance in general surgery and pathology. Open operations are done freely; many deformities are cured by operative means alone; the X ray has made the diagnosis of bone and joint lesions more exact and the results of treatment more satisfactory. The transplantation of bone, fascia, muscle, tendon, and nerve, for the restoration of function of disabled or the replacement of destroyed tissue, and the re-forming of joints that have become ankylosed (as a result of some infection, injury, or other pathologic process), are now commonplace achievements.

Deformities coming particularly under the observation and care of the orthopedic surgeon include tuberculosis, syphilis, rickets, arthritis, infantile paralysis, and congenital deformities.

ORTHOPTERA, a large and important group of insects comprising the forms known as the straight-winged insects and including the grasshoppers or true locusts, long-horned grasshoppers (including katydids), crickets, cockroaches, walking sticks and leaf-insects, and the praying mantis or rearhorse. The mouth parts are fitted for biting, and the metamorphoses are incomplete, the young when first hatched closely resembling the adult insects except in lacking wings. The eggs are few in number and as a rule are laid in specialized egg cases, although with some they are deposited without such cases and with a few are scattered singly. About 10,000 species exist; but, in spite of the comparatively small number of eggs, many of the species are tenacious of life and apparently very prolific, and swarm in enormous numbers of individuals, as in the case of the destructive and migratory locusts. The ability to produce sounds of a more or less musical character by rubbing one part of the body, modified for the purpose, upon another, is highly developed. The capability to make such sounds is confined to the male sex, and its object is to attract the female; and this ability belongs only to the families which jump (the Saltatoria). The runners, walkers, and graspers (Cursoria, Gressoria, and Raptoria) make no sound, but in these groups, especially in the tropical forms, the wings seem to be of little use as organs of flight, but they are of striking value in ornamentation and in concealment. This is especially true with the Phasmidae and Mantidae. Even the eggs resemble the seeds of plants.

ORURO, capital of the department of Oruro, Bolivia, on a saline plain 11,960 ft. above the sea, near the salt lake of Aullagas. Mines of silver, gold, and tin are located there. The department, bordering on Peru, has an area of 20,657 sq.m. and a population (1950) of 210,260. Pop. of city (1950) 62,975.

ORVIETO, city in Italian province of Terni, 78 miles N.N.W. of Rome. The city is on an isolated tufa rock, which rises 765 ft. above the river Paglia, and 1327 ft. above sea level. It has a beautiful cathedral (1290-1580) with paintings by Fra Angelico. St. Patrick's Well (1527-40), with its 250 steps, and the former papal palace are also noteworthy. Pop., about 20,000.

ORWELL, GEORGE, real name ERIC ARTHUR BLAIR (1903–50), British author, born in Motihari, India, and educated at Eton. He served with the Indian Imperial Police in Burma from 1922 to 1927, when he returned to Europe. In poor health, and striving to become a writer, he lived for several years in poverty, first in Paris and then in London. His first works entitled *Down and Out in Paris and London* (1933) and *Burmese Days* (1934) are largely autobiographical. Having become an anti-imperialist while serving in Burma, Orwell had meanwhile joined the Marxist movement, and from 1936 to 1937 he fought for the Republican cause in the Spanish Civil War. He described his war experiences in *Homage to Catalonia* (1938). In the most significant phase of his literary career, Orwell's political convictions underwent a profound change. Becoming increasingly anti-Stalinist and anti-totalitarian, he developed an overriding concern for the future of individual liberty. His condemnation of a regimented society is expressed in the satirical *Animal Farm* (1945) and *Nineteen Eighty-Four* (1949). The latter work presents a terrifying picture of life in a completely authoritarian society. Among his other writings are *Coming Up for Air* (1939), *Critical Essays* (1946), *The English People* (1947), and *Shooting An Elephant* (posthumously published, 1950).

OSAGE, a North American Indian tribe of Siouan stock (q.v.), formerly holding an extensive territory between the Missouri and Arkansas rivers in Oklahoma. Their culture was typical of that of the Plains Indians (q.v.). Their first contact with white men occurred in the 17th century, when they were discovered by French explorers; the Osage subsequently allied themselves to the French in warfare with other tribes, including the Cherokee and Chickasaw to the east and the Kiowa, Cheyenne, and Pawnees on the plains. Between 1808 and 1870 they sold most of their land to the United States. In 1870 they entered their present reservation in northeastern Oklahoma, securing favorable terms in land leases and interest derived from trust funds held for them by the U.S. government. Subsequently, oil was discovered on their lands, and with the royalties on the oil wells to supplement their incomes they became one of the wealthiest communities per capita in the world. Their population was estimated at 6000 in the early 19th century; in a recent year they numbered over 4500.

OSAGE ORANGE or **BOWWOOD,** an American tree, *Maclura pomifera,* belonging to the Mulberry family, so called because its bright-orange wood was used by the Osage Indians for bows and because its nonedible fruit superficially resembles an orange. The plant is dioecious, bearing male flowers in racemes and female flowers in heads. The male flowers have a four-parted calyx and four stamens; the female flowers have a four-cleft calyx and a solitary pistil. Flowers of both sexes lack petals. The fruit is an achene. The Osage orange is widely cultivated in the warmer parts of the United States as a hedge tree; its wood is used for fence posts.

OSAGE RIVER, river rising in Lyon Co., Kan., and flowing into Missouri. It joins the Missouri R. 10 miles E.S.E. of Jefferson City. The length of the river is 500 m., its course lying chiefly in Missouri. The stream is also called Marais des Cygnes.

OSAKA, or OZAKA, important city of central Japan, situated at the head of the gulf of the same name, and at the mouth of the Yodo River, which issues from Lake Biwa, and is intersected with canals. Its fine castle was constructed by Hideyoshi's orders in 1583. By absorbing its suburbs, the industrial city Osaka has become the second largest city in Japan, both as to area and population. Osaka has improved its harbor works, stimulating trade. Its airdrome is s. of the harbor. It is equipped to accommodate both landplanes and seaplanes. The airport is the key point in the air routes of the empire. Regular passenger, mail, and freight services are operated. The port now occupies about 1800 acres. There are modern apartment houses, and the streets have been widened and railways improved. The center of the textile export trade for Japan, and of the trade with China and Korea, Osaka is also the center of the Japanese automobile import industry. An international fair is held there annually. Osaka is also the headquarters of the rice and tea trade. In the earthquake of October 28, 1891, of which Osaka was the center, nearly 10,000 lives were lost. A great fire in 1909 destroyed 12,120 buildings, and another occurred in 1912. Pop. (1950) 1,956,-136.

OSBORN, HENRY FAIRFIELD (1857–1935), American paleontologist, born in Fairfield, Conn., and educated at Princeton University. He was professor of comparative anatomy at Princeton University from 1883 to 1890, when he joined the faculty of Columbia University, serving as professor of biology from 1891 to 1895 and thereafter until his death as professor of zoology; from 1892 to 1895 he was dean of the Faculty of Sciences. In 1891 Osborn was appointed curator of vertebrate paleontology at the American Museum of Natural History, and served as president of the museum's board of trustees from 1908 to 1933. From 1924 until his death he was senior geologist of the United States Geological Survey. Osborn was one of the leading paleontologists of the 20th century, making significant contributions to the study of evolution in animals. He wrote *The Age of Mammals* (1910), *Origin and Evolution of Life* (1917), and *Creative Education* (1927).

OSBORNE, THOMAS BURR (1859–1929), American biochemist, born in New Haven, Conn., and educated at Yale University. He conducted extensive studies of vegetable proteins and nutritional problems at the Carnegie Institution of Washington, D.C., and at Yale University. In 1926, through use of information obtained from experiments in selective breeding and diet conducted jointly with the American physiological chemist Lafayette Benedict Mendel, he succeeded in accelerating the normal growth rate of certain experimental animals by one third. He also discovered the presence of vitamin D in cod-liver oil. In addition to many papers on nutrition, he was the author of *Proteins of the Wheat Kernel* (1907) and *The Vegetable Proteins* (1909).

OSBORNE, THOMAS MOTT (1859–1926), American penologist, born in Auburn, N.Y., and educated at Harvard University. He was elected chairman of the New York State Commission for Prison Reform in 1913, and had himself committed to Auburn Prison for one week in order to study prison conditions at first hand. In 1914 he was appointed warden of Sing Sing Prison at Ossining, N.Y., where he introduced a number of reforms aimed generally at allowing the prisoners a measure of self-government and at substituting educational for merely punitive measures. Osborne was indicted for alleged misconduct in 1915; after winning a dismissal of the case in the courts he was reinstated, but he resigned soon afterward. He was commandant of the Portsmouth Naval Prison from 1917 to 1920. His writings include *Within Prison Walls* (1914), *Society and Prisons* (1916), and *Prisons and Common Sense* (1924).

OSCAR I (1799–1859), King of Sweden and Norway, son of Marshal Bernadotte, born in Paris. He reigned over Norway and Sweden from 1844 to 1859, having been made Duke of Södermanl when his father was elected crown prince of Sweden. He married the granddaughter of Empress Josephine of France, Josephine Beauharnais.

OSCAR II (1829–1907), King of Sweden and Norway, fourth of the Bernadotte monarchs, and third son of King Oscar I. He succeeded his brother Charles XV (1872). The chief event of his reign was the severance of the union between the two countries of Scandinavia, which had existed since the Napoleonic era. He was judge in the Venezuelan Dispute between the United States and Great Britain (1895–96).

OSCEOLA (1800?–38), Seminole Indian leader, born near the Chattahoochee River, Georgia. See SEMINOLES. His father was an English trader and his mother was the daughter of a Creek chief. His mother took him to live in northern Florida while he was still very young, and there he became a leader of the Seminoles, heading the opposition to the cession of tribal territories to the United States. In 1835 Osceola's wife was seized as the daughter of a runaway slave, and carried into slavery. He denounced the U.S. Indian agent for this act, and was briefly imprisoned. A few months after his release he killed the Indian agent and began attacks on the Americans which precipitated large-scale warfare between the Seminoles and the United States. In 1837 he was seized while conferring under a flag of truce with the American military commander, General Thomas Sidney Jesup (1788–1860), and was imprisoned first at St. Augustine, Fla., and then at Fort Moultrie, S.C., where he died.

OSCILLATION, term applied to any type of back-and-forth or vibratory motion. Typical mechanical oscillations are the motion of a pendulum and the motion of a single particle of water under the influence of waves or ripples. In electricity, an oscillating current is one which changes direction, rising to a peak positive value, falling to zero, rising to a peak negative value, and falling to zero again. The alternating current used for power and lighting is an oscillating current which changes direction 120 times per second; see ELECTRICITY. Alternating currents of extremely high frequencies—200,000 changes of direction per second and up—are used in the generation of the electromagnetic waves of radio transmitters; see RADIO.

OSHAWA, a city and port of Ontario County, Ontario, Canada, on Lake Ontario, 34 miles N.E. of Toronto. It has automobile factories and manufactures textiles, woolens, pianos, metal shingles, culverts, malleable iron, and leather. Pop. (1951) 41,545.

OSHKOSH, county seat of Winnebago Co., Wis., situated on the w. shore of Lake Winnebago, at the mouth of the Fox R., 75 miles N.N.W. of Milwaukee. Transportation facilities include three railroads, river steamers, and a municipal airport. Oshkosh is the center of a farming, dairying, and lumbering region. The principal industries are brewing, the processing of dairy products, and the manufacture of boats, woodwork, furniture, trunks, matches, sash and doors, Venetian blinds, foundry products, motor trucks, agricultural equipment, pumps, marine engines, concrete mixers, rugs, and overalls. The city is the site of a State teachers college and of a State hospital for the insane. In addition, Oshkosh is a popular summer resort and winter sports center. The site of the present city was an important trading station for French fur trappers in the 18th century. It was first permanently settled about 1835 and in 1840 the settlement was named Oshkosh in honor of a chief of the Menominee Indians. Oshkosh became a city in 1853. Pop. (1950) 41,084.

OSIER. See WILLOW.

OSIJEK, city of Croatia, Yugoslavia, situated on the right bank of the Drave, 13 m. above its confluence with the Danube. It is strongly fortified. The manufactures include silk and flour. The town is a busy trade center. It occupies the site of the Roman *Mursa,* the former capital of Lower Pannonia. Pop. (1948) 50,400.

OSIRIS, in the religion of ancient Egypt, one of the principal deities. Originally the local god of Abydos and Busiris, Osiris, who represented the male productive force in nature, became identified with the setting sun. Hence, he was regarded as the ruler of the realm of the dead in the mysterious region below the western horizon. Osiris was the brother and husband of Isis (q.v.), goddess of the earth and of the moon, who represented the female productive force in nature. According to legend Osiris, as king of Egypt, found his people plunged in barbarism, and he taught them law, agriculture, religion, and other blessings of civilization. He was murdered by his evil brother Set, who tore the body to pieces and scattered the fragments. However, Isis found and buried his scattered remains, and each burial place was thereafter revered as sacred ground. Their son Horus (q.v.) avenged his father's death by killing Set, and then ascended the throne. Osiris lived on in the underworld as the ruler of the dead, but he was also, through Horus, regarded as the source of renewed life.

OSLER, SIR WILLIAM (1849–1919), British physician, born in Tecumseh, Ontario, Canada, and educated at Trinity College and McGill University in Canada, University College in London, and the universities of Berlin and Vienna. He was professor of the institutes of medicine, McGill University (1874–84), professor of clinical medicine, Pennsylvania University (1884–89), professor of medicine, Johns Hopkins University (1889–1904), and Gladstonian lecturer, Royal College of Physicians, London, England (1885). He was then appointed regius professor of medicine, Oxford (1905) and honorary professor of medicine, Johns Hopkins University. He was a physician of the first rank, and a stimulating teacher. He was made a baronet in 1911. In 1914–15 Osler was engaged in supervising the general medical preparedness of the British forces in the European War, and helped to organize and equip the Queen's Canadian Military Hospital. He wrote *The Principles and Practice of Medicine* (1893; 10th ed., 1925), *A Concise History of Medicine* (1919), and *The Evolution of Modern Medicine* (1921).

OSLO, formerly CHRISTIANIA or KRISTIANIA, the capital, largest city, chief seaport, and one of the twenty administrative divisions of Norway, situated on the Aker R. at the N. end of Oslo Fiord, about 80 miles N. of the Skagerrak. The city lies in a basin rimmed by forested hills. Around Oslo proper are a number of suburbs, notably Ullevaall, Lille-Thöien, Lindern, and Thorshaug, which have been built to keep pace with the city's growth and are noted for their large, modern apartment houses. Notable buildings in the city include the Storting (Parliament) building, the royal palace, the National Theater, the State Gallery of Fine Arts, the University of Oslo, and the 13th-century citadel of Akershus, now a prison and arsenal. Several museums contain collections of Viking relics. The Oslo quays have a total length of 34,000 ft. and the adjacent pier areas comprise about 360,000 sq. yds. Hydroelectric plants on the Aker R. furnish power for shipyards and factories producing chemicals, machinery, paper, pulp, glass, alcoholic beverages, textiles, and flour.

The first settlement on the site was established as Oslo by Harold Haardraade, King of Norway, in 1048. During the 13th and 14th centuries Oslo became a great trading center. It was frequently burned and plundered during Norwegian dynastic wars. After a fire which completely destroyed the town, Christian IV of Denmark, then ruler of Norway, forbade the inhabitants to rebuild on the old site. They were commanded to build their dwellings on the other side of the bay and to name the city Christiania, in the king's honor. The new city grew rapidly; in 1769 its population numbered 7500, and in 1886 its population was 134,000. Christiania, the new town, was extended to include the site of the old Oslo and incorporated, as Kristiania, in 1878. In 1925 the name of the municipality was changed to Oslo. In World War II Oslo was occupied by German troops on April 9, 1940, the first day of the invasion of Denmark and Norway, and held until May, 1945. Pop. (1951 est.) 420,000.

OSMIRIDIUM. See IRIDIUM; OSMIUM.

OSMIUM, a metallic element, member of the platinum group, of atomic number 76, atomic weight 190.2, and symbol Os. It was discovered in 1803 by the English chemist Smithson Tennant (1761–1815). The metal occurs native in platinum ores and as an alloy, osmiridium, with iridium. Osmium has the greatest density of any known substance; its specific gravity ranges from 21.3 to 24. It is a bluish-white, brittle metal, with hardness 7 and m.p. 2700° C. (4892° F.). It is not attacked by ordinary acids, but dissolves in aqua regia or fuming nitric acid. It forms salts in which it has valences of 2, 3, 4, 6, and 8. The chief use of the metal is in the alloy osmiridium; see IRIDIUM. It is also used, alloyed with platinum, for standard weights and measures.

OSMORHIZA. See SWEET CICELY.

OSMOSIS, diffusion through a semipermeable membrane of a component of a solution from a region of higher concentration to a region of lower concentration. When two solutions of different strength are separated by a semipermeable membrane, the solvent in the more dilute solution will diffuse through the membrane into the more concentrated solution until the concentration of the two solutions is equalized. To a lesser degree, dissolved material will diffuse from the region of high concentration to that of low concentration. In a classic demonstration of osmosis a vertical tube containing a solution of sugar is placed, with its lower end closed off by a semipermeable membrane, in a container of water. The level of the sugar solution in the tube increases visibly as the water from the container passes through the membrane into the tube. A very small amount of the sugar also passes from the tube into the water container. The passage of a substance from the outside to an inside system (water diffusing from the container to the tube) is called *endosmosis*. If the sugar water were in the container and the water in the tube, the process would be called *exosmosis*. Osmosis is an extremely important process in the physiology of plants and animals. It is involved in the passage of water and dissolved salts from the earth into the roots of plants and in the flow of water and sap through plant tissue. Similarly, in animals, the passage of dissolved food material contained in the blood stream from the capillaries to the tissue is partially dependent on osmosis. The term *dialysis* is used to describe the separation by means of a semipermeable membrane of colloidal material from dissolved substances; see COLLOIDAL DISPERSION.

OSMUNDA, genus of ferns, commonly called "flowering ferns", and belonging to the family Osmundaceae. The genus is widely distributed in temperate regions. It is also widely cultivated for the matted roots of its members; the roots are used as a growing medium for the cultivation of orchids. Flowering ferns are so called because they produce spore-bearing leaves which resemble sprays of small flowers. The plants grow to a height of about five feet. The cinnamon fern, *Osmunda cinnamomea,* characterized by cinnamon-colored sporophylls, the royal fern, *O. regalis,* characterized by sporophylls which form a paniclelike inflorescence, and the interrupted fern, *O. claytonia,* characterized by brown, drooping sporangia, are common in wet woods of the United States.

OSNABRÜCK, city of the State of Lower Saxony, West Germany, 75 miles s.s.w. of Bremen. Its great Catholic cathedral, in the style of the first half of the 13th century, is rich in relics and monuments; and the town hall (1486–1512) contains portraits of all the plenipotentiaries who here, on October 24, 1648, signed the peace of Westphalia. Osnabrück has important iron and steel works, and manufactures of railroad plant, agricultural machinery, gas meters, chemicals, paper, and tobacco. Pop. (1950) 109,533.

OSPREY, FISH HAWK, or GLEDE, common name applied to a cosmopolitan bird, *Pandion haliaëtus,* of the Hawk family. The bird, which is about two feet long, is dark brown above and white below. The undersurface of the female is streaked with brown. The osprey, when seeking food, hovers over a body of water, and dives beneath the surface to capture fish in its talons. Ospreys build huge,

basketlike nests of sticks in trees, sometimes close to human habitations, and breed in the same nests for many years. The characteristic cry of the osprey is a thin, shrill whistle.

OSSETIANS, OSSETS, or **OSSETES,** a people descended from the Alani (q.v.) or Alans, speaking Ossetic, a language of the Iranian branch of the subfamily of Indo-Iranian languages (q.v.) and inhabiting Ossetia, a region in the central Caucasus, U.S.S.R. Ossetia comprises the South Ossetian Autonomous Region, created in 1922, and lying within the boundaries of the Georgian Soviet Socialist Republic; and the North Ossetian Autonomous Soviet Socialist Republic, created in 1936 and a part of the Russian Soviet Federated Socialist Republic. Christianity was introduced among the Ossetians in the 12th century; subsequently, a large number of Ossetians adopted Mohammedanism. They were conquered by the Russians in 1802. At the present time the North Ossetians export timber and cultivate a number of crops and vegetables, principally corn. Dairy farming is also common. The South Ossetians, fewer in number than the northern, are chiefly pastoral, herding sheep and goats in the east, and cattle in the west. Peasant industries include the manufacture of leather goods, fur caps, daggers, and metalware. The two chief dialect groups of the Ossetic language are the Digor in the north and the Iron in the south. Since the Ossetians received political and cultural autonomy the Latin alphabet has been adopted for the writing of the Ossetic language, formerly written in the Armenian alphabet. In a recent year the population of the North Ossetian Autonomous Soviet Socialist Republic numbered about 350,000; the population of the South Ossetian Autonomous Region numbered about 100,000.

OSSIAN or **OISIN,** Gaelic poet. Ossian was the son of Fionn MacCumhail, a hero who flourished in the 3rd century A.D.

To the majority of people Ossian is known through the publications of James Macpherson. Between 1760 and 1763 he published *Fingal,* an epic poem in six books, purporting to be translations of poems composed by Ossian, son of Fingal. The translations were probably the compositions of James Macpherson. See MACPHERSON, JAMES.

OSSINING, a town in Westchester Co., N.Y., on the Hudson River, 30 miles N. of New York. The 88-ft. span of the Croton aqueduct is located there, with an adjacent arched bridge, and also Sing Sing Prison. The name was changed in 1901, and in 1906 a new

The osprey

charter went into effect. Settled about 1700 on part of the Philipse Manor, Sing Sing, named from the Sin Sincks Indians, was incorporated as a village in 1813. Pop. (1950) 16,098.

OSSIPEVSK, formerly BERDICHEV, town in Russia, 115 m. by railroad w.s.w. of Kiev. The principal manufactures include tobacco, oil products, and leather. Pop., about 65,000.

OSTADE, ADRIAEN VAN (1610–85), Dutch painter and engraver, elder brother of Isaac van Ostade, born in Haarlem. He studied with the Dutch artist Frans Hals and later came under the influence of Rembrandt. He painted many small genre pictures, lively and vigorous and full of subtle effects of light and shade. His subject matter was tavern scenes, peasants drinking and smoking, itinerant musicians, village festivities, and quaint village characters. He also executed fifty etching plates depicting peasant life. His work is represented at The Hague, and in the Louvre, Paris, the Metropolitan Museum of Art, New York City, and the Philadelphia Museum of Fine Arts.

OSTEND, a summer resort in the Belgian province of W. Flanders, on the North Sea, 77 miles w.n.w. of Brussels. Its digue, or sea wall, 3 m. long, 40 ft. high, and 35 yds. broad, forms a favorite promenade. From July to September it is frequented by visitors from all over the world. It is an important fishing

station, and it has a school of navigation.

In World War I, British forces, in August 1914, occupied the city, to which the Belgian government removed at the beginning of October. The Germans entered two weeks later and made it an important submarine base. The city was repeatedly bombarded from the sea and air. Simultaneously with the attack on Zeebrugge, April 22–23, 1918, blockships attempted to reach the entrance to Ostend harbor but failed when the wind changed and lifted the smoke screen. An attempt the following month was more successful when H.M.S. *Vindictive*, filled with cement, was sunk in the fairway but did not completely block it. During the final operations in Belgium (in which the 37th and 91st American divisions figured) the Germans evacuated Ostend and King Albert re-entered on Oct. 19, 1918. Dating from 1072, the city is noted for the protracted siege by the Spaniards which it underwent from July 7, 1601, to Sept. 20, 1604. Pop. (1951 est.) 51,156.

OSTEND MANIFESTO, the title of a document drawn up by James Buchanan, John Y. Mason, and Pierre Soulé, the American ministers to Great Britain, France, and Spain, respectively, at Ostend, Belgium, in October, 1854. Shortly prior to that date, Soulé had entered into negotiations with the Spanish government for the purchase of Cuba by the United States, although he had not been authorized to do so by the U.S. government. This action incurred the censure of his superiors, who ordered him to consult with the other envoys named above. The result of this conference was the Ostend Manifesto, which urged Spain to sell Cuba to the United States and advocated the use of force by the United States if Spain refused. Publication of the Manifesto caused a sensation among the antislavery forces in the United States, who feared that the acquisition of Cuba, where slavery was a well-established institution, would strengthen the proslavery forces. The sensation soon abated, however, and the establishment of new grounds for North-South conflict was avoided, when the U.S. government repudiated the Manifesto.

OSTENSO, MARTHA (1900–), American novelist, born in Norway and reared in Minnesota and South Dakota, and in Canada. She is noted for her novels dealing with the lives and problems of the farmers of Scandinavian ancestry in Middle Western United States. Her best-known novel is *Wild Geese* (1926); among her other works are *The Mad Carews* (1927), *The Mandrake Root* (1930), *Stone Field* (1937), *O, River, Remember* (1943), and *Sunset Tree* (1949).

OSTEOLOGY, the scientific study of bones. See BONE; SKELETON.

OSTEOMYELITIS, term applied to any inflammation of bone or bone marrow, usually caused by infection by such microorganisms as *Staphylococcus aureus,* various streptococci or the typhoid bacillus. The microorganisms reach the bone through the blood stream after systemic infection has occurred. Occasionally, osteomyelitis occurs by direct infection after surgery or after a compound fracture, or as a result of trauma. Osteomyelitis most often occurs in boys from two to twelve years old; it may, however, occur in persons of any age or either sex, especially if systemic infection has been immediately preceded by a blow to a bone. Common symptoms include chills followed by fever, and pain and swelling above the site of inflammation. Because osteomyelitis usually first appears near a joint at the end of a long bone in the lower limb, the condition is often mistaken for arthritis. The inflammation begins in the soft parts of the long bones, often with the formation of pus-containing abscesses, and soon spreads over the entire bone, with consequent death of the hard portions of the bone. If the pus is not drained quickly, the pressure caused by accumulation within a limited space results in the extrusion of pus from the weakened outer surface of the bone into the region below the membrane covering the bone, causing the membrane to be stripped away. Further extension of the suppurative process results in metastasis (q.v.) to other bones, and often in death. Osteomyelitis is treated by injections of antibiotics such as penicillin, and by concurrent surgery to open the affected bone and drain the pus and dead tissue. Incomplete drainage results in chronic inflammation of the bone. Bacteriophage and maggots (q.v.) are sometimes used to kill bacteria within the infected bone and to eat away necrotic tissue. The affected limb is immobilized by traction prior to surgery, and is placed within a plaster cast after surgery to insure immobilization.

OSTEOPATHY, a school of medicine whose thesis is twofold: (1) It is natural for the living body to protect itself against disease; and (2) The power to do this depends upon the normal relationships of the component parts of the body machine. The influence of climate, age, sex, and physical and mental habits are also recognized. Osteopathy includes the specialties relating to the diagnosis and treatment of diseases of women and children,

of the eye, ear, nose, and throat, of the heart and blood vessels, and of the various other organs, and insanity. Obstetrics and surgery are included. Physical disturbances interfering with the defensive mechanism are said to be found in bones, muscles, ligaments, tendons, or fasciae. They result from accident, postural faults, malnutrition, bad habits of work or play, even from congenital causes such as abnormal length, size, or shape of bones. They often result from reflexes caused by inflammation or infection. These physical disturbances cause the circulation to slow up, causing congestion of blood and lymph and resulting in relative acidosis in local tissues. This irritates the nerves passing through and distant organs are affected, directly and through their circulation.

This influences the natural functions of the organs and also interferes with the making of remedies to fight infection. Of course such physical disturbances also have their part in many conditions of crippling resulting from industrial conditions and sports, including the states commonly referred to as rheumatism, neuralgia, sciatica, and lumbago. Osteopathic physicians use the standard scientific methods of diagnosis—physical, chemical, and microscopic. They go beyond this to study the physical disturbances already referred to, determining gait, posture, and joint and tissue conditions by observation and the sense of touch. Osteopathic treatment majors in the specific correction of these physical disturbances, including surgery, the correction of errors in hygiene and sanitation, and in mental and physical habits.

OSTIA, a city of ancient Latium, situated at the mouth of the Tiber R., about 14 miles s.w. of Rome. Reputedly founded about 640 B.C. by Ancus Marcius, the fourth legendary king of Rome, Ostia was regarded as the oldest Roman colony. It was famed for its salt works, and was the port where grain from Sicily, Sardinia, and Africa was landed. Ostia was long the chief base of the Roman navy, but its harbor finally became filled with silt. In the 1st century A.D., Emperor Claudius dug a new harbor 2½ miles N. of Ostia and connected it with the Tiber by a canal. A new town, commonly called Portus, developed around the new harbor. At the height of its prosperity Ostia had a population of about 75,000, but the city declined rapidly after the fall of the Roman Empire, and by the 8th century was in ruins. These ruins, systematically excavated after 1880, are second in importance only to those of Pompeii (q.v.)

Comprising a forum, temples, baths, villas, warehouses, and blocks of flats, called insulæ, the ruins provide invaluable data on the nature of a prosperous seaport of the imperial age. Modern Ostia, a small village built during the Middle Ages, is about ½ mile N. of the ancient site.

OSTIAKS. See OSTYAKS.

OSTRACISM, in Greek antiquity, a political procedure providing for the temporary banishment of any citizen whose presence appeared to endanger the stability of the state. The law of ostracism is thought to have been first promulgated in Athens by the statesman Cleisthenes (q.v.) about 508 B.C., but the first record of its enforcement dates from 488–87 B.C., when Hipparchus, a member of the powerful Pisistratus family, was banished. Every year the Athenian assembly decided by a show of hands whether or not an ostracism was to take place. If the assembly decided in the affirmative, a date for public voting was set and the citizens, voting by tribes, deposited their ballots in boxes in the market place. Each voter wrote the name of the person whom he wished exiled on a fragment of pottery, or *ostrakon*. The man who received the most votes out of a required minimum of 10,000 total ballots cast had to leave Athens within ten days and remain away for ten years. Ostracism did not inflict any stigma upon the victim, and neither his property nor his civil rights were in any way disturbed. The ostracized man might be recalled by vote of the assembly. Among the prominent statesmen who suffered ostracism were Aristides, surnamed "The Just", Themistocles, and Hyperbolus. In the case of the last-named demagogue, whose ostracism took place in 418–17, the vote had been intended to decide between Nicias and Alcibiades (q.v.), but they combined their forces against the much less influential Hyperbolus. This occurrence resulted in the abandonment of the system. More than 1500 *ostraka* have been found in recent years in the vicinity of the Athenian Acropolis and the market place, including many which bear the names of the statesmen known from literary sources to have been ostracized. More than 500 *ostraka* bearing the name of Themistocles, ostracized in 471 B.C., have been discovered.

OSTRICH, common name applied to any of four species of large, flightless birds constituting the genus *Struthio* and the order Struthioniformes. The birds are native to Africa and the Near East. Ostriches are the largest and strongest of living birds, attaining a height from crown to foot of about eight

Canadian Pacific Railway

Above: Ostriches in Cape Province, South Africa. Left: The head of an ostrich.

feet. They have small heads, with large eyes and short, broad beaks, long necks, comparatively small wings which they spread when running, and long, powerful legs which they use in defense. The feet bear only two toes, the outer of which is rudimentary. The feathers, especially of the tail, are large and soft. Male ostriches are black in color, with white wings and tail. The white feathers of the male are the ostrich plumes of commerce. The female is dull grayish brown.

Ostriches are rapid runners, often attaining a running speed of about twenty-five miles per hour. The males are polygamous and travel about in hot, sandy areas with three or four females, or in groups of four or five males accompanied by mates and young. The mates of a male ostrich lay their white or yellowish-white eggs together in a single large depression in the sand. The eggs weigh about three pounds each and have a volume of about three pints. To guard the eggs against destruction the male sits on them at night; the females take turns sitting on them during part of the day. Actual incubation of the eggs is performed by the heat of the sun. Contrary to popular belief, ostriches do not bury their heads in the sand when frightened.

In the last half of the 19th century ostrich farming (the breeding of domesticated ostriches for their plumes) was carried on extensively in South Africa, Algiers, Australia, France, and the United States. Ostrich plumes were used in hatmaking and dressmaking. Toward the end of the 19th century, annual world income from ostrich farming amounted to about $10,000,000. Today, ostrich farming is an extremely small-scale industry, the demand for ostrich plumes being almost negligible.

The common African ostrich or "camel bird" is *Struthio camelus.* The so-called "American ostrich" is actually a rhea (q.v.).

OSTRICH FERN, common name applied to ferns of the genus *Matteuccia,* so called because their sporophylls (spore-bearing leaves) resemble small ostrich plumes. Ostrich ferns are native to cool, damp, sandy areas in the Northern Hemisphere, and are cultivated for ornament. The nonfertile leaves are tall and graceful, thin near the roots and broad distally, growing in a vaselike cluster. The plant grows to a height of from 7 to 10 feet. The American ostrich fern, *M. nodulosa*, is common in northeastern United States; the European ostrich fern is *M. struthiopteris*.

OSTROGOTHS. See GOTHS.

OSTROVSKI, ALEXANDER NIKOLAYEVITCH (1823–86), Russian dramatist, born in Moscow. He wrote some fifty comedies. Ostrovski, while idolized at Moscow, found scant recognition in St. Petersburg. Just before his death he was appointed director of the Moscow theaters. Among his plays the best are *Poverty Is Not a Fault, A Profitable Position, Innocent Culprits* (trans., New York, 1906), and *The Storm* (1860). The last-named play, generally considered his masterpiece, was presented, in an English translation, by Constance Storm, in New York (1900). His plays embrace all types of middle-class life.

OSTWALD, WILHELM (1853–1932), German physical chemist, born in Riga, Latvia, and educated at the University of Tarty. In 1882 he was appointed professor in the Riga Polytechnicum, and from 1887 to 1906 served as professor of physical chemistry and director of the Physico-chemical Institute at the University of Leipzig. Ostwald is generally considered to be one of the founders of modern physical chemistry, and is especially known for his contributions to the field of electrochemistry, including important studies of the electrical conductivity and electrolytic dissociation of organic acids. He invented a viscometer which is still used for measuring the viscosity of solutions. In 1900 he discovered a method of preparing nitric acid by oxidizing ammonia; this method was used by Germany during World War I for manufacturing explosives after the Allied blockade had cut off her regular supply of nitrates, and is still used in several countries under the name of the Ostwald-Brauer process. Ostwald received the 1909 Nobel Prize for chemistry. His works include *The Scientific Bases of Analytical Chemistry* (1894), *Electrochemistry* (1895), *Fundamental Principles of Chemistry* (1909), and *Colour Science* (1931).

OSTYAKS or **OSTIAKS,** the name of a western Siberian tribe speaking Ostyak, a language of the Ugric branch of the Finno-Ugric (q.v.) family of languages, and inhabiting the upland valleys of the Ural Mountains, principally the basin of the Ob River. The name is sometimes also applied to a group of tribes of different languages who inhabit the region between the Urals and the Yenisei River. All Ostyaks are short and spare in body, with white skin and brown eyes and hair. They live chiefly by hunting and fishing. Their handicrafts include carving in wood, bone, and birch bark. In a recent year the Ostyaks as a whole numbered more than 22,300; members of the Ostyak tribe numbered about 1500.

OSWEGO, lake port and capital of Oswego Co., N.Y., on the mouth of Oswego River, Lake Ontario, at the end of the Oswego Canal, 326 miles N.W. of New York City. It is one of the chief ports on the lake, with a breakwater, large grain elevators, and several miles of wharves, and carries on a brisk trade. The river falls here 34 ft., and the water power is utilized in flour mills, knitting mills, and other industries. Oswego starch and corn flour are as well known in Europe as in America. Other manufactures are knit goods, car springs, boilers, engines, and oil-well supplies; sashes and blinds, lumber and perfumery are among the leading industries. The soil is fertile, rich crops of grain are raised, and iron and salt are mined. Owing to its location it was an important post in King George's War and the French and Indian War. Pop. (1950) 22,647.

OSWEGO TEA. See MONARDA.

OTALGIA. See EAR, DISEASES OF.

OTARU, seaport of Hokkaido Prefecture, Japan, 100 miles N. of Hakodate. Timber and agricultural produce are exported. It is a herring fishing center. Pop., about 165,000.

OTHMAN, or OSMAN I (1259–1326), founder of the Ottoman power, born in Bithynia. On the overthrow of the sultanate of Iconium in 1299 by the Mongols, he seized upon a portion of Bithynia. Then he took possession of the territory of Nicæa, and gradually subdued a great part of Asia Minor, and so became the founder of the Turkish Empire.

OTIS, ELISHA GRAVES (1811–61), American inventor and manufacturer, born in Halifax, Vt. He was a pioneer in the construction and manufacture of steam-powered elevators and elevator devices. In 1853 at the World's Fair in the Crystal Palace in New York City he demonstrated his most important invention, an automatic safety device for stopping an elevator when its supporting cables have broken; see ELEVATOR. Four years later he designed and installed the first passenger elevator in the United States. Shortly before his death he patented a steam elevator which became the basis of the world-famous Otis Elevator Co.

OTIS, JAMES (1725–83), American Revolutionary statesman, born in West Barnstable,

Mass., and educated at Harvard College (now Harvard University). He entered the legal profession in Boston in 1750, and was later appointed king's advocate general. In 1760 he resigned from that office to appear as counsel for the merchants of Boston, in opposition to the issuance of writs of assistance enabling the royal customs collectors to search the establishments of merchants suspected of violating the Sugar Act of 1733. In a brilliant address to the court, Otis declared that any act passed by Parliament contrary to the "natural rights" of the American colonists was invalid. Although he failed to prevent the issuance of the writs, he was recognized thereafter as one of the ablest pleaders of the cause of freedom for the colonists. He was elected to the Massachusetts legislature in 1761, and three years later became the head of the Massachusetts branch of the Committees of Correspondence (q.v.). In 1764 he also prepared a cogent summary of the colonists' grievances against the mother country, *The Rights of the British Colonies Asserted and Proved.* From 1766 to 1769, in association with Samuel Adams (q.v.) and Joseph Hawley, Otis directed the opposition within the Massachusetts legislature to the oppressive revenue measures of the British government. In the latter year he was violently attacked by a customs collector who opposed his published statements; the injuries sustained by Otis were so severe that he was compelled to withdraw from public life.

OTITIS. See EAR, DISEASES OF.

OTO or **OTOE,** the name of a small North American Indian tribe of Siouan stock (q.v.), formerly holding the territory west of the Missouri River and south of the Platte River in southeastern Nebraska. Since the early 19th century the Oto have been confererated with another small tribe called the Missouri. The two tribes speak the same language, and reside together on a reservation in eastern Oklahoma. In a recent year the Oto numbered more than 880.

OTOLITHS. See EAR: *Equilibrium.*

OTOMACO, OTOMACA, or **OTOMAC,** a South American Indian tribe comprising an independent linguistic stock, and living in Venezuela in the forests along the Orinoco River near its junction with the Meta River. They follow an agricultural economy in which the fields are cultivated communally. The principal crops are manioc and corn. The tribe also engages in hunting and fishing. Game, fish, and farm produce are divided among the community by the chief. A peculiarity of their

diet is the eating of an oily clay, which they often mix into their bread. Marriage is monogamous, and women have equality in tribal ceremonies.

OTOMI, an ancient people of central Mexico, comprising an independent linguistic stock, and inhabiting most of the area of the States of Querétaro and Guanajuato, and considerable portions of the States of Hidalgo, Michoacán, and Mexico. The Otomi are below medium stature and darker in color than the Indians of neighboring tribes. They were originally agriculturalists, wove cotton clothing, and worked in gold, copper, and stone. They were noted for their songs and musical ability, and had elaborate religious ceremonies. The Aztecs subjugated them, and the Spanish, during the conquest of Mexico in the 16th century and subsequently, sent a number of expeditions against them. They were not reduced to submission by the Spanish until 1715. At the present time they still form a substantial part of the working-class population of their former territories, and their language, which is monosyllabic and consists of several major dialects, continues to be spoken over a wide area.

OTRANTE, DUC D'. See FOUCHÉ, JOSEPH, DUC D'OTRANTE.

OTSU, city and capital of Shiga Prefecture, Honshu Island, Japan, situated on Lake Biwa, about 10 miles E. of Kyoto. It lies in a rich farming region and is a resort center, with excellent transportation facilities. Points of interest include the biological laboratory of Kyoto Imperial University and the grave of the celebrated Japanese poet Basho (1640–94). For periods during the 2nd and 7th centuries A.D. Otsu was the site of the imperial court. Pop., about 80,000.

OTTAWA, a North American Indian tribe belonging to the Algonquin linguistic family (see ALGONQUIN), and formerly living in the region of the upper Ottawa River, Canada. In culture, the Ottawa were similar to the several other tribes inhabiting the same area; see AMERICAN INDIANS: *Eastern Woodland Area.* They carried on an extensive trade along the water routes between the tribes to the east of them and the tribes of the Great Lakes. The Ottawa had a moral rule of conduct, embodied in twenty-one precepts, which strikingly resembles the code of the Biblical Ten Commandments.

About 1645 the tribe was driven out of their territory by the Iroquois, and took refuge on Manitoulin Island in Lake Huron. They later

Aerial view of Ottawa, capital of the Dominion of Canada

moved to the south shore of Lake Superior, but were obliged to return to Manitoulin Island when they were attacked by the Sioux. Subsequently they extended their territory until they controlled all of lower Michigan, parts of Ohio and Illinois, and an area on the Canadian side of Lake Huron. During the colonial period the Ottawa fought on the side of the French and one of their chiefs, Pontiac (q.v.), achieved wide renown as a leader in warfare against the English. In the American Revolutionary War and the War of 1812, the tribe was allied with the English against the Americans. In 1870 several bands of Ottawa Indians moved to the Indian Territory (q.v.) and soon lost their tribal identity. The majority of the Ottawa remained in Michigan, first on reservations, and then in scattered communities where many still reside.

OTTAWA, capital of the Dominion of Canada and county seat of Carleton County, Ontario, situated in the E. part of the province of Ontario, on the s. bank of the Ottawa R. at its confluence with the Rideau R., 101 miles w. of Montreal. At the w. end of the city the Ottawa R. forms the rapids known as Chaudière Falls, the major source of hydroelectric power for the factories of the city. The Rideau Canal, extending from Ottawa to Kingston on Lake Ontario, divides the city into the Upper Town, which is predominantly English, and the Lower Town, predominantly French. The streets of Ottawa are wide and laid out regularly in a gridiron pattern, with about 1500 acres of park. The chief architectural features are the Gothic-style parliament and departmental buildings, occupying three sides of a quadrangle on Parliament Hill, 125 ft. above the Ottawa R. Other notable buildings include the Roman Catholic Cathedral of Notre Dame, the Anglican Christ Church Cathedral, the official residence of the governor general, known as Rideau Hall, the National Museum, the Dominion Observatory, and the National Art Gallery. Among the notable educational institutions are the University of Ottawa, several collegiate institutes, and St. Patrick's College. Because of the abundant hydroelectric power Ottawa is a large manufacturing city. The chief products are paper and pulp, wood products, matches, cement, carbide, iron and foundry products, mica, and clothing.

The city was founded in 1827 by Col. John By, an English engineer who supervised the building of the Rideau Canal. The settlement, named Bytown, grew rapidly as a result of the development of the lumber trade. It was incorporated as a city under its present name in 1854 and four years later was selected by

N.Y. Zoological Society

Otter (Lutra canadensis)

Queen Victoria as the capital of Canada. Pop. (1951) 202,045.

OTTAWA RIVER, the principal tributary of the St. Lawrence. It rises 160 miles north of Ottawa, on the Laurentian divide, and flows generally southeast until after a course of about 685 miles, most of it along the boundary between the provinces of Ontario and Quebec, it falls into the St. Lawrence by two mouths which form the island of Montreal. During its course it is fed by many important tributaries, such as the Madawasca and Rideau on the right and the Gatineau and the Rivière du Lièvre on the left. These, with the Ottawa itself, form the means of transit for a large lumber trade. The Ottawa is connected with Lake Ontario at Kingston by the Rideau Canal and is navigable for 250 miles.

OTTAWA, UNIVERSITY OF, a partly coeducational Catholic institution of higher learning, situated in Ottawa, Ontario, Canada, founded as the College of Bytown about 1848 and granted university status in 1866. It was recognized by the Holy See in 1899, and is now one of the four North American pontifical universities. In 1933 its power to grant degrees in all branches of learning was confirmed by the Ottawa legislature. The divisions of the University are schools of theology, philosophy, canon law, political science, arts, music, medicine, and nursing. All courses are given in both English and French. Bachelor's, master's and doctor's degrees are granted. In 1953 the enrollment, including almost 1375 full-time students, was more than 4600, and the faculty numbered about 325.

OTTER, any aquatic carnivore of the genus *Lutra*, belonging to the family Mustelidae, which also includes the badgers and weasels. In the common species, *L. lutra,* distributed through Europe and Asia, the body may attain a length of 2½ ft., and the tail half as much; the head is broad and flat, with short, rounded ears; the blunt snout bears lateral slitlike nostrils, closed during diving; the long body is covered with chestnut fur; the legs are short, but strong; the feet are clawed as well as webbed. The otter lives in a hole by the stream side, and feeds especially on fish, but also on small mammals, birds, frogs, and crayfish. A similar species, *L. canadensis,* is found in North America. The otters of North America were once abundant, but owing to the value of their fur and the subsequent trapping, they are comparatively rare, except in the Hudson Bay region. See SEA OTTER.

OTTER HOUND, a special breed of dog descended from the old Southern hound of Great Britain. It has large broad feet, a rough, grizzly coat varying in color, and good sight and a keen scent. It is a powerful swimmer, has great endurance, and is of a savage disposition. The average height is 23 to 25 inches, and weight 50 to 75 pounds.

OTTER SHREW. See INSECTIVORA.

OTTO, the name of four Holy Roman emperors. **1.** OTTO, called THE GREAT (912–73), King of Germany from 936 to 973 and Emperor from 962 to 973, son of Henry I, the Fowler. After subduing an uprising of nobles incited by his brother Henry, he consolidated his kingdom by granting duchies to faithful relatives and followers. In 951 he marched to Italy to assist Adelaide, Queen of Lombardy, against Berengar II of Italy. Otto defeated Berengar and married Adelaide, thereby becoming ruler of northern Italy. When he returned to Germany, he again overcame a rebellion of nobles, and halted a Hungarian invasion in 955. Berengar took arms against the newly installed pope, John XII, and Otto conquered him in 961. The next year he was crowned Holy Roman Emperor, reviving Charlemagne's empire, which had been divided since 814. In 936 he deposed Pope John and had Leo VIII elected in his stead. Otto sought to make the Church subordinate to the authority of the empire, but assisted in spreading Christianity throughout his domain. He negotiated unsuccessfully with the Eastern Roman emperor Nicephorus II for an alliance between the Eastern and Western Roman empires, but was able to arrange a marriage between his son Otto and Theophano, daughter of the emperor Romanus II.

2. OTTO II (955–83), King of Germany from 861 to 983 and Emperor from 973 to 983, son of Otto I, with whom he ruled jointly from 967 to 973. In 976 he suppressed the rebellion led by his cousin Henry II of Bavaria, and two years later, having been attacked by Lothair, King of France, drove the French out of Lorraine but was unsuccessful in besieging Paris. Later Lothair renounced Lorraine and peace was established. Otto next invaded southern Italy, gaining possession of Naples, Salerno, and Taranto, but was overwhelmingly defeated by the Greeks and Saracens at Cotrone in 982, and died shortly after the planning of a new campaign. His wife Theophano brought Byzantine refinement and culture into the German court.

3. Otto III (980–1002), Emperor from 983 to 1002, son of Otto II. During his minority the empire was governed by a co-regency of his mother, Theophano, and his grandmother, Adelaide, until 991, and under the regency of a council headed by Willigis, Archbishop of Mainz, from 991 until 996, when Otto assumed control. In the last-named year, having been crowned King of the Lombards, he went to Rome and established his cousin Bruno as Pope Gregory V; he later defended Gregory against John Crescentius, self-styled patrician of the Romans, and after Gregory's death made his own former tutor pope as Sylvester II. Otto remained in Rome until his death, striving to make the city the capital of the Western Empire and to restore many of the customs of the ancient Roman Empire.

4. Otto IV of Brunswick (1175–1218), Emperor from 1198 to 1215, son of Henry the Lion, Duke of Bavaria, and of Matilda, daughter of King Henry II of England. He was educated in England at the court of his uncle, Richard I, and was supported by the Guelphs (see Guelphs and Ghibellines) as successor to the imperial crown in opposition to Philip, Duke of Swabia. Otto fought Philip for ten years and was finally crowned in 1209, a year after the latter's assassination. When Otto seized papal territory in 1210 he was excommunicated by Pope Innocent III and a year later was proclaimed deposed by a council of German princes, who invited Frederick of Hohenstaufen (later Holy Roman emperor as Frederick II) to take the throne. Otto, supported by King John of England, continued to fight against Frederick and against Philip II Augustus of France, who was supported by the pope. In 1215, after being defeated by the French army at Douvines, Otto retired to his estates in Brunswick, where he remained until his death.

OTTOMAN EMPIRE, an empire founded by Othman, who died at Pausa, in Bithynia, in 1326. Othman was succeeded by a race of the

most warlike princes of history. They greatly extended the bounds of the Turkish dominion, and about 1357 crossed the Hellespont into Europe, when Amurath I made Adrianople the seat of the Turkish Empire, gradually reduced the dominions of the Greeks, and, after a long siege, Mahomet II took Constantinople in 1453. See Othman; Turkey.

OTTUMWA, county seat of Wapello Co., Iowa, on both sides of the Des Moines River, 75 miles N.W. of Burlington, in the heart of the State's bituminous coal fields. Extensive dams furnish water power; the industrial works include foundries, agricultural implement, candy, cigar, and furniture factories, stove and boiler works, and meat packing. Pop. (1950) 33,631.

OTUS and **EPHIALTES,** in Greek mythology, two giants, the twin sons of Aloeus, or, by some accounts, of Poseidon, god of the sea, and of Imphimedia, the wife of Aloeus. They are often called Aloidæ (or Aloadæ). Renowned for their strength and daring, Otus and Ephialtes at the age of nine declared war upon the Olympian deities. As a means of reaching the deities, they tried to pile Mount Ossa upon Olympus (q.v.), and Pelion upon Ossa. They were slain by Apollo, god of medicine, music, and light, before they grew to manhood. According to another legend, the twins imprisoned Ares, god of war, for thirteen months.

OTWAY, Thomas (1652–85), English dramatist, born in Trotton, Sussex, England.

Photo by Mary Eleanor Browning
Otter hound

In 1673 he settled in London, and produced *Alcibiades,* in which Mrs. Barry made her first appearance. In 1680 he produced *The Orphan,* and in 1682, *Venice Preserved.* His other works include *Don Carlos* (1676), *Friendship in Fashion* (1678), *The Soldier's Fortune* (1679), and *The Atheist* (1684).

OUACHITA RIVER, or WASHITA RIVER, river rising N. of Mena, Polk Co., Ark., and flowing S.E. through Arkansas and into Louisiana, where under the name of the Black River it passes through Caldwell, Catahoula, and Concordia parishes, joining the Red River before its junction with the Mississippi after a course of 550 m.

OUD, JACOBUS JOHANNES PIETER (1890–), Dutch architect, born in Purmerend, and educated at the Technische Hoogeschool, Delft. He studied architecture in Amsterdam and Munich, became interested in developing a modern building style free of traditional elements, and joined the *de Stijl* group, an association of modernist artists, architects, and writers. He was the leading architect of this group, and designed a great number of simple, cubelike buildings and housing projects. From 1918 to 1933 he was city architect of Rotterdam. His best-known work includes housing projects for workers at Hoek van Holland and Rotterdam, and middle-class housing at Stuttgart, Germany.

OUDH or **OUDE.** See UTTAR PRADESH.

OUDRY, JEAN BAPTISTE (1686–1755), French painter, born in Paris. He learned painting chiefly from the French court painter Nicolas de Largillière, who taught him to paint portraits, landscapes, and animal scenes. In 1717 he painted a portrait of Czar Peter the Great, then on a visit to Paris. Louis XV commissioned him to record scenes of the royal hunts, and appointed him superintendent of the Gobelins' tapestry works (see TAPESTRY), where Oudry's hunting designs were woven. His work was classical in style and displayed subtlety in the use of light and shadow. Examples of his work are in the Louvre, Paris, the Wallace Collection, London, and the Metropolitan Museum of Art, New York City.

OUIDA. See RAMÉE.

OUISTITI. See MARMOSET.

OULU (Sw. *Uleaborg*), coastal city and capital of the department of the same name, Finland, situated on the Gulf of Bothnia. The department comprises N. Finland, or almost half the area of the country. It is a forested region, drained by the Torne, Tana, and Kemi rivers. In the N. are the Lapland Mts., rising to a height of 4438 ft. above sea level in Halditsjokko, the highest point in Finland. By the peace treaty of 1947, following World War II, the department lost the Petsamo and Karelian regions to the Soviet Union (see FINLAND: *History*). The capital was founded in 1375 by the Swedes as a fortified center to be used against the Russians. It is a seaport, exporting tar, leather, timber, wheat, wood products, and fish. Oulu is also the center of a dairying region and is a resort town. Area of department, 21,887 sq.m.; pop. (1950 prelim.) 360,078. Pop. of city (1950 prelim.) 37,896.

OUNCE or **SNOW LEOPARD,** a wild, carnivorous mammal, *Felis uncia,* of the Cat family, found in the mountains of Central Asia. The animal, which attains a body length of about four feet, is white and bluish gray in color, spotted with black. Its large eyes are usually bluish gray. The ounce subsists on large, wild, mountain animals, such as mountain sheep and ibexes. The ounce is not ferocious; it does not ordinarily attack man, and is easily domesticated in captivity.

OUNCE. See WEIGHTS AND MEASURES.

OUR LADY OF MERCY. See LADY OF MERCY.

OURSLER, CHARLES FULTON, pseudonym ANTHONY ABBOT (1893–1952), American editor and author, born in Baltimore, Md., and educated in the public schools of that city. He joined the newspaper *Baltimore American* as a reporter in 1910 and two years later became its drama and music critic. Removing to New York City in 1918, he served on the editorial staff of a music publication there for a period and between 1913 and 1944 was successively editor of the *Metropolitan* and *Liberty* magazines. After 1943 he was a senior editor of the periodical *Reader's Digest.* Oursler attained success as a novelist and dramatist in the 1920's, but he is best remembered for *The Greatest Story Ever Told* (1949), a popular biography of Jesus Christ; *The Greatest Book Ever Written* (1951), a version of the Old Testament in narrative form; and *The Greatest Faith Ever Known* (with Grace Oursler Armstrong, posthumously published, 1953), a history of Biblical events. Among his other works are the plays *The Spider* (1927) and *All the King's Men* (1929); the novels *Poor Little Fool* (1928) and *The Great Jasper* (1930); and *Why I Know There Is a God* (1950).

OUSE, chief river of Yorkshire, England. It is formed by the confluence of two streams, the Ure and the Swale, near Boroughbridge, West Riding, and flows s.e. until it joins the Trent to form the Humber. Its total length is 61 miles, and it is navigable for 45 miles.

OUSE, GREAT, a river of England rising in Bedford and flowing N.E. into the Wash below King's Lynn. It is 160 m. in length.

OUTCAULT, RICHARD FELTON (1863–1928), American newspaper artist and humorist, originator of colored comic sheets, born in Lancaster, Ohio. While drawing comic pictures for the New York *World* in 1895, he adopted the suggestion that vivid color would make his pictures more popular, and thenceforth the hero of *Hogan's Alley,* a figure he had created, appeared in a bright yellow dress, becoming widely known as the "Yellow Kid", and giving rise to the phrase *yellow journalism.* He transferred this one-toothed creation to the New York *Journal* in 1896, going, the following year, to the *Herald,* where he started *Buster Brown* in 1902.

OUZEL. See DIPPER, RING OUZEL.

OVARY, in anatomy, the organs of female animals and humans which produce female reproductive cells, called eggs or ova. The ovaries are analogous to the testes in the male. They are two oblong flattened vessels, about one and one half inch long in the human subject, on either side of the uterus, to which they are connected by ligaments and by the Fallopian tube. The ovary is composed of two portions, a superficial or cortical portion, and a deep or medullary portion. The cortical portion in the adult contains an enormous number of vesicles varying greatly in size. They are the *Graafian vesicles* or *follicles,* and contain the ova or germs, the female element of reproduction.

The ovary is the subject of several diseased conditions. It is the seat of acute and chronic inflammation. This may arise from injuries during labor, operations in the pelvis, or gonorrheal infection, spreading from the vagina. The ovary also is the seat of new growths, which may be of several varieties. Some represent enlargements of one or more Graafian follicles, and attain an enormous size, sometimes weighing 100 lb. or more. These are known as *ovarian cysts.* Other tumors are of a more or less solid nature, and contain portions of hair, teeth, and bone, and are known as *dermoid tumors.*

The treatment of ovarian disease by ovariotomy, removal of the offending organ, is one of the triumphs of modern surgery. Formerly relief in cystomata was only obtained by tapping, i.e., withdrawing some of the fluid

by means of a trocar and canula. But the tumor almost always filled again, and, though tapping might be repeated time after time, the patient ultimately succumbed. The operation for extirpation of ovarian cystoma was first performed by Ephraim M'Dowell of Kentucky in 1809, but was established in England as a regular operation by Charles Clay of Manchester, who operated on his first case in 1842.

OVARY, in botany. See FRUIT; OVULE.

OVEN, a heated, insulated chamber used for baking food, or for purposes such as firing pottery. A primitive type of cooking oven, which was used by the Egyptians in ancient times and is still used in some parts of the East, consists of an earthenware crock in which the food is placed after a fire has been built in it and allowed to burn out. The crock is sunk in the ground, which serves as an insulator. Another type of primitive oven consisted of a pot or jar half filled with heated bricks.

The modern household oven is incorporated in the stove. The oven is heated uniformly by the circulation of hot air, the air being heated by a source of heat, i.e., electricity, gas, or other fuel, which is located outside the oven. Most ovens are provided with regulators for controlling and adjusting the temperature. Large-scale commercial baking is done in large ovens with mechanisms for controlling the heat to a fraction of a degree and for unloading, loading, and conveying baking pans; see BREAD.

OVERBECK, JOHANN FRIEDRICH (1789–1869), German religious painter, born in Lübeck. He studied at the Academy of Art in Vienna until 1810, when he went to Rome. There he became the leader of a group of Pre-Raphaelite (q.v.) artists known as the "Nazarenes", who believed that German painting should emulate the work of the Italian painters of the Early Renaissance in simplicity and unworldliness. They became converted to Catholicism, studied only early Christian art, and lived in an abandoned monastery in Rome, spending their time in work and meditation. Overbeck's work showed nobility and purity but a lack of strength or solidity. His drawings were unusually sensitive. The two principal works on which the group collaborated were frescoes in the sumptuous private Roman homes the Casa Bartholdi and the Villa Massini; the first series, representing the history of Joseph and his brethren, is now in the Kaiser Friedrich Museum, Berlin.

OVERBURY, Sir Thomas (1581–1613), English courtier, murdered at the instigation of the Countess of Essex, born in Compton-Scorpion, Warwickshire. In 1601, at Edinburgh, he met Robert Carr, who became Viscount Rochester, the minion of James I. The two became friends, and Overbury was, through Carr's influence, knighted (1608). He incurred the anger of the Countess of Essex by opposing her marriage to Robert Carr, and was, on a trivial pretext, confined to the Tower of London, where he was poisoned. Overbury holds a minor place in English literature, his work including *The Wife* (1614) and *Characters* (1614).

OVERIJSSEL, or Overyssel, province of the Netherlands on the east side of the Zuider Zee, separated from Guelderland on the south by the river Yssel. Meadows cover almost one third of the province, moors are extensive, and the province is intersected by canals. The chief cities are Zwolle, Deventer, and Kampen. Area, 1301 sq.m.; pop. (1951 est.) 691,473.

OVERTURE, in music, originally, an instrumental introduction to an opera. The term was later used to denote an independent orchestral composition. The earliest operas had no overture, but began either directly with the action or with a vocal prologue. The overture developed out of the instrumental preludes of the late 16th and early 17th centuries (often called sinfonias or toccatas), which were designed to serve as introductions to Italian operas or operatic scenes. The form of this dramatic prelude was first standardized by the French composer Jean Baptiste Lully in the middle of the 17th century, and has since become known as the French overture. It consisted of a slow introduction, often repeated, followed by a lively allegro in imitative style. A moderately slow dance form such as the minuet was sometimes added. This form became popular throughout Europe and served as a model for composers of succeeding generations. It competed for popularity with the style known as the Italian overture, which was developed in the late 17th century by the Italian composer Alessandro Scarlatti. The Italian operatic overture was of three sections: a quick allegro, an adagio (or *grave*), and another allegro (or *presto*). Both Italian and French overtures were composed during the early half of the 18th century. They had little relevance to the operas, oratorios, plays, and ballets of which they were a part. The Italian overture was soon adapted for concert performances and as such

presaged the growth of the symphony and sonata forms. It finally superseded the French overture, which was taken over into the orchestral suite as the first movement, particularly by the German composers Johann Josef Fux, Georg Philipp Telemann, and Johann Sebastian Bach.

Among the reforms in operatic music initiated by Christoph Willibald Gluck, which were discussed by him in the famous preface to his opera *Alceste* (1767), was a closer identification between the overture and the rest of the opera. This unity was achieved by the use of material from the opera in the overture itself, and by the foreshadowing, in the overture, of the mood of the opera. A particularly fine illustration of the latter principle occurs in the overture to Gluck's opera *Iphigénie en Aulide* (1774). The influence of Gluck's ideas upon Wolfgang Amadeus Mozart are evident in Mozart's opera *Don Giovanni* (1787), wherein music from late scenes is first heard in the overture. The extensive use of music from the opera itself can be found in Ludwig van Beethoven's first three *Leonore* overtures. The overture had, by the 19th century, developed into a single movement, similar to the first movement of the sonata or symphony. The form was further extended by Richard Wagner; the overtures to his operas review the dramatic action of the plot as well as incorporate its themes. Wagner also discarded the sonata form for that of the free *Vorspiel*, or prelude, which led directly into the first scene of the opera. This style is preferred by modern operatic composers.

The 19th century also saw the growth of the concert overture, an independent orchestral composition utilizing the principles of the operatic overture either as a free "prelude" or as a single sonata-form movement. Felix Mendelssohn's *Hebrides (Fingal's Cave)* overture (1830), Louis Hector Berlioz' *Roman Carnival* (1844) overture, and Johannes Brahms' *Academic Festival* and *Tragic* overtures (both 1881) are popular examples. The form also was used as an introduction to a play. Beethoven's *Coriolanus* overture (1808) to Johann von Goethe's drama of the same name, Mendelssohn's overture (1826) to the *Midsummer Night's Dream* of Shakespeare, and, in the 20th century, David Diamond's overture to Shakespeare's *Tempest* and Samuel Barber's overture (1933) to Richard Brinsley Sheridan's *School for Scandal* attest to the continued popularity of this use of the concert overture.

OVERWEIGHT. See OBESITY.

OVERYSSEL. See OVERIJSSEL.

OVID, in full PUBLIUS OVIDIUS NASO (43 B.C.–17? A.D.), Roman poet, born in Sulmo (modern Sulmona), in central Italy. Educated for the bar, he became highly proficient in the art of declamation, but his genius was essentially that of the poet, and he devoted most of his time and energy to the writing of verse. After inheriting his father's property, Ovid went to Athens for the completion of his education. He later traveled in Asia and Sicily with his friend the poet Æmilius Macer (d. 16 B.C.). By the age of thirty, Ovid had been thrice married and twice divorced, and he may have carried on an intrigue with the woman whom he celebrated in his poetry as Corinna. His private life was that of a gay, well-to-do, and somewhat licentious man of letters. At Rome, where he resided until his fiftieth year, he was assiduously courted by the distinguished and fashionable society of the city, including Emperor Augustus and the imperial family. In 8 A.D. Ovid was banished by an edict of the emperor to Tomi (modern Constanta), near the mouth of the Danube River. According to Ovid, one reason for his banishment was the publication of *Ars Amatoria,* a poem on the art of making love. Since the poem had been in circulation for almost ten years, there is a strong possibility that it served merely as a pretext. A second reason, never disclosed by Ovid, may have been his knowledge of a scandal involving the emperor's granddaughter Julia. Ovid did not lose his citizenship, nor did he give up hope of repatriation, a hope that is frequently revealed in the many poems written to his friends during his exile at Tomi, but his entreaties and those of his friends were unavailing. He died at Tomi, an honored citizen of the town.

The poetry of Ovid falls naturally into three divisions, the works of his youth, of his middle age, and of his years of exile at Tomi. In the first period, Ovid continued the elegiac tradition of the poets Sextus Propertius and Albius Tibullus (qq.v.), both of whom he knew and admired. The *Amores,* originally in five books, but revised and abridged to three, are erotic poems centering about Corinna, but they display little real feeling and are characterized by artificiality and cleverness. Other works of this period reveal Ovid as a didactic poet imparting instruction on love. Among these poems are *Medicamina Faciei,* a fragment on cosmetics; the *Ars Amandi,* or

Ars Amatoria, in three books; and a kind of recantation in one book, the *Remedia Amoris.* *Medea,* a tragedy highly praised by ancient critics, has not been preserved. Ovid's interest in mythology first becomes apparent in his *Heroides,* or *Epistulæ Heroidum,* twenty-one fictional love letters, mostly from mythological heroines to their lovers.

To Ovid's middle period belongs his masterpiece, the *Metamorphoses,* in fifteen books. The work deals with all the transformations recorded in mythology and legend from the creation of the world down to the time of Gaius Julius Cæsar, whose change into a star marks the last of the series. Deservedly famous as a handbook of Greek mythology, it is composed in a witty and, at times, almost burlesque spirit. The other work of the middle period is the *Fasti,* a poetic calendar describing the various Roman festivals and the legends connected with each. Of the projected twelve books, one for each month of the year, only the first six are extant, and it is believed that these are probably all that Ovid completed.

The works which Ovid composed during the period of his exile are pervaded by a spirit of melancholy and despair. These works include five books of elegies, namely the *Tristia,* which are descriptive of his unhappy existence at Tomi and contain numerous appeals to the clemency of Augustus; the *Epistulæ ex Ponto,* poetic letters similar in theme to the *Tristia;* the *Ibis,* a short invective invoking destruction upon a personal enemy; and the *Halieutica,* a poem extant only in fragments, about the fish of the Euxine (now the Black Sea). The *Nux* and the *Consolatio ad Liviam* are usually considered spurious. With the exception of the *Metamorphoses* and the fragmentary *Halieutica,* both of which are in the dactylic hexameter meter, all the poetry of Ovid is composed in the elegiac couplet, a meter which he brought to its highest degree of perfection.

Ovid was one of the most popular and influential of Roman poets during the Middle Ages and the Renaissance. Lodovico Ariosto and Giovanni Boccaccio, in Italy, and Geoffrey Chaucer and John Gower, in England, found in his mythological narratives a rich quarry of romantic tales. Edmund Spenser, William Shakespeare, John Milton, and many other English poets were indebted to him. Although Ovid was at times superficial, he was a born storyteller, and his ingenuity, cleverness, and gaiety have endeared him to generations of modern readers.

OVIEDO (anc. *Ovetum*), city and capital of the province of the same name, Spain, situated about 15 miles s.w. of Gijón. It is a transportation and industrial center of the surrounding agricultural and mining region. The principal manufactures include ordnance, chemicals, matches, ceramics, distilled beverages, and processed dairy products. Oviedo is famed as the site of many architectural landmarks, including several medieval churches and the Gothic cathedral. Begun in 1388, the latter contains a number of royal Asturian tombs and priceless relics and manuscripts. The adjoining *Cámara Santa,* part of the original chapel, dates from 802. The city is the site of a university established in 1604.

Oviedo was founded in the middle of the 8th century. It reached the height of its importance during the 9th and 10th centuries, when it was the capital of the kingdom of Asturias. Oviedo Province, which is coextensive with the Asturian region, was constituted in 1833.

Area of province, 4207 sq.m.; pop. (1950) 888,149. Pop. of city (1950) 106,002.

OVULE, in botany, name applied to immature seeds, which are produced within the ovary of a flower (q.v.). In ordinary flowering plants the history of the ovule is as follows. On a special leaf called a carpel a mass of tissue grows called the nucellus; this becomes covered by two integuments which grow up from its base, but leave an opening at the top called the micropyle. A cell near the top of the nucellus represents the mother cell of the female spore of the vascular cryptogams. It divides into two and then into four; one of these becomes the female spore; it is called the embryo sac because the embryo will be formed in it. The male spores of the vascular cryptogams are represented by the pollen grains contained in special leaves called stamens; a pollen grain being placed on a part of the ovary sends out a tube which enters the micropyle. The nucleus of the embryo sac now divides into two, one daughter nucleus traveling to each end of the sac; it there divides into two, then into four, daughter nuclei. Fertilization is effected by the pollen tube entering by the micropyle and touching one of the outer archegonia, which then breaks up and becomes attached to the oosphere; this is now called oospore, and grows into the embryo, while the secondary nucleus of the embryo sac by repeated division gives rise to a tissue which fills up the embryo sac, called endosperm, rich in food materials upon which the embryo feeds. The embryo sac at the same time grows, displacing the tissue of the nucellus.

OWEN, SIR RICHARD (1804–92), English zoologist, born in Lancaster, and educated at the universities of Edinburgh and London. In 1856 he became superintendent of the natural history department of the British Museum, where he made investigations on living and fossil animals.

OWEN, ROBERT (1771–1858), British social reformer, born in Newtown, Montgomeryshire, Wales. Owen had little opportunity for schooling, and began work in a draper's shop at the age of ten. His progress was rapid and he became manager of one of the largest Manchester cotton mills by the time he was nineteen. In 1794, he helped establish an independent company; and in 1799, he and his associates purchased the famous New Lanark mills in Manchester. Here, at the age of twenty-eight and already one of the most respected textile merchants in England, Owen put into effect the social theories for which he later became famous. About two thousand people were connected with his mills, five hundred of whom were children from Scottish poorhouses. The great majority lived in the same squalor and demoralization that characterized all industrial communities of that period; see FACTORIES AND THE FACTORY SYSTEM. Believing that character is formed by early environment and training, Owen paid particular attention to the establishment of schools in his community, and caused the first nursery school in Britain to be established there. He also instituted housing and sanitation improvements, and opened a store at which goods could be bought for little more than cost.

The New Lanark experiment was highly successful in both its business and social aspects, and it drew visitors from all over Europe. Encouraged by this success, Owen began a campaign in 1815 for legislation prohibiting employment before the age of ten and night work before eighteen, and establishing a ten and one-half hour maximum working day for children under eighteen. This effort met with only limited success and the bill which finally passed Parliament enacted few of Owen's proposals into law. Owen became disillusioned with reform schemes and began to campaign for immediate changes to transform the social structure of England. He urged the establishment of thousands of co-operative communities of about twelve hundred persons each, who would conduct their own agriculture and industry, living communally and sharing the product of their labor. This suggestion was strongly opposed by other businessmen, and Owen determined to put it into practice in the United States, where he hoped it would be received more favorably. In 1825, he purchased thirty thousand acres of land in Indiana, and founded a community called New Harmony (q.v.). An unbalanced selection of personnel, among whom several necessary occupations were inadequately represented, caused the dissolution of the community in 1828, and Owen returned home. Other Owenite communities, established in Britain, were somewhat successful. In London Owen found himself the leader by popular acclaim of a new and powerful labor movement, and he began a campaign for the establishment by unions of their own industries.

The Labor Exchange (q.v.) was founded in 1832 to market the products of these industries; and a National Operative Builders Union was set up to take over the construction industry. However, governmental opposition was so intense that Owen was forced to dissolve the movement in 1834; and he withdrew from active participation in labor affairs.

During the rest of his life, Owen devoted himself to general propaganda on behalf of his theories. Owen is noted both for his contributions to educational practice, particularly through his belief in the importance of early training, and for his socialist ideas and experiments. He is generally classed as a "utopian" socialist, after the derisive application of this term by Friedrich Engels (q.v.), who contrasted Owen and his followers with the Marxian, or self-styled "scientific", socialists.

At the present time Owen's influence is more apparent in the co-operative movement (q.v.) which began at Rochdale, England, than in modern socialist movements. See also SOCIALISM; UTOPIA; ROCHDALE SOCIETY OF EQUITABLE PIONEERS.

OWEN, ROBERT DALE (1801–77), American legislator and diplomat, son of Robert Owen (q.v.), born in Glasgow, Scotland. Owen accompanied his father on a trip to the United States in 1825 to help in the founding of the short-lived colony at New Harmony (q.v.), Indiana. He remained in the United States, settling first in New York City in 1829 and becoming the editor of the socialistic newspaper, the *Free Inquirer*. In 1832 he returned to Indiana and was elected to the State legislature as a Democrat in 1835. He was elected to Congress in 1842, and again in 1844. In 1853, he was appointed United States chargé d'affaires at Naples, Italy, and he became minister at Naples in 1855. After his return to the United States in 1858, he took an active part in the abolitionists' (q.v.) campaigns. Owen's writings include a book on spiritualism, *Footprints on the Boundary of Another World* (1859), and an autobiography, *Threading My Way* (1874).

OWENS, JESSE, real given name JAMES CLEVELAND (1914–   ), American Negro athlete, born in Decatur, Ala., and educated at Ohio State University. He competed in interscholastic track meets while attending secondary school, excelling in the running broad jump, the 100-yard dash, and the 220-yard dash and setting new records for these events in 1933. In 1935, as a member of the Ohio State University track squad, he established a new world record (26 ft. 8¼ in.) for the running broad jump; the next year he set a new world record (10.2 sec.) for the 100-meter dash. On the U.S. track team in the Olympic Games of 1936, Owens became the first American and the second athlete in history to win three Olympiad events. He won the 100-meter dash in 10.3 sec., equalling the Olympiad record; the 200-meter dash in 20.7 sec., setting a new Olympiad and world record; and the running broad jump with a leap of 26 ft. 5⁵⁄₁₆ in., setting a new Olympiad record. In addition, the U.S. 400-meter relay team, of which he was a member, set a new Olympiad and world record of 39.8 sec.

OWENSBORO, capital of Daviess Co., Ky., on the Ohio River, 50 miles S.W. of Brandenburg. It has flour and lumber mills; iron, lead, and coal mines; and manufactures furniture. It is one of the largest leaf and strip tobacco markets in the United States. Pop. (1950) 33,651.

OWEN SOUND, town of Grey Co., Ontario, Canada, situated on Georgian Bay, Lake Huron, 120 miles N.W. of Toronto. The chief industries are iron and wood working, cement making, lumbering, and wool manufacture. There are several grain elevators here. Pop. (1951) 16,423.

OWL, formerly regarded as of the order Accipitres or Raptores (birds of prey), but now placed in the Coraciiformes as the suborder Striges. The head is large, the skull broad, the cranial bones highly pneumatic, and the facial region flattened; the beak is short, hooked, strong, and sharp. The eyes are large, directed forward, only slightly

Top: Left, great gray owl; right, barred owl. Bottom: Left, Richardson's owl; middle, screech owl; right, saw-whet owl.

movable; the upper eyelid is large, and both eyelids are ciliated with barbed plumelets, and have a broad, thin, bare margin; the third eyelid, or nictitating membrane, is conspicuous. The iris is unusually broad, and is capable of being greatly expanded and contracted.

Owls range over the whole globe from the polar regions to the oceanic islands. They are generally nocturnal; their flight is noiseless and buoyant; their eyesight is acute, as is also their sense of hearing. They are either solitary or live in pairs, and although often regarded with superstitious aversion, they are nearly always harmless and useful birds. Their food consists of small mammals, birds, and insects, especially nocturnal lepidoptera; some species prey on fish, either habitually or occasionally. If found abroad they are persecuted by smaller birds, being bewildered and rendered helpless by the unaccustomed glare of daylight. When surprised, owls hiss like a cat and make a clicking noise with their bills; some have a harsh shrieking cry, others a not unmusical *hoot.*

The long-eared and short-eared owls of America, Europe, and Asia, *Asio otus* and *A. accipitrinus,* have the ear peculiarly developed, the opening on one side looking upward, and on the other downward. The specialization of ear structure is carried to its greatest known limit in Tengmalm's owl, *Nyctala tengmalmi,* where the bones of the head are developed differently on each side. Of American species belonging to this family, one of the most noteworthy is the burrowing owl, *Speotylo* or *Athene cunicularia.* On the prairies of North America it shares the burrows of the prairie dog and other mammals, while on the pampas of South America it lives in the holes of the viscacha, armadillos, and large lizards, or makes a hole for itself, which is often invaded by rattlesnakes. Among the best known of North American owls are the little mottled owl, *Mega-scops asio,* the great horned or hoot owl, *Bubo virginianus,* and the grayish barred owl, *Syrnium nebulosum.*

The tawny owl, wood owl, ivy owl, or

brown owl, *Strix stridula* or *aluco*, or *Syrnium aluco*, is a common British species. Its cry *hoo-hoo*, or, as rendered by Shakespeare, *tu-whit, tu-whoo*, at night makes it easily recognized. The snowy day owl, the *Harfang* of the Swedes, *Nyctea scandiaca*, is a circumpolar bird, breeding chiefly within the Arctic Circle, and common in parts of Greenland and Iceland, Russia, and North America. See BARN OWL.

OX. See CATTLE.

OXALIC ACID. See DICARBOXYLIC ACIDS.

OX BOT or **CATTLE GRUB,** common name for the larva or bot of any of several species of flies, commonly known as "heel flies", "warble flies", and "ox botflies", and constituting the genus *Hypoderma* of the family Oestridae. The insects are found throughout the United States and Europe. In the United States they cause annual damage of about $75,000,000, ruining cattle hides, and irritating cattle so that they lose weight and produce less milk. The female lays its eggs in early spring on the hairs about the hoofs of cattle. The yellowish-white eggs hatch in about three to four days, and the bots or grubs burrow into the skin of the infested animal, working their way through the muscles to the esophagus and the back. When the bots reach the skin of the back (about seven to eight months after entering the body) they bite holes in the skin and then molt, using the openings they have created as breathing holes. After the first molt, the body of the bot is studded with sharp spines. The bot develops in the back of the infected animal for a period of from thirty-five to one hundred days, widening the breathing holes in the animal's back as it grows larger. At the end of this period it works its way out of the animal's back and falls to the ground, pupating about a day later. The length of pupation varies from fifteen to seventy-seven days and is dependent upon climatic conditions. The adult fly lives for about two weeks, and does not feed, living on reserve energy stored in the bot stage. Ox botflies may be controlled by spraying cattle with insecticide during the egg-laying season of the fly.

The common American ox botfly is *H. lineatum*, about ½ in. long. It is black and hairy, with bands of orange and yellow hair running transversely across its body. The common European ox botfly, also found in northeastern United States, is *H. bovis*, which is somewhat larger. Compare HORSE BOT; SHEEP BOT.

OXENSTIERNA, OXENSTJERNA, or **OXENSTIERN,** COUNT AXEL GUSTAFSSON (1583-1654), Swedish statesman, born in Fönö, and educated at the universities of Rostock, Jena, and Wittenberg. In 1612 he was appointed chancellor of Sweden by Gustavus II (q.v.). He negotiated peace settlements with Denmark in 1613, with Russia in 1617, and with Poland in 1623 (see SWEDEN: *History*), and was appointed governor general of the province of Prussia in 1626. Oxenstierna became the most powerful statesman in Swedish history in January, 1633, when the king designated him legate plenipotentiary in Germany, with absolute power over the vast territories conquered by the Swedish armies. In the same year he organized the Protestant leaders of Sweden and Germany into a mutual-assistance organization known as the Evangelical League. In 1636 he negotiated the Treaty of Wismar with France, whereby Sweden, whose resources had been severely strained as a result of her recurring wars, gained the promise of aid from France while making no major concessions or sacrifices. Another of his brilliant achievements was the planning of the Danish War of 1643-45, which resulted in the Peace of Brömsebro, whereby Denmark, Sweden's hereditary enemy, was stripped of her power. After the accession of the young Queen Christina in 1644, he wielded almost absolute power in the foreign and domestic policies of his country. He was created a count in 1645.

OXFORD, municipal county and parliamentary borough, the capital of Oxfordshire, England, the seat of the university, and the see of the bishopric of the same name, located at the confluence of the Cherwell and Isis rivers, so called as a tributary of the Thames, 52 miles w.n.w. from London.

The center of the town is at a place called "Carfax" (derived from *quadrifurcus*, "four-forked"), from which four main streets run to the four points of the compass. The main street is High Street (the "High"), a part of London Road with Carfax at one end and Magdalen Bridge at the other. St. Mary's Church in High Street is the church of the university. Off Broad Street is the Bodleian Library next to the Sheldonian Theatre.

Oxford was a center of the Wycliffite movement in the 14th century, and in the 17th century it became a high church and loyalist center. King Charles I made it his capital from 1642 to 1645. The chief industries are brewing, printing, and automobile manufacturing. It is also a market center for cattle. Pop. (1951 est.) 98,675.

OXFORD AND ASQUITH, EARL OF. See ASQUITH, HERBERT HENRY.

OXFORD MOVEMENT, the name commonly applied to the revival of the doctrines and practices of an earlier age which took place in the Church of England in the early years of the Victorian era. It covered a period of twelve years, beginning with a sermon preached by the English clergyman John Keble on national apostasy at Oxford in 1833 and ending with the defection of the English theologian John Henry Newman in 1845. See ANGLICAN CHURCH; KEBLE, JOHN; NEWMAN, JOHN HENRY; PUSEY, EDWARD BOUVERIE.

OXFORDSHIRE, or OXON, inland county of England, bounded on the N. by Warwickshire and Northants, on the E. by Bucks, on the S. by the river Thames, and on the W. by Gloucestershire. It is watered by the Thames, with its affluents the Windrush, Evenlode, Cherwell, and Thame. The Oxford and Birmingham Canal affords access to the midland coal fields. The soil is fertile, and the state of agriculture advanced, producing barley, oats, and wheat; livestock, cattle, sheep, and pigs are raised. Ironstone is worked near Banbury. The manufactures include blankets, paper, and gloves. Area, 751 sq.m.; pop., (1951 est.) 275,765.

OXFORD UNIVERSITY, the oldest institution of higher learning and one of the two most important universities of England (compare CAMBRIDGE UNIVERSITY), situated at Oxford (q.v.), Oxfordshire. Although legendary accounts of its foundation by King Alfred in 872 exist, the University first appears in historical records of the early 12th century. As early as 1117 Continental scholars are known to have lectured at Oxford, possibly attracted by the nearness of the palace of the scholarly King Henry I. About 1167 the expulsion of foreigners from the University of Paris (see PARIS, UNIVERSITY OF), as one of the results of the quarrel between King Henry II and Thomas à Becket (qq.v.), caused a migration of English students to Oxford; by 1185 Oxford was considered an established center of learning, possessing organized faculties granting regular degrees, and in the reign of Richard I scholars were maintained there by the royal bounty. Before the end of the 12th century the existing schools at Oxford came to be considered a *Studium Generale*, at which students and doctors from all the great universities of Europe congregated. In 1214, by order of the papal legate, a chancellor of the University was chosen to preside over a self-governing guild of masters. Like the University of Paris,

Oxford was divided into "nations": the North, including Scotch students; and the South, including Irish and Welsh students. The faculty of arts was of chief importance, overshadowing those of law, medicine, and theology.

Separate colleges were gradually established, composed of voluntary associations of students who joined together in renting houses, instead of living separately at their own expense in the town. These voluntary student associations then obtained licenses from the University. The development of the colleges was further strengthened by the arrival, in the mid-13th century, of the mendicant orders of Dominicans, Franciscans, Carmelites, and Augustinians, who acquired property in the town, built houses, and soon gained influence among the students. About the same time, colleges began to be established by private benefaction; the earliest of these colleges were University College (1249), founded by William of Durham; Balliol College (between 1263 and 1269), founded by Devorguila, wife of John de Baliol; and Merton College (1264), founded by Walter de Merton. The last-named college was the first of its kind in the modern sense of the term, and served as a model for subsequent colleges at both Oxford and Cambridge. Thenceforth more and more students became members of individual colleges, in which instruction was given within the college walls, and a comparable decrease took place in the number of students living alone in the town, or in religious houses or independent student halls.

The new learning of the Renaissance (q.v.; see also HUMANISM) was warmly received at Oxford, and the earliest Greek students in England were Oxford scholars. Notable among contemporary Oxford scholars and students were Desiderius Erasmus, William Grocyn, Thomas Linacre, John Colet, and Sir Thomas More (qq.v.). During the Reformation (q.v.) the severing of ties with the Roman Catholic Church put an end to the scholastic methods of teaching at Oxford and Cambridge, and both universities suffered loss of land and revenues. In 1570, during the reign of Elizabeth, an act was passed incorporating and reorganizing the University, and in 1636, during the reign of Charles I, the University's statutes were codified by William Laud, Archbishop of Canterbury, who was then chancellor of Oxford; these two sets of codes remained the official governing statutes of the University until the middle of the 19th century. Oxford was a center of the Royalist party during the Civil War, from 1642 to 1645, although the

Aerial view of Oxford University, England

town of Oxford favored the Parliamentary cause; see GREAT REBELLION. Oliver Cromwell was chancellor of the University from 1651 to 1657, after the town was taken by the Parliamentarians, and was responsible for preventing both Oxford and Cambridge from being closed down by the Puritans, who distrusted university education on the grounds that it was dangerous to religious belief. During the 18th century the University was largely Jacobin in sentiment, while the town took the part of the Hanoverians, but after 1785, in the reign of George III, Oxford took little part in politics. In the latter half of the 18th century, academic conditions, which had been neglected since the Civil War, improved. During the 19th century written examinations for admission replaced oral tests; the University also became more liberal in regard to admission of religious dissenters. The first of the four colleges for women, all established before the beginning of the 20th century, was founded in 1879.

At the present time Oxford University is organized as a federation of colleges, each with its own internal organization and laws, united under the University itself, which maintains separate officials and legislative bodies. The chief officer of the University is the chancellor, its nominal head, elected for life by members of the House of Convocation (see below), who are graduates of the University holding the degree of M.A.; the chancellor is generally a peer of the realm. The actual head of the University is the vice-chancellor, nominated annually by the chancellor from among the heads of the colleges. Two proctors, charged with the responsibility of disciplinary measures regarding the junior members of the University (the undergraduates), are elected annually from two colleges, with the various colleges electing in rotation.

The business of the University is transacted by four bodies: the *Ancient House of Congregation,* consisting of masters of arts of less than two years' standing, heads of colleges, deans of degrees of colleges, professors, examiners, and other lesser officials, which exercises authority as a body conferring ordinary degrees; the *Congregation of the University,* constituted by act of Parliament in 1854 and consisting of University officers, professors, and resident graduates, which discusses and votes on proposed statutes submitted by the Hebdomadal Council (the most influential body of the University in regard to practical administration; see below) prior to their submittal to the House of Convocation; the *House of Convocation*, consisting of all graduates who have kept their names on the books of the University, which is in theory the supreme governing body of the University and which elects the two members of Parliament by whom the University has been represented since 1604; and the *Hebdomadal Council*, a body of practical educators which promulgates legislation and controls University policy, and is composed of the vice-chancellor, the retiring vice-chancellor, the proctors, and eighteen other members elected by the Congregation of the University from among heads of the colleges, professors, and members of the House of Convocation.

Each college is organized under a head (variously called warden, provost, principal, president, or master in different colleges) and is composed of fellows and tutors, and scholars or undergraduates. The officer charged with the internal discipline is usually known as the dean. All members of a college above the undergraduates are known collectively and colloquially as "dons". Each undergraduate is assigned a tutor, who is responsible for him during his residence at the college and may or may not be concerned with his academic work. Formal teaching is chiefly by means of lectures, which are usually given by the college or by combinations of colleges; exceptions to this rule are the lectures of the professors, who are University functionaries and whose lectures are public.

Examinations are conducted and degrees granted by the University, rather than by the individual colleges. Three examinations for the degree of bachelor of arts are required: the first, known as *responsions* and colloquially called "smalls", is now always taken before matriculation; the second, known as *moderations* or "mods", is taken after one or two years, according to whether or not the candidate seeks honors in his subject; and the third, taken two years after the moderations, is known as *final schools* or "greats" for honors candidates and *pass schools* for ordinary students. The degree of master of arts requires no further study or examination, but is granted after the name of the recipient of a B.A. has remained on the University's books for three or four years and the recipient has paid quarterly dues and graduation fees. The University also grants bachelor's and doctor's degrees in divinity, law, medicine, literature,

science, music, and other fields. In contrast to Cambridge, which became noted for its concentration in the fields of mathematics and science, Oxford University long maintained a close adherence to traditional classical education. In recent years, however, its curricula have been expanded to include a larger variety of subjects, particularly modern languages and economics, and emphasis has been placed upon scientific and medical research.

Approximately 7000 students, including about 1000 women, were registered at the University in 1952–53. Oxford has a famous library (see BODLEIAN LIBRARY) and its own press, Clarendon Press. The principal colleges, the majority of which are described in separate articles are as follows.

COLLEGE	FOUNDED
All Souls	1437
Balliol	1263–69
Brasenose	1509
Christ Church	1525–46
Corpus Christi	1546
Exeter	1314
Hertford	1874
Jesus	1571
Keble	1870
Lincoln	1427
Magdalen	1458
Merton	1264
New College	1379
Oriel	1326
Pembroke	1624
Queen's	1340
Saint John's	1555
Trinity	1555
University	1249
Wadham	1612
Worcester	1714

OXIDATION, in chemistry, a term originally used to express a reaction involving direct combination of an element or compound with oxygen, but more precisely used to express a reaction in which an element or group of elements loses one or more electrons from the outer shell of each atom. Charcoal, which is composed of carbon, reacts with oxygen to form carbon monoxide, which in turn is further oxidized to carbon dioxide. The rusting of iron is an oxidation process in which iron, exposed to air in the presence of water, forms the compound Fe_2O_3. From a more general point of view each atom of iron has lost three electrons and the valence (q.v.) of the iron has changed from zero to $+3$. Iron also combines with fluorine and chlorine to form ferric fluoride and ferric chloride, respectively, and these reactions are oxidation reactions although no oxygen is present. Substances which oxidize other substances are called *oxidizers* or *oxidizing agents;* among the common oxidizing agents are chlorine, hydrogen peroxide, nitric acid, oxygen, ozone, sulfuric acid, and salts, such as nitrates and permanganates.

Oxidation is always accompanied by the reverse process, called reduction. The word was originally used by metallurgists to describe the reduction of an ore, such as hematite, Fe_2O_3, to the metal (iron) by removing the oxygen. More precisely, in the process of reduction each atom of an element gains electrons. In the reaction of iron with chlorine the iron is oxidized and the chlorine is reduced; each atom of chlorine gains one electron and the valence changes from 0 to -1. Among the common reducing agents are carbon, carbon monoxide, and hydrogen.

OXIDE. See OXYGEN.

OXNARD, city in Ventura Co., Calif., 66 miles N.W. of Los Angeles. There are machine and woodworking shops and a beet sugar industry. Pop. (1950) 21,567.

OXUS, the ancient name of the Amu River, also called Jihun by Arabic writers. See AMU DARYA.

OXYGEN, a gaseous element, atomic number 8, atomic weight 16, symbol O. It was discovered in 1774 by the English chemist Joseph Priestley and, independently, by the Swedish chemist Karl Wilhelm Scheele; it was shown to be an elemental gas by the French chemist Antoine Lavoisier in his classic experiments on combustion; see CHEMISTRY: *History.* Oxygen is the most abundant of all the elements. In combination it comprises 88.8 percent by weight of the earth's water and, as a constituent of many minerals, 50 percent by weight of the rocks and soils of the earth; in the free state it comprises one fourth of the volume of the atmosphere (q.v.). It is a constituent of all living tissues; almost all plants and animals require oxygen, in the free or combined state, to maintain life; see RESPIRATION.

Ordinary oxygen is a colorless, odorless, tasteless, slightly magnetic, nontoxic gas, with specific gravity 1.105. It can be condensed to a pale-blue liquid, b.p. $-183°$ C. ($-297°$ F.), which is strongly magnetic. Pale-blue solid oxygen, produced by compression of the liquid, has a melting point of $-218.4°$ C. ($-361.3°$ F.). Three allotropic forms of oxygen are known to exist: ordinary oxygen, containing two atoms per molecule, formula O_2, ozone (q.v.), containing three atoms per molecule, formula O_3, and a pale-blue, nonmagnetic form, O_4, containing four atoms per molecule, which readily breaks down again into ordinary oxygen. Three stable isotopes of oxygen are known. O-16 (oxygen of atomic mass 16) is the most abundant isotope; it comprises 99.76% of ordinary oxygen.

Oxygen is prepared in the laboratory from salts, such as potassium chlorate, barium peroxide, and sodium peroxide. The most important industrial methods for the preparation of oxygen are the electrolysis of water and the fractional distillation of liquid air. In the latter method air is liquefied and allowed to evaporate. The nitrogen in the air is more volatile and boils off first, leaving the oxygen. Oxygen is stored and shipped in either liquid or gaseous form.

Oxygen is a component of a great number of organic and inorganic compounds, in which it has a valence of two. It forms compounds, called *oxides,* with all elements except the inert gases. The rate of the reaction, called *oxidation,* varies with different elements. Ordinary combustion, or burning, is an intense form of oxidation. Phosphorus combines so vigorously with oxygen that the heat liberated in the reaction causes the phosphorus to melt and burn; elements such as sulfur, hydrogen, sodium, and magnesium combine with oxygen less energetically and burn only after ignition. Some elements, such as copper and mercury, form oxides slowly, even when heated. Inactive metals, such as platinum, iridium, and gold, form oxides only through indirect methods. For discussion of oxides of elements see individual articles on the elements.

Large amounts of oxygen are used in various types of high-temperature torches, in which a mixture of oxygen and another gas produces a flame of much higher temperature than is obtained by burning gases in air. Oxygen is administered medicinally to patients whose respiratory functioning is impaired. It is also supplied to persons in aircraft flying at high altitudes where concentration of oxygen is insufficient to support normal respiratory processes. Oxygen-enriched air is used in open-hearth furnaces for steel manufacture; see IRON, METALLURGY OF.

OYAMA, PRINCE IWAO (1842–1916), Japanese military leader, born in Statsuma. In 1894, upon the outbreak of the Chinese-Japanese War, he was appointed commander of the Second Army Corps, which under his leadership captured Port Arthur and the fortress of Weihaiwei. At the end of the war

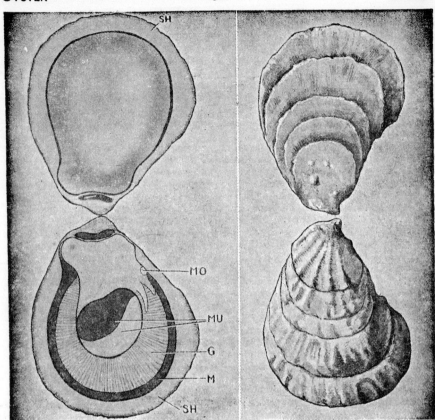

Left: The internal anatomy of the oyster. MO, mouth; MU, muscle; G, gill plate; M, mantle; SH, shell. Right: The exterior of an opened oyster.

he was created a marquis, and in 1898 he was elevated to the rank of field marshal. He was given command of the Japanese armies in Manchuria at the beginning of the Russo-Japanese War in 1904, and inflicted decisive defeats on the Russians in the battles of Liaoyang, the Shaho R., and Mukden. Oyama was given the rank of prince in 1907.

OYSTER, edible sessile bivalve mollusk of the family Ostreidae, especially any of the numerous species of the genus *Ostrea.* The shells are irregular and unequal; the fixed left valve is generally spacious, strongly convex without and excavated within; the right valve is generally plane or concave externally, always less convex than its fellow. The shells are lateral and hinged anteriorly, an elastic pad (ligament) causing them normally to gape. Closely applied to their inner faces and extensible beyond their margins are two thin folds (mantle) of the body wall, which secrete the shell in successive layers within and on the margins. The mantle incloses a chamber (mantle cavity), open ventrally and posteriorly, into which project on each side a pair of gills, commonly called the beard, and in front of these a pair of smaller fleshy lobes (palps). Above the gills and palps lies the body, containing the digestive, reproductive, circulatory, excretory, and nervous systems, and the adductor muscle which closes the shells.

The oyster feeds on microscopic organisms which are washed into the gaping shell and on to the mouth by the ciliary activity of the gills and palps. They live in "beds" or "banks" at depths of 3 to 20 fathoms.

There are many interesting facts connected with the life history of the oyster. Thus, *O. eduiis* is hermaphrodite, being first an egg-laying female, afterward a sperm-producing male, while *O. angulata* and the American *O. virginica* have the sexes separate. Maturity is attained in the third or fourth year and the maximum fertility is between the fourth and seventh year. The reproductive season generally begins in May and continues till the beginning of autumn. The embryos are about one-one hundred and fiftieth of an inch in length, but the numbers which rise from an oyster bank are so immense that the water seems to be clouded. They swim actively for some days by means of a protrusible ciliated cushion or *velum,* and then settle on stones or shells.

Oysters are represented by several widely distributed species, e.g., the European *O. edulis* and *O. angulata,* the American *O. virginica* with several varieties, and two others from the western coasts, *O. conchophila* and *O. lurida,* all of them edible, while others are found in the Cape of Good Hope, Australia, and Japan. The usual size is 3 to 6 in. but much larger ones are occasionally found. Fossil remains of the oyster date to the Carboniferous period.

Many cases of enteric illness and death have been referred to the eating of oysters, and it appears that oysters contaminated by sewage can and do transmit disease.

In the United States the largest beds are found in Long Island Sound and Chesapeake Bay. The bivalve is found, however, from the Gulf of St. Lawrence to and along the N. shore of the Gulf of Mexico, and, at points on the w. coast, as in Puget Sound and Juan de Fuca Strait.

Artificial oyster culture is now successfully practiced on various plans throughout the world, American and British methods substantially agreeing, while French, Dutch, and Japanese systems are more elaborate.

OYSTER CATCHER, genus of birds of the family Charadriidæ, closely allied to the plovers, and distinguished chiefly by the long, wedge-shaped bill, legs of moderate length, and feet with only three toes. The genus embraces nine species. The common American species is *H. palliatus,* found in the South Atlantic States and tropical America. Its head, neck, and mantle are black, its other parts mostly white, and its length is about 19 in. It lives on shore mollusks and marine worms.

OYSTERFISH. See Tautog.

OYSTER MUSHROOM. See Fungi.

OYSTER PLANT. See Salsify.

OZARK MOUNTAINS, a heavily timbered range in the Mississippi Valley, stretching from Jefferson City, Mo., in a southwesterly direction through Missouri and Arkansas into Oklahoma. The average height is about 2000 ft.

OZENFANT, Amédée (1886–), French painter, born in Saint-Quentin, and educated at the University of Paris. He studied art at the Académie La Palette, Paris. In 1915 he became influenced by cubism (q.v.) and wrote *Après le Cubisme* (1918) with the painter-architect Charles Édouard Jeanneret (known as Le Corbusier). Feeling that cubism was too undisciplined in character, Ozenfant formulated the idea of *Purism,* the use of abstract, universal symbols in art to emulate the pure, emotional quality of music. He subsequently came to America, where in New York City he lectured at the New School for Social Research (1938–41) and founded (1939) the Ozenfant School of Fine Arts. In 1944 he became a U.S. citizen. He also wrote *La Peinture Moderne* (1924) and *Journey Through Life* (1939), contributed many articles on modern art to periodicals, and founded (1915) the revue *L'Élan.*

OZONE (Gr. *ozein,* "to smell"), an allotropic form of oxygen having three atoms in each molecule, formula O_3. Ozone is pale blue in color and possesses a penetrating odor; it has a specific gravity of 1.66, b.p.—112° C. (—170° F.), and m.p. —251° C. (—420° F.). Liquid ozone is a deep-blue, strongly magnetic liquid. Minute amounts of ozone are present in the atmosphere, particularly in the upper regions. Ozone is formed when an electric spark is passed through oxygen, and causes a detectable odor around electrical machinery. The commercial method of preparation consists of passing cold, dry oxygen through a silent electrical discharge. Ozone is much more active chemically than ordinary oxygen, and is a better oxidizing agent. It has been used in purifying water, sterilizing air, and bleaching certain foods, but large-scale industrial use of ozone is still in the experimental stage.

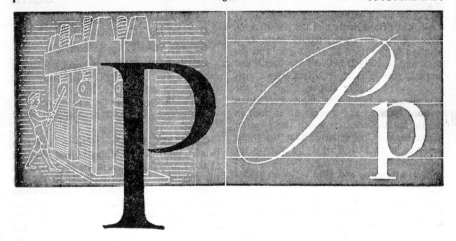

P, the sixteenth letter and twelfth consonant of the English alphabet. The modern form of the letter first appeared in the Latin alphabet as an adaptation of the Greek letter *pi,* which was in turn derived from the Phenician *pe.* The Phenician letter originated in an Egyptian hieratic character based upon an Egyptian hieroglyph representing a shutter. The historical development of the letter may be summarized as: Roman, P ; < Early Greek, Ꝓ or Γ ; < Phenician, Ꝓ ; < Egyptian hieratic, ✍ < Egyptian hieroglyph, ▦ .

The voiced *p* sound is pronounced by closely compressing the lips, and then strongly emitting the breath so as to separate them. The sound is technically called voiceless or mute, and is related to the voiced *b.* Most English words beginning with the *p* sound are of Greek, Latin, or French origin. In a number of English words *p* stands for the *b* sound in cognate Indo-European languages, as in the word *pool,* which is translated as *bala* in Lithuanian. In cognate words English *p* generally corresponds to German *pf* and *f,* Latin *b,* and Greek *b.* The letter *p* is often silent in English words of Greek derivation, particularly when it is part of initial combinations such as *pn, ps,* and *pt.* Examples include *pneumonia, psychic,* and *ptarmigan.* The digraph *ph,* corresponding to the Greek *phi,* is pronounced *f* as in *pharmacy* and *phonetic.*

As an abbreviation, the capital P is used for names beginning with P, such as Peter and Priscilla, for titles such as Pope, and for the pawn in chess. The capital or lower-case P is used for pastor, priest, president, and proconsul. Lower-case P may stand for page or pages, penny, peseta, peso, or population; in music it denotes *piano,* or "softly".

As a symbol, capital P is used in chemistry for phosphorus, in electricity for power, in physics for pressure, and in logic for predicate. In either capital or lower-case form, P is a symbol for the fifteenth or (when J is included) sixteenth in a series, class, order, or group.

PABIANICE, city in the Polish department of Lodz, 10 miles s.s.w. of the city of Lodz. It has textile, paper, chemical, and machine industries. Pop., about 35,000.

PACARAIMA, SIERRA, range of mountains separating Venezuela from Brazil. They have a length of 300 m., and reach a height of about 9000 ft. in Mt. Roraima.

PACHMANN, VLADIMIR DE (1848–1933), Russian pianist, born in Odessa, and educated by his father and at the Vienna Conservatory. He made his debut in Odessa in 1869. Although he was favorably received, de Pachmann was dissatisfied with his performance, and studied for eight years before making another public appearance. After a few European concerts, he retired again for two more years of further study. Following his second period of retirement he rapidly became an extremely popular concert pianist. He was in constant demand in Europe and frequently toured the United States, where he made his first visit in 1891 and his last in the 1924–25 season. De Pachmann frequently appeared in concerto performances with orchestras but was at his best in his interpretations of short pieces, particularly those of the Polish composer Frédéric Chopin.

PACHOMIUS (b. 292?), Egyptian monk, the first to substitute for the free asceticism of the solitary recluse a regular cenobitic system. About 340 he founded the first monastic community at Tabenna, an island in the Nile, where 1400 monks were assembled.

PACHUCA, capital of Hidalgo State, Mexico, 55 miles N.E. of Mexico City. There are rich silver mines in the district, said to have been worked before the Spanish conquest. The *patio* ore reduction process was invented here by Bartolomé de Medina in 1557. Pop. (1951) 58,698.

PACIFIC OCEAN, the portion of the water envelope of the earth lying between America on the E. and Australia, the Malay Archipelago, and Asia on the w. The name Pacific was given to it by the Portuguese navigator Ferdinand Magellan. On the north it connects with the Arctic by the Bering Strait, and southward it merges into the great expanse of water formerly called the Southern Ocean, the parallel of lat. 40° S. having been commonly taken as the limit in this direction. Present-day geographers consider the southern boundary to be the Antarctica. The Pacific is the largest and deepest of the oceans. Exclusive of dependent seas, it has an area of 63,801,668 square miles, greater than the entire land surface of the globe. Its greatest length from north to south is about 8300 nautical miles, and the greatest breadth, along the parallel of lat. 5° N. is about 9300 nautical miles.

The mean depth of the Pacific is about 14,000 feet. Its western basin is the more diversified, shallow water and immense depths occurring irregularly; the greatest depth yet found is in the Marianus Trench, southwest of Guam, where in 1951 a sounding of 35,-640 was obtained.

The Pacific Ocean is remarkable for the innumerable small islands and island groups which stud its surface, but the area occupied by the truly oceanic islands is very small; they are principally situated toward the central and western portions of its basin. There archipelagos are numerous.

In the trade-wind belts of the Pacific the winds are generally uniform except when such belts approach the western coasts, where they are modified by monsoon influences. In Polynesia hurricanes called typhoons are of frequent occurrence. North and south of the tropical zone the winds exhibit little regularity, though a westerly direction is most frequent. The currents of the Pacific Ocean are less marked in character than those of the Atlantic. Their movement and direction generally follow prevailing winds.

PACIFIC UNION COLLEGE, a coeducational, privately controlled institution of higher learning, situated at Angwin, Calif. It was founded in 1882 as Healdsburg College under the auspices of the Seventh Day Adventist Church; its present name was adopted in 1909. The College offers courses leading to the degrees of bachelor and master of arts, and bachelor of science. In 1953–54 the total enrollment was 809, including 607 full-time students; the faculty numbered 72.

PACIFISM, a political attitude opposing warfare between nations under any and all circumstances; or, opposition to the use of force for any purpose whatever. Pacifism has been propounded throughout history; and arguments have been advanced for it on grounds of philosophy, morality, divine will, and economic and social utility.

The problem faced by pacifists in attempting to prevent war is believed by most political scientists to contain four principal divisions, which roughly parallel comparable divisions of the problem faced by government, or any other social organization, in the maintenance of internal peace. A climate of feeling favorable to peace must be established; the potential causes of conflict, inherent in such factors as economic competition, the quest for power, and fear of foreign domination, must be eliminated or minimized; means for the settlement of disputes must be provided, as in mediation, arbitration, and trial procedures; and, finally, means must be provided to insure observance of the settlements that are made.

Six distinctive approaches to the problems of pacifism have been advanced. The first is the absolute pacifism of some religious sects, members of which believe they can convert aggressors to peaceful ways by setting an example of friendly behavior; see FRIENDS, SOCIETY OF. This is the attitude expressed in the Sermon on the Mount; but it is much older than Christianity, permeating the teaching of Buddha (see BUDDHISM), Confucius (q.v.), and other ancient philosophers. Absolute pacifism assumes both that its practitioners will be able to maintain an unusual degree of moral courage in face of prolonged aggression and provocation, and that its violators will be affected by a constant return of good for bad. Such pacifism has never been entirely successful, however; and though the early Christians consistently maintained this attitude through several generations, their uncompromising opposition to the use of force disappeared after the Church became allied with the Roman state in the 4th century. The second approach bars the use of force and urges moral persuasion, but also envisages passive resistance such as the resistance offered to British rule in the 20th century by Hindus who lay in the streets and blocked military traffic. Critics of this view contend that resistance in any form destroys the possibility of convincing an aggressor of his victim's friendliness, and that even passive resistance provokes frustration, resentment, and further oppression. The same arguments are usually applied to the third theory, which favors active, though nonviolent, resistance, including such acts as sabotage and agitation against an invader.

Each of the remaining three approaches to the problem of peace involves a readiness to use force in certain circumstances, usually characterized as defensive. The first of these positions permits armed defense against attack, but not assistance to other nations being attacked. Adherents of another theory, that of collective security, claim this simple defensive approach assists an aggressor to accumulate strength through conquest, thus making more difficult the defense of all potential victims; and they urge a policy of defensive combination of peace-loving nations against violators of the peace. If such a policy is not to result merely in a system of rival alliances, it must be implemented by an effective international machinery able to make and enforce settlements. Advocates of collective security accordingly support all movements toward establishing international organizations such as the Permanent Court of Arbitration, the League of Nations, and the United Nations. The last position, which accepts use of force as necessary to the establishment of peace, is that of revolutionary socialism, which claims that the capitalist system will never permit the development of a workable international security organization because it promotes international rivalry and conflict. The revolutionary socialists assert that only socialism (q.v.) can eliminate the economic rivalries which breed war, and thus make possible an effective international government.

Although organized peace movements did not appear until the 19th century, the modern search for a means of preventing war began with the rise of national states at the end of the Middle Ages. In the 14th century, the Italian poet Dante Alighieri proposed a world empire to abolish war; in the 15th century Georg von Podiebrad, King of Bohemia, proposed an international parliament; in the 16th century, King Henry IV of France made a similar suggestion; in the 17th century, William Penn wrote *An Essay towards the Present and Future Peace of Europe* (1694); and, in the 18th century, the Abbé St. Pierre greatly influenced readers of his time with his proposals for the securing of "perpetual peace". The first peace society in history was organized in New York in 1815 by David Low Dodge (1774–1852); another was organized in Massachusetts in the same year by Noah Worcester; and both were incorporated into the American Peace Society founded by William Ladd (q.v.) in 1828. Other peace societies were established in European countries later in the century; and, in 1848, Elihu Burritt founded the League of Universal Brotherhood which established branches in the United States, France, England, and Holland. These early groups attempted to mobilize a general opposition to war, but they did not formulate specific plans for domestic policy or international organization to prevent it. The problem of attitudes regarding wars against obvious and grave injustices eventually gave rise to serious dissension, and the American peace movement fell apart during the Civil War, when many of its adherents maintained that preservation of the Union and the abolition of slavery were primary considerations.

Many new groups were organized toward the end of the 19th century, including the International Workingmen's Association (q.v.), which advocated workers' strikes to prevent wars; two juridical organizations, the Institut de Droit International and the International Law Association; and the Inter-Parliamentary Union of peace advocates in the various parliaments of Europe. Frequent meetings and congresses and the announcement of such awards as the Nobel peace prize (see NOBEL PRIZES) stimulated public interest in the peace movement; and the formation of an international postal union in 1874 was considered an important milestone in practical co-operation between nations. Nevertheless, wars multiplied in frequency and intensity during the same period. At the end of the century the impact in Britain of the Boer War and in the United States of the Spanish-American War caused grave setbacks to peace groups in those countries. Finally, World War I broke out in 1914 despite the signing of 163 arbitration treaties between 1903 and 1913, and despite the promises of leaders of the Second (Socialist) International to do everything in their power to avert war. The peace movement as it had existed for almost a century was all but destroyed; and most socialist and other pacifists hastened to support the war efforts of their respective governments.

Following World War I, peace efforts were directed toward collective security through the League of Nations. This organization was loosely constructed, however, providing no really effective means of preventing war; and it proved unable to prevent the Japanese seizure of Manchuria in 1931, the Italian invasion of Ethiopia in 1935, or the German absorption of Austria and Czechoslovakia in 1938 and 1939 respectively. World War II was followed in turn by the establishment of the United Nations which shortly after its birth proved unsuccessful in preventing conflict in Palestine (see ISRAEL: *History*) and in Greece (see GREECE: *History*), and which was considerably weakened by a growing power struggle between the Western democracies and the Soviet Union and its satellites. Many peace organizations, including the American Peace Society, continue in existence; but their work now is oriented principally toward the strengthening of the United Nations, upon which much hope for peace now rests See DISARMAMENT; HAGUE CONFERENCES.

PACIUS, FREDRIK (1809–91), Finnish violinist and composer, born in Hamburg, Germany, and educated under the German violinist and composer Ludwig Spohr. At the age of twenty-five he went to Helsinki, where for many years he served as instructor in music at the University of Helsinki. Pacius enjoyed a considerable reputation in his day as a violin virtuoso; he is best known at the present time, however, as one of the leaders of the 19th-century national school of Finnish music. Among his works are the Finnish national anthem, *Maamme;* some of the most popular national songs of Finland, including *Vårtland, Suomis Sång,* and *Soldatgossen;* the grand operas *Kung Karls Jakt* and *Lorelen;* and an operetta, *Prinsessan of Cypern.*

PACKARD, JAMES WARD (1863–1928), American inventor and manufacturer, born in Warren, Ohio. In 1890 he founded the Packard Electric Co., and subsequently invented and manufactured several electric-lighting devices. He began the manufacture of automobiles in 1897 with his organization of the Ohio Automobile Co. Two years later he designed and built the first Packard automobile, and renamed his company the Packard Motor Car Co., serving as its president until 1903 and chairman of the board until 1915. Packard contributed one million dollars to Lehigh University for the establishment of an engineering laboratory.

PACKING INDUSTRY, a large industry concerned with slaughtering and processing of cattle, sheep, and hogs. It is one of the most important industries in the U.S., having large centers in Chicago, Kansas City, Milwaukee, and other cities of the Middle West. Many parts of the animals are shipped for consumption as fresh meat, while other parts, especially in the case of the hog, are cured and smoked. The fatty portions are converted into lard and commercial grease by rendering processes. The bones are converted into glue, fertilizers, animal feeds, and other usable products, and the hoofs and horns are used or sold for other purposes. The term "meat-packing industry", which was originally applied to the curing and packing of the flesh of the hog, has been extended, with the development of the industry, to include all the operations connected with the utilization and transformation into merchantable form of the different parts of animals slaughtered for food, in so far as these operations are conducted in a single plant.

Before cold storage of meat was introduced it was customary to ship the living animals to Eastern markets. Now the meat, after thorough chilling, is shipped in refrigerator cars to consuming cities and placed in cold-storage warehouses owned by the packing companies, from which it is delivered to dealers.

Labor-saving devices have been adopted at every step in the industry. The carcasses of hogs killed are hooked by the foot to an endless chain, passed through scalding vats, and then through an automatically adjusted scraper which deprives them of hair and bristles. The animals are then hoisted, head down, upon an inclined rail and disemboweled, beheaded, washed, trimmed, and whirled to the chill rooms at a rate as high as 20 to a minute. In dressing hogs about 20 percent is offal and the rest is used as meat, of which only about 10 percent is sold as fresh meat. The other parts are cured, usually by salting in brine, and then smoked for 24 hours. For the manufacture of sausage the meat used is chiefly trimmings, which are obtained from all parts of the establishment.

Legislation. While inspection by the Federal government of meat used in the packing in-

Polish Research & Information Service
Ignace Jan Paderewski

of the port of Telukbayur (formerly Emma-haven). It is the shipping center of a region noted for the production of coal, rubber, copra, coffee, spices, and tea. The city has an airport and is the site of Panchasila University, founded in 1951. Dutch traders established a settlement at Padang about 1680. It was largely under British control between 1781 and 1819, when the Dutch regained possession. The Japanese occupied the city during World War II; in 1945 it passed to Indonesian sovereignty. Pop. (1951 est.) 108,728.

PADDLE STEAMER. See SHIPBUILDING; STEAM NAVIGATION.

PADEREWSKI, IGNACE JAN (1860–1941), Polish pianist, composer, and statesman, born in Podolia, and educated at the Warsaw Conservatory and in Berlin and Vienna. Shortly after making debuts in Vienna in 1887 and in Paris in 1889, he established himself as one of the greatest masters of the piano. He made the first of his many tours of the United States in 1891. His compositions include the opera *Manru* (1901), a symphony, concertos, and orchestral and piano pieces, among which is his popular *Minuet in G.* Between 1910 and 1920 Paderewski devoted himself to the cause of Polish independence; he aided in organizing a committee for the assistance of the victims of World War I in Poland and made concert tours in the United States to raise funds for Polish relief. At the end of the war he was elected prime minister of foreign affairs in the Polish republic and he held office for ten months, from January, 1919 to November, 1919.

PADUA, a province of Venetia in North Italy, watered by the Adige and other rivers, and intersected by a network of canals. Mineral springs are numerous, and wheat, hemp, wine, and silk are produced. Area, 826 sq.m.; pop., about 630,000.

PADUA, the capital of Padua province, Italy, 23 miles s.w. of Venice. The first place among the public buildings belongs to the municipal palace (1172–1219). Its cathedral (1552–1754) contains a collection of valuable miniatures. Donatello's equestrian statue of Gattamelata, the Venetian captain, stands in front of the church of St. Anthony. Padua has enjoyed her greatest fame from her university, founded by the emperor Frederick II in 1221. To it is attached one of the oldest botanical gardens in Europe, an observatory, and a library of 250,000 volumes. The chief industrial establishments are breweries, foundries, corn and saw mills, and motor car and chemical works. Padua's most famous natives were Livy

dustry was provided for in earlier acts of Congress (1890–91 and 1895), it was not until 1906 that comprehensive legislation was introduced. By the Act of 1906 all cattle, sheep, goats, and hogs became subject to ante-mortem and post-mortem examination when the meat is to be used in interstate or foreign commerce, while later it was further extended to include reindeer.

By these means about 60 percent of the total meat supply of the United States was brought under inspection. The Packers and Stockyards Act of 1921 added further control, directed against trust activities. See MEAT.

PACT OF LONDON, an agreement concluded on September 5, 1914, shortly after the outbreak of World War I (q.v.), by the governments of France, Great Britain, and Russia, who pledged that they would not make peace separately. The signatories further agreed that each would demand only those peace terms to which the others had agreed. Japan entered into the agreement in October, 1915, and Italy became the fifth signatory about one month later.

PADANG, city of the Republic of Indonesia, situated on the w. coast of Sumatra, at the base of the Padang Highlands, 4 miles N.

and Mantegna. Pop. (1951 prelim.) 172,692.

PADUCAH, county seat of McCracken Co., Ky., on the Ohio River, 48 miles above its mouth, 226 miles w.s.w. of Louisville. It has a large trade by river and railroad, and contains shipyards, foundries, railroad shops, flour, saw, and planing mills, and manufactures soap, vinegar, ice, furniture, and tobacco. Large quantities of tobacco, corn, and other products are exported. Pop. (1950) 33,828.

PAEAN, an ancient Greek god of healing; the name later became an epithet of Apollo, god of medicine, music, and light. Paean appears in the works of Homer and other early poets as a personal god, a divine physician who was invoked to cure disease and also to avert threatened destruction from other causes. The term eventually became the name for a recognized division of Greek choral lyric poetry. Paeans were composed by the ancient lyric poets, especially Bacchylides and Pindar (qq.v.). Prayers or hymns accompanying the libation at a sacrifice or sung to the gods with

the libation at the marriage feast were also known as paeans.

PAESTUM, a Greek city-colony of ancient Lucania, in s. Italy, on what is now the Gulf of Salerno. The site, occupied by the modern village of Pesto, is 24 miles s.e. of Salerno. Founded by colonists from Sybaris between 650 and 600 B.C., the city was originally called Posidonia. It was subdued by the Lucanians and, subsequently, by the Romans, who established a colony there about 273 B.C. In the 1st century B.C. Paestum was famous for its roses, which were mentioned by several Roman poets, including Vergil. The town was sacked by the Saracens in the 9th century A.D. and finally abandoned in the 16th century. Paestum is famed today for the fine ruins of three large Doric temples, namely the temple of Poseidon (see POSEIDON, TEMPLE OF), god of the sea; the Basilica; and the temple of Ceres, the Roman deity corresponding to Demeter, Greek goddess of agriculture. The temple of Poseidon is one of the most perfectly preserved of all ancient Greek temples.

Italian National Tourist Office

Aerial view of the church of St. Anthony in Padua, Italy

Nicolò Paganini (drawing by Ingres)

PAEZ, mountain tribe of Colombia, occupying about 20 villages in the high Central Cordilleras, westward from Bogotá. They are believed to be the principal modern representatives of an ancient group of allied tribes, hostile to the more civilized Chibcha and constituting a distinct linguistic stock.

PAÉZ, JOSÉ ANTONIO (1790–1873), Venezuelan revolutionist and political leader, born in Acarigua. He was a commander of the Venezuelan revolutionary armies during the War of Independence (1810–22), and inflicted a series of defeats upon the Spanish which culminated in their expulsion in 1822. In the same year he concluded the negotiations whereby Venezuela was incorporated into the federated state of Great Colombia, which had been established in 1819 by Simón Bolívar (q.v.). Paéz later fomented a revolt against Bolívar and in 1830 set up an independent Venezuelan government with himself as president and dictator; he retained these posts until 1846. In 1847 he led a revolt against his elected successor, José Tadeo Monagas; the uprising was quickly suppressed, and Paéz was captured and imprisoned for three years. He lived in exile, chiefly in the United States, from 1850 to 1858, and then returned to Venezuela. In 1861 he reestablished himself as dictator, but was forced to resign two years later because of popular pressure for a constitutional government. He spent the remainder of his life in the United States.

PAGANINI, NICOLÒ (1782–1840), Italian violin virtuoso and composer, born in Genoa, and educated in Genoa and in Parma. He made his first public appearance at the age of nine, playing his own set of variations on a French air, and made his first tour of several Italian cities at thirteen. He left home at fifteen, and for several years led a dissipated life, giving only occasional recitals. After retiring from the concert stage in 1801, he resumed public performances in 1804 and was received with great enthusiasm throughout Italy. In 1805 he was made court musician at Lucca, and while he held that position he also toured Italy. After 1827 he played in Vienna, Berlin, London, and Paris. Paganini was the greatest violin virtuoso of his day, and is often considered the greatest virtuoso of all time. He performed sensational feats on the violin, such as playing an entire piece on one string, but many of the special techniques and effects which he developed, particularly in his exploitation of the harmonic effects of playing on two strings simultaneously, were not only feats of virtuosity but proved revolutionary to the art of violin playing. He composed many works for the violin, including eight concertos, twenty-four caprices, and many sonatas.

PAGE, THOMAS NELSON (1853–1922), American novelist, born on Oakland Plantation, Hanover County, Va. In 1893 he moved to Washington, D.C., where he resided thereafter. He was honored with degrees from several universities and with membership in the American Academy of Arts and Letters. He was appointed ambassador to Italy by President Wilson in 1913 and served in that capacity until 1919. Aside from some dialect poetry, his first noteworthy literary venture was the tale *Marse Chan*, published in 1884 and incorporated, with *Meh Lady* and other stories, in the volume entitled *In Ole Virginia* (1887). Other works include *Two Little Confederates* (1888); *The Old South* (1892); *The Southerner's Problem* (1904); *Robert E. Lee, Man and Soldier* (1911); and *Italy and the World War* (1920). A collective edition of his works was published in 1906 (12 vols., New York).

PAGE, WALTER HINES (1855–1918), American journalist, publisher, and diplomat, born in Cary, N.C., and educated at Randolph-Macon College, Va., and at Johns Hopkins University. From 1887 to 1895 he was on the staff of the *Forum*, a monthly periodical published in New York City. He then joined the *Atlantic Monthly*, of which he was editor in chief in 1898–99. In 1899, in association with Frank N. Doubleday, he founded the publishing firm of Doubleday, Page & Company. Page established the *World's Work*, a monthly magazine of general commentary, in 1900, and was its editor until 1913. In that year he was appointed ambassador to Great Britain by President Woodrow Wilson, whose Presidential candidacy he had previously supported. After the outbreak of World War I in 1914, Page maintained an overt attitude of strict diplomatic neutrality, but in his letters to the President he strongly urged that the United States enter the war on the side of the Allies. He viewed the American declaration of war in April, 1917, as the climax and justification of his career. Page was the author of *The Rebuilding of Old Commonwealths* (1902); an autobiography *A Publisher's Confession* (1905); and, under the pen name Nicholas Worth, a novel, *The Southerner* (1909).

PAGE, WILLIAM (1811–85), American portrait and historical painter, born in Albany, N.Y. He studied painting at the National Academy of Design, New York City, and was elected a National Academician in 1836. From 1849 to 1860, he lived in Rome, where he painted portraits of his close friends Elizabeth Barrett Browning and Robert Browning. He was president of the National School of Design from 1871 to 1873, and was a leading figure in literary and artistic circles. His works include portraits of John Quincy Adams and William Lloyd Garrison in the Boston Art Museum, "Ruth and Naomi" in the New York Historical Society Museum, and "The Young Merchants" in the Pennsylvania Academy of Fine Arts, Philadelphia.

PAGODA. See CHINESE ART; INDIAN ART AND ARCHITECTURE; JAPANESE ART AND ARCHITECTURE.

PAGO-PAGO, a United States port and coaling station on the S.E. coast of Tutuila in Samoa. It became an American coaling station in 1887, and has been under the protection of the United States since 1900.

PAHANG, one of the Federated Malay States on the east coast of the Malay Peninsula, since 1889 under British protection. The products comprise gold, lead, rattans, guttapercha, dammar, and tin. The latter is mostly exported to Singapore. Area, 13,820 sq.m.; pop. (1947) 250,178.

PAHLAVI LANGUAGE AND LITERATURE, the language and literature of the middle Persian period, extending from the 3rd to the 9th or 10th century A.D. Yet the origin of Pahlavi may be traced back with probability, through coins and incidental allusions, to preceding Parthian times. The language is closely akin to Old Persian and Modern Persian in direct line of descent, although it stands much nearer to the latter than to the former.

PAINE, ROBERT TREAT (1731–1814), American jurist and Revolutionary leader, born in Boston, Mass., and educated at Harvard College (now Harvard University). He was one of the leading exponents of the cause of American independence. From 1774 to 1778 he served as a member of the Continental Congress, and in 1776 was among the signers of the Declaration of Independence. Paine was attorney general of Massachusetts from 1777 to 1790, and judge of the Massachusetts Supreme Court from 1790 to 1804.

PAINE, THOMAS (1737–1809), Anglo-American political philosopher and writer, born in Thetford, Norfolk, England. In 1774, with introductions from Franklin, he sailed for Philadelphia. On January 1, 1776, appeared his pamphlet *Common Sense,* which argued for complete independence. In 1778 Congress appointed him secretary of the committee of

Thomas Paine

foreign affairs. He lost that post in 1779 for divulging state secrets, but was appointed clerk of the Pennsylvania legislature, and in 1785 received from Congress $3000 and from New York a confiscated royalist farm at New Rochelle. In 1787 he returned, by Paris, to England, where in 1791–92 he published *The Rights of Man*, the most famous of all the replies to Burke's *Reflections upon the French Revolution*. The work, of which a million and a half copies were sold in England alone, involved many in heavy penalties. Paine, however, had slipped off to Paris, having been elected by the department of Pas-de-Calais its deputy to the National Convention. Here he voted with the Girondists. He offended the Robespierre faction, and in 1794 was thrown into prison, just before his arrest having written Part I of *The Age of Reason*, against atheism and against Christianity, and in favor of deism. Part II appeared in 1795, and a portion of Part III in 1807. The book alienated Washington and most of his old friends; and it was not till after an imprisonment of eleven months that he was released and restored to his seat in the Convention. He became, however, disgusted with French politics, and occupied himself chiefly with the study of finance, till in 1802 he returned to America in a ship placed at his service by President Jefferson.

PAINLEVÉ, PAUL (1863–1933), French statesman and mathematician, born in Paris, and educated at the École Normale Supérieure. He taught mathematics at the École Normale and at the Sorbonne between 1892 and 1903, when he was appointed professor of general mathematics at the University of Paris. His career as a statesman began in 1906 with his election as an independent socialist to the Chamber of Deputies. During World War I he served from 1915 to 1916 as minister of public instruction and inventions, and in 1917 as minister of war and premier of France, holding these two offices concurrently. In March, 1917, he appointed General Henri Philippe Pétain commander in chief of the French army, and in October he took part in discussions with the English and Italian prime ministers which resulted in the formation of the Supreme Allied Council of War at Versailles. The following month he resigned from the cabinet after being criticized for tolerating defeatism in the French conduct of the war. In 1924 he returned to government service as president of the Chamber of Deputies, and the next year, succeeding Édouard Herriot (q.v.), again became premier. He also took the portfolio of minister of finance in addition to his other position, but was forced to resign his offices in November because of opposition in the Chamber of Deputies to his socialistic financial policies. In the cabinets of 1926 and 1928 he served as minister of war, and was minister of air from 1930 to 1931 and from 1932 to 1933. Among his mathematical works are *Leçons sur le Frottement* (1895), *Leçons sur la Théorie Analytique des Équations Differentielles* (1897), and *L'Aviation* (with Émile Borel, 1910).

PAINTED BEAUTY. See NYMPHALIDAE.

PAINTED CUP or **INDIAN PAINTBRUSH,** common name applied to annual, biennial, and perennial herbs constituting the genus *Castilleja* of the Figwort family. The genus, which contains about fifty species, is native to the cooler portions of North America and Asia. Because plants in this genus are parasitic on the roots of other plants, painted cups have not been naturalized and have rarely been cultivated away from their native habitat. The plants have long, hairy, unbranched stems bearing showy, alternate leaves. The flowers, which are borne in spikes, have a two-lobed calyx, a two-lobed corolla, four stamens, and a solitary pistil. The corolla, which is usually yellow, is encased within the calyx, and is usually indiscernible. The fruit is a two-celled, many-seeded, loculicidal capsule. The common painted cup, *Castilleja linariaefolia,* is the State flower of Wyoming. The calyx of this plant is greenish white, tipped with intense vermilion. The scarlet paintbrush, *C. coccinea,* is a common wild plant of northeastern United States. Common Indian paintbrush, *C. pallida,* is a hardy herb found in Canada and in the mountainous regions of northern United States from New England to the Rocky Mountains; its calyx is greenish white tinted with purplish red.

PAINTED DESERT, a name given to the plateau region of Arizona, bordering upon the Colorado and Marble cañons, and derived from the brilliant coloring of the rock surfaces.

PAINTER, WILLIAM (1540–94), born of Kentish stock in London. He published the first volume of *The Palace of Pleasure* in 1566, and the second in 1567, but the definitive edition of the whole work (1575) has additions from other sources. His work is alleged to have furnished several of Shakespeare's plots.

PAINTING. See separate articles on various techniques, such as FRESCO, MURAL PAINTING, and TEMPERA; the sections on painting in the articles on the art of various cultures, such as

Met. Mus. Art; Boston Mus. Fine Arts

AMERICAN PAINTING. *Above: "Mrs. Paul Revere," by Gilbert Stuart. Right: "Mrs. Epes Sargent," by John Singleton Copley.*

BYZANTINE ART, MOHAMMEDAN ART AND ARCHITECTURE, and RENAISSANCE ART AND ARCHITECTURE, and the art of various countries, such as ITALIAN ART AND ARCHITECTURE and PERSIAN ART AND ARCHITECTURE; the articles on various schools of painting, such as BARBIZON SCHOOL, FLORENTINE SCHOOL, and HUDSON RIVER SCHOOL; the articles on various movements in modern art, such as CUBISM and IMPRESSIONISM; and individual biographies of famous painters.

PAINTING, AMERICAN. Art during the early history of the American colonies found its chief outlet in the form of handicrafts: furniture, woodwork, metal work, and glassware. Early Colonial furniture, particularly from Pennsylvania and the New England States, represented work of exceptional utility and a high esthetic order, but the earliest native paintings were made by self-taught itinerant artists or sign painters; although crude and remote from the formal traditions of European art, these simple portraits often displayed a homely charm.

The English tradition was the dominant influence on all American art forms during the 17th and 18th centuries, and many of the most important American portrait painters were trained in England. John Singleton Copley, who worked in the second half of the 18th century, was the first American to raise the art of portrait painting to a distinguished level. Benjamin West, the first American painter to achieve a European reputation, opened a studio in London in 1763 and trained many of his younger contemporary compatriots. The finest portraitist of the late 18th and early 19th centuries, Gilbert Charles Stuart, became noted for his excellent likenesses of President George Washington and for his lovely, silvery-toned portraits of women. The classically disciplined style of the late 18th-century and early 19th-century French painter Jacques Louis David influenced the art of Rembrandt Peale and the painter and inventor Samuel Finley Breese Morse, two noteworthy portrait painters. Besides portraiture, battle scenes and historic public assemblages were characteristic subjects of the time. Another important contemporary painter was John Trumbull, who became known for his historical subjects.

The Romantic movement which raised landscape painting to an important position in European art found its reflection in America in the formation, about 1830, of the Hudson River School (q.v.); its chief exponents,

Whitney Museum of American Art; Metropolitan Museum of Art

AMERICAN PAINTING. *Top: "The Bridle Path, White Mountains," by Winslow Homer. Bottom: Left, "Charlotte Louise Burkhardt," by John Sargent; right, "Theodore Duret," by Whistler.*

Phillips Memorial Gallery; Met. Mus. of Art; Whitney Mus. of American **Art**

AMERICAN PAINTING. *Top: "Six O'Clock," by John Sloan. Bottom, left: "Mother and Child," by Mary Cassatt. Bottom, right: "Laughing Child," by Robert Henri.*

Metropolitan Museum of Art

AMERICAN PAINTING. *Above: "Max Schmitt in a Single Scull," by Thomas Eakins. Left: "Toilers of the Sea," by Albert Ryder.*

Thomas Doughty, Thomas Cole, and Asher Brown Durand, found their inspiration in the scenery of the Hudson River valley. Portraiture declined in the period before the Civil War, and landscape art flourished throughout the country, with such painters as Frederick Edwin Church, Albert Bierstadt, and Thomas Moran depicting the grand vistas of the Colorados mountains, Niagara Falls, the Yosem-

ite River, and Yellowstone Falls. William Morris Hunt and George Inness were deeply influenced by the warmly poetic landscape art of the French impressionists of the Barbizon School (q.v.), though Inness' sense of color helped him create one of the most brilliant and original concepts of landscape art in America. Alexander Helwig Wyant and Homer Dodge Martin were other outstanding landscape masters of the second half of the 19th century. Winslow Homer worked with a fresh and vital realism, giving a new impetus and direction to American painting. His vigorous seacoast paintings and his frank approach to nature broke away from the general European traditions. Albert Pinkham Ryder was the counterpart in painting of the contemporary idealistic tradition in American literature known as Transcendentalism (q.v.). Ryder's romantic seascapes were among the most intensely moving examples in the entire range of American painting. The sober realism of Thomas Eakins probed such subjects as the prize ring and the medical clinic. His large-scale portraits displayed an acute observation and solid mastery of treatment unexcelled in

American art. These three last-mentioned painters are regarded as the chief exponents of the native tradition. John La Farge was important in promoting mural and decorative art in America, and became the first president of the Society of American Artists, established in 1877.

Among notable 19th-century American expatriate painters, Mary Cassatt studied and worked in France under the influence of the French impressionist painter Hilaire Degas, creating sensitive studies of women and children; and James Abbott McNeil Whistler, working in England and France, skillfully adapted Oriental design and the quiet, grey harmonies of the work of the 17th-century Spanish painter Velásquez to works such as his "Nocturnes" and "Arrangements". His "Portrait of the Artist's Mother" and "Thomas Carlyle" were notable achievements. John Singer Sargent, utilizing a brilliant and facile style of painting, became the most celebrated and fashionable portrait painter of his day. William Merritt Chase and Frank Duveneck, working in Munich and other European cities, helped guide and teach a full generation of young American painters who went abroad to study.

AMERICAN PAINTING. *Right: "Egg Beater Number Five," by Stuart Davis. Below: "Italian Landscape," by Ben Shahn.*

Warren Stokes; Metropolitan Mus. of Art

The chief American impressionists of the late 19th and early 20th centuries were John Henry Twachtman, Childe Hassam, Maurice Brazil Prendergast, Ernest Lawson, Julian Alden Weir, and William James Glackens. In 1910 an important exhibition was organized

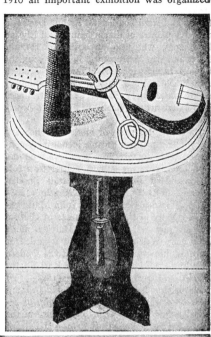

by a group called "The Eight", who opposed the academic conventions, and advocated a vital art portraying scenes of everyday life. The leaders of this group were Robert Henri, George Benjamin Luks, John Sloan, and George Bellows. Their subjects included city streets, saloon and tenement scenes, prize fights, and slum characters. Arthur Davies, a sensitive painter of dream figures and Elysian landscapes, was also an artist of catholic taste, and was instrumental in organizing the famous International Exhibition of Modern Art at New York City in 1913, popularly called the Armory Show, which introduced the modern art movements of France to America.

Under the influence of modern French art, the younger painters became increasingly concerned with organization, structure, and design, often reducing subject matter to a role of secondary importance. Charles Sheeler, Georgia O'Keeffe, Charles Demuth (1883–1935), Marsden Hartley, and John Marin exploited many of the new elements of Cubism and abstract art. Marin and Hartley, along with Max Weber, are generally regarded as the most important exponents of the modern American tradition. Stuart Davis, Karl Knaths (1891–   ), and Milton Avery (1893–   ) made original use of flat space and brilliant color schemes in their work. A group of regional painters made their appearance in the 1930's, led by Thomas Hart Benton and Grant Wood, who exploited picturesque rustic material and popular Western scenes for paintings and murals. Charles Ephraim Burchfield executed many studies of the old-fashioned architecture in small towns. Social realism is best represented in the work of Ben Shahn and Philip Evergood (1901–   ). Alexander Brook, Eugene Edward Speicher, and Yasuo Kuniyoshi were the leading representatives of the Woodstock School of painting, which occupied an important middle-of-the-road position in American painting during the third, fourth, and fifth decades of the 20th century. For further information see separate articles on most of the above-mentioned painters.

PAINTS, colors or pigments either dry or mixed with oil, and used as decorative or protective coatings for various surfaces. The chief pigments are white lead, zinc oxide, lithopone, and titanium oxide. The desired color is obtained by using natural earth colors. In making prepared paint the pigments and a small quantity of oil are thoroughly mixed by machinery into a paste. To the paste is added linseed oil, turpentine, liquid drier, coloring pigments, and sometimes plasticizers to give flexibility to the film. *Enamel paints* consist of zinc oxide and lithopone in brown linseed oil and high-grade varnish. *Luminous paints* contain various phosphorescent sulfur compounds of barium, strontium, and calcium. *Water colors* for artists are finished either in dry cake or moist condition. In both cases they contain the finest pigments ground in gum arabic or dextrin. For the moist form glycerin is added.

Among the new types of paint are various synthetic resins (see PLASTICS) and the water-thinned latex paints, introduced in 1949. Most of the latex paints are limited (1955) to interior use, and are increasingly popular because of the lack of odor and the ease of application.

PAISIELLO or **PAESIELLO,** GIOVANNI (1740–1816), Italian composer, born in Taranto, and educated in Naples. As a student he composed religious music, but it was as a composer of opera that he became famous. At the invitation of the empress Catherine II of Russia he stayed at the Russian court between 1776 and 1784, and during that period wrote many operas, including his most popular work, *The Barber of Seville* (1780). In 1784 he became court conductor to King Ferdinand IV of Naples, and his highly successful operas *La Molinara* (1788), *Nina* (1789), and *I Zingara in Fiera* (1789) were first presented in court productions. From 1802 to 1804 he lived in Paris, where he organized and directed the music for Napoleon Bonaparte's chapel. The remainder of his life was spent in Naples. He composed altogether about one hundred operas and a great variety of other works, including twelve symphonies and six piano concertos. His music is highly melodic, and notable for its simplicity, grace, and charm.

PAISLEY, a manufacturing town of Renfrewshire, Scotland, situated on the White Cart, 7 miles s.w. of Glasgow. The linen, lawn, and silk-gauze industries, important during the 18th century, are now extinct; Paisley shawls, so celebrated between 1805 and the middle of the century, are no longer made. There are works for dyeing, bleaching, tartans, woolen shawls, carpets, distilling and brewing, chemicals, starch, corn flour, preserves, engineering, and cotton thread, besides shipbuilding yards. Pop. (1951 est.) 93,704.

PAKISTAN, a self-governing Dominion of the British Commonwealth of Nations, situated in the subcontinent of India (q.v.), and comprising, with the Union of India (see

INDIA, UNION OF), the territories formerly included in British India (q.v.) and the Native States (Princely States) of India (see INDIA, NATIVE STATES OF). Under the provisions of the Indian Independence Act, Pakistan achieved its present status on August 15, 1947. The dominion consists of two groups of provinces in N. India, separated by more than 700 m. of territory of the Union of India. The Pakistani provinces in N.W. India include Baluchistan, North-West Frontier Province, Punjab (Pakistan), and Sind (qq.v.). The N.E. province of East Pakistan includes East Bengal and most of the Sylhet (q.v.) District of Assam (q.v.). The capital and chief port of Pakistan is Karachi (q.v.); other important cities include Lahore, Dacca, Multan, Rawalpindi, and Chittagong (qq.v.). Area, 365,907 sq.m.; pop. (1951) 75,687,000.

Pakistan is essentially an agricultural country, with about 56,000,000 acres under cultivation in 1951–52. Among the principal crops, with estimated production figures for 1952–53, are rice, 8,147,000 tons; wheat, 2,-417,000 tons; and cotton, 235,000 tons. Pakistan also grows most of the world supply of jute; production in 1952–53 was 6,800,000 bales. The industry of the country was dislocated by the partition of India in 1947. Mills for processing jute were all in the Union of India, as were all Indian steel and paper factories; only fourteen spinning and weaving mills were situated in Pakistan after the partition. However, the country has extensive petroleum and water-power resources and coal and iron deposits for potential industrialization. In 1948 all ammunition, hydroelectric, transport, and communications industries were placed under government control and operation. Pakistan has (1953) about 7000 m. of railroad and 58,084 m. of highway. There are four Pakistani air lines operating, of which two are privately owned. More than 85% of the inhabitants are Moslems, their predominance having been the principal basis of the partition. The executive power of Pakistan is vested in a governor general, assisted by a cabinet; the legislative body is the constituent assembly, which was in session at the time of partition.

History. For the history of the territory now Pakistan before August 15, 1947, see INDIA: *History.* At the inception of the new state, Mohammed Ali Jinnah (q.v.) became the first governor general. Although the beginning of independence was celebrated with rejoicing in both Pakistan and the Union of India, strife between the newly created dominions began almost immediately thereafter. The first great conflict centered on the persecution of religious minorities where areas predominantly Hindu were awarded to Pakistan, or the reverse. About half the population of Lahore, the largest city in Pakistan, were Hindus or Sikhs, nearly all of whom emigrated to India. At the same time Moslems from East Punjab began moving into Pakistan. Rioting and bloodshed between the two great religious groups became common. The influx of Moslem refugees into West Punjab became a major concern and, on August 27, 1948, the dominion government invoked emergency powers, ordering its various provinces and states to take assigned numbers of refugees. By Feb. 26, 1949, 5,100,000 Moslems from India had emigrated to West Punjab, and 3,565,000 Pakistani Hindus had been resettled in the Union of India.

A second grave problem arose in Princely States ruled by Moslems or Hindus in which the majority of the population followed a religion different from that of the ruler. In Kashmir (q.v.), the Hindu maharajah agreed to join the Union of India in late 1947, against the will of his predominantly Moslem subjects. Both Pakistan and India sent in troops and in 1948 India referred the situation to the United Nations Security Council. On April 21, 1948, the Council agreed to hold a plebiscite in Kashmir to determine the ultimate disposition of that state. The situation was reversed in Junagadh where, after an almost unanimous plebiscite in favor of annexation by India, the Moslem ruler retired to Karachi, leaving the succession to the throne to be determined by the provisional government.

Economic problems provided a third source of conflict between the two dominions. Pakistani-Indian conferences were held in 1947 concerning Indian processing of Pakistani jute. The negotiations were ineffective after Pakistan initiated export duties on jute, which were necessary as a primary source of revenue for the comparatively poor Moslem state. In 1948 Pakistan began to invite foreign investors to aid in the development of its natural resources. With Pakistan and India holding irreconcilable viewpoints regarding the proposed plebiscite, U.N. attempts to arbitrate the Kashmir dispute met with systematic failure during 1949 and 1950. Pakistan approved (April 2, 1951) a new U.N. plan to end the dispute. India rejected certain features of the plan, however, further aggravating the protracted crisis. Pakistani-Indian relations improved somewhat during 1951 as a result of

Ewing Galloway

A letter writer plying his trade on a street in a town in Pakistan

full resumption (February) of trade between the two countries. On Oct. 16 Prime Minister Liaquat Ali Khan was assassinated by a political fanatic. Kwaja Nazimuddin, the governor-general, was named to succeed him in office.

The government announced in June, 1952, that at the end of the first year of the six-year, national-development program progress was being made toward industrialization and the expansion of hydroelectric facilities. To finance the program, part of the Colombo Plan for the development of South and Southeast Asia, the government encouraged investment of private capital and negotiated loans from the United States, Canada, and the International Bank. Toward the end of the year Pakistan was threatened by famine, as the result of a prolonged drought, and by grave financial difficulties consequent on the fall in world commodity prices.

The deadlock over Kashmir continued to center around Indian refusal to recognize Pakistani demands for the equal right to station troops in the area. In December the U.N. Security Council requested the two countries to negotiate directly on the Kashmir issue.

The economic situation deteriorated during 1953. The lack of sufficient foreign exchange necessitated barter agreements, such as one signed (March) with Communist China, whereby Pakistan would receive coal in exchange for its cotton. Also in March, the government was forced to ban imports from so-called dollar countries of more than 200 items, including much-needed machinery, chemicals, electrical equipment, and other manufactures. The imminent threat of famine, coupled with Moslem factional disputes, caused the downfall of the Nazimuddin government on April 17. Mohammed Ali, Ambassador to the United States, became prime minister. The new government planned drastic cuts in expenditures in a desperate attempt to improve the economic situation.

In July part of 1,000,000 tons of U.S. wheat, allocated by the Congress on a loan basis, reached Pakistan, relieving the severe food shortage. Further international assistance included a $28 million loan from Great Britain for the purchase of British capital goods, and approximately $26 million in U.S. Point-Four aid.

The Kashmir question was no nearer solution by the end of 1953. In December direct negotiations on proposals for a plebiscite were terminated following disagreement on the number and composition of forces to be stationed in Kashmir during the voting. Pakistani-Indian relations were further strained, beginning late in 1953, after publication of reports that Pakistan had begun to negotiate with the United States for military aid. The Indian government lodged vigorous protests with both countries. Pakistan rejected the protest, and the United States, in an official statement, declared that military assistance to Pakistan, if granted, would be comparable to aid furnished Iran.

Pakistan and Turkey signed a treaty on April 2, 1954, establishing a mutual-defense alliance. Because it brought Pakistan indirectly into the Western defense system, the treaty was hailed by the United States and denounced by the Soviet Union. Egypt and the Indian Union also denounced the alliance. On May 19 the United States agreed to furnish Pakistan military aid costing $27 million during the 1954–55 fiscal year.

On the Pakistani domestic scene meanwhile an opposition coalition, including communists, had triumphed in provincial elections held in East Pakistan on March 19. The East Pakistani labor movement became increasingly restive after the coalition government assumed office, and on May 30 Prime Minister Mohammed Ali, accusing the coalition cabinet of moves to establish a separate East Pakistani state, removed it from office. On July 24 the Pakistani government imposed a nationwide ban on the Communist Party.

On Sept. 8 Pakistan became a signatory of the Southeast Asia Treaty, a U.S.-sponsored document providing for the collective defense of "the general area of Southeast Asia . . . and the Southwest Pacific . . .", excluding Formosa (q.v.). Besides Pakistan and the United States, signatories were Great Britain, France, Australia, New Zealand, the Philippines Republic, and Thailand.

The Pakistani governor general dissolved the Constituent Assembly on Oct. 24, charging it with having "lost the confidence of the people".

Members of the provincial legislatures elected a new constituent assembly on June 21, 1955. The Moslem League won 35 of the 80 seats and the two Bengali (East Pakistan) parties known as the United Front and the Awami (People's) League together won 38 seats. The election ended the one-party rule of the Moslem League, which had been in power

since the inception of Pakistan as an independent state. Prime Minister Mohammed Ali resigned on Aug. 7. He was succeeded by the former finance minister Chaudri Mohammed Ali (1905–), who also succeeded him as head of the Moslem League. Members of the Moslem League and of the United Front comprised the coalition cabinet formed on Aug. 11. Pakistan joined the Turkish-Iraqi-British mutual-defense alliance on Sept. 23.

PALACKY, FRANCIS (1798–1876), Bohemian historian, born in Moravia. In 1825 he became the first editor of the *Journal of Bohemian Museum;* in 1839 Austrian authorities confirmed his appointment as historiographer of Bohemia. He also served in the Austrian parliament where he upheld the cause of autonomy for a federated Czech state, consisting of Bohemia, Moravia, and Silesia. His chief work is *The History of the Bohemian People* (5 vols., 1836–67).

PALÆOLOGUS, the name of an illustrious Byzantine family which founded the last dynasty of the East Roman emperors (1261–1453), in the person of Michael VIII, Emperor of Nicæa. He was a soldier and administrator, who tried to heal the breach between the Eastern and Western churches. The last member of the family was Constantine Palæologus, with whom the East Roman Empire came to an end in 1453.

PALAMAS, KOSTES (1859–1943), Greek poet, born in Patras, and educated at Missolonghi and the University of Athens. His first important work, written in demotic speech, the vernacular as compared to the literary language (see GREEK LITERATURE: *The Modern Period*), was *Tragoudia tes Patridos Mou* ("Songs of My Fatherland", 1886), an expression of his aim to revive Greek literary eminence. Philosophy and reason rather than lyricism distinguish his verse, which glorifies the Hellenistic spirit and traditions.

His poetry includes *Taphos* ("The Tomb", 1898), *Assalephti Zoi* ("Immutable Life", 1904), *Dodekalogos tou Yiphtou* ("The Gypsy's Decalogue", 1907), *Phloyera tou Vasilia* ("The Flute of the King", 1910), *Dekatertraticha* ("Fourteen Verses", 1919), and *Royal Blossom* (1923).

PALAMEDES, in Greek legend, the son of King Nauplius of Eubœa and his wife Clymene. Palamedes is not mentioned by Homer. However, he plays a prominent part in post-Homeric literature on the Trojan War, in which he is depicted as a man of cunning and resourcefulness, and the reputed inventor of weights, measures, money, dice, and some of the letters of the Greek alphabet. When the Ithacan hero Ulysses (q.v.) feigned madness, that he might not be compelled to sail to Troy, Palamedes detected the deception by placing Ulysses' infant son Telemachus in front of the hero's plow in order to ascertain whether Ulysses was sane enough to change direction and avoid the child. For this trick Palamedes was thereafter hated by Ulysses, who also turned the Greek leaders Agamemnon and Diomedes against him. Versions concerning his death differ, but he was apparently the victim of a plot by Ulysses and Diomedes, was accused of treasonable correspondence with the Trojans, and was stoned to death. His father Nauplius avenged his death after the fall of Troy by luring the returning Greek fleet onto the rocks of the Eubœan coast by means of false beacons.

PALATINATE, THE, historical region of Germany, situated w. of the Rhine R., and now forming part of the West German State of Rhineland-Palatinate. Originally a countship ruled by a count palatine, The Palatinate began to figure in German history in the 11th century. After many vicissitudes, including a number of partitions, most of the region was united with Bavaria; following the adherence of Bavaria to the Weimar Republic The Palatinate comprised two State government districts, officially known as The Palatinate (sometimes Lower Palatinate) and Upper Palatinate. Allocated to the French Zone of Occupation after the defeat of Germany in World War II, the two government districts were incorporated (1947) in the newly created State of Rhineland-Palatinate. Aggregate area of two former districts, 5854 sq.m.; pop., about 1,500,000.

PALATINE HILL (*Mons Palatinus*), one of the famous seven hills of Rome, and, according to tradition, the site of the earliest Roman settlement. On its N.W. slope was the Lupercal, the cave where Romulus and his twin brother Remus were said to have been suckled by a she-wolf. On this hill, according to legend, Romulus founded the city of Rome. In late Republican days, several temples and some of the finest private homes in Rome stood upon the summit of the Palatine or on its slopes; under the Empire the hill became the site of the imperial residences, and the emperor Nero included the entire hill within the precincts of his *aurea domus* (Golden House), erected after the disastrous fire of 64 A.D. From the time of Alexander Severus, Roman emperor from 222 to 235 A.D., the Palatine Hill ceased

to be the official place of residence of the emperors.

PALAWAN, or PARAGUA, an island and province of the Philippines, situated in the extreme w. of the group, in the Sulu Sea. The island is about 280 m. long and 25 m. broad with a mountain chain running through the center culminating in Mt. Mantalingajan, 6843 ft. The vegetation is tropical, the mountains being covered with vast forests of ebony, sandalwood, and logwood. Coffee, cacao, sugar cane, and vegetable gum are abundant, and there is a trade in livestock. The province includes the Calamian and Cuyo groups, and the islands of Dumaran and Balabac. Area, 4550 sq.m.; pop., about 30,000.

PALAZZO VECCHIO. See FLORENCE.

PALEARCTIC REGION. See GEOGRAPHICAL DISTRIBUTION OF ANIMALS.

PALEMBANG, river port and the largest city of Sumatra, Republic of Indonesia, situated on the Moesi R. The principal industries are silk weaving, wood and ivory carving, and the manufacture of weapons and gold articles. Pop., about 108,000.

PALENCIA (anc. *Pallantia*), a walled city of Spain, in Old Castile, 29 miles N.N.E. of Valladolid. The Gothic cathedral was built 1321–1504. Blankets and coarse woolen cloths are manufactured. The vine is cultivated, and there is a trade in wool. Pop., about 20,000. Area of province of Palencia, 3093 sq.m.; pop. (1950) 232,680.

PALEOGRAPHY, in its widest signification, the science that treats of the writing of the ancients and that of the Middle Ages, whether on materials regarded as destructible or indestructible; in its restricted sense, paleography denotes only the study of writing on such destructible materials as wax, papyrus (q.v.), parchment (q.v.) or vellum, and paper. Inscriptions engraved on stone or metal provide the material for the science of *epigraphy*. Latin paleography owes its origin to the study of diplomatics, or ancient legal documents, and in turn led to the study of ancient Greek writing, through the investigation of the manuscripts of the Greek Church Fathers of the early Christian Era.

Ancient writing materials included leaves, bark, clay, and leaden tablets, but the most commonly used were the wax tablet, the papyrus roll, and later the parchment book. Wax tablets were convenient for letters, accounts, and writing of a temporary nature. Papyrus sheets, made into rolls from twenty to thirty feet in length, provided the most common writing material of classical antiquity, being in constant use from about 500 B.C. to 300 A.D., and even later for nonliterary purposes. The papyrus roll had several disadvantages; because it had to be rerolled after each reading, it was extremely awkward to use for reference, and often from excessive wear the beginning and end of a roll would be torn or mutilated. This mutilation caused the lacunæ, or gaps, which sometimes appear in the works of classical authors. Parchment, known to have been employed for literary works at Rome as early as the 1st century A.D. and used by the Greeks much earlier, became increasingly popular, and by the 4th century, Greek and Latin literature was generally transferred from the papyrus roll to the parchment codex, made into book form in imitation of the wax tablet. The codex was much more suitable for long works and lent itself more readily to convenient reference. Some pagan works, however, were not transcribed, and many losses occurred in this period, especially among the works of Greek writers. The pages of the early codices were large, and the practice of writing in columns, usually two, but sometimes three or four, was taken over from the papyri; poetry was transcribed with each verse written continuously across the page. In both the papyrus rolls and the parchment books which supplanted them, the regular practice was not to separate words, although in some writing, both inscriptions and literary works, dots or points were used as divisions. Word division did not become common until about the 9th century, when many wrong divisions were made; for instance, *opsonatu redeo*, a phrase in the *Menæchmi* of Titus Maccius Plautus, was divided as *opso nature deo* and then corrupted into *ipso naturæ deo*.

The two styles of penmanship in antiquity are known as the formal literary, or *book*, hand and the more rapid *cursive* hand, which was employed for nonliterary, everyday purposes. The extant manuscripts of the classical authors exhibit either the ancient book hands or various scripts which developed later, in the Middle Ages, under cursive influence. All Greek and Roman manuscripts, ancient and medieval, are classified either as *majuscule*, that is, written in large letters, or as *minuscule*, written in small letters. Majuscule writing is subdivided into (1) *capitals*, either square capitals, carefully formed with angles to resemble inscriptions carved on stone, or rustic capitals, drawn with somewhat greater freedom with oblique and short cross strokes; and (2) *uncials*, modified capitals, in which curves are favored and angles avoided as much as

possible; originally, the shape of both types of majuscule letters was dictated by the materials used, capitals having been incised on hard stone on which a chisel could not easily make curves, and uncials having been written on such nonresistant surfaces as papyrus. Minuscules, or small letters, resulted from the rapid and inartistic writing of majuscules under cursive influence; the letters became changed in form and reduced in size, but minuscule writing is in most instances distinct from cursive writing.

The science of paleography as applied to the study of Greek writing on papyrus is of modern date. Previous to the discoveries of the past seventy-five years (see PAPYRI, DISCOVERIES OF), Greek papyri were customarily classified according to the style of writing, as the literary, or book, hand or the cursive hand. Although these styles are sharply differentiated, there is no set form for either one. Writing on vellum may be classed as uncial or minuscule, and this distinction can be sharply drawn in the Middle Ages, when the literary hands were settled. The uncial of the medieval period is a lineal descendant of the literary style in the papyri, but the medieval minuscule is a new letter, based on the cursive but molded into an exact form and becoming finally the regular hand of the literary style.

Present knowledge of Greek writing is dependent upon the evidence of inscriptions, the study of which is the science of Greek epigraphy. The earliest literary papyrus, that of the *Persæ* by the Greek poet Timotheus (446?–357? B.C.), is written in capital letters very similar to those of inscriptions. By the 3rd century B.C. the book hand had become uncial, and a handsome broad uncial continued in use on papyri until the 6th or 7th century A.D. Three periods in the history of Greek writing on papyrus may be recognized: the Ptolemaic, from 330 to 23 B.C., marked by freedom and breadth of style; the Roman, from 27 B.C. to 305 A.D. (the reigns of Augustus to Diocletian), marked by roundness and curved, flowing strokes; and the Byzantine, from 360 A.D. to the Arab conquest of Egypt in 640, marked by a large, handsome style.

The oldest vellum manuscripts are the great uncial codices of the Bible, the *Codex Vaticanus* and the *Codex Sinaiticus*, both probably of the 4th century A.D.; these manuscripts have essentially the uncial characters of the papyrus rolls. About the 7th century a slanting uncial came into popularity; this type of uncial became pointed, with a strong contrast between heavy and light strokes, and is known as the Slavonic uncial, because it formed the basis of the Slavic alphabet. When the Greek uncial was taken over in the 9th century by the Slavs, the Greeks developed for their formal book hand a minuscule writing based upon cursive. Manuscripts written in Greek minuscules are very numerous. They are classified as the *vetustissimi,* from the 9th to the middle of the 10th century, distinguished for their purity and simplicity; the *vetusti,* from the middle of the 10th to the middle of the 13th century, in which contractions and abbreviations become more frequent; the *recentiores,* from the middle of the 13th to the middle of the 15th century, written with great carelessness, as were the contemporary Gothic scripts of western Europe; and the *novelli,* comprising the manuscripts written after the fall of Constantinople in 1453.

The study of the history of Latin paleography begins with majuscule writing as found in the earliest Latin manuscripts extant, such as the Vergil manuscripts of the 4th and 5th centuries A.D., which are written in square or rustic capitals. As a literary hand, uncial writing extends from the 5th to the 8th century; uncial was predominantly the writing used for Biblical and patristic works and seems to have been developed by the Christians, perhaps formalized by the early copyists of the Bible under the influence of Greek uncials. The cursive hand in general use influenced the literary majuscule hand, so that a style designated as half-uncial became a popular book hand, and this, being a clear and beautiful script, had an important effect upon some of the medieval book hands. The contest between formal majuscule and cursive minuscule ended, however, in the victory of the latter. After the 7th century, the various book hands were all minuscule, developed by scribes from the cursive with an admixture of uncial or half-uncial forms. The earliest examples of the cursive style are the wall inscriptions and wax tablets of Pompeii, written before 79 A.D. The minuscule scripts which developed from cursive became the so-called national hands of the Middle Ages, each assuming an individuality according to the locality in which it prevailed.

The important national hands are seven in number. The Beneventan, or Lombardic, script is the writing of s. Italy, as practiced in the monasteries of Monte Cassino and La Cava from the 9th to the 13th century. The Visigothic was employed for books and documents of Spain from the 8th to the 12th century. The Insular scripts, those of Ireland and

England from the 7th to the 11th century, differ from the Continental forms of writing in that they were not derived from the cursive style, but from the half-uncial, which had been taken to Ireland by missionaries in the 4th and 5th centuries. Manuscripts written in the Insular scripts are noted for their calligraphic forms and their ornamentation. The script written in France during the 7th and 8th centuries is called Merovingian, or pre-Carolingian; this hand never reached the calligraphic form, which marked the highest development of the other national hands, for it was supplanted by the round minuscules of the Carolingian reform. The reform of writing which marked the reign of Charlemagne had its origin in the monasteries of France, where much attention was given to the copying of earlier manuscripts. The scribes wrote in a plain, simple, and beautiful script that was strongly influenced by the earlier half-uncial characters. A new hand was the result, which is known as the Carolingian minuscule, and which became the literary hand of the Frankish Empire. In the 11th century the Carolingian began to assume an individual form in the various nations of w. Europe. This period was the starting point of the history of modern hands, which are traced to the Roman alphabet. In the 12th century appeared the so-called Gothic writing, which is simply the Carolingian minuscule with angles replacing the curves. Excessive angularity and compression, and the use of numerous contractions and abbreviations, made the Gothic script difficult to read, and it was often artistically awkward as well as illegible. A renaissance of the Carolingian style took place in Italy in the 14th century, developing a very regular and beautiful style, which led to the Humanistic script of the 15th century. The Humanistic hand served as the model for the early typesetters, and so preserved the clear and simple Roman letters which go back through the Carolingian script to the half-uncials of the earlier period. These minuscule letters were the ancestors of the lower-case letters of the modern Roman type; the Gothic script was used for the lower case of German type.

The difficulty of deciphering medieval manuscripts arises largely from the contractions, abbreviations, and ligatures which were employed to economize labor and parchment. In the early manuscripts, written in capitals and uncials, abbreviations were rarely used, but they became more frequent in the 6th and 7th centuries. More than 5000 contractions of Latin words were used in France between the

7th and the 16th centuries; in England more than 1000 are found in official Latin documents of the Tudor period alone. Fortunately, the Carolingian scribes, who copied many of the best medieval manuscripts of Latin authors, employed abbreviations somewhat sparingly. In Gothic writing, abbreviations of every kind appeared with the greatest frequency.

PALEOLITHIC PERIOD. See STONE AGE.

PALEONTOLOGY, the study of fossil animal and plant life which existed in remote geological times. The study of such remains is important not only in tracing the evolutionary history of organisms which now exist but also in the determination of the relative ages of geological deposits.

The term *fossil* is applied to actual remains of living organisms preserved and protected from decay by enclosure in the earth's crust. Commonly only the harder and more resistant parts of organisms, such as bones, shells, and teeth of animals and woody tissue of plants, were preserved in this manner. In some cases the original materials underwent little change in shape after they were embedded in mineral deposits, but the original substance of the organism was petrified (turned into stone). Petrification took place in either of two ways. The open spaces of porous materials such as bone and some types of shell were filled with mineral solutions which dried and hardened, leaving a stonelike fossil which is heavier and more compact than the original material. Calcium carbonate and silica are the most common mineral materials which formed this type of fossil. In some instances, organic material was completely replaced chemically by an inorganic material, usually silica. In such fossils no trace of the original organic matter remains, but the entire structure of the organism was preserved, including the microscopic details of individual cells. The fossil forests of western U.S. are well-known examples of this form of petrification.

Outlines of softer and more delicate animal and plant tissues were frequently preserved in the form of carbon prints in stone when the tissues were subjected to heat while in contact with a stone surface. Natural molds were formed when an animal or plant was enclosed in a sedimentary deposit which later hardened. Water seeping through the stone dissolved the original material, leaving a natural mold. Sometimes these molds were later filled with mineral material, forming replicas of the original organisms. The footprints and body prints which prehistoric animals left on soft surfaces such as mud flats are also sometimes preserved in stone, as are fossil animal droppings.

The true nature of fossils was not generally understood until about the beginning of the 19th century, when the basic principles of modern geology were established. From about the year 1500, scholars engaged in a bitter controversy over the origin of fossils. One group held the modern view that fossils are the remains of prehistoric plants and animals, but this group was opposed by another which declared that they are either freaks of nature or creations of the devil. In the 18th century, many believed that all fossils are relics of the Biblical flood, and that fossils of such diverse animals as mastodons and salamanders are the remains of men who perished in that disaster.

The fossils of ancient animals and plants are usually incomplete, but paleontologists, aided by their knowledge of living forms and of comparative anatomy, are usually able to reconstruct the form of an organism as it appeared in life.

Paleozoic Life: Cambrian. Almost no fossils belonging to the Archeozoic or Proterozoic eras of geological history are known, and the first abundant fossil deposits appear in the rocks of the Cambrian period at the beginning of the Paleozoic era. The earliest of the fossils date from approximately 450,000,000 years ago. The reason for the scarcity of earlier fossils is not fully understood, but geologists believe that in pre-Cambrian times most species of animals were soft-bodied, and that shells and other hard body parts adapted to preservation first developed in the Cambrian period.

At the beginning of the Paleozoic era, animal life was entirely confined to the seas. With the exception of the vertebrates all the phyla of the animal kingdom existed in Cambrian times, and the first vertebrates, which were primitive fishes, appeared in the Ordovician period which followed the Cambrian. The characteristic animals of the Cambrian period were the *trilobites,* a primitive form of crustaceans which reached their fullest development in this period and became extinct in Permian times. Among the *mollusks,* the earliest snails appeared in this period, as did the *cephalopods.* Other groups represented in the Cambrian were *brachiopods, bryozoans,* and *foraminifers.* The flora of the Cambrian was entirely confined to such low forms as seaweeds in the oceans and lichens on land.

Ordovician. The most characteristic ani-

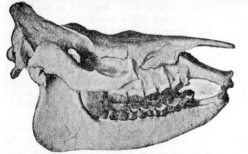

PALEONTOLOGY

Top: A dinosaur skeleton found in the upper chalk strata of Alberta, Canada. Above, left: A trilobite fossil found in a shale quarry at Field in British Columbia, Canada. Above: A fossil leaf from the Miocene shale beds of Baden, Germany. Left: The skull of a huge hornless rhinoceros, found in the Bad Lands of South Dakota.

mals of this period were the *graptolites*, which were small, colonial coelenterates. The first vertebrates and the earliest corals emerged during the Ordovician. The largest animal of the period was a cephalopod mollusk which had a shell about 10 ft. in length. The flora of this period resembled that of the Cambrian.

Silurian. The most important evolutionary development of this period was the first air-breathing animal, a scorpion, fossils of which have been found in Scandinavia and England. Most paleontologists believe that the primitive mosses emerged in this period. The remaining fauna and the flora of the period resembled that of earlier Paleozoic times.

Devonian. The dominant forms of animal life in this period were fishes of various types, including sharks, lungfishes, armored fishes, and primitive forms of ganoid fishes which are believed to have been the evolutionary ancestors of the amphibia. Fossil remains found in Pennsylvania and Greenland indicate early forms of amphibia may have existed during the period. Lower animal forms included corals, starfishes, sponges, and trilobites. The earliest known insect was found in Devonian rock.

The Devonian is the first period from which any considerable number of fossilized plants have been preserved. During this period the first woody plants developed, and before the period had closed the land-growing forms included seed ferns, ferns, scouring rushes, scale trees, and primitive cone-bearing trees called *Cordaites.* Fossil evidence indicates that forests existed in Devonian times, and petrified stumps of certain of the larger Devonian plants are two feet in diameter.

Mississippian. The seas of this period contained a variety of *echinoderms* and *foraminifers* as well as most of the forms of animal life appearing in the Devonian. A group of sharks, the *Cestraciontes* or "shell crushers" were dominant among the larger marine animals. The predominant group of land animals was the *Stegocephalians,* a class of primitive, lizardlike amphibians which developed from the lungfishes. During the Mississippian the various forms of land plants became diversified and grew larger, particularly those which grew in low-lying swampy areas.

Pennsylvanian. This period saw the evolution of the first reptiles, a group which developed from the amphibians and which was completely independent of a water environment. Other land animals included spiders, snails, scorpions, more than 800 species of

cockroaches, and the largest insect ever evolved, a species resembling the dragonfly with a wingspread of about 29 in. The largest plants were the scale trees, the tapered trunks of which were as much as 6 ft. in diameter at the base and 100 ft. high. *Cordaites,* which had pithy stems surrounded by a woody shell, was more slender but even taller. The first true conifers also developed during the Pennsylvanian period.

Permian. The chief features of the animal life of the Permian period were the disappearance of many forms of marine animals and the rapid spread and evolution of the reptiles. In general the Permian reptiles were of two types: lizardlike reptiles which lived wholly on land, and sluggish, semiaquatic types. A comparatively small group of reptiles which evolved in this period, the *Theriodontia,* was the group from which mammals later developed. Among the plants the scale trees became more rare, and the predominant vegetation was composed of ferns and conifers.

Mesozoic Life: Triassic. The Mesozoic era as a whole is often called the Age of Reptiles because the reptile phylum was dominant throughout the entire age. The most notable of the Mesozoic reptiles were the *dinosaurs,* which first evolved in Triassic times. The Triassic dinosaurs were not as large as their descendants in later Mesozoic times, and were comparatively slender animals which ran on their hind feet, balancing their bodies with heavy, fleshy tails. They seldom exceeded 15 ft. in length. Other reptilian forms of the Triassic included such aquatic reptiles as the *ichthyosaurs,* and a group of flying reptiles, the *pterosaurs.* During this period the first mammals appeared. The fossil remains of these animals are fragmentary, but they were apparently small in size and reptilian in appearance. Among the other land animals were insects and snails, and in the sea the first ancestors of the modern bony fishes, *Teleostei,* made their appearance. The plant life of the Triassic seas included a large variety of marine algae. On land, the dominant vegetation was composed of evergreens such as ginkgos, conifers, and palms. Small scouring rushes and ferns still existed, but the larger members of these groups had become extinct. A great portion of the semiarid plains of this period were entirely without vegetation of any kind.

Jurassic. In the Jurassic period the evolution of the dinosaurs produced four distinct types or tribes: heavy four-footed *sauropods* such as *Brontosaurus;* two-footed carnivorous dinosaurs such as *Tyrannosaurus;* two-footed

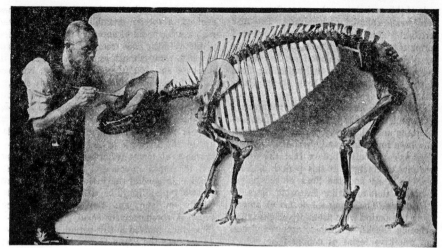

Smithsonian Institution, U.S. National Museum

Mounting the skeleton of a Palaeosyops paludosus, an Eocene mammal found in Wyoming

vegetarian dinosaurs such as *Trachodon;* and four-footed armored dinosaurs such as *Stegosaurus*. The winged reptiles were represented by the *pterodactyls* which, during this period, ranged in size from extremely small species to others which had wingspreads of 4 ft. Marine reptiles included pliosaurs, a group which had broad, flat bodies like those of turtles, with long necks and large flippers for swimming; icthyosaurs, which had scaly bodies; and primitive crocodiles. During the Jurassic the first true bird, *Archaeopteryx,* evolved from the reptiles. Although this animal, which was about the size of a modern crow, had feathers, its toothed jaw and the structure of its wings clearly indicate its reptilian origin. The mammals of the Jurassic period comprised four orders, all of which were smaller than small modern dogs. In this period the evolution of the insects resulted in the development of a number of the modern orders, including moths, flies, beetles, grasshoppers, and termites. Shellfish included lobsters, shrimps, and ammonites, as well as the extinct group of *belemnites* which resembled squids and had cigar-shaped internal shells. The flora of the Jurassic period was dominated by *cycads*. Fossils of most species of Jurassic plants are widely distributed in the temperate zones and polar regions, indicating that the Jurassic climate was uniformly mild.

Cretaceous. The reptiles were still the dominant form of animal life in the Cretaceous period. The four tribes of dinosaurs found in the Jurassic also lived during this period, and in addition a fifth tribe, horned dinosaurs like *Triceratops,* appeared. The largest of the pterodactyls, *Pteranodon,* lived in this period. This flying reptile, which had a wingspread of 24 ft., is the largest flying animal known. The pliosaurs also increased in size during Cretaceous times and reached a maximum length of 50 ft. Among the other reptiles of the period were the first snakes and lizards. Several types of Cretaceous birds are known, among them *Hesperornis,* a diving bird about 6 ft. in length, which had only vestigial wings and was unable to fly. Mammals of the period included the first marsupials, which strongly resembled the modern opossum, and the first placental mammals, which belonged to the group of *insectivores*. Among the shellfish, the first crabs developed at this time. A number of the modern varieties of fishes also evolved during the Cretaceous period.

The most important evolutionary advance in the plant kingdom during this period was the development of deciduous woody plants, which first appeared in early Cretaceous rock formations. Figs, magnolias, sassafras, and poplars were among the earliest to evolve, and by the end of the period virtually all the modern varieties of trees and shrubs had made their appearance, and represented more than ninety percent of the known plants of the period. Mid-Cretaceous fossils include remains of beech, holly, laurel, maple, oak, plane tree, and walnut. Some paleontologists believe that these deciduous woody plants first evolved in Jurassic times but grew only in upland areas where conditions were unfavorable for their preservation as fossils.

Cenozoic Life: Paleocene and Eocene. The first portion of the Cenozoic era represents a transition in the animal kingdom from the Age of Reptiles to the Age of Mammals. The large dinosaurs and other reptiles which had dominated the life of the Mesozoic era disappeared abruptly, and the only important members of the group appearing among the fossils of early Cenozoic times were crocodiles, turtles, lizards, and snakes, all essentially similar to the modern representatives of these groups. With the decline of the reptiles the mammals suddenly increased in number and variety of types. Seven groups of Paleocene mammals are known, all of which appear to have developed in northern Asia and to have migrated to other parts of the world. These primitive mammals had many features in common. All of them were small, with no species exceeding the size of a small modern bear. All were four-footed, having five toes on each foot and walking on the soles of the feet. Almost all the Paleocene mammals had slim heads with narrow muzzles and small brain cases. The predominant mammals of the period were members of three groups that are now extinct. These were the *creodonts,* which were the ancestors of the modern *carnivores;* the *amblypods,* which were small, heavy-bodied animals; and the *condylarths,* which were light-bodied herbivorous animals with small brains. The Paleocene groups which have survived are the marsupials, the insectivores, the primates, and the rodents, all of which were represented during this period by small, primitive species.

In the Eocene epoch a number of direct evolutionary ancestors of modern animals appeared. Among these animals, all of which were small in stature, were horses, rhinoceroses, camels, rodents, and monkeys. The creodonts and amblypods continued to develop during the epoch, but the condylarths became extinct before its close. The first aquatic mammals, the ancestors of the modern whales, also appeared in Eocene times, as did such modern birds as eagles, pelicans, quail, and vultures. The flora of the early Cenozoic era did not differ substantially from that of the late Mesozoic.

Oligocene. In this epoch most of the archaic mammals which characterized the earlier portion of the Cenozoic era disappeared and in their place appeared representatives of a large number of the modern mammalian groups. The creodonts became extinct, and the first

true carnivores, resembling dogs and cats, evolved. Other animals of the period included beavers, camels, mice, rabbits, rhinoceroses, and squirrels. The first anthropoid apes also lived during this time but became extinct in North America during the epoch. Two extinct groups of animals flourished in Oligocene times: the *titanotheres,* related to the rhinoceros and the horse; and the *oreodonts,* small, doglike grazing animals. Plant life showed no striking evolutionary changes during the Oligocene epoch.

Miocene. The development of the mammals during the Miocene epoch was conditioned by an important evolutionary development in the plant kingdom, the first appearance of the grasses. These plants, which were ideally suited for forage, encouraged the growth and development of grazing animals such as horses, camels, and rhinoceroses, which were abundant during the period the *mastodon* evolved, and in Europe and Asia a gorilla-like ape, *Dryopithecus,* was common. Various types of carnivores, including cats and wolflike dogs, ranged over many parts of the world. Besides the grasses, the flora of the period included such modern trees as elms and sumacs.

Pliocene and Pleistocene. The paleontology of the Pliocene epoch does not differ in any marked extent from that of the Miocene, although the period is regarded by many zoologists as the climax of the Age of Mammals. The Pleistocene epoch in both Europe and North America was marked by the abundance of large mammals, most of which were essentially modern in type. Among them were buffaloes, elephants, mammoths, and mastodons; the latter two became extinct before the close of the epoch. In Europe antelopes, lions, and hippopotamuses also appeared. Carnivores included badgers, foxes, lynxes, otters, pumas, and skunks, as well as such extinct species as the giant saber-toothed tiger. In North America the first bears made their appearance, apparently as migrants from Asia. Other migrants included armadillos and ground sloths, which came to North America from the South American continent, and musk oxen, which ranged southward from the arctic regions. An important development of the Pleistocene epoch was the emergence of the first primitive men; see MAN, ANCIENT.

See articles on most of the animal and plant groups mentioned, and also GEOLOGY, SYSTEMATIC.

PALEOZOIC, scientific name applied to the lowest division of the fossiliferous rocks, which contain the earliest forms of life, for merly known as the Primary rocks. The systems included under this title are the Cambrian, Ordovician, Silurian, Devonian, Carboniferous (Mississippian and Pennsylvanian), and Permian (qq.v.). See GEOLOGY, SYSTEMATIC.

PALERMO, a province of Sicily on the Tyrrhenian Sea. Area, 1927 sq.m.; pop., about 845,000. The capital and chief seaport is Palermo (anc. *Panormus;* pop. in 1951, 501,005). The oldest public buildings date from the Norman period, and belong to two styles of architecture, Saracen and Byzantine. The most conspicuous is the cathedral of St. Rosalia (1169–85). Industry is little developed; but trade is carried on in oranges, lemons, dried fruits, sumach, tartar, grain, oils, manna, sulfur, wine, and animal produce.

Palermo was founded as Panormus by the Phenicians, and was a strong Carthaginian colony until taken by the Romans (254 B.C.). It subsequently passed into the hands of the Goths (440 A.D.), the Byzantines (535), the Saracens (830), the Normans (1072), and the Hohenstaufens (1194). In 1282 it was the scene of the massacre of the French rulers, known as the Sicilian Vespers; under Spain it was the residence of a viceroy, and a place of great magnificence. It was liberated by Garibaldi in 1860.

PALERMO STONE, a fragmentary block of hard black diorite inscribed with the annals of ancient Egyptian history, and preserved at the present time in the Museum of Palermo, Palermo, Italy. One of the earliest known historical records, it was inscribed during the Vth Dynasty, between 2750 and 2625 B.C., with annals of the Egyptian kings from predynastic times to the first half of Dynasty V. The Palermo stone is about 17 in. long, 9½ in. wide, and 2½ in. thick. Four fragments originally forming part of this stone are in the Cairo Museum, Cairo, Egypt.

PALES, a pre-Roman deity, adopted by the Romans, who presided over cattle and pastures and was worshiped by herdsmen. The sex of the divinity was uncertain; the scholar Marcus Terentius Varro referred to Pales as a god, and the Roman poets Vergil and Ovid considered the deity a goddess. According to a recent theory, the Pales were two in number, a god and a goddess, divinities of such antiquity that the Romans themselves had forgotten that they were a pair. The festival of Pales, the *Parilia* or *Palilia*, was celebrated by the Romans on April 21 as a ritual purification of flocks and herds.

PALESTINE (fr. Heb. *Pelishti,* "Philistine"), the designation, since ancient times, for a region of w. Asia bordering the E. Mediterranean Sea, of varying extent; and also, in modern times, for a territory under the mandate of Great Britain from July 22, 1922, to May 15, 1948. For the history of the region since the termination of this mandate, see ISRAEL. At a very early date the name Palestine was applied to the portion of the Mediterranean littoral occupied by the Philistines (q.v.), a martial people who emigrated either from the island of Crete or from the s. coast of Asia Minor; later, however, the term came to include the land of the Israelites (see JEWS). At the time of the creation of the British mandate, Palestine had been reduced in size by the establishment (1920) of the British satellite state of Trans-Jordan (see JORDAN.) The mandated territory was bounded on the N. by Lebanon and Syria, on the S. by the Egyptian province of Sinai, on the w. by the Mediterranean Sea, and the E. by the Dead Sea and the Jordan R., which divides the territory from Trans-Jordan. The area of the Palestinian mandate was 10,429 sq.m., comprising 10,157 sq.m. of land area and 272 sq.m. of inland water area.

Physical Features. The distinctive physiography of Palestine is due to the deep depression through which the Jordan R. (q.v.) flows. This depression is the result of a geological cataclysm by which the entire plateau E. of the Mediterranean Sea was sundered from N. to s. as far as the Red Sea. In Palestine the earth's crust immediately w. of the fault broke and fell precipitously toward the deep valley formed by the upheaval. Throughout almost the whole course of the Jordan R. this valley is now lower than the level of the Mediterranean Sea. Thus the Waters of Merom (Bahr el Hule) are about seven ft. above sea level; but the Sea of Galilee (Lake of Gennesaret), some ten m. farther s., has a surface elevation 682 ft. below sea level; and the Dead Sea, 65 m. south of the Sea of Galilee, has a surface elevation 1292 ft. below sea level.

The land surface of Palestine falls generally into four parallel zones, namely, the seacoast plain, the hills and mountains w. of the Jordan R., the valley of the Jordan, and the plateau region E. of the great depression. The hilly range w. of the Jordan R. is broken and irregular, and may be divided into several distinct regions. At the extreme south is the Negeb (q.v.), a desert steppe region or tableland, 1500 to 2000 ft. above sea level, inter-

Ewing Galloway

IN PALESTINE

Above: Ancient walls surrounding the city of Jerusalem. Right: A camel driver.

sected by wadies, or ravines, running E. toward the Dead Sea or N.W. toward the Mediterranean Sea. The largest of these ravines is the Wadi es Saba, which passes ancient Beersheba (q.v.) and enters the Mediterranean as Wadi Gaza a few miles s. of ancient Gaza (q.v.). The N. part of the Negeb is higher than that of the s. (about 2500 ft. above sea level), and marks the beginning of the highland or mountain region of the ancient Kingdom of Judah (q.v.). The greatest elevation of the Judæan Range is reached near the subdistrict of Hebron (3370 ft.). Toward Jerusalem (q.v.) the altitude diminishes in places to about 2400 ft., but becomes higher again to the north. The crest of the Judæan highland averages nearly 15 m. in breadth, the descent thence to the Dead Sea, some 10 or 15 m. away, being rapid and terminating in steep cliffs. The whole region bordering on the Dead Sea is wild, barren, and rocky. It was known In Biblical times as Jeshimon (the desert waste). West of the Judæan highland the country sinks gradually toward the coastal plain. From the coastal plain several large valleys lead up into the interior highlands.

The central highland of Palestine continues N. of Jerusalem for more than forty miles. The descent to the valley of the Jordan is in places very abrupt, though traversed by a number of passable valleys. One of these val-

leys, the Wadi Fara, pierces far into the interior. Near Nablus (Shechem), situated in a beautiful valley between Mount Gerizim (2849 ft.) on the s. and Mount Ebal (3077 ft.) on the N., several valleys have their origin. Among them is the Wadi es Shair, which opens out N.W. into the plain in which the ancient city of Samaria (q.v.) was situated, and continues thence to the coast. Another valley opens into the Wadi Fara and thus affords a connection with the valley of the Jordan. To the N. of Samaria the country takes on a new character. The low-lying Plain of Dothan connects the seacoast region with the great Plain of Esdraelon (q.v.), or Plain of Jezreel, a triangular-shaped expanse, about 16 m. across, situated midway between the Jordan R. and the Mediterranean Sea, with an average elevation of about 250 ft. This district is sepa-ated from the seacoast plain to the w. by a series of low hills running n.w. from the Plain of Dothan and culminating in the Carmel Range (1500 to 1800 ft.), which juts out into the Mediterranean Sea in a promontory 556 ft. high. The Esdraelon is shut in on the e. by the Gilboa Mountains (1300 to 1650 ft.) and by the hills near the sites of ancient Shunem and Nain. Between these two ranges the deep valley of Jezreel, all of which lies below sea level, leads down to the Jordan R. The n.e. corner of the Esdraelon opens into another precipitous valley, across which rises Mount Tabor (1843 ft.).

North of the Esdraelon, in lower Galilee (q.v.), the terrain becomes mountainous again. The entire region between the Sea of Galilee and the Mediterranean Sea is relatively open. The peaks are less than 2000 ft. above sea level, and are for the most part isolated and interspersed with valleys and plains. Two main systems of hills run through lower Galilee. One bounds the Plain of Esdraelon on the n., extending from the Kishon R. just opposite Mount Carmel to the Sea of Galilee. North of this first system, extending from the n.w. coast of the Sea of Galilee to the Mediterranean coastal plain, is a long, low plain broken into several portions by low hills crossing it from n. to s. The e. end of the plain as it descends to the Sea of Galilee forms the land of Gennesaret, a region of great fertility. The second line of hills, n. of the long plain, completes the hill system of lower Galilee. To the n. upper Galilee consists of a high central plateau with a general elevation of 2000 to 3000 ft. This plateau is narrower in its northern than in its southern portion and is terminated by the Leontes Mountains, which, rising among the Lebanon Mountains in s.w. Syria, make a sharp turn to the w. and enter the Mediterranean Sea just n. of the ancient city of Tyre, in Lebanon.

Across the valley through which flow the upper courses of the Jordan R. stands Mount Hermon, the summit of which is 9056 ft. above sea level. From the base of this mountain issue most of the springs which combine to form the Jordan. At the point where these streams converge the valley is from 8 to 10 m. wide and only a little above sea level. Thereafter it becomes marshy and at length opens into the Waters of Merom. Thence the valley narrows, the stream descending rapidly to the Sea of Galilee. From the Sea of Galilee to the Dead Sea, a distance of 65 m., the valley of the Jordan varies from 3 to 14 m. in width. It is only about 4 m. wide at the point

at which it leaves the Sea of Galilee, but broadens to the point at which it joins the valley of Jezreel, 13 m. below. It narrows once more, but after receiving the waters of the Jabbok R., widens steadily until, at Jericho (q.v.), it attains its maximum breadth. On either side of the Jordan valley the ascent to the highlands is generally steep. The western side is broken by many ravines and passes; the eastern side, however, has a more uniform character, being intersected only at long intervals by large streams. The Dead Sea marks the deepest part of the Jordan valley. It has no outlet, and the constant evaporation, together with the saline character of many of the springs which empty into it, make its waters so salty that they are exceedingly bitter in taste and of high specific gravity. In some places the shores are heavily lined with deposits of salt. The Dead Sea is also notable for the petroleum springs below its surface; from these springs come the lumps of bitumen (asphalt) often found floating on the waters. Hence the Dead Sea was known in ancient times as the *Lacus Asphaltites* (Asphalt Lake). The sea is deepest at its northern end (about 1300 ft.), the southern portion being quite shallow. It lies 1292 ft. below the level of the Mediterranean Sea, is surrounded by hills rising 3000 to 4000 ft. above its surface, and is one of the hottest regions of the world.

Across the deep, hot valley of the Jordan lies e. Palestine, which falls physiographically into three regions. From Mount Hermon to the Yarmuk R., a large stream traversing the e. plateau and emptying into the Jordan, extinct volcanoes abound, the lava soil rendering the region exceptionally fertile. South of the Yarmuk R. to the Jabbok R. and from the Jabbok to the Arnon R., a total distance of nearly 100 m., lie the ancient city of Gilead (q.v.) and the Plains of Moab, both of which are coextensive with the Perea of New Testament times. The soil in this vicinity is not as fertile as that found in the region n. of the Yarmuk R., and is consequently less fitted for agriculture. The region has always been noted, however, for its excellent pasturage. The terrain takes the form of a high rolling plateau broken only by large wadies running to the Jordan. North Gilead is not as high as s. Gilead and the Plains of Moab, but it is more heavily wooded and better supplied with water. The most southerly portion of Gilead, s. of the Arnon R., the site of the ancient Kingdom of Moab, is even more barren and dry, but is nevertheless suitable for pasturage.

The water supply of Palestine is not abun-

Ewing Galloway

View along the shore of Galilee, Palestine

dant. Heavy rains occur during the winter, but the numerous wadies are for the most part dry in the summer months. The only large river is the Jordan; other rivers include the Yarmuk, the Jabbok, the Kishon, and the Zerka. Palestine has two seasons. The rainy or winter season begins in late October. Rain falls more or less continuously until February, when the intensity of the downfall diminishes, permitting the farmers to sow their crops. By May the rains are over and the long hot summer (May to October) begins. The highlands, with a mean annual temperature of 63° F. and a range from 34° F. to 100° F., are dry and healthful. The lowlands are moist and humid. The prevailing winds are from the Mediterranean Sea, N.W. in summer, W. or S.W. in winter. The *sirocco,* a hot wind carrying clouds of dust from the desert regions to the E. and S., frequently inflicts damage and severe discomfort.

The flora of Palestine is remarkably rich and diversified, considering the limited area of the country and the many barren tracts of land. The luxuriance of Palestinian flora is due to the fact that Palestine is the center of three great floral regions, namely, the Mediterranean flora, the Asiatic steppe flora, and the tropical flora of Arabia and Egypt. The last-named type is confined to the valleys.

Mediterranean flora in Palestine includes date, banana, fig, olive, and almond trees and acacia and azalea bushes. Patches of dense forest cover the mountain slopes N. of Judea. On the lower slopes the trees are deciduous, notably oak, beech, maple, poplar, and mulberry; on the higher slopes are found evergreen forests containing spruce, cypress, juniper, and cedar trees. The fauna of Palestine is also varied, including over 100 species of mammals and several hundred types of birds. The large wild animals, however, such as the lion, bear, and leopard, are virtually extinct. The most characteristic surviving mammals are the mountain goat and the hyrax, a small, thickset animal with short legs and ears.

The mineral resources of Palestine, with few exceptions, are insufficient to repay commercial exploitation. A concession for the extraction of salt, bromides, and carnallite from the Dead Sea was granted to a British company in 1930. Other minerals found in the country are limestone, sandstone, gypsum, sulfur, and potash. The chief industry of Palestine is agricultural; major crops are almonds, barley, corn, figs, lemons, olives, oranges, potatoes, rice, tobacco, and wheat. Important machine industries include diamond-cutting, the manufacture of soap, shoes, and glass, and the refining of petroleum.

History. The earliest history of Palestine, down to the 16th century B.C., is exceedingly obscure, although archeological investigation has produced much material relating to the civilization of the primitive inhabitants. According to ancient Egyptian records, Palestine was originally a part of the land of the Amu, a people dwelling to the N.E. of Egypt. The Amu called Palestine *Lotan* or *Ruten*, reserving the name *Kharu* for the S. part of the country and *Amor* or *Amur* for the N. district and the region around what is now Lebanon. Until the 18th century B.C. the dominant power in Palestine, as in all of S.W. Asia, was the Babylonian. This supremacy was destroyed by the incursion of great numbers of Semitic tribesmen from the Arabian desert. Between 1500 and 1450 B.C. Egypt established its overlordship in Palestine. The Tell el-Amarna (q.v.) letters, which make up the correspondence between the Egyptian pharaoh Amenhotep IV (Ikhnaton) and his father Amenhotep III, disclose that the common name for Palestine at the time of the 18th Egyptian Dynasty was Canaan (see CANAAN; CANAANITES) and that the language of its people was an earlier form of the tongue known later as Hebrew (see HEBREWS; SEMITIC LANGUAGES). This tongue was spoken not only by the Israelites but also by the Edomites (see EDOM), the Moabites (q.v.), and the Phenicians (see PHENICIA). The Tell el-Amarna letters show further that under the lax rule of Amenhotep IV Palestine passed from Egyptian control. The Hittites (q.v.) from the N. and the Habiru (an ethnic subdivision of the great Aramæan group to which the Israelites belonged) in the central and S. portions then fought to gain possession of the country. This era of conflict was ended by the revival of Egyptian supremacy under the 19th Dynasty, the kings of which, Seti I and Ramses II, drove back the Hittites and once more subjugated Palestine. The succeeding Egyptian dynasty was weak, with the result that Palestine broke up into a number of petty kingdoms.

About this time (1300-1100 B.C.) two peoples of markedly different origin and character sought to make Palestine their home. These peoples were the Philistines and the Israelites. The former acquired dominion over the whole Mediterranean coastal plain; the latter undertook a series of conquests which at length gained them full control of Palestine. The Canaanites appear to have offered little united opposition to the Israelites. The work of conquest was long and gradual, the Israelite tribes being finally settled in the following

manner. East of the Jordan R. between the Arnon and Jabbok rivers the Gadites and Reubenites (see GAD; REUBEN) had their homes. The Reubenites soon lost their identity, either because they were absorbed by the Gadites, who finally occupied Reubenite territory, or because they drifted further eastward and merged with other tribes near the great Arabian desert. The W. highland from Jerusalem southward constituted the home of the tribes of Judah. Southwest of Judah lay the territory of Simeon (q.v.). Between Judah and the Plain of Esdraelon the country was occupied for the most part by members of the house of Joseph (q.v.), that is, the tribes of Benjamin (q.v.) N.E. of Judah, the tribes of Ephraim (q.v.) in the central portion, and the tribes of Manasseh in the north. A tiny district N.W. of Judah was occupied by the small tribe of Dan (q.v.); a considerable portion of this tribe subsequently migrated to the extreme N. near the sources of the Jordan R. In the valley and plain of Jezreel lay the territory occupied by the tribes of Issachar (q.v.) and the tribes of Zebulon (q.v.), the former in the E., the latter in the west. Part of southern and all of northern Galilee was inhabited by the tribes of Naphtali (on the E.) and of Asher (on the W. behind the Phenician maritime cities of Sidon and Tyre).

About 1030 B.C. the various Israelite tribes were confederated into a kingdom under Saul (q.v.), of the tribe of Benjamin. Saul's successor, David (q.v.), of the tribe of Judah, completed the establishment of Israelite supremacy in Palestine. Under David and his son Solomon (q.v.), Palestine was the home of a free people united under a central government. About 933 B.C. this united kingdom was split into two kingdoms, Israel in the N. and Judah in the S. Israel was conquered by Assyria in 722 B.C. The annals of Sargon II, King of Assyria, record that Sargon deported over 27,000 persons from Israel and sent a number of Aramæans into the country from Babylonia. This Aramæan colony, subsequently augmented, merged with the remaining Israelites. Thus a mixed population, still essentially Semitic, came to occupy the old Ephraim-Manasseh territory. Galilee was gradually filled with a hybrid Phenician-Syrian population, which, with the exception of the Ituræan occupation (see ITURÆA), remained substantially intact until about 100 B.C. The Kingdom of Judah came to an end when Nebuchadnezzar II, King of Babylon, captured and destroyed Jerusalem in 586 B.C. During the next half century Nabatæan Arabs (see NABATÆANS) pressed in from the deserts to the E. and S.E., occupied much of the old Moabite territory, and, forcing the Edomites out of their abode, drove them northward into S. Judah, which then became Edomite territory. The Jewish exiles who returned to Palestine from Babylon by permission of Cyrus the Great in 536 B.C. settled only in the northern part of the old Kingdom of Judah.

Under the Persian Empire (see PERSIA) Palestine was a part of the satrapy, or province, of Syria. The satrapy was subdivided into a number of districts, of which Judah, Phenicia, and Samaria (q.v.) were administered by separate governors. Through the efforts of the leaders Ezra and Nehemiah (qq.v.) the Judæan community was thoroughly consolidated, Jerusalem was fortified, and foreigners were expelled. The inhabitants of Judah constantly encroached on Samaritan territory and gradually extended their frontier toward the N.W. The Samaritans (q.v.) also became more closely united through the founding of the Samaritan religion, based exclusively on the Pentateuch (q.v.), or first five books of the Old Testament (see SAMARITAN PENTATEUCH), and through the building of a temple on Mount Gerizim. During the Persian period the language of the Jewish community became assimilated by the Aramaic tongue spoken throughout the region, and Hebrew gradually ceased to be the language of colloquial speech.

The conquest of the Near East by Alexander the Great (q.v.) resulted in the introduction of Greek influence into Palestine. Samaria was razed and rebuilt as a Macedonian city. In the struggles of Alexander's successors, Palestine came into the possession of Ptolemy I of Egypt, and until 197 B.C. was under Egyptian control. It then passed to Antiochus III (the Great) of Syria. The attempt of Antiochus IV to destroy the Jewish religion in Palestine (168 B.C.) precipitated the great Jewish War of Independence (see JEWS; MACCABEES). When the conflict came to an end, a free Judæa under the Hasmonæan or Maccabean priest-princes controlled all of S. Palestine from the Jordan R. to the Mediterranean coast. The rest of the country, nominally under the power of Syria, was actually in a state of anarchy. East of the Jordan R. the Nabatæan Arabs were in possession of all territory but that occupied by the Greek cities. Under the Hasmonæan rulers John Hyrcanus, Aristobulus I, and Alexander Jannæus, the Jews subjugated Idumæa (Edom), Samaria,

Galilee, and virtually all of the old East Jordan territory.

Quarrels among rival Jewish factions afforded Rome the opportunity of extending its conquests into Palestine. In 63 B.C. the Roman general and statesman Gnæus Pompeius Magnus, known as Pompey the Great, annexed Syria and Palestine to the Roman Empire. From 63 B.C. until 67 A.D. Palestine was a part of the Roman province of Syria. During most of this time Judæa and other districts were administered by Herod the Great (q.v.) and his successors. The greater part of the country was included in the four districts of Judæa, Samaria, Galilee, and Peræa. The territory north of the Jabbok R. was broken up into minor divisions, such as Gaulanitis, Auranitis, Trachonitis, and Batanæa, administered by tetrarchs, or petty governors. With the outbreak of the Jewish rebellion against Roman rule (66-73 A.D.), Palestine was detached from Syria and made a separate province under the Roman general and statesman (later emperor) Titus Flavius Sabinus Vespasianus. The war against Rome ended disastrously for the Jews with the capture and ruin of Jerusalem in 70 A.D., the destruction of the Temple, and the dissolution of the Jewish state. Thereafter new cities sprang up, fostered by Rome. Another Jewish insurrection against the Romans (132-35) led by Simon Bar Cocheba (see BAR COCHEBA), though at first successful, was finally put down with great bloodshed and devastation. The Roman emperor Publius Ælius Hadrianus, familiarly known as Hadrian, rebuilt Jerusalem, changed its name to Ælia Capitolina, and forbade any Jew to live in it.

Palestine remained an integral part of the Roman Empire, and afterward of the Byzantine Empire, until the invasion of the Persian king Khosrau II in 614. In 628, however, the Byzantine emperor Heraclius utterly defeated Khosrau and expelled him from Palestine. With the advent of Christianity to Palestine it became customary to speak of the country as divided into Palestina Prima (Judæa and Samaria), Palestina Secunda (Galilee), and Palestina Tertia (Idumæa and Moab). Each of these districts was subdivided ecclesiastically into bishoprics. The Latin Kingdom of Jerusalem (see JERUSALEM), founded by the Crusaders (see CRUSADES) in 1099 and overthrown by Saladin, Sultan of Egypt and Syria, in 1187, was merely a passing phase in the history of Palestine, although it left its imprint in the form of churches, monasteries, and shrines throughout the land. After the

Ewing Galloway

A Jewish co-operative settlement at Beth Alpho, Palestine

conquest by the Ottoman Turks (see OTTO-MAN EMPIRE; TURKEY: *History*) in 1516, Palestine became a vilayet, or administrative division, of the Turkish province of Syria.

In World War I (q.v.) the immediate object of Turkey was to seize the Suez Canal in order to block communications between Great Britain and India. Accordingly, Turkish troops were dispatched to the Sinai peninsula and Suez. The British garrison of Egypt was thereupon reinforced. Turkish divisions occupied the Sinai peninsula (belonging to Egypt) from which the British had withdrawn, and early in 1915 launched an attack upon the British positions on the Suez Canal. The British decided to reoccupy the peninsula, an operation requiring a large and well-equipped army. Faced with the problem of maintaining such an army in the desert, the British boldly undertook an extensive engineering program. El Qantara on the Suez Canal was converted into a railroad and water terminus; a broad-gauge railroad was built across the desert; and hundreds of miles of water pipes were laid. In the course of this construction work the British met with a military reverse at Katia, 25 miles E. of the Suez Canal (April, 1916). The Turks were decisively beaten at Romani on August 4th, however, and driven back from their stronghold at El Arish on the Sinai Peninsula. The British then forced the Turks from Rafal on the Egypt-Palestine frontier, January 9, 1917. They attacked Gaza

in March, and again in April, incurring heavy losses but failing to capture the town. Sir Archibald Murray, the British commander in chief, was then superseded by General Edmund Henry Hynman Allenby, who trained his troops intensively before resuming the offensive against the Turks. Cavalry was sent into action on the approaches to Gaza (October 27) in a diversionary feint, a main attack being simultaneously delivered to the left of the Turkish line on the town of Beersheba, which fell on October 31st. Gaza was captured on November 7th, and Jaffa three days later. Two British columns, one inland and one on the coast, moved northward, driving the Turkish army before them. Ascalon, Ashdod, and Gath capitulated in quick succession, and by November 25th, after a victory at El Maghar, Jerusalem was virtually surrounded. The city was not fired upon, however, and after the negotiation of surrender terms, British forces entered Palestine on December 11, 1917.

On July 22, 1922, the League of Nations (q.v.) assigned to Great Britain the mandate for Palestine. From that time until the establishment of the Jewish state of Israel on May 15, 1948, the conflicting claims of Arabs and Jews resulted in perpetual tension in the Middle East, punctuated by frequent armed clashes. The Arabs maintained that in 1914–15 the British gave pledges to the Sherif of Mecca which were in direct contravention of the Balfour Declaration (q.v.) of November 2, 1917. This instrument pledged the British government to the "establishment in Palestine of a national home for the Jewish people". For an account of the rivalry between Arabs and Jews in Palestine and a survey of proposals leading to the establishment of the Jewish homeland, see ISRAEL: *History;* ZIONIST MOVEMENT.

PALESTRINA (anc. *Præneste*), an Italian town, 22 miles s.e. of Rome. It is built almost entirely upon the foundations of the ancient Temple of Fortune, one of the greatest religious edifices in all Italy.

PALESTRINA, GIOVANNI PIERLUIGI DA (1526?-94), Italian composer of church music in the polyphonic style, born in the town of Palestrina, southeast of Rome. Nothing is known of Palestrina's musical education or teachers. The first positive information concerning him is that he was organist and choirmaster at the principal church in Palestrina from 1544 to 1551. During this period he attracted the attention of the chief prelate of the town, Giovanni del Monte, who afterward became Pope Julius III. When Del Monte assumed the papacy in 1551, he appointed Palestrina choirmaster at Cappella Giulia in Rome. Palestrina held similar posts at the church of St. John Lateran from 1555 to 1561 and, from 1561 until his death, at the church of Santa Maria Maggiore. In 1564 Pope Pius IV appointed a committee of cardinals to investigate and, if possible, reform the condition of church music, ridding it of the polyphonic displays with which it had become encumbered. Palestrina was asked to support the argument of those who opposed the rigid application of the pope's radical views. Palestrina responded by submitting three masses (among them the great *Missa Papæ Marcelli,* now usually considered his masterpiece) which, though polyphonic in character, were free of the musical vices condemned by the pope. The first performance of these masses in 1565 completely vindicated the position of Palestrina and his associates; Pius IV was won over to their views, and appointed Palestrina composer to the papal chapel. The remainder of Palestrina's life witnessed an ever-increasing recognition of his genius. In 1571 he was appointed master of music at Cappella Giulia; six years later he was commissioned by Pope Gregory XIII to assist in a complete revision of the Gregorian chant (q.v.). He died in Rome, accepted by his contemporaries as the greatest master who had appeared up to that time in the history of music.

Palestrina represents the most perfect expression of an entire epoch in musical style, that of polyphonic composition in the medieval church modes (see MODE). He both sums up and exhausts the possibilities of this style, an achievement comparable to that of Johann Sebastian Bach in the field of contrapuntal composition in the major and minor modes over two centuries later. The impersonality and lack of emotional expressiveness characteristic of music in the older modes were eminently suited to Palestrina's style, which was formed for the expression of a severe, noble, and majestic religious sentiment. In the musical currents of his day Palestrina's influence was enormous. He brought to an end the unnecessarily complex polyphonic displays into which the music of northern Europe and in part of Italy had degenerated, employing his stupendous technique only as a legitimate means toward artistic ends. A typical example of Palestrina's contribution is the care taken in his compositions to ensure the proper declamation and enunciation of the words of his texts, in contrast to the meaningless flourishes and polyphonic excesses of his immediate predecessors. Palestrina composed in every form of church music current in his time, and also left a small number of secular madrigals; his religious works include masses, hymns, motets, litanies, and magnificats.

PALEY, WILLIAM (1743-1805), celebrated English divine, born in Peterborough. In 1785 he published his *Principles of Moral and Political Philosophy,* in which he propounds his ethical theory, a form of what is usually known as utilitarianism. In 1790 appeared his *Horæ Paulinæ,* the aim of which is to prove, by "undesigned coincidences", the improbability of the belief that the New Testament is a fable. It was followed in 1794 by his *View of the Evidences of Christianity.* In 1802 he published the most popular of all his works, *Natural Theology, or Evidences of the Existence and Attributes of the Deity,* based largely on the *Religious Philosopher* of Nieuwentyt, a Dutch disciple of Descartes.

PALGHAT, a town of Malabar district, Madras, India, 68 miles s.e. of Calicut. Its old fort was of strategic importance, as it commanded the Palghat Pass of the Nilgiri Hills, the great route from the w. coast to the interior. Pop., about 45,000.

PALGRAVE, FRANCIS TURNER (1824-97), English poet and critic, born in Great Yarmouth. He studied at Charterhouse and Balliol College, Oxford, and became professor of poetry at Oxford (1886-95). He is best known as the editor of the *Golden Treasury of English Lyrics* (1861 and 1897), *The Children's Treasury of Lyrical Poetry* (2 vols., 1875), *The Sonnets and Songs of Shakespeare* (1877), and *Treasury of Sacred Songs* (1889).

PALI, an ancient Indian language, of the Prakrit group, descended from Vedic Aryan; Pali was formerly widespread as the sacred language of Buddhism, and is in limited use at the present time in Ceylon, Burma, and Siam. (See INDIAN LANGUAGES.) Strictly speaking, Pali (Skr. *pali*, "row", "line", "series") refers to the written language, so called because it is applied to a series of sacred texts; spoken Pali was called *Palibhāsā* ("language of the series"). Ancient Pali is divided into two groups, that found in inscriptions and that used in literature, inscriptional Pali being the older. The earliest writings in Pali occur in the inscriptions of Asoka (q.v.), and date from the third quarter of the 3rd century B.C.; the latest date from the 10th century A.D. Pali literature is almost entirely religious. The best-known works are the *Tripitaka*, three collections of rules, doctrines, and analyses pertaining to Buddhism; the *Visuddhi Magga*, a Buddhist treatise by Buddhaghosa (q.v.); and the *Milindapañha*, a series of questions and answers on Buddhism. A number of historical and grammatical works also exist. Pali has no distinctive alphabet, but is written according to locality in Ceylonese, Burmese, or Cambodian script. See SANSKRIT LANGUAGE.

PALIMPSEST, a manuscript of parchment, papyrus, or other writing material, from which an early text was removed and which was then covered with a second writing. The term means "scraped again" and, in its strict sense, applies only to waxen tablets or to vellum books. It was also applied to papyrus manuscripts by ancient writers, although papyrus was too delicate to bear scraping or erasing; writing on papyri could be washed off, somewhat imperfectly, with a sponge, but because the writing on papyri was usually on only one side, the back of the papyrus sheet could be used for a second writing. In the case of books of parchment, which by the 4th century A.D. had become the more popular material for literary works, erasure was necessary for a second use. In the early Middle Ages, as the number of books increased and material for making them became scarce, numerous earlier manuscripts of classical authors were employed for later works. Often the earlier writing was incompletely erased or scraped away, and the more ancient and

more valuable work of literature can be deciphered. The great importance of palimpsest manuscripts lies in the ancient works which they preserve and the degree of legibility which the original writing still retains. Usually the more ancient writing, being in capitals or uncials (see PALEOGRAPHY), is larger than the later writing.

Among the most important Greek palimpsests are the *Fragments of the Gospel of Saint Matthew*, the original writing dating from the 6th century A.D.; and the *Codex Nitriensis*, containing part of the Gospel of Saint Luke, part of Homer's *Iliad*, and the *Elements* of Euclid, all used by a monk as material for a copy of a Syriac treatise. Latin palimpsests include the *Codex Ambrosianus* of the Roman dramatist Titus Maccius Plautus, in rustic capitals of the 4th or 5th century A.D., over which were written portions of the Bible in the 9th century, a manuscript of special value because it provides a text of Plautus about 600 years older than any other existing Plautine manuscript; the *De Republica* of Marcus Tullius Cicero, over which was written Saint Augustine's commentary on the Psalms; and the *Institutiones* of the 2nd-century A.D. Roman jurist Gaius, discovered at Verona in 1816 by Barthold Georg Niebuhr. Occasionally a palimpsest was written over twice; a manuscript of the British Museum contains as its original writing the *Annals* of Gaius Granius Licinianus, a writer of the 2nd century A.D., over which was written a grammatical treatise, the third writing being in Syriac.

PALINURUS, in ancient Roman legend, the helmsman of the Trojan hero Æneas. The Roman poet Publius Vergilius Maro, usually known as Vergil, describes in his *Æneid*, Book V, how Palinurus was lulled to sleep at his post and fell overboard near the coast of Lucania. In the following book, the ghost of Palinurus relates to Æneas that he was washed ashore and murdered by the natives. His body later received suitable burial.

PALISADES, a cliff of traprock, from 200 to 500 feet high, in Rockland County, N.Y., and Bergen and Hudson counties, N.J., forming the western bank of the Hudson River from Fort Lee about 20 miles to the north. See HUDSON RIVER.

PALISSY, BERNARD (about 1510–89), French potter, born probably near Agen. He experimented for many years in an effort to discover the secret of making white enamel and, although he did not succeed, his productions of enamelware, with sculptured plants and animals colored to resemble nature, made him famous as one of the foremost French ceramists. He was imprisoned as a Huguenot in 1562 during the French oppression of Protestants, but was set free by royal edict, and was shortly afterward appointed "inventor of rustic figurines" to the queen-mother Catherine de Médicis. In 1588 he was betrayed by a fellow-Huguenot and imprisoned in the Bastille, Paris, where he died. Fine specimens of his work are in the Louvre (Paris), the museums of Cluny and of Sèvres, the Victoria and Albert and British museums, London, and the J.P. Morgan Collection in New York City.

PALIURUS, a genus of trees and shrubs of the Buckthorn family. *P. spinacristi* is often called Jew's thorn or Christ's thorn, from the fancy that it supplied the crown of thorns with which Jesus Christ was crowned. It is a deciduous shrub, with three-nerved leaves, each of which has two sharp spines at the base.

PALLADIO, ANDREA (1518–80), Italian architect of the High Renaissance, born in Vicenza, and trained as an architect in his native city and in Rome. His first important work was a two-storied arcade around the basilica at Vicenza, begun in 1549, in which the composition, proportion, and details were based upon Roman architectural design adapted to the requirements of the time. A distinguishing feature of this arcade and of many of Palladio's later works was an opening, such as a door or window, with an arched top, flanked by two flat-topped openings. This motif became popular as the "Palladian motif", and was widely employed by Renaissance and later architects. Palladio designed many buildings in and near Vicenza. The best known of these are the Barbarano, Chieregati, Tiene, Porto, and Valmarana palaces and the Villa Capra or Villa Rotunda. From about 1560 to 1580 he built a number of churches in Venice, including San Francesco della Vigna, San Giorgio Maggiore, and the church of Il Redentore. His last great work was the Teatro Olimpico, a theater at Vicenza, which was completed after his death. Palladio's work represents the Classisima or Palladian phase of the High Renaissance; see ITALIAN ART AND ARCHITECTURE. He was the author of a scientific treatise on architecture, *I Quattro Libri dell' Architettura* (1570), which was translated into many European languages and influenced many later architects. The precise rules and formulas given in the book were widely adopted, especially in England, and were basic in the formation of the Georgian style; see GEORGIAN ARCHITECTURE.

PALLADIUM, a metallic element of the platinum group, of atomic number 46, atomic weight 106.7, and symbol Pd. It was discovered in 1804 by the English chemist William Hyde Wollaston. The metal occurs in the pure state in platinum ores; and occurs in the combined state in Canadian nickel ore. Palladium is a silvery-white metal of hardness 4.8, specific gravity 12.0, and m.p. 1553° C. (2827° F.). Like platinum it is ductile, malleable, and resistant to corrosion; it fuses more easily than platinum, and can be welded easily. Finely divided palladium is an excellent adsorbent for some gases; it adsorbs one thousand to three thousand times its volume of hydrogen or acetylene gas when heated to 100° C. (212° F.). Palladium is dissolved readily by aqua regia. It forms bivalent and quadrivalent compounds and resembles platinum chemically. The metal is used in dentistry, for nonmagnetic springs in clocks and watches, for coating special mirrors, and in jewelry, alloyed with gold, in what is called white gold.

PALLADIUM, among the ancient Greeks and Romans, an image of Pallas Athena, Greek goddess of wisdom and the protectress of cities. The safety of a city was believed to depend upon the careful preservation of the image in the sanctuary of the goddess. The most famous Palladium was that of ancient Troy; it was said to have fallen from heaven, and according to Greek legend to have been stolen by the Greek leaders Diomedes and Ulysses. Its subsequent fate was the subject of many different tales, since various cities desired to claim possession of the Palladium. The Romans, tracing their ancestry from the Trojans, believed that the Palladium, which was kept at Rome in the temple of Vesta, goddess of the hearth, was the Trojan original, which had been brought to Italy by the hero Æneas. According to other versions, two images existed at Troy, one of which was stolen and the other brought to Italy by Æneas. According to a third group of Roman versions Æneas brought the real Palladium, and the statue stolen by Diomedes and Ulysses was only a copy.

PALLAS, one of the planetoids (q.v.), the second to be discovered, first observed by the German astronomer H.W.M. Olbers (q.v.) in 1802. It revolves about the sun in 1684 days.

PALL MALL, a street of London, famous for its clubs and palaces. Among the prominent clubs are the Athenæum, Traveller's, Reform, Carlton, Army and Navy, Oxford and Cambridge, White's Royal Automobile, and the

Left: Royal palm trees. Right: Betel palm (Areca catechu), source of the betel nut.

Devonshire. The Crimean Monument, the York Column, and the statues of George III and Sir John Franklin are the principal works of sculpture on the thoroughfare; nearby, in the Haymarket, are Her Majesty's Theatre and the Haymarket Theatre. The London House, the Winchester House, and the Marlborough House, St. James's Palace, and the Spencer House are the principal places of note. See LONDON.

PALM, common name for any plant of the family Palmaceae, comprising the order Palmales. The family, which includes about 170 genera and 1500 species, is native to all tropical and subtropical regions of the world. Plants of the Palm family are monocotyledons characterized by a simple stem, a terminal crown of large leaves which are usually pinnate of palmately cleft with deep wedge-shaped notches, and perfect or polygamous flowers. The typical genus of the family is *Areca* (q.v.; see also separate articles on most of the genera and species mentioned below). In most species the stem is long and undi-

vided; stems of the *jupati, buriti,* and *palmyra* palms are sufficiently large and strong to be used for timber. Species of the genus *Chamaerops* have short stems, and the *doom* palm is unusual in having branched stems. In the *rattan* palm the stem is exceptionally long and flexible, sometimes reaching a length of 600 feet, and climbing upon other plants by means of hooked spines. Palm leaves have a strong sheathing, and are often a source of fiber. Plants of the genus *Astrocaryum,* among many others, furnish fiber for cordage; leaves of the *gebang* palm are used for thatching and making baskets, and single leaves of the *talipot* are used for umbrellas and parasols. The enormous leaves of the *bussu* palm of Central and South America are atypical in being undivided; one or two leaves suffice to cover the entire roof of a native hut. Wax is obtained from the leaves of some species of *wax* palm, other species produce a resinous wax from the stem. The stem produces a form of starch in species of the *sago* palm; in species of the genus *Caryota* and other types of *jaggery* palm the sap is sweet and furnishes palm sugar. The sap of these and related species is used as a refreshing beverage, which sometimes is fermented to make palm wine. The terminal bud of the cabbage palm, or *assai*, is valued for food and, like the cabbage, is used either cooked or raw. The fruit of various species of palm range in form from that of the date palm to that of the coconut. The sweet, fleshy part of the date corresponds botanically to the fibrous husk surrounding the shell of the coconut, and the hard stone of the date is homologous with the sweet, oily flesh of the coconut. The seeds of species of *oil* palm produce palm oil, as in species of the genus *Elaeis* and of the *grugru* palm. Fruits of the *ivory* palm produce vegetable ivory (q.v.), used in the manufacture of buttons and other small turned or carved products. Many palms produce a variety of products; the *gomuti* palm, for example, yields cordage fiber from the leaves, sago from the pith, and sugar and palm wine from the sap. Species of the genus *Attalea* produce piassava (q.v.) fiber; some species also yield oil from the fruit, called cohune nuts, others produce coquilla nuts, resembling a brown variety of vegetable ivory.

Most palms are ornamental in cultivation, and many of the smaller species are grown as pot or greenhouse plants in cool climates. See also PALMETTO.

PALMA, capital of the island of Majorca and of the Balearic Islands, on the Bay of Palma. The city is surrounded by orange plantations and is walled and fortified. The houses are mostly in the Moorish style of architecture. Palma is the see of a bishop and has a Gothic cathedral which has a spire so delicate that it is called the Angel's Tower. The chief manufactures are alcohol, liquors, chocolate, starch, sugar, flour, soap, leather, and glass. Pop., about 90,000.

PALMA, JACOPO, called IL VECCHIO ("the Elder") or PALMA VECCHIO (1480?–1528), Italian painter of the Venetian School, born in Serina, near Bergamo. His work was allied in spirit and treatment to that of the Venetian masters Giorgione and Titian. His forms were large and ample; his color rich and warm. He used a remarkable brilliance of color in portrayal of beautiful women, and in his "Holy Conversations", a subject which he painted many times, the groupings of figures in a quiet landscape setting were suffused with a golden glow. Among his most noted portraits are those of Francesco Querini (Querini Stampalia Gallery, Venice) and "The

Poet" (National Gallery, London). "The Three Sisters", in the Dresden Gallery, is generally called the "Three Graces" because of the great beauty and dignity of its subjects.

PALMA, JACOPO, called IL GIOVANE ("the Younger") or PALMA GIOVANE (1544–1628), Italian painter of the Venetian School. He was the grandnephew of Jacopo Palma the Elder, and studied under Titian. Though he utilized characteristic rich Venetian coloring in his work, he fell under the influence of classical Roman grandeur, and his art, which combined both sources, marked the transition to the decadence of Venetian painting. After the death of the great Venetian painters Titian and Veronese, Palma was the sole heir of the tradition, and received many important commissions, painting a "Last Judgment" in the hall of the Doges' Palace, and other scenes in the Great Council Hall in Venice.

PALMA, TOMAS ESTRADA (1835–1908), Cuban revolutionist and statesman, born near Bayamo. He joined the Cuban patriot forces in 1868 upon the outbreak of a revolt against the Spaniards, and subsequently rose to the rank of general. In 1877, shortly after he had been elected president of the Cuban provisional government, he was captured by the Spaniards, who imprisoned him for about one year. After his release Palma spent some years in Honduras and then settled in the United States, where he established a school for Latin-Americans at Central Valley, N.Y. In 1895, when a second Cuban revolution began, he was designated minister to the United States for the Republic of Cuba, and became the head of the Revolutionary Junta in New York City, which purchased arms and secured American aid for the insurgents. He was elected the first president of the Cuban Republic in 1901, and was re-elected in 1906; soon after his re-election he was charged with corrupt practices and was compelled to resign.

PALMAS, CAPE. See CAPE PALMAS.

PALMAS, LAS. See LAS PALMAS.

PALM BEACH, a city of Palm Beach Co., Fla., situated on an island between the Atlantic Ocean and Lake Worth, opposite the city of West Palm Beach, with which it is connected by bridges, and 300 miles s.s.e. of Jacksonville. Transportation facilities include two railroads, steamship lines, and craft on the Inland Waterway. Palm Beach is one of the most noted and fashionable winter resorts in the world. The Gulf Stream runs less than 3 miles offshore, providing a mild climate and excellent deep-sea fishing. The city provides exceptional facilities for bathing and boating, including a yacht basin on Lake Worth, an extensive public beach, and several private beaches. The resident population of the city is increased each winter by a transient population of over 16,000. Pop. (1950) 3886.

PALMER, GEORGE HERBERT (1842–1933), American scholar and writer, born in Boston. At Harvard, he was assistant professor of philosophy (1873–83), professor (1883–89), and Alford professor of natural religion, moral philosophy, and civil polity (1889–1913). In 1887 he married, as his second wife, Alice Freeman. His publications include *The Nature of Goodness* (1904) ; *The Life and Works of George Herbert* (3 vols., 1905) ; *The Life of Alice Freeman Palmer* (1908) ; *The Problem of Freedom* (1911) ; *Formative Types of English Poetry* (1918) ; a notable prose translation (1884) of Homer's *Odyssey;* and a translation (1899) of the *Antigone* of Sophocles.

PALMER, SAMUEL (1805–81), English painter and etcher, born in London. He studied art at the Antique School of the British Museum, and from 1837 to 1839 in Rome. Palmer was deeply influenced by the romantic and mystical qualities in the work of his friend the poet and artist William Blake, and his best pictures, such as "Dream on the Apennines" (1864) and "The Waters Murmuring" (1877), are imbued with an intense poetic feeling. His noted illustrations for John Milton's *L'Allegro* and *Il Penseroso* display his poetically idealistic manner of treating landscapes. Among his graceful etchings, which display a masterful treatment of light, are "The Early Plowman", "The Skylark", and "The Herdsman's Cottage". Palmer devoted himself chiefly to water color, however, and became a member of the Society of Water Colour Painters in 1854. His English blank-verse translation of Vergil's *Eclogues* was published posthumously in 1883.

PALMER LAND, peninsula forming the most northerly part of the continent of Antarctica, discovered (1820) by N.B. Palmer and thereafter known under that name. Directly south of South America, Palmer Land is flanked on the east by Weddell Sea and on the west by Bellinghausen Sea. See ANTARCTIC EXPLORATION.

PALMERSTON, HENRY JOHN TEMPLE, 3rd VISCOUNT (1784–1865), English statesman, born near Romsey, in Hants, England, and educated at Harrow School and at St. John's College, Cambridge University. He entered Parliament for Newton, on the Isle of Wight, in 1807, and he won the seat for Cambridge University in 1811. Offered the chancellorship of the exchequer in 1809, Palmerston refused, and took, instead, a position as supervisor of the financial business of the army, in which he remained, without cabinet rank and refusing every offer of promotion, until 1827. During this period Palmerston attained more fame as a man of fashion and as a writer of satirical poetry than as a political figure. In 1827, however, he became a member of the Tory cabinet formed by the Duke of Wellington. In 1828 he resigned and joined the Opposition, becoming foreign secretary of the Whig government formed in 1830, and remaining in this post, except for a brief interval, until 1841. Palmerston re-entered the cabinet as foreign secretary under the prime ministership of Lord John Russell in 1846. He was dismissed in 1851 for having supported the coup d'état of Louis Napoleon (see NAPOLEON III) in France. He became prime minister in 1855, following the success of British forces in the Crimean War (1854–56), in which he had initiated British participation, and remained in that post until his death ten years later.

Palmerston was noted for his vacillation between Whig and Tory sentiments, which made it impossible for him to be completely in accord with either party. During his leadership of British foreign policy, he supervised the annexation of Hong Kong and the opening of five other Chinese ports by the Treaty of Nanking (1842) ; supported movements for constitutional government in Spain and Portugal ; fought the international slave trade (see SLAVERY) ; and supported British neutrality in the American Civil War. See also GREAT BRITAIN: *History.*

PALMETTO, common name of a species of palm, *Sabal palmetto,* a native of maritime parts of North America, from Florida to North Carolina. It attains a height of 40 to 50 feet and has a crown of large palmate leaves, the blade from 1 foot to 5 feet in length and breadth and on a long petiole.

PALMISTRY, or CHIROMANCY (Gr. *cheir,* "hand"; *manteia,* "divination"), the art of characterization and foretelling the future through the study of the palm of the hand. Palmistry was known among the Chaldaeans, Assyrians, Egyptians, and Hebrews, and was recognized by the philosophers Plato, Aristotle, and Antiochus. Palmistry was seriously practiced and widely accepted during the Middle Ages, and was revived as a serious art during the 19th century, especially in France. Since the turn of the century it has been regarded as a branch of fortunetelling (q.v.), without scientific basis. Palmistry is chiefly concerned with the mounts of the palm, the lines on the mounts, and the lines interlacing the palm. The left hand supposedly reflects inbred and the right hand acquired characteristics. The presence of each mount signifies a certain personality trait and the absence of a particular mount indicates the lack of a corresponding trait. The mount of Jupiter denotes honor and a happy disposition; of Saturn, prudence and therefore success; of Apollo, appreciation of beauty; of Mercury, scientific, industrial, and commercial interests; of Mars, courage; of the Moon, a dreamy disposition; and of Venus, an amorous nature. The four most important lines represent life, intelligence, the heart or sensation, and personal fortune. Markings known as squares, stars, circles, points, triangles, crosses, rings, branches, and islands corroborate or modify by their positions in the palm the deductions made from the mounts and lines.

PALM SUNDAY, the Sunday before Easter, so called from the custom of blessing palms and of carrying the portions of branches in procession, in commemoration of the entry of our Lord into Jerusalem. The date of this custom is uncertain, and cannot be traced beyond the 8th century.

PALMYRA, in ancient times, a wealthy and magnificent city of N. Syria, situated in an oasis on the northern edge of the Arabian desert, about 150 miles N.E. of Damascus. According to the old tradition, it was founded by Solomon. After the decline of Petra in 105 A.D., Palmyra took its place as the chief commercial center in N. Arabia. Its merchant aristocracy reaped great advantage from the long-protracted wars between Rome and Parthia by acknowledging the supremacy of Rome. When the Moslems conquered Syria, Palmyra also submitted to them. From the 15th century it began to sink into decay, along with the rest of the Orient. Of the remains of the ancient city the temple of the Sun (or Baal) and the colonnade, nearly 1 m. long, originally of some 1500 Corinthian columns, still stand. Near the ancient city a modern town has been built on the Bagdad-Beirut-Haija mail-service route.

PALO ALTO, BATTLE OF. After the United States had annexed Texas, General Taylor received orders to advance to the Rio Grande. On the advance, however, Arista, the Mexican commander, crossed the river and fought a battle with Taylor's army at Palo Alto (May 8, 1846), and at Resaca de la Palma (May 9). These actions were regarded as acts of aggression by President Polk, and Congress decided on war.

PALOMAR OBSERVATORY, MOUNT. See MOUNT PALOMAR OBSERVATORY.

PALSY. See PARALYSIS.

PALSY, CEREBRAL, term applied to any of five paralytic conditions of the human body, caused by damage to the brain before, during, or immediately following birth, and almost invariably accompanied by impaired sensation, especially in the sense of hearing and sight. The five conditions are all characterized by various degrees of loss of muscular control resulting in facial grimaces, drooling, and awkward gait and speech in its victims. This awkwardness of manner has led many people to classify victims of cerebral palsy as feebleminded; actually, only about one third of them have suffered damage to the thinking centers of the brain.

Two of the cerebral-palsy conditions, the *athetoid* and the *spastic,* account for about eighty-five percent of all victims. The athetoid palsied manifest involuntary uncontrolled movements of the affected muscles; such movements are accentuated in states of excitement. Children with this condition tense their muscles in an effort to stop the movements, sometimes resulting in permanent muscular tenseness. The spastic palsied do not manifest involuntary movements; however, when they attempt to move, their movements are exaggerated. All forms of cerebral palsy are popularly, but erroneously, called "spastic paralysis". The other three cerebral-palsy conditions are *ataxia,* in which balance is disturbed, *tremor,* in which involuntary rhythmic contractions of the muscles occur, and *rigidity,* in which the muscles are stiff and inelastic.

About 550,000 individuals in the United States suffer from cerebral palsy; each year, about 10,000 children develop one or more of the five cerebral-palsy conditions as a result of trauma at birth, congenital malformation of the brain, blood disturbances such as those caused by incompatible Rh factors (q.v.) in the mother and child, or infectious diseases such as encephalitis or meningitis. One out of seven of these children die before the age of six. Educational and rehabilitational programs instituted between 1945 and 1950 have resulted in increased acceptance of the intelligence of most of the cerebral palsied, and in training of victims of these conditions in speech and the pursuance of normal activities.

PAMIRS, a lofty plateau region which forms with the Bolor-Tagh the nucleus of the Central Asian highland system. It has a mean elevation of 13,000 ft., uniting the western terminations of the Himalaya and the Tian-Shan mts., and both with the Hindu-Kush. It is traversed by mountain ridges that rise from 4000 to 5000 ft. above the plateaus, and the culminating points attain in some cases about 26,000 ft. above sea level (Mustagh Ata). The Great Pamir is the name given to the south-central part of the plateau, while Little Pamir lies to the s. of this in the upper Ak-su valley. There are some 70,000 inhabitants of the Pamir region, and almost the whole territory belongs to Russia, although small sections are held by the Chinese and Afghans. The great-horned sheep of the Pamirs is the most famous of all the fauna of the region.

PAMLICO SOUND, a shallow body of water, some 75 m. by 10 to 25 m. in size, on the coast of N. Carolina, separated from the ocean by long, narrow islands of sand, with narrow passages. The Pamlico and Neuse rivers empty into the sound, which communicates in the N. through Croatan Sound with Albermarle Sound. A thriving fishing industry is carried on here.

PAMPAS, a term properly confined to the immense treeless plains of the Argentine Republic, which rise, almost imperceptibly, in a series of terraces from the coast to the base of the Cordilleras. Extending some 2000 by 500 m., they differ greatly in various districts. The northeastern portion, in the Paraná basin, is one of the most fertile regions in the republic. Stretching from this through Buenos Aires and the s. of Cordova and Santa Fé is the rich grassy pampas-land proper, supporting great herds of cattle, horses, and sheep. The name "pampas" is given also to the level districts of Peru, where those of the Sacramento occupy an area estimated at 180,000 sq.m. The term is derived from Peruvian *pampa* ("plain").

PAMPHYLIA, in ancient geography, a country on the s. coast of Asia Minor, between Lycia and Cilicia. The inhabitants, a mixed race of aborigines, Cilicians, and Greek colonists, spoke a language which was probably Greek in origin but which was disfigured and corrupted by the infusion of barbaric elements. The country was freed from Persian domination by the conquests of Alexander the Great in the 4th century B.C., and after his death it passed into the hands of the Seleucid kings of Syria. Later becoming a part of Pergamum (q.v.), it fell to the Romans along with the rest of the kingdom by the bequest of Attalus III in 133 B.C.

PAMPLONA, or PAMPELUNA, a city of northern Spain on a tributary of the Ebro River, 11 miles N.W. of Saragossa. Its known history goes back to 68 B.C., in the time of Pompey the Great. It has manufactures of linen, flour, soaps, leather, and paper. Pop. (1950) 72,394.

PAN, in Greek mythology, the great god of pastures, forests, and flocks, described as the son of Hermes, god of commerce, invention, and athletics, and of a Dryad, or as the son of Zeus, father of the gods, and the nymph Callisto. Pan seems originally to have been a god of Arcadia (q.v.), which remained the principal seat of his cult, although his worship spread over the Peloponnesus and to Athens. From early times reference is made to the *panic* fear which he inspired by his unexpected appearance. Various stories are related about Pan. The nymph Syrinx fled from him and was transformed into a bed of reeds, whereupon Pan took reeds of unequal length and invented the syrinx (q.v.), or shepherd's pipe. When he challenged Apollo, god of music, medicine, and light, to a musical contest, the victory was awarded to Apollo, and Midas, King of Phrygia, had his ears changed to those of an ass by Apollo for objecting to the decision. In the reign of the Roman emperor Tiberius, the passengers of a ship heard, or thought that they heard, a voice shouting that Pan was dead; the early Christians saw in this story a reference to the birth of Christ and an indication that a new era was beginning. In art Pan is depicted in two ways: as a handsome youth with short horns growing from his forehead; and as a more animal-like figure, with horns, a goat's beard, a crooked nose, pointed ears, a tail, and goat's feet. In the latter form Pan seems to have contributed to the development of the popular conception of the devil.

C